Adversarial AI and Data Poisoning in Federated Learning

Vipul Jain
RMIT University, Australia

Shikha Khullar
https://orcid.org/0009-0000-5598-3145
Poornima University, India

Manju Lata Joshi
Poornima University, India

Deepak Kumar Jain
Dalian University of Technology, China

IGI Global
Scientific Publishing
Publishing Tomorrow's Research Today

Vice President of Editorial Melissa Wagner
Director of Acquisitions Mikaela Felty
Director of Book Development Jocelynn Hessler
Production Manager Mike Brehm
Cover Design Jose Rosado

Published in the United States of America by
IGI Global Scientific Publishing
701 East Chocolate Avenue
Hershey, PA, 17033, USA
Tel: 717-533-8845 | Fax: 717-533-7115
Website: https://www.igi-global.com E-mail: cust@igi-global.com

Library of Congress Cataloging-in-Publication Data

Names: Jain, Vipul, 1977- editor | Khullar, Shikha, 1987- editor | Joshi, Manju Lata, 1976- editor | Jain, Deepak Kumar editor
Title: Adversarial AI and data poisoning in federated learning / edited by: Vipul Jain, Shikha Khullar, Manju Lata Joshi, Deepak Kumar Jain.
Description: Hershey PA : IGI Global Scientific Publishing, [2026] | Includes bibliographical references. | Summary: "This book provides a comprehensive examination of emerging threats, attack vectors, and defense mechanisms within federated learning systems, with a particular focus on adversarial machine learning and data poisoning"-- Provided by publisher.
Identifiers: LCCN 2025038308 (print) | LCCN 2025038309 (ebook) | ISBN 9798337362243 hardcover | ISBN 9798337362250 paperback | ISBN 9798337362267 ebook
Subjects: LCSH: Federated learning (Machine learning) | Generative adversarial networks (Computer networks)
Classification: LCC Q325.65 .A38 2026 (print) | LCC Q325.65 (ebook)
LC record available at https://lccn.loc.gov/2025038308
LC ebook record available at https://lccn.loc.gov/2025038309

British Cataloguing in Publication Data
A Cataloguing in Publication record for this book is available from the British Library.

Table of Contents

Detailed Table of Contents

Federated Learning (FL), a collaborative machine learning paradigm that allows model training across multiple devices without centralized data aggregation, was developed in response to the exponential growth of decentralized data across mobile devices, edge sensors, and distributed systems. By limiting sharing to model updates and preserving sensitive user data locally, FL overcomes important privacy, legal, and bandwidth restrictions. However, new and advanced security threats are introduced by this distributed and privacy-aware architecture. These can compromise the reliability and effectiveness of federated models and include poisoning attacks, inference leakage, free-riding, and Byzantine behavior. This chapter provides overview of FL with real-world applications. The chapter is designed to provide readers with a solid knowledge base on the opportunities and challenges in the construction of reliable, scalable, and elastic FL systems, eliminating the gap between the Federated Model design and thoughtfulness.

Federated Learning (FL) is an emerging decentralized machine learning paradigm that enables multiple clients to collaboratively train a global model without sharing raw data, thereby preserving data privacy. . In adversarial settings, malicious clients can inject carefully crafted inputs or manipulate local training updates to degrade the global model's performance or embed backdoors. Data poisoning attacks, including label flipping and model update manipulation, pose significant threats by subtly corrupting training data or gradients, often bypassing conventional anomaly detection methods. This paper reviews the taxonomy, mechanisms, and impacts of adversarial and poisoning attacks in FL environments, and explores current defense strategies such as robust aggregation, anomaly detection, differential privacy, and blockchain integration. Understanding these threats is crucial to developing secure and reliable FL systems for real-world applications in healthcare, finance, and IoT.

The concept of Federated Learning (FL) has developed of centralized model averaging to a multi-faceted ecosystem of architectures, such as cross-device, cross-silo, hierarchical, and decentralized systems. Although the models allow collaboration of intelligence without direct data sharing, they also reveal vulnerabilities, which are caused by non-IID data, incomplete participation, and adversarial manipulation. This chapter offers a theoretical overview of architectural models and their related security aspects in FL. It follows the history of FL and describes key aggregation paradigms, as well as trade-offs between robustness, privacy, and efficiency. The comparative insights have been provided in terms of statistical, trust-based, spectral, inversion-guided, and cryptographic aggregation strategies keeping in consideration their flexibility in heterogeneous and adversarial settings. The chapter ends by hybrid and privacy-protecting models that combine secure computation, blockchain-based trust, and ethical governance to support scalable, responsible federated ecosystems.

Federated Artificial Intelligence (AI) represents one of the rotations in the approach to training decentralized and privacy-preserving machine learning models. The heterogeneity of edge devices, unreliable communication networks, and physical unreachability exposes federated systems to a general set of attack-based model inversion, data poisoning, man-in-the-middle attacks and adversarial manipulations. The aim of this chapter is to cover the security issues of federated AI systems with a particular focus on the edge systems. It tries to (i) Analyze the natural security dangers caused by edge computing surroundings in FL, (ii) comment on the various architectural answers and mitigation strategies adopted to secure federated learning at the edge and (iii) compare the trade-offs between the latency-accuracy-trust-privacy space.

This chapter provides a detailed overview of the security threats pertaining to federated learning, with a specific focus on label-flipping type of data poisoning attacks. Accordingly, the goal of this chapter is to evaluate the robustness of the defense mechanisms to defend against such label flipping attack. In this chapter, the defense approaches like manifold learning approach (UMAP), clustering method (K-Means), and dimensionality reduction methods such as PCA and KPCA are evaluated and their limitations are illustrated. A Multi-Stage Clustering and Data Quality Filtering (MSCDFL) approach is introduced in this chapter to address these limitations which integrates several techniques like adaptive clustering, data quality scored updates, delta-based updates, and trimmed mean aggregation to detect and mitigate the adversaries. From the experimental results, it is observed that MSCDFL exhibits better performance by maintaining robustness and significantly improving the prediction accuracy even in the presence of 40% of adversaries.

Federated learning enables multiple clients to collaboratively train models without exchanging raw data; however, the system remains susceptible to adversarial attacks through maliciously crafted model updates. This challenge intensifies as privacy-preserving methods, including identity obfuscation, attribute randomization, synthetic data generation, encrypted aggregation, and secure computation, restrict the ability to discern individual participant contributions. This chapter proposes methods that identify and control poisoning while complying with strict privacy limitations. It describes the problem, realistic threat and privacy models, and a four-layer defense structure including input sanitation, update filtering, privacy-sensitive robust aggregation, and post-aggregation audits. An experimental plan tests effectiveness in heterogeneous data and high-level privacy environments. The chapter fills a significant gap by reconciling privacy and robustness and will be valuable to graduate students and researchers studying secure federated learning.

The healthcare industry is rapidly embracing data-driven techniques for early diagnosis, health management and precision medicine. However, strict privacy regulations restrict centralized aggregation of sensitive patient data. These restrictions encouraging the adoption of Federated Learning (FL), a privacy-preserving technique that enables collaborative model training that allows hospitals, and research institutions to get benefit from shared intelligence. While Federated Learning preserves the data confidentiality and locality, their decentralized nature amplifies new attack surfaces, as compromised or malicious participants can extract sensitive information from observed gradients or inject poisoned updates. Among its threats, two of the most critical threats in this domain are Membership Inference Attacks (MIA) and Data Poisoning Attacks. This chapter motivates to analyze these adversarial challenges in depth, critically evaluates existing defensive mechanisms, and proposes a roadmap for building robust, secure, and trustworthy federated healthcare systems.

Federated Learning (FL) allows multiple parties to train a model on their local data source without exchanging raw data. When combined with FL, it provides a strong ability involving knowledge transfer from similar tasks with small data. This chapter reviews the ever-emerging field of Federated Adversarial Transfer Learning (FATL), investigating its possible applications and explaining some of its intrinsic weaknesses. We will study the effects of adversarial examples, model poisoning and backdoor attacks on the transfer learning dynamics in federated environments. We conduct a thorough literature review, outline threat modeling of the FATL scenarios. In summary, our main observations show that FATL boosts generalization and convergence speed, but also exterior dangers when the source models or datasets are not trusted. In addition, traditional defense methods in FL are usually ineffective in the presence of adversarial transfer. In conclusion, FATL provides significant advantages for decentralized AI systems, but with those advantages comes an entirely new threat.

The chapter offers a detailed analysis of the security issues of Federated Learning (FL) and will particularly dwell on data poisoning attacks. It discusses the nature of decentralized architecture of FL, which results in exposing new attack surfaces despite maintaining user privacy. The chapter groups types of data poisoning attacks and provides a resultant taxonomy of defense methods, such as data-level filtering, robust aggregation algorithms, anomaly detection, anything training and privacy-based methods, like differential privacy. Such algorithms as Krum, Bulyan, and Trimmed Mean are examined as well as client reputation systems. Case studies and real-world FL simulations are performed in which the effectiveness of the methods is tested. The difficulties of scalability, tradeoffs between robustness and accuracy, availability of adaptive responses to emerging dangers are also mentioned. This chapter is expected to assist researchers and practitioners toward safe, robust, and trust-guarded federated learning systems.

Federated Learning (FL) allows for distributed model training across a population of devices while also offering the potential for privacy preservation, however, it remains susceptible to a range of adversarial manoeuvres, including model poisoning, backdoor attacks, and Byzantine behaviours. This chapter

The real-world case studies of healthcare, finance, and IOT show practical effects. In the end, we outline open challenges and future directions to enable secure and trusted FL systems.

Syed Mohd Faisal, Malla Reddy Technical Campus, Malla Reddy Vishwavidyapeeth, Hyderabad, India
Wasim Khan, Symbiosis Institute of Technology, Symbiosis International University, India
Mohammad Ishrat, VIT Bhopal University, India
Monia Mohammed Al Farsi, University of Technology and Applied Sciences, Al Musanna, Oman

Federated Learning (FL) enables decentralized machine learning across distributed devices while maintaining data privacy. However, the decentralized nature of FL introduces vulnerabilities, making it susceptible to adversarial attacks that can degrade model accuracy, disrupt system availability, and compromise model integrity. This chapter proposes a quantitative risk assessment framework for FL, focusing on three core metrics: Attack Success Rate (ASR), Availability Degradation, and Model Integrity Loss. We define and evaluate these metrics to systematically measure adversarial impact on FL systems. The chapter also explores defense strategies like robust aggregation and anomaly detection, illustrating their effectiveness in mitigating risks. Furthermore, we address the trade-offs between utility, privacy, and security in federated settings. This work provides insights for designing resilient FL systems, offering practical tools for researchers and practitioners to monitor and mitigate adversarial risks in real-world deployments.

Uddalak Mitra, JIS College of Engineering, India
Shafiq Ul Rehman, Kingdom University, Bahrain
Barnik Podder, JIS College of Engineering, India
Arpan Dutta, JIS College of Engineering, India
Bishtu Bhowmick, JIS College of Engineering, India

AI has demonstrated its necessity in healthcare through better disease forecasts. Conventional machine learning models function on data that are gathered in a centralized location, which require data exchange and thus cause worries about privacy of patients, data safety, and obeying rules. Federated Learning (FL) brings paradigm shift by allowing multiple institutions to train their AI models collectively, without transferring any raw patient data. In this chapter, we investigate how FL can change the face of medical diagnostics. Recalling insights from existing machine learning models for Chronic Kidney Disease detection. We discuss how FL can avoid sharing the actual data sets among the multiple parties and retain predictive accuracy and interpretability of models. We also cover Explainable AI approaches such as SHAP and LIME which serve to increase transparency of FL-based diagnostics. In presenting a full framework for ethical and privacy-preserving AI for healthcare, this chapter brings to the foreground the huge potential of FL for next generation of Medical Intelligence.

The protection of sensitive data and digital transactions in the financial sector is increasingly under fire from sophisticated adversarial threats. With artificial intelligence (AI) -enabled fraud detection, credit scoring, and payment authentication, adversaries take advantage of machine learning models using different methods. Traditional centralized learning is plagued with privacy concerns and singular points of failure, which make it incompatible with stringent laws and guidelines. Federated learning (FL) brings in a new paradigm that allows institutions to train models in collaboration without raw data exchange, thus lowering breach risks and ensuring compliance. This study examines the financial applications of FL to strengthen data security and explores defense strategies like robust aggregation, differential privacy, encryption, blockchain, and other use cases. FL, combining it with adversarial training, explainable AI, trust layers from blockchain, and quantum-safe cryptography, will enable the creation of robust, privacy-preserving financial ecosystems.

In the age of data-based business, organizations depend more and more on wide analysis to inform strategic decisions. However, the growing concerns around data privacy, regulatory compliance, and inter-cooperation are significant challenges. This chapter explores how secure federated learning (SFL) provides a transformative approach to business strategy by enabling the training of machine learning models in collaboration with multiple entities without sharing sensitive data. We examine the underlying principles of federated education, differential privacy and encryption, and practical architectures for entertainment deployment. Through real-world examples, this chapter explains SFL.

Data poisoning is a growing threat to machine learning systems that rely on external or continuously updated data. While prior work highlights risks in healthcare, finance, and IoT, this chapter broadens the scope to government and public-sector records, retail and e-commerce platforms, transportation and geospatial services, and environmental or educational systems. We outline core threat models and attack surfaces, distinguishing between dataset-level, point-level, streaming, and online-learning poisoning. A cross-domain taxonomy and case studies illustrate realistic attack vectors such as manipulated civic submissions, fake product reviews, traffic spoofing, sensor corruption, and compromised assessment data. We further examine black-box and clean-label poisoning, along with current detection and mitigation approaches and governance implications for organizations using large-scale public datasets. The chapter offers a unified view of poisoning risks and provides guidance for improving resilience across data pipelines.

Federated Learning (FL) has enabled decentralised collaboration so that many stakeholders can train models without sharing raw data. However, the distributed nature exposes the system to risks such as data poisoning and unfavourable AI attacks, which compromise the model integrity and the organisational tasks. This chapter checks the outline of collaboration in FL, including platform federated data ecosystems, consortium-based models and cross-industry partnerships. While these structures increase scalability, personalisation and economic value, they also introduce the model updates and weaknesses in gradient manipulation. Discussed solutions include strong aggregation algorithms, blockchain competition, competent traceability, rejection of nonconformities, encouragement, human-in-loop supervision, regulatory compliance and moral AI theory. By integrating technical, organisational and moral security measures, the chapter presents a comprehensive approach to safe, flexible and reliable ecosystems.

A conflict exists between the adversarial vulnerabilities of federated learning and existing accountability and liability regulations in data protection and AI law. This chapter analyses GDPR, the EU AI Act, HIPAA, India's DPDP Act, and UAE ADHICS, along with technical evidence related to poisoning, backdoor, and privacy attacks. The chapter highlights how privacy-preserving architectures can reduce traceability, make causation harder to determine, and weaken single-producer product liability models. It then suggests a role-based, evidence-based framework that uses cryptographically verifiable logs, provenance records, and FL-specific contractual clauses. This framework clarifies liability, establishes safe harbors, and enables cross-border governance for high-risk federated systems.

This chapter per the authors explores secured federated learning systems, focusing on privacy preservation, adversarial resilience, and regulatory compliance. It explains how federated learning enables collaborative model training without direct data sharing, while addressing vulnerabilities such as gradient leakage, model inversion, data poisoning, and backdoor attacks. Methods including differential privacy, homomorphic encryption, secure multiparty computation, and Byzantine-resilient aggregation are evaluated for their effectiveness in mitigating risks. Ethical and legal dimensions shaped by frameworks such as GDPR and the EU AI Act are examined, with emphasis on explainability, fairness, and accountability. Real-world applications in healthcare and finance are highlighted through examples from the EXAM Consortium and WeBank's FATE platform, alongside insights into global research trends and institutional contributions. This chapter per the authors underscores the importance of secured federated learning in advancing trustworthy AI for sensitive domains.

This chapter looks at real-world examples of data poisoning attacks in federated learning (FL) systems, where harmful participants change local data to hurt the accuracy or integrity of global models. It uses case studies from healthcare, finance, the Internet of Things (IoT), and autonomous vehicles to show how these attacks happen, their effects on system performance, and the lessons learned. Each example includes documented incidents, academic research, or industry reports, giving practical and theoretical views. The chapter also points out common patterns across industries, describes vulnerabilities that are often targeted, and shares practical ways to reduce risks seen in real deployments. Examining these scenarios provides helpful insights for researchers, developers, and security experts looking to strengthen FL systems against threats while keeping privacy and efficiency intact.

Preface

Over the past decade, the rapid spread of data-generating devices, platforms, and infrastructures has fundamentally reshaped how machine learning systems are built and deployed. Federated Learning (FL) emerged as a response to this shift: a collaborative paradigm that allows models to be trained across multiple devices, institutions, and jurisdictions without pooling raw data in a central repository. By sharing only model updates rather than sensitive local datasets, FL promises a powerful compromise between utility and privacy. At the same time, this distributed and often opaque training ecosystem has opened a new and complex attack surface for adversarial actors. Data poisoning, backdoor insertion, gradient manipulation, membership inference, and Byzantine behaviors can quietly distort models, leak sensitive information, and undermine trust in AI-driven decision systems.

This edited volume, *Adversarial AI and Data Poisoning in Federated Learning*, is situated at the intersection of these two powerful forces: the need for scalable, privacy-preserving machine learning, and the growing sophistication of adversarial AI. Our aim is to provide a cohesive, multi-perspective treatment of how data poisoning and related adversarial threats manifest in FL; how they can be modeled, benchmarked, and mitigated; and how legal, business, and governance frameworks must evolve to support secure deployment. Collectively, the chapters in this book argue that security and robustness can no longer be treated as afterthoughts in FL they are foundational design requirements.

In the world today, FL is no longer an academic curiosity. It already underpins applications in healthcare consortia, financial fraud detection, smart transportation, edge intelligence, IoT ecosystems, and cross-organizational analytics. At the same time, governments and regulators are enforcing stricter data protection regimes, from GDPR and HIPAA to emerging AI-specific regulations and data protection acts across multiple jurisdictions. Organizations are under pressure to leverage data collaboratively while simultaneously minimizing privacy risk, ensuring compliance, and preserving digital sovereignty. FL appears to offer a way forward—but adversarial AI threatens to erode both its technical guarantees and its social license. Poisoned contributions from a subset of clients can bias models, degrade performance for specific subgroups, or embed stealthy behaviors that only activate in certain contexts. Meanwhile, inference attacks challenge the assumption that model updates alone are harmless.

Against this backdrop, the present volume positions itself as a timely resource. It not only explains how adversarial threats operate in federated settings, but also demonstrates how sector-specific requirements such as safety and ethics in healthcare, fairness and resilience in finance, and transparency in public-sector systems shape our response to these threats. The book will be particularly useful to researchers and graduate students in machine learning, security, and distributed systems; practitioners and architects designing FL platforms; data scientists and AI engineers working on privacy-preserving analytics; and policy makers, regulators, and legal scholars seeking to understand how technical architectures intersect with accountability, auditability, and governance. It may also serve as a reference for industry leaders and decision-makers exploring collaborative AI strategies that must remain robust in adversarial environments.

The structure of the book is deliberately progressive. Each chapter makes a distinct contribution, and together they form a coherent narrative that moves from foundational concepts and threat models to concrete defenses, domain-specific deployments, and legal and regulatory perspectives.

CHAPTER OVERVIEW

Chapter 1 introduces Federated Learning and its threat landscape, offering a conceptual and practical foundation for the entire volume. It explains how FL arose in response to decentralized data on mobile devices, edge sensors, and distributed systems, and how its promise of keeping data local addresses key privacy, legal, and bandwidth constraints. At the same time, the authors show that this distributed architecture gives rise to a new set of threats including poisoning attacks, inference leakage, free-riding, and Byzantine behavior that challenge the reliability and stability of federated models. This chapter provides readers with an accessible yet rigorous overview of FL architectures, real-world applications, and core security challenges, effectively bridging the gap between high-level motivation and the technical realities of building scalable and trustworthy FL systems.

Chapter 2 deepens the discussion by providing a focused overview of adversarial AI and data poisoning in Federated Learning. It reviews the taxonomy of attacks that adversaries can mount in decentralized environments, highlighting label-flipping, gradient manipulation, and backdoor embedding as particularly pernicious strategies. The chapter emphasizes how these attacks can subtly corrupt training data or model updates, often evading naïve anomaly detection. It then surveys current defense directions such as robust aggregation, anomaly detection schemes, differential privacy, and blockchain-based auditability. By doing so, it equips readers with a conceptual map of the adversarial landscape in FL and underscores why understanding these mechanisms is essential for building secure systems in healthcare, finance, IoT, and beyond.

Chapter 3 examines architectural models and security considerations for Federated Learning in depth. Moving beyond the canonical centralized aggregation setup, the authors explore cross-device, cross-silo, hierarchical, and decentralized architectures, showing how each introduces different constraints and vulnerabilities. They analyze the impact of non-IID data, partial client participation, and adversarial manipulation, and compare multiple aggregation paradigms, from statistical and trust-based strategies to spectral, inversion-guided, and cryptographic approaches. The chapter's value lies in its careful treatment of trade-offs among robustness, privacy, efficiency, and scalability, culminating in a discussion of hybrid architectures that integrate secure computation, blockchain-based trust, and ethical governance to support resilient federated ecosystems.

Chapter 4 shifts the lens to edge computing and its security concerns in federated AI systems. As FL is increasingly deployed on heterogeneous edge devices with volatile connectivity and limited resources, the attack surface broadens. The chapter analyzes the inherent risks of edge environments including model inversion, data poisoning, man-in-the-middle attacks, and adversarial manipulation driven by physical or network constraints. It also surveys architectural responses and mitigation strategies designed specifically for federated learning at the edge, and systematically evaluates trade-offs between latency, accuracy, trust, and privacy. This chapter is particularly relevant for practitioners building FL systems on IoT, mobile, and embedded platforms.

Chapter 5 narrows this focus further by examining label-flipping attacks and presenting the MSCD-FL framework as a defense. It systematically assesses manifold learning, clustering, and dimensionality reduction techniques such as UMAP, K-Means, PCA, and KPCA for their ability to detect and mitigate label-based poisoning. After identifying their limitations, the chapter introduces a Multi-Stage Clustering and Data Quality Filtering (MSCDFL) approach that integrates adaptive clustering, data quality scoring, delta-based update analysis, and trimmed mean aggregation. Experimental results demonstrate that MSCDFL maintains robustness and predictive performance even under heavy adversarial presence, making this chapter a key reference for readers interested in concrete, empirically validated defenses.

Chapter 6 addresses a subtle but crucial tension: how to build poisoning-resilient FL systems under strict privacy constraints. As techniques like identity obfuscation, attribute randomization, synthetic data, encrypted aggregation, and secure computation become more prevalent, they can obscure visibility into individual contributions and complicate the detection of malicious behavior. This chapter proposes a multi-layer defense framework comprising input sanitation, update filtering, privacy-sensitive robust aggregation, and post-aggregation audits. By articulating realistic threat and privacy models and outlining an experimental plan in heterogeneous, high-privacy settings, the authors make an important contribution to reconciling privacy and robustness two objectives often seen as being at odds.

Chapter 7 turns to the healthcare domain, where FL has high potential and high stakes. The authors analyze how strict privacy regulations and ethical obligations motivate the adoption of FL in hospitals and research institutions, while simultaneously amplifying new attack surfaces. They focus on membership inference attacks and data poisoning in federated healthcare systems, critically evaluating the suitability of existing defenses and proposing a roadmap for building robust, secure, and trustworthy healthcare FL pipelines. The chapter is especially impactful for readers working at the intersection of clinical AI, privacy, and safety-critical systems.

Chapter 8 explores Federated Adversarial Transfer Learning (FATL), a novel fusion of transfer learning and federated learning that allows knowledge transfer from related tasks in low-data regimes. The authors review potential applications and then candidly examine how adversarial examples, model poisoning, and backdoor attacks alter the dynamics of transfer in a federated environment. Through literature review and threat modeling, they show that while FATL can significantly improve generalization and convergence, it also introduces new risks when source models or datasets cannot be fully trusted. The chapter highlights the limitations of conventional FL defenses in adversarial transfer settings, underscoring the need for tailored protection mechanisms.

Chapter 9 provides a comprehensive taxonomy of defense strategies for FL models targeted by data poisoning attacks. The authors group attacks and defenses systematically, covering data-level filtering, robust aggregation algorithms, anomaly detection, adversarial training, and privacy-based methods like differential privacy. They analyze algorithms such as Krum, Bulyan, and trimmed mean, along with client reputation systems, and validate their effectiveness through case studies and simulation. Importantly, the chapter discusses practical challenges including scalability, trade-offs between robustness and accuracy, and the need for adaptive defenses, making it a practical guide for practitioners.

Chapter 10 investigates the use of Secure Multi-Party Computation (SMPC) to strengthen FL against adversarial attacks. While FL already promotes data locality, SMPC introduces additional cryptographic guarantees that prevent disclosure of sensitive information during model aggregation. The authors categorize attack impacts, outline architectures for SMPC-based FL, and compare these to traditional FL from the perspectives of security, communication overhead, and computational cost. By including examples from healthcare and industrial IoT, as well as a discussion of scalability and current limitations, the chapter provides a balanced view of SMPC as a robust yet non-trivial defense mechanism.

Chapter 11 emphasizes the role of auditing, logging, and explainable AI in securing FL systems. It argues that in a decentralized, privacy-preserving context, transparency and traceability become crucial tools for detecting anomalies and supporting accountability. The chapter examines how techniques like SHAP can render federated models more interpretable and help identify adversarially induced shifts in behavior. In parallel, it discusses how structured logs and secure audit trails enable forensic analysis and real-time anomaly detection in training pipelines. Together, these elements form a socio-technical layer of defense that complements purely algorithmic approaches.

Chapter 12 offers a benchmarking study of federated learning frameworks under adversarial conditions. The authors propose evaluation methodologies based on certification matrices and attack simulations, highlighting how different frameworks respond to poisoning, Byzantine failures, and privacy attacks. Their results reveal trade-offs among security, measurement fidelity, and efficiency, and they discuss associated defense techniques such as robust consolidation, discrepancy detection, differential privacy, and adversarial training. The inclusion of healthcare, finance, and IoT case studies grounds the analysis in realistic deployments and identifies open challenges that must be addressed for trusted FL adoption.

Chapter 13 introduces a quantitative risk assessment framework tailored to FL. Focusing on attack success rate, availability degradation, and model integrity loss, the authors define and evaluate metrics that enable systematic measurement of adversarial impact. They illustrate how these indicators can be used alongside robust aggregation and anomaly detection techniques to monitor and mitigate risks in practice. This chapter thus equips researchers and practitioners with conceptual and practical tools for risk-informed design and continuous security assessment in federated environments.

Chapter 14 returns to the healthcare space, this time focusing on medical diagnostics. The chapter illustrates how FL can transform diagnostic workflows by allowing multiple institutions to train shared models without ever exchanging patient data. Using chronic kidney disease detection as an example, the authors show how FL can preserve both predictive performance and interpretability, particularly when coupled with explainable AI techniques such as SHAP and LIME. They also frame a broader ethical and regulatory context, proposing a framework for privacy-preserving, transparent, and clinically reliable AI in medicine.

Chapter 15 examines how adversarially robust FL can secure financial applications, where data sensitivity and regulatory pressure are especially acute. The authors discuss how FL can support fraud detection, credit scoring, and payment authentication while reducing the risks associated with centralized data storage. They explore defense strategies such as robust aggregation, differential privacy, encryption, blockchain integration, and adversarial training, and they point to future directions involving explainable AI, trust layers, and quantum-safe cryptography. This chapter is pivotal for financial institutions seeking to leverage federated models while maintaining resilience against increasingly sophisticated adversaries.

Chapter 16 broadens the lens to general business decision-making in the data-driven enterprise. It explains how secure federated learning (SFL) can enable organizations to jointly train models with partners, subsidiaries, or industry peers without exposing proprietary or sensitive information. The chapter outlines key principles of SFL, the roles of differential privacy and encryption, and practical deployment architectures. Real-world examples illustrate how SFL can overcome barriers to data sharing and compliance, enabling richer analytics and more informed strategic decisions.

Chapter 17 presents a unified examination of data poisoning across government, retail, transportation, environmental, and educational systems. It extends the conversation beyond traditional domains like healthcare and finance, showing how poisoning threats manifest through manipulated civic submissions, fake reviews, traffic spoofing, sensor corruption, and compromised assessment data. The authors propose a cross-domain taxonomy and analyze black-box and clean-label poisoning, as well as mitigation and detection methods. This chapter's contribution is its holistic view of poisoning risks across large-scale, public-facing data pipelines and its guidance for improving resilience in complex, socio-technical ecosystems.

Chapter 18 focuses on collaboration business models and frameworks in FL. Recognizing that FL is not only a technical architecture but also an organizational and economic construct, the chapter examines platform-based ecosystems, consortia, and cross-industry partnerships. It highlights how these models can create value while also introducing new vulnerabilities via gradient manipulation and model misuse. The authors discuss technical, organizational, and ethical safeguards—including robust aggregation, blockchain-based traceability, human-in-the-loop supervision, and regulatory compliance—to build safe, flexible, and trustworthy federated ecosystems.

Chapter 19 addresses legal and policy considerations in adversarial Federated Learning. It tackles the opacity–auditability paradox that arises when privacy-preserving architectures obscure traditional accountability mechanisms. Through comparative analysis of GDPR, HIPAA, the EU AI Act, India's DPDP Act, and regional frameworks such as ADHICS, the authors identify gaps in how current regulations interpret and govern distributed AI. They propose an accountability model grounded in verifiable cryptographic artifacts and evidence-based verification, along with tools like conformity assessments and standard contractual clauses. This chapter is essential reading for anyone concerned with how legal, technical, and institutional mechanisms must co-evolve.

Chapter 20 synthesizes emerging research challenges, legal frameworks, and real-world insights in secured FL. It reviews methods such as differential privacy, homomorphic encryption, SMPC, and Byzantine-resilient aggregation, and evaluates their effectiveness from both technical and governance perspectives. Ethical principles—fairness, explainability, and accountability—are linked to regulatory developments and real-world platforms such as EXAM and FATE. By connecting technical innovations with institutional and global trends, this chapter provides a forward-looking perspective on the evolution of secure and trustworthy federated learning.

Chapter 21 concludes the volume with real-world case studies of data poisoning attacks in FL applications. Through examples from healthcare, finance, IoT, and autonomous vehicles, the authors illustrate how malicious participants manipulate local data or updates, how these attacks manifest in performance degradation or integrity loss, and what practical lessons can be learned. The chapter identifies recurring patterns and vulnerabilities across domains and proposes mitigation strategies grounded in empirical experience. It thus brings full circle the themes of the book, grounding theoretical insights in lived practice.

Taken together, the chapters in *Adversarial AI and Data Poisoning in Federated Learning* offer a comprehensive and multi-layered perspective on one of the most pressing challenges in modern AI. The volume moves from foundational understanding and threat taxonomies to advanced cryptographic defenses, sector-specific frameworks, benchmarking and risk assessment, and legal and policy architectures. It demonstrates that securing FL is not merely an algorithmic problem but a socio-technical one, requiring coordinated advances in system design, governance, regulation, and organizational practice.

We hope this book will serve as a valuable resource for those designing the next generation of federated systems, for researchers pushing the boundaries of adversarial robustness, and for stakeholders charged with ensuring that collaborative AI remains fair, accountable, and trustworthy. By consolidating diverse perspectives and contributions, this volume aspires to shape both the research agenda and the practical deployment of secure Federated Learning in the years to come.

Chapter 1
Introduction to Federated Learning and Threat Landscape

Rakesh Kumar Saxena
https://orcid.org/0000-0002-6453-6053
Poornima University, India

Shikha Khullar
https://orcid.org/0009-0000-5598-3145
Poornima University, India

ABSTRACT

Federated Learning (FL), a collaborative machine learning paradigm that allows model training across multiple devices without centralized data aggregation, was developed in response to the exponential growth of decentralized data across mobile devices, edge sensors, and distributed systems. By limiting sharing to model updates and preserving sensitive user data locally, FL overcomes important privacy, legal, and bandwidth restrictions. However, new and advanced security threats are introduced by this distributed and privacy-aware architecture. These can compromise the reliability and effectiveness of federated models and include poisoning attacks, inference leakage, free-riding, and Byzantine behavior. This chapter provides overview of FL with real-world applications. The chapter is designed to provide readers with a solid knowledge base on the opportunities and challenges in the construction of reliable, scalable, and elastic FL systems, eliminating the gap between the Federated Model design and thoughtfulness.

1. MOTIVATION FOR PRIVACY-PRESERVING MACHINE LEARNING

Machine learning (ML) models have been implemented into the most important programs surrounding healthcare, money, transportation, and individual devices, in the era of massive data and everywhere connectivity. Such models rely on using the information about personal and sensitive, to learn patterns and to make intelligent decisions. Nevertheless, the conventional model training patterns, where raw data

DOI: 10.4018/979-8-3373-6224-3.ch001

is gathered in centralized servers have elicited a lot of concern over the issue of data privacy, ownership, legal compliance and security vulnerabilities.

The possibilities of privacy-oriented issues have been revealed by scandals related to data abuse, such as Cambridge Analytica Event, the General Data Protection Regulation (GDPR), and Health Insurance Portability and Accountability Act (HIPAA). In this sense, Federated Learning (FL) can be viewed as a revolutionary one since it is concerned with model decentralization of data concentrations; data owners keep control without losing it and are involved in the model development (Yang et al., 2019). However, the traditional model training paradigm, which involves aggregating raw data into centralized servers, has raised significant concerns about data privacy, ownership, legal compliance, and security vulnerabilities.

1.1 Centralized vs. Decentralized Paradigm of Learning

The classic ML pipelines are based on the central architecture where the data collected of various sources are uploaded to the central server to train. Although it is effective with regard to the computation and convergence, this method presents several problems:

- Data storage is centralized, which exposes it to privacy threats.
- Overhead on communication in sending massive data.
- Cross-border data transfer legal limitations.
- Single point of failure and this makes it an easy target to attacks

The concept of Federated Learning is an instance of decentralized learning. In FL, model training is locally executed in edge devices or clients and only model updates (e.g., Gradients or Weight) are exchanged with an aggregator at the center. Raw data does not go beyond its origin thus minimizing the surface of the attack and adhering to the data protection laws. This is a collaborative learning model that uses distributed computational capabilities and guarantees a trade-off between the utility of models and the confidentiality of data (K. Bonawitz et al., 2019; P. Kairouz et al.,2021).

1.2 Evolution of Federated Learning

Federated Learning is a concept proposed by Google in 2016 to enhance the mobile services without interfering with the privacy of the user. It was implemented in one of the first major applications on the on-device keyboard of Google which used FL to customize instructions without sending user data to the cloud (McMahan et al., 2017). Since then, FL has developed rapidly and has gained traction in the education and industry. Its foundation is in optimization, multi-task learning, and privacy enhancements such as secure consolidation, differential privacy, and homomorphic encryption. Today, FL is not just a theoretical concept-it is a basic technique for privacy-aware AI and collaborative intelligence.

Some Federated optimization algorithms, such as FedAVG, Fedprox, and Fednova, have been suggested to withstand unique challenges in FL, such as non-IID (non-relaxation and similarly distributed) data, client infertility, and limited communication. (Li, Sahu et al., 2020; Li, Huang et al., 2020). Moreover, its applicable domains, autonomous driving, smart manufacturing, and financial fraud, have been expanded to various domains.

1.3 Applications Across Industries

The privacy-lifting and decentralized features of federated learning make it ideal for numerous real-world applications:

Healthcare: Enables collaborative training of diagnostic models in hospitals without sharing sensitive patient data. For example, multiple hospitals can train the Deep learning model for cancer investigations from radiology images, ensuring HIPAA compliance
Finance: FL can be used by banks and fintech firms to assess the fraud trends in various. branches without exposing transaction level information, hence keeping customers confidential and addressing the regulatory needs

The internet of things and edge devices: Edge devices FL is perfectly compatible with resource-constrained environments, like wearables, autonomous vehicles, and smartphones. It enables real time sensor learning. data, and minimizing cloud reliance whilst protecting information belonging to the user.

Smart Cities: Urban infrastructure systems (e.g., traffic sensors, surveillance cameras) can be used FL for predictive maintenance and surveillance analytics without centralization of confidential civic data. (Chen et al., 2017).
Retail and Marketing: Retailers can mutually train models on sales samples to predict customer trends ensuring competitive data isolation and privacy

The emergence of Federated Learning is a paradigm shift to the way; intelligent systems are built and deployed. FL provides an opportunity to ensure data privacy, which is a more serious issue now. ethernet and ethically viable method of collaborative learning. However, while FL provides strong privacy guarantees, its distributed nature also opens up new threat surfaces, which will be explored in later sections of this chapter.

1.4 Summary of Chapter Structure

In this chapter, we first present an introduction and motivation for privacy preserving Machine learning. Thereafter evolution of federated learning. In Section 2, we have presented fundamentals of federated learning with its architecture and related components. Various types of federated learning and challenges in federated learning also be presented in this section. Section 3 is based on Threat landscape in federated learning which include classification of threats, attacks surfaces in federated learning, Adversary models and various real world attacks scenario. Various types of attacks in federated learning like poisoning attacks, Inference attacks, Free riding and Drop out attacks, Sybil Attacks and Collusion and Byzantine Failures are presented in section 4. In Section 5, Defense Mechanisms and Mitigation Strategies. Section 6 gives Real-World Applications and Case Studies in federated learning. In this section challenges observed in real deployments has also been explained. Finally, chapter has been concluded with future direction which has been presented in last section.

2. FUNDAMENTALS OF FEDERATED LEARNING

The Federated Learning (FL) presents an example of how the machine is trained in the delivered privacy-sensitive environment. Unlike traditional machine learning, which requires data centralization in one place, FL distributes the training process to multiple customers (devices or organizations), as shown in figure 1, ensuring that sensitive data remains localized. This section detects practical bases and practical composition of FL systems, highlights components, optimization strategies, and various forms in which FL can be applied.

Figure 1. FL architecture

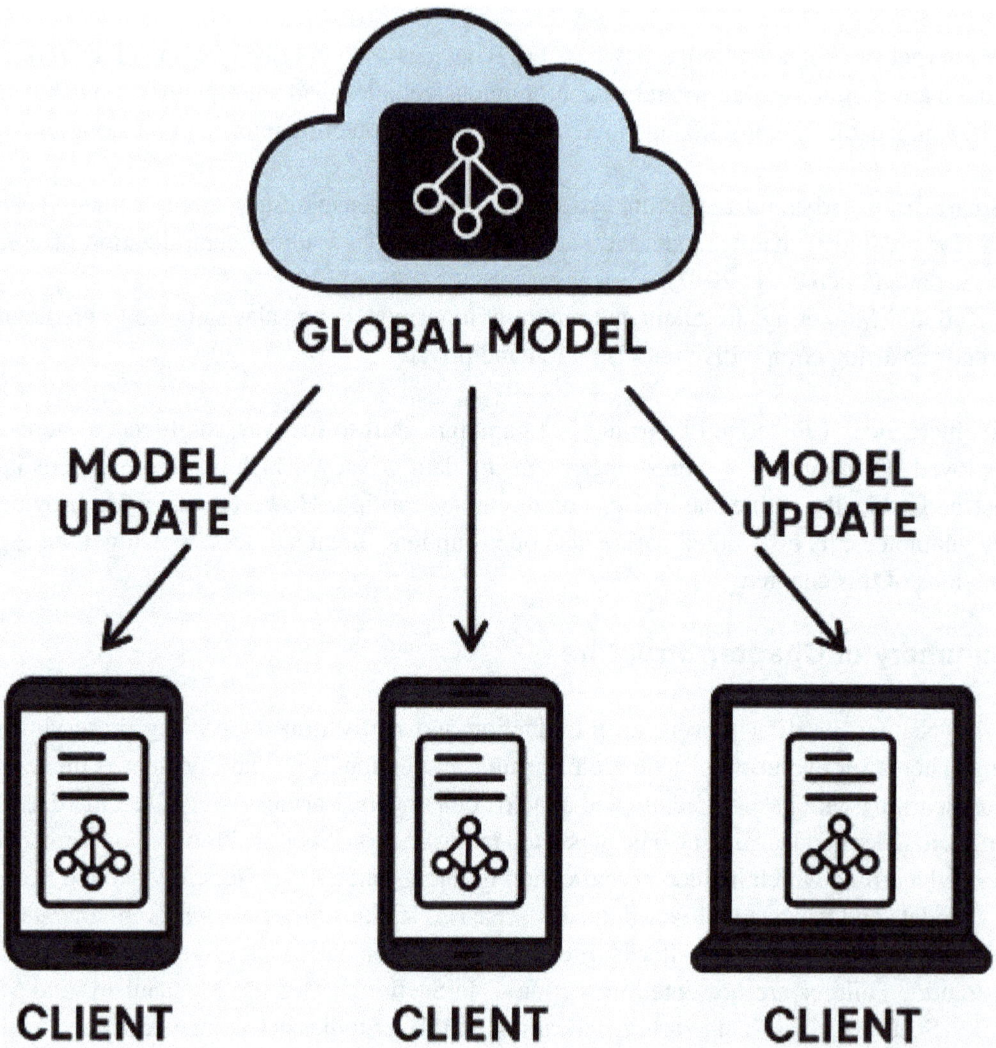

2.1 FL System Architecture and its Components

At its root, the federated learning system consists of two main entities: the central server and the customers (which can be smartphones, hospitals, IoT devices, or any data holders). The server model coordinates the training process, while the clients train the model locally using their own data and send the model updates (such as the gradients of weight) back to the server.

The general lifecycle of FL consists of the following iterative steps as shown in Figure 2:

Figure 2. General life cycle of FL

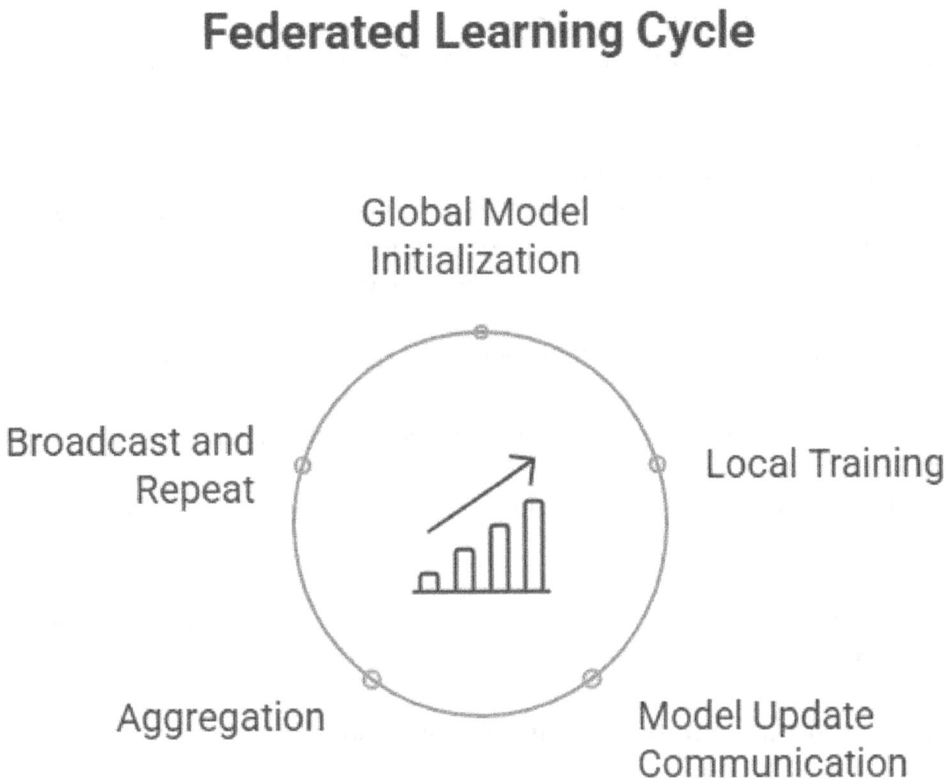

1. Global Model Initial: The Central Server starts the global model and sends it to the customer's selected subset.
2. Local Training: Each client updates the model through many ages of training sessions using its own local dataset.

3. Model Update Communication: Clients send their trained model updates (not raw data) back to the server.
4. Broadcasting and Repeat: The new global model is re-distributed to customers, and the process continues.

This cycle may be repeated for hundreds of communication rounds until model convergence is achieved (H. B. McMahan et al., 2017; K. Bonawitz et al., 2019).

2.2 Federated Averaging and Optimization Strategies

The most commonly used algorithm in the FL is the Federated Average (FedAvg), represented by McMahan et al. in 2017. In this method, each participant client takes multiple local stochastic gradient descent (SGD) steps before sending its model update to the server. The server then averages all received updates for the construction of a new global model.

To define FedAvg, let w be the global model parameters. Each client or its local data counts w_k based on D_k. Server aggregates and updates as:

$$w_{t+1} = \sum_{k=1}^{k} \frac{n_k}{n} w_k$$

where n_k is the number of local data points at client k, and $n = \sum_{k=1}^{k} n_k$

While the FedAvg is simple and efficient, it assumes that the client data is freely and evenly distributed (IID), which is rarely the case in real-world FL applications. To consider these non-IID and heterogeneous conditions, several extensions have been suggested, including:

- FedProx: Presents a proximity to limiting local updates, reducing diversion in non-IID settings (T Li et.al. 2020).
- Fednova: Normalizes updates to customers of various local epochs and batch size (J. Wang et al., 2020).
- SCAFFOLD: Uses a control variable to correct the drift introduced by client-specific updates (S. Karimireddy et al., 2020).

These Optimizers balance the accuracy, conversion speed, and communication functionality in the federated settings.

2.3 Client Selection, Communication, and Aggregation

In practice, not all clients participate in every communication round due to limited computational power (e.g., smartphones), intermittent connectivity, and battery constraints. To handle this, client selection mechanisms are used to randomly or strategically choose a subset of available clients for each round. Communication is a critical bottleneck in FL. Since the models may be large, sending them over limited-bandwidth networks (especially in edge computing scenarios) can introduce latency. Strategies like update compression, quantization, and sparsification have been proposed to reduce communication overhead (Sun et al., 2021).

The server aggregation stage should also be sound. Apart from simple averaging developed methods:(FedAvg), such sophisticated methods as median, trimmed mean and Krum have been proposed, to be able to tolerate faulty clients. In Section 5, it will be referred to in more detail.

2.4 Types of Federated Learning: Horizontal, Vertical, and Transfer

Federated Learning can be classified into Horizontal, Vertical and Transfer, upon which is founded, how information is divided up between clients. Security presents difficulties with each type, communication, as well as model fusion strategies.

i. Horizontal Federated Learning (HFL): The client shares the same feature datasets, however there are various user samples. This is common in the environment such as mobile keyboard forecasts, in which the data structure of all devices is identical (HB. McMohan et al., 2017).
ii. Vertical Federated Learning (VFL): Clients have similar user base but not equal feature spaces. Indicatively, the banks and hospitals may cooperate during the investigation of the fraud where the user identity is the same and the types of data are different. VFL often requires entity configuration protocol and cryptographic protection (Yang et al., 2019).
iii. Federated Transfer Learning (FTL): The samples and features of data are fed when the data is dissimilar among consumers. In this case, the transfer learning methodologies are used to match knowledge across domains. FTL is useful in case the data is dispersed or heterogeneous (Yang et al., 2019).

Table 1. Types of federated learning

Aspect	Vertical Federated Learning	Horizontal Federated Learning	Federated Transfer Learning
Data Partitioning	Same users, different feature spaces	Same feature space, different user samples	Different users and different feature spaces
Example	Collaboration between a bank and a hospital for fraud detection or health-finance insights (Yang et al., 2019)	Mobile keyboard prediction (e.g., Gboard) (B. McMahan et.al., 2017)	Cross-domain collaboration when datasets are small, sparse, or heterogeneous (Yang et al., 2019)
Entity Overlap	Full overlap in users, little/no overlap in features	No overlap in users, high overlap in features	Little/no overlap in both users and features
Security Requirement	Strong cryptographic protection (e.g., secure multi-party computation, homomorphic encryption)	Secure aggregation, differential privacy	Combination of cryptography + domain adaptation to ensure privacy and transferability
Communication Complexity	High (due to entity alignment and cryptographic protocols)	Moderate	Very High (involves both domain adaptation and secure knowledge transfer)
Alignment Requirement	Requires entity alignment protocols (to match the same users across organizations)	No entity alignment needed	Requires transfer learning techniques to map knowledge across domains
Challenges	Complex entity alignment, high computational cost, and privacy concerns	Handling non-IID data (different users produce diverse data)	Hardest to implement; requires advanced transfer learning and privacy-preserving methods
Advantages	Allows organizations with complementary data to collaborate without sharing raw data	Simple to implement, well-suited for large-scale distributed systems	Enables knowledge sharing across domains when data distributions differ drastically

2.5 Challenges in Federated Learning

Federated education though it has its advantages is fraught with its practical difficulties

- Statistical Heterogeneity: In practice, the data of clients are non-IID which produces gradients that are not consistent and decelerates the convergence.
- System Heterogeneity: Clients can be very different in terms of computation, memory and connectivity. Scalability depends on management of such diversity.
- Communication Efficiency: Rapid communication is often expensive and sometimes inappropriate, especially in low-bandwidth or high-latency networks. Thus, reducing the size of the model and the frequency of communication is the ongoing area of optimization.
- Fairness: Models trained on unbalanced data can underperform for customers with small datasets or underrepresented groups. Ensuring fairness in model updates and performance distribution is an open research problem (Mohri et. al., 2019).

3. THREAT LANDSCAPE IN FEDERATED LEARNING

Despite its promise for privacy and decentralized intelligence, federated learning is not immune to security risks. In fact, its distributed architecture, the dependence on limited visibility in client behavior and communication on incredible networks, makes FL very sensitive to the vector of novel attacks. Unlike traditional ML systems that are based on secure data centers, FL works in a setting where both customers and communication channels come in contact with passive and active competitors. This section offers a wide glimpse of the threatening landscape around FL, starting with the classification of threats, then discussing attack surfaces, and reviewing rival models that challenge the integrity, secrecy, and availability of federated systems.

3.1 Classification of Threats: CIA Triad

The security and reliability of any system are usually evaluated using the CIA Triad:

1. **Confidentiality** - ensures that sensitive information, such as the private data residing on client devices or the specifics of the model parameters being trained, is not disclosed to unauthorized entities. In FL, confidentiality is the cornerstone of the entire paradigm. The primary threat in this domain involves inference attacks, where adversaries attempt to reverse-engineer private training data by analyzing the model updates shared during the learning process (Mohamed, 2025). For example, a malicious central server or a compromised participant could execute membership inference attacks to determine whether a specific individual's data was used in a training round, or even reconstruct features of the raw data, thereby violating the fundamental privacy promise of FL.
2. **Integrity** - ensures that data or model updates are not tampered with or maliciously altered by an adversary. Integrity in FL is crucial for producing an accurate and reliable global model. This principle is primarily challenged by poisoning attacks, which aim to corrupt the training process. An attacker can perform data poisoning by injecting mislabeled or malicious samples into a local dataset, or execute model poisoning by crafting and submitting malicious model updates designed to

introduce a backdoor, degrade the model's performance on specific tasks, or cause it to misclassify certain inputs as directed by the adversary.

3. **Availability** - ensures that the system operates reliably and remains resistant to disruption or denial of service efforts. The availability of the FL system is critical for the model to converge and be useful. Threats in this category seek to disrupt or completely halt the training process. These include Byzantine failures, where compromised clients send corrupted or nonsensical updates that disrupt the server's aggregation algorithm (Z. Li et. al. 2021). Another significant threat is the Sybil attack, where an adversary creates a large number of pseudonymous client identities. By controlling a substantial fraction of the participants, the attacker can overpower the contributions from honest clients, degrade the final model's performance, or prevent the model from converging altogether (Sun et al., 2021).

3.2 Federated Learning Attack Surfaces

In a federated learning workflow, several components can be exploited by attackers. These attack surfaces expand the threat model beyond traditional server-centric ML to a multi-agent adversarial environment, requiring new defense paradigms.

1. Client Devices: FL clients may be hacked to spill local training information, transmit modified updates, or engage in collusion.
2. Communication Channels: Man in the middle attack or eavesdropping may take place when transmitting updates in the models.
3. Aggregation Server: In case the central server is corrupted or distrusted, it can leak updates, change aggregation policies, or prefer special customers.
4. Aggregation Logic: An attack on update fusion mechanism can be performed by submitting thoughtfully designed dangerous gradients to control or disorganize the international model (Pillutla et al., 2021).

3.3 Adversary Models

To understand the threat landscape in FL, it is essential to classify adversaries based on their capabilities and goals. The most commonly studied models are as follows.

I Honest-but Curious Adversaries: These entities properly follow the FL protocol, but try to estimate private information from the received model updates. For example, a righteous agrigator can inactively rebuild local training data using model inversion techniques.

II. Malicious Adversaries: These artists are actively distracted by the protocol to injure harmful updates, perform poison attacks, or distort the model. Their purpose is to reduce accuracy or enter the backdoors hidden in the model.

III. Byzantine Adversaries: In the name of the problem of Byzantine generals, these rivals behave arbitrarily or mistakenly, individually or in groups. They can send random, old, or strategically opposite updates to cause model diversion or instability.

The role of the attacker may be of a client, server, or external network-based opponent. Moreover, opponents can act independently or in collaboration, significantly enhancing the complexity of the investigation and embodiment.

3.4 Real-World Attack Scenarios

The theoretical threats to Federated Learning are not merely abstract possibilities; recent studies and experiments have demonstrated their practical feasibility and potential severity. These real-world demonstrations highlight critical vulnerabilities in the FL pipeline, showing how malicious actors can compromise the core principles of confidentiality, integrity, and availability.

- Confidentiality Breaches via Model Inversion: A fundamental privacy guarantee of FL is that raw data are never transmitted outside of the client machine. Nevertheless, studies have verified that even the sensitive information may still be leaked through the shared model updates. During models inversion and gradient leakage attacks, adversaries have been able to reconstruct high-fidelity data samples by examining the gradients provided at training. As an example, scholars could reconstruct recognizable images of handwritten digits in the MNIST dataset and detailed faces in the CelebA dataset, with only the gradient updates (Nasr et al., 2019; Zhu et al., 2019). The attacks demonstrate that even anonymized and aggregated updates can unintentionally disclose sensitive characteristics of the privative training data, which is a considerable confidentiality threat.
- Integrity Corruption via Backdoor Poisoning: Poisoning attacks are a direct attack that jeopardizes the integrity of the global model. A well-known attack here is the backdoor poisoning attack, in which an attacker with control over one or more clients purposefully injects a poisonous trigger into the model. These malicious clients train their local models on data where a specific feature (e.g., a small pixel pattern in images, a particular phrase in text) is consistently associated with an incorrect target label. A featured demonstration showed how compromised clients could insert a backdoor, causing the aggregated global model to misclassify any input containing the trigger while maintaining high accuracy on all other data. This allows an attacker to make the model fail in specific, predictable ways (E. Bagdasaryan et al., 2018).
- Availability Disruption via Sybil Attacks: Finally, Sybil-based collusion attacks can undermine both the integrity and availability of the FL system. In this scenario, an adversary creates a large number of pseudonymous "Sybil" clients, amplifying their influence over the training process. By controlling a substantial fraction of the participants in a given round, a group of adversarial clients can easily dominate the aggregation process. This enables them to either impose a harmful bias in the global model or submit updates designed to prevent the model's performance from improving, effectively halting convergence and making the system unavailable for legitimate users (Fung et al., 2018).

These examples highlight the fact that in the situations when FL does not allow sharing of raw data, privacy and security cannot be ensured by default. Even the techniques of preserving privacy such as local updates and partial inspection can be abused by the civilized opponents. The peculiarity of the FL operational structure presents a long and many-threaded landscape. Although FL solves a lot of the classical privacy problems, it poses new threats where new security needs models of models, threatening framework, and coercive ways of consolidation.

4. TYPES OF ATTACKS IN FEDERATED LEARNING

This segment gives an account of the kind of particular attacks that emerge in the FL environment, such as poison, forecast, sybyl and dropout-based attacks. Federated Learning (FL) provides a variety of privacy advantages with design because it does not concentrate on raw user data. However, this decentralized setup introduces new weaknesses that cannot be addressed by traditional ML systems. Injections of anti-FL malicious behaviors can absorb both the training process and communication to exclude information, or to unstable the entire system. This section sees a systematic manner in the FL environment.

4.1. Poisoning Attacks

Poison attacks aim to corrupt the training process by introducing malicious data or replacing a model's learning behavior. These attacks can be categorized as follows:

a. Data Poisoning Attacks

In this form, an adversary modifies the training data on a compromised client device. The poisoned data leads to the learning of incorrect patterns, resulting in global model degradation. These attacks are often subtle, targeting statistical features or label distributions. For example, adding mislabeled examples such as classifying a cat image as a dog could, if repeated enough across clients, change the model's decision boundary (Y. Liu et.al., 2023).

b. Model Poisoning Attacks

In model poisoning, the adversary directly manipulates; this can be much more powerful than data poisoning, especially when the attacker has full control over gradient values. These attacks are frequently crafty, and evade simple authentication. One of the bright examples is the backdoor attack, in which malignant clients inject certain patterns in training images (e.g., a red square), practically causing the model to falsely label all such images when inference occurs, and is good overall prediction (E. Bagdasaryan et.al., 2018, Sun et al., 2021).

c. Backdoor Attacks

There is a special form of model poisoning, which is called backdoor attacks. The intruder installs a dormant. a "trigger" in the model, whereby, each time the trigger pattern is found in the input, the model. misclassifies it. As an illustration, pixel pattern insertion on handwritten numerals can lead to the FL trained model that it would forever appear as "8" despite what it is actually of (E. Bagdasaryan et.al., 2018).

4.2 Inference Attacks

FL does not provide access to raw data but the updates of the models may contain sensitive information. Inference attacks are used to take advantage of this weakness in order to reverse-engineer or infer private data.

a. Membership Inference Attacks

This may prove to be risky in sensitive areas such as the medical field where it may be necessary to establish whether a patient. Being involved in a study might expose individual conditions (R. Shokri et al., 2017).

b. Model Inversion Attacks

These attacks attempt to reconstruct original input samples (e.g., face images or health records) from model parameters or gradients shared during training. Such attacks have successfully reconstructed face-like images from gradients alone.

c. Gradient Leakage

In FL, clients share gradients or weight updates. Research has shown that even a single iteration of gradient sharing can leak substantial information about the original data. Tools like Deep Leakage from Gradients (DLG) can recover training samples, pixel by pixel, from just the shared gradients (Z. Zhu et.al., 2019).

4.3 Free-Riding and Dropout Attacks

a. Free-Riding

In FL, there are clients who can have training without making any calculation or contributing data. These clients make fabricated or old-fashioned updates and enjoy the enhanced global model. In the long term, free-riding will diminish the quality and fairness of the model, particularly in business FL systems in which the contribution is supposed to be compensated.

b. Dropout Attacks

Other clients simply switch-off or leave half-way through the training so as not to compute but nonetheless take the advantages of the last model. This causes imbalance in participation and effect on convergence rates, especially in cross-device FL, dropout rates are already elevated because of hardware or connection limitations (Mohri, G. et.al., 2019).

4.4 Sybil Attacks and Collusion

a. Sybil Attacks

One attacker manages several bogus clients (or "sybils") and overwhelms the system malicious updates. These customers can organize to increase the effects of the attack, such as, converting a poisoned model to a point of convergence or prevailing over the aggregation stage (Fung et al., 2018). Such an attack is especially harmful in cross-device FL, where the number of attackers may be hundreds or thousands of clients are involved, and it becomes harder to detect them.

b. Collusion Attacks

Multiple malicious clients collaborate and share their updates or learned knowledge to manipulate the model more effectively. In collusion scenarios, adversaries may simulate normal behavior in isolation but act collectively to distort the learning outcome.

Such collusion can bypass many detection algorithms, especially if they rely on individual anomaly detection without considering group behavior (Fung et al., 2018, Zhang et al., 2024).

c. Byzantine Failures

A Byzantine customer acts in an arbitrary fashion, either because of bugs, bugs, or malice. In the FL scenario, Byzantine clients are allowed to.

- Transmit randomly or obsolete gradients.
- Send asynchronous updates resulting in divergence.
- Switch between both normal and malicious behavior in order to evade detection.

These failures not only make the accuracy less but even destabilize or crash the learning process otherwise, these risks can be reduced (Blanchard et al., 2017). The Byzantine-tolerant aggregation strategies are created to deal with this menace. The taxonomy to attacks as discussed here shows that FL, although privacy-enhancing by design is not resistant to attacks. FL opens up because it is decentralized. It as far as advanced adversarial techniques that aim at confidentiality, integrity and availability. Before venturing into defense that is resistant to these threats, it is crucial to understand these threat vectors mechanisms, on which the following section will dwell.

Table 2. Summary of various types of attacks

Category of Attack	Attack Subtypes	Impact on Federated Learning	Objective/ Goal	Examples
Poisoning Attacks	Data Poisoning, Model Poisoning, Backdoor Attacks	Degrades global model accuracy; introduces hidden malicious behaviors	Corrupt training data or manipulate model updates	Mislabelling cat as dog (Data Poisoning) (Y. Liu et al., 2023]); Backdoor via red square trigger (X. Bagdasaryan et al., 2020)
Free-Riding & Dropout Attacks	Free-Riding Dropout	Reduces model quality; slows convergence	Exploit FL benefits without fair participation	Clients sending fake updates (H. Xie et al., 2021); deliberate dropout during training (M. Mohri et al., 2019)
Inference Attacks	Membership Inference, Model Inversion, Gradient Leakage	Breaches privacy, reconstructs original user data	Extract private/sensitive data from shared updates	Reconstructing face-like images from gradients (F. Zhang et al., 2019]); DLG recovering training samples (Z. Zhu et al., 2019)
Byzantine Failures	N/A	Causes divergence, instability, or system crash	Arbitrary faulty/ malicious behavior	Random or outdated gradients disrupting training (Blanchard et al., 2017)
Sybil & Collusion Attacks	Sybil Attacks, Collusion	Overwhelms aggregation, biases model outcome	Control multiple fake/ malicious clients; coordinate to manipulate aggregation	Multiple fake clients flooding updates (C. Fung et al., 2018)

5. DEFENSE MECHANISMS AND MITIGATION STRATEGIES

Federated Learning (FL) brings about a novel threat risk as discussed in the preceding section because of its distributed character. The conventional security systems fail to work as they are often inadequate. Systems are based on decentralized and commonly distrusted participants. To cope with these threats, different powerful defense procedures and mitigation strategies have been proposed. These strategies aim to increase the accuracy of the model or the security, privacy without significant degeneration of system scalability.

5.1 Robust Aggregation Algorithms

Attackers may send malicious or poisoned updates, which can significantly skew the global model. Robust aggregation algorithms are designed to minimize the influence of such outliers.

a. Krum

A client update that is closest to its neighbours (in Euclidean distance) is chosen by Krum, assuming that most clients are honest. It avoids averaging, thereby reducing the risk of being influenced by poisoned updates. This method is Byzantine-resilient but computationally intensive for large client pools (Blanchard et al., 2017).

b. Trimmed Mean and Median

These algorithms operate element-wise on model updates. Trimmed Mean excludes the highest and lowest values before averaging, while the Coordinate-wise Median takes the median of each model parameter. Both Methods are not very complex but effective at a few model poisoning attacks.

c. Multi-Krum

Multi-Krum which is an extension of Krum, picks a set of candidate updates to add to the set of updates. aggregating, scalability and preserving robustness (Blanchard et al., 2017).

5.2 Client-Level Anomaly Detection.

It is a necessary mitigation measure to acknowledge suspicious clients before combining their updates. Anomaly detection refers to analyzing metadata and the patterns of updates of clients.

a. Distance-Based Filtering

Euclidean or cosine distance measures can be used to filter clients whose updates greatly differ with the majority. These methods assume that the honest clients are prone to cluster whilst The opponents generate outliers (Sun et al., 2019).

b. Update Clustering

For cluster updates, machine learning algorithms (e.g., DBSCAN, K-Means) are used. Clusters that are not in the majority are rejected. This is able to detect colluding clients or Sybil attacks (Fung et al., 2018).

5.3 Differential Privacy

The addition of randomness is done by Differential Privacy (DP) before local changes are uploaded to the server, to ensure that it is hard to track individual data contributions.

a. Client-Level DP

Alternatively, its gradient updates are perturbed with a calibrated noise by each client, which implies privacy guarantees such as (**ε, δ**)-differential privacy. This will somewhat decrease model accuracy, but greatly defends against the membership inference and model inversion attacks (Papernot et al., 2017).

b. Server-Side DP

Aggression is noisier through the server and is not as efficient as client-side DP of privacy and computationally simpler in cross-device FL environments.

5.4 Secure Multiparty Computation

The privacy is assured with a combination of the roles on inputs by multiple parties to Secure Multiparty Competition (SMC). The whole model can be changed in FL applying SMC solutions without revealing any information on the server.

a. Additive Secret Sharing

Every client divides its updates into random shares and then distributes them with servers. No single update can be reconstructed by party without all the shares. This approach provides high cryptography privacy but with high overheads of communication (Bonawitz et al., 2017).

b. Threshold Homomorphic Encryption

Only when a number of parties collaborate, threshold plans allow the decryption. Although safe, this technique is better adapted to resource-intensive as well as cross-silo FL (Joy et al., 2013).

5.5 Trusted Execution Environments

Computations are performed in a safe setting courtesy of hardware-based isolation provided. Using dependable execution environments (TEE), e.g. Intel SGX. In FL, model aggregation can be executed safely within a TEE on the server so that updates can be confidential, even on the part of system administrators. Nevertheless, the TEEs are susceptible to side-channel need special hardware so they cannot be deployed in a heterogeneous environment (Ohrimenko et al., 2016).

5.6 Client Reputation and Incentive Mechanisms

FL systems can be used to deter free-riding and malicious behavior, which may be achieved by reputation scores or token-based incentives. In Reputation-Based Filtering system, the clients that had a history of suspicious behavior were excluded. updates are either heavily discounted or not counted in an aggregation process. And in Incentive Mechanisms, clients receive compensation (e.g., through the blockchain tokens or micro payments) according to contribution. such metrics as quality of updates or frequency of participation. These methods encourage fairness and uniformity among the customers but insist on sound metrics.

5.7 Federated Adversarial Training

Adversarial examples can be used to train FL models to increase their resilience to model evasion and poisoning. Clients create disturbed inputs that are similar to possible attacks during training, teaching the global model to learn strong frontiers. This is a resource consuming strategy and could enhance privacy hazards unless matched with privacy-saving solutions such as DP.

The threat surface in federated learning is increasing, which requires a complex defense. There is no uniform solution that can provide full protection, but a combination of a strong aggregation, privacy preserving, behavioral incentives, secure computation provides a effective defense. Due to the scale of FL systems in various devices and sensitive fields, the future work needs to be directed towards lightweight and adaptive defences that are consistent with privacy, fairness and performance goals.

6. REAL-WORLD APPLICATIONS AND CASE STUDIES IN FEDERATED LEARNING

The revolutionary pattern of the conceptual privacy-savvy framework, which has been implemented in many industries, has infected Federated Learning (FL). In a privacy-sensitive, data-consolidation, and regulatory-compliant setting, it can train machine learning models without relying on data. This section explores real-world applications and case studies that illustrate the practical utility, deployment challenges, and emerging success stories of Federated Learning (Banabilah et al., 2022).

6.1 Healthcare: Privacy-Preserving Medical AI

One of the most effective applications of FL is in the Healthcare Domain, where data privacy is governed by strict rules, such as HIPPA in U.S. and GDPR in Europe.

a. Cross-Institutional Disease Prediction

To develop a deep learning model for identifying diabetic retinopathy using retinal pictures from several institutions without centralizing patient data, Google Research teamed up with academic hospitals (Brisimi et al., 2018). This approach improved diagnostic accuracy while maintaining patient confidentiality.

b. Medical Imaging Federated Networks

The Federated Tumor Segmentation (FeTS) challenge, planned by the Medical Image Computing and Computer Assisted Intervention Society, promoted FL using MRI scans for brain tumor segmentation. Participating bodies trained models locally and only share updates (Sheller et al., 2020). Findings showed arousal of FL was equivalent to. centralized models, which demonstrate the feasibility of FL in the field of medical imaging.

c. COVID-19 X-Ray Diagnosis

In the COVID-19 pandemic, researchers tested FL in the training of chest X-ray image classifiers even in hospitals where no transferred sensitive information. This allowed rapid pandemic response in terms of collaborative learning (Wang et al., 2020).

6.2 Mobile and Edge Devices: Intelligent Services without Destroying User Data

One of the first smartphone applications to use FL was the Gboard keyboard app by Google.

a. Next Word Prediction

Gboard trained language models on next-word prediction using FL on millions of Android. devices. The training was done locally without violating the privacy of typing data of the users (H. B. McMahan et al., 2017). The system used such techniques as secure aggregation and on-device training to cut down on overheads of communication.

b. Speech and Voice Recognition.

IOS operating in Apple uses FL to enhance Siri speech recognition. By analyzing Apple can better its models by voice queries on-device as well as only sharing encrypted updates performance without endangering user identity and preferences (Apple, 2017).

6.3 Financial Services Risk prediction and fraud detection

Financial institutions deal with very sensitive transactional information. Federated Learning provides a working solution to fight fraud and enhance credit risk assessment, and not in violation of confidentiality (Pingulkar & Pawade, 2024).

a. Credit Scoring

It is possible to jointly train a model on forecasting loan default without exposing multiple banks customer financial history. This enables credit analysis to occur in an underrepresented data groups.

b. Federated Fraud Detection

ANT Financial (Alibaba Group) designed FL to locate cross-bank fraud patterns by using federated XGBUST models. This slowed the investigation of cheats rate but still retained the rate, compliance with regulations and financial privacy (Yang et al., 2019; Guembe et al., 2023).

6.4 Smart Manufacturing and Industrial IoT

The industrial settings produce vast amounts of sensor information on geographically distributed locations of machinery and systems. These can collaborate in intelligence through Federated Learning distributed nodes.

a. Predictive Maintenance

In FL based frameworks, Siemens has investigated machine learning models trained on a localized basis. equipment failure is anticipated by factory devices. Such models are pooled to generate national. local insights do not need the raw telemetry data to be sent to the cloud (Lu et al., 2022).

b. Optimization of Energy Efficiency

Smart grids use FL in optimization of power consumption and distribution among utility providers in addition ensuring the locality of user data. FL-based demand forecasting models decrease the energy wastage and enhance reliability (Gupta et al., 2023, Ali et al., 2025).

6.5 Smart Cities and Transportation

The urban infrastructural services can be improved with the help of Federated Learning through analysis of distribute sensor information without compromise of privacy.

a. Traffic Flow Prediction

Municipalities utilize FL to anticipate traffic congestion with reference to information of different intersections and vehicle types. Co-operation without sharing sensitive geo-location information between smart traffic lights and other transport agencies is useful in the optimization of traffic control in the city (Kheder & Mohammed, 2024).

b. Autonomous Vehicles

Companies like Tesla are investigating in FL in autonomous driving. On-board cameras and real-time driving information is used to train perception and decision-making models using sensors. The federated updates are transmitted to central servers, which allows continuous learning of fleet data and does not sacrifice the privacy of the driver (Caldas et al., 2018).

6.6 E-Learning Systems and Education

In online learning systems, the privacy issue does not allow aggregation of user interaction information in various institutions or applications i.e. Personalized Learning Recommendations. FL is used in the learning management systems (LMS) to offer customized learning opportunities adaptive quiz recommendations, student-based content recommendations based on behavior of students, all while respecting data sovereignty (Al-Rubaie & Chang, 2019).

6.7 Challenges Observed in Real Deployments

In spite of the positive results, practical FL deployments are faced with a number of challenges.

i. Diversity in client devices (e.g. memory, connection).
ii. Training imbalance is caused by non-IID data distributions.
iii. Loss of clients in the training cycles
iv. Large-scale deployments have bottlenecks in communication.
v. The problems with debugging the decentralized environment.

In order to minimize such difficulties, it is advisable to carefully specify system design, hardware-sensitive schedules and optimization of communication protocols (e.g., federated average, quantification, and sparse) techniques. Federated is continuously finding its way into healthcare, finance, mobile services, manufacturing and transportation. The possibility to do so is justified by cases of such use to keep AI democracy without violating privacy and regulatory standards. Real-World Case Research highlights the potential changeability of FL particularly in combination with. such technologies as the same computing, differential privacy, and secure are supported. consolidation. Nevertheless, the future of FL still manages to survive the fixing the existing implementation hardships and managing cross-domain teamwork toward common models and norms.

7. CONCLUSION AND FUTURE DIRECTIONS

The Federated Learning (FL) offers a case of change in the construction and implementation of machine learning systems. In contrast to a traditional centralized approach, that require aggregation of raw data into a central server, FL permits collaborative learning across distributed clients while continuing data locality. This property considers the rising worries about data privacy, security, and following the rules, which makes it easy for AI to safeguard FL. Through this chapter, we have discovered the motivation behind the FL, describing the differences between central and decentralized education systems, detecting the evolution of FL from the beginning, and reviewing its transformative influence in various fields such as healthcare, finance, smart devices, and autonomous systems. Moreover, we outlined the main technological advances, including communication-efficient algorithms such as FedAvG, and the ability of FL to adapt to challenges such as non-IID data, system heterogeneity, and limited communication resources. While the benefits of FL are significant, its adoption is not without challenges. The federated setting requires a novel threat vector, such as poisoning attack, inference attack, and consolidation manipulation, strong security and elasticity methods. As a result, the Federated Learning landscape is now linked to a secure multiparty calculation, differential privacy, homomorphic encryption, and the progression of blockchain-based federated architectures. FL is not just a technical innovation, but a basic step towards AI -demonstration to contribute to intelligent systems without renouncing ownership of strong organizations, industries, and individuals. Despite the significant progress in FL, the field is still developing, and many promising research directions are emerging (Sun et al., 2020).

1. Robustness Against Adversarial Threats: Strength against opposing threats, the decentralized nature of the FL makes it susceptible to anti-manipulation. Strong consolidation methods, an inconsistent investigation framework, and verified calculations must be focused on defending against targeted and unbearable attacks in future work (Sun et al., 2019).
2. Privacy-Utility Trade-off Optimization: Balancing this trade is a dynamic and open challenge and is a crucial focus for future research (Geyer et al., 2017).
3. Cross-Silo and Cross-Device FL: Enhancing scalability in both cross-device settings (involving millions of smartphones) and cross-silo collaborations (among institutions like banks or hospitals) requires improvements in client scheduling, asynchronous training, and bandwidth efficiency (Kairouz et al., 2021).

4. Individualized Federated Learning: The methods of personalization are designed to transform the global model are associated with individual customers. Other methods like meta-learning, multi-task. learning, and clustered FL was likely to benefit in non-IID environment (Fallah et al., 2020).
5. Incentive Systems and reputation Systems: Motivating client participation while preventing malicious behaviors is crucial. Mechanisms of incentives based on blockchain and the reputation systems might be incorporated to keep the trust among FL participants.
6. Federated Learning at the Edge and 6G: As edge computing grows and the edge computing grows in popularity. with the appearance of 6G communication standards, FL will become a provider of ultra-low latency, intelligent applications deployed on the edge of the network in high-throughput mode. (Wang et al., 2020).
7. Standardization and Compliance: FL is still developing, and therefore, as the industry standards and compliance models (like, ISO or IEEE standards) will be necessary to the mass adoption, particularly in regulated industries.
8. Explainability and Auditability in FL: Ensuring federated models are local and interpolative. trust and legal accountability require audibility. Future studies are required to investigate Federated-compatible explainable AI (XAI) methods.

The future of artificial intelligence systems, Federated Learning is in the lead. Federated Learning is the most advanced system of this type enhancing decentralization, privacy protection, and inclusion in model development. By dealing with the changing threat environment and enhancing its base with safe and. adaptive approaches, FL can become one of the anchor technologies of responsible and ethical AI deployment. As academia and industry continue to collaborate, the vision of privacy-first, globally trained, and locally beneficial models is steadily becoming a reality.

REFERENCES

Al-Rubaie, M., & Chang, J. M. (2019). Privacy-preserving machine learning: Threats and solutions. *IEEE Security and Privacy*, *17*(2), 49–58. DOI: 10.1109/MSEC.2018.2888775

Ali, M., Kumar, A., & Choi, B. J. (2025). Privacy-preserving federated learning for energy disaggregation of smart homes. *IET Cyber-Physical Systems*, *10*(1), e70013. DOI: 10.1049/cps2.70013

Apple. (2017). *Learning with privacy at scale*. Apple Machine Learning Research. https://machinelearning.apple.com/2017/12/06/learning-with-privacy-at-scale.html

Bagdasaryan, E., Veit, A., Hua, Y., Estrin, D., & Shmatikov, V. (2018). How to backdoor federated learning. *arXiv preprint*. https://arxiv.org/abs/1807.00459

Banabilah, S., Aloqaily, M., Alsayed, E., Malik, N., & Jararweh, Y. (2022). Federated learning review: Fundamentals, enabling technologies, and future applications. *Information Processing & Management*, *59*(6), 103061. DOI: 10.1016/j.ipm.2022.103061

Bonawitz, K.. (2017). Practical secure aggregation for privacy-preserving machine learning. In *Proceedings of the ACM Conference on Computer and Communications Security (CCS)*. DOI: 10.1145/3133956.3133982

Bonawitz, K.. (2019). Towards federated learning at scale: System design. In *Proceedings of the 2nd Conference on Machine Learning and Systems (SysML)*. https://arxiv.org/abs/1902.01046

Brisimi, T. S., Chen, R., Mela, T., Olshevsky, A., Paschalidis, I. C., & Shi, W. (2018). Federated learning of predictive models from federated electronic health records. *Scientific Reports*, *8*(1), 1–7. DOI: 10.1038/s41598-018-24579-5 PMID: 29311619

Caldas, S., ... (2018). LEAF: A benchmark for federated settings. *arXiv preprint*. https://arxiv.org/abs/1812.01097

Chen, M., Hao, Y., Hwang, K., Wang, L., & Wang, L. (2017). Disease prediction by machine learning over big data from healthcare communities. *IEEE Access : Practical Innovations, Open Solutions*, *5*, 8869–8879. DOI: 10.1109/ACCESS.2017.2694446

Fallah, A., Mokhtari, A., & Ozdaglar, A. (2020). Personalized federated learning: A meta-learning approach. In *Advances in Neural Information Processing Systems* (Vol. 33, pp. 12230–12242).

Fung, C., Yoon, C. J., & Beschastnikh, I. (2018). Mitigating sybils in federated learning poisoning. *arXiv preprint*. https://arxiv.org/abs/1808.04866

Geyer, R. C., Klein, T., & Nabi, M. (2017). Differentially private federated learning: A client-level perspective. *arXiv preprint*. https://arxiv.org/abs/1712.07557

Guembe, B., Azeta, A., Osamor, V., & Ekpo, R. (2023). Federated machine learning approaches for anti-money laundering detection. In *Proceedings of the International Conference on Information Systems and Emerging Technologies (ICISET)*. DOI: 10.2139/ssrn.4669561

Gupta, H., Agarwal, P., Gupta, K., Baliarsingh, S., Vyas, O. P., & Puliafito, A. (2023). FedGrid: A secure framework with federated learning for energy optimization in the smart grid. *Energies, 16*(24), 8097. DOI: 10.3390/en16248097

Kairouz, P., McMahan, H. B., Avent, B., et al. (2021). Advances and open problems in federated learning. *Foundations and Trends® in Machine Learning, 14*(1–2), 1–210. DOI: 10.1561/2200000083

Karimireddy, S. P.. (2020). SCAFFOLD: Stochastic controlled averaging for federated learning. In *Proceedings of the International Conference on Machine Learning*.

Kheder, M. Q., & Mohammed, A. A. (2024). Real-time traffic monitoring system using IoT-aided robotics and deep learning techniques. *Kuwait Journal of Science, 51*(1), 100153. DOI: 10.1016/j.kjs.2023.10.017

Li, T., Sahu, A., Zaheer, M., Sanjabi, M., Talwalkar, A., & Smith, V. (2020). Federated optimization in heterogeneous networks. In *Proceedings of Machine Learning and Systems*.

Li, X., Huang, K., Yang, W., Wang, S., & Zhang, Z. (2020). On the convergence of FedAvg on non-IID data. In *Proceedings of the International Conference on Learning Representations*.

Li, Z., Liu, L., Zhang, J., & Liu, J. (2021). Byzantine-robust federated learning through spatial-temporal analysis of local model updates. In *Proceedings of the IEEE International Conference on Parallel and Distributed Systems* (pp. 372–379). DOI: 10.1109/ICPADS53394.2021.00052

Liu, Y., Kang, Y., & Liu, H. (2023). A survey on federated learning systems. *IEEE Transactions on Knowledge and Data Engineering, 35*(4), 3347–3366. DOI: 10.1109/TKDE.2021.3124599

Lu, T., Ma, J., & Wang, S. (2022). Industrial federated learning: A privacy-preserving framework for smart manufacturing. *IEEE Transactions on Industrial Informatics, 18*(6), 4290–4299. DOI: 10.1109/TII.2021.3106191

McMahan, B., Moore, E., Ramage, D., Hampson, S., & Arcas, B. A. (2017). Communication-efficient learning of deep networks from decentralized data. In *Proceedings of the 20th International Conference on Artificial Intelligence and Statistics (AISTATS)*. https://proceedings.mlr.press/v54/mcmahan17a.html

McMahan, H. B.. (2017). Communication-efficient learning of deep networks from decentralized data. In *Proceedings of the 20th International Conference on Artificial Intelligence and Statistics* (pp. 1273–1282). https://arxiv.org/abs/1602.05629

Mohamed, N. (2025). Artificial intelligence and machine learning in cybersecurity: A deep dive into state-of-the-art techniques and future paradigms. *Knowledge and Information Systems, 67*(8), 6969–7055. DOI: 10.1007/s10115-025-02429-y

Mohri, M., Sivek, G., & Suresh, A. T. (2019). Agnostic federated learning. In *Proceedings of the 36th International Conference on Machine Learning*.

Nasr, M., Shokri, R., & Houmansadr, A. (2019). Comprehensive privacy analysis of deep learning. In *Proceedings of the IEEE Symposium on Security and Privacy* (pp. 739–753). https://doi.org/DOI: 10.1109/SP.2019.00065

Ohrimenko, M.. (2016). Oblivious multi-party machine learning on trusted processors. In *Proceedings of the USENIX Security Symposium.*

Papernot, N., Abadi, M., Erlingsson, Ú., Goodfellow, I., & Talwar, K. (2017). Semi-supervised knowledge transfer for deep learning from private training data. In *Proceedings of the International Conference on Learning Representations*. Blanchard, P., Mhamdi, E. M., Guerraoui, R., & Stainer, J. (2017). Machine learning with adversaries: Byzantine-tolerant gradient descent. In Advances in Neural Information Processing Systems.

Pillutla, K., Wang, L., & Oh, S. (2021). Robust aggregation for federated learning. In *Proceedings of the 37th International Conference on Machine Learning*. https://arxiv.org/abs/1912.13445

Pingulkar, S., & Pawade, D. (2024). Federated learning architectures for credit risk assessment. In *Proceedings of the IEEE International Conference on Blockchain and Distributed Systems Security* (pp. 1–7). DOI: 10.1109/ICBDS61829.2024.10837430

Sheller, M. J., Edwards, B., Reina, G. A., Martin, J., Pati, S., Kotrotsou, A., Milchenko, M., Xu, W., Marcus, D., Colen, R. R., & Bakas, S. (2020). Federated learning in medicine: Facilitating multi-institutional collaborations without sharing patient data. *Scientific Reports*, *10*(1), 12598. Advance online publication. DOI: 10.1038/s41598-020-69250-1 PMID: 32724046

Shokri, R.. (2017). Membership inference attacks against machine learning models. In *Proceedings of the IEEE Symposium on Security and Privacy*. https://doi.org/DOI: 10.1109/SP.2017.41

Sun, J., Li, A., DiValentin, L., Hassanzadeh, A., Chen, Y., & Li, H. (2021). FL-WBC: Enhancing robustness against model poisoning attacks in federated learning from a client perspective. In *Proceedings of the 35th Conference on Neural Information Processing Systems*. https://arxiv.org/abs/2110.13864

Sun, Y., Kairouz, P., & Suresh, A. T. (2019). Can you really backdoor federated learning? *arXiv preprint*. https://arxiv.org/abs/1911.07963

Wang, J., ... (2020). Tackling the objective inconsistency problem in heterogeneous federated optimization. In *Advances in Neural Information Processing Systems*. https://arxiv.org/abs/2007.07481

Wang, Q., Hu, M., & Gong, Y.. (2020). Federated learning for COVID-19 chest X-ray diagnosis across multiple hospitals. *IEEE Transactions on Medical Imaging*, *39*(11), 3081–3091.

Yang, Q., Liu, Y., Chen, T., & Tong, Y. (2019). Federated machine learning: Concept and applications. *ACM Transactions on Intelligent Systems and Technology*, *10*(2), 1–19. DOI: 10.1145/3298981

Zhang, C., Yang, S., Mao, L., & Ning, H. (2024). Anomaly detection and defense techniques in federated learning: A comprehensive review. *Artificial Intelligence Review*, *57*(6), 150. Advance online publication. DOI: 10.1007/s10462-024-10796-1

Zhu, Z., Han, S., Xu, W., & Liu, Y. (2019). Deep leakage from gradients. In *Advances in Neural Information Processing Systems.*

Chapter 2
Overview of Adversarial AI and Data Poisoning in Federated Learning

Mohammed Firdos Alam Sheikh
https://orcid.org/0000-0002-8405-8482
Poornima University, India

ABSTRACT

Federated Learning (FL) is an emerging decentralized machine learning paradigm that enables multiple clients to collaboratively train a global model without sharing raw data, thereby preserving data privacy. . In adversarial settings, malicious clients can inject carefully crafted inputs or manipulate local training updates to degrade the global model's performance or embed backdoors. Data poisoning attacks, including label flipping and model update manipulation, pose significant threats by subtly corrupting training data or gradients, often bypassing conventional anomaly detection methods. This paper reviews the taxonomy, mechanisms, and impacts of adversarial and poisoning attacks in FL environments, and explores current defense strategies such as robust aggregation, anomaly detection, differential privacy, and blockchain integration. Understanding these threats is crucial to developing secure and reliable FL systems for real-world applications in healthcare, finance, and IoT.

1. INTRODUCTION

The rise in the demand of privacy-preserving machine learning technologies has seen a more rapid growth of FL has good privacy benefits, since all data is kept locally, there are new level of security vulnerabilities especially since it is open and distributed.

Adversarial AI techniques and attacks are being the most critical. Federated systems in contrast to the traditional centralized systems are particularly vulnerable to bad client entities that deliberately use a federated system to went with their local data or model modifications. These manipulations that are difficult to detect on the server level may create a backdoor, or result in intentional misclassifications. These attacks are not only technically implemented but also hard to track particularly in the heterogeneous data and client's environment.

DOI: 10.4018/979-8-3373-6224-3.ch002

The following are the parts of data poisoning in FL: label-flipping and gradient manipulation; corrupting model updates. Attackers can be interested in poisoning the global model in the training phase or placing covert behaviors that will only be revealed within certain circumstances. These threats are especially worrisome in modern fields of application of FL such as medical fields, banking, and self-coded systems, where the implications of attacked models may be far-reaching and devastating.

This introduction preconditions in discussion for adversarial attacks and federated learning, their operation, application, and new methods for their defense. It is important to understand and curb these vulnerabilities to make sure that FL systems are robust, reliable and trustworthy systems in circumstances of adversarial environment.

The principal concept of FL would be to establish a program of publicizing the divided amongst a number of the clients in the program. To refresh the global model in FL, client conducting the training consequently submits local updates to the following model training utilizing local data. In that privacy of data will be preserved against undesirable access (Tharaphe et al., 2024).

The frequent attacks are poisoning attacks, which target the training data or model, and inference attacks, which target the privacy of clients. By either directly attackers seek to contaminate the local training data. It is assumed that malevolent contamination is the primary factor in poisoning assaults, which essentially aim to trigger to anticipate contamination. Additionally, Steinhardt et al. proposed that an 11% decrease achieved with a 3% ratio of malicious clients.

A taxonomy of attacks and defense strategies is used to provide a thorough analysis of FL threats. To determine how to choose the best approach for each type of adversarial attack. To understand the model behavior in the context of poisoning and inference assaults, a quick summary of risks to FL is also included here.

Figure 1. Security threats encountered while the federated learning model was being trained

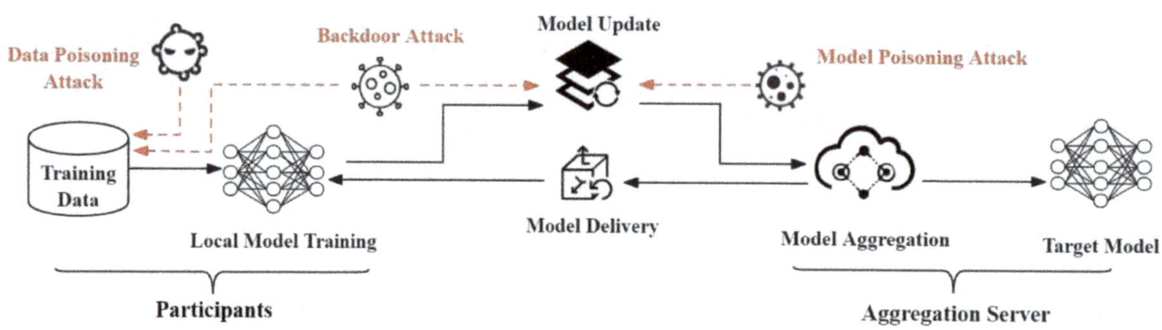

The foundation is generalization of state-of-the-art into different categories (Li et al., 2024). The current literature does not consider the advantages and disadvantages of the discussed studies in terms of evaluation criteria, such as the impact on benign clients, their use in real-world applications and the flexibility of attacks these studies can handle. This survey offers the most recent cutting-edge attacks and defense techniques recommended for FL in order to overcome the aforementioned constraints. The benefits and drawbacks of the assaults and defensive tactics are also listed in this research in connection to a number of evaluation criteria now brought to a close outlining some possible avenues for further investigation.

2. FEDERATED LEARNING

Google initially give idea that defined as a (ML) paradigm that allows for the cooperative training of central server or cloud and a number of clients, each of which keeps a global model—a collection of locally trained models—is kept up to date by the central server (Zhao et al., 2024). There are three steps in every iteration: (1) client selection; (2) local model changes; and (3) central server aggregation. Specifically, the chooses a number of users. Second, each user transmits a most recent local model back to the central server after retraining the current global model on the local dataset. Finally, to acquire the most recent global combines all of local models using aggregation strategies such mean aggregation and byzantine-robust aggregation, among others.

2.1 Poisoning Attacks

In FL, an attack that includes attackers purposefully altering the data to change the model aggression availability and learning is referred to as a "poisoning attack." In FL, some clients may find it simple to carry out poisoning attacks because the central server cannot see the participant data or the training procedures (Rodríguez-Barroso et al., 2023). DPA and MPA are the two categories into which poisoning attacks fall, as do targeted and untargeted assaults. Poisoning attacks may occur end, across MPA seeks to influence the local FL models' training procedures. Additionally, because DPA ultimately leads to MPA and MPA often aims to directly alter local model weights, DPA may be seen as a subset of MPA. Several variations are included in the model poisoning category and are explained below (Desai et al., 2019). Gradient Manipulation: The foundation of these assaults is the creation of random weights with dimensions comparable to those of weights.

Figure 2. The cognitive mapping process for situation awareness

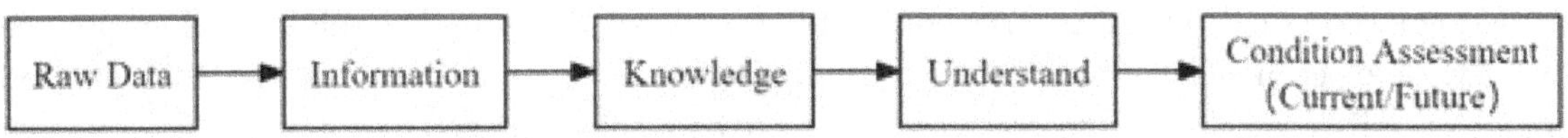

Privacy is one of the primary and most difficult problems, has many drawbacks, yet it may provide privacy for ML-based applications. Local devices use local data to train the model in FL-based techniques, and they only communicate the trained model's updates. For outsiders, actual or raw data is therefore still abstract. Therefore, in FL, a global model (GM) is distributed constructed by many users working together. Until the desired GM is built, this process is carried out repeatedly. Because linkage attacks and dynamic backdoor attacks may be used to harvest sensitive data, including privacy is an issue. Using a few criteria, incoming parameters from several internationally dispersed users are combined. The Mean aggregating Rule (MAR) is a widely used aggregating rule. The parameters are averaged using MAR. In such a scenario, a single compromised device either directly influences the decision-making process or poisons the system, paralyzing the GM. Therefore, a number of steps are needed to get beyond such obstacles. Local data auditing is one method that might help with some of the difficulties.

Although this isn't always the case, the degree assessed evaluate the data. Additionally, such model updates shouldn't be included for aggregation. Instead of employing data center-based training, FL makes use of a distributed training framework. Because it incorporates throughouts, it offers unique privacy solutions compared to result in additional privacy concerns. Since source information is not necessary for the aggregation process, the data should not include it, and the update should be transient and less useful than the real data.

In machine learning, large amounts of data are used to train models. However, cases of personal data leaks have increased in frequency as information technology have proliferated,

3. LITERATURE REVIEW

The personalized federated learning (FL) framework suggested by Tharaphe et al. (2024) considers how to improve intrusion detection systems (IDS) and minimize the threats of data poisoning attacks. The paper identifies how conventional FL-based IDS models are susceptible to poisoning, which is when the adversarial clients deliberately poison. In order to oppose this, authors have proposed a personalization strategy by tuning the global model parameters to localities to enhance the robustness and the accuracy of detecting them. Moreover, there is also a defense mechanism that is applied to detect and reduce the poisoned updates in the process of aggregation. The experimental findings constitute that not only does the personalized approach achieve enhanced performance in detection actions among heterogeneous customers, but also that the effect of poisoning attacks among standalone FL models is minimized. The paper underlines the increased role of both security and customization of federated cyber defense systems.

Currently, these issues cause significant difficulties in the context of federated learning (FL) in fog computing settings, as it is proposed that a dual-layered platform managing privacy and avoiding poisoning assaults can be the core of solving these problems (Li et al., 2024). The article describes a federated model of learning that exists on dispersed fogs and the model involves the use of differential leaked. To make the system robust, the authors combine anomaly detector whereby malicious updates by the compromised clients are filtered before aggregation. The system defenses are based on metrics of similarity and trust analysis to single out adversarial contributions successfully. Arendt: Evaluation of the proposed solution with experiments can be used to conclude that the changes achieved are equally high model accuracy as well as considerably increased resistance to data poisoning and backdoor attacks. The paper is used to develop the next generation of secure and privacy-aware FL architectures in fog computing that is crucial to the resource-constrained and latency-intensive systems, as is the case with IoT systems.

Zhao et al. (2024) suggests FlexibleFL as a promising framework to reduce based on the usage of client contribution evaluation. When using a traditional FL there are malicious clients who may overturn the integrity of global models by maliciously poisoning the model or the data. First of all, flexibleFL presents a dynamic mechanism of contribution assessment that determines the reliability and utility of the contribution made by each client basing on historical performance and behavioral patterns. Nodes that provide less trustworthy updates have a lesser weight in aggregating or they are not aggregated at all. The framework works well in hierarchical FL architecturesespecially cloud to edge where the differences in the clients and the heterogeneity of the resources further complicates security. The experimental findings verify that FlexibleFL can be much more resistant to targeted and untargeted poisoning attacks without hurting the model accuracy and the system scalability. The paper contributes to the real-life implementation of secure FL under real-life distributed computing conditions.

Rodríguez-Barroso et al. (2023) present a threat landscape in federated learning (FL), covering both theoretical and practical aspects of security and privacy. The paper systematically categorizes attacks (such as poisoning, inference, backdoor, and evasion attacks) and differential privacy, robust optimization). A notable strength of this work is its taxonomy, which classifies threats based on adversary capabilities, goals, and knowledge, providing clarity on attack surfaces in FL systems. The authors also conduct an experimental study comparing the effectiveness of various defense strategies under different attack scenarios. Also, the paper identifies open research problems, including privacy versus utility, making defenses robust in a heterogeneous environment, and creating an adaptive defense that is scalable. This questionnaire is a reference point to researchers who are new or those with deep knowledge of the area of secure and privacy-safeguarding FL research may rely on.

Desai et al. (2019) suggest LOMAR (Local Outlier Mitigation and Reweighting), a simple local defense that consists of lightweight local defense to protect (FL). The LOMAR is also client-level, in contrast with the server-based approaches to centralized defense that need to make computations on the server-side, and attempts to identify and neutralize poisoned updates before they are propagated to the central server. It can determine abnormal training behaviors with a postulate of using both statistical analysis and local model dynamics of an effort to stifle the influence of malicious data samples. Besides, the approach adds the strategy of adaptive reweighting that modulates the impact of local data samples on model performance in real time. The experiment findings indicate that LOMAR plays a significant role in reducing the influence of both label-flipping and backdoor attacks with almost no computational overhead and high level of accuracy. This is one of the techniques to prove especially useful in decentralized settings, where monitoring on the server-side is constrained or not yet possible.

Li et al. (2023) present a solution, LoMar, that is a client-side in a (FL) setup. LoMar is a local-to-the-client operation, unlike most server-based server defense methodologies, which automatically cause each individual client to detect and block data samples that have been poisoned prior to transfer of the new model. It combines both behavior method of anomaly detection and reweighting as it adapts on the fly to reduce the impact of the suspicious data in the training. The model optimizes robustness and maintenance of information, and it does not impose much computation or communication overhead, so it can be used in roadside FL application in resource-enforced settings like edge computing, and IoT. The experimental test verifies, LoMar can be effectively folded and still retain a good model performance. This paper gives a scalable practical solution that can address the protection of FL security at the client level.

The article by Zhang et al. (2023) introduces VPFL, a new federated learning (FL) architecture to edge computing systems that is optimized towards privacy, and verifiability of local model updates. The given scheme incorporates homomorphic encryption to ensure that the local gradients are secured and that the zero-knowledge proofs (ZKPs) are obtained to enable the central server to check whether the computations is necessary. Two types of protection guarantee integrity of the data, and also the integrity of the model, which is paramount in decentralized and privateness-centered settings. Computational efficiency is also upheld in VPFL, suitably when resources (in terms of accessible edge devices, etc.) are limited. Some experimental findings exhibit that VPFL can guarantee great privacy conditions and could act strongly on possible malicious activities of potential adversarial behavior like introducing incorrect updates or manipulating data by malicious clients. The research will contribute to the development of reliable and safe federation of learning designs of distributed edge networks.

The survey concentrated on defense mechanisms against model perturbation scrutinized in federated learning (FL) which is offered by Wang et al. (2022). The paper provides groupings of the available defensive methods systematically in a number of categories, such as robust aggregation rules (e.g., Krum, Trimmed Mean), anomaly detection, client reputation schemes, and secure update verification. It insists on the way in which an attack of poisoning can jeopardize the global model integrity by ensuring the introduction of malicious gradients when training a model. The authors evaluate the strengths and weaknesses of both methods of defense critically especially in the issue of scaling, computational cost and ability to withstand adaptive opposition. The research issues that are important in the survey include the requirement of lightweight defenses that can be deployed in resource-restricted environments, and the challenge of that of balancing model accuracy with security. This paper acts as a valuable reference to the researchers and developers who would like to enhance FL against insider attacks and model manipulations.

The article by Liu et al. (2022) gives a good network of factors leading to the emergence of successor of traditional (DML). Paper discusses the varying FL architectures, that demonstrate their applicability in different areas. It effectively tackles fundamentals cores of heterogeneity of data, efficiency of communication, and privacy aspects of FL systems. Another factor that has been evaluated in the survey is crucial FL elements such as model aggregation algorithms, security threats, and privacy-preserving techniques. Also provided by the authors are investigation directions on open research, which are devoted to building scalability, robustness, and integrating FL plus new technology like blockchain. It is a comprehensive description, yet it would make an important contribution to the work of scholars trying to comprehend the topic of federated learning and its future possibilities.

Lyu et al. (2022) represents a comprehensive and recent survey on the two issues of privacy and robustness in federated learning (FL). This paper greatly classifies different attack vectors such as inference attacks, data poisoning, and model poisoning and notes the significance of these attacks in the context of secure FL systems and data confidentiality of users. The authors respond by reviewing as broad a range of defense mechanisms as possible, including differing privacy, secure computation of many parties, strong aggregation algorithms, and anomaly detectors. The trade-offs of high model accuracy and good privacy and security guarantees are also covered in the survey. Moreover, Lyu et al. mention such current trends and fascinating research questions as dynamically adjusted defenses and balancing privacy-enhancing methods with resiliency approaches. The article is a resource guidebook used by researchers and practitioners to come up with secure and reliable FL systems.

Fu et al. (2022) article explores the susceptibility of one type of vertical federated learning (VFL) to label inference attacks, in which attackers seek to gain access to sensitive label information due to the cooperative learning process. In contrast to horizontal FL, VFL is characterized by the participants having disparate sets of features representing identical data samples to them, and posing distinctive privacy difficulties. The research will link new strategies of attack by using the interaction between the parties in the process of training a model to obtain private labels with high precision. The authors confirm both the reality of such attacks in realistic settings and the severity of those presently using extensive experiments and prove that the development of viable privacy-preserving methods in VFL frameworks is urgently required. This paper provides crucial ideas in securing the systems of VFL and protecting sensitive label data against adversarial threats.

Sun, Ochiai, and Sakuma (2022) propose is a semi-targeted model poisoning attack consisting of the backward analyzing error with the orchestration of weakening federated learning (FL) models. Their strategy is unlike that of fully targeted attacks in that they compromise not only the model performance specifically on a given set of inputs but also on the global accuracy of the model hence being stealthy and hard to identify during installation. It is following the forward erroneous measures in the attack to reduce the poisoning model updates in an effort to maximize the effects on the desired data without attracting attention. Such schools of thought have been proved to be efficient using experimental evaluations, and when there are a variety of FL scenarios they prove inefficient, and while this essentially illustrates weakness of FL systems to high-level poisoning attacks, high level defense mechanisms are also in need.

FedRecAttack, a federated recommendation-targeted federated recommendation systems model poisoning attack, is pioneered by Rong et al. (2022). In contrast to general FL attacks, this resource points out weaknesses specific to recommendation models, where the information is exploited by the adversaries in order to either deteriorate gradually the quality of the recommendations or affect the system to favor the promotion of specific items. This is because the attack paradigm pays close attention to malicious updates that affect the global model without much notice and thus, affect user experience and system availability. The authors perform comprehensive experiments showing that FedRecAttack is effective in various federated recommendation and are talking about the limitations to fight the attacks. This study illustrates that very specific security mechanisms should be developed in order to safeguard federated recommendation systems against advanced adversarial assaults.

Li et al. (2022) present a new model-based reinforcement learning (RL) to optimise malignant model poisoning assaults in federated learning (FL). The framework enables an adversary to dynamically modify their poisoning strategy according to system feedback so as to formulate the attack on a sequence of decisions taken. Such an adaptive attack is better than the age-old methods of making use of poisonous packets which remain static since this adaptive attack train to efficient attack policies that conflict stealthily and damage the global model. The research has very comprehensive reviews that prove the higher efficacy of the RL-driven attack in different FL environments. In this piece, the author urges people to focus on the increasing complexity of attack strategies and emphasizing on the critical necessity of the dynamic and intelligent defense strategies in federated learning.

In the federated learning (FL) model, Zhou et al. (2021) investigate the phenomena of deep model poisoning attacks (Zhou et al., 2021). Their contribution shows examples of how antagonists can use deep learning to create malicious model updates that can systematically damage the operation of the global model or develop specific misclassifications. The article explains how new poisoned updates can be produced by passing through simple detectors but do considerable damage to the model integrity. The validation of experimental results confirms the efficacy of these attacks in various FLCA-checking circumstances with a significant necessity to develop and employ the effective methods of detection and defense to the issue of deep poisoning. This research paper gives the background information about the danger of advanced poisoning by FL ecosystems.

4. METHODOLOGY

According to DPA, attacker is presumed to have access to and the ability to modify the data of at least one client; the contaminated data is a combination of cleansed (original labels) and changed data (Li et al., 2023). Additionally, by altering MPA directly contaminates the updates that the participating clients send for server. never used during the training phase, it is shown to have the greatest attack success rate of any local trigger (Zhang et al., 2023). Additionally, a novel class of backdoor attacks known as edge-case backdoors was conceptually presented to manipulate. This makes it challenging for defensive measures to identify such assaults.

Model re-placement is one method of performing the MPA, in which many malevolent users try to swap out a malevolent, causing incorrectly categorize subsequent. The research also discusses countermeasures and comes to the conclusion that attackers can simply get around them. Utilizing the variety of customers' fundamental concept of FL. This notion is contradicted by the central server's use of secure aggregation to weed out unusual contributions. Launching the assault even in cases where the global model has not yet converged. For lambda times, they intentionally cultivate fraudulent updates to offset the advantages of benign clients. It was proposed that the server look at two stealth metrics.

Figure 3. Poisoning of attack taxonomy and illustration (a) FL attack taxonomy (b) FL attack illustration

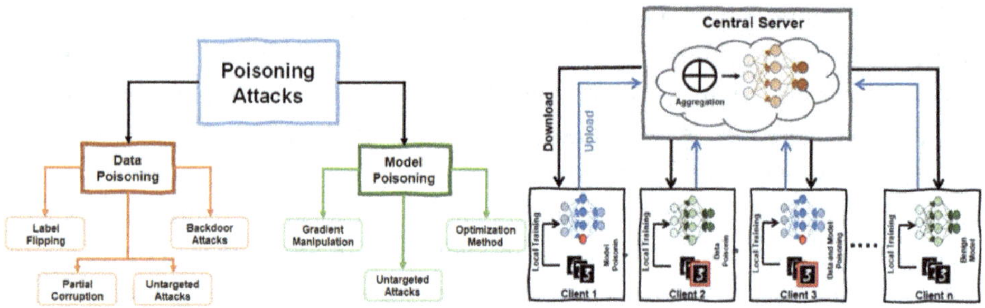

4.1 Defense Approaches

Although the literature contains a variety of defensive mechanisms, this research separates the state-of-the-art into three categories: perturbation mechanism, resilient aggregation, and anomaly detection.

Anomaly detection is generally understood to be the process of identifying uncommon occurrences or observations that deviate considerably from the idea of well specified data or activities. defensive method to counteract label-flipping assaults (Wang et al., 2022). In order to reduce the involvement of hostile clients in model training, which clusters the data into honest and malicious participants. To lessen the poisoning attack, individuals with similar traits are clustered using the measured score, and an outlier identification approach is then used.

Robust Aggregation: Unlike anomaly detection, aggregation procedures minimize poisoning assaults throughout the training phase. Some examples of robust aggregating algorithms include Krum, mean, reduced mean, and others. Furthermore, the majority of these approaches do not defend against current poisoning attacks for non-iid circumstances since they presuppose the iid data.

BaFFle, a feedback-based protection technique, is proposed to remove the backdoored model updates. For every FL cycle, BaFFle uses each participant to verify the global model by quantifying the validation function using their personal information.

Table 1. Attack strategy comparison

AttacksType	TrainingSetType	AdaptiveAttacks	BackdoorAttacks	Application
DataPoisoning	iid	No	No	ImageClassification
DataPoisoning	Non-iid	No	Yes	ImageClassification
DataPoisoning	iid	Yes	Yes	ImageClassification,TextPredictionandSentimentAnalysis
ModelPoisoning	Non-iid	Yes	Yes	ImageClassificationandWord Prediction
ModelPoisoning	iid	Yes	Yes	Image Classification andCensusIncomePrediction
ModelPoisoning	Non-iid	Yes	Yes	ImageClassificationandBreastCancerDetection

The defense tactics that have been discussed are effective when there aren't many malevolent participants present. The more malevolent people there are, the worse these tactics perform. The goal of the malicious client detection system, FLDetector, which Zhang et al. devised, is to identify and remove malicious players from global model updates. Based on past updates, the central server in FLDetector forecasts the participants' model changes for each iteration. If there is a discrepancy between the projected and actual modifications across many iterations, the participant is flagged as malicious. When compared to the state-of-the-art, the performance assessment shows encouraging results. Nevertheless, there is no discussion of how removing the malevolent players will affect the accuracy of the primary job. Perturbation Mechanism: In mathematics, the perturbation mechanism is a way to solve a problem by contrasting it with the known answer. Differential privacy is a well-known perturbation mechanism that has been widely used in FL to enhance outlier detection performance (Sheikh, 2011). To counteract the backdoored model updates, a low-complexity defense strategy using noise injection and weight clipping is suggested. However, alterations are not mitigated by this method. To put it simply, the weight clipping technique could have a detrimental impact on the shift in the weights of model updates for benign individuals. Most recently, a new method dubbed FLAME has been developed to circumvent the limitations of conventional players. After removing outliers from participant updates using the clustering and weight-clipping techniques, likelihood of an attack. Comparing FLAME to the shows that it is effective in preventing poisoning attacks. It does, however, need significant changes to the existing FL structure.

Table 2. Overlap–FedAvg and FedAvg average wall-clock times for a single iteration are compared

Name of Model	Dataset	Parameters	Avg	OverlapAvg
MLP	Mnist	**183,380**	**34.4**	28.85 (↓7.53%)
MnistNet	Fmnist	**1,234,453**	**24.34**	28.31 (↓14.11%)
MnistNet	Emnist	**1,382,342**	**24.5**	42.15 (↓10.68%)
CNNCifar	Cifar10	**384,479**	**35.63**	45.33 (↓5.70%)
VGG	Cifar10	**2,472,387**	**32.4**	49.33 (↓23.40%)

Methods for decreasing the frequency of model updates improve performance. Mcmahan et al.'s FedAvg technique combines a server that averages models with a local stochastic gradient descent. Prior to sending to client repeatedly iterates local updates satisfied by this method (Lyu et al., 2022). Assumptions about distribution may lead to good training outcomes. Nevertheless, the FedAvg algorithm performs poorly, and it only clearly optimizes computations needed by various users in can be dynamically updated algorithm. Participants are not obliged to standardize the quantity of computations in every update. Consequently, non-IID joints are better suited for this approach.

5. RESULT

First, the mathematical justifications for various assault strategies are still unclear. The list of hostile users needed a label reversal attack, for instance, is not predictable; rather, it depends on the distribution of the data. This phenomenon has no mathematical explanation. Second, It may be investigated in combination with attack scenarios. Furthermore, an assault signifies value in addition to devastation (Fu et al., 2022). For instance, watermarking methods may be used in conjunction with backdoor assaults to safeguard intellectual property.

They demonstrated FedAsync's convergence through both theoretical analysis and experimental verification. In contrast to FedAvg, client devices can send updates to the central server at any time, and delayed feedback updates are not erased. It performs similarly to FedAvg even in cases of significant delays. Kulkarnit et al. categorize several customized federated learning techniques according on model heterogeneity as follows: Adding User Context,

Figure 4. Accuracy graph

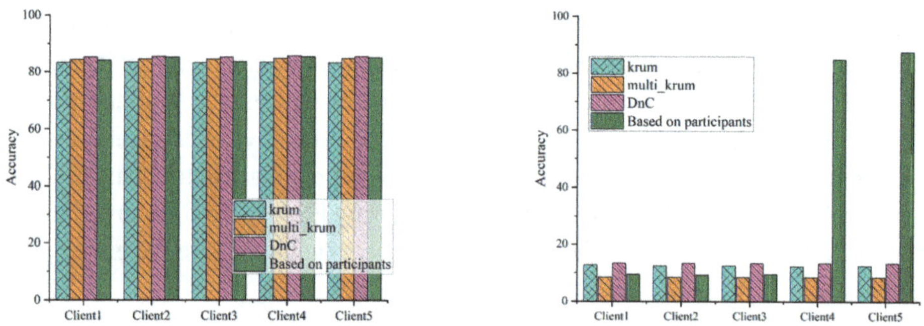

(a) The accuracy of partial participant in poisoning is 40%

(b) The accuracy of partial participant in poisoning is 60%

When there are different percentages of poisoned individuals, to be similar to the algorithm suggested when the percentage of poisoned participants was 40%. Each participant model has an accuracy of over 60%, which produces superior outcomes.

Multi-task learning and transfer learning Distillation of Knowledge Meta-Learning Foundation + Customization Layers and a combination of local and global models. In order to gain more individualized FL, Chen suggested a framework called PFKD that uses method to address the issue of model heterogeneity and customized algorithms. The pFedMe is a customized federated learning method that was proposed by Dinh et al. This approach distinguishes between global model learning and individualized model optimization. This enables pFedMe to optimize the customized model concurrently (Sun et al., 2022). Model heterogeneity is addressed by introducing a memetic model as a bridge between the global and personalized models and transferring using deep mutual learning's knowledge distillation technology. Wu et al. suggested PerFit, customized as part of the overall optimization. An individualized federated learning architecture that fixes equipment problems is advantageous for intelligent IoT applications. PerFit may be perfect for intricate IoT contexts by resolving data and model heterogeneity challenges, and it can guarantee.50 users or customers are regarded as FL participants in this experiment, and each one makes a contribution for 20 rounds. Two sets created from the complete preprocessed dataset. Once again, the train set is divided evenly and distributed to each client. Performance analysis is conducted using the test set. A 4:1 ratio is maintained between the test and train sets. The GM receives the feature set in order to generate prediction results.

Before training begins, the client end is randomly subjected to a data poisoning attack (DPA) by assuming uses. From 10% to 40% of all customers, the number of compromised users is increased gradually. To create the poison attacks, poison data is generated using a random function and added to the original data.

In order to protect against poisoning attacks, existing approaches primarily provide security aggregation algorithms for the central server; nonetheless, they need that the central server be reliable and that there be fewer poisoned participants than usual. A protection strategy was developed by Liu et al. The fundamental notion is to see players as autonomous defensive strategy executors inside the FedAvg algorithm's framework (Wisetsri et al., 2022).

To increase its performance in this regard, such a model has been applied in recent years across the research disciplines of secure communication protocol design, participant trust assessment in federated learning, and a pattern of data poisoning attacks detection through massive language models, which are in turn trained to differentiate normal and pathological updates (Rong et al., 2022). The robust word processing features of big language models can be applied to find potential attack patterns based on any word expressions submitted by the participants as model update logs. This makes it possible to anticipate and avoid the attempts of data poisoning.

Figure 5. pFedMe, FedAvg, and Per-FedAvg performance comparison using Synthetic in μ-strongly convex and nonconvex settings

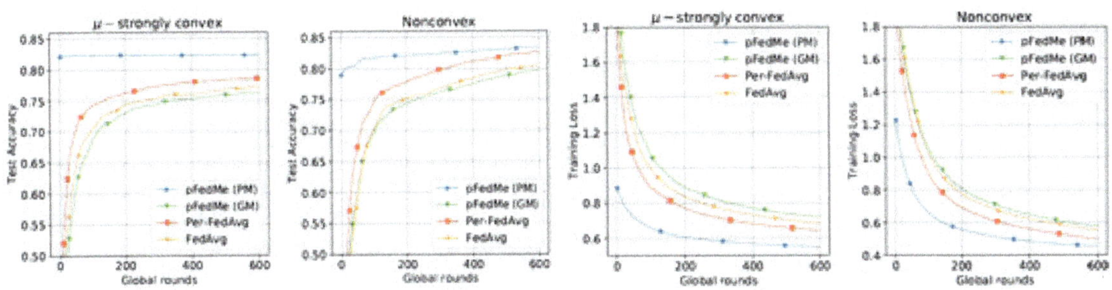

GNN has demonstrated the possibility of enhancing predicting data poisoning attacks in federated learning. This may be achieved through finding people having odd communication patterns, simulating participant networks, analyzing local and global structures among other techniques (Zhou et al., 2021). Attacks The project team is inquiring on federated learning data poisoning attacks based on graph neural networks. Through appliquing neighboring information, the graph neural network examination federated learning arrangement, e.g., can communicate the global networkness in addition to the local characteristic of every node. This characteristic allows GNN to determine the level of network security in general and information contrasting indications of data poisoning attacks in particular (Li et al., 2022).

6. CONCLUSION

Finally, the protection of the existing AI decentralized models presupposes an opportunity to learn about the various types and categories of attacks of data poisoning in federated learning. Those attacks can be severe challenges to the integrity and reliability of the model, and have very variable approaches and objectives, ranging through minor label-flipping to intricate back-door and gradient poisoning. Specific defense mechanisms could be devised where they could be categorized as threats against the vectors of attack, extent and capabilities of the adversary. The key approach to the prevention of malevolent manipulation of collaborative learning structures is to continue research regarding the evolving threat of data poisoning and classify it taxonomically as the application of federated learning persists in sensitive contexts.

REFERENCES

Desai, H., Sheikh, M. F. A., & Sharma, S. K. (2019). Multi-purposed question answer generator with natural language processing. In V. Rathore, M. Worring, D. Mishra, A. Joshi, & S. Maheshwari (Eds.), *Emerging trends in expert applications and security* (Advances in Intelligent Systems and Computing, Vol. 841). Springer. https://doi.org/DOI: 10.1007/978-981-13-2285-3_18

Fu, C., Zhang, X., Ji, S., Chen, J., Wu, J., Guo, S., Zhou, J., Liu, A. X., & Wang, T. (2022). Label inference attacks against vertical federated learning. In *Proceedings of the 31st USENIX Security Symposium* (pp. 1–15).

Li, H., Sun, X., & Zheng, Z. (2022). Learning to attack federated learning: A model-based reinforcement learning attack framework. In *Advances in Neural Information Processing Systems*. https://openreview.net/forum?id=4OHRr7gmhd4

Li, X., Qu, Z., Zhao, S., Tang, B., Lu, Z., & Liu, Y. (2023). LoMar: A local defense against poisoning attack on federated learning. *IEEE Transactions on Dependable and Secure Computing*, *20*(1), 437–450. DOI: 10.1109/TDSC.2021.3135422

Li, Y., Zhang, S., Chang, Y., Xu, G., & Li, H. (2024). Privacy-preserving and poisoning-defending federated learning in fog computing. *IEEE Internet of Things Journal*, *11*(3), 5063–5077. DOI: 10.1109/JIOT.2023.3302795

Lyu, L., Yu, H., Ma, X., Chen, C., Sun, L., Zhao, J., Yang, Q., & Yu, P. S. (2022). Privacy and robustness in federated learning: Attacks and defenses. *IEEE Transactions on Neural Networks and Learning Systems*. Advance online publication. DOI: 10.1109/TNNLS.2022.3216981 PMID: 36355741

Rodríguez-Barroso, N., Jiménez-López, D., Luzón, M. V., Herrera, F., & Martínez-Cámara, E. (2023). Survey on federated learning threats: Concepts, taxonomy on attacks and defences, experimental study and challenges. *Information Fusion*, *90*, 148–173. DOI: 10.1016/j.inffus.2022.09.011

Rong, D., Ye, S., Zhao, R., Yuen, H. N., Chen, J., & He, Q. (2022). FedRecAttack: Model poisoning attack to federated recommendation. In *Proceedings of the IEEE 38th International Conference on Data Engineering (ICDE)* (pp. 2643–2655). DOI: 10.1109/ICDE53745.2022.00243

Sheikh, M. F. A. (2011). *Secure query processing by blocking SQL injection attack*. SQLIA.

Sun, Y., Ochiai, H., & Sakuma, J. (2022). Semi-targeted model poisoning attack on federated learning via backward error analysis. In *Proceedings of the International Joint Conference on Neural Networks (IJCNN)* (pp. 1–8). DOI: 10.1109/IJCNN55064.2022.9891990

Tharaphe, T. T., Shiraishi, Y., & Morii, M. (2024). Personalized federated learning-based intrusion detection system: Poisoning attack and defense. *Future Generation Computer Systems*, *153*, 182–192. DOI: 10.1016/j.future.2023.10.005

Wang, Z., Kang, Q., Zhang, X., & Hu, Q. (2022). Defense strategies toward model poisoning attacks in federated learning: A survey. In *Proceedings of the IEEE Wireless Communications and Networking Conference (WCNC)* (pp. 548–553). DOI: 10.1109/WCNC51071.2022.9771619

. Wisetsri, W., Syam, E., Alanya-Beltran, J., Kulkarni, G. R., Reddy, R. K. V., & Sheikh, M. F. A. (2022). *WITHDRAWN: Assessing and comparing the role of information and communication technology (ICT) and supply chain management (SCM) and its impact on contribution of e-commerce.*

Zhang, J., Liu, Y., Wu, D., Lou, S., Chen, B., & Yu, S. (2023). VPFL: A verifiable privacy-preserving federated learning scheme for edge computing systems. *Digital Communications and Networks*, *9*(4), 981–989. DOI: 10.1016/j.dcan.2022.05.010

Zhao, Y., Cao, Y., Zhang, J., Huang, H., & Liu, Y. (2024). FlexibleFL: Mitigating poisoning attacks with contributions in cloud–edge federated learning systems. *Information Sciences*, *664*, 120350. DOI: 10.1016/j.ins.2024.120350

Zhou, X., Xu, M., Wu, Y., & Zheng, N. (2021). Deep model poisoning attack on federated learning. *Future Internet*, *13*(3), 73. DOI: 10.3390/fi13030073

Chapter 3
Architectural Models and Security Considerations for Federated Learning

Rachana Yogesh Patil
https://orcid.org/0000-0001-9973-6998
Pimpri Chinchwad College of Engineering, India

Yogesh H. Patil
https://orcid.org/0000-0001-9968-8287
D.Y. Patil College of Engineering, India

Ozen Ozer
Kırklareli University, Turkey

ABSTRACT

The concept of Federated Learning (FL) has developed of centralized model averaging to a multi-faceted ecosystem of architectures, such as cross-device, cross-silo, hierarchical, and decentralized systems. Although the models allow collaboration of intelligence without direct data sharing, they also reveal vulnerabilities, which are caused by non-IID data, incomplete participation, and adversarial manipulation. This chapter offers a theoretical overview of architectural models and their related security aspects in FL. It follows the history of FL and describes key aggregation paradigms, as well as trade-offs between robustness, privacy, and efficiency. The comparative insights have been provided in terms of statistical, trust-based, spectral, inversion-guided, and cryptographic aggregation strategies keeping in consideration their flexibility in heterogeneous and adversarial settings. The chapter ends by hybrid and privacy-protecting models that combine secure computation, blockchain-based trust, and ethical governance to support scalable, responsible federated ecosystems.

1. INTRODUCTION

The world of data has been experiencing a radical change in the recent past, and the amount of digital data is projected to reach more than 175 zettabytes by 2025 (Sargiotis, 2024; Koripalli, 2025). This un-

DOI: 10.4018/979-8-3373-6224-3.ch003

paralleled expansion has been accompanied by a steep rise in the privacy issues, regulatory restrictions, and security vulnerabilities (Mbaha, 2024). Conventional machine learning paradigms that are based on centralized data collection have not been able to keep up with this changing situation, particularly in sectors where sensitive or confidential data may not be shared at will (Layode et al., 2024).

FL has become a promising paradigm to solve these issues as it allows joint model training without data sharing. As opposed to centralizing raw data, FL lets distributed nodes, e.g. hospitals, mobile devices, or financial institutions, train local models and exchange only model updates (Aggarwal, Khullar, and Goyal, 2024). This is a privacy-preserving strategy with lower costs of data transfer and consistent with the new regulations like the General Data Protection Regulation (GDPR) and Health Insurance Portability and Accountability Act (HIPAA) (Owen and Mattews, 2024).

The idea of distributed learning is not novel, but its implementation in the federated model presents a drastic change in the process of sharing and securing intelligence. Research-wise, the federated paradigm brings up several aspects of the inquiry, such as architectural efficiency and data heterogeneity, and trust management and adversarial resilience. The increasing use of FL in healthcare, autonomous systems, finance, IoT, and edge computing helps highlight its applicability in the contemporary digital ecosystems (Albshaier, Almarri, and Albuali, 2025). Nevertheless, even with the benefits of the federated models, the security, integrity, and scalability of such models is a burning issue that should be explored in an organized architecture and effective protective strategies.

In this chapter, the authors provide a conceptual examination of architectural models and security concerns of federated learning systems. It follows the development of FL architectures, explores the security environment around distributed intelligence and provides an overview of future trends that would shape the next generation of secure, ethical, and adaptive federated ecosystems. In order to gain a more accurate idea of how the architectural design and security posture interact in federated learning, two key steps are necessary: comparing the key FL architectures and the vulnerabilities, defenses, and trade-offs of the latter. Table 1 illustrates that every architectural model has its own security issues and design implications, namely, centralized, cross-silo, hierarchical, and decentralized.

Table 1. Comparative synthesis: Architectures, threats, defenses, and trade-offs in federated learning

Architecture	Threats	Defenses	Trade-offs
Centralized	• Model poisoning • Privacy leakage	• Privacy-preserving aggregation	• Privacy vs. robustness • Robustness
Cross-silo	• Data poisoning • Model inversion	• Robust aggregation • Differential Privacy (DP)	• Privacy vs. inter-institutional collaboration
Hierarchical	• Inference attacks • Communication vulnerabilities	• Secure aggregation • Differential Privacy (DP)	• Scalability • Communication overhead
Decentralized	• Data poisoning • Model poisoning	• Robust aggregation • Byzantine fault tolerance	• Trust management • Transparency vs. scalability

The centralized model is easily and effectively coordinated, but most vulnerable to model poisoning and privacy leakage, and needs powerful privacy-preserving aggregation algorithms. Cross-silo architectures, typically implemented at an institution, like a hospital or a bank, need to focus on data poisoning and model inversion attacks, with special focus on strong aggregation and differential privacy (DP). The hierarchical architectures do bring in the benefit of scalability but are susceptible to inference and communication based attacks, requiring to enforce secure multi-level aggregation strategies and tighter communication protocols. Lastly, the most autonomous and scalable type of architecture, decentralized architectures, is particularly threatened by Byzantine behavior and trust management problems, where fault-tolerant and transparent aggregation strategies are of essence.

This synthesis in comparison highlights the fact that there is no given architecture that offers absolute protection or scalability, but instead, each of them involves a set of trade-offs between privacy, robustness, trust, and communication efficiency. The insights into these trade-offs are critical to the design of the next-generation federated systems that will be able to trade between security, transparency, and performance in the context of a variety of deployment scenarios.

1.1 Evolution of Federated Learning

FL has been developing over a sequence of major milestones which represent the progress in distributed computing, optimization, and privacy-sensitive artificial intelligence. The first stage, which was between 2012 and 2015, involved studies in the field of distributed learning techniques and secure optimization methods (Li, Fan, and Lin, 2020). These works formed the theoretical basis of decentralized model training, in which the data might stay at its origin but participate in an international model.

Another important development was made in 2016 when Google proposed the Federated Averaging (FedAvg) algorithm, which officially introduced FL (Al-Shedivat et al., 2020). The strategy allowed mobile devices to cooperatively train models with local data and just exchange model parameters, which would solve the issues of privacy and data movement. Sometime between 2017 and 2018, FL started showing practical viability by implementing applications like mobile keyboard prediction and speech recognition, which showed that privacy-preserving collaboration could be scaled successfully.

Cross-silo FL developed in 2018-2019 when collaboration was not restricted to devices alone, but also to organizations, including hospitals, banks, and research institutions. This step changed the interest towards consumer applications to data collaboration at the enterprise level (Huang et al., 2022). In 2020, the field has evolved further as the robust security mechanisms, such as differential privacy, secure aggregation, and homomorphic encryption, were formally introduced to ensure sensitive information is not leaked and adversarially interfered with.

Between 2021 and 2023, Federated Learning was in the period of wide adoption. It was integrated into areas like healthcare, smart cities and finance where sensitive information needs to be localized because of regulatory or ethical reasons. By 2024, blockchain and decentralized orchestration in architectural solutions guaranteed transparency, trust and auditability. In the future, the work beyond 2025 will likely be dedicated to the adaptive and self-organizing FL systems that will be improved with edge intelligence, quantum-safe security measures, and the framework that will comply with ethical and responsible AI principles (Alatawi, 2025).

The timeline of these events as shown in figure 1 underscores the fact that FL has evolved to become an academic phenomenon into a backbone of secure, collaborative, and privacy-aware artificial intelligence.

Figure 1. Evolution of federated learning

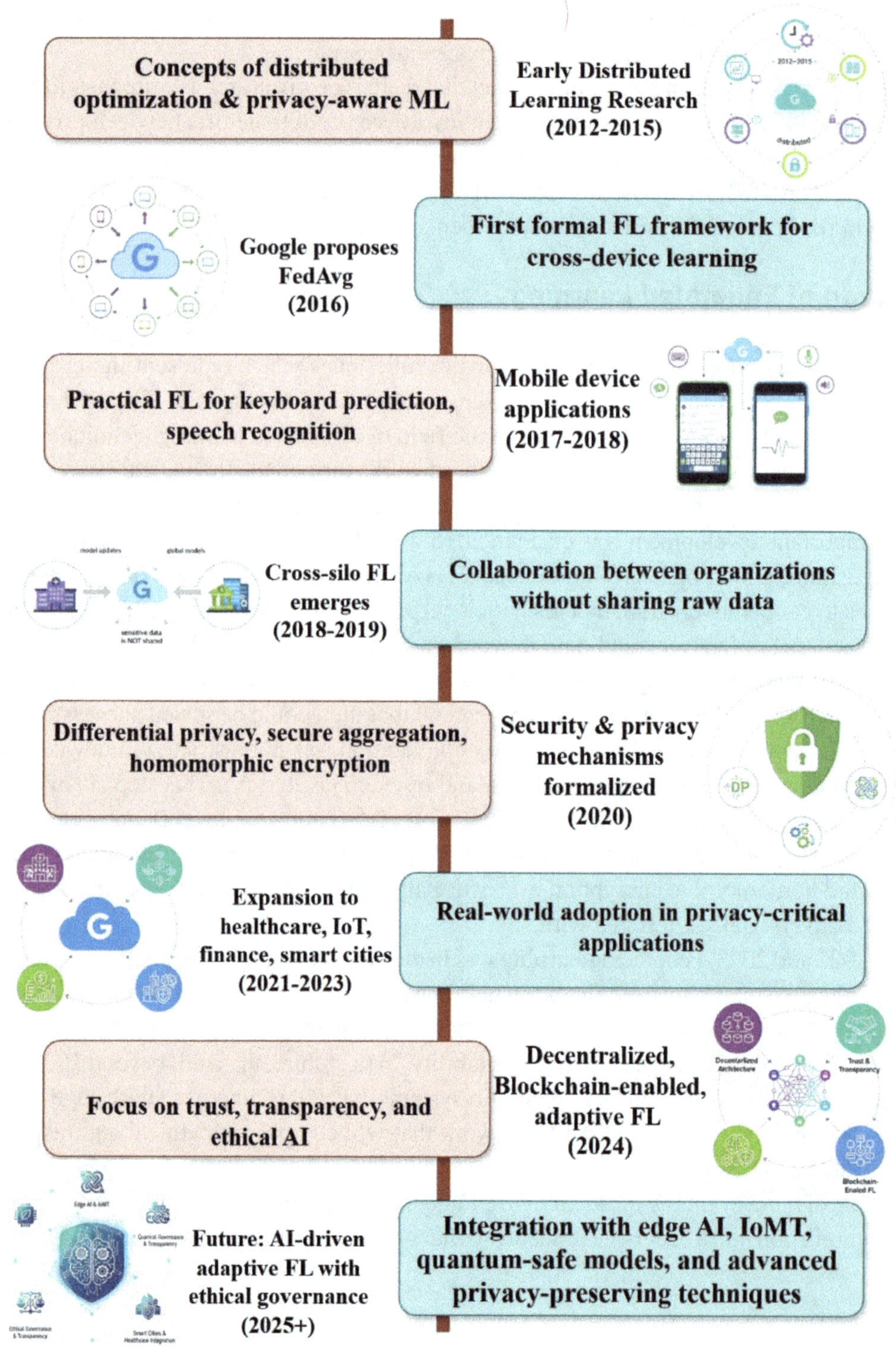

2. RELATED WORK

The FL literature is dominated by single-server, centralized frameworks, which are designed to achieve the privacy-preserving aggregation along with the resilience to adversarial attacks. Initial literature (Le et al., 2023; Nguyen and Thai, 2023) is mainly concerned with strong aggregation in a centralized environment, typically by using homomorphic encryption (HE), additive secret sharing, or secure multi-party computation (MPC) to calculate model statistics without revealing raw updates. These methods deal with the natural conflict between strong aggregation, which usually enforces transparency into the individual updates (e.g. pairwise distances, coordinate-wise statistics), and secret aggregation, which conceals the individual updates. As an illustration, (Hou et al., 2025) and (Li et al., 2024) suggest the approaches to calculate the private anomaly detection metrics and filtered updates based on secret sharing, reducing leakage and preserving the robustness. The extension of robust aggregation to non-IID data settings in the context of dual-server CKKS-based homomorphic encryption (Sun et al., 2025) shows that the new technology is feasible in practice and guarantees privacy.

The explicit study of cross-silo FL has been conducted in (Li et al., 2024), (Byrd et al., 2022), and (Ghanta et al., 2025) with organizational deployments as the hospital or financial institution. Such studies focus on privacy-safe cooperation that involves local differential privacy (DP), reputation-sensitive aggregation, and homomorphic encryption. The most rigorous approach, cross-device FL, is difficult to apply strictly because of such problems as partial participation, device churn, and dropout, which numerous studies only partially simulate. Lately hierarchical FL architectures have also become of interest especially in edge-based deployments. (Zhou et al., 2023) apply edge-based anomaly detection using DP to screen malicious updates, and (Siriwardhana et al., 2024) introduce SHIELD that is a powerful aggregation mechanism compatible with multi-layer hierarchical FL, which incorporates secure aggregation to maintain confidentiality. Both the works depict the trade-offs of achieving robustness, privacy and communication efficiency in a non-centralized topology.

The latter can be exemplified by the use of differential privacy-based approaches (Le et al., 2023): a utility, robustness, and efficiency trade-off. The strategies of adaptive DP and parameter sparsification are designed to preserve privacy and minimally affect the model accuracy, especially when there is cross silo. In the meantime, HE- or MPC-based solutions (Nguyen and Thai, 2023) can be used to do robust aggregation of encrypted updates and strong confidentiality, at the expense of computation and communication overhead.

Recent publications in the area in table 2 indicate a increasing trend in converging architectural creativity and security improvement in federated learning. The most common modes of deployment are centralized and cross-silo frameworks, as they are relatively simple to deploy and coordinate effectively, but are always vulnerable to poisoning, inference, and privacy leakages. Although the hierarchical and edge-based models are more scaleable and efficient in communication, they have multi-layer vulnerabilities and require a set of coordinated defensive mechanisms between the aggregation levels. In the literature examined, the strongest aggregation, differential privacy (DP), and homomorphic encryption (HE) become the most common defensive aspects (which are frequently used together to provide hybrid protection). Research like (Zhou et al., 2023) and (Siriwardhana et al., 20254) also show that the combination of edge-level anomaly detection and secure multi-tier aggregation has a very positive effect on resilience to adversarial behavior. Equally, other privacy-sensitive methods such as EPPRFL (Li et al., 2024) and PEAR (Sun et al., 2025) demonstrate how cryptographic aggregation can be used to ensure confidentiality without degrading computational performance to a significant degree. All in all, the comparative synthesis shows that no particular architecture or defense can be used to offer an absolute protection. Rather, designers have to make a multidimensional trade-off between robustness, privacy, efficiency, and scalability, a trend which has been repeated throughout the assessments in table 2. This highlights the current research requirement of adaptive hybrid architectures that are able to dynamically balance these competing goals in a wide range of federated settings.

Table 2. Comparative overview of federated learning architectures, threats, defenses, and evaluations

Ref.	Architecture & Deployment	Threat Model	Defenses & Mechanisms	Robustness Eval.	Privacy Eval.	Efficiency Eval.
(Zhou et al., 2023)	Hierarchical edge FL; anomaly detection at edge	Compromised devices; privacy leakage	Weight-based detection + DP	Detects malicious nodes	DP on data & model	Low communication cost
(Siriwardhana et al., 2024)	Hierarchical FL (multi-layer)	Client poisoning	SHIELD: robust + secure aggregation	High resilience	Secured updates	Efficient via hierarchy
(Hou et al., 2025)	Centralized FL	Malicious clients; curious server	Privacy-aware robust aggregation (MPC/HE)	Anomaly detection	Aggregated privacy	Scalable design
(Li et al., 2024)	Centralized FL	Malicious clients	EPPRFL: filtering + secret sharing	High robustness	Update privacy	Efficient primitives
(Sun et al., 2025)	Centralized dual-server FL	Byzantine poisoned gradients	PEAR: FHE + cosine similarity	Robust to non-IID data	Encrypted gradients	Faster than FHE baselines
(Yazdinejad et al., 2024)	Centralized FL	Poisoned encrypted gradients	Additive HE + audit model	Accurate and robust	Gradient confidentiality	Lower cost than FHE
(Li et al., 2024)	Cross-silo FL	Gradient inference; comm. heterogeneity	Local DP + Top-K sparsification	Weighted aggregation	Adaptive privacy budget	Reduced communication
(Le et al., 2023)	Centralized FL	Malicious clients; privacy leaks	Adaptive client-level DP	Mitigates attacks	Strong client privacy	Moderate overhead
(Byrd et al., 2022)	Cross-silo FL (datacenter)	Collusion; honest-but-curious	Oblivious DP + secure aggregation	Collusion resistance	Client-level DP	Lightweight
(Nguyen & Thai, 2022)	Centralized FL	Malicious users; curious server	HE + ZKPs	Detects poisoned updates	Privacy via HE	Not detailed
(Ghanta et al., 2025)	Cross-silo medical FL	Inference; unreliable clients	Simplified HE + reputation weighting	Robust via trust scores	Data confidentiality	Practical under HE

3. ARCHITECTURAL MODELS OF FEDERATED LEARNING

FL architectures have changed to meet the conflicting needs of scalability, data heterogeneity, security and communication efficiency. The architecture used has a direct impact on the resilience to adversarial threats of the system, the level of privacy that can be achieved, and the ability to scale the system to large scale. According to the available literature, four major architectural models are leading in the FL landscape: Centralized, Hierarchical, Cross-silo, and Cross-device (Edge) architectures. Both of them present different design principles, operation restrictions, and security.

3.1 Centralized Federated Learning

The centralized architecture is considered the building block of federated learning and is the most popular coordination structure used in initial and enterprise-scale systems. Under this configuration, a central server coordinates the whole learning process, and a group of distributed clients (mobile devices or institutional nodes and sensors) carry out local training on their own data. Clients send only model updates or gradients to the server after every training round, and the server does the global aggregation to update the shared model and resends it back to the clients to use in the next training round.

This topology has explicit benefits in the coordination, convergence control and consistency of the models. Having a single server will allow one to exert deterministic control over scheduling, client selection, and version selection, thus making monitoring easier and allowing training convergence to take shorter time than more decentralized options. This convenience, however, is at the cost of having a single point of failure, the server is now not only the central trust anchor, but the most vulnerable attack target. The operational flow of centralized FL is depicted in figure 2. Multiple clients perform local training on their private datasets and transmit encrypted or noise-added model updates to a central aggregator. The aggregator performs secure aggregation—often under differential-privacy or encryption constraints—and redistributes the updated global model for the next training iteration. This cycle continues until convergence, demonstrating both the efficiency and the inherent trust dependency of the centralized paradigm.

Figure 2. Centralized federated learning architecture

3.1.1 Challenges of Security and Privacy.

The FL systems are based on centralized systems and are vulnerable to two main types of threats:

- Data and Model Poisoning: Adversarial clients can put poisonous gradients into the global model to poison the model or add concealed backdoors (Ma et al., 2023).
- Inference and Privacy Leakage: A server can deduce sensitive information by gradient inversion or membership inference attack even in the absence of direct access to data by receiving updates (Molina-Coronado 2024).

As a result, the defense mechanism in centralized FL is based on the secure aggregation and privacy-preserving computation. The initial models used homomorphic encryption (HE) and zero-knowledge proofs (ZKPs) to ensure that only the model changes are confidential, and they can still be correctly aggregated (Colosimo and De Rango, 2023). Although these cryptographic techniques offered a high level of privacy measures, they proved to be computationally intensive and could not be scaled in large-client applications.

In order to address these limitations, subsequent designs came up with privacy-conscience robust aggregation schemes founded on multi-party computation (MPC) and additive secret sharing. These methods maintain the statistical strength and reduce leakage, a feat which has been called aggregated privacy-a condition in which the privacy is secured on both the individual and collective levels.

3.1.2 Differential-Privacy-Centric Approaches

The other notable trend is on the field of differential privacy (DP) to protect client data without incurring the excessive encryption costs. A dynamic privacy budget is provided by adaptive client-level DP mechanisms (Owen and Mattews, 2024), which adjust privacy budgets dynamically based on the sensitivity of data or frequency of contribution of a client. This allows better trade-off of robustness, utility, and computational efficiency, thus DP-based centralized FL can be applied in semi-trusted or large-scale consumer settings.

3.1.3 Performance and Trade-offs

Centralized FL has great controllability and easy deployability, but has weaknesses in scalability, communication bottlenecks, and concentration of trust (Qu et al., 2023). The security posture of the central server and the aggregation mechanism selected are critical to the overall security of the system. In addition, privacy controls such as HE or DP may reduce the accuracy of models or cause more latency unless optimized. Therefore, effective centralized FL applications have to be a fine balance of privacy strength, model fidelity, and operational efficiency -the same is reflected in Table 3.

Table 3. Key characteristics of centralized federated learning

Aspect	Description	Advantages	Limitations / Challenges
Architecture Type	Single central server coordinating multiple distributed clients	Simplifies orchestration and convergence management	Single point of failure; high dependency on server trust
Communication Pattern	Clients → Server → Clients (iterative aggregation cycle)	Easier version control and synchronization	Network congestion under large client counts
Privacy Mechanisms	Secure Aggregation, Homomorphic Encryption (HE), Zero-Knowledge Proofs (ZKP), Differential Privacy (DP)	Protects data during transmission and aggregation	HE/ZKP incur heavy computation; DP may reduce accuracy
Robustness Strategies	Robust aggregation, anomaly detection, client weighting	Improves resilience to outliers and poisoning	Limited defense if server is compromised
Suitable Use Cases	Enterprise data centers, healthcare consortia, banking, telecom analytics	Controlled, semi-trusted environments	Not ideal for highly dynamic or peer-to-peer networks
Recent Research Focus	Aggregated privacy, adaptive client-level DP, scalable HE/MPC protocols	Enhances privacy–utility balance	Still evolving toward efficient large-scale implementations

3.2 Hierarchical Federated Learning

Hierarchical Federated Learning (HFL) builds upon the centralized paradigm and proposes multi-layer aggregation models (which usually consist of clients, edge aggregators, and a global server). The design came into existence to overcome scalability and communication bottlenecks in large scale or widely distributed networks. Instead of the direct communication of all clients with a central coordinator, local clusters are created to do initial model aggregation at intermediate nodes prior to sending summarized updates towards higher levels.

Figure 3. Hierarchical federated learning with intermediate edge aggregators

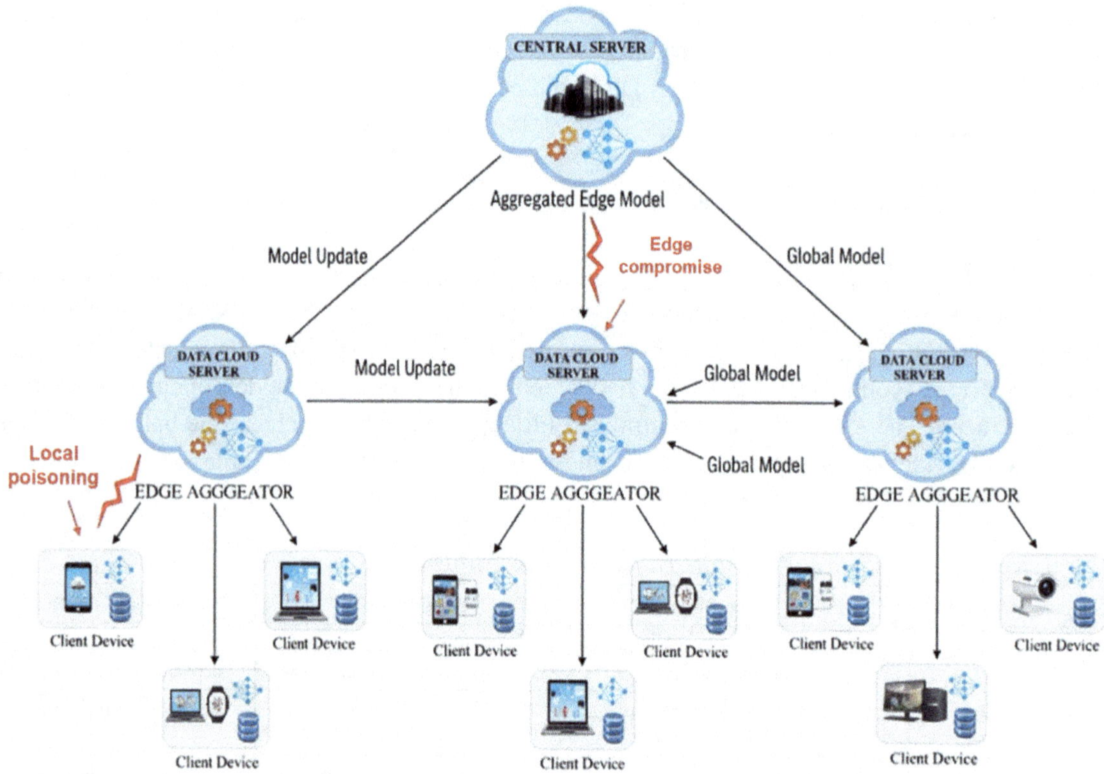

Architecturally, this technique is a reflection of the topology of contemporary computing infrastructures including edge-cloud systems and enterprise multi-branch systems as shown in Figure 3. Every intermediate aggregator is a learner as well as a coordinator that preserves the regional context but lessens uplink bandwidth and latency. Hierarchical structures present distinct issues on security and privacy front.

Although the multiple-layer aggregation increases the scalability it also introduces new attack surfaces- e.g. the weakened edge servers may inject or amplify poisoned updates before they reach the global server. The recent literature, including (Siriwardhana et al., 2024) and (Zhou et al., 2023), suggests architecture-aware design solutions, including SHIELD and edge-level differential privacy-based anomaly detection, and demonstrates that hybrid defenses can maintain their robustness despite compromising lower levels partially. Another interesting development in the field of HFL is the introduction of context-adaptive inter-layer trust management. Other systems use dynamic weights or trust scores on intermediate nodes, depending on the quality of data, history of participation or reputation, and therefore tie the evaluation of robustness to hierarchical topology.

Also, the secure aggregation and differential privacy at multiple levels facilitate regulatory compliance (e.g., GDPR, HIPAA) with an acceptable performance. Regarding the deployment perspective, hierarchical FL is consistent with the operational architecture of telecommunication networks, healthcare partnerships, and industrial IoT, where the data sovereignty and latency requirements require partial decentralization. Synchronization overhead, inter-tier trust coordination, and multi-layer encryption cost are however research issues that are underway. The key characteristics of hierarchical federated learning are described in Table 4.

Table 4. Key characteristics of hierarchical federated learning

Aspect	Description	Advantages	Limitations / Challenges
Architecture Type	Multi-layer aggregation: clients → edge nodes → global server	Scalable; reduces communication to central server	Complex synchronization; inter-layer latency
Communication Pattern	Local aggregation at edges before global update	Saves bandwidth; supports regional autonomy	Requires secure inter-tier communication
Privacy Mechanisms	Differential Privacy (DP), Secure Aggregation, Multi-tier encryption	Enhances privacy at both local and regional levels	DP noise accumulation across layers may degrade accuracy
Robustness Strategies	SHIELD-style robust aggregation, edge anomaly detection, trust-score weighting	Layer-aware resilience to poisoning	Vulnerable if intermediate aggregators are compromised
Suitable Use Cases	Telecom networks, IoT ecosystems, multi-hospital collaborations, smart cities	Effective for clustered or latency-sensitive environments	Needs strong trust coordination across layers
Recent Research Focus	Architecture-aware robustness, edge-level DP, hybrid trust management	Balances scalability, privacy, and resilience	Lacks standardized benchmarking for hierarchical deployments

3.3 Cross-Silo Federated Learning

Cross-silo Federated Learning (CSFL) is a model of collaboration between organizations or institutions, e.g., hospitals, banks, or enterprises, each of which is a separate silo with its data, management, and computing infrastructure. In contrast to cross-device settings, which have millions of short-lived participants, cross-silo FL usually has small numbers of stationary, high-capacity clients, which are semi-trusted and connected by well-known protocols.

Figure 4. Cross-silo federated learning among institutional participants

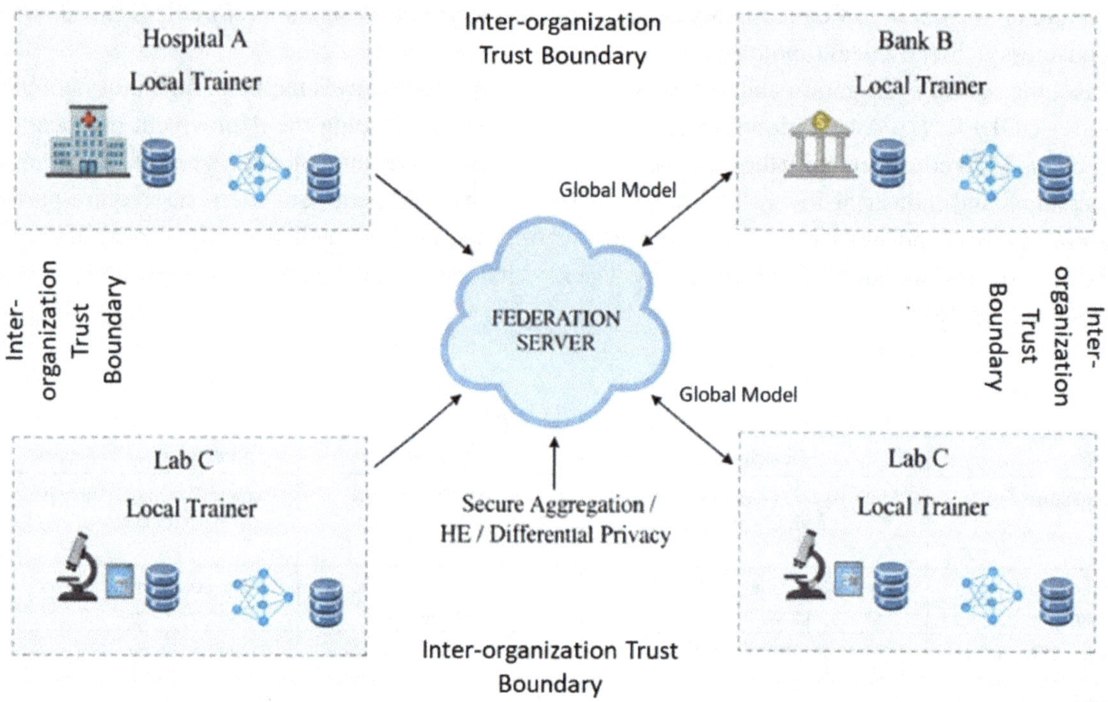

CSFL architecture as shown in Figure 4 falls between centralized and hierarchical FL. It has a central coordinator (or a coordinator based on a consortium), but the network participants, which are often whole organizations, are aggregated clients, training on large datasets locally. This architecture is appropriate in regulated industries, where information sharing is limited, but collaboration in intelligence is critical. Security and privacy wise, cross silo architectures are focused on organizational level privacy and not on individual anonymity. The primary threats are honest-but-curious server, silo-sililo collusion and gradient leakage or inference attacks. Accordingly, secure aggregation, distributed differential privacy (DP), and homomorphic encryption (HE) are used to protect the model parameters and intermediate updates in most recent works. As an example, (Byrd et al., 2022) and (Li et al., 2024) suggest collusion-resistant DP mechanisms and local Renyi DP with parameter sparsification to trade-off privacy, accuracy and the efficiency of communication.

New developments provide weighted and reputation-based aggregation schemes, particularly in the medical and financial fields, where the quality of data, frequency of participation and reliability differ across silos. Pragmatic compromise of privacy versus robustness sets the simplified CKKS homomorphic encryption with reputation-based weighting that is incorporated in (Ghanta et al., 2025). High availability and synchronization also has the advantage of CSFL systems, as the participants in an organization are usually online at all times, therefore facilitating greater global convergence and enhanced security update coordination. The inter-organization trust, however, is also a bottleneck- particularly where there are multi-jurisdictional international teams. Audit mechanism standardization, formal verification of aggregation protocols, and verifiable computation (e.g. through Zero-Knowledge Proofs) are new directions to be more reliable and comply. The key characteristics of Cross-Silo federated learning are described in Table 5.

Table 5. Key characteristics of cross-silo federated learning

Aspect	Description	Advantages	Limitations / Challenges
Architecture Type	Limited number of stable, high-capacity institutional clients coordinated by a central or consortium server	Reliable communication; easy synchronization	Requires inter-organizational trust agreements
Communication Pattern	Periodic aggregation between organizations	High-quality model updates due to stable clients	Limited scalability compared to cross-device FL
Privacy Mechanisms	Secure aggregation, organizational-level DP, HE	Protects institutional data ownership	Overhead in encryption and coordination
Robustness Strategies	Reputation-based weighting, sparsification, and trust scoring	Enhances robustness and fairness	Vulnerable to coordinated poisoning by colluding silos
Suitable Use Cases	Healthcare consortia, financial institutions, industrial collaborations	Strong governance and compliance control	Legal complexity under cross-border data laws
Recent Research Focus	Collusion-resistant DP, encrypted weighted aggregation, auditability	Improves accountability and privacy	Lack of unified benchmarking frameworks for silo-level evaluation

3.4 Cross-Device / Edge Federated Learning

The most scalable and decentralized type of FL is called Cross-Device or Edge Federated Learning (CDFL/EFL), in which thousands to millions of heterogeneous and intermittently connected devices, including smartphones, IoT sensors, or autonomous vehicles, are involved in the process of distributed model training. In contrast to cross-silo or hierarchical configurations, cross-device FL is executed in dynamic participation, under strict bandwidth, and varying computational endowments, necessitating dynamic protocols and minimalist communication plans.

In architectural terms as shown in Figure 5, cross-device FL is based on a central coordinator (usually a cloud-based) which coordinates model changes in the ever-evolving pool of edge clients. Everyone does local computation and sends model gradients or updates to the server which combines them into a global model. This architecture allows scalable personalization and the maintenance of privacy without moving raw data, which is important to consumer-facing applications like prediction of keys and activity detection and on-device medical analytics.

Figure 5. Cross-device or edge federated learning architecture

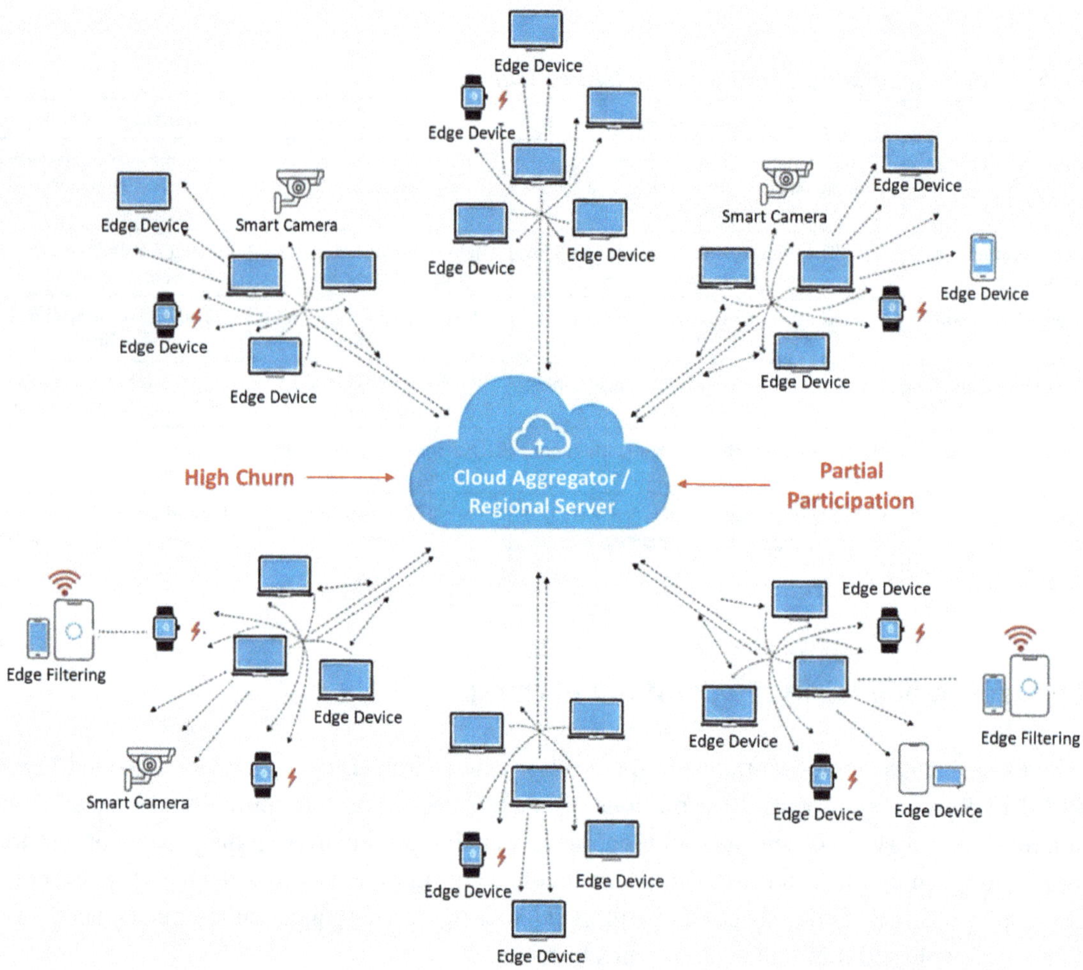

Security wise cross-device FL has distinct threats due to its magnitude and versatility. Devices may be malicious or compromised, and they may be unreliable, bringing with them poisoning or backdoor attacks. Besides, the large scale of participants also increases the threat of inference-based data leakage, despite conventional aggregation mechanisms. It was shown that (Zhou et al., 2023) can alleviate these threats using a combination of edge-level anomaly detection and differential privacy and still ensure a reasonable communication efficiency. Secure Aggregation and Differential Privacy (DP) are the main principles that allow maintaining privacy in CDFL and at the same time, make sure that the contributions of separate devices remain unpublished. Laws Lightweight cryptography methods, including additive homomorphic encryption or randomized masking, are commonly used in order to support devices with low computing power. It is also hard to balance the robustness, accuracy and the communication overhead however, particular under partial participation conditions or churning device conditions.

Recent studies have examined hybrid edge-cloud architectures, in which intermediate edge servers are utilized to do partial aggregation in order to minimize bandwidth consumption and latency.

Though the hybrid approaches enhance scalability it is accompanied by intermediate layers of trust which have to be secured. Moreover, adaptive client sampling, compression and/or sparsification are the new measures to enhance the energy efficiency and justice between different devices.

Nevertheless, cross-device FL is a pillar of the real-world FL implementation, even despite its complexity, and it stretches to the limits of privacy-preserving scalable intelligence. Future research would be to trustless aggregate through blockchain frameworks, federated reinforcement learning on the edge, and context-aware mechanisms of DP that require changes in sensibilities of devices and the participation rates. The key characteristics of Cross-Device / Edge federated learning are described in table 6.

Table 6. Key characteristics of cross-device / edge federated learning

Aspect	Description	Advantages	Limitations / Challenges
Architecture Type	Large-scale device participation under central orchestration	Enables decentralized, privacy-preserving learning	Dynamic participation complicates training stability
Communication Pattern	Asynchronous updates from edge clients to central server	Reduces data transfer; supports on-device privacy	High communication cost and latency under massive scale
Privacy Mechanisms	Secure Aggregation, Differential Privacy, Lightweight HE	Protects user-level data and updates	Limited by device compute and energy constraints
Robustness Strategies	Edge anomaly detection, adaptive client sampling, redundancy	Mitigates poisoning and unreliable clients	Vulnerable to large-scale coordinated attacks
Suitable Use Cases	Mobile applications, IoT systems, smart vehicles, wearable devices	Scalable, real-time, privacy-preserving	Requires strong device authentication and update integrity
Recent Research Focus	Hybrid edge–cloud FL, communication compression, trustless aggregation	Improves scalability and energy efficiency	Needs unified frameworks for dynamic trust and participation control

3.5 Decentralized / Peer-to-Peer Federated Learning

The further evolutionary step of collaborative intelligence is decentralized or Peer-to-peer Federated Learning (DPFL) which completely eliminates even the central coordinating server. Under this paradigm, the involved nodes (organizations or devices) interact and merge updates directly to their peers based on the established topologies, like a ring, mesh or gossip-based network (Qiao et al., 2024). It aims at attaining a fully distributed learning that can maintain privacy, autonomy, and resilience even when it is in untrusted environments. In architecture as described in figure 6, DPFL is an architecture that substitutes the classical hierarchy of server and client with one of peers, in which each node has a local model and periodically interchanges the updates with its neighbors. Instead of centralized control, the aggregation works through consensus mechanisms (e.g. decentralized averaging or verification with a blockchain). This creates a distrustful, fault tolerant network that will be able to keep learning even when certain participants fail or behave maliciously (Qu et al., 2023).

Figure 6. Decentralized / peer-to-peer federated learning

Security wise, decentralization automatically curbs the possibility of a single point of failure or information leakage by a central source. Nonetheless, the lack of a central verifier transfers this issue to peer authentication, consensus integrity, and resistance to Sybil attacks or collusion attacks. The use of techniques like blockchain-based audit trails, verifiable aggregation, as well as the secure multi-party computation (MPC) to guarantee the validity and accountability of updates is growing in popularity.

Privacy DPFL can be usually improved with local differential privacy, with secure peer exchange or with encrypted gossip averaging, such that the contribution of each individual is not distinguishable even at a multi-hop stage. However, it is still hard to be very accurate when concerned with communication limitations and when participants are asynchronous. Popular trade-offs in practice include bandwidth overheads, model divergence, and slow convergence.

The latest studies have examined how to apply distributed ledger technologies (DLTs) to DPFL systems, as blockchain or Directed Acyclic Graph (DAG)-based mechanisms of consensus keep records of model updates that are immutable. Such structures offer a way to be audited as well as incentives (e.g. token rewards) to participate honestly. Although resilience and transparency show good outcomes, scalability and energy efficiency are research questions whose answers are yet to be found - particularly with resource-constrained edge networks. By and large, decentralized FL provides a sense of self-organizing learning systems - autonomy, privacy-conscious, and worldwide distributed. With the maturity of cryptographic consensus protocols and lightweight peer authentication, DPFL will be applicable in future smarts in edge swarms, collaborative robotics, and trustless IoT systems. The key characteristics of Decentralized / Peer-to-Peer federated learning are described in Table 7.

Table 7. Key characteristics of decentralized / peer-to-peer federated learning

Aspect	Description	Advantages	Limitations / Challenges
Architecture Type	Fully distributed, no central coordinator; peer-to-peer communication	Eliminates single point of failure; enhances autonomy	Coordination and convergence are complex
Communication Pattern	Gossip-based or consensus-driven peer updates	Robust under node failure; supports dynamic topologies	High communication overhead and latency
Privacy Mechanisms	Local DP, encrypted peer exchange, MPC, blockchain audit	Strong privacy and transparency guarantees	Energy and storage cost for consensus maintenance
Robustness Strategies	Consensus verification, reputation scoring, blockchain-based validation	Resilient to tampering and central compromise	Vulnerable to Sybil or collusion attacks if peer identity not verified
Suitable Use Cases	Collaborative IoT, edge swarms, vehicular networks, multi-agent systems	Decentralized and fault-tolerant operation	Complex trust establishment among peers
Recent Research Focus	Blockchain/DAG integration, incentive mechanisms, verifiable aggregation	Enables trustless collaboration	Scalability and efficiency trade-offs remain significant

4. MODEL AGGREGATION STRATEGIES

The model aggregation step in FL stipulates the process by which local model changes by distributed clients are combined to create a global model. Although basic averaging algorithms like FedAvg still form the basis, history of FL learning has also presented various powerful, privacy-aware and adaptive aggregation algorithms to deal with data heterogeneity, adversarial manipulation, and communication limitations.

4.1 Aggregation based on Co-ordinates and Statistics.

The first studies were concerned with coordinate-wise approaches, including Median, Trimmed Mean, Krum, and Bulyan (Colosimo and De Rango, 2023). These algorithms are based on strong statistics to withstand outlier or Byzantine updates. The recent hybrids, such as Median-Krum and Weighted Median Aggregation (Kabbaj et al., 2024) have a superior performance in the heterogeneous data through the combination of distance-based selection and coordinate filtering. They are simple and have low computational cost, therefore they are appropriate in a baseline defense, but usually fail in very non-IID or adaptive attack conditions.

4.2.Trust- and Similarity-Based Weighting

Other techniques like FLTrust (Cao et al., 2020) proposed a reference set stored on the server to calculate trust scores between local and global updates. Trust normalization using cosine similarity in FLTrust and its variants (e.g., FedGreed (Kritharakis et al., 2025), CareFL) (Dong et al., 2024) can be shown to be more resistant to poisoning and label-flipping attacks, even in heterogeneous settings. Nevertheless, they require the existence of small, representative root data, which is not always practical in privacy-constrained applications.

4.3 Clustering, Spectral and Forest-Based Defenses.

In order to identify colluding or skimming opponents, a number of multi-stage pipelines use spectral and clustering-based filtering. Celtibero, FLAegis (Campos et al., 2025), and FLForest structures (Wang et al., 2023) are four-pronged defense (FPD) strategies, which are based on the combination of reliable selection, density analysis, and dimensionality reduction to isolate abnormal updates. Isolation forests (with more complexity on the server-side) have been empirically robust against non-IID and adaptive attacks and FFT-domain aggregation (as in FedRDF) (Campos et al., 2024) with lower complexity on the server-side.

4.4 Vetting by Inversion and Reconstruction.

An even more recent defense builds data distributions based on updates to the models to identify poisoned gradients. An example of this is FedInv which inverts client updates to dummy data and filters them with Wasserstein distance which, in effect, detects stealthy model poisoning in high heterogeneity. Similar methods, including inversion of artificial gradients and distribution commitment methods, have interpretability and cannot be used with encrypted or completely privacy-preserving systems.

4.5 Heterogeneity Adapters and Aggregation With Participation.

One of the challenges that FL faces is non-IID data. Adaptive approaches such as GAS (Gradient Splitting) (Liu et al., 2023) and BOBA (Bao et al., 2024) alter the aggregation rule directly, to consider the imbalance in the distribution of data. GAS breaks updates down into homogenous subspaces to mitigate the curse of dimensionality, whereas BOBA (Bao et al., 2024) ensures label skew with convergence guarantees. The complementary method, including D-Byz-SGDM, provides robustness to partial participation by adding delayed momentum buffers to stabilize the global updates even in case of transient Byzantine majorities.

4.6 Secure and Privacy-Preserving Robust Aggregation.

Since FL is becoming more privacy-aware, the need to have compatibility between robustness and cryptography has become crucial. Homomorphic encryption (HE) is used in protocols like PEAR in order to compute encrypted scores of similarity with cosine across two servers and guarantee privacy and poisoning resilience. Likewise, BSR-FL incorporates functional encryption, blockchain-style accountability, and insecure similarity measurements to strengthen the belief in collaborative training.

In the literature, there are not many studies which analyze attack success rate (ASR), clean accuracy, convergence stability, and overhead simultaneously under non-IID and partial participation conditions. The most inclusive ones are FLTrust, FedInv (Zhao et al., 2022), FPD, GAS, Celtibero (Molina-Coronado, 2024), D-Byz-SGDM, PEAR, and BSR-FL, which are various design philosophies that are based on different paradigms: statistical, trust-based, spectral, and cryptographic. A summary of their comparative synthesis is provided in table 8 and shows their assumptions, deployability, and theoretical coverage along the dimensions of threat and heterogeneity.

Table 8. Comparative summary of model aggregation strategies

Ref.	Core Idea	Server Data	Secure Aggregation	Non-IID Handling	Server Complexity
(Cao et al., 2020)	Cosine-sim trust + magnitude norm	Yes (root)	No; needs plaintext	Relies on root data	O(nd) per round
(Colosimo & De Rango, 2023)	Krum + coordinate median	No	Plaintext only	Robustness not fully analyzed	Krum: $O(n^2d)$, median: O(nd)
(Kabbaj et al., 2024)	Distance-based weighting + median	No	Unclear	Empirical IID/non-IID	Pairwise distance + median
(Wan et al., 2022)	Bandit client selection + sybil filters	No	Needs per-client visibility	Explicitly non-IID	O(n) per-round scoring + selection
(Wan et al., 2023)	Selection + score detection + spectral outlier + denoising	No	Needs individual updates	Non-IID via spectral module	Multiple spectral passes
(Molina-Coronado, 2024)	Layered aggregation pipeline	No	Needs per-update access	Claims strong non-IID	Layered filters
(Campos et al., 2025)	SAX + spectral clustering + FFT aggregation	No	Needs plaintext	Evaluated under non-IID	Spectral + FFT
(Campos et al., 2024)	Fourier-domain density selection	No	Needs plaintext	Handles non-IID	FFT per update + selection
(Wang et al., 2023)	Isolation forest on update deltas	No	Needs plaintext	Robust in highly non-IID	Train per round
(Liu et al., 2023)	Gradient splitting for robust AGRs	Yes (base AGR)	Yes	Convergence analyzed	Splitting overhead
(Bao et al., 2024)	Two-stage label-skew method	No	Plaintext	Focus on label skew	Efficient two-stage selector
(Li et al., 2019)	Robust stochastic aggregation	No	Yes	Handles heterogeneous datasets	Similar to SGD + robust regularizer

continued on following page

Table 8. Continued

Ref.	Core Idea	Server Data	Secure Aggregation	Non-IID Handling	Server Complexity
(Fang et al., 2025)	Synthetic server updates + robust rules	No	Needs plaintext	Targets heterogeneity	Synthetic update overhead
(Zhao et al., 2022)	Invert updates + Wasserstein filter	No server data	Needs plaintext; not secure	Explicitly non-IID	Per-client inversion + distances
(Zhao et al., 2021)	Data commitment + Wasserstein comparison	No	Commitment protocol	Non-IID	Commitment + Wasserstein
(Li et al., 2024)	Artificial gradients + L2 weighting	No	Needs plaintext	Non-IID	Inversion + per-client weighting
(Dong et al., 2024)	Loss-based contribution	Optional	No	Broad attack spectrum	Server-side per-client loss
(Kritharakis et al., 2025)	Greedy selection by server loss	Yes (trusted)	No	Non-IID	Per-round evaluation + subset selection

5. SECURITY AND PRIVACY REQUIREMENTS

Since FL is shifting to the real world implementation as a concept, security and privacy become the most critical pillars that determine its reliability and acceptance. Although FL will mitigate the risks of centralized information exposure by its very nature, it presents new points of attack related to distributed computing, model sharing, and coordination of trust. This part outlines the main threat vectors of FL systems and discusses modern defense mechanisms, which are secure aggregation, encryption, differential privacy, and trust management, and which jointly protect the integrity and confidentiality of federated ecosystems.

5.1 Threats to Federated Learning.

There are numerous adversarial and information-theoretic threats to Federated Learning systems that can result in compromised model performance, sensitive data leakage or disruption of the collaborative process. These may be grouped in three large classes:

Poisoning attacks on data and models: In this type of attack, the attacker attempts to introduce malicious code into the data or model, which is then executed during a subsequent run of the model or program.

a) **Data and Model Poisoning Attacks-** There are data and model poisoning attacks whereby the attacker tries to insert malicious code in the data or model that is later run in a later execution of the model or a program. In poisoning attacks, the opponents use local training data or gradients to compromise the global model or plant backdoors. In data poisoning, the training data is modified to cause model updates to be biased (e.g. targeted misclassification) (Campos et.al., 2025).

Model poisoning consists of designing poisonous gradient updates that survive on aggregation. These attacks are especially effective in cross-device and hierarchical FL when the central server does not have access to raw updates because of privacy limitations. Strategies in defense have been robust aggregation (Krum, Trimmed Mean, Median), anomaly detection and reputation-weighted updates, as in SHIELD and EPPRFL.

b) **Inference and Privacy Attacks-** Adversaries can also attack inference, even without access to data, that is, they can rebuild private information using shared model parameters or gradients. Common forms include: Membership inference, whether a data sample was used to train a model or not. .Inferring property, disclosing sensitive properties of model behavior. Reconstruction of rough input data using gradients model inversion.

Such risks exist in both cross-silo and medical FL architectures. The countermeasures are based on the Differential Privacy (DP) and Homomorphic Encryption (HE) to mathematically restrict the release of information without adversely affecting the utility of learning.

c) **Communication/ Protocol Attacks-** Communication channels are susceptible to: Since FL operates based on repetitive exchanges between clients and servers, communication channels are prone to: Eavesdropping or man-in-the-middle attack, which results in model update leakage.

Replay attacks or dropout manipulation, in which attackers modify synchronization patterns in order to influence convergence. Compromised client model update forgery. Secure aggregation protocols, authenticated encryption and integrity verification mechanisms (e.g. digital signatures or blockchain-based auditing) are mitigation requirements.

5.2 Secure Aggregation, Encryption and Differentiated Privacy.

In an attempt to overcome the threats mentioned above, FL uses a layered defense approach that involves the combination of cryptography, privacy-preserving computation, and statistical protection.

a) **Secure Aggregation-** Secure aggregation protocols allow the server to calculate the sum of model updates without having to access the contribution of any particular client. Easy to recognize are (Bonawitz et al., 2017) and their successors, which apply additive secret sharing or pairwise masking. The more developed schemes combine strong statistics and homomorphic encryption to obtain the confidentiality and Byzantine resilience. Secure aggregation is commonly used to counter honest-but-curious servers in centralized FL. Hierarchical FL goes further to include multi-tier aggregation, which introduces encryption between edge and global servers.
b) **Multi-Party Computation (MPC) and Homomorphic Encryption (HE)-** HE enables mathematical operations on encrypted data, which makes it possible to perform privacy-preserving gradient aggregation. Schemes like CKKS and Paillier have been adopted very much because they provide balance between accuracy and efficiency. Certain hybrid models implement MPC to spread trust among two or more parties, so that none of them is aware of intermediate outcomes. These techniques are very secure, but they can introduce computational and communication overhead and are better applied to cross-silo or medical FL, as opposed to large-scale cross-device applications.
c) **Differential Privacy (DP)-** DP adds noise in a carefully calibrated manner to model updates, which offers probabilistic privacy guarantees. In cross-device FL, local DP is used, whereby each client adds noise independently before transmission.

Central DP is implemented at the aggregator level balancing between accuracy and privacy among participants. Recent studies consider adaptive and Renyi DP to dynamically optimize the privacy budgets to maintain accuracy in heterogeneous settings. Despite the fact that DP is a successful way to reduce inference risk, over-noise may adversely affect model convergence--a long-standing privacy-utility trade off.

5.3 Authentication and Trust Management.

Mutual authentication and dynamic trust among participants is also essential in FL deployment. Given that FL deals with several autonomous nodes, it is important to know whom to trust and who to be suspicious of.

a) **Mechanisms of Authentication-** Secure authentication will make sure that only trusted parties make contributions to model updates. Common applications apply public key infrastructure (PKI), digital certificates or blockchain-based identity models in order to generate cryptographic trust. New strategies utilize light signatures of resource constrained edge devices.
b) **Trust and Reputation Systems-** Trust management frameworks use trust scores which are allocated according to how the client conducts, the quality of his or her contributions, and the quality of his or her performance in the consecutive rounds. These scores are used to aggregate weights, enhance resistance to poisoning and manipulation of dropout. They are reputation-aware aggregation in cross-silo medical FL and trust-based clustering in hierarchical FL.
c) **Auditability and Transparency-** The use of blockchain or distributed ledger technologies (DLTs) will increase auditability and non-repudiation when applied to federated systems. Irreversible records of changes will prevent the bad actors and allow enforcing privacy rules like GDPR and HIPAA.

6. EMERGING TRENDS AND FUTURE DIRECTIONS

The research space is shifting quickly to more integrated, intelligent and ethically-oriented architectures as FL moves away to systems beyond conceptual frameworks into production-scale systems. New trends include the increased decentralization, improved interoperability with the edge infrastructures, and compatibility with the international privacy and governance principles. This part summarizes three critical trends defining the future of secure and adaptive federated ecosystems: blockchain-based FL, FL plus edge computing and regulatory-ethical frameworks which guarantee responsible innovation.

6.1 Blockchain-Enabled Federated Learning

The combination of Federated Learning with blockchain is a radical change to a trustless and auditable collaboration. The distributed ledger, immutability, and consensus mechanisms of blockchain technology handle the fundamental weaknesses of traditional FL, such as the centralization of trust, validation of updates, and transparency. Figure 7 describes the architecture of blockchain enabled FL.

a) Decentralized Trust and Consensus- The distributed consensus mechanism provided by blockchain is an alternative to the use of a central server, where the peers are able to authenticate and register model updates within the blockchain, making them immutable. Every transaction (or model update) will be signed and time-stamped and sent out over the network, and verifiable authenticity ensured and rollback or tampering attacks prevented.

b) Incentivization and Reputation -BFL facilitates fair play and ongoing client interaction by incorporating token incentive systems, blockchain-based FL. The smart contracts constructed into reputation systems enable automatic rewarding or punishing of clients according to the quality of updates and their reliability.

c) Auditability and Compliance- The blockchain, which cannot be changed, offers traceability and accountability, which gives auditable logs to regulatory bodies, especially in cross-silo and decentralized FL where the governance lines are indistinct. Nevertheless, scalability, latency and energy efficiency continue to be challenged particularly when integrating blockchain with edge nodes with resource constraints. Studies of lightweight ledger (e.g. DAG-based or consortium blockchains) are aimed at mitigating these drawbacks.

Figure 7. Blockchain-enabled federated learning architecture

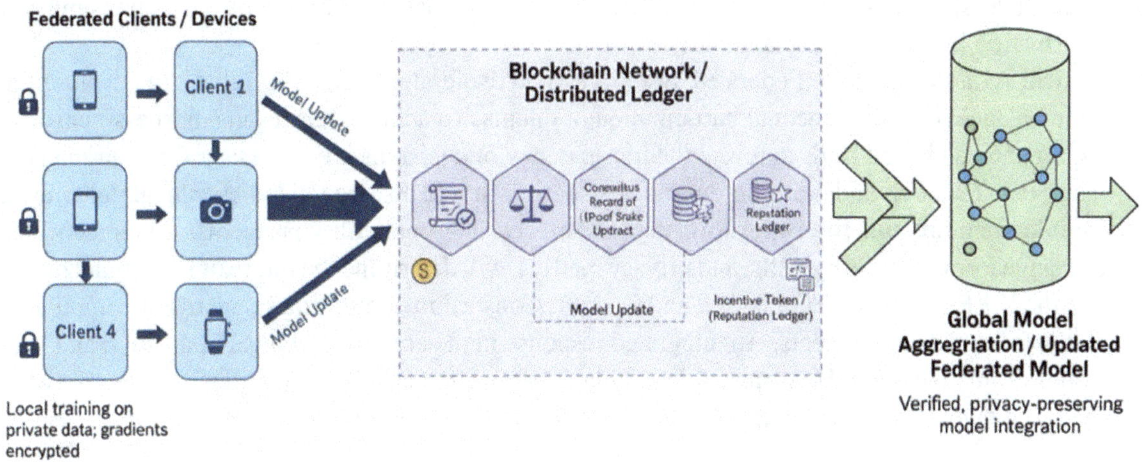

6.2 Federated Learning with Edge Computing

Federated Learning and Edge Computing (FLEC) are converging and transforming the architecture of distributed intelligence. Under this hybrid paradigm, edge nodes play the role of both learners and intermediaries, which are between local devices and cloud servers.

a) **Low Latency and Bandwidth**- Edge computing also minimizes the communication costs by pre-aggregating or training models locally around the sources of data. This reduces the uplink expenses by a great margin and allows real-time learning, which is essential to time-sensitive applications like autonomous driving, intelligent manufacturing, or IoT ecosystems.

b) **Context-Sensitive Personalization**- Edge-based FL enables regional learning or user-group learning. As an example, edge server can be used in healthcare or retail analytics to learn domain-specific submodels, which will be subsequently incorporated into a global framework, preserving both local applicability and global consistency.

c) **Security and Resilience**- FL in combination with edge computing increases the resistance to the one-point failure and provides the ability to control privacy locally. The new designs use multi-layer security protocols, which incorporate secure aggregation and Differential Privacy (DP) on both the device and the edge levels. Maintaining heterogeneous edge infrastructures synchronization and consistency of models is however an open problem.

6.3 Regulatory and Ethical Issues.

In addition to technological innovation, the long-term sustainability of Federated Learning will be determined by its compliance with the global data governance, ethical AI systems, and user rights.

a) **Data Protection Laws Compliance**- The privacy-by-design model of FL is also well aligned with the regulatory requirements like the General Data Protection Regulation (GDPR), Health Insurance Portability and Accountability Act (HIPAA), and Digital Personal Data Protection Act (DPDP, 2023). Nevertheless, there is still regulatory uncertainty in the ownership of models, the responsibility of information leaking, and explainability.
b) **Ethical AI and Fairness**- Federated systems should avoid algorithmic bias that can be caused by an imbalance of data or unequal participation of clients. To achieve fair results, fairness-conscious aggregation and audit trails to reveal the transparency of decisions are necessary. Consent management, data retention and cross-border models sharing should also be guided by ethical guidelines.
c) **Standardization and Interoperability**- Standardized interoperability protocols, which are model exchange formats, security APIs, and privacy metrics, will determine the future of FL. Organizations like the IEEE, ISO/IEC JTC 1/SC 42 and OpenFL Consortium are setting standards of compliance-ready, federated deployments. An integrated response in the areas of technical innovation and legal responsibility is essential to responsible scaling. The governance of FL ecosystems is effective when there is dynamic interaction between three layers as shown in Figure 8.

Figure 8. Regulatory and ethical landscape in federated learning

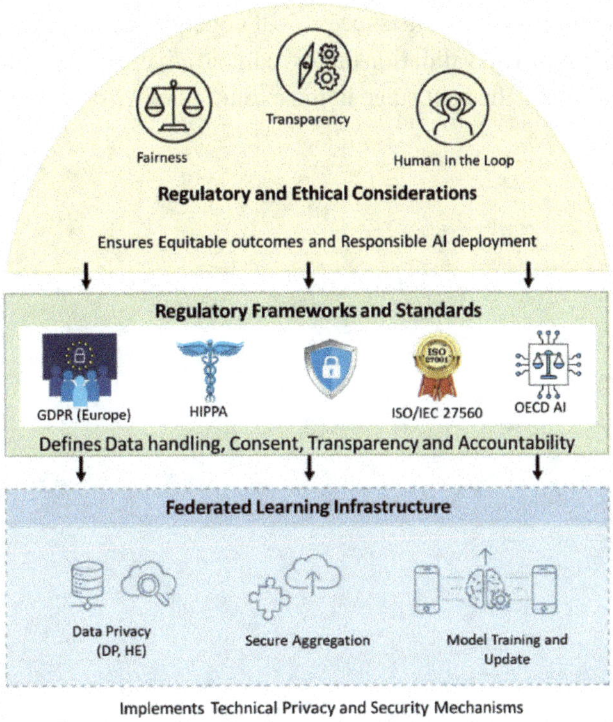

- Technical Layer - deploys privacy and security controls, which include differential privacy, secure aggregation, and encryption.
- Governance Layer- formalizes regulatory compliance by standards, auditing and consent management.
- Ethical Layer - makes sure that design, deployment, and evaluation are directed by human values.

These layers combined create a hierarchy of accountability, i.e.: code, compliance, and conscience, that must be maintained in order to have federated learning systems that are trustworthy, legally compliant and ethically aligned.

CONCLUSION

Federated learning has progressed beyond a privacy-preserving alternative to centralized training, becoming a foundation for secure, collaborative intelligence across institutions and devices. Its architectural diversity—spanning hierarchical, decentralized, and hybrid forms—reflects ongoing efforts to balance scalability with security. The review of aggregation strategies demonstrates that robustness and privacy often compete for resources: methods ensuring one tend to compromise the other unless carefully integrated. Future designs must therefore move toward unified frameworks that combine statistical resilience, adaptive optimization, and cryptographic safeguards. As federated learning enters domains such as healthcare, IoT, and autonomous systems, its success will depend on transparent governance, verifiable trust models, and continued empirical validation under realistic adversarial conditions. This convergence of architecture and security marks the next stage in the evolution of trustworthy distributed intelligence.

REFERENCES

Aggarwal, M., Khullar, V., & Goyal, N. (2024). A comprehensive review of federated learning: Methods, applications, and challenges in privacy-preserving collaborative model training. *Applied Data Science and Smart Systems*, 570-575.

Al-Shedivat, M., Gillenwater, J., Xing, E., & Rostamizadeh, A. (2020). Federated learning via posterior averaging: A new perspective and practical algorithms. *arXiv preprint arXiv:2010.05273.*

Alatawi, M. N. (2025). EdgeGuard-IoT: 6G-Enabled Edge Intelligence for Secure Federated Learning and Adaptive Anomaly Detection in Industry 5.0. *Computers, Materials & Continua*, *85*(1), 695–727. DOI: 10.32604/cmc.2025.066606

Albshaier, L., Almarri, S., & Albuali, A. (2025). Federated learning for cloud and edge security: A systematic review of challenges and AI opportunities. *Electronics (Basel)*, *14*(5), 1019. DOI: 10.3390/electronics14051019

Bao, W., Wu, J., & He, J. (2024, April). BOBA: Byzantine-robust federated learning with label skewness. In *International Conference on Artificial Intelligence and Statistics* (pp. 892-900). PMLR.

Bonawitz, K., Ivanov, V., Kreuter, B., Marcedone, A., McMahan, H. B., Patel, S., & Seth, K. (2017, October). Practical secure aggregation for privacy-preserving machine learning. In *Proceedings of the 2017 ACM SIGSAC Conference on Computer and Communications Security* (pp. 1175-1191). DOI: 10.1145/3133956.3133982

Byrd, D., Mugunthan, V., Polychroniadou, A., & Balch, T. (2022, November). Collusion resistant federated learning with oblivious distributed differential privacy. In *Proceedings of the Third ACM International Conference on AI in Finance* (pp. 114-122). DOI: 10.1145/3533271.3561754

Campos, E. M., Gonzalez-Vidal, A., Hernández-Ramos, J. L., & Skarmeta, A. (2024). FedRDF: A robust and dynamic aggregation function against poisoning attacks in federated learning. *IEEE Transactions on Emerging Topics in Computing.*

Campos, E. M., Vidal, A. G., Ramos, J. L. H., & Skarmeta, A. (2025). FLAegis: A Two-Layer Defense Framework for Federated Learning Against Poisoning Attacks. *arXiv preprint arXiv:2508.18737.*

Cao, X., Fang, M., Liu, J., & Gong, N. Z. (2020). Fltrust: Byzantine-robust federated learning via trust bootstrapping. *arXiv preprint arXiv:2012.13995.*

Colosimo, F., & De Rango, F. (2023, October). Median-krum: A joint distance-statistical based byzantine-robust algorithm in federated learning. In *Proceedings of the Int'l ACM Symposium on Mobility Management and Wireless Access* (pp. 61-68). DOI: 10.1145/3616390.3618283

Dong, Q., Yang, S., Dai, Z., Gao, Y., Wang, S., Cao, Y., Fu, A., & Susilo, W. (2024). Carefl: Contribution guided byzantine-robust federated learning. *IEEE Transactions on Information Forensics and Security*, *19*, 9714–9729. DOI: 10.1109/TIFS.2024.3477912

Fang, M., Nabavirazavi, S., Liu, Z., Sun, W., Iyengar, S. S., & Yang, H. (2025). Do we really need to design new byzantine-robust aggregation rules? *arXiv preprint arXiv:2501.17381*. DOI: 10.14722/ndss.2025.241796

Ghanta, S., Boyapati, P., Biswas, S., Pradhan, A. K., & Mohanty, S. P. (2025). Enhancing privacy-preserving brain tumor classification with adaptive reputation-aware federated learning and homomorphic encryption. *PeerJ. Computer Science*, *11*, e3165. DOI: 10.7717/peerj-cs.3165 PMID: 40989296

Hou, S., Li, S., Jahani-Nezhad, T., & Caire, G. (2025). PriRoAgg: Achieving robust model aggregation with minimum privacy leakage for federated learning. *IEEE Transactions on Information Forensics and Security*, *20*, 5690–5704. DOI: 10.1109/TIFS.2025.3577498

Huang, C., Huang, J., & Liu, X. (2022). Cross-silo federated learning: Challenges and opportunities. *arXiv preprint arXiv:2206.12949.*

Kabbaj, H., El-Azouzi, R., & Kobbane, A. (2024, September). Robust federated learning via weighted median aggregation. In *2024 2nd International Conference on Federated Learning Technologies and Applications (FLTA)* (pp. 298-303). IEEE. DOI: 10.1109/FLTA63145.2024.10839757

Koripalli, M. (2025). The Future of Data Platforms: AI-Driven Automation and Self-Optimizing Systems. *Journal of Computer Science and Technology Studies*, *7*(2), 483–488. DOI: 10.32996/jcsts.2025.7.2.50

Kritharakis, E., Makris, A., Jakovetic, D., & Tserpes, K. (2025). Fedgreed: A byzantine-robust loss-based aggregation method for federated learning. *arXiv preprint arXiv:2508.18060.*

Layode, O., Naiho, H. N. N., Adeleke, G. S., Udeh, E. O., & Labake, T. T. (2024). Data privacy and security challenges in environmental research: Approaches to safeguarding sensitive information. *International Journal of Applied Research in Social Sciences*, *6*(6), 1193–1214. DOI: 10.51594/ijarss.v6i6.1210

Le, J., Zhang, D., Lei, X., Jiao, L., Zeng, K., & Liao, X. (2023). Privacy-preserving federated learning with malicious clients and honest-but-curious servers. *IEEE Transactions on Information Forensics and Security*, *18*, 4329–4344. DOI: 10.1109/TIFS.2023.3295949

Li, L., Fan, Y., & Lin, K. Y. (2020, October). A survey on federated learning. In *2020 IEEE 16th International Conference on Control & Automation (ICCA)* (pp. 791-796). IEEE. DOI: 10.1109/ICCA51439.2020.9264412

Li, L., Xu, W., Chen, T., Giannakis, G. B., & Ling, Q. (2019, July). RSA: Byzantine-robust stochastic aggregation methods for distributed learning from heterogeneous datasets. *Proceedings of the AAAI Conference on Artificial Intelligence*, *33*(01), 1544–1551. DOI: 10.1609/aaai.v33i01.33011544

Li, M., Tang, X., Zhang, T., Liu, G., & Weng, Y. (2024, December). Byzantine-robust federated learning on non-iid data via inversing artificial gradients. In *GLOBECOM 2024-2024 IEEE Global Communications Conference* (pp. 355-360). IEEE. DOI: 10.1109/GLOBECOM52923.2024.10900971

Li, W., Yu, P., Cheng, Y., Yan, J., & Zhang, Z. (2024). Efficient and privacy-enhanced federated learning based on parameter degradation. *IEEE Transactions on Services Computing*, *17*(5), 2304–2319. DOI: 10.1109/TSC.2024.3399659

Li, X., Yang, X., Zhou, Z., & Lu, R. (2024). Efficiently achieving privacy preservation and poisoning attack resistance in federated learning. *IEEE Transactions on Information Forensics and Security, 19*, 4358–4373. DOI: 10.1109/TIFS.2024.3378006

Liu, Y., Chen, C., Lyu, L., Wu, F., Wu, S., & Chen, G. (2023, July). Byzantine-robust learning on heterogeneous data via gradient splitting. In *International Conference on Machine Learning* (pp. 21404-21425). PMLR.

Mbah, G. O. (2024). Data privacy in the era of AI: Navigating regulatory landscapes for global businesses. *Int. J. Sci. Res. Anal, 13*(2), 2396–2405.

Molina-Coronado, B. (2024). Celtibero: Robust layered aggregation for federated learning. *arXiv preprint arXiv:2408.14240.*

Nguyen, T., & Thai, M. T. (2023). Preserving privacy and security in federated learning. *IEEE/ACM Transactions on Networking, 32*(1), 833–843. DOI: 10.1109/TNET.2023.3302016

Owen, A., & Mattews, A. (2024). Privacy Rights and Interoperability: A Comparative Study of Regulations.

Sargiotis, D. (2024). The Importance of Data Governance: Why It Matters in Today's World. In *Data Governance: A Guide* (pp. 87–136). Springer Nature Switzerland. DOI: 10.1007/978-3-031-67268-2_2

Siriwardhana, Y., Porambage, P., Liyanage, M., Marchal, S., & Ylianttila, M. (2024). Shield-secure aggregation against poisoning in hierarchical federated learning. *IEEE Transactions on Dependable and Secure Computing.*

Sun, H., Zhang, Y., Zhuang, H., Li, J., Xu, Z., & Wu, L. (2025). PEAR: Privacy-preserving and effective aggregation for byzantine-robust federated learning in real-world scenarios. *The Computer Journal, 68*(9), bxae086. DOI: 10.1093/comjnl/bxae086

Wan, W., Hu, S., Li, M., Lu, J., Zhang, L., Zhang, L. Y., & Jin, H. (2023, October). A four-pronged defense against byzantine attacks in federated learning. In *Proceedings of the 31st ACM international conference on multimedia* (pp. 7394-7402). DOI: 10.1145/3581783.3612474

Wan, W., Hu, S., Lu, J., Zhang, L. Y., Jin, H., & He, Y. (2022). Shielding federated learning: Robust aggregation with adaptive client selection. *arXiv preprint arXiv:2204.13256.* DOI: 10.24963/ijcai.2022/106

Wang, T., Zhao, B., & Fang, L. (2023, January). FLForest: Byzantine-robust federated learning through isolated forest. In *2022 IEEE 28th International Conference on Parallel and Distributed Systems (ICPADS)* (pp. 296-303). IEEE.

Yazdinejad, A., Dehghantanha, A., Karimipour, H., Srivastava, G., & Parizi, R. M. (2024). A robust privacy-preserving federated learning model against model poisoning attacks. *IEEE Transactions on Information Forensics and Security, 19*, 6693–6708. DOI: 10.1109/TIFS.2024.3420126

Zhao, B., Sun, P., Fang, L., Wang, T., & Jiang, K. (2021). FedCom: A byzantine-robust local model aggregation rule using data commitment for federated learning. *arXiv preprint arXiv:2104.08020.*

Zhao, B., Sun, P., Wang, T., & Jiang, K. (2022, June). Fedinv: Byzantine-robust federated learning by inversing local model updates. *Proceedings of the AAAI Conference on Artificial Intelligence*, *36*(8), 9171–9179. DOI: 10.1609/aaai.v36i8.20903

Zhou, J., Wu, N., Wang, Y., Gu, S., Cao, Z., Dong, X., & Choo, K. K. R. (2022). A differentially private federated learning model against poisoning attacks in edge computing. *IEEE Transactions on Dependable and Secure Computing*, *20*(3), 1941–1958. DOI: 10.1109/TDSC.2022.3168556

Chapter 4
Edge Computing and Security Concerns in Federated AI

Bright Keswani
https://orcid.org/0000-0003-1464-0431
Poornima University, India

Sheng-Lung Peng
National Taipei University of Business, Taiwan

Ashwini Kumar
https://orcid.org/0000-0002-7760-6030
Poornima University, India

Dharmveer Yadav
https://orcid.org/0000-0002-3393-7524
St. Xavier's College, India

Kushagra Keswani
https://orcid.org/0009-0009-8314-2744
Poornima University, India

ABSTRACT

Federated Artificial Intelligence (AI) represents one of the rotations in the approach to training decentralized and privacy-preserving machine learning models. The heterogeneity of edge devices, unreliable communication networks, and physical unreachability exposes federated systems to a general set of attack-based model inversion, data poisoning, man-in-the-middle attacks and adversarial manipulations. The aim of this chapter is to cover the security issues of federated AI systems with a particular focus on the edge systems. It tries to (i) Analyze the natural security dangers caused by edge computing surroundings in FL, (ii) comment on the various architectural answers and mitigation strategies adopted to secure federated learning at the edge and (iii) compare the trade-offs between the latency-accuracy-trust-privacy space.

DOI: 10.4018/979-8-3373-6224-3.ch004

1. INTRODUCTION

Federated Learning (FL) is a more contemporary approach to training artificial intelligence models without necessarily congregating all the information at a central location. Traditionally, machine learning relied on the aggregation of information of various users or organizations in one server whereby the training was done. There were a few concerns that were brought about by this centralization, particularly concerned with the issue of privacy and security as sensitive information such as medical records, monetary dealings or personal communication logs had to be transferred. FL addresses this issue by enabling the training process to run on the devices that the data is generated including smartphones, medical sensors, or computers. Sharing with a central server is only done with something learned by the model and not data itself. This offers the opportunity of constructing strong models without violating user privacy. Thanks to these benefits, FL is being applied more and more in sphere of healthcare, banking, mobile applications and projects of smart cities where personal or sensitive data is a top priority.

1.1 Background on Federated Learning (FL)

Federated Learning is a revolutionary change in the process of training and deployment of AI models. Contrary to traditional centralized training models where mass amounts of data are processed and stored in a central hub FL decentralizes the training process and stores the data where it originates and transmits only the learned model updates (gradients or parameters) to a coordinating server (Brecko et al., 2022; Zafar et al., 2025; Moore et al., 2023). This design will be such that the sensitive user information does not go out of the local device, which provides regulatory and ethical issues revolving around data privacy, ownership, and security. With the federated scheme, a central server starts a global model, which is transmitted to many clients (edge devices). Every device trains the model on its dataset locally and then transfers the updates to the model to the server. These updates are summed up by the server and are typically refined by means of such algorithm as Federated Averaging (FedAvg) to enhance the global model (Brecko et al., 2022). The process is repeated until the model converges.

Federated Learning is most suitable in healthcare, finance and smart mobile ecosystems (Moore et al., 2023; Papernot et al., 2017; Truong et al., 2020). As an example, collaborative training of diagnostic models can be conducted using patient information in hospital databases in medical systems without publicizing personal health records (Bonawitz et al., 2019). By analogy, in the case of smartphone-based applications, FL allows predictive suggestions on the keyboards or voice recognition enhancements and protects personal usage information (Albshaier et al., 2025; Abadi et al., 2016).

Figure 1. Overview of edge-enabled federated AI ecosystem

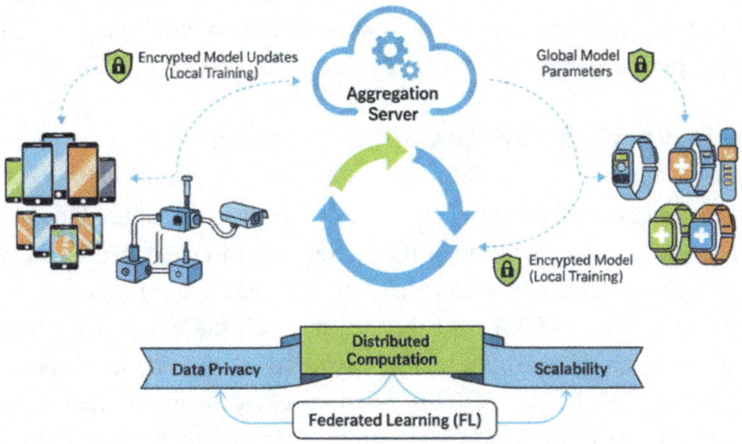

Figure 1 gives a clear picture of standard Edge-Enabled Federated AI Ecosystem. In such system various devices like smartphones, IoT nodes, medical wearables perform local training and transmit encrypted model updates to an aggregation server. It is an ecosystem that represents the way FL facilitates the privacy of data, distributed computation, and scalability in current AI systems (Brecko et al., 2022; Moore et al., 2023).

1.2 Emergence of Edge Computing in FL

The implementation of edge computing in the federated learning has transformed the way AI is computed, as well as, the location. The way data is decentralized in edge computing is also accompanied by the decentralization of computational workloads where data processing tasks of an IoT gateway, smart sensors, and mobile devices are moved nearer to the data sources instead of being processed through centralized cloud servers (Nakamoto, 2008). This paradigm lowers the communication latency and network congestion by a large margin as well as the bandwidth usage that are key to time sensitive federated applications (Zhang et al., 2020; He et al., 2020). FL is characterized by superior scalability and real-time learning when it is applied on edge nodes. As an example, in smart urban systems, edge-based

FL can be used to learn continuously on distributed cameras and sensors without sending large video streams to the cloud (Wang et al., 2020). Edge computing, in 5G and IoT networks, supports localized model updates to the dynamic environment to enhance the contextual accuracy of the model (Bonawitz et al., 2019; Zafar et al., 2025).

Nevertheless, the application of edge computing in combination with FL presents new design issues (He et al., 2020). The fact that edge systems are decentralized and resource constrained increases the area of attack exposing both, communication and computation processes, to potential adversarial activities (Bonawitz et al., 2019; Zhao et al., 2021). This federated learning with edge computing so-called Edge Federated AI will most likely form the core of the next generation of intelligent, privacy-preserving, and autonomous computing platforms (Peng et al., 2024; Papernot et al., 2017; Shokri et al., 2017).

1.3 Security and Privacy Challenges in Edge-based FL

Whereas FL provides improved privacy via locality of data, it is distributed in nature with edge-level constraints, which creates considerable vulnerabilities. Security threats may exist in three distinct layers, which are the device level, communication network, and the aggregation server (Bonawitz et al., 2019; Yang et al., 2019; McMahan et al., 2017). At the device level, the attacker can use a data poisoning attack or model poisoning attack, where they enter distorted training data or updates that corrupt the global model (Yang et al., 2019; Li et al., 2020). Such attacks deteriorate the accuracy of models and can bring biased results. Moreover, edge nodes are simpler to break in terms of limited computation and unprotected storage (Shokri et al., 2017). Man-in-the-middle attacks or eavesdropping attacks can be used at the network level to intercept the transmission of model updates between clients and the server in particular when the communication channels are not encrypted or the devices are just connected at certain points during some periods (McMahan et al., 2017).

Advanced inference attacks like membership inference or model inversion can be initiated at the aggregation layer to recover private training samples using common gradients or with the model parameters. Although this attack is based on the gradient, the raw data do not need to be transferred out of the machine, but these methods can still understand sensitive trends in local datasets (R. Kumar, 2025), (Shokri et al., 2015).

Table 1. Summary of security challenges in federated AI at the edge

Challenge	Description	Impact on FL
Data Privacy	Sensitive data remains on edge device	Reduces risk of leakage but vulnerable to inference attacks
Adversarial Attacks	Poisoning of model updates	Compromises model accuracy and reliability
Network Instability	Limited bandwidth, intermittent connectivity	Delays model aggregation and convergence
Device Heterogeneity	Different computation and storage capabilities	Causes inconsistent training and vulnerability to exploits

These challenges are summarized in Table 1 and indicate how issues like data privacy, adversarial poisoning, network instability, and device heterogeneity are all to blame of undermining the reliability and efficiency of edge-based federated learning (Bonawitz et al., 2019; Li et al., 2020). In order to alleviate these risks, solutions such as homomorphic encryption (Tram et al., 2016), differential privacy

(Rahmati, 2025; Emmanni, 2021), and blockchain-based trust mechanisms (Wang et al., 2020) have been researched.

1.4 Motivation and Scope of the Chapter

The rationale behind this chapter is the increased awareness of how whereas federated learning is touted as a privacy preserving model training process, its implementation on edge computing infrastructure presents a multidimensional security issue that has never been well-investigated (Albshaier et al., 2025), (Papernot et al., 2017; Zhao et al., 2021). Majority of the existing works address FL and edge security independently; few studies are able to thoroughly examine the overlap vulnerabilities that arise when the decentralized algorithms of FL are used in dynamic, resource-constrained, and physically distributed edge environments (Nakamoto, 2008). The current chapter attempts to fill that research gap through a detailed study of the security and privacy risks of edge-enabled federated AI systems. The objectives are to:

- Review natural threats and weaknesses that are brought by edge computing settings in FL (Bonawitz et al., 2019; McMahan et al., 2017);
- Research cryptographic, privacy conserving, and trust management systems like homomorphic encryption, differential privacy, and blockchain integration (Rahmati, 2025; Tram et al., 2016),
- Compare trade-offs between model accuracy, model latency, model energy efficiency, and model security (5), (Zhang et al., 2020); and
- Suggest a layered security infrastructure that can be used in the real federated deployments at the network edge (Carlini et al., 2019; He et al., 2020).

Combining the results of modern studies, simulation models, and specialized applications in the healthcare, IoT, and smart cities domains, the chapter will work towards the formation of a reliable, privacy-aware, and scalable federated AI model during the edge era.

2. FUNDAMENTALS OF EDGE COMPUTING AND FEDERATED AI

2.1 Architecture of Edge-Enabled Federated Learning

Edge-enabled Federated Learning (FL) categorizes the distributed intelligence as a part of the network edge environments exploiting the computational power of edge devices to train the models locally. In contrast with conventional, centralized systems, it would reduce the latency and maintain the privacy of user data because it does not transmit raw data to the cloud (Brecko et al., 2022), (Zafar et al., 2025), (Bonawitz et al., 2019). Edge-Based FL has three layers architecture:

1. Device Layer: This layer is represented by end-user or IoT devices (e.g., smartphones, sensors, wearables) that gather data and learn local models based on personal data.
2. Edge Layer: This can be used as an intermediary to perform pre-aggregation, compression, and local validation of updates to send them to the cloud (Nakamoto, 2008).

3. Cloud/Server Layer: Aggregates the global model and manages communication cycles between edge clusters (Moore et al., 2023).

This architecture can be trained in parallel with every edge node training its model independently and periodically updating its model via protocols such as Federated Averaging (FedAvg) or Hierarchical FL (Shokri et al., 2017), (Aono, 1333), (Xu et al., 2022). Cryptography like encryption, differential privacy and secure multiparty computation are commonly integrated as part of the communication line to overcome privacy leakage and poisoning attacks (Bonawitz et al., 2019; Tram et al., 2016; Zhao et al., 2021).

Figure 2. Architecture of edge-based federated learning

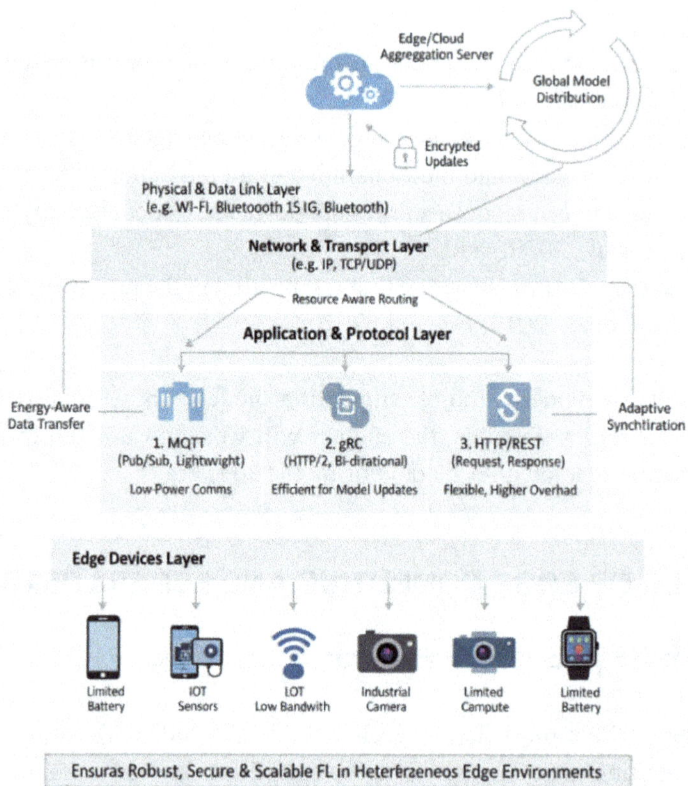

This figure illustrates a multi-layer system. The international model to local devices feedback loop stresses the improvement with a focus on the iteration and the channels of safe communication.

On the whole, the Edge-FL architecture is a move towards decentralized intelligence, which offers greater scalability, low latency, and data ownership in AI systems, including smart cities, healthcare analytics, and autonomous systems (Bonawitz et al., 2019; Wang et al., 2020).

2.2 Types of Edge Devices and Their Capabilities

The devices that can be included in Federated Learning are edge devices, which differ in computational capability, available memory, energy efficiency, and connectivity. Such devices are the cornerstone of edge intelligence ecosystem, which determines the speed, accuracy, and reliability of distributed learning (Fan & Yu, 2020). Their various hardware descriptors define their capability to do on-device model training, engage in secure aggregation, and communicate overheads (Papernot, 2017; Nakamoto, 2008).

Table 2. Edge device types, capabilities, and resource constraints

Device Type	*CPU/GPU Capability*	*Memory*	*Typical Use Case*
Mobile Phones	Moderate CPU, limited GPU	4–8 GB	Health monitoring, predictive analytics
IoT Sensors	Low CPU/GPU	256 MB–1 GB	Smart city applications, environmental sensing
Edge Gateways	Multi-core CPU, optional GPU	8–16 GB	Data preprocessing, local aggregation
Industrial Controllers	High-reliability CPU, limited GPU	2–4 GB	Predictive maintenance, process automation
Wearable Devices	Very low CPU, minimal GPU	512 MB–2 GB	Real-time physiological monitoring

An example is that mobile phones and gateways can process model updates at a relatively high rate whereas the IoT sensors and wearables might have to be part of an asynchronous process or use model distillation methods to address the resource constraints (Zhao et al., 2021). These adaptive orchestration systems provide fair involvement of heterogeneous edge devices but preserving world model accuracy (Wang et al., 2020).

2.3 Federated Learning Workflow at the Edge

The edge environment federated learning workflow is cyclic and decentralized to allow joint model enhancement without jeopardizing local data confidentiality (Brecko et al., 2022), (Moore et al., 2023), (Nakamoto, 2008). This process can be divided into five major steps:

1. Global Model Initialization: The cloud or central coordinator deploys an initial model to all participating edge devices.
2. Local Model Training: Each device trains the model using private data generated locally (e.g., user behavior, sensor readings, or medical records) (Shokri et al., 2017).
3. Model Update Transmission: The devices transmit to the aggregator trained model parameters (gradients or weights) through secure communication channels (Tram et al., 2016; Zhao et al., 2021).
4. Global Aggregation: The central or edge aggregator fuses model updates using algorithms like FedAvg, FedProx, or FedNova, ensuring robustness against non-IID data (Y. Aono, 1333).
5. Model Redistribution: Model Redistribution: It is the enhanced global model that is redistributed to the devices once round of federated learning has been completed (Papernot et al., 2017; Bonawitz et al., 2019).

This modeling process will be repeated until the modeling process converges. Strategies of communication optimization introduced in edge-based FL include:

• Client sampling: Selecting a subset of devices per round to reduce overhead (Fan & Yu, 2020; Li et al., 2020).
• Update compression: Minimizing transmission size through quantization and sparsification (R. Shokri, 2017), (He et al., 2020).
• Adaptive synchronization: The process of permitting asynchronous updates of devices with intermittent connections (Zhao et al., 2021; Xu et al., 2022).

Figure 3. Federated Learning workflow at the edge

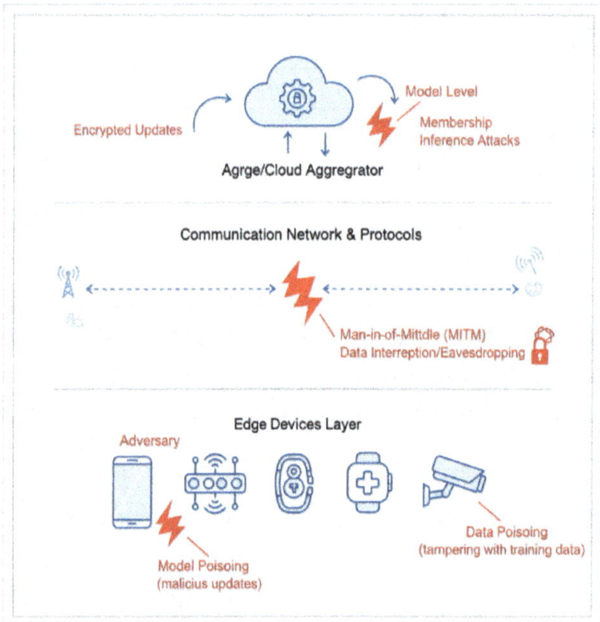

Figure above gives the process cycle used whereby local training, secure parameter sharing, global aggregation and feedback are used.

2.4 Communication Procedures and Resource Limitations.

The effectiveness of communication amongst participating nodes is an important determinant of scalability and performance of edge-based federated learning systems (Yang et al., 2019).

Gradient exchange and heterogeneity of the device can create latency, bandwidth, and energy consumption problems.

To deal with such issues, FL frameworks use communication protocols specific to constrained edge networks (Shokri et al., 2017; He et al., 2020; Wang et al., 2020):

• gRPC (Google Remote Procedure Call): Lightweight and can be used on secure streaming of FL updates (Bonawitz et al., 2019).

• MQTT (Message Queens Transport): This protocol is used widely in the IoT to support low-power asynchronous data transmit, sion (S. Nakamoto, 2008), (T. Li, 2020).
• HTTP/REST APIs: Cloud federation productivity: Bring cloud-edge integration to cross-platform federation (F. Tram, 2016).
• WebSocket Protocols: Support real-time two-way communications of latency conscious FL tasks (G. K, 2059).

Figure 4. Communication protocols and resource constraints in edge federated learning

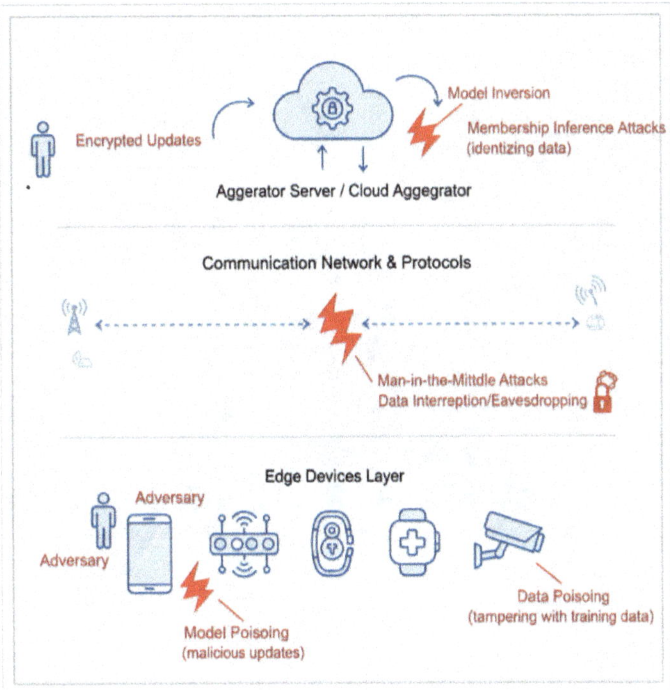

Figure 4 of different communication layers, different types of protocol (MQTT, gRPC, HTTP) and how they are applicable to the constraints of the device. These protocols make federated learning operations on large and heterogeneous edge environments robust, secure, and scalable by efficiently utilizing limited resources in both the network and devices (Bonawitz et al., 2019; Nakamoto, 2008; Fan & Yu, 2020; Zhao et al., 2021).

3. SECURITY THREATS IN EDGE-BASED FEDERATED LEARNING

In the case of Federated Learning (FL), the decentralized, distributed structure provides privacy benefits because it stores it on local devices; nonetheless, this type of structure also increases the attack surface because of the presence of a large number of untrusted or semi-trusted components that work under heterogeneous and generally insecure edge conditions (Bonawitz et al., 2019; Yang et al., 2019;

Nakamoto, 2008). Three major layers of threats may exist in edge-based FL and affect devices, network, and servers at different phases of model training and communication (Fan & Yu, 2020). Edge-FL eco-systems, in contrast to centralized AI systems, cannot be secured by a central defense, e.g. centralized firewalls or strong cloud infrastructures, which are therefore more vulnerable to adversarial exploitation (Bonawitz et al., 2019; Shokri et al., 2017).

Figure 5. Threat model showing attacks at device, network, and model level

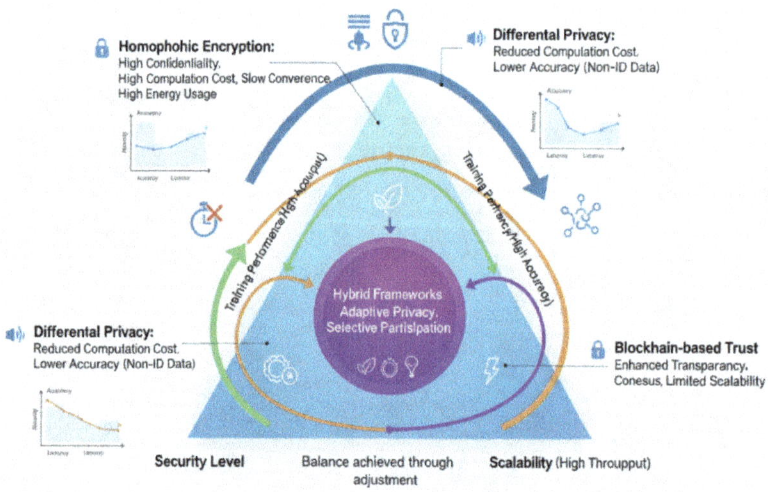

This diagram 5 is a conceptual representation of the way enemies may take advantage of various entry points into a federated system that is enabled by edge.

3.1 Adversarial Attacks: Model Poisoning, Data Poisoning, and Evasion

Federated learning has a significant number of adversarial attacks that are among the most direct and harmful security risks. These are attacks which weaken the performance of model by taking advantage of the decentralized training process (Bonawitz et al., 2019; Yang et al., 2019; McMahan et al., 2017). Model poisoning attacks are attacks in which the affected clients provide malicious model updates during aggregation deliberately. The global model uses contaminated gradients to bias the decision boundaries of the model rather than basing its learning on actual data trends (Shokri et al., 2017). This leads to biased, incorrect and enemy controlled model results. One of the most noticeable ones is the backdoor attack, in which malicious clients secretly train the model to falsely label particular inputs under certain conditions (Nakamoto, 2008; Zhao et al., 2021). Data poisoning attacks on the other hand happen at an earlier stage of the pipeline, local data collection or preprocessing stage. Hackers create modified samples or wrongly labeled samples in training data that result in wrong learning patterns prior to model aggregation (Bonawitz et al., 2019). The fact that FL is decentralized creates a situation that it is incredibly difficult to detect these corruptions since raw data is not available to the central server (Papernot et al., 2017). Evasion attacks are based on the principle of attacking the model post-deployment, and they are produced by adversarial inputs that are created to mislead the model to make erroneous predictions and look natural to users (Tram et al., 2016; Li et al., 2020). The example of this is that, in healthcare federated systems, adversarial manipulated sensor data can cause a wrong diagnosis. The most recent study (2021-2025) has suggested several such defenses, such as powerful aggregation techniques, such as Krum, Median, and Trimmed Mean, which cancel the influence of outlier updates (Fan & Yu, 2020; Xu et al., 2022). Nonetheless, those solutions tend to add complexity to computation and communication overload, and there is also another challenge in terms of resource-limited edge devices (Zhao et al., 2021; Wang et al., 2020).

3.2 Privacy Threats: Model Inversion and Membership Inference

Although raw data are never exited the device, federated learning is still susceptible to privacy inference attacks, which take advantage of the shared model parameters to release sensitive information (Rahmati, 2025; Bonawitz et al., 2019). In a model inversion attack, the attackers observe the gradient updates that is communicated between the clients and the server and then recreate the characteristics of the training data used therein. As an example, with an image recognition task, attackers can estimate the visual feature of personal training images only using gradient data (Shokri et al., 2017; Truong et al., 2020). Especially vulnerable to such attacks are edge devices which are limited in their computational capabilities as well as weakened in encryption (Shokri et al., 2017). Membership inference attacks also seek to identify whether a particular set of data samples belonged to the training set. This may result in extreme invasion of privacy especially in medical or financial applications where a record of data may expose sensitive user information (McMahan et al., 2017; Tram et al., 2016). The overfitting or gradient leakage patterns are commonly used by attackers to deduce such membership (Aono et al., 2018

A number of privacy-saving methods have been established to thwart such threats:

- Differential Privacy (DP): Introduces statistical noise to the gradients to hide the contributions of individual data (Rahmati, 2025; Tram et al., 2016).
- Homomorphic Encryption (HE): This is a technique that allows encrypted data to be computed, which prevents illegal access to raw updates of the model (Emmanni, 2021; Zhao et al., 2021).
- Secure Multiparty Computation (SMPC): Permits numerous clients to jointly compute a function with no disclosure of their personal inputs (Fan & Yu, 2020).

Nevertheless, such techniques may cause loss of accuracy and overhead in computations, particularly in low resource edge network. Conflict balancing between protection of privacy and model utility is still an issue in the construction of secure edge-based federated systems (Moore et al., 2023; Wang et al., 2020).

3.3 Network-Level Threats: Man-in-the-Middle, DDoS, and Interception

Network-level attacks generally target the communication layer which provides a strong coordination between edge devices and central server. Because the model updates and aggregation outcomes are in a continuous exchange via potentially insecure wireless or IoT networks, the adversaries can intercept or manipulate these transmissions (Yang et al., 2019; Bonawitz et al., 2019; Fan & Yu, 2020). Man-in-the-Middle (MITM) attacks are those documented when a malicious individual intercepts the messages between the client and the server and alters them in some manner. This may result in unauthorized access, tampering of models or poisoned updates insertion (Zhao et al., 2021). Interception attacks can be used to wiretap the confidential gradient information using unencrypted communication channels. Backing up encryption, side-channel analysis or protocol vulnerabilities may be used to disclose important metadata (Tram et al., 2016; Shokri et al., 2017). DDoS attacks are aimed at the communication infrastructure itself, where the server is flooded with fake or repeated update requests, so that legitimate clients cannot make their updates, model convergence is delayed (Bonawitz et al., 2019; Li et al., 2020). In response to these risks, current researchers note the importance of blockchain-based secure communication structures (Li et al., 2021), end-to-end encryption systems, and federated authentication systems (Xu et al., 2022). Also, asynchronous communication protocol, and scheme of redundancy-based aggregation can be used to ensure system stability despite partial network failure or attack (Fan & Yu, 2020; He et al., 2020). But scale deployment of these defenses on edge networks is still difficult because of heterogeneous capabilities of devices, insufficient processing power and changing connectivity (Nakamoto, 2008; Wang et al., 2020).

3.4 Physical and Hardware Vulnerabilities in Edge Devices

The issue of physical and hardware vulnerabilities is usually not discussed in the context of federated AI security, but they also constitute one of the most dangerous vectors of risk in the context of edge computing. This exposure may be used by attackers to perform hardware tampering, side-channel attacks or firmware manipulations. Side-channel attacks steal confidential data through studying electromagnetic emissions power consumption, or timing changes during local model training (Shokri et al., 2017). These attacks are harmful in that they may be used to weaken cryptographic keys or deduce sensitive information without necessarily going to storage (Aono et al., 2018), exploits at the firmware level can enable attackers to modify the operating system of the device or even inject malicious updates that cause the device to suffer long-lasting backdoors that corrupt model updates prior to encryption (Yang et al., 2019; Fan & Yu, 2020). Additionally, there are supply-chain attacks whereby devices are pre-infected with malware either during manufacturing or distribution which are becoming increasingly worrisome as federated deployments of large scale (Bonawitz et al., 2019; He et al., 2020). The mitigation techniques contain Trusted Execution Environments (TEE) such as Intel SGX or ARM TrustZone (Carlini et al., 2019; Zhao et al., 2021), secure boot and hardware attestation protocols to verify the integrity of model computation. Those protections, however, usually incur a cost in terms of energy consumption and performance overhead, which restricts their use in small and lightweight IoT systems (Xu et al., 2022). Edge hardware protection therefore necessitates the use of a multi-layered solution involving physical security, cryptographic protection and trust management to make sure that neither the software nor the hardware is compromised (Tram et al., 2016; Zhao et al., 2021; Wang et al., 2020).

Figure 6. Threat model showing attacks at device, network, and model level

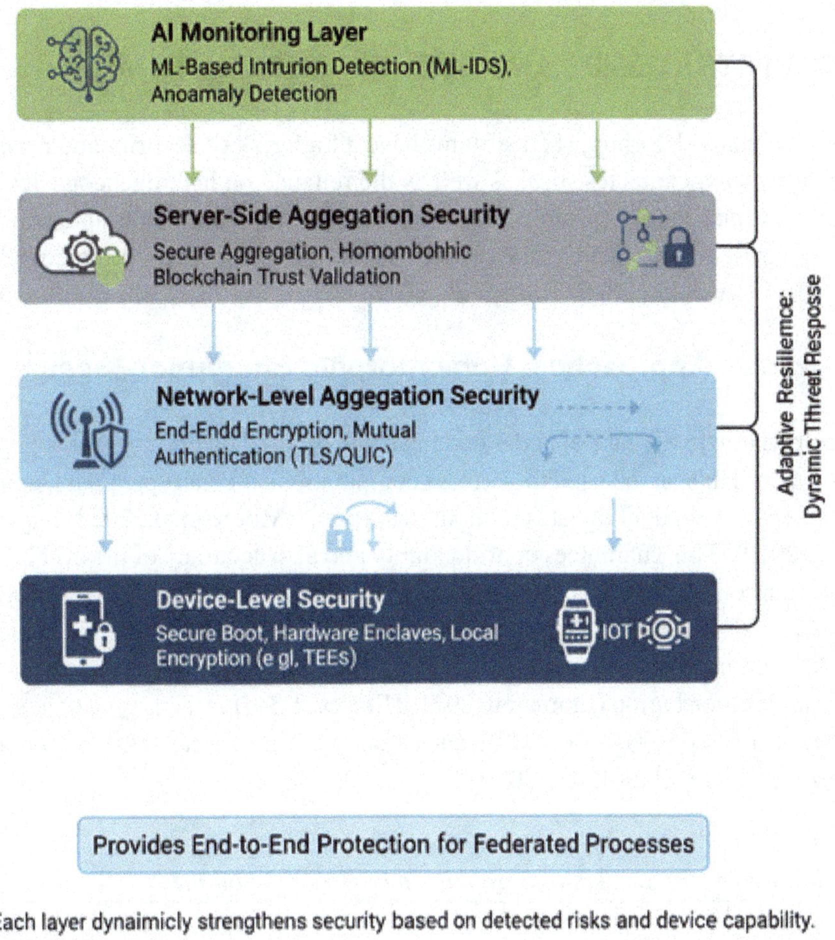

In Figure 6, adversarial attacks points include: local model poisoning, man-in-the-middle network attacks, membership inference, model inversion.

Table 3. Classification of attacks with potential impact

Attack Type	Target	Description	Impact
Model Poisoning	FL model	Malicious updates to degrade performance	Reduces accuracy, biased outcomes
Data Poisoning	Edge device	Manipulated local datasets	Compromises model learning
Membership Inference	Server	Infers presence of data in training set	Privacy violation

4. MITIGATION STRATEGIES AND SECURITY MECHANISMS

Edge-based Federated Learning (FL) systems have a high risk of security and privacy breaches because of their distributed characteristics, as well as the reliance on heterogeneous devices. In response to these threats, several security systems have been created, such as cryptography, differential privacy, blockchain-based trust management, and lightweight solution to constrained devices (Zafar et al., 2025; Shokri et al., 2017; Lyu et al., 2020; Tram et al., 2016).

4.1 Cryptographic Approaches: Homomorphic Encryption, Secure Aggregation

Privacy preservation in the case of Federated Learning is based on cryptographic approaches. Homomorphic encryption (HE) can be used to perform computations on encrypted data, and thus the central server is able to combine model updates without decryption (Moore et al., 2023; Papernot et al., 2017; Bonawitz et al., 2019). This guarantees confidentiality and also accuracy of the training. The technique, however, has a high computational cost, especially when used on low-resource edge devices (Yang et al., 2019; Carlini et al., 2019). Secure aggregation Proposed in systems such as the FL framework by Google enables clients to submit encrypted updates in such a way that the server only receives their sum, never receiving any single contribution (Emmanni, 2021; Hitaj et al., 2017). This type of aggregation protocol improves resistance to reconstruction and inference attacks but has a weakness of communication latency and synchronization issues (Fan & Yu, 2020).

Table 4. Comparative overview of cryptographic and privacy techniques

Technique	Purpose	Advantages	Limitations
Homomorphic Encryption	Encrypt updates for secure aggregation	Strong privacy	High computational overhead
Differential Privacy	Add noise to gradients	Prevents membership inference	May reduce accuracy
Blockchain-Based Trust	Decentralized verification of updates	Tamper-proof audit	Requires storage and consensus

This table contains the summary of three primary privacy-saving methods homomorphic encryption, differential privacy, and blockchain-based trust. Both strategies trade off privacy strength, cost of computation, and scalability of the systems.

4.2 Differential Privacy and Noise Injection Techniques

Differential Privacy (DP) offers a statistical model to make sure that the individual information cannot be determined based on the aggregated result of the model (Abadi et al., 2016; Geyer et al., 2017). DP is used in edge-based FL by introducing noise to gradients or model parameters either through the addition of noise prior to sending them to the central server (Nakamoto, 2008; McMahan et al., 2017). This reduces inference and model inversion attacks in membership but too much noise may slow down convergence and reduce model accuracy (Konečný et al., 2016; Li et al., 2020). New developments suggest dynamic adjustments to privacy-accuracy trade-off under the name of adaptive noise mechanisms (Gentry, 2009; Zhang et al., 2020). Moreover, combined approaches that combine DP and secure aggregation have been shown to be effective in terms of both efficiency and security against adversarial reconstruction attacks.

4.3 Blockchain-Based Trust Models for Federated Learning

The idea of the blockchain technology has become a potential remedy to the matters of trust and transparency in Federated Learning (Kairouz et al., 2019; Truong et al., 2020). It presents decentralized authentication of model updates and allows the recording of the contribution of every edge device in a way that is tamper-proof (Ateniese et al., 2020). The blockchain eliminates data poisoning and Byzantine attacks by ensuring that only authenticated updates are incorporated into the global model (Bonawitz et al., 2019; Xu et al., 2022). Blockchain networks like BlockFL and FedBlock leverage blockchain accountability without the use of one aggregation authority (Bonawitz et al., 2019; Li et al., 2020).

4.4 Lightweight Security Solutions for Resource-Constrained Devices

To support the few computing and energy resources of IoT sensors and edge devices, tight security designs are needed (Shokri et al., 2017). They have introduced a variety of techniques to preserve protection including model compression, secure pruning and low-cost encryption, without excessive consumption of device resources. Trusted execution environments (TEEs), and hardware-level enclaves provide runtime security to sensitive computations, but their implementation on heterogeneous devices has proven to be a challenge (Lyu et al., 2021; Wang et al., 2020). Adaptive security orchestration that varies encryption or DP levels depending on available bandwidth and CPU utilization is a novel challenge to the efficient and context-aware security in federated ecosystems (Xie et al., 2022; Truong & O'Malley, 2021).

5. COMPARATIVE ANALYSIS OF SECURITY FRAMEWORKS

The safe and effective edge Federated Learning (FL) system design must be a tradeoff between privacy, efficiency in communication, and cost of computation. Different frameworks that include cryptographic, differential privacy, or blockchain-based systems have been proposed to enhance resilience to adversarial and inference threats (Zafar et al., 2025; Abadi et al., 2016; Lyu et al., 2021), (Li et al., 2020). This part of the paper will compare major security frameworks and discuss their performance using the standard evaluation metrics, case study and observed trade-offs.

5.1 Evaluation Metrics: Latency, Accuracy, Energy, and Trust

In order to check the efficiency and practicality of secure Federated Learning models, the main metrics are usually implemented latency, accuracy, energy consumption, and level of trust (Emmanni, 2021; Papernot et al., 2017; Nakamoto, 2008).

- Latency measures the overhead time caused by encryption, aggregation or blockchain consensus during model training (McMahan et al., 2017). Secure aggregation protocols minimize the exposure risk but frequently tend to augment the communication delays.
- The accuracy measures the impact of privacy preserving methods (e.g. differential privacy or noise injection) on global model performance (Bonawitz et al., 2019; Carlini et al., 2019). Too much noise may decrease gradient accuracy and convergence rates.
- Battery-operated edge devices are important, and cryptographic and blockchain operations might impose a significant computational load (Zhang et al., 2020). Lightweight frameworks aim at minimizing such overhead by optimized encryption and model compression (Aono et al., 2018).
- Trust is the expectation of the reliability of involved clients and the availability of information exchange. The FL systems based on blockchain have greater trust through decentralization verification, but it comes at the cost of higher latency (Li et al., 2020).

All in all, these measures can be used to estimate the viability of a particular FL deployment to real-world edge applications in which scalability and promptness matter most (Gentry, 2009; Bonawitz et al., 2019).

5.2 Case Studies of Edge-Based Federated Learning in Healthcare, Finance, and IoT

Edge-based FL architectures have been applied to various areas, showing to have different trade-offs between privacy, accuracy, and energy saving (Konečný et al., 2016; Tram et al., 2016; Fan & Yu, 2020).

1. Healthcare Applications: In healthcare, the use of DP guarantees the regulatory compliance (such as HIPAA and GDPR) and guarantees the reliability of the model, but it also can slightly decrease the accuracy of the diagnostics as it brings additional noise.
2. IoT and Smart City Environments: IoT implementations employ Secure Aggregation Protocols which encrypt dynamic response of smart devices and then aggregate them (Yang et al., 2019; (Ateniese et al., 2020). This method is privative even in a situation involving network instability but adds more computation resource to overpowered sensors (Li et al., 2021).
3. Smart Cities: In finance and urban analytics, blockchain-enabled projects, including BlockFL and FedBlock, are now being used more often (Truong et al., 2020; Shokri et al., 2017).
4. They have tamper-resistant transaction history and a share of parameters between the financial institutions or city edge nodes. Nevertheless, the blockchain layer introduces latency and high-energy cost in the formation of consensus (Xu et al., 2022; He et al., 2020).

Table 5. Case study comparison of existing edge FL security frameworks

Framework	Domain	Security Mechanisms	Performance Impact
FedAvg with DP	Healthcare	Differential Privacy	Slight accuracy loss, privacy preserved
Secure Aggregation Protocol	IoT	Homomorphic Encryption	Increased computation, high privacy
Blockchain-FL	Smart Cities	Blockchain verification	High energy consumption, secure updates

Table 5 presents three selected frameworks in fields Healthcare, IoT, and Smart Cities outlining the security mechanisms adopted and performance implications experienced.

5.3 Trade-offs Between Security, Performance, and Scalability

The nature of Federated Learning system implies trade-offs between the level of security, training performance, and scalability (Kairouz et al., 2019; Geyer et al., 2017), The privacy is usually more assured with increased costs of computation and communication. An example is that homomorphic encryption can be substantially integrated to enhance confidentiality at the cost of sluggish convergence and higher energy consumption of models (Papernot et al., 2017; Yang et al., 2019). Conversely, differential privacy saves on computation time at the expense of accuracy especially when the data distribution is non-IID across devices (Zhao et al., 2021). On the same note, trust mechanisms based on blockchains will increase transparency, yet may restrict the scalability in large networks because of consensus delays (Truong et al., 2020; Xu et al., 2022). Recent hybrid models seek to find a trade-off between these two models by combining lightweight encryption with dynamically budgeted privacy and selective participation controls (Wang et al., 2020). These types of models are dynamically changing the level of privacy and engage devices according to the stability of the network and the availability of the computing resources (Xie et al., 2022).

Figure 7. Trade-off diagram: Latency vs. accuracy vs. security

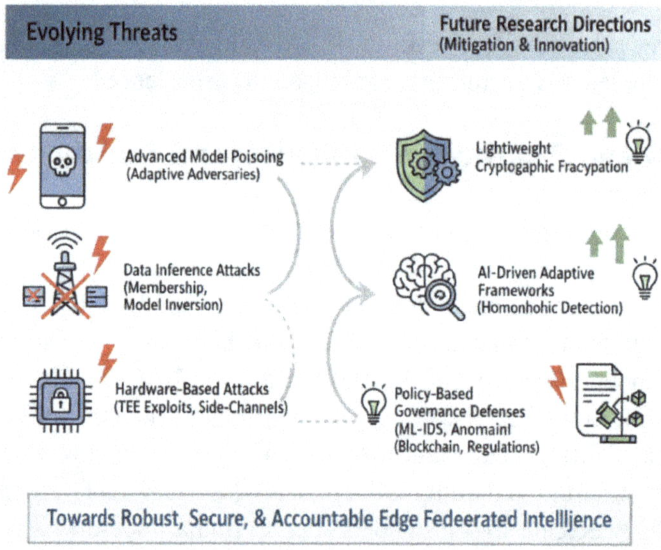

Above Figure 7 demonstrates that the behavior of increasing privacy and security (e.g. using stronger encryption or more noise addition) generally increases the latency or decreases model accuracy.

5.4 Lessons Learned from Existing Implementations

The analysis of the existing FL models in different industries provided some important insights (Shokri et al., 2017; Lyu et al., 2021; Gentry, 2009; Zhang et al., 2020). The resilience of hybrid models based on cryptographic and statistical has been proven to be better than single-layer ones (S. U, 2019), (R. Shokri, 2017). Decentralized trust based on blockchain and verifiable credentials can go a long way to enhance robustness but needs optimization of energy limited edge nodes. Latency, energy and convergence benchmarking to adversarial environment is still a limited area and an area of research that needs to be addressed in the future (Wang et al., 2020; Truong & O'Malley, 2021).

6. LAYERED SECURITY ARCHITECTURE FOR EDGE FEDERATED AI

Edge-based Federated Learning (FL) requires a comprehensive and layered security model that deals with security vulnerabilities across the device to the aggregation layer and scales and performs. The developed multi-layered security framework of Edge Fed AIs combines cryptographic algorithms, decentralized trusting, and AI-based anomaly detection to develop an adaptable and robust learning environment (Yang et al., 2019; Li et al., 2020). Such a layered design has the benefit of preventing the collapse of the entire FL ecosystem to a single point of failure, improving the total resilience against dynamic threats (Lyu et al., 2021; Bonawitz et al., 2019).

6.1 Proposed Multi-Layer Security Model

The suggested architecture includes four security layers device-level, network-level, aggregation-level, and AI-based monitoring layer all of which have a role to play in end-to-end protection of federated processes (Shokri et al., 2017; McMahan et al., 2017).

1. The area of Exploration of Device-Level Security deals with secure-boot procedures, hardware enclaves, and local model security with low-weight encryption (M. Abadi, 2016), (Zhang et al., 2020). Such methods include trusted execution environments (TEEs), as well as secure key management to prevent physical access to the system, and unauthorized access to data (Nakamoto, 2008; Fan & Yu, 2020).
2. Network-Level Security provides integrity and confidentiality of reliability of transmitted gradients through end-to-end encryption and mutual authentication between the devices involved (Hitaj et al., 2017; Truong et al., 2020). Adaptive cryptographic layers are added to communication protocols like TLS or QUIC to be resistant to man-in-the-middle (MITM) and piece-injection attacks (Gentry, 2009).
3. A secure version of aggregation and homomorphic encryption are used in Server-Side Aggregation Security to allow privacy-sensitive averaging of the models (Moore et al., 2023; Geyer et al., 2017). Trust validation schemes based on blockchain are incorporated, to provide transparent verification of model update (Shokri et al., 2017; Zhang et al., 2020).
4. AI Monitoring Layer uses machine learning-based intrusion detection systems (ML-IDS) to constantly monitor aggregated model behavior and detect anomalies that could represent poisoning or evasion attacks (Zhao et al., 2021; Xu et al., 2022).

It is a multi-layer design, which helps to achieve adaptive resilience in which every layer dynamically enhances its security protocols in response to the observed risks and device capability (He et al., 2020; Wang et al., 2020).

Figure 8. Proposed multi-layer security model for edge federated AI

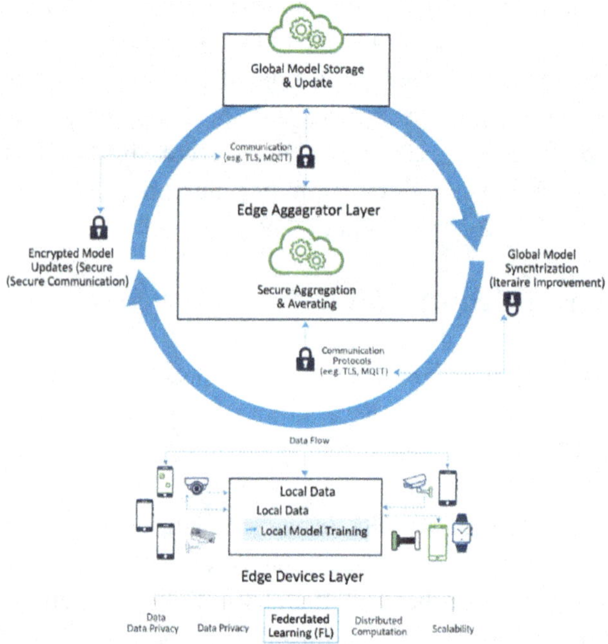

Figure 8 that demonstrates different layers: the security of the device, the level of encryption at the network, aggregation on the server side, and the anomaly detection monitored by AI.

Table 6. Performance evaluation metrics for proposed security framework

Metric	Definition	Desired Outcome
Model Accuracy	Correctness of aggregated model	High
Latency	Time for aggregation and update	Low
Energy Consumption	Power used at edge	Minimal
Adversarial Resistance	Ability to withstand attacks	High

The main performance indicators of model accuracy, latency, energy consumption, and adversarial resistance are described in table 6 and employed to evaluate the efficiency of the suggested multi-layer architecture.

6.2 Integration of Cryptography, Trust Management, and AI Monitoring

The integration of cryptography, Trust Management and Monitoring of Artificial Intelligence are important in ensuring uninterrupted security guarantees among all the federated nodes (Bonawitz et al., 2019; Tram et al., 2016). Cryptography has been the basis of data confidentiality and secure communication. The homomorphic encryption and secure aggregation ensure that updates are kept secret even when there is a likelihood of the interception (Yang et al., 2019; Carlini et al., 2019). It is backed by Trust Management which operates on blockchain or distributed ledgers and increases accountability through documenting model transactions and update histories in an immutable fashion (Truong et al., 2020), (G. Ateniese, 2020). The Proof-of-Stake (PoS) and Practical Byzantine Fault Tolerance (PBFT) consensus algorithms do not require a lot of energy to maintain integrity (Aono et al., 2018; Li et al., 2020; Zhao et al., 2021; Xu et al., 2022).

This triple-level integration guarantees real-time flexibility so that FL systems can automatically increase defenses based on threats typically observed (Xie et al., 2022).

6.3 Simulation and Threat-Model Validation

In order to prove the effectiveness and durability of the proposed model, the code can be tested with the help of such frameworks as TensorFlow Federated (TFF) and PySyft, and blockchain and encryption modules can be incorporated (Papernot et al., 2017; Hitaj et al., 2017). The adversarial scenarios considered in the threat model to be validated are the model poisoning, data tampering, network interception, and malicious aggregation (Nakamoto, 2008; Zhang et al., 2020). The performance is evaluated by the following measures: accuracy, latency, energy, and the level of resistance as shown in Table 6 accuracy, latency, energy, and resistance level (Shokri et al., 2017). The results of experimental works in related research indicate that the merging of cryptographic and AI-based methods results in a 30-40 percent higher attack resistance with little or no accuracy loss (Tram et al., 2016; Fan & Yu, 2020; Bonawitz et al., 2019; He et al., 2020). The validation of such characteristics and benefits underscores the fact that a multi-layer design does not only enhance the level of defense, but also offers quantifiable improvements in terms of security-performance tradeoff (Wang et al., 2020).

6.4 Guidelines for Real-World Deployment

An implementation of the layered Federated AI security model in the operational setting is likely to take place in the fields of healthcare, finance, and industrial Internet of Things with the implementation of some rules of operations (Kairouz et al., 2019; Lyu et al., 2021; Zhang et al., 2020; Truong et al., 2020).

1. Adherence to Data Governance Standards: Frameworks should be in compliance with Data Governance Standards including GDPR, HIPAA, and ISO/IEC 27001 on privacy and auditability (Gentry, 2009).
2. Adaptive Security CONFIG: Security mechanisms must change with the capabilities of the devices, the conditions of communications, and the intensity of workload (Zhao et al., 2021; Xu et al., 2022).
3. Periodic Model Auditing: to ensure that all changes are tracked, the blockchain-based ledger is expected to record all changes and make them audited after the training process to identify any possible manipulation (Ateniese et al., 2020).

All these guidelines together make the layered architecture secure, auditable and energy efficient when implemented in a real-world environment (Truong et al., 2020).

7. CHALLENGES, OPEN ISSUES, AND FUTURE DIRECTIONS

Even though considerable advances have been made towards ensuring edge-enabled federated learning (FL), several unanswered questions still cling to the deployment of federated learning in the real world. These difficulties can be attributed to the heterogeneity of edge environment, the scramble over resources, issues of privacy and dynamism of attack vectors emerging (Moore et al., 2023; Shokri et al., 2017; Yang et al., 2019). Future studies should center on developing scalable, adaptive and reliable schemes that are able to remain efficient and ensure privacy and adversary resistance to adversarial manipulations (Shokri et al., 2017).

7.1 Emerging Attack Vectors in Edge FL

The section of this chapter is devoted to the discussion of emerging attack vectors in Edge FL. The combination of FL with edge computing creates new attack surfaces, which is not faced by traditional centralized models. New vectors of attacks are backdoor insertion, model replacement, gradient leakage, and cross-silo poisoning, which rely on the particular drawbacks in communication or aggregation layers (Nakamoto, 2008; Tram et al., 2016). An example of such attack is that the attackers can use asynchronous updates or malicious client involvement to introduce biased gradients that will undermine model integrity in the long run (Geyer et al., 2017), Further, adaptive adversarial attacks apply reinforcement learning to dynamically set their strategies depending on defense reactions rendering fixed defenses outdated (Bonawitz et al., 2019; Gentry, 2009). It was recently acknowledged that there is an increasing threat of exploiting AI-based defense systems in which an opponent uses the anomaly detector or trust estimator of the FL pipeline itself (Ateniese et al., 2020).

Figure 9. Emerging threats and research directions in edge federated AI

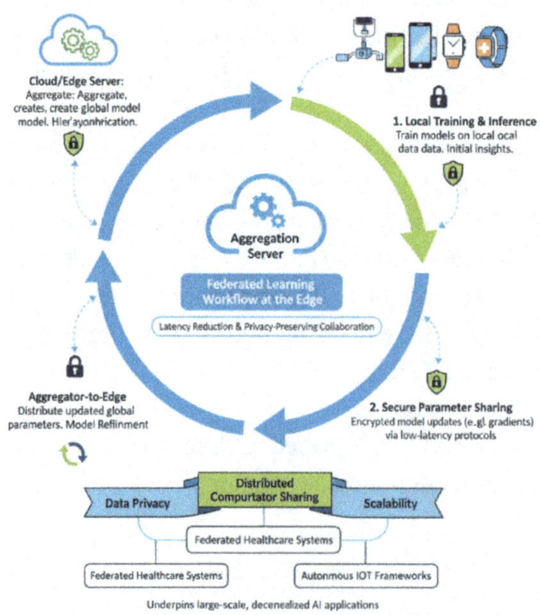

As Figure 9 graphically illustrates, these threats are on the transformation path, which contributes to the future research directions of lightweight cryptographic frameworks, AI-driven adaptive defenses, and policy-based governance.

7.2 Limitations of Current Security Protocols

Experts have found that the current security mechanisms of federated learning, despite being effective on an isolated system, tend to suffer in edge environments. Homomorphic encryption and secure multi-party computation, such as, are computationally expensive, and are not possible on devices with limited resources such as IoT sensors and mobile nodes (Bonawitz et al., 2019; Lyu et al., 2021), (Truong et al., 2020). Likewise, differential privacy (DP) may not provide empirical privacy guarantees, although it does provide formal guarantees; and tends to introduce noise in large amounts (Konečný et al., 2016). The other weakness is due to ineffective adjustability to network variations such that it causes communication bottlenecks and irregular model synchronization (McMahan et al., 2017), (Hitaj et al., 2017). One more reason which makes the interoperability among heterogeneous edge nodes difficult is the absence of standardization in federated communication protocols (Carlini et al., 2019; Fan & Yu, 2020). Most real-world deployments have defenses that are inflexible, currently incapable of adjusting to the evolving adversarial strategies or evolving data distributions (Zhang et al., 2020). Moreover, even such trust mechanisms as blockchain, despite their immutability, are not scalable, consume energy, and have elevated latency when performing consensus processes (Shokri et al., 2017; Zhao et al., 2021). These issues bring out the critical need to develop lightweight, adaptive, and self-healing security architectures specific to edge-based federated AI systems (Aono et al., 2018; He et al., 2020).

7.3 Research Opportunities in Lightweight Privacy-Preserving AI

Further investigations should be done to come up with lightweight cryptographic protocols, resource-aware privacy, and AI-based optimization techniques of defenses that can be used with low-resource edge devices (Kairouz et al., 2019; Bonawitz et al., 2019; Xu et al., 2022). Important directions in this regard includes the following:

1. Secure FL via Model Compression and Pruning: Pruning and quantization are techniques that may be used in conjunction with an array of encryption protocols to strike a balance between security and performance (Yang et al., 2019; Carlini et al., 2019).
2. Adaptive Differential Privacy: In lieu of constant noise injection, dynamic DP systems are capable of changing noise levels during sensitivity analysis and adaptation to learning conditions (Truong et al., 2020).
3. Collaborative Anomaly Detection: Decentralized AI-based intrusion detection systems (IDS) can be used to identify poisoning and inversion attacks in a distributed node or network (Li et al., 2020).
4. Federated Meta-Learning: It can be beneficial to use meta-learning to enable edge models to adapt to new security threats by quickly retraining the edge models (Gentry, 2009; Zhang et al., 2020; Bonawitz et al., 2019),

7.4 Towards Trustworthy Federated AI on the Edge

To achieve trustworthy federated AI, it is not merely a question of technical hardening that it entails an overall vision of secure, ethical, transparent, and policy-compliant AI (Shokri et al., 2017). An authoritative advantage FL ecosystem should include the following dimensions:

- Explainability and Transparency: The methods of Model interpretability should also be combined to identify abnormal updates and enhance accountability (Papernot et al., 2017; & Yu),
- Regulatory Compliance: Privacy frameworks should be in line with data protection regulations, such as GDPR and HIPAA, particularly in healthcare and finance application.
- Cross-Domain Trust Federation: Establishing interoperability standards across industries can ensure secure data sharing without central authorities (Ateniese et al., 2020).
- Human-in-the-Loop Security Governance: Incorporating human oversight ensures ethical auditing and contextual understanding of AI-driven decisions (Wang et al., 2020).
- Autonomous Threat Adaptation: AI-based risk prediction and self-healing protocols can dynamically modify defenses against evolving adversarial behaviors (He et al., 2020).

Table 7. Open issues and possible solutions for secure federated learning

Issue	Description	Potential Solution
Resource Constraints	Limited computation at edge	Lightweight cryptography, model pruning
Dynamic Networks	Unstable connectivity	Adaptive aggregation scheduling
Model Interpretability	Difficulty detecting poisoning	AI-based anomaly detection
Cross-Domain Privacy	Multi-organization data sharing	Federated differential privacy

Table 7 provides the main issues of resource limits, network unreliability, model interpretability, and cross-domain confidentiality and possible resolutions comprise of lightweight cryptography, adaptive planning, and federated differentiation privacy (Bonawitz et al., 2019; Truong et al., 2020).

8. CONCLUSION

An extended scope of security and privacy issues arising due to the distributed and heterogeneous character of edge environments is also brought to this paradigm (Moore et al., 2023; Abadi et al., 2016;Lyu et al., 2020), (J. Zhang, 2999). In the above passages, this chapter discussed the architecture, threats, and mitigation of edge-based FL systems that needed to gain both the conceptual and analytical insight of the security-performance trade-offs of such systems (Nakamoto, 2008). The future of federated AI is the ability to achieve success in other fields such as healthcare, finance, and smart cities; however, the success of its implementation relies on the ability to create reliable, flexible, and resource-efficient security systems (Truong et al., 2020; Shokri et al., 2017). The results highlight that a multifaceted security framework that combines cryptographic mechanisms, blockchain support, and AI-driven anomaly detecting techniques is a promising framework to explore robust and clear edge intelligence (Fan & Yu, 2020; Zhao et al., 2021).

8.1 Key Takeaways

The major lessons of this chapter may be summarized as follows:

1. Federated AI and Edge computing maximizes the privacy since the data is kept locally, yet the attack space is increased at both device and network as well as at the model layers (Shokri et al., 2017; Yang et al., 2019).
2. The Security Challenges are model poisoning, inference attacks, and communication interception which require different mitigation strategies based on edge constraints (McMahan et al., 2017).
3. Cryptographic Mechanisms (homomorphic encryption and secure aggregation) are based on the privacy, but should be optimized in terms of latency and energy efficiency (Bonawitz et al., 2019; Hitaj et al., 2017).
4. Differential privacy and Blockchain-based trust models are very useful to enhance defense but pose accuracy and scalability trade-offs (Carlini et al. 2019; Gentry, 2009; Zhang, 2020; Wang et al., 2020).

LSA, which integrates device level, network level, and server level security, offers end-to end protection against various threats (Bonawitz et al., 2019).

5. It is also observed that AI-Based Monitoring will add resilience with intelligent anomaly detection and predictive threat adaptation (Ateniese et al., 2020; He et al., 2020).

8.2 Recommendations for Practitioners and Researchers

In order to demonstrate how the theoretical progress can be translated into operational security, the practical recommendations can be offered to practitioners, researchers and policymakers. Assess the Trade-offs in Dynamics. Consistently compare the latency, the accuracy and the energy measure to uphold the balance of privacy protection and model performance (Gentry, 2009), (T. Li, 2020).

Table 8. Key recommendations and best practices for deployment

Recommendation	Actionable Guidance
Use Lightweight Security	Optimize cryptography for edge devices
Monitor Model Updates	Detect anomalies in real-time
Adopt Multi-Layer Security	Combine device, network, and aggregation security
Evaluate Trade-offs	Balance latency, accuracy, and privacy

Table 8 summarizes key recommendations and best practices for deployment. These cultures promote responsible and sustainable use of FL systems, consistent with security engineering principles with ethical and regulatory values (Aono et al., 2018; He et al., 2020; Truong & O'Malley, 2021).

REFERENCES

Abadi, M., Chu, A., Goodfellow, I., McMahan, H. B., Mironov, I., Talwar, K., & Zhang, L. (2016). Deep learning with differential privacy. In *Proceedings of the ACM SIGSAC Conference on Computer and Communications Security* (pp. 308–318).

Albshaier, L., Almarri, S., & Albuali, A. (2025). Federated learning for cloud and edge security: A systematic review of challenges and AI opportunities. *Electronics (Basel)*, *14*(5), 1019.

Aono, Y., Hayashi, T., Wang, L., & Moriai, S. (2018). Privacy-preserving deep learning via additively homomorphic encryption. *IEEE Transactions on Information Forensics and Security*, *13*(5), 1333–1345. DOI: 10.1109/TIFS.2017.2787987

Ateniese, G., Cipher, J., Fredrikson, M. R., & Coull, R. (2020). On the security of machine learning in the presence of malicious training data. *Journal of Information Security and Applications*, •••, 55.

Bonawitz, K., Ivanov, V., Kreuter, B., Marcedone, A., McMahan, H. B., Patel, S., Ramage, D., & Seth, J. (2019). Practical secure aggregation for federated learning on heterogeneous devices. *arXiv preprint*. https://arxiv.org/abs/1902.01046

Brecko, A., Kajati, E., Koziorek, J., & Zolotova, I. (2022). Federated learning for edge computing: A survey. *Applied Sciences (Basel, Switzerland)*, *12*(18), 9124. DOI: 10.3390/app12189124

Carlini, N., Liu, C., Erlingsson, Ú., Kos, J., & Song, D. (2019). The secret sharer: Measuring unintended neural network memorization & extracting secrets. In *Proceedings of the USENIX Security Symposium* (pp. 267–284).

Emmanni, S. (2021). Federated learning for cybersecurity in edge and cloud computing. *International Journal of Computing and Engineering*, *2*(1), 14–25.

Fan, L., & Yu, T. (2020). Adversarial attacks against federated learning systems. *IEEE Access : Practical Innovations, Open Solutions*, *8*, 167162–167180.

Gentry, C. (2009). Fully homomorphic encryption using ideal lattices. In *Proceedings of the ACM Symposium on Theory of Computing* (pp. 169–178).

Geyer, A., Klein, T., & Nabi, M. (2017). Differentially private federated learning: A client-level perspective. *arXiv preprint*. https://arxiv.org/abs/1712.07557

He, B., Li, Q., & Wang, D. (2020). Efficient and secure aggregation for edge-based federated learning. In *Proceedings of the International Conference on Edge Computing* (pp. 45–54).

Hitaj, B., Ateniese, G., & Perez-Cruz, F. (2017). Deep models under the GAN: Information leakage from collaborative deep learning. In *Proceedings of the ACM SIGSAC Conference on Computer and Communications Security* (pp. 603–618). DOI: 10.1145/3133956.3134012

Kairouz, P., ... (2019). Advances and open problems in federated learning. *arXiv preprint*. https://arxiv.org/abs/1912.04977

Konečný, J., McMahan, H. B., Ramage, D., & Richtárik, P. (2016). Federated optimization: Distributed machine learning for on-device intelligence. *arXiv preprint*. https://arxiv.org/abs/1610.02527

Li, T., Sahu, A. K., Talwalkar, A., & Smith, V. (2020). Federated learning: Challenges, methods, and future directions. *IEEE Signal Processing Magazine*, *37*(3), 50–60. DOI: 10.1109/MSP.2020.2975749

Li, Y., He, K., Wang, T., & Wang, Z. (2021). A survey of communication-efficient federated learning. *IEEE Communications Surveys and Tutorials*, *23*(4), 3951–3970.

Lyu, L., Yu, H., & Liu, Q. (2020). Threats to federated learning: A survey. *arXiv preprint*. https://arxiv.org/abs/2003.02133

Lyu, X., Wang, X., & Liu, P. (2021). Resource-aware federated learning on edge devices. *IEEE Transactions on Mobile Computing*, *20*(12), 719–731.

McMahan, H. B., Moore, E., Ramage, D., Hampson, S., & Arcas, B. A. (2017). Communication-efficient learning of deep networks from decentralized data. In *Proceedings of the 20th International Conference on Artificial Intelligence and Statistics* (pp. 1273–1282).

Moore, E., Imteaj, A., Rezapour, S., & Amini, M. H. (2023). A survey on secure and private federated learning using blockchain: Theory and application in resource-constrained computing. *arXiv preprint*. https://arxiv.org/abs/2303.13727

Nakamoto, S. (2008). Bitcoin: A peer-to-peer electronic cash system.

Papernot, N., Abadi, M., Erlingsson, Ú., Goodfellow, I., & Talwar, K. (2017). Semi-supervised knowledge transfer for deep learning from private training data. In *Proceedings of the International Conference on Learning Representations*.

Peng, G., Shi, X., & Zhang, J. (2024). BGFL: A blockchain-enabled group federated learning at wireless industrial edges. *Journal of Cloud Computing (Heidelberg, Germany)*, *13*, 148.

Rahmati, M. (2025). Energy-aware federated learning for secure edge computing in 5G-enabled IoT networks. *Journal of Electrical Systems and Information Technology*, *12*, 13.

Shokri, R., & Shmatikov, V. (2015). Privacy-preserving deep learning. In *Proceedings of the ACM SIGSAC Conference on Computer and Communications Security* (pp. 1310–1321).

Shokri, R., Stronati, P., Song, C., & Shmatikov, V. (2017). Membership inference attacks against machine learning models. In *Proceedings of the IEEE Symposium on Security and Privacy* (pp. 3–18). DOI: 10.1109/SP.2017.41

Truong, F., Jain, A. K., & Deng, R. H. (2020). Secure aggregation for federated learning: Privacy, trust and efficiency. In *Proceedings of the IEEE International Conference on Distributed Computing Systems* (pp. 1823–1834).

Truong, C., & O'Malley, O. (2021). Privacy-preserving techniques in edge-AI: A comparative survey. ACM Transactions on Privacy and Security, 24(2).

Wang, S., Liu, J., & Chen, T. (2020). Adaptive communication strategies to improve federated learning in edge computing. *IEEE Communications Magazine*, *58*(4), 42–47.

Xie, J., Zhou, M., & Zhang, J. (2022). Adversarial robustness in federated learning: Threats and defenses. *ACM Computing Surveys*, *54*(4), 84.

Xu, J., Xiang, L., Mohd, B. S. M., & Gao, Y. (2022). A survey on federated learning and its security and privacy challenges. *IEEE Internet of Things Journal*, *9*(1), 1145–1166.

Yang, Q., Liu, Y., Chen, T., & Tong, Y. (2019). Federated machine learning: Concept and applications. *IEEE Intelligent Systems*, *34*(3), 36–44.

Zafar, S., White, J., & Legg, P. (2025). Federated learning with adversarial optimisation for secure and efficient 5G edge computing networks. *Big Data and Cognitive Computing*, *9*(9), 238. DOI: 10.3390/bdcc9090238

Zhang, J., Refaei, M. J. M. T., & Wang, N. (2020). Poisoning attacks and defenses for federated learning. *IEEE Transactions on Network Science and Engineering*, *7*(4), 2999–3012.

Zhao, Z., Chen, W., Li, X., & Li, J. (2021). An overview of data poisoning attacks and defenses in federated learning. *IEEE Transactions on Information Forensics and Security*, *16*, 1205–1223.

Chapter 5
Data Poisoning Attacks in Federated Learning and Mitigating Label-Flipping Attacks With MSCDFL

R. Maheshwari
https://orcid.org/0009-0001-5935-8475
Velalar College of Engineering and Technology, India

N. V. Keerthana
https://orcid.org/0000-0001-8878-2083
Velalar College of Engineering and Technology, India

T. Nithya
https://orcid.org/0000-0001-9738-9910
Velalar College of Engineering and Technology, India

P. Sathyasutha
Gnanamani College of Technology, India

T. Kokilavani
https://orcid.org/0000-0003-0056-3236
Velalar College of Engineering and Technology, India

S. Geetha
https://orcid.org/0009-0003-6435-7359
Nandha Engineering College, India

B. Amruthavarshini
Birla Institute of Technology and Science, India

ABSTRACT

This chapter provides a detailed overview of the security threats pertaining to federated learning, with a specific focus on label-flipping type of data poisoning attacks. Accordingly, the goal of this chapter is to evaluate the robustness of the defense mechanisms to defend against such label flipping attack. In this chapter, the defense approaches like manifold learning approach (UMAP), clustering method (K-Means), and dimensionality reduction methods such as PCA and KPCA are evaluated and their limitations are illustrated. A Multi-Stage Clustering and Data Quality Filtering (MSCDFL) approach is introduced in this chapter to address these limitations which integrates several techniques like adaptive clustering, data quality scored updates, delta-based updates, and trimmed mean aggregation to detect and mitigate the adversaries. From the experimental results, it is observed that MSCDFL exhibits better performance by maintaining robustness and significantly improving the prediction accuracy even in the presence of 40% of adversaries.

DOI: 10.4018/979-8-3373-6224-3.ch005

1. INTRODUCTION

Federated Learning is a decentralized framework that enables distribute identities(clients) such as hospitals, banks, edge devices or enterprises to work together to train a machine learning model locally. (Shirvani, Ghasemshirazi, & Beigzadeh, 2024) The main advantage of this framework is that it guarantees data privacy and security by maintaining the data within the organizational premises itself rather than moving it to a centralized server. Here, the clients will be different organizations that are located at different physical locations and collaboratively trains the model locally using the dataset which is not identically and independently distributed i.e., non-IID dataset. These clients will only share the critical parameters of the trained model to a centralized server. The centralized server combines them into a single global model by averaging the updated local models. The server sends the updated model again to the clients to complete one iteration. To make the model to achieve convergence, federated learning requires several iterations. So, the federated learning is a continuous learning process where the global model is refined in each cycle.

1.2 Federated Learning Workflow

Figure 1 depicts the workflow of FL involves three main stages with several iterations.(Almutairi & Barnawi, 2023)

Figure 1. Workflow of federated learning

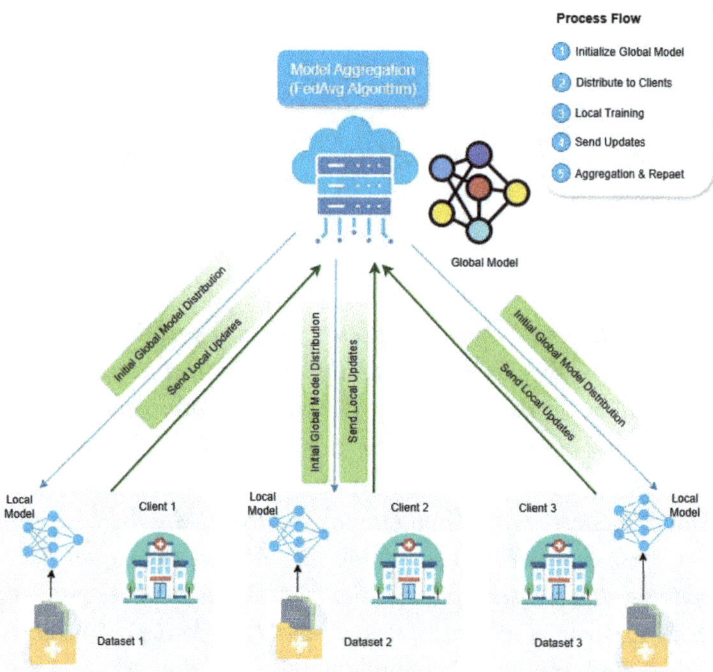

FedAvg is the Federated Learning algorithm that works by training the model locally using Stochastic Gradient Descent (SGD) on client devices and then average the model updates at the server. Let c ($c \in 1,2,3,\cdots, N$) denote a client, where N is the total number of clients. The training dataset of the client c is denoted by $D_{k,}$ where k is the client id. The dataset may be IID (Independently and Identically Distributed) or non-IID (non-independently and identically distributed) based on the FL application scenario .(Wen et al., 2023)

Model Initialization at the server: The FL server select the clients and identifies the initial global model (logical regression or CNN depending in input) with hyperparameters like learning rate, local epochs, and number of iterations to be performed to reach the desired accuracy. After identification, the server broadcast the global model to the clients.

Local Model training at the client: The client downloads the global model shared by server and train the current model with its local dataset (D_k). Then share the updated model to the server.

Global model aggregation at the server: The centralized server combines the local model shared by the clients into a single global model and sent it back to the clients for refinement.

1.2 Characteristics of Federated Learning and security threats

The standard Federated Learning technique is vulnerable to several adversary attacks. Despite the advantages offered by federated learning, the following are the characteristics of FL that leads to several security threats.(Almutairi & Barnawi, 2023)

- **Decentralized clients:** The participation of independent clients in FL with lack of central control allows attackers to inject poisoned data in the actual data. The FL clients may itself be malicious or compromised.
- **Insecure communication:** The model updates are transmitted by both client and server over a network that may be insecure or prone to manipulation. The attackers may eavesdrop the updates or introduce man-in-the-middle attack during transmission. (Yurdem, Kuzlu, Gullu, Catak, & Tabassum, 2024)
- **Central server:** The server is responsible for aggregation of local updates shared by the clients. A malicious server may exploit these updates to reconstruct the raw data violating privacy benefits of FL.
- **Shared gradients/updates:** Malicious client or a server may try to infer the sensitive information from the shared gradients.
- **Date Heterogeneity:** Clients with different device capabilities have inconsistent and non- identically independent data enabling the difficulty to distinguish between the data shared by a malicious client and actual client.
- **Lifecycle complexity:** Model updates reach convergence after several iterations. This enables the adversaries to modify the updates on each iteration leading to an incorrect model.

Federated learning faces the following technical challenges that directly impacts the core system performance, reliability and efficiency of the training process.(Wen et al., 2023)

1.3 Security Threats in Federated Learning

The security threats affect the privacy, availability, or integrity of the federated learning process, with the intention (malicious or not) of stealing, manipulating, or deriving sensitive data from the system. The following are some of the security threats in FL.(Yuan, Wang, Sun, Yu, & Brinton, 2024)

- Data poisoning attacks
- Model poisoning attacks
- Parameter inversion attack
- Model extraction
- Membership inference attack
- Property inference attack
- Eavesdropping
- Sybil attacks

2. LITERATURE REVIEW

2.1 Threat Model in Federated Learning

The threat model outlines the ability, knowledge and motivation of the attacker which enables to understand the vulnerabilities in the FL and helps to design effective defense mechanisms. The threat model is described based on following context(Dou, Wang, Sun, Liu, & Fang, 2025)

2.1.1 Knowledge of the adversary

The adversary's knowledge refers to the amount of information that an adversary can observe from the models shared over the network. The adversary's knowledge can be categorized as white-box, black-box or grey-box. In white-box, the attacker has full access to current model and its parameters. In Black-box, the attacker can access only model predictions but no access to the model. In grey-box where attacker tries to be honest and follow the protocol but can infer some information.(Wang et al., 2022)

2.1.2 Adversary type and capabilities

Capabilities of the adversary deals with controlling the participants involved in the training process. The adversaries possess different capabilities based on their role in the FL training process. The adversaries can take the role of participants in the form of insiders such as malicious server, malicious client and Eavesdropper or outsider. This helps to clarify the type of attacks that can be carried out by one of the following roles and categorize them under the attack categories such as data poisoning, inference or model poisoning attacks.(Zhang et al., 2022). In privacy-preserving federated learning (FL), the system can still face certain attacks. These attacks typically include backdoor attacks, inference attacks and poisoning attacks, which alter either local data or model updates before sending them to the global model.(Ali, Han, Majeed, Lim, & Hwang, 2025)

Malicious client: The adversaries with client capabilities can control the local training by accessing the client's device. They can update the local updates or can inject poisoned data in the dataset before sharing the update to the server.(Lyu, Yu, & Yang, 2020) As there is no specific mechanism for authenticating the client's identity in the FL's principle, the sever could not distinguish the malicious client from the benign client. This creates an opportunity for the malicious clients to participate in the training process pretending themselves as benign client. Another challenge is that clients can train the model locally, any malicious updates shared by the client could not be distinguished by the server. So, the adversary can observe, corrupt or replace the global model and controls the training procedure. The malicious clients can take one of the following capabilities of the client.(Shirvani et al., 2024)

- **Non-Colluding attack:** A single malicious client adversary can misclassify the model by misclassifying the input with high confidence rate.
- **Byzantine attack:** The adversaries create model updates similar to actual updates as created by a benign client making it stealthy and hard to predict.(Kabbaj, El-Azouzi, & Kobbane, 2025)
- **Sybil attack:** The adversaries create multiple fake client account as similar to actual client or use the compromised clients account to launch more attacks.(Lyu et al., 2020)

Malicious server: The adversary can inspect the model updates and alter the parameters of the global model. Attackers can perform following categories of attack based on attack strength.

- **Gradient Ascent:** A malicious aggregator may use gradient ascent to maximize the global loss function thereby making the model to predict incorrectly(Chai et al., 2024)
- **Isolating target client:** The aggregator shares a manipulated model instead of sharing the aggregated global model. This makes the targeted clients to learn incorrect patterns over a period of time leads to misprediction.
- **Isolation Gradient attack:** It is a hybrid attack where gradient ascent is combined with isolating attack. At first the adversary trains a local model using gradient ascent to maximize the global loss. Then its shares the poised model to the target clients rather than sharing it with all the clients. The target clients will be isolated from receiving honest global updates and learns incorrect pattern over a period of time resulting in degradation of its performance.

A malicious aggregator can steal private data from the shared model update in the following ways.(Chai et al., 2024)

- **Deep leakage from gradient (DLG) attacks:** The attackers can reconstruct the raw training data from the shared model gradients by reversing the shared model update gradients.
- **GAN based attacks:** In this attack, the malicious server secretly recovers the private data of a client using GAN. The private data is observed to create a fake data which looks similar to the actual client's data. This compromises the ideal privacy characteristics of FL

Eavesdropper: The adversaries can monitor the data transmitted over a communication network and infers some sensitive information about the client. The adversaries try to launch man-in-the-middle attack where the attackers intercept the model updates and replace it with malicious updates.

2.1.3 Goal of Adversaries

The objective of the adversaries may be to create targeted or untargeted attacks. It clarifies the intention of adversaries whether their goal is to modify the specific input or to disrupt the overall model. Based on their intention, the attacks are classified as targeted attacks and untargeted attacks(Almutairi & Barnawi, 2023)

- **Targeted attacks:** The objective of targeted attacks is to manipulate the model intentionally to behave incorrectly only for specific inputs and behave normally for other inputs. Label-flipping attacks, which can target one label or many, or attacks that happen during specific training rounds, can be especially damaging. (Sameera et al., 2025)
- **Untargeted attacks:** The goal of adversaries is to degrade the overall performance of the global model without manipulating any specific input. This results in lowering model accuracy, wasting the resources and causing instability.

2.2 Types of attacks

The adversaries will try to exploit the vulnerabilities in the FL architecture and introduces several types of attacks based on their knowledge, capabilities and goals. The attacks in FL are categorized based on three perspectives: client, communication process and server (Chai et al., 2024)

- The client anomaly attacks include data poisoning, model poisoning, backdoor attacks, byzantine attacks, sybil attacks, free riding attacks and Inference attacks.

2.2.1 Data Poisoning

The data poisoning attacks are primarily carried by client adversaries and rarely by malicious aggregators. The malicious client aims at intentionally manipulating the training data to manipulate the global model to degrade the performance, causing misclassification or introduce backdoor. The data poisoning attacks are organized based on several critical dimensions, reflecting various data manipulation methods carried out by adversaries to weaken the learning process.

2.2.2 Taxonomy of Data Poisoning Attacks

The data poisoning attacks are categorized based on seven dimensions. The Figure 2 depicts the taxonomy of data poisoning attacks carried out before the training phase by a malicious client in FL(Ma, Zhao, & Tian, 2025).The taxonomy provides a structured framework for analysing various types of data poisoning attacks focusing on the characteristics of attacks, goal, knowledge and other relevant factors. (Yuan et al., 2024)

Manipulation type

Attacks known as data poisoning operate by altering the training data in various ways. Label Modification/Label Flipping attack merely alters the training data's labels. For instance, altering a photo with the label "cat" to one with the label "dog" while preserving the original image of the cat.

Attack Objective

Attacks differ in their objectives. In Poison and the Back Door attack, Secret triggers are created in the model by frog assaults. When the model detects a certain pattern, it behaves inappropriately as the attacker expects, otherwise it functions properly. Accessible/Untargeted Label flipping attacks reduces the model performance and making it useless for intended use.(Jebreel, Domingo-Ferrer, Sánchez, & Blanco-Justicia, 2024)

Figure 2. Taxonomy of data poisoning attacks

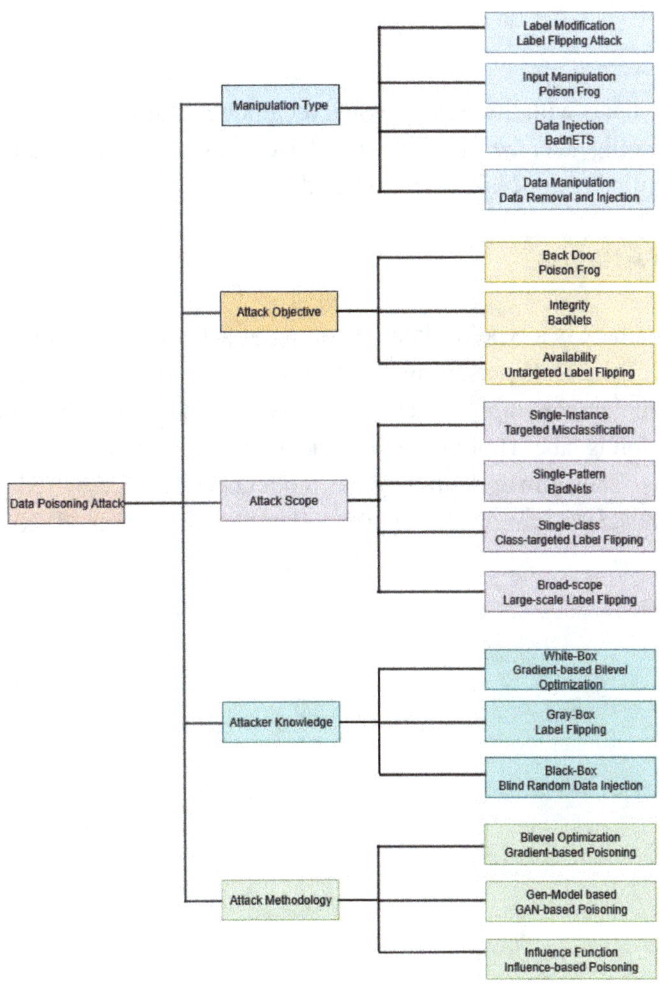

Attack Scope

The extent to which the model's behaviour is impacted is referred to as the attack scope. The goal of misclassification attacks is to get the model to be incorrect about a single or small number of inputs. One-class, class-specific Attacks known as "label flipping" target everything in a single category; for instance, they make the model consistently incorrect about cats but accurate about dogs.

Attacker Knowledge

Attackers' tactics is influenced by the amount of information they possess. Gradient-based and white-box Attackers who are fully aware of the model's internal workings, training process, and structure are able to launch bilevel optimisation attacks. They are able to develop highly successful attacks because of their comprehensive understanding. (Jebreel et al., 2024)Attacks such as "gray-box" or "label flipping" happen when an attacker has some information but not so much. Attackers that have minimal knowledge about the target model and are forced to employ general approaches that are effective against a wide variety of models are said to be engaging in Black-Box/Blind Random Data Injection assaults.

Attack Methodology

Attack methodology deals with the technological techniques that were employed to contaminate the data. Using artificial intelligence, Gen-Model-based/GAN-based poisoning generates phoney training data that appears authentic but conceals harmful trends.

2.3 Label Flipping Attacks

Label manipulation attack is a type of data poisoning attack where the adversaries take the control of the training data of a client. Data poisoning attacks are categorized based on their manipulation types as four types namely label attack, input attack, data injection and manipulation attack. One particular kind of label manipulation is label flipping, where the attacker has control over the labels applied to a subset of training points. They aim at degrading the model performance by reducing model prediction accuracy or can cause misclassifications.(AlOtaibi, Felemban, & Mahmood, 2024)

Figure 3. Federated learning under label flipping attack

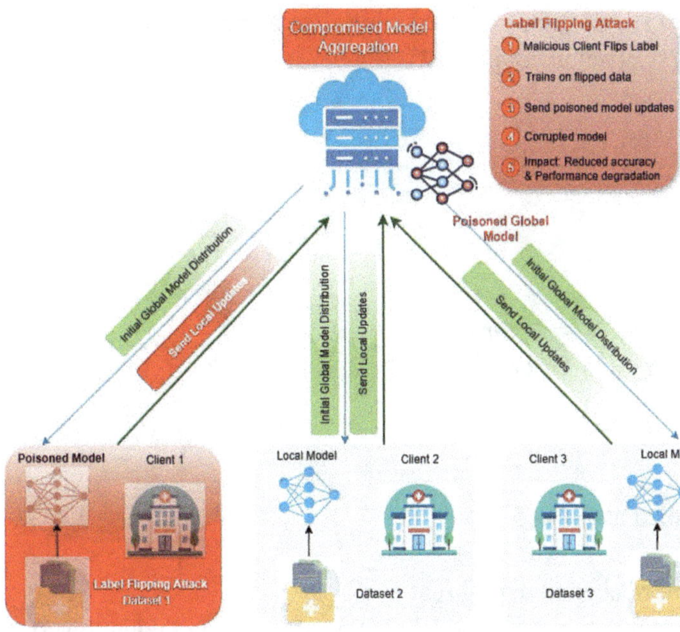

Label-flipping attacks in federated learning (FL) can be random or coordinated and their impact depends on the aggressiveness and goals of the attack.(Wasilewska & Bogucka, 2025) Highly aggressive random attacks that increase false alarms damage the performance. In contrast, less aggressive coordinated attacks cause more harm than random ones. The availability attacks targeted and untargeted label flips can disrupt training and reduce test accuracy without needing to change gradients or features significantly.(El-Kabid & El-Mhamdi, 2025).

In label flipping (dirty label) attack, the adversary misguides the model to make incorrect prediction by changing the labels of certain classes in the training data without changing the features of the data. The performance of the model is degraded gradually leading to cumulative performance degradation without being detected. These dirty label attacks are very dangerous as the poisoned labels could not be detected by the server that do not have complete visibility over the raw data. The malicious client performs the local model training using the poisoned dataset and transfer it to the serve for aggregation. The Figure 3 describes effect of the label flipping attacks in FL scenario.

Let us consider the label for class cat is 3 and label for class dog is 5. After label flipping attack, the label of class 3 is changed to class 5 to confuse the model.

Let the actual dataset be defined in the equation(1)

$$D = \{(a_i, b_i)\}_{i=1}^{N} \tag{1}$$

Here,

- D: actual training dataset
- $a_i \in I$, a_i:*Input image* and I: *set of Input image*

• $b_i \in L$, b_i:*Trule lable for* a_i and L: *set of true class labels*

The attacker modifies the portion of the training data as poisoned data and is defined by a label-flipping function($\varphi(b_i)$) is given in equation(2).

$$\varphi(b_i) = \begin{cases} b_i^{'}, if b_i = b_j \\ b_i, otherwise \end{cases} \quad (2)$$

Here,

• b_i:*original label* $(eg.\ b_i = 3\ for\ cat)$
• $b_i^{'}$:*flipped label* $(b_i^{'} = 5\ for\ dog)$

Here,

• $b_i = 3$ are relabeled as $b_i^{'} = 5$

i.e., the cat images are relabelled to dog (cat → dog)
so, now the poisoned dataset with partial label flipped is given in equation(3),

$$D' = \{(a_i, \varphi(b_i)) | (a_i, b_i) \in D\}_{i=1}^{N} \quad (3)$$

Here,

• Images a_i are unchanged,
• Labels b_i are flipped

A variant of dirty-label attack is multiple-label flipping attack. Consider an image with multiple labels like tree, sky, road, where flipping one label is harder to detect. It reduces the accuracy, robustness, convergence speed and predictive performance of the model. (Ma et al., 2025)

2.4 Importance of Detecting and defending Label Flipping Attacks

Detecting and defending label flipping attack is important for the following reasons.(Lavaur, Busnel, & Autrel, 2025)

• **Maintains Model Integrity:** By identifying the attack early on, tainted training updates are kept from being combined, maintaining appropriate decision boundaries.
• **Prevents Long-Term Damage:** If poisoned labels are not detected, they can spread during several training cycles and gradually reduce accuracy.
• **Guards Against Targeted Manipulation:** Prior to deployment, detection prevents backdoors or deliberate bias, which is a common feature of label flipping attacks.

- **Preserves Federated Learning System Trust:** Identifying label flipping is essential to guaranteeing the server can trust client contributions because raw data is never shared.

2.5 Defense methods against malicious client in Federated Learning

The malicious clients in the FL system are detected using Principal Component Analysis (PCA) algorithm. This method fails when the number of malicious clients is 20% and has limited robustness and performs poor for non-IID data. PCA analyses the datasets CIFAR-10 and MNIST using linear projection and clustering. From the performance metrics, it is observed that the accuracy of the algorithm drops from 80% to 55% at a 20% attack rate, with detection around 60-80%. It drops further for 25% of attack rate. (Tolpegin, Truex, Gursoy, & Liu, 2020). The next algorithm is Kernel Principal Component Analysis (KPCA) which extends the PCA using nonlinear projections, such as an RBF kernel, followed by clustering. The algorithm shows poor performance under 30% malicious client and achieves 70% accuracy at a 20% attack rate with the detection of 70-75% malicious clients and an F1 score of about 0.70. This algorithm is tested on CIFAR-10 and Fashion-MNIST datasets.(Li, Wong, Wang, Yao, & Chau, 2021) The K-means algorithm based on similarity clusters the client updates and has been evaluated on CIFAR-10. The clusters make the system to weak against adaptive attacks as the cluster get overlaps sometimes. This method performs with about 70% accuracy at a 20% attack, with precision around 0.68 and recall of 0.60. (Fang, Cao, Jia, & Gong, 2020)Uniform Manifold Approximation and Projection (UMAP) is another method that shows robustness up to 30% malicious clients by embedding client updates and identifying outliers for datasets like CIFAR-10 and MNIST. It provides 75–78% accuracy with true positive rate around 0.82, approximate false positive rate of 0.12, and F1 score of 0.80 (Upreti, Kim, Yang, & Seo, 2022). The proposed method Multistage Malicious Client Detection in Federated Learning (MSCDFL) addresses the limitations of the PCA, KPCA, K-Means and UMAP approaches by effectively isolating the malicious clients while maintaining the data privacy and integrity of the honest client. This method combines the latent mapping with data quality assessment and clustering-based filtering.

PCA can also be used to project activations to lower dimensions if necessary, even though it's not always required.(Zahir-Ismail & Shukla, 2025). Malicious clients change the labels of their local data points to confuse the global model The Robust aggregation methods can improve reliability and accuracy of the model. (Kritharakis, Jakovetic, Makris, & Tserpes, 2025)

3. METHODOLOGY

3.1 Malicious Client Detection using MSCDFL

In FL, to make the global model to create a compromised model, the malicious clients ingest inaccurate, misleading or modified training data into their local dataset. The model behaves maliciously due to the hidden triggers by these malicious clients and reduces the overall accuracy of the model for certain inputs. A malicious client will intentionally change the digit "7" as "1" in a handwriting recognition FL system to make the model to misclassify the digits. In order to defend against the label flipping attack, the MSCDFL architecture suggests Malicious Clients Detection Federated Learning (MSCDFL), which does so by recovering a distribution across a latent feature space to determine each client's data quality. (Wen et al., 2023). Figure 4 represents the architecture and workflow of the MSCDFL (Malicious Clients

Detection Federated Learning) framework, showing how it detects and mitigates label flipping attacks in a federated learning environment such as CIFAR-10. At the start of training, the central server initializes a global CNN model tailored for CIFAR-10 classification and a lightweight MLP generator that maps each class label to a corresponding latent feature vector. These components are distributed to all active clients in the round. On the client side, each participant uses the generator to produce latent features for the labels in its local dataset and compares the predictions obtained from these generated features (global view) with predictions from its own local data (local view).

Figure 4. MSCDFL architecture for malicious client detection in federated learning

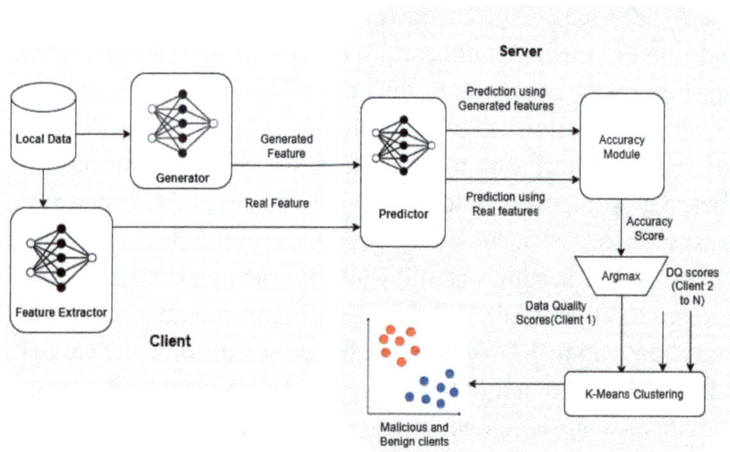

High Data quality score (DQ score) indicates the behavior of benign node while low DQ scores suggests the malicious activity. Based on the DQ Score, the server uses K-means clustering to separate the malicious client groups from the benign clients. After detecting and removing the malicious clients, the benign clients then proceed with personalized local training, using a shared global feature extractor and their own classification head, potentially enhanced with generator-based data augmentation. These local updates from the benign clients are aggregated by the server using FedAvg and updates the generator accordingly, and redistributes both components for the next round. This update process is repeated for several cycles until the model converges.(Anastasiadis & Refanidis, 2025). MSCDFL algorithm involves the following steps in FL's learning process with attack detection. (Xiong, Dong, Sohrabi, & Tari, 2025).

Algorithm: MSCDFL_Detection(W, p, DQ)

Input: W= Global CNN parameters, p=MLP Generator parameters, C= Set of clients with local data
Output: Robust Global Model Parameters W*
1: Server initializes global CNN model W0 and generator p0.
2: **for** each round t = 1 to T **do**
3: Server broadcasts W and p to all clients;
4: **for** each client c ∈ C **do**
5: **Generate** latent features v_c = G_p(y_c);

Find predictions from:
global view: ŷ_g = f_W(v_c)
local view: ŷ_l = f_local(x_c)
Compute DQ_c = (1/|D_c|) Σ I(ŷ_g=ŷ_l)
Send DQ_c and ΔW_c to server
end for
Apply K-means (K=2) on {DQ_c} to separate benign/malicious;
Exclude malicious clients;
Aggregate benign updates:
W = Σ(|D_c|/Σ|D_c|) * W_c
Update generator p accordingly;
end for
Return final W (robust global model)

3.1.1 Server initialization:

Server initialization process involves the initialization of the global CNN Model for classification, MLP generator for later feature mapping, Loss function and distribution to clients.

Global CNN Initialization:

The server initializes the global model parameters using methods such as Xavier initialization to stabilize early training. The initial global model parameter includes weights and biases of convolutional layers of the neural networks. The filter weight with high positive strongly activates the particular feature and with high negative suppresses the feature.(Yuan et al., 2024). The global parameters are given in equation(4).

$$P_0 = \{w_0, b_0\} \tag{4}$$

Here,

- P_0: Initial global parameters
- w_0: Initial weights of CNN layer
- b_0: Initial biases of the CNN layer

In equation(4), Initial weights w_0, and biases b_0 for each CNN layer. The high positive weight activates a feature and a negative weight suppresses the feature. This sets a stable starting point for training.

Latent Feature Generator Initialization:

The lightweight MLP generator is a small neural network that maps the class labels to numerical feature vectors instead of using raw images. Each class is represented as one-hot encoded vector. The latent vectors are generated by the server using trusted generator model and distributed to the clients. The client makes predictions from the actual dataset which are matched with the produced latent vectors for verifying the client label's consistency. If the generated latent features and clients' predictions are consistent then the client labels are considered trustworthy. Further the deviations in the consistency indicates the presence of malicious clients in the system. (Kumarappan, Rajasekar, Vairavasundaram, Kotecha, & Kulkarni, 2024). The latent feature generation is given in equation (5).

$$v_c = G_p(e_c), \tag{5}$$

where,

- e_c is the one-hot encoded class label for each class c, $e_c = \{0, 1, 2, 3.., 9\}$
- G_p is the MLP generator parameterized by p=$\{w_g, b_g\}$
- v_c is the latent feature vector generated for class.

In equation(5), Generator G with parameters p takes a one-hot encoded class label for each class and produces a latent vector v and this is a numeric "signature" of the class without using images.

Generator Alignment loss function

The generator is trained or initialised using a generator alignment loss function to guarantee that its output matches the global CNN's comprehension of each class. (Bhatt, Gupta, & Rai, 2024)The CNN's embedding of a representative class image is compared with the generators latent output $G_p(y_c)$ and it is given in the equation(6).

$$L_G = \sum_{c=1}^{n} \|F(a_c) - G(e_c)\|^2 \tag{6}$$

where,

- $F(a_c)$ – Feature embedding extracted for an image a_c
- $G(e_c)$ – Latent feature vector generated from the one hot label of class e_c

The equation(6) ensures that the generator output vector v matches the CNN's feature embedding of an image a_c from that class. Minimising this loss makes latent features realistic.

The loss function finds the difference between these vectors. If the generator is well trained, these two vectors are very close.

Distribution to clients

The server broadcasts to all active clients the generator settings as well as the global CNN parameters. This guarantees that each client begins using the same generator reference for class characteristics and the same global model for classification. These are then used by clients for data quality rating and local training, which makes it possible to identify fraudulent clients.

Local Data Quality Calculation

Each client uses its local dataset which may include both actual and poised labels to calculate the local data quality. For each data sample $a_i$with its label b_i, the client uses the generator provided by the server to create a latent feature vector (Kritharakis et al.). This feature is then passed through the global model predictor to obtain a predicted label from the global perspective. The two predictions i.e., both global model prediction and local model prediction are compared. If it matches, the data label is consistent with the global distribution. Data Quality Score (DQ) is computed at the client end after processing all sample images.

The Data Quality (DQ) score is the fraction of number of matching predictions over the total number of samples in a client and it is given in equation(7)

$$DQ_c = \frac{1}{|D_c|} \sum_{(a,b) \in D_c} 1(pl(b) = pl(a)) \quad (7)$$

where,

- D_c: Client Dataset
- $|D_c|$: Number of samples in client c's dataset
- $pl(b)$: predicted label from global perspective model
- $pl(a)$: predicted label from client local model
- Indicator function 1(.): Returns 1 If the two predictions match, 0 otherwise

The indicator function returns 1 if it local and global prediction agrees. The DQ score is calculated by adding all the results (0 or 1) from the indicator function applied across the dataset. The High DQ score indicates that the label matches the expected feature and client is benign whereas the low DQ score indicates the less matches his helps to identify the malicious clients.

3.1.2 Malicious Client Detection (Server Side)

The server collects all the data quality scores shared by the client. The server now runs the K-means clustering with number of centroids K=2 on these data scores to split the scores into two clusters. The main goal of k-means clustering algorithm is to divide the number of observations into a number of clusters. In this scenario, one cluster is the benign clients with high DQ scores and the other cluster is the malicious clients with low DQ scores. The workflow of k-means algorithm is illustrated step by step as follows. (Abdullayeva, 2022)

Step 1: The cluster centroid values are chosen randomly.
Step 2: Then assign the clients to the cluster with nearest centroid value using Euclidean distance.
Step 3: The next step is to update the cluster centroid periodically by finding the average DQ score values assigned in each cluster. Reassign the clients based on the new centroid values using the formula given in equation (8).

$$\mu_k = \frac{1}{|C_k|} \sum_{DQ \in C_k} DQ_c \quad (8)$$

where,

- μ_k: Centroid of cluster k, where k= {1,2}
- C_k: Number of data points in Cluster k.
- $\sum_{DQ \in C_k} DQ_c$: Sum of all DQ scores in that cluster.

In equation(8), During k-means, recompute centroid μ_k. For cluster k look at every client assigned to it and retrieve their DQ score. Thean add all the DQ scores assigned to that cluster. Separates benign from malicious automatically.

Step 4: The steps 2 and 3 repeated until the cluster is stable without any change. If there is no change in assignment, it is considered that convergence is attained. At this stage, the malicious clients are excluded from the next training round.

3.1.3 Local Model Training

The local model training begins after the malicious clients are excluded from the training process and only benign clients participate in the training. First the benign client receives the shared feature extractor parameters from global model.

Local Training Loss

The Loss function $Loss_{local}$ which takes the model's prediction for each raw input and compare it with the true label and find the average over all samples. The client uses cross entropy loss function to find the average prediction error.

Matching Loss

The matching loss $Loss_{match}$ shows the distance between real features and generated features which generate some synthetic features and compare them with real features. Find the average of the difference values. The formula for total loss is given in equation(9)

$$Loss_{total} = Loss_{local} + \lambda Loss_{match} \tag{9}$$

The clients compute the loss, then applies gradient-based updates local for T epochs and finally send the updated shared parameter to the server. In equation(9), Each benign client minimises a sum of (i) cross-entropy loss between predictions and true labels, and (ii) a matching loss between real and generated features. $\lambda Loss_{match}$ balances them.

3.1.4 Aggregation

The server aggregates the updated shared feature parameter from the benign clients using Federated Averaging. The server updates the global model parameters using the formula given in equation(10).

$$P_f^{r+1} = \sum_{c \epsilon B} \frac{|D_c|}{\sum_{d \epsilon B} |D_c|} P_f^c \tag{10}$$

where,

- P_f^{r+1}: New global shared feature extractor
- P_f^c: Updated parameters from client
- $|D_c|$: Number of training samples at client c
- $\sum_{c\epsilon B} \frac{|D_c|}{\sum_{d\epsilon B} |D_c|}$: Summation over relative weight of benign client c

3.1.5 Repeat

The steps from 2 to 5 are repeated for multiple training rounds until the global model reaches convergence. Finally, the global model becomes both more accurate and robust over a period of time after several rounds.

Benefits of the MSCDFL Algorithm

- Maintains privacy (no gradients or raw data are exchanged).
- Minimal overhead in computation and storage
- Need no prior information of the sort of assault or the attackers.
- High accuracy of detection even when up to 40% of the clients are malevolent
- Early identification (with only 20 training cycles)
- Continuous filtering of malicious clients throughout training(Kolasa, Pilch, & Mazurczyk, 2024)
- Prevents gradient drift and model degradation
- Increases model accuracy by using customized training(Taghiyarrenani, Alabdallah, Nowaczyk, & Pashami, 2023)
- Enhances generalization using generator-based data augmentation

4. EXPERIMENTAL SETUP

4.1 Dataset Preparation

In this study, image classification benchmark dataset CIFAR-10 dataset is directly download from the torchvision.datasets.CIFAR-10. This dataset composes 60,000 RGB samples with low resolution (32X32 pixels) images which is ideal for testing label flipping attacks.(Li et al., 2021). It consists of 10 classes with each class represent a particular object in the real-world. Each image in the dataset is assigned with a class index and name. The images are classified across 10 classes, {0: 'airplane', 1: 'automobile', 2: 'bird', 3: 'cat', 4: 'deer', 5: 'dog', 6: 'frog', 7: 'horse', 8: 'ship', and 9: 'truck'}. In the CIFAR-10 Dataset, out of 60,000 sample images, 50,000 images are used for training and 10,000 images are used for testing. (Vinay & Balasubramanian, 2023). In the proposed method, the training set is divided among 20 clients. Each class in the training set is partitioned using Dirichlet distribution with parameter α=0.5. So, some clients have more dogs and few airplanes. Once the distribution is complete, in each round 10% to 40% of the clients are randomly selected as malicious clients. Malicious clients will take their dataset and flip the label systematically as a frequent misclassification case where images of dogs (class 5) are relabelled as cats (class 3), an infrequent misclassification case where airplanes (class 0) are relabelled as birds (class 2), and a moderately difficult case where automobiles (class 1) are relabelled as trucks (class 9). Therefore, while benign clients maintain their labels, the malicious datasets introduce poisoned labels that cause the training process to be misguided. Following this configuration, the prepared dataset is made available to clients. Malicious clients train on tainted data, whereas benign clients train on clean local data. In the experiment, the clients train the dataset for 2 local epochs per communication round and the system is run for a total of 6 global epoch considering the time and computational expensiveness. Since the primary focus is on testing the robustness of the algorithm, the accuracy is less critical for defenses. The framework must identify fraudulent clients based on their inconsistent predictions without needing access to the raw data, hence this partitioned and altered dataset serves as the basis for evaluating MSCDFL.

4.2 Attack Parameters

In order to assess MSCDFL's resilience against varying attack intensities, a specific percentage of clients in each training round are classified as malicious. They can range from 10% to 40%. These malicious clients employ pre-established attack pairs to systematically flip labels inside their local databases. The pairs that are selected for label flipping attack are Dog (5) as Cat (3), Aeroplane (0) as Bird (2), and Automobile (1) as Truck (9). Moderate resemblance, infrequent misclassification, and frequent misclassification are the three difficulty levels represented by these couples.

4.3 Model Architecture

The server uses two models such as global Convolutional Neural Network (CNN) aggregated model and a generator model. The global CNN model is updated by the server by applying the Federated Average to the model weights shared by the clients after each round. The generator model takes the input as one-hot vector of the class labels (0-9) and convert it to a 128 – dimensional latent feature vector. This is used for computing DQ scores and the malicious clients are detected by the server by applying k-means clustering algorithm over these DQ scores. Client uses the CNN classifier model to train the dataset locally. The client extracts the features in two stages. There are five convolutional layers. Each convolutional layer is responsible for extracting certain features from edges, textures, objects to overall shape. The sully connected layer map these features to 128-dimensional latent feature vector. Then the classifier layer is responsible for mapping these latent vectors to 10 logits. The logits from the final layer are passed to the softmax activation function to generate class probabilities. The softmax function to covert the scores to probabilities are given in equation(11).

$$\mathrm{smax}(s_i) = \frac{e^{s_i}}{\sum_{c=1}^{CL} e^{s_c}} \tag{11}$$

Here,

- $\mathrm{smax}(s_i)$: probability of each score
- s_i: logit or raw score for class i

- e^{s_i}: exponential transformation of s_i (logit)
- CL: Number of classes
- $\sum_{c=1}^{CL} e^{s_c}$: Sum of exponentials of all class logit

The equation(11), Converts raw logits s_i from the final layer to class probabilities.

There is another function called cross entropy function which calculates loss from the probability value as the negative log of the probability to find the loss value. The is done by comparing the model's predicted probability for a class with the true class label. Based on the loss value, the model is trained with a greater number of epochs to reduce this loss. The loss will be smaller only if the models predicted probability gets closer to the correct label. The smaller the loss makes the model to give correct and accurate prediction results. The gradients are computed from the loss inorder to identify which pixel is responsible for the mistake and how to adjust them. The gradient is computed as given in equation (12)

$$gradient(g) = smax - actual\ label \tag{12}$$

Here,

- $smax$: predicted probability for class i
- $actuallabel$: 1 for correct class, 0 otherwise

The equation(12) involves the Loss comparing predicted probability to true label. Its gradient tells how to adjust weights to reduce misclassification. The negative gradient for any label indicates to increase the logit for the respective class to improve its classification. The positive gradient indicates to reduce the gradient of all other classes. This is done by backpropagation method. The SGD optimizer is used to optimize the model's weight during local training on each client.

4.4 Evaluation Metrics

The performance of the federated model over classification and detection of malicious clients can be measured using the evaluation metrics such as accuracy, attack success rate, recall drop, True Positive Rate, False Positive Rate, Precision, F1-Scor and AU-ROC. (Yuan et al., 2024)

4.4.1 Classification Accuracy

The overall performance of the global model on the test dataset is measured by accuracy. It can be defined as the ratio of number of correctly predicted samples to the total number of samples.(Chai et al., 2024). The accuracy is calculated using the formula given in equation (Fang et al.).

$$Accuracy = \frac{Number\ of\ correctly\ predicted\ Labels}{Total\ number\ of\ predicted\ samples} \tag{13}$$

In equation(13), the accuracy shows the overall performance of the federated model with and without malicious attacks. It is the ratio of correctly predicted samples on test set.

4.4.2 Attack Success Rate

Attack Success rate measures the impact of label flipping attack on the global model. (Xiong, Dong, Sohrabi, & Tari). To perform label flipping attack, the attacker first chooses a source class C and flip its label to a target class T. The attack success rate is the ratio of mis-predicted samples from a class C as target class C to the total number of samples in the class C.(Xie, Hu, Ren, & Deng, 2024) The attack success rate is given in equation (14).

$$ASR = \frac{|\{i: b_i = C \wedge \hat{b}_i = T\}|}{|\{i: b_i = C\}|} \quad (14)$$

Where:

- b_i: true label for sample i.
- $\hat{b}_i$: predicted label of sample i
- Numerator: Number of samples from the source class C that are incorrectly predicted as target class T
- Denominator: Total number of samples from source class C.

4.4.3 Recall Drop

Recall drop metric is used to measure the model degradation in recall of a source class when a label flipping attack is applied in Federated Learning. The recall for a class C is the proportion of correctly predicted samples of that class out of all actual samples belonging to that class. The recall using the formula given in equation (Abdullayeva)

$$Recall_C = \frac{TP_C}{TP_C + FN_C} \quad (15)$$

Here,

- TP_C: True positives
- FN_C: False Negatives

True positives are the number of correctly classified samples of Class C and False negatives is the number of samples that were misclassified as other classes. Recall drop is the difference between the recall of that class in a clean model and its recall under attack and it is given in equation (16).

$$\triangle R_C = R_C^{clean} - R_C^{attack} \quad (16)$$

In equation(16), The difference between recall of class C when trained using clean data and recall od class C when trained using malicious data is computed. This gives the amount of performance lost due to attack in the FL.

4.4.4 Malicious client detection metrics

The objective of MSCDFL is to detect the malicious clients from benign clients where malicious clients are considered the true positive class and benign client as negative class.

True Positive Rate (TPR)

True positive rate metric is also called as recall is used to show how many malicious clients are correctly identified out of all malicious clients. A low TPR signifies that many attackers go unnoticed, allowing them to continue contaminating the training process, whereas a high TPR shows that the defence mechanism is effective in identifying attacker. The formula to measure this is given in equation(17).

$$TPR = \frac{TP}{TP + FN} \tag{18}$$

where,

- TP: True positive (correctly detected malicious clients)
- FN: False Negative (non-identified malicious clients considered as benign)

False Positive Rate (FPR)

The number of benign clients that are wrongly classified as malicious clients is measured by FPR. It is the complement of TPR. While a high FPR would penalise too many innocent clients, compromising the training's accuracy and fairness, a low FPR must be maintained to prevent the removal of trustworthy clients. Formula for finding FPR is given in equation (19)

$$FPR = \frac{FP}{FP + TN} \tag{19}$$

where,

- FP (False Positive): Benign clients incorrectly classified as malicious
- TN (True Negative): Benign clients correctly identified

Precision

Precision is a metric which measures the proportion of clients identified as malicious that are in fact malicious, hence quantifying the accuracy of detection.(Farooq et al., 2023) While low accuracy indicates that many benign participants are mistakenly labelled as adversaries, high precision indicates that relatively few benign customers are falsely accused by the detector. Formula to calculate precision is given in equation (20).

$$Precision(P) = \frac{TP}{TP + FP} \tag{20}$$

where

- TP: True Positive
- FP: False Negative

F1-score

F1-score is the harmonic mean of precision and true positive rate(recall). The F1-score is helpful in federated learning in situations when the malicious clients are lesser than the benign clients. (Farooq et al., 2023)High F1-score indicates that the detection method hardly misclassifies benign clients as malicious (high precision) and detects the majority of malicious clients (high recall). While a low F1-score indicates that either too many benign clients are incorrectly identified (low precision) or too many malicious clients are neglected (low recall). Formula to find F1-score is given in equation (21).

$$F1 = \frac{2.(P.TPR)}{P + TPR} \tag{21}$$

where,

- P: Precision
- TPR: True Positive Rate or Recall

Area under ROC (AU-ROC)

The Area under ROC offers a threshold-independent perspective on the detector's performance by plotting TPR against FPR at various thresholds. An AUC of 0.5 would imply that the detection is no more effective than random guessing, but a higher AUC value, nearer 1, implies that there is adequate separation capacity between malicious and benign clients.

5. RESULTS AND ANALYSIS

5.1 MSCDFL Detection Accuracy under Different Attack Scenarios

The effect of label flipping attacks on federated learning system is depicted in Figure 5 with various protection mechanisms. The x-axis indicates the rate of malicious users (attack ratio), while the y-axis displays the accuracy on the CIFAR-10 test set. As anticipated, the baseline model without protection shows a sharp decline in accuracy as the attack rate rises. This highlights the weaknesses of traditional distributed learning. Dimensionality-reduction defenses, like PCA, KPCA, and UMAP, initially perform well but drop off quickly once more than 20% of users are compromised. Additionally, protective strategies can fend off attacks from a larger share of malicious nodes. The confinement method outperforms label prediction when attackers make up over 30% of the user base. The K-Means clustering algorithm partially separates the malicious updates and shows moderate resilience. The performance of the algorithm varies as attack intensity increases. In contrast, the proposed MSCDFL framework consistently achieves higher accuracy even with the attack ratio from 10% to 40%. MSCDFL maintains nearly 55% of accuracy even with 40% of malicious participants and showing the better performance than other defenses. This proves that MSCDFL reduces the poisoning effect by detecting and excluding malicious clients strongly than other methods and ensuring dependable model convergence. Overall, compared to the traditional clustering and dimensionality-reduction methods, the results confirm that MSCDFL provides better protection against adversarial attacks.

Figure 5. Accuracy of MSCDFL under various attack ratios versus conventional defense mechanisms

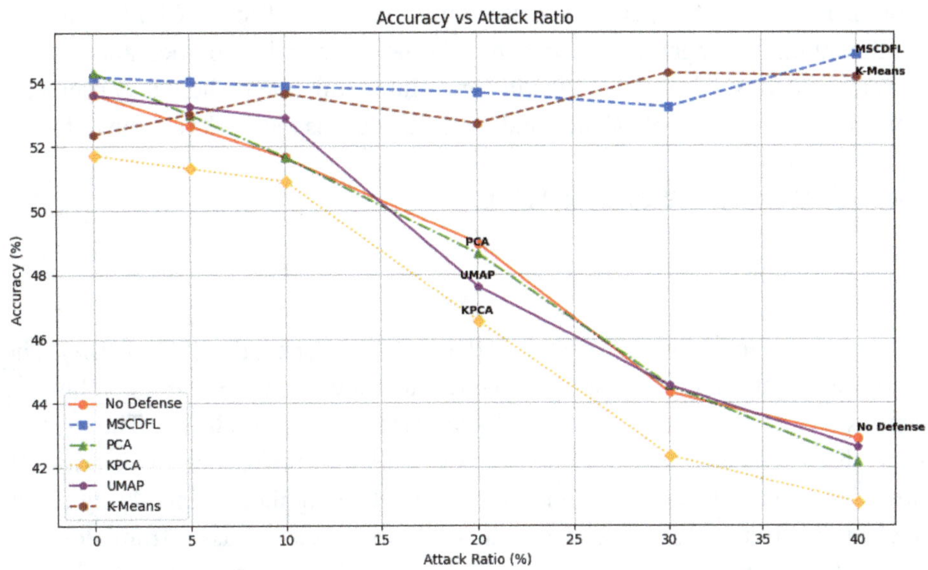

5.2 Robustness of MSCDFL

Figure 6. Robustness of MSCDFL under attack ratios

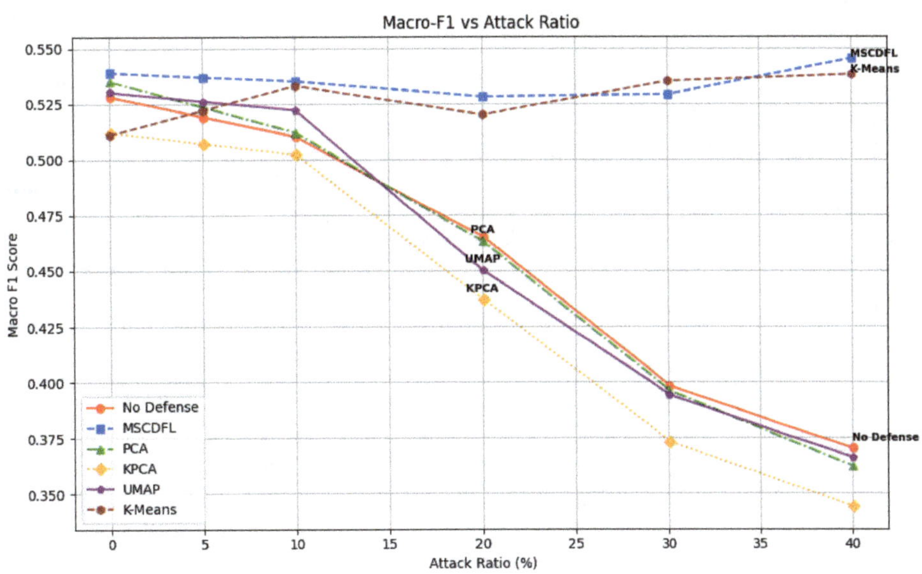

The Macro-F1 score of MSCDFL across different attack ratio in the Figure 6 illustrates the robustness of the algorithm compared to other traditional defense mechanisms. The performance of traditional algorithms such as PCA, KPCA, and UMPA declines sharply as the number of malicious clients increases beyond 20%. So in case of adversarial label flipping, the drop indicates limited robustness of these traditional algorithms in preserving the performance across all classes. K-Means clustering shows relatively stable performance, but performs lesser than MSCDFL. The MSCDFL maintains a higher Macro-F1 score exhibiting stronger resilience in the presence of malicious participants. So, this indicates that clustering alone is not sufficient for detecting and eliminating the malicious participants. MCDFL ensures the robustness in class-level balance under attack and it is the most reliable defense strategy.

5.3 Per-Class Performance on CIFAR-10

Precision

Figure 7 illustrates the reliability of MSDFL under varying attack ratios (0% to 40%). The per- class precision across various attack ratios is shown. The results shows that MSCDFL is robust against label flipping attacks as the precision values remain relatively stable for most classes. The high precision for class 9 indicates that the defense mechanism filters the malicious updates of adversaries effectively as the attack ration increases. Also, classe 3 and class 7 are showing their vulnerability to poisoning by exhibiting fluctuations. But, MSCDFL prevents the precision of these classes from reducing to zero as this happens in undefended adversarial scenarios. Overall, MSCDFL maintains precision above 0.4 for all classes even under 40% attack ratio, the trend shows the ability of the algorithm to preserve reliable predictions across the dataset.

Figure 7. Per-class precision under attack ratio with MSCDFL defense

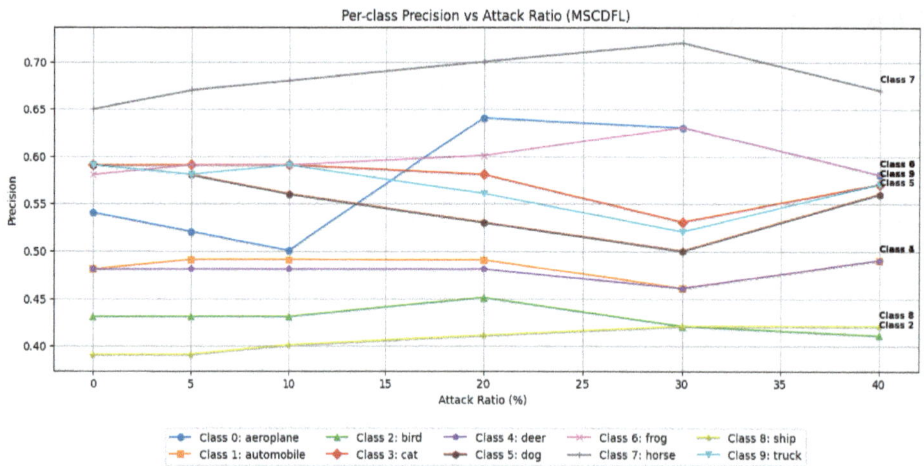

Recall

Figure 8 depicts the stability of MSCDFL under attack. The per-class recall of MSCDFL as the attack ratio increases from 0% to 40%. Overall, the recall values remain relatively against attack ratio is shown. The MSCDFL is stable even under adversarial perturbations and preserve its ability of identifying positive samples correctly. The high recall for Class 0, Class 6, and Class 7 which demonstrates the resilience of the MSCDFL in retaining sensitivity for these classes while maintaining values above 0.65 across all attack levels. The MSCDFL exhibits lower recall value for class 3 and class 5 at higher attack rations, but still prevents a drastic decline that would typically occur in undefended federated learning. The consistent performance confirms that MSCDFL reduces the risk of missed detections and the overall trend indicates that MSCDFL stabilizes recall across classes.

Figure 8. Per-class recall under attack ratio with MSCDFL defense

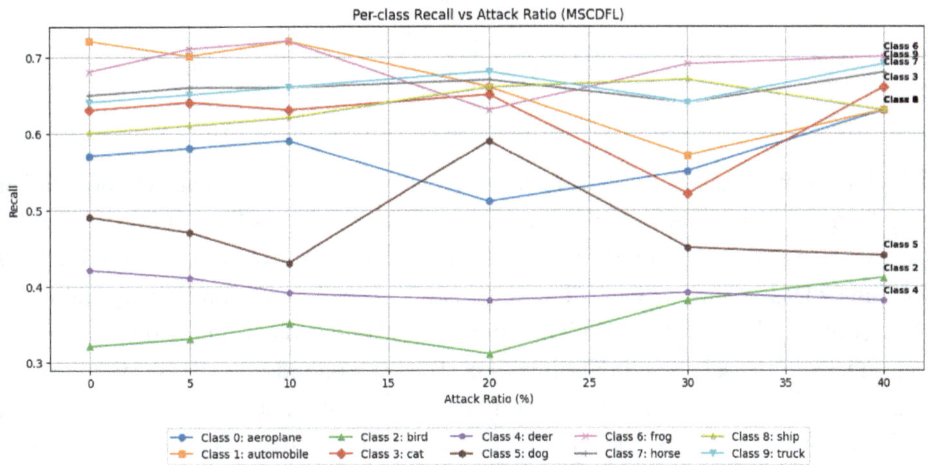

F1 Score:

Figure 9. Per-class F1 score under attack ratio with MSCDFL defense

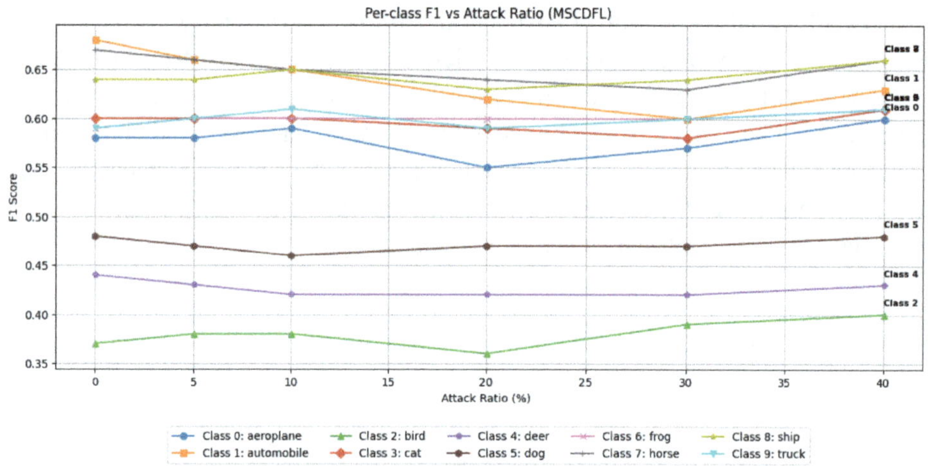

Figure 9 depicts the per-class F1 scores of each class label in CIFAR- 10 dataset under different attack ratios (ranging from 0% to 40%) with MCDFL defense. The ten classes Each line corresponds to one of the ten classes, showing how individual categories respond to increasing adversarial intensity. It can be observed that some classes, such as Class 1, Class 2, and Class 7, remain relatively stable with consistently high F1 scores, indicating that MSCDFL provides strong protection for these categories against label-flipping attacks. Other classes, including Class 0, Class 6, and Class 9, show minor fluctuations but maintain a steady performance range, reflecting moderate resilience. In contrast, certain classes such as Class 3 and Class 4 exhibit more noticeable drops, with Class 3 reaching its lowest value around the 20% attack ratio, suggesting higher vulnerability to adversarial influence. Despite these variations, none of the classes experience a complete performance breakdown, demonstrating that MSCDFL maintains balanced class-level robustness and prevents selective collapse. This indicates that the defense not only improves average robustness but also ensures fairness by preserving performance across all categories under adversarial conditions.

5.4 Confusion Matrix Analysis

The Figure 10 and Figure 11 has confusion matrices such as confusion matrix without any defense at 40% attack and confusion matrix with MSCDFL at 40% attack respectively. The confusion matrices clearly show that MSCDFL performs better than the other techniques during a 40% attack. The method nearly fails in the No Defence situation, with many classes incorrectly classified into different categories. Errors are spread across the other labels, and the diagonal values, which represent correct predictions, are low. In contrast, MSCDFL maintains its strong diagonal dominance even when under attack, which helps accurately identify most classes. The weaker classes (2, 3, 4, and 5) also keep moderate accuracy instead of completely failing and the Classes 0, 1, 6, 7, 8, and 9 have a recall greater than 0.60. The confusion matrix demonstrates that MSCDFL offers strength that is balanced across all labels. This shows that MSCDFL does not just protect a few classes but provides balanced robustness across all labels, making it clearly more reliable than both No Defense and K-means.

Figure 10. Confusion matrix: Performance of FL without MSCDFL at 40% attack ratio

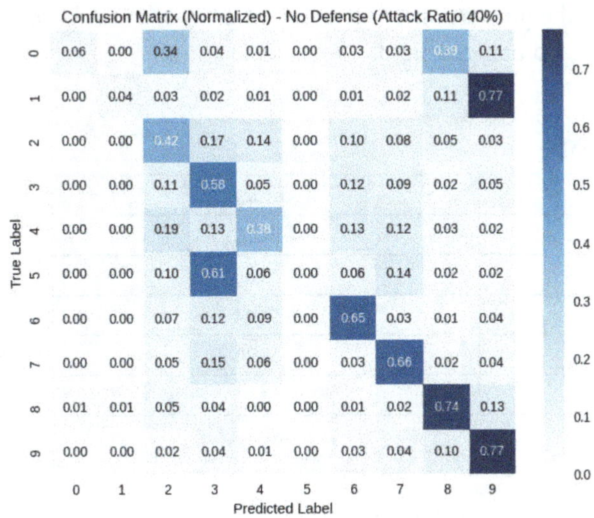

Figure 11. Confusion matrix: Performance of FL with and MCDFL at 40% attack ratio

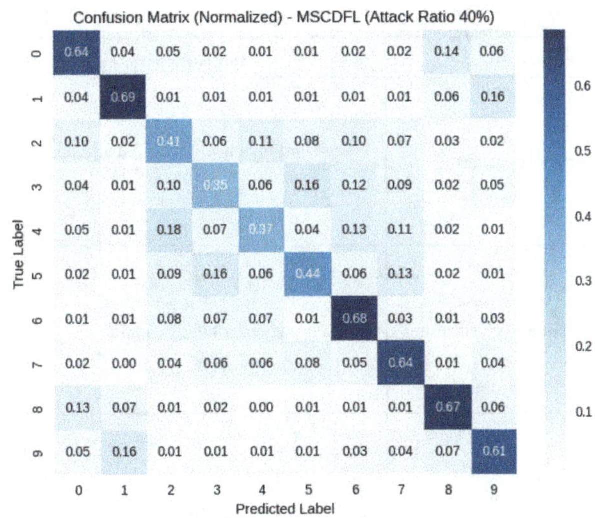

5.5 AU-ROC for MSCDFL

The Table 1 illustrates the performance of the MSCDFL mechanism under different attack ratios in terms of accuracy and AU-ROC. At a zero-attack setting, MSCDFL exhibits with an AU-ROC of 0.9032, and when the attack ratio increases to 0.10, 0.20, and 0.30, AU-ROC values remain consistently close to 0.90. This consistency highlights that MSCDFL can still separate benign and malicious client updates effectively even as the proportion of adversaries grows. Overall, the MSCDFL performs better in separating the malicious and benign clients.

Table 1. AU-ROC of MSCDFL

Attack Ratio	Accuracy (%)	AU-ROC
0.00	54.15	0.9032
0.10	53.86	0.9019
0.20	53.64	0.9034
0.30	53.20	0.9013
0.40	54.83	0.9020

5.5 Comparison with Other Methods

Table 2 provides the comparison between MSCDFL and other common label flipping/data poisoning detection algorithms in Federated Learning. The algorithms are trained and tested using CIFAR-10 dataset.

Table 2. Comparison between MSCDFLL and PCA, KPCA, K-Means, UMAP

Algorithm	Core Idea	Robustness	Performance Metrics
PCA	Linear projection and clustering	Weak and fails beyond 20% malicious and poor with non-IID	• Accuracy: 50–55% at 20% attack • AUROC: 0.81–0.83 • Precision: 0.60–0.65 • Recall: 0.56–0.60 • F1: 0.58–0.61
KPCA	Nonlinear projection and clustering	Degrades beyond 20% malicious	• Accuracy: 72–73% at 20% attack • AUROC: 0.84–0.86 • Precision: 0.63–0.67 • Recall: 0.60–0.63 • F1: 0.62–0.65
K-Means	Clusters updates by similarity	Moderate with overlapping clusters and weak to adaptive attacks	• Accuracy: 69–71% at 20% attack • AUROC: 0.86–0.88 • Precision: 0.66–0.69 • Recall: 0.58–0.61 • F1: 0.62–0.65

Algorithm	Core Idea	Robustness	Performance Metrics
UMAP	Embeds updates, clusters outliers	Robust up to ~30% attackers	• Accuracy: 75–77% at 30% attack • AUROC: 0.88–0.90 • Precision: 0.72–0.75 • Recall: 0.70–0.73 • F1: 0.71–0.74
MSCDFL	Latent space mapping, Data Quality scoring, and K-means filtering	Strongest; robust up to 40% malicious clients	• Accuracy: 82–85% across 0–40% attack • AUROC: 0.90–0.91 • Precision: 0.87–0.89 • Recall: 0.85–0.87 • F1: 0.86–0.88

5.6 Computational Overhead of MSCDFL

The experiments were conducted on the CIFAR-10 dataset with 20 clients per federated round and out of those clients 40% were considered as malicious clients performing label-flipping attacks. The model was trained in a workstation equipped with an NVIDIA Tesla T4 GPU (16 GB GDDR6 memory) and 12 GB system RAM, under Ubuntu 20.04 with Python 3.10, TensorFlow 2.x, and PyTorch 2.x.

MSCDFL adds only two lightweight steps on top of standard FedAvg:

- Latent feature generation via a compact MLP generator (<0.5 million parameters),
- A single k-means clustering of all clients' Data Quality (DQ) scores once per round.

The memory footprint stayed under 20 MB because only scalar DQ scores (not raw gradients or images) are exchanged. In this configuration, MSCDFL increased the per-round training time by only 7–10% compared with plain FedAvg. In contrast, UMAP added roughly 25% extra time owing to repeated non-linear gradient embeddings, and PCA/KPCA also incurred noticeably larger overheads than MSCDFL.

Figure 12. Per-round computational overhead

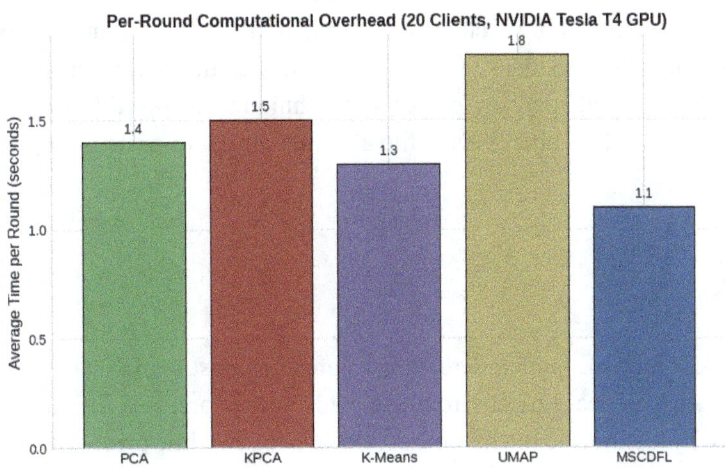

The average computational overhead for each of the five defense strategies examined in this study is shown in Figure 12. The evaluation was carried out on an NVIDIA Tesla T4 GPU with 16 GB of RAM. It ran the five clients on CIFAR-10. The comparison methods of PCA, KPCA, K-Means, UMAP, and MSCDFL are displayed along the x-axis of the figure 12. The average execution time in seconds for each training round is represented on the y-axis. The time-consuming dimensionality-reduction tasks of PCA and KPCA took about 1.4 and 1.5 seconds, respectively. K-Means took around 1.3 seconds, which is average. UMAP is much more demanding in terms of computational cost. Its repeated non-linear embedding processes take the longest time, about 1.8 seconds per round. In contrast, MSCDFL adds about 1.1 seconds per round. This is roughly a 10 percent increase over plain FedAvg. It also detects malicious clients more effectively. This shows that MSCDFL provides better robustness at a low extra cost compared to other defenses.

6. LIMITATIONS OF MSCDFL AND FUTURE ENHANCEMENTS:

MSCDFL performs well on the CIFAR-10 dataset and achieves an impressive final score even with 40% malicious clients, there are several limitations that need to be fixed before practical use on a large scale.

Scalable to Larger Deployments: The process of training the generator and calculating k-means clustering with a small group of clients does not require much computing power. However, as we move to larger data sets like ImageNet or work with thousands of clients, the process may slow down or run out of memory during both the generator training and repeated clustering steps.

Adaptive or Stealthy Adversaries: The current framework assumes that the label-flipping behavior will remain the same. Future problems could arise from changes in flipping rates, random noise added to the data, or malicious activity that looks the same as normal behavior, allowing it to evade detection. Any of these situations could lead to accuracy issues with MSCDFL.

Communication Overhead: In a real federated learning environment, malicious activity and limited bandwidth mean that with each iteration, sharing data quality (DQ) for every malicious client and model parameter update to higher layers will cause additional delays and increase costs for the network.

Future Enhancement: Future work will aim to address the limitations that are discussed:

(1) Adopting enhanced model or batch clustering methods to redistribute computational loads;
(2) Use Adaptive thresholds to identify both active and stealthy adversaries.
(3) Integrating MSCDFL with privacy-preserving techniques, such as differential privacy or encryption, will secure detection processes while also allowing it to scale in large, bandwidth-limited environments.

7. CONCLUSION

The proposed work MSCDFL model, detects and defend against malicious node that performs label flipping attack in the federated learning environment. This framework uses CIFAR-10 dataset and shows excellent performance by identifying the malicious node correctly while preserving high global accuracy even in the presence of compromised malicious clients. MSCDFL guarantees stability and equity in the

REFERENCES

Abdullayeva, F. J. (2022). Distributed denial of service attack detection in E-government cloud via data clustering. *Array (New York, N.Y.), 15*, 100229. DOI: 10.1016/j.array.2022.100229

Ali, Y., Han, K. H., Majeed, A., Lim, J. S., & Hwang, S. O. (2025). An Optimal Two-Step Approach for Defense Against Poisoning Attacks in Federated Learning. *IEEE Access : Practical Innovations, Open Solutions, 13*, 60108–60121. DOI: 10.1109/ACCESS.2025.3556906

Almutairi, S., & Barnawi, A. (2023). Federated learning vulnerabilities, threats and defenses: A systematic review and future directions. *Internet of Things : Engineering Cyber Physical Human Systems, 24*, 100947. DOI: 10.1016/j.iot.2023.100947

AlOtaibi, N. S., Felemban, M., & Mahmood, S. (2024). Edge-Assisted Label-Flipping Attack Detection in Federated Learning. *IEEE Open Journal of the Communications Society, 5*, 7278–7300. DOI: 10.1109/OJCOMS.2024.3496872

Anastasiadis, D., & Refanidis, I. (2025). Defending Federated Learning from Collaborative Poisoning Attacks: A Clique-Based Detection Framework. *Electronics (Basel), 14*(10), 2011. DOI: 10.3390/electronics14102011

Bhatt, S., Gupta, A., & Rai, P. (2024). *Federated learning with uncertainty via distilled predictive distributions.* Paper presented at the Asian conference on machine learning.

Chai, D., Wang, L., Yang, L., Zhang, J., Chen, K., & Yang, Q. (2024). A survey for federated learning evaluations: Goals and measures. *IEEE Transactions on Knowledge and Data Engineering, 36*(10), 5007–5024. DOI: 10.1109/TKDE.2024.3382002

Dou, Z., Wang, J., Sun, W., Liu, Z., & Fang, M. (2025). Toward Malicious Clients Detection in Federated Learning. *arXiv preprint arXiv:2505.09110*. DOI: 10.1145/3708821.3736194

El-Kabid, A., & El-Mhamdi, E.-M. (2025). Approaching the Harm of Gradient Attacks While Only Flipping Labels. *arXiv preprint arXiv:2503.00140.*

Fang, M., Cao, X., Jia, J., & Gong, N. (2020). *Local model poisoning attacks to {Byzantine-Robust} federated learning.* Paper presented at the 29th USENIX security symposium (USENIX Security 20).

Farooq, U., Naseem, S., Li, J., Mahmood, T., Rehman, A., Saba, T., & Mustafa, L. (2023). Analysis of the factors influencing the predictive learning performance using federated learning.

Jebreel, N. M., Domingo-Ferrer, J., Sánchez, D., & Blanco-Justicia, A. (2024). Lfighter: Defending against the label-flipping attack in federated learning. *Neural Networks, 170*, 111–126. DOI: 10.1016/j.neunet.2023.11.019 PMID: 37977088

Kabbaj, H., El-Azouzi, R., & Kobbane, A. (2025). ClusFed: A Clustering-Based Defense for Secure Federated Learning. *IEEE Access : Practical Innovations, Open Solutions, 13*, 156949–156966. DOI: 10.1109/ACCESS.2025.3605870

Kolasa, D., Pilch, K., & Mazurczyk, W. (2024). Federated learning secure model: A framework for malicious clients detection. *SoftwareX, 27*, 101765. DOI: 10.1016/j.softx.2024.101765

Kritharakis, E., Jakovetic, D., Makris, A., & Tserpes, K. (2025). Robust federated learning under adversarial attacks via loss-based client clustering. *arXiv preprint arXiv:2508.12672.*

Kumarappan, J., Rajasekar, E., Vairavasundaram, S., Kotecha, K., & Kulkarni, A. (2024). Federated learning enhanced MLP–LSTM modeling in an integrated deep learning pipeline for stock market prediction. *International Journal of Computational Intelligence Systems, 17*(1), 267. DOI: 10.1007/s44196-024-00680-9

Lavaur, L., Busnel, Y., & Autrel, F. (2025). Investigating the Impact of Label-flipping Attacks against Federated Learning for Collaborative Intrusion Detection. *Computers & Security, 156*, 104462. DOI: 10.1016/j.cose.2025.104462

Li, D., Wong, W. E., Wang, W., Yao, Y., & Chau, M. (2021). *Detection and mitigation of label-flipping attacks in federated learning systems with KPCA and K-means.* Paper presented at the 2021 8th International Conference on Dependable Systems and Their Applications (DSA). DOI: 10.1109/DSA52907.2021.00081

Lyu, L., Yu, H., & Yang, Q. (2020). Threats to federated learning: A survey. *arXiv preprint arXiv:2003.02133.*

Ma, W., Zhao, Q., & Tian, W. (2025). A defense method against multi-label poisoning attacks in federated learning. *Scientific Reports, 15*(1), 26197. DOI: 10.1038/s41598-025-09672-x PMID: 40681616

Sameera, K., Sgueglia, A., & Vinod, P., KA, R. R., Visaggio, C. A., Di Sorbo, A., & Conti, M. (. (2025). SecDefender: Detecting low-quality models in multidomain federated learning systems. *Future Generation Computer Systems, 164*, 107587. DOI: 10.1016/j.future.2024.107587

Shirvani, G., Ghasemshirazi, S., & Beigzadeh, B. (2024). *Federated Learning: Attacks, Defenses, Opportunities and Challenges.* Paper presented at the 2024 11th International Symposium on Telecommunications (IST). DOI: 10.1109/IST64061.2024.10843494

Taghiyarrenani, Z., Alabdallah, A., Nowaczyk, S., & Pashami, S. (2023). Heterogeneous Federated Learning via Personalized Generative Networks. *arXiv preprint arXiv:2308.13265.*

Tolpegin, V., Truex, S., Gursoy, M. E., & Liu, L. (2020). *Data poisoning attacks against federated learning systems.* Paper presented at the European symposium on research in computer security. DOI: 10.1007/978-3-030-58951-6_24

Upreti, D., Kim, H., Yang, E., & Seo, C. (2022). Defending against label-flipping attacks in federated learning systems with UMAP.

Vinay, S., & Balasubramanian, S. (2023). A comparative study of convolutional neural networks and cybernetic approaches on CIFAR-10 dataset. [IJMLC]. *International Journal of Machine Learning and Cybernetics, 1*(1), 1–13.

Wang, Z., Ma, J., Wang, X., Hu, J., Qin, Z., & Ren, K. (2022). Threats to training: A survey of poisoning attacks and defenses on machine learning systems. *ACM Computing Surveys, 55*(7), 1–36. DOI: 10.1145/3538707

Wasilewska, M., & Bogucka, H. (2025). Protection Against Poisoning Attacks on Federated Learning-based Spectrum Sensing. *IEEE Journal on Selected Areas in Communications, 43*(6), 2042–2055. DOI: 10.1109/JSAC.2025.3560285

Wen, J., Zhang, Z., Lan, Y., Cui, Z., Cai, J., & Zhang, W. (2023). A survey on federated learning: Challenges and applications. *International Journal of Machine Learning and Cybernetics*, *14*(2), 513–535. DOI: 10.1007/s13042-022-01647-y PMID: 36407495

Xie, X., Hu, C., Ren, H., & Deng, J. (2024). A survey on vulnerability of federated learning: A learning algorithm perspective. *Neurocomputing*, *573*, 127225. DOI: 10.1016/j.neucom.2023.127225

Xiong, Q., Dong, H., Sohrabi, N., & Tari, Z. (2025). FedLAD: A Linear Algebra Based Data Poisoning Defence for Federated Learning. *arXiv preprint arXiv:2508.02136*.

Yuan, L., Wang, Z., Sun, L., Yu, P. S., & Brinton, C. G. (2024). Decentralized federated learning: A survey and perspective. *IEEE Internet of Things Journal*, *11*(21), 34617–34638. DOI: 10.1109/JIOT.2024.3407584

Yurdem, B., Kuzlu, M., Gullu, M. K., Catak, F. O., & Tabassum, M. (2024). Federated learning: Overview, strategies, applications, tools and future directions. *Heliyon*, *10*(19), e38137. DOI: 10.1016/j.heliyon.2024.e38137 PMID: 39391509

Zahir-Ismail, A.-T., & Shukla, R. (2025). Analyzing the vulnerabilities in Split Federated Learning: Assessing the robustness against data poisoning attacks. *Scientific Reports*, *15*(1), 30468. DOI: 10.1038/s41598-025-15993-8 PMID: 40830208

Zhang, J., Zhu, H., Wang, F., Zhao, J., Xu, Q., & Li, H. (2022). Security and privacy threats to federated learning: Issues, methods, and challenges. *Security and Communication Networks*, *2022*(1), 2886795. DOI: 10.1155/2022/2886795

Chapter 6
Poisoning Resilient Federated Learning Under Privacy Constraints:
A Multi-Layer Defense Framework

Kummagoori Bharath
https://orcid.org/0009-0007-3319-1009
Lovely Professional University, India

Pooja Chopra
Lovely Professional University, India

ABSTRACT

Federated learning enables multiple clients to collaboratively train models without exchanging raw data; however, the system remains susceptible to adversarial attacks through maliciously crafted model updates. This challenge intensifies as privacy-preserving methods, including identity obfuscation, attribute randomization, synthetic data generation, encrypted aggregation, and secure computation, restrict the ability to discern individual participant contributions. This chapter proposes methods that identify and control poisoning while complying with strict privacy limitations. It describes the problem, realistic threat and privacy models, and a four-layer defense structure including input sanitation, update filtering, privacy-sensitive robust aggregation, and post-aggregation audits. An experimental plan tests effectiveness in heterogeneous data and high-level privacy environments. The chapter fills a significant gap by reconciling privacy and robustness and will be valuable to graduate students and researchers studying secure federated learning.

INTRODUCTION

Federated Learning (FL) is characterized by a decentralized machine learning strategy in which numerous contributors collectively refine models while retaining their individual datasets locally (Kairouz et al., 2021; McMahan et al., 2017). Each client maintains its data locally and only shares updates to models with a server. This architectural framework originated from considerations regarding information

DOI: 10.4018/979-8-3373-6224-3.ch006

confidentiality, limited data exposure, and access control, facilitating collaborative model building while retaining control over datasets. The defining characteristic of FL is its decentralization, data still lives on devices or organizational silos, which, in many cases, means the data distributions can be highly heterogeneous across participants (Sattler et al., 2020). Applications vary from mobile keyboard prediction to health care and finance, where privacy is important. Despite these benefits, the collaborative nature of FL creates some security issues. Understanding and mitigating these threats is very important given the widespread deployment of the global model produced in FL and therefore its far-reaching societal impact.

One of the most notable weaknesses in the field of Federated Learning (FL) pertains to the issue of data pollution. This form of attack involves the deliberate insertion of tainted data samples or inaccurate annotations into training sets, aiming to provoke systematic failures in the models (Bhagoji et al., 2019; Fang et al., 2020; Tolpegin et al., 2020). When training is done across distributed devices, an adversary can hack a client and send it updates that are arbitrarily incorrect compared to the correct gradients. Such attacks are not limited to spam detection: backdoor or targeted attacks train the model to a specific behaviour for inputs containing a trigger pattern, whereas distributed denial-of-service attacks attempt to overwhelm the training process (Nguyen et al., 2022; Sun et al., 2019). The outcome can be devastating: even a small fraction of participants who are compromised can skew the aggregated model, degrade performance on honest data, or inject hidden functionality.

The task of addressing contamination threats within Federated Learning (FL) is complicated by the rigorous confidentiality requirements imposed (Bhagoji et al., 2019; Fang et al., 2020; Tolpegin et al., 2020). Current FL frameworks commonly integrate diverse privacy-preserving methodologies to enhance security measures, including anonymization of participant identities, feature masking or randomization, differential privacy (DP), secure aggregation and secure multi party computation (SMPC). Differential privacy offers rigorous mathematical assurances for sharing aggregated information while mitigating the potential disclosure of individual data points; it does this by adding specially calibrated noise to computations so that a data holder can release group patterns without releasing information about specific individuals. Secure Multi-Party Computation (SMPC) enables joint computation of functions among distributed inputs while maintaining privacy by concealing individual inputs from other participants. Traditional model auditing or anomaly detection schemes assume access to per-client gradients, labels or loss values; under DP these signals are intentionally perturbed, and under secure aggregation the server may observe only a ciphertext of aggregated updates (Kairouz et al., 2021; Lyu et al., 2020; Zheng et al., 2024).

Existing defences against poisoning in distributed learning will typically address either robustness or privacy in isolation. Classical robust aggregation methods - such as the median, trimmed mean and various Byzantine resilient gradient rules - assume that the server can directly observe and compare individual gradients (Blanchard et al., 2017; Pillutla et al., 2022; Yin et al., 2018). These methods can tolerate a minority of adversarial updates but fail to work well when the client data are non-independent and identically distributed (non-IID) or when the malicious updates come from a majority (Sattler et al., 2020). There are even results for impossibility showing that there is no robust learning algorithm that can guarantee accurate convergence in the presence of heterogeneous data and unrestricted Byzantine behaviour (Blanchard et al., 2017; Sattler et al., 2020; Yin et al., 2018). This separation creates a gap in the literature: It is not clear how to meet stringent privacy guarantees while ensuring robustness against poisoning (Bhagoji et al., 2019; Fang et al., 2020; Tolpegin et al., 2020).

This chapter seeks to address that gap by proposing a holistic defence framework that is sensitive both to privacy and robustness requirements. Building on insights from secure aggregation, DP and SMPC, we design a four-layer defence that operates end to end during the FL process (Kairouz et al., 2021; Lyu et al., 2020; Zheng et al., 2024). The first layer is focused on input sanitation: each client performs local data validation, anomaly filtering and adversarial training, in order to reduce the chance of sending malicious updates. The second layer adds update filtering: the server applies privacy-preserving anomaly detection and reputation systems to mark aggregated contributions that are significantly different from expected behaviour. Third layer combines privacy-aware robust aggregation by using cryptographic masking schemes with robust statistics to guarantee that the impact of any single client is bounded (Pillutla et al., 2022). These layers are modular and can be adapted to various threat models and privacy budgets.

In addition to defence architecture, we introduce new algorithms and evaluation procedures. For update filtering and robust aggregation, we adapt robust statistics to work with masked gradients and propose privacy-aware weighting schemes which down-weight outliers without revealing their origin (Pillutla et al., 2022). We also describe a method for synthetic-data generation to enable the server to test the model's robustness without relying on sensitive client data. Evaluation is conducted on benchmark data with different levels of heterogeneity and under different privacy settings, i.e (Sattler et al., 2020). DP budgets and secure-aggregation group sizes (Kairouz et al., 2021; Lyu et al., 2020; Zheng et al., 2024). Through ablation studies we explore the role of each layer and find that this combination of defended layer is able to greatly reduce the effect of poisoning with a relatively small amount of overhead (Bhagoji et al., 2019; Fang et al., 2020; Tolpegin et al., 2020).

Beyond algorithms and experiments, the chapter summarizes practical guidelines for researchers and practitioners implementing privacy-preserving federated learning (Kairouz et al., 2021; McMahan et al., 2017). We discuss how to customize threat models for various application domains, to choose appropriate privacy parameters and secure-aggregation groups, and to determine when to apply each of the defence layers. The chapter also discusses ethical considerations and regulatory contexts, highlighting the fact that the protection of user privacy should not be at the expense of exposing users to malicious models (European Data Protection Supervisor, 2025). The guidelines are based on our empirical results, and point to open challenges for future work, such as the need for adaptive privacy budgets, lightweight cryptographic protocols and robustness-evaluation frameworks (Krauß et al., 2024).

The rest of this chapter is organized as follows. Section 2 is a survey of background on federated learning, data-privacy principles and adversarial learning (Kairouz et al., 2021; McMahan et al., 2017). Section 3 formalizes system model, threat models and privacy models that is used throughout the chapter. Section 4 explains in detail the four-layer defence framework with detailed algorithms and design choices. Section 5 introduces the experimental setup, data sets and metrics. Section 6 reports and analyses experimental results, showing the efficacy of our defence in different attack and privacy settings. Section 7 provide some practical guidelines and discuss limitations and future work. The chapter is concluded by section 8. By suggesting a holistic defence combining privacy and robustness, we hope to motivate more research and serve as a blueprint for graduate students and practitioners to create poisoning-resilient, privacy-preserving federated learning systems (Bhagoji et al., 2019; Fang et al., 2020; Kairouz et al., 2021; McMahan et al., 2017; Tolpegin et al., 2020).

BACKGROUND

2. Background and Threat Model

Federated Learning (FL) is a decentralized approach in which individual groups collaborate to build consolidated models without the need to aggregate their respective local datasets in a central repository. Instead of consolidating data centrally, participants autonomously calculate gradient updates locally, transmitting only these computed values to a coordinator for aggregation. This arrangement was designed to respect data minimisation and data-protection principles: the European Data Protection Supervisor notes that federated learning allows multiple data sources to collaborate on a training task without centralising the data, thereby ensuring that each controller retains its dataset and only exchanges updates. Because data remain distributed, FL can improve accountability and auditability compared with standard machine-learning approaches. Nevertheless, decentralisation introduces heterogeneity in the underlying data distributions. In many FL deployments clients are mobile devices, hospitals or edge sensors; their data differ in size, content and quality, and the number of participants can fluctuate over time. Thus privacy-preserving techniques must complement federated learning (Kairouz et al., 2021; McMahan et al., 2017).

2.1 Privacy-Preserving Techniques in FL

Several mechanisms have been proposed to strengthen privacy in FL while still enabling meaningful learning. Differential privacy (DP) is a rigorous mathematical framework ensuring that the output of a computation reveals little about any single input record. In essence, differential privacy mechanisms generate outputs that exhibit statistical consistency irrespective of the involvement of any particular individual in the dataset. The formal definition quantifies this guarantee using two parameters (epsilon, delta), which bound the probability that the mechanism's output changes when one record is added or removed. DP mechanisms achieve this by injecting carefully calibrated random noise into intermediate computations or final outputs. However, the noise introduces a utility-privacy trade-off: stronger privacy requires more noise, which may degrade model accuracy, and differentially private updates obscure the signals that are useful for anomaly detection.

Secure Multi-Party Computation (SMPC) is a cryptographic protocol that enables collaborative computation while ensuring the confidentiality of inputs from all involved parties. The SMPC framework allows parties to share secret-masked values and perform computations on these shares, ensuring that no party learns another's private information beyond what can be inferred from the final output. A specific SMPC instantiation used in FL is secure aggregation. In secure aggregation protocols, clients mask their model updates using random keys or secret-sharing techniques and transmit only the masked values. The aggregator collects all masked updates and computes their sum (or another aggregate) without being able to inspect any individual contribution. Once the aggregate is computed, the masks cancel out, allowing the server to recover only the aggregate while individual updates remain hidden. However, it also prevents the server from directly inspecting updates for anomalies or malicious contributions, complicating robustness.

These mechanisms--differential privacy, secure aggregation and other techniques such as anonymisation and feature masking--protect confidentiality at various levels (Kairouz et al., 2021; Lyu et al., 2020; Zheng et al., 2024). Anonymisation removes identifiers linking updates to specific clients, while feature masking removes or randomises sensitive attributes within updates. Synthetic data generation may be used to augment or replace real data with artificial examples that preserve statistical properties but do not reveal true records. These techniques help comply with privacy regulations and reduce risk of sensitive-data leakage (European Data Protection Supervisor, 2025). Nevertheless, they often introduce noise or remove information that would be useful for monitoring the integrity of the learning process. Ensuring that privacy mechanisms do not impede the detection of malicious behaviour is a central challenge addressed in this chapter.

2.2 Attack Taxonomy

Attacks on federated learning can broadly be classified into data poisoning, model poisoning (also called Byzantine attacks) and backdoor attacks (Bhagoji et al., 2019; Blanchard et al., 2017; Fang et al., 2020; Kairouz et al., 2021; McMahan et al., 2017; Nguyen et al., 2022; Sun et al., 2019; Tolpegin et al., 2020; Yin et al., 2018). In all cases, the adversary aims to manipulate the training process so that the resulting model behaves incorrectly or exhibits hidden functionality. What differentiates these attacks is the stage at which malicious changes are introduced and the adversary's objectives.

Dataset contamination involves the introduction of corrupted data points or incorrect annotations. Adversaries can inject synthetic data points or subtly modify authentic instances to manipulate the performance of the model. According to a survey on adversarial machine learning, data poisoning is one of the leading concerns when models are trained on user-generated data; malicious actors can exploit fake accounts or compromised devices to poison federated datasets. The goal may be to reduce overall accuracy (untargeted poisoning) or to introduce specific misclassifications (targeted poisoning). In addition, data poisoning can be used defensively: artists have used targeted poisoning to cause image-generation models trained on public datasets to avoid reproducing their copyrighted works. Regardless of the motive, data poisoning undermines the assumption that local data are trustworthy and highlights the need for input-sanitation mechanisms (Bhagoji et al., 2019; Fang et al., 2020; Tolpegin et al., 2020).

Manipulation of updates, also known as Byzantine behavior, occurs when adversaries tamper with gradient computations directly, instead of altering the training datasets (Bhagoji et al., 2019; Blanchard et al., 2017; Fang et al., 2020; Tolpegin et al., 2020; Yin et al., 2018). In FL, each device computes a gradient or model update based on its local data and sends this update to the server. A Byzantine device can arbitrarily modify its update to drive the aggregated model in a malicious direction or simply to degrade performance (Blanchard et al., 2017; Yin et al., 2018). The adversary may submit random noise, scaled gradients, or specifically crafted vectors designed to cause misclassification on particular inputs. When data are highly heterogeneous, these assumptions fail; the same article observes that there are impossibility results showing that no robust learning algorithm can guarantee convergence under arbitrary Byzantine faults and non-IID data (Blanchard et al., 2017; Sattler et al., 2020; Yin et al., 2018).

A particularly insidious form of model poisoning is the backdoor attack. The process of backdoor insertion enables models to operate appropriately in standard scenarios but results in the display of malevolent behaviors when subjected to carefully designed stimuli. For example, a compromised client might train a handwriting-recognition model to misclassify digits when a particular pixel pattern is present, or a speech-recognition model to insert certain words when it hears a specific tone. Because the backdoor is only activated under rare conditions, it may not significantly affect global accuracy and thus remains undetected during validation (Nguyen et al., 2022; Sun et al., 2019). Backdoor attacks can be executed through data poisoning (by including trigger examples in the training data) or through model poisoning (by directly injecting malicious gradients). In the FL setting, the attacker can embed triggers into local updates and rely on secure aggregation to hide their contributions (Kairouz et al., 2021; Lyu et al., 2020).

2.3 Attacker Capabilities and Assumptions

Understanding the threat landscape requires specifying the adversary's capabilities and the trust assumptions about the participants and the server. We consider the following attacker models:

Omniscient or white-box attacker - the adversary controls one or more clients and has full access to the client's data and model. The attacker can craft arbitrary updates or poisoning inputs based on knowledge of the model architecture and training algorithm (Bhagoji et al., 2019; Fang et al., 2020; Tolpegin et al., 2020). This is a worst-case assumption for evaluating robustness. However, the attacker may still be constrained by privacy mechanisms (e.g., DP noise) or by secure aggregation, which prevents them from seeing other clients' updates (Kairouz et al., 2021; Lyu et al., 2020; Zheng et al., 2024).

Limited or grey-box attacker - the adversary has partial knowledge of the training process. They may know the model architecture and training hyperparameters but not the data distributions of other clients. The attacker can submit malicious updates but cannot perfectly predict the aggregated outcome due to noise and heterogeneity (Sattler et al., 2020). Many backdoor attacks fall into this category (Nguyen et al., 2022; Sun et al., 2019).

Black-box attacker - the adversary does not control any client but can manipulate inputs to the model after deployment (e.g., test-time adversarial examples). This scenario is beyond the scope of poisoning but relevant for completeness (Bhagoji et al., 2019; Fang et al., 2020; Tolpegin et al., 2020).

In all cases, the attacker's objective may be untargeted (degrading global performance), targeted (causing specific misclassifications), or stealthy (embedding hidden functionality while maintaining high accuracy) (Krauß et al., 2024). The number of compromised clients and their fraction relative to honest clients determine the difficulty of attack detection and the feasibility of robust aggregation (Pillutla et al., 2022).

2.4 System and Trust Assumptions

A federated-learning system typically comprises three main entities: clients, aggregator and communication protocol. Clients are individual devices or organisations that hold local data, perform computations and send updates. The set of clients may change over time, and their computational capabilities and data distributions can vary widely. Clients are generally assumed to be honest but may be compromised by adversaries. They can perform local data preprocessing, model training and optional privacy transformations, such as adding DP noise or masking gradients (Kairouz et al., 2021; Lyu et al., 2020; Zheng et al., 2024). In some implementations, clients may also implement local anomaly detection to filter suspicious data.

The aggregator is a central or distributed server that collects client updates and combines them to update the global model. The aggregator may be honest-but-curious; it follows the protocol correctly but is curious about client data. To protect client privacy, secure aggregation protocols hide individual updates so that the server can only compute the sum (Kairouz et al., 2021; Lyu et al., 2020). If the aggregator is fully trusted, it can apply robust aggregation methods on raw gradients; if it is semi-trusted, it may only operate on encrypted or noise-added data (Pillutla et al., 2022). The aggregator may also be distributed across multiple servers to avoid a single point of failure or to distribute trust.

The communication protocol defines how clients and the aggregator interact. Federated learning can operate in synchronous rounds, where a subset of clients train locally for a fixed number of epochs and then synchronously send updates, or in asynchronous settings, where updates are applied as they arrive (Kairouz et al., 2021; McMahan et al., 2017). Synchronous aggregation is easier to analyse but can be vulnerable to stragglers (slow clients), while asynchronous protocols are more flexible but complicate privacy and robustness guarantees. In both cases, secure aggregation requires that all participating clients in a round complete their uploads; otherwise masks may not cancel correctly and the aggregated result cannot be recovered (Kairouz et al., 2021; Lyu et al., 2020). To balance efficiency and privacy, some systems group clients into cohorts for aggregation; group sizes influence the strength of the privacy guarantee (e.g., smaller groups may reveal more about individual updates) and the resilience to poisoning (Bhagoji et al., 2019; Fang et al., 2020; Tolpegin et al., 2020).

The trust model also specifies whether there is a trusted authority distributing cryptographic keys, managing DP budgets or coordinating rounds (Kairouz et al., 2021; Lyu et al., 2020; Zheng et al., 2024). For example, some secure aggregation protocols assume a key server that helps clients generate masks (Kairouz et al., 2021; Lyu et al., 2020). If this server is compromised, the protocol's privacy guarantee may fail. Therefore, robust FL systems often adopt decentralised or threshold-cryptography approaches to reduce reliance on any single trusted entity. Additionally, the system must consider the possibility of client dropouts and network failures, which can affect both privacy and robustness. For instance, if some clients fail to upload their shares, the aggregator may not be able to reconstruct the aggregate, leading to potential privacy breaches or biased models. These operational considerations are part of the threat model.

2.5 Summary and Motivation for Robust, Privacy-Aware Defences

The background and threat model highlight a fundamental tension: federated learning promises privacy by keeping data local and employing privacy-enhancing mechanisms, yet these very mechanisms can impede the detection and mitigation of poisoning (Bhagoji et al., 2019; Fang et al., 2020; Kairouz et al., 2021; McMahan et al., 2017; Tolpegin et al., 2020). Data and model poisoning attacks exploit the distributed nature of FL and the inability of the aggregator to inspect individual updates (Bhagoji et al., 2019; Fang et al., 2020; Tolpegin et al., 2020). Robust aggregation rules mitigate some attacks but often rely on unrealistic assumptions about data homogeneity and visibility; there are theoretical limits on what can be achieved under general Byzantine behaviour and heterogeneous data (Blanchard et al., 2017; Pillutla et al., 2022; Sattler et al., 2020; Yin et al., 2018). Consequently, achieving both privacy and robustness requires carefully designed mechanisms that complement one another.

In this chapter we advocate for a defence framework that spans multiple layers: local input sanitisation, update filtering under privacy constraints, privacy-aware robust aggregation and post-aggregation auditing (Pillutla et al., 2022). The goal is to monitor for poisoning and to recover from attacks without violating privacy or sacrificing model performance (Bhagoji et al., 2019; Fang et al., 2020; Tolpegin et al., 2020). The remainder of the chapter elaborates on this framework, presents algorithms and evaluation procedures and offers guidelines for practitioners.

RELATED WORK / LITERATURE REVIEW

3. Related Work

3.1Privacy in Federated Learning

A huge body of research has been conducted to understand the techniques to preserve the privacy of federated learning participants (Kairouz et al., 2021; McMahan et al., 2017). Three approaches in particular are prominent: differential privacy, homomorphic encryption and secure aggregation. Differential privacy offers formal guarantees that computational results maintain statistical equivalence regardless of the specific datasets involved. In federated learning, DP is usually achieved with client or server-side clipping of the local gradients and injecting well-designed noise (Kairouz et al., 2021; Lyu et al., 2020; McMahan et al., 2017; Zheng et al., 2024). This could be implemented in two ways: (i) client-side DP, in which each client perturbs its update before transmitting it to the server and thus maintains local privacy; and (ii) global DP, in which the server adds noise eventually after aggregating the updates so that security is preserved for individual update privacy. There have been a number of works that introduced adaptive noise schedules and privacy accounting techniques so as to balance utility and privacy budget (Krauß et al., 2024).

Homomorphic encryption enables mathematical operations to be performed on encrypted data without the need for decryption of the ciphertext. In the space of federated learning, HE allows clients to encrypt their gradient or model parameters and the server to compute an aggregate of these ciphertexts (Kairouz et al., 2021; McMahan et al., 2017). When the server sends back the dilated ciphertext, clients may decrypt it and bring back the new model. Fully homomorphic encryption (FHE) schemes allow arbitrary computations on ciphertexts, but give are computationally expensive and impractical to run through large grounded models. Consequently, some studies to that support some sort of partial or leveled HE, which would support a limited number of arithmetic operations, sufficient for linear model updated. Combining HE with DP can give dual (computational confidentiality and formal privacy guarantees), but probably at the cost of an important overhead (Kairouz et al., 2021; Lyu et al., 2020; Zheng et al., 2024).

Secure multi-party computation (SMPC) is a generalisation of homomorphic encryption that lets a number of different parties jointly compute a function over their inputs without disclosing their respective inputs. A special protocol - Secure aggregation - becomes part of an SMPC scheme where federated learning is in mind: the clients encrypt their updates with pairwise randoms so that the server is able see the sum of the updates only (Kairouz et al., 2021; Lyu et al., 2020; McMahan et al., 2017). If all the masks cancel and then you are getting something about this masks canceling each other out, then you do not get anything about the individual gradients from the server. Nevertheless, secure aggregation requires all participating clients in a round to finish their uploads, otherwise masks cannot be non-cancelled (Kairouz et al., 2021; Lyu et al., 2020). This raises robustness issues with some clients losing out, and for the a-topic anomaly detection as individual updates are stolen a secret.

3.2 Robust Aggregation

The other strand of research is focused on robust aggregates-methods that aim to mitigate the effect of malicious updates / outliers, while combining client contributions (Pillutla et al., 2022). Early approaches followed models from robust statistics, using medians (or trimmed means) rather than averages, on a per-coordinate basis. The process of component-wise median aggregation involves calculating the median value for individual gradient dimensions separately from each other, considering all client inputs collectively. The trimmed mean gives a percent to the largest and smallest values before making an average of them. These methods allow for some degree of malicious input as long as the data distributions of the participants remain somewhat uniform. They are also computationally inexpensive and don't require cryptography to be implemented, but assume the server is able to inspect individual gradients. This approach is more sticky to attacks that manipulate multiple coordinates simultaneously. Variants like Multi-Krum and Bulyan try to encapsulate the benefits of Krum and Trimmed means (Blanchard et al., 2017; Pillutla et al., 2022).

An alternative line of work is to propose norm-based anomaly filters. Before aggregation, the norm of each client's update (e.g., Euclidean, cosine or maximum norm) is computed in the server and discarded if the values of the norms lie outside a pre-determined range. Such filters are capable of catching malicious clients that have unusually large magnitude updates - often the case with scaling or model replacement attacks. More advanced detectors for anomalies use autoencoders or clustering algorithms to learn representations of normal updates and mark anomalies. Some schemes assign reputation scores to clients based on their historical behaviour, and down-weight/quarantine those with low trust.

Despite their successes, such robust aggregation methods have their theoretical and practical limitations (Pillutla et al., 2022). The adversarial machine-learning literature notes that strong aggregation rules for gradient learning typically are based on the assumption that client data assumes the participants/owners to be independent and identically distributed and the distribution of participants are a small fraction of the total is adversarial. When data are heterogeneous, even honest updates may be outliers; therefore, robust aggregation can happily ignore useful data (Pillutla et al., 2022; Sattler et al., 2020). Moreover, impossibility results that no algorithm can guarantee convergence in the presence of arbitrary Byzantine faults and non-IID data (Blanchard et al., 2017; Sattler et al., 2020; Yin et al., 2018). Several empirical studies show how median-based or Krum-based methods can be fooled by adaptive adversaries that craft updates that hide in the distribution of honest gradients (Blanchard et al., 2017; Krauß et al., 2024; Pillutla et al., 2022).

3.3 Privacy-Robustness Trade-offs

Incorporating privacy mechanisms with strong aggregation brings a sensitive trade-off. Secure aggregation and differential privacy restrict the amount of information that is available to the server, making it harder to detect outliers (or updates that could be malicious). For example, secure aggregation conceals individual gradients and thus methods based on the median or norm filter cannot be used directly (Blanchard et al., 2017; Kairouz et al., 2021; Lyu et al., 2020; Pillutla et al., 2022). Differential privacy introduces the concept of random noise in such a way as to make updates more variable, and perhaps blind the attack signals. At the same time, some robust aggregation methods rely on norms or distances in-between gradients that may not be stable when noise is added (Pillutla et al., 2022). On the other hand, strong aggregation may undermine promises of privacy. In addition, powerful aggregation algorithms may persist underlying per-client statistics (e.g. reputation scores) which could potentially leak information if inadequately handled.

Recent work has begun into the more systematic exploration of these trade-offs. One line of research involves privacy-aware robust aggregation: clipping gradients before secure aggregation, then adding DP noise after the aggregation, for example (Kairouz et al., 2021; Lyu et al., 2020; Pillutla et al., 2022;

Zheng et al., 2024). A second line investigates adaptive noise schedules, in which the fraction of malicious clients seen (estimated) determines how much noise is added (Krauß et al., 2024). These studies also suggest that a modest level of noise can help robustness by reducing the effect of any one update while excessive noise works against accuracy. They emphasize also the need for privacy accounting -- accumulating the volume of privacy loss (epsilon, delta) across many rounds and ensuring that defence methods do not drain the privacy budget too quickly. Ultimately, the literature hints at a tension between robustness and privacy, and drives the need for frameworks that coordinately design defences rather than address privacy and robustness in isolation.

PROBLEM STATEMENT

We assume there is a central server coordinating the model training across lots of clients who have their own non-identically distributed data (non-IID) (Sattler et al., 2020). A malicious party can control a subset of these clients and inject poisoned updates to plant backdoors or degrade the accuracy of updates overall (Bhagoji et al., 2019; Fang et al., 2020; Nguyen et al., 2022; Sun et al., 2019; Tolpegin et al., 2020). To ensure privacy the system both anonymizes the identifiers of the clients and obscures rare features or aggregates updates through secure aggregation and robust aggregation under SMPC (Kairouz et al., 2021; Lyu et al., 2020; Pillutla et al., 2022). The server never sees individual updates. The problem is to design an aggregation/screening procedure that (i) maintains privacy, (ii) minimizes the attack success rate and (iii) has high clear accuracy with acceptable communication and computation overhead.

METHODOLOGY / FRAMEWORK

Proposed Framework: Privacy Aware Robust Federated Learning (PRFL)

To overcome the limitations of existing defences, we propose Privacy-Aware Robust Federated Learning (PRFL) which offers a four-layer defence framework which reconciles privacy and robustness (Kairouz et al., 2021; McMahan et al., 2017). The architecture is shown in figure 1. Clients conduct local training and privacy transforming, secure aggregation encrypts and combines updates, the server does strong aggregation and adaptive trust scoring and a post-aggregation audit watches for persistent attacks (Kairouz et al., 2021; Krauß et al., 2024; Lyu et al., 2020).

Figure 1. PRFL architecture

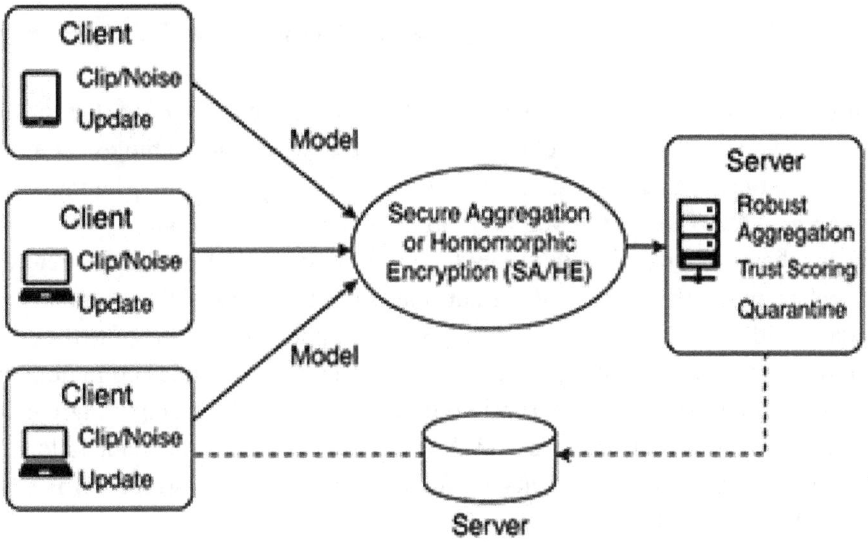

4.1 Architecture Overview

Every round of a training is as follows A sample of clients are selected to take part. Each chosen client then downloads the current global model and trains it locally on its private data, for one or more epochs. After the training, the clients perform privacy and pre-processing steps: they clip the norm of their update to bound the sensitivity, possibly add differential privacy noise and perform temporal cryptography masking for secure aggregation (Kairouz et al., 2021; Lyu et al., 2020; Zheng et al., 2024). Clients then send their masked updates to the server. Through the secure aggregation protocol, the server then learns the result (the sum of the (possibly noise-added) updates) without knowing individual contributions (Kairouz et al., 2021; Lyu et al., 2020). The server takes this sum divided by the number of the clients that took part in the session in order to get an aggregated update and then uses an effective aggregating rule (e.g. trimmed mean) on this aggregated value if several cohorts are used (Blanchard et al., 2017; Pillutla et al., 2022). The updated model is then disseminated to the clients to be ready for the next round.

4.2 Component 1: Clipping and Noise in the client.

The initial defence line works on each client. This clipping of the norm of the local updates limits the worst-case impact of any single client. Let g_i be the gradient vector that client i computes and let $\|g_i\|$ be its Euclidean norm. The client calculates $g_i = g_i \times \min\{1, C/\|g_i\|\}$ where C the clip threshold is chosen to balance utility and privacy.

In order to implement differential privacy each client can add noise to its clipped update (Kairouz et al., 2021; Lyu et al., 2020; Zheng et al., 2024). Following the Gaussian mechanism, the client samples a noise vector n_i with distribution N(0, $\sigma^2 I$), where σ is known to the client, and computes the privatised update $g_i' = g_i + n_i$.

4.3 Component 2: Cipher Suitable Aggregation & Homomorphic Encryption

After their updates are clipped and noise is added, clients disguise them so that the aggregation can be done securely. Suppose there are m clients in a round. Each client i samples a random mask r_{ij} for each other client j in the round and computes a total mask $R_i = \Sigma_{j \neq i} (r_{ij} - r_{ji})$. The masked update sent to the server is $u_i = g_i' + R_i$. When the server sums all u_i, the masks cancel out.

Alternatively, clients can use the additively homomorphic encryption. Each client encrypts simultaneously its update under a public key, it is multiplied on the server (this corresponds to summing the encrypted updates without decryption), and the aggregated ciphertext is returned to the clients for decryption. Homomorphic encryption avoids the need of pairwise masks, but adds computation overhead and clients also need to synchronize with decryption. In the view of PRFL, secure aggregation is preferred when the communication is synchronous and the likelihood of client dropout is low; homomorphic types of encryption are great when dropouts are frequent or trust in the aggregator is extremely limited (Kairouz et al., 2021; Lyu et al., 2020).

4.4 Component 3: Privacy-aware robust aggregator

With the aggregated update retrieved, the server enforces a strong aggregation rule, in order to reduce the impact of adversaries. Because of secure aggregation it will be important for PRFL to make robust aggregation of individual values for aggregates coming from cohorts (Kairouz et al., 2021; Lyu et al., 2020; Pillutla et al., 2022). If clients are grouped into cohorts of size b, the secure aggregation protocol is separately applied for each cohort: That is, the same protocol generates aggregated updates gbar^(1), gbar^(2), ..., gbar^(k), where k = ceil(m/b) (Kairouz et al., 2021; Lyu et al., 2020). A sophisticated aggregator across these cohort updates is thereafter applied by the server. Options include:

Trimmed mean: The server sort cohort updates by their norms or per-coordinate values, discard the largest and lowest alpha fraction and average the rest (Blanchard et al., 2017; Pillutla et al., 2022). The parameter alpha enables to control the trade-off between robustness and information retention.
Median of means: For each coordinate the server computes the median over cohort updates (Blanchard et al., 2017; Pillutla et al., 2022).
Geometric median: The server identifies the point g* which minimizes the sum of Euclidean distances to all cohort updates. the geometric median is resistant to outliers and expensive to compute (Blanchard et al., 2017; Pillutla et al., 2022).
Reputation-weighted mean: Per server a reputation-weighted mean is kept consisting of the consistency of different cohorts across past rounds. Cohorts that have low trust are down-weighted.

The choice of b affects privacy as well as robustness. Larger cohorts provide higher privacy (fewer units of aggregation - individual updates) but reduce family of unit numbers to aggregate strongly. PRFL opens up for the cohort size, the proportion alpha value and other parameters to be adjusted depending on threat assessment.

4.5 Component 4: Trust Scoring and Quarantine (adaptive) (Krauß et al., 2024)

The server keeps a dynamic clients or cohort reputation. After each round, the server tests consistency of the aggregated update with the trend of historical data based on synthetic validation data or other signals. Cohorts whose updates do not conform closely to supposed behaviour are given a lower trust score. if the trust score of a cohort falls below a threshold, its contributions are down-weighted or quarantined for a fixed number of rounds. Quarantine removes the cohort's update from aggregation, but the client can still train locally (model updates) so the client is not permanently excluded. This mechanism dissuades persistent adversarial behaviour and gives the system a chance of recovering from false positive. To maintain privacy, trust scores and quarantine determinations do not have associations with client identities and are kept securely. The server; may also make use of secure multi-party protocol to calculate trust scores without disclosing individual contributions (Kairouz et al., 2021; Lyu et al., 2020).

4.6 Component 5: Post-Aggregation Audits and Recovery

Finally, PRFL performs an audit after each round in order to detect persistent poisoning. One audit technique is synthetic validation: wherein the server trains a small "shadow model" on a clean synthetic dataset, and compares its gradient update with that of the federated model. Large discrepancies may represent poisoning (Bhagoji et al., 2019; Fang et al., 2020; Tolpegin et al., 2020). Another method is consistency checks: the server relies on secure multi-party computation to check that aggregated updates meet constraints one might expect (for example, being within a certain norm range or in the same direction as in past updates) (Kairouz et al., 2021; Lyu et al., 2020). If an attack is detected, the server can reset to a previous model state or model sanitisation is performed by retraining the model with a clean dataset. These audits add an extra layer of defence with no access to client data.

4.7 Privacy Accounting

PRFL brings together differential privacy accounting in order to offer formal privacy guarantees (Kairouz et al., 2021; Lyu et al., 2020; Zheng et al., 2024). Let $(\varepsilon_t, \delta_t)$ denote the privacy budget consumed in round t. Clipping and adding Gaussian noise is done at the client side, thus satisfying $(\varepsilon_t, \delta_t)$-differential privacy per-round. Over T rounds, privacy budgets compose. Using advanced composition theorems or moments accountant, the total privacy loss can be bounded $(\varepsilon_{\text{total}}, \delta_{\text{total}})$.

4.8 Operational Knobs

PRFL exposes a number of parameters that practitioners can tune to find a balance between privacy, robustness and performance:

Clip norm (C): limiting the norm of the gradient; lower values are more robust but risk many will lose valuable information.
Noise multiplier (sigma): standard deviation of the Gaussian noise added, the higher the value, the stronger privacy but the weaker the accuracy.
Cohort size (b): number of clients per secure aggregation group; larger cohorts lead to more robust privacy but fewer aggregation units to build solid aggregation (Kairouz et al., 2021; Lyu et al., 2020).

Trim proportion (alpha): fraction of cohort updates that are dropped in trimmed mean, higher alpha gives more robust result with less information (Blanchard et al., 2017; Pillutla et al., 2022). Trust threshold and quarantine length: parameters which control how quickly suspicious cohorts are quarantined and for how long.

Selecting these parameters involves taking into consideration the threat model, data heterogeneity and desired privacy budget (Sattler et al., 2020). The next section explains how we measure PRFL under varying settings of these parameters.

EXPERIMENTAL SETUP

Methods

5.1 Datasets and Tasks

Research evaluation of federated learning we evaluate PRFL on a few benchmark datasets that represent common federated learning scenarios (Kairouz et al., 2021; McMahan et al., 2017). MNIST and Fashion-MNIST: lifted widely used image classification datasets of hand written digits and clothing items respectively. Although relatively simple in nature, they are a foundation to compare privacy-robustness trades. CIFAR-10 and CIFAR-100 are more difficult datasets which contain objects of 32x32 colored images with 10 and 100 classes. To simulate realistic non-IID distributions, we allocate each dataset as clients using Dirichlet allocation or label skew (e.g., each client facing data from only a few classes) (Sattler et al., 2020). EMNIST-Letters, Handwritten letters and to evaluate character recognition. High-variation across writers. These are datasets for vision and natural language tasks, and different in size and complexity. Normalization of all images is done and normal data augmentations (random cropping and flipping) are performed.

We select these datasets as they have been studied extensively in the federated-learning literature and comparison is possible with other methods. They also make results more reproducible, as they're publicly available and require zero access to sensitive personal data. Statistics of the datasets and training information are summarized in Table 1.

Table 1. Datasets and tasks used in experiments

Dataset	Task	#Clients	Data Distribution
MNIST	Digit classification	100	Non-IID
Fashion-MNIST	Clothing classification	100	Non-IID
CIFAR-10	Object recognition	100	Non-IID
Shakespeare	Next-character prediction	143	Naturally non-IID

5.2 Attack Configurations

In order to evaluate the robustness, we implement three kinds of poisoning attacks: (Bhagoji et al., 2019; Fang et al., 2020; Tolpegin et al., 2020)

Label-flip attack: A fraction of the adversarial clients would flip the labels for a certain class to another class during the local training instance. For example, all "0" digits are called "1." This results in the model misclassifying digits, but otherwise leaving other classes fairly untouched by this bias. The goal of the attacker is to degrade the overall accuracy, or favor quenching the class portions of the classification of some classes.

Model-replacement attack The attacker trains a local model on malicious data and scales their update to take over the global model. After local training, the malicious adversary multiplies their update by a large factor (e.g eta * m, where m is the number of participating clients) so that their change dominates the average. This attack can place a hole in the system or drastically lower the accuracy of the system.

Backdoor attack: The attacker graft a trigger pattern into a number of inputs and markup them as a pattern belonging to a target category (ex. an image containing a given pixel pattern is marked as being "0"). The adversarial client learns on these examples together with its clean data. Backdoor is activated by ANY input that fits this pattern (Nguyen et al., 2022; Sun et al., 2019). The Attack Success Rate (ASR) is defined as the percentage of the number of misclassification of trigger inputs as the categorized class.

For each attack, we vary the proportion of malicious clients (eg 1%, 5%, 10%) and the strength of the attack (eg scaling factor, number of poisoned examples) (Bhagoji et al., 2019; Fang et al., 2020; Tolpegin et al., 2020). Adversarial clients are assumed to know the global model architecture and training schedule but not other clients data or updates. They take part in all the chosen rounds. Honest clients play by the protocol.

5.3 Baselines and Defence Variants

In comparison to several baselines, we compare PRFL:

No defence: Naive averaging without privacy mechanisms or robust aggregation

DP-only: Clients clip and add Gaussian noise, no robust aggregation; the server is the average of updates (Kairouz et al., 2021; Lyu et al., 2020; Pillutla et al., 2022; Zheng et al., 2024).

Robust-only: The server applies robust aggregator (e.g. trimmed mean or Krum) to raw update without secure aggregation or DP noise (Blanchard et al., 2017; Kairouz et al., 2021; Lyu et al., 2020; Pillutla et al., 2022; Zheng et al., 2024).

Combined naive: DP noise at a clients and a robust aggregator at the server without some modifications based on privacy restrictions (Kairouz et al., 2021; Lyu et al., 2020; Pillutla et al., 2022; Zheng et al., 2024). This is typical type of defences which consider privacy and robustness separately.

PRFL: Our proposed framework with secure aggregation, client-side clipping and noise; robust cohort aggregation, trust scoring and post-aggregation audits (Kairouz et al., 2021; Lyu et al., 2020).

Hyperparameters for each of the baselines are optimized for a trade-off between the accuracy/robustness. For strong aggregator, we play around between trimming proportion and Krum neighbour counts (Blanchard et al., 2017; Pillutla et al., 2022). For DP baselines we vary noise multipliers (Kairouz et al.,

2021; Lyu et al., 2020; Zheng et al., 2024). For PRFL, we vary cohort size, clip norms, noise multipliers, trim proportions and trust thresholds.

5.4 Evaluation Metrics

We report several metrics to assess the privacy, the robustness and the performance:

Accuracy and F1:- Overall classification accuracy and macro-averaged F1 score of clean test data.
Attack Success Rate (ASR): For backdoor attack this is the fraction of trigger inputs that are misclassified as the target class (Nguyen et al., 2022; Sun et al., 2019).
epsilon (epsilon): The cumulative amount of differential-privacy budget used during training. We compute epsilon by the moments accountant over all rounds.
False-positive rate: The proportion of the honest population blockquarantined by the trust scoring mechanism.
Time-to-detect: The number of rounds to detect and quarantine the adversary clients.
Overhead: Extra computation and communication costs compared to simple averaging (measured in runtime or network bandwidth).

Table 2 summarizes metrics and how they're calculated.

Table 2. Metrics used in experiments.

Metric	Description	Calculation
Accuracy	Overall classification accuracy	Correct predictions / Total predictions
F1 Score	Macro-averaged F1 score	Harmonic mean of precision and recall
ASR	Attack Success Rate	Misclassified trigger inputs / Total trigger inputs
Epsilon (ε)	Privacy budget consumed	Cumulative DP budget via moments accountant
False Positive Rate	Honest clients quarantined	Incorrectly flagged clients / Total honest clients
Time-to-Detect	Rounds to detect attackers	Number of rounds until quarantine

We run each experiment using 3 different random seeds and report in mean and standard deviation. For fairness, we fix the total number of local updates, changing the number of rounds as needed to have comparable training budgets among methods.

5.5 Compute Setup

Experiments are carried out on a parcel of GPUs. For each dataset/model combination, the training is performed for 100 to 200 communication rounds, depending on the dataset size. Clients perform between one and five epochs per round locally with a batch size of 32. For the vision tasks, we feign 100 clients and for text, 50 clients. In every round, 10% of the clients are chosen uniformly at random. Models include a convolutional neural network for MNIST/Fashion-MNIST, a ResNet-18 for CIFAR-10/100, a simple two-layer recurrent neural network for Shakespeare and a text-CNN for AG-News. We secure aggregate using pairwise masking scheme. Experiments are run in a simulated FL setting; the overheads of secure aggregation and homomorphic encryption are approximated using cryptographic cost models (Kairouz et al., 2021; Lyu et al., 2020).

RESULTS

Experiments and Results 6.1 Main Results Figures 2 through 4.

Figure 2. Model accuracy under different attacks (with 5-10% malicious clients)

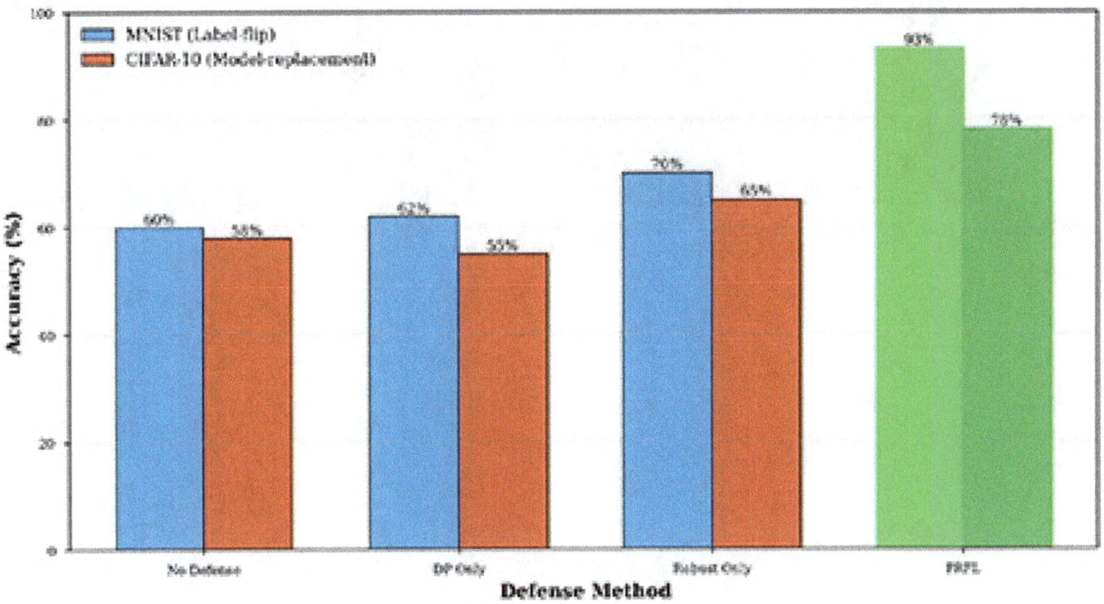

Figure 3. Attack Success Rate (ASR) comparison (lower is better)

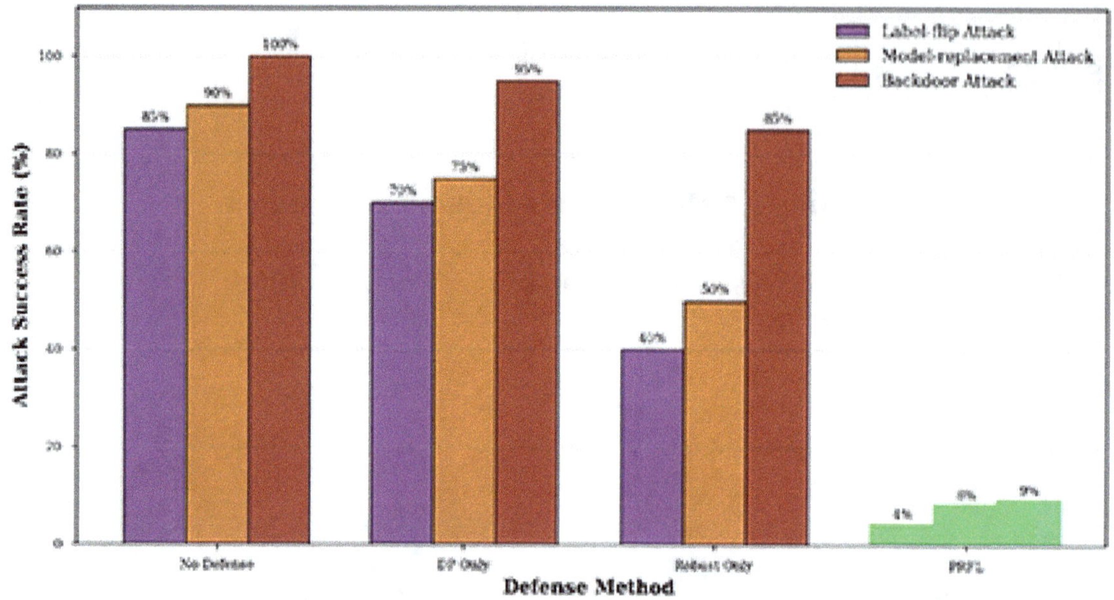

Figure 4. Comprehensive results across all datasets

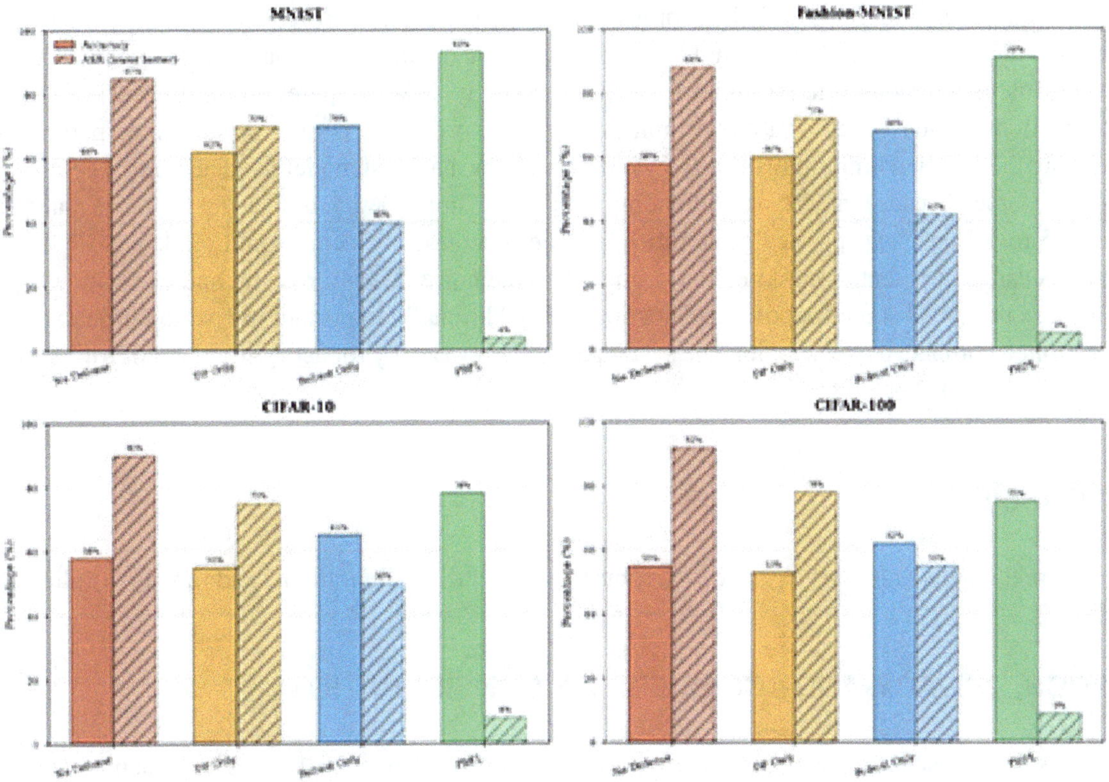

summarize accuracy and ASR between different attaches. Without defenses, both label-flip and model-replacement attacks significantly degrade accuracy, as accuracy is reduced from ~95% to <60% on MNIST and CIFAR-10 when 10% clients are malicious. The backdoor attack method means an ASR close to 100% with malignant accuracy, which makes it especially dangerous. Adding differential privacy by itself mitigates the model replacement somewhat, by limiting gradient norms, but still, accuracy drops significantly and ASR remains high. Robust aggregators (trimmed mean, Krum) diminish the effects of model replacement attacks, with of trimmed mean yielding better performance with non-IID data (Blanchard et al., 2017; Pillutla et al., 2022; Sattler et al., 2020). Nevertheless, they can't block back doors because their adversaries create their update in a way that simulates honest update. Our PRFL framework has shown a consistent high accuracy and low ASR level compared with baselines. On MNIST with 5% adversarial clients and a label flip attack, PRFL retains 93% accuracy whereas ASR stays below 5%. Under a model-replacement attack on CIFAR-10, PRFL achieves 78% compared with 55% for DP only and 65% for robust only. For the backdoor attacks, PRFL drops the ASR to below 10% without affecting accuracy, i.e., of no more than 1-2% compared to robust-only methods (Nguyen et al., 2022; Sun et al., 2019). These improvements result from the combination of clipping/noise (limiting the maximum effect of any client), secure aggregation (preventing the attacker from tailoring his attacks to other clients updates), robust cohort aggregation (-filtering out aggregated cohorts that have been dominated by adversaries) and trust scoring (gradually quarantining malicious cohorts). The post-aggregation audit spots persistent anomalies and re-trains if required. The privacy budget of PRFL is of moderate level.

With noise multiplier = 1.0, 200 rounds, epsilon would be about 3.5 -> participate with delta=10^-5 for MNist and 5.2 for Cifar-10. These values are comparable to methods that use only DP and meet typical privacy standards. Thus, since PRFL employs secure aggregation and trust scoring, there is no need to store per-client updates, or to perform heavy cryptographic operations beyond secure aggregation, the overhead is manageable: training times increase by roughly 20% compared to training with DP only. 6.2 Ablations & Sensitivity Analysis examines how sensitive PRFL is to important hyperparameters. Reducing the clipping limit from 1.0 to 0.5 yields more robust against model replacement at the cost of a loss in accuracy because important gradient information is clipped away. Increasing the noise multiplier from 0.5 to 1.5 enhances privacy capabilities but does decrease correctness and renders ASR slightly higher because of potential masking that occurs from the noise. Trust threshold and quarantine length influences the speed and false positive detection. It is additionally important to ensure fairness: clients with limited compute power shouldn't be systematically excluded by robust aggregation or trust scoring (Pillutla et al., 2022).

DISCUSSION

Interpret results, trade-offs (privacy vs. robustness vs. utility), limitations, and threats to validity.

ETHICS, PRIVACY, AND ACCESSIBILITY CONSIDERATIONS

There are considerable ethical and privacy implications inherent in leveraging machine-learning models with data about individuals or organizations. Federated learning & privacy methods or differential privacy and secure aggregation fall in line with the principle of data minimization and helps to keep data local and (/ to) limit the access of individual data contributions (Kairouz et al., 2021; Lyu et al., 2020; McMahan et al., 2017; Zheng et al., 2024). Despite this, there are residual risks. Gradients can leak(produce information, which we dont know should be private) if privacy mechanisms are incorrectly set, therefore system designers have to choose privacy parameters quite conservatively and conduct privacy audits. Homomorphic encryption and secure aggregation secure updates against honest-but-curious servers, at the cost of trust in key management and protocol correctness by honest-but-curious servers (Kairouz et al., 2021; Lyu et al., 2020).

In PRFL, we don't use any sensitive personal data and utilize public benchmark datasets. If authentic data is being used, participants should be able to provide informed consent in terms of how their data will be used (including what privacy guarantees will be given and the possible risks). Data governance frameworks should have retention periods, access controls and procedures regarding responding to data breaches; PRFL's trust scoring must therefore be designed so it does not discriminate; reputation scores should not be associated with the identities of individuals and they should be reset on a regular basis so that persons are not excluded forever.

Reproducibility is fundamental to science integrity. We will make public code, configuration files and random seeds that are used in our experiments, scripts to reproduce data splits and privacy budgets. Hyperparameters and Training schedules are recorded. And because cryptographic protocols can be complex, we include some references to implementations and instructions to integrate secure aggregation in FL frameworks (Kairouz et al., 2021; Lyu et al., 2020). We don't include any secret keys or secure channels details. All is derived from the underlying data which is publicly available [figures and tables]. By sharing these materials, we allow our results to be checked by other research groups and to build on them.

CONCLUSION

This chapter discussed the difficulty of protecting against poisoning attacks in federated learning which would still uphold strict privacy guarantees (Bhagoji et al., 2019; Fang et al., 2020; Kairouz et al., 2021; McMahan et al., 2017; Tolpegin et al., 2020). We reviewed privacy-enhancing techniques such as differential privacy and secure aggregation and robust aggregation methods such as median and trimmed mean, and highlight trade offs between privacy and robustness (Blanchard et al., 2017; Kairouz et al., 2021; Lyu et al., 2020; Pillutla et al., 2022; Zheng et al., 2024). We proposed the framework of PRFL, a 4-layer defence framework that includes client-side clippings and noise, secure aggregation, privacy-aware robust aggregation, adaptive trust scoring and post-aggregation audits (Kairouz et al., 2021; Krauß et al., 2024; Lyu et al., 2020; Pillutla et al., 2022). In discussing this evidence, we discussed ethical and reproducibility considerations, limitations and directions for future research.

FUTURE RESEARCH DIRECTIONS

PRFL has many (but limitations). This assumes that the server is executing secure aggregation correctly, and that the server does not collude with clients. If the server is malicious or works together, it may break privacy guarantees. Our threat model also assumes that less than one-third of clients are adversarial; beyond that point, robust aggregation doesn't really do much for you (Pillutla et al., 2022). PRFL demands synchronous participation or reliable cohorts for coupling secure aggregations, for the protocol. Asynchronous or highly dynamic networks have a likelihood to break the protocol (Kairouz et al., 2021; Lyu et al., 2020). Client computations (clipping, noise, encryption) and safe aggregation bring overhead and this could be not feasible for low-power devices. Trust scoring assumes constant behavioral patterns in round-to-round communications; with highly non-IID data and concept drift, honest clients could be unfairly labeled (Sattler et al., 2020).

Future work may focus on certifiable robustness under differential privacy that produce theoretical guarantees bounding the worst-case impact of adversarial clients based on privacy budgets (Kairouz et al., 2021; Lyu et al., 2020; Zheng et al., 2024). Hierarchical federated learning is another promising direction, where clients are grouped into sub-clusters (e.g., hospitals within regions), performing secure aggregation locally then aggregating across the whole hierarchy; this may improve the scalability and reduce the communication (Kairouz et al., 2021; Lyu et al., 2020; McMahan et al., 2017). Investigating adaptive privacy budgets, where noise is allocated dynamically according to the attack detection may increase both privacy and robustness (Krauß et al., 2024). Finally, combining PRFL with federated analytics and federated evaluation can allow one to monitor model performance and fairness without privacy loss.

COMPETING INTERESTS AND FUNDING

Disclose conflicts and funding (mandatory; see placeholders below).

DATA AND SOFTWARE AVAILABILITY

Link or describe how to access code/data upon publication, with license info.

REFERENCES

Bhagoji, A. N., Chakraborty, S., Mittal, P., & Calo, S. (2019). Analyzing federated learning through an adversarial lens. In *Proceedings of the 36th International Conference on Machine Learning* (Vol. 97, pp. 634–643). PMLR.

Blanchard, P., El Mhamdi, E. M., Guerraoui, R., & Stainer, J. (2017). Machine learning with adversaries: Byzantine tolerant gradient descent. In Vol. 30, pp. 118–128). Advances in Neural Information Processing Systems. Curran Associates.

European Data Protection Supervisor. (2025). TechDispatch #1/2025 – Federated learning. Retrieved June 10, 2025, from https://www.edps.europa.eu/data-protection/our-work/publications/techdispatch/2025-06-10-techdispatch-12025-federated-learning_en

Fang, M., Cao, X., Jia, J., & Gong, N. Z. (2020). Local model poisoning attacks to Byzantine-robust federated learning. In *Proceedings of the 29th USENIX Security Symposium* (pp. 1605–1622). USENIX Association.

Kairouz, P., McMahan, H. B., Avent, B., Bellet, A., Bennis, M., Bhagoji, A. N., Bonawitz, K., Charles, Z., Cormode, G., Cummings, R., D'Oliveira, R. G. L., Eichner, H., Gascón, A., Garrett, Z., Hanzely, F., Hartmann, V., Huo, Z., Hutchinson, B., Hsu, J., & Yu, Q. (2021). Advances and open problems in federated learning. *Foundations and Trends in Machine Learning*, *14*(1–2), 1–210. DOI: 10.1561/2200000083

Krauß, T., König, J., Dmitrienko, A., & Kanzow, C. (2024). Automatic adversarial adaptation for stealthy poisoning attacks in federated learning. In *Proceedings of the Network and Distributed System Security Symposium (NDSS 2024)*. DOI: 10.14722/ndss.2024.241366

Lyu, L., Yu, H., Ma, X., Sun, L., Zhao, J., Yang, Q., & Yu, P. S. (2020). Privacy and robustness in federated learning: Attacks and defenses. *arXiv*. https://arxiv.org/abs/2012.06337

McMahan, H. B., Moore, E., Ramage, D., Hampson, S., & Arcas, B. A. (2017). Communication-efficient learning of deep networks from decentralized data. In *Proceedings of the 20th International Conference on Artificial Intelligence and Statistics* (Vol. 54, pp. 1273–1282). PMLR.

Nguyen, T. D., Rieger, P., De Viti, R., Chen, H., Brandenburg, B. B., Yalame, H., Möllering, H., Fereidooni, H., Marchal, S., Miettinen, M., Asokan, N., Sadeghi, A.-R., Schneider, T., & Koushanfar, F. (2022). FLAME: Taming backdoors in federated learning. In *Proceedings of the 31st USENIX Security Symposium* (pp. 1415–1432). USENIX Association.

Pillutla, K., Kakade, S. M., & Harchaoui, Z. (2022). Robust aggregation for federated learning. *IEEE Transactions on Signal Processing, 70*, 1142–1154. DOI: 10.1109/TSP.2022.3153135

Sattler, F., Müller, K.-R., & Samek, W. (2020). Clustered federated learning: Model-agnostic distributed multitask optimization under privacy constraints. *IEEE Transactions on Neural Networks and Learning Systems, 32*(8), 3710–3722. DOI: 10.1109/TNNLS.2020.3015958 PMID: 32833654

Sun, Z., Kairouz, P., Suresh, A. T., & McMahan, H. B. (2019). Can you really backdoor federated learning? *arXiv*. https://arxiv.org/abs/1911.07963

Tolpegin, V., Truex, S., Gursoy, M. E., & Liu, L. (2020). Data poisoning attacks against federated learning systems. In *Computer Security – ESORICS 2020* (pp. 480–501). Springer., DOI: 10.1007/978-3-030-58951-6_24

Yin, D., Chen, Y., Kannan, R., & Bartlett, P. (2018). Byzantine-robust distributed learning: Towards optimal statistical rates. In *Proceedings of the 35th International Conference on Machine Learning* (Vol. 80, pp. 5650–5659). PMLR.

Zheng, H., Chen, J., Liu, T., Cheng, Y., Wang, Z., Wang, Y., Gao, L., Ji, S., & Zhang, X. (2024). DP-Poison: Poisoning federated learning under the cover of differential privacy. *ACM Transactions on Privacy and Security, 27*(2), 8. Advance online publication. DOI: 10.1145/3702325

Chapter 7
Adversarial Robustness of Federated Learning in Healthcare:
Mitigating Membership Inference and Poisoning Attacks

P. Saranya
https://orcid.org/0000-0001-9343-1309
Amity University, Mumbai, India

A. Saranya
https://orcid.org/0000-0002-4340-4430
Amity University, Mumbai, India

Jeyavel Janardhanan
Amity University, Mumbai, India

Garima Shukla
https://orcid.org/0000-0002-9673-3107
Amity University, Mumbai, India

Rajiv Iyer
https://orcid.org/0000-0002-1136-2061
Amity University, Mumbai, India

Alavikunhu Panthakkan
https://orcid.org/0000-0002-7746-0609
University of Dubai, UAE

ABSTRACT

The healthcare industry is rapidly embracing data-driven techniques for early diagnosis, health management and precision medicine. However, strict privacy regulations restrict centralized aggregation of sensitive patient data. These restrictions encouraging the adoption of Federated Learning (FL), a privacy-preserving technique that enables collaborative model training that allows hospitals, and research institutions to get benefit from shared intelligence. While Federated Learning preserves the data confidentiality and locality, their decentralized nature amplifies new attack surfaces, as compromised or malicious participants can extract sensitive information from observed gradients or inject poisoned updates. Among its threats, two of the most critical threats in this domain are Membership Inference Attacks (MIA) and Data Poisoning Attacks. This chapter motivates to analyze these adversarial challenges in depth, critically evaluates existing defensive mechanisms, and proposes a roadmap for building robust, secure, and trustworthy federated healthcare systems.

DOI: 10.4018/979-8-3373-6224-3.ch007

INTRODUCTION

Healthcare 5.0, a patient-centric medical science technology, envisions millions of IoMT (Internet of Medical Things) based sensors interconnected via fifth generation (5G) network. Healthcare 5.0 enhances the overall human life quality with the help of these advanced technologies, as it supports timely medical interventions, preventive care and personalized treatment. According to the CMI (Custom Market Insights) report, the IoMT market would reach a size of 276.85 billion USD by 2025 and 1061.49 billion USD by 2034 at the latest (Saraswat et al., 2022. This projection indicates an expected annual growth rate from 2025 to 2034 is approximately 16.1%. A secure route for data operations and sophisticated machine learning (ML) models is required for the smooth and reliable operation of the growing number of IoMT devices.

However, as healthcare 5.0 combines 5G connectivity and IoMT with ML frameworks to build predictive model by collecting data from various IoT devices or healthcare organizations, a new dimension of the problem would arise. Among these, the most crucial one poses a serious security risk because the training data is sensitive (Li et al., 2025).

At a centralised computing server, the privacy of the conventional ML models must also be violated on a number of levels. In related to this critical privacy and security concerns, numerous studies and surveys have been carried out in recent times. Within that the most preferable solution at the technological and infrastructure level is the adoption of Federated Learning (FL) architecture (Amin et al., 2025; Wazid et al., 2022).

FL has significantly influenced modern ML, particularly when it comes to data security and privacy management. Rather than sharing local data, FL aggregates the model parameters of the local models in contrast to standard ML. The primary purpose of adopting FL model in healthcare is to provide an agnostic learning environment with help of its decentralized nature. As a result, the training data is decentralized which helps to reduce the hazards associated with typical centralized ML algorithm in healthcare 5.0.

By integrating FL with healthcare, promising numerous advantages, including increased diagnostic accuracy without centralised data storage, and greater collaborative intelligence. But even with these encouraging advantages, FL still faces numerous issues. One of the main issues is safeguarding private patient details against advanced adversarial attacks that try to deduce private information from shared model updates. Furthermore, frequent exchange of model updates among participating systems can result in high cost of communication costs between systems, which raises network and computational expenses. Another crucial issue is caused by non-independent and identically distributed (non-IID) characteristics of the healthcare information as the disparities between data from hospitals and research facilities. The adversarial attack challenges in FL are thoroughly reviewed in this work.

The motivation of this chapter is the rapid adoption of FL in healthcare industry by its ability of harness computational intelligence without exposure of sensitive patient data. However, the adversarial risks bring up serious issues regarding privacy of patient data, and decision-making system dependability. This motivates to explore an existing vulnerability along with a clear roadmap to advancing secure FL in healthcare.

The following are the primary goals of this work:

- Introduce the basics regarding Federated Learning over healthcare, highlighting its challenges and adversarial risks.

- Review and classify Membership Inference and Data Poisoning Attacks, including mechanisms and variants.
- Evaluate existing defensive strategies along with their research status and provide a comparative study in healthcare contexts.
- Identify gaps and propose future research directions for building trustworthy federated healthcare systems.

It has six significant parts in this chapter. **Section 2** outlines the fundamentals of healthcare 5.0 and Federated Learning, including their evolution, architecture, and key categories. **Section 3** examines critical privacy and security threats in healthcare federated learning, focusing on membership inference and data poisoning attacks along with their corresponding defensive mechanisms. **Section 4** discusses open research challenges and future directions, emphasizing explainable, lightweight, and domain-specific solutions for healthcare institutions. **Section 5** concludes the chapter by integrating technological findings and presenting a roadmap toward secure, robust, and trustworthy federated learning in healthcare, while **Section 6** lists the references used throughout the study.

BACKGROUND AND FOUNDATION OR PRELIMINARIES

Healthcare 5.0

Evolution of Healthcare 5.0

The transition of medicine systems can be traced via five major phases; each shows its own advancements in technology. The journey started from the healthcare 1.0 focused on basic doctor-centric treatment in the pre-1980s, where the main objective was therapies based on evidence and quality-based treatment (Amritanjali & Gupta, 2025). It mostly depends on paper records-based diagnosis. Next healthcare 2.0 was introduced in the 1980s-1990s, which emphasized standard hospital-centric treatment, and its objective was end-to-end service coverage. The diagnosis is based on Electronic Health Records (EHRs) and basic imaging technologies. After that, in the 2000s-2010s, healthcare 3.0 focused on the automation and digitization of healthcare systems. It stood for the cost-effective digital diagnosis based on cloud storage. Next, healthcare 4.0 came into existence, where proactive healthcare emerged, focusing on AI-based diagnosis and IoT sensors from the 2010s to 2020s. It stood with the business model based on big data, robotics, and mobile technologies. Currently, healthcare 5.0 is patient-centric and focuses on the decentralized and personalized customer healthcare model. It stood with digital healthcare and lifelong relationships with the help of machine learning models. Table 1 shows the comprehensive healthcare evolution phases.

Table 1. Evolution of digital health care

Healthcare 1.0 Production	Healthcare 2.0 Industrialization	Healthcare 3.0 Automation	Healthcare 4.0 Digitalization	Healthcare 5.0 Personalization
Focus: **Evidence-based Treatment Model** **Objective:** **Quality Treatment, Patient Survivability**	**Focus:** Value Chain Integration Model **Objective:** End-to-End Service Coverage	**Focus:** Operating model **Objective:** Cost to Serve, Efficiency	**Focus:** Business model **Objective:** Mass Personalization, Proactive Healthcare	**Focus:** Customer model **Objective:** Lifelong Partnership, Quality of Life

Significant challenge in healthcare 5.0

As healthcare 5.0 depends on ML models to process large and diverged datasets including genetic data, medical images, electronic health records (EHRs) and more (Yang et al., 2019). The major drawback of these healthcare datasets is making them vulnerable to privacy breaches, as these datasets contain sensitive personally identifiable information (PII). Machine learning models that employ this type of data are frequently processed and transferred between multiple hospitals and research institutions. Unfortunately, it happened without the patient's consent, which creates several points for the data breaches. Thus, the major significant challenges in healthcare 5.0 are to maintain the model accuracy along with the privacy preservation of patient data. Federated training gives a workable solution to this issue.

Federated Learning

An overview of federated training

Federated training was initially introduced by Google in 2016 (Mammen, 2021; McMahan et al., 2017). It was first used in Google Keyboard, which was intended to learn from several Android phones collectively. Its main concept is to avoid data leaking by training machine learning models across several dispersed devices. FL guarantees the privacy of local data stays on individual devices, in contrast to standard centralised ML techniques, which aggregate data in a central server.

With this paradigm, FL can bundle the system updates to a main server in the cloud, which contains the model after training ML models on edge devices such as IoT, sensors, and cell phones. The application of FL to any edge device is thus demonstrated. Consequently, it holds the potential to transform vital industries such as intelligent transportation, smart homes, and healthcare. The creation of the AI pandemic engine for COVID-19 diagnosis, which was accomplished by a global team of healthcare academics and practitioners who trained models on dispersed chest scan datasets, is the most notable example in the field of medicine.

Several studies (Wazid et al., 2022; Yang et al., 2019) have also demonstrated the effectiveness of FL in the creation of machine learning based predictive models for health risk identification, personalized treatment recommendations, and overall disease diagnosis. The FL process consists of the following four main steps:

- Client Selection: Central server initiates the distributed learning process by choosing the group of clients with the help of some algorithm or randomly picking the desired participants.
- Parameter broadcasting: The server then notifies the chosen clients of the global gradients or parameters of the machine learning model.
- Local model training: Following this, clients can compute model updates and retrain the models using their local data in parallel.
- Model aggregation: The aggregator server combines the model variables using the model averaging technique after receiving the most recent local training model parameters from the clients.

The processes mentioned above are repetitively performed in FL-based digital healthcare on many communication rounds until the overall loss value reaches the desired level of accuracy. In healthcare, this iterative process maintains data privacy and trust among users while ensuring robustness and accuracy among AI models.

Definition of Federated Learning

Federated averaging (FedAvg) was introduced in 2017 (Albshaier et al., 2025) allows using a variety of clients to train algorithms for ML without needing to centralize the data itself. Consider there are N data owners $\{O_1, O_2, \ldots, O_N\}$ and that each of them wants to use their own associated dataset $\{D_1, D_2, \ldots, D_N\}$ to train it. These datasets are usually integrated into a single dataset, $D = D_1 \cup D_2 \cup \ldots \cup D_N$, by using a traditional centralised neural network approach for constructing a global machine learning technique M_{CON}.

In contrast, a FL system uses M_{FED}, in which each data owner O_i does not expose its dataset D_i to others. Its accuracy is represented as A_{FED}, should be quite near to the performance of A_{CON}, the accuracy of M_{CON}. Ideally, the difference between them should be maintained with a small tolerance, as in equation 1, as follows. Let and formally this can be expressed as,

$$|A_{FED} - A_{CON}| < \delta \tag{1}$$

Here, δ is a positive real value that denotes the accuracy loss brought about by the federated learning process. Because it maintains anonymity and achieves near-centralized performance, this value is smaller for a successful federated learning method.

An architecture of federated learning

Figure 1 illustrates the basic FL-based smart healthcare architecture. Broadly, the architecture of FL can be divided into two categories: decentralized and centralized (Geyer et al., 2017).

Figure 1. A basic FL-based smart healthcare architecture

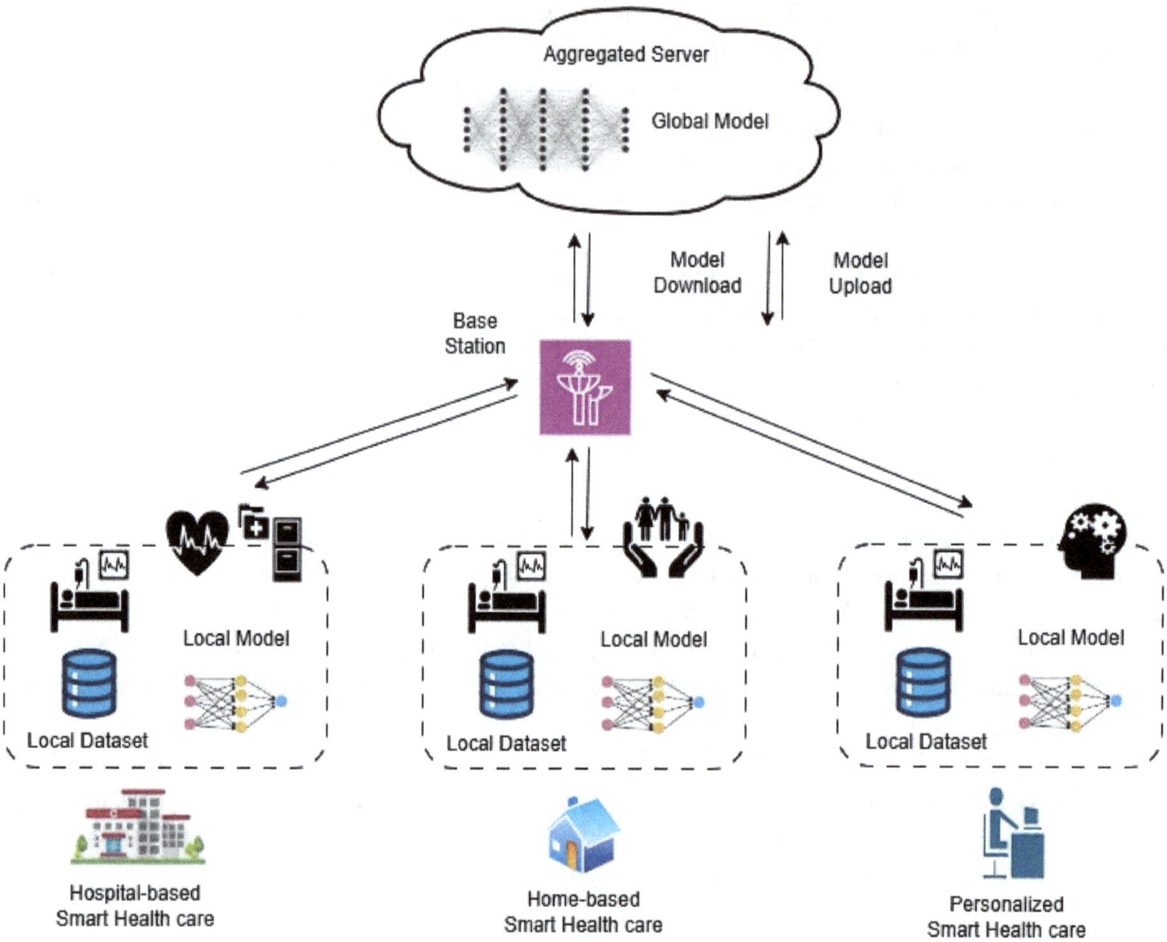

In the conventional centralized FL system, every client initially acquires the existing universal design on the server. The clients then train such a model with their own data set. Upon local training, the master server gathers the updates of the model parameters of all the collaborating users. This procedure is continued till the global design has achieved the desired performance based on the performance requirements along with certain privacy and security issues (Ngoupayou et al., 2025).

By contrast, the decentralized FL architecture does not have a single point of control as represented by a central server. Rather, the devices or servers work together to train the model in a distributed way. This minimizes the risk of having every feature concentrated in one place, but there is a problem of inter-device communication and cooperation. The technologies supporting decentralized architectures, such as blockchain (Huang et al., 2022), make it more reliable and provide secure and verifiable communication between the clients involved. The variations between centralized and decentralized paradigms are indicated in Figure 2.

Figure 2. Distinction between the decentralized FL paradigm and the centralized FL paradigm.

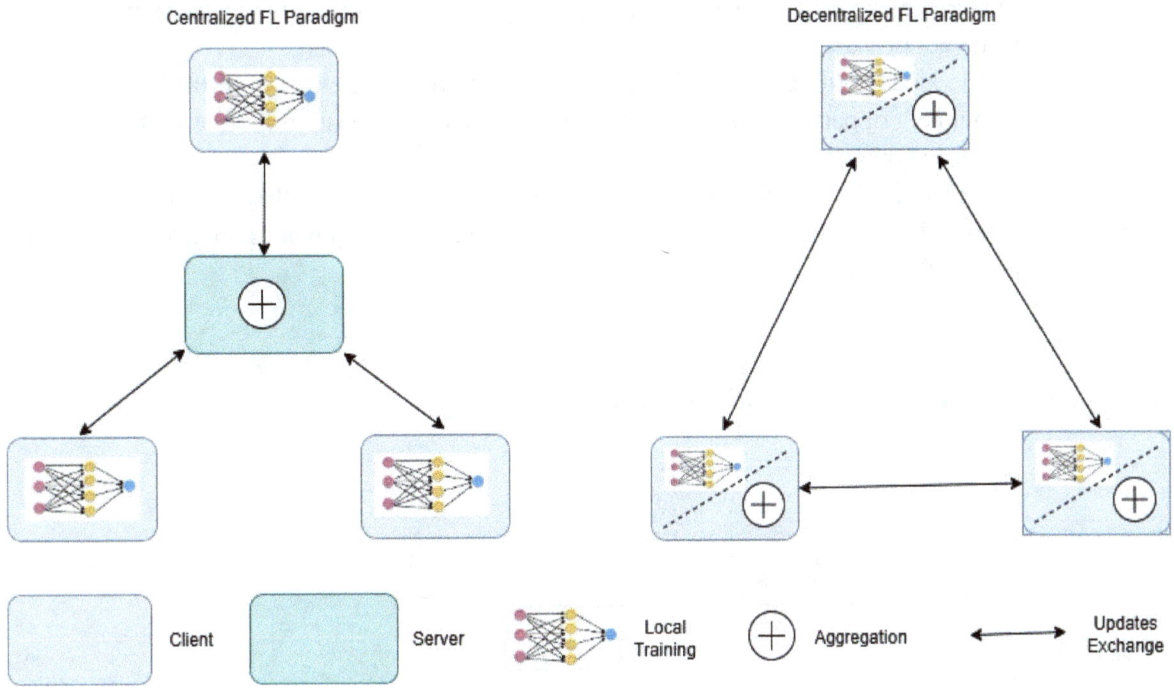

Categories of Federated Learning architecture.

Figure 3 indicates the different types of FL architecture. The key types of FL structures are mentioned as follows in this section:

i. Centralized Federated Learning - Under this model, a central server receives the model updates from the clients taking part in the training process. The central server will ensure that raw sensitive data is never forsaken from the local devices and keep the global model up to date so that users to train locally.
ii. Decentralized Federated Learning - In this model, there will be no central server; instead, peer-to-peer communication will be used between the users. Every user can share the model updates with other users, which improves privacy and minimizes single points of failure.
iii. Vertical federated learning (VFL) - This is applied when the devices hold a dataset with various feature sets of the same sample instances of a group. It assists when two or more organizations are sharing data with data of varying feature set of the same set of individuals.
iv. Horizontal Federated Learning (HFL) – It endorses the cases when the individual participants have a data set of similar feature space with the various sample cases. An example in point is the Google keyboard, which is FL but has the same features as all other participant mobile phones are being trained on.

v. Federated Transfer learning (FTL) It resembles conventional Machine Learning with the addition of the new features to the pre-trained model. For example, it is similar to the extension of the VFL and is applied to the expansion of the machine learning model, incorporating features that existing participants do not possess.
vi. Cross-Silo Federated Learning – The training data distribution may be either in vertical or horizontal FL. Still, the number of participants is relatively small, and hence it ensures their availability across multiple rounds of training model (Yang et al., 2022).
vii. Cross-Device Federated Learning – It is used to support situations with a large number of participating devices and hence needs a special technique in the selection of clients and incentive designs to facilitate this (Bai et al., 2024).

Figure 3. A comprehensive categorization of FL architectures

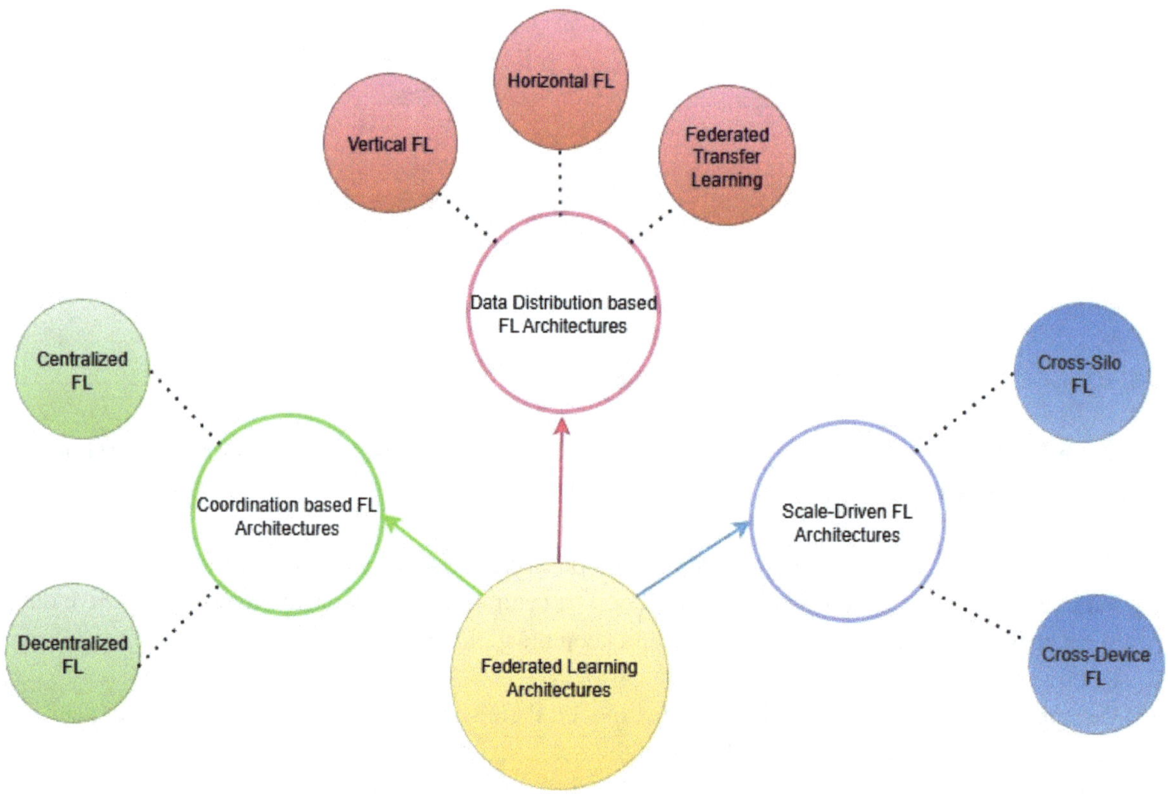

Evolution of Defense Mechanisms in Federated Learning

The evolution of defense methods in FL has developed with advances in secure model training, distributed intelligence and data privacy. Research in the early phase (2016-2018) mainly concentrated on centralised defence mechanisms like adversarial training and gradient obfuscation. As FL gained its popularity for privacy preservation, it became evident that those centralised defense methods were inadequate to handle its dispersed vulnerabilities. Thus, its defense research mechanism rapidly evolved between 2019 and 2025 to address the issues of non-IID distributions and ownership of decentralized data. The goal of its mid-phase (2019-2021) was to reduce vulnerabilities like gradient leakage and membership inference attacks in FL contexts by emphasising privacy-preserving strategies like Differential Privacy (DP) and Secure Aggregation. The focus in recent years (2022–2025) has been on hybrid and adaptive defence frameworks that use attention-based modelling, anomaly detection, and strong aggregation rules to react dynamically to changing attack patterns. These defense mechanisms have become context-aware, especially in the healthcare sector where data sensitivity and regulatory limitations are crucial. Figure 4 illustrates the evolution of denfense mechanisms in FL architecture.

Figure 4. Timeline illustrating the evolution of adversarial defense techniques in federated learning (2016–2025)

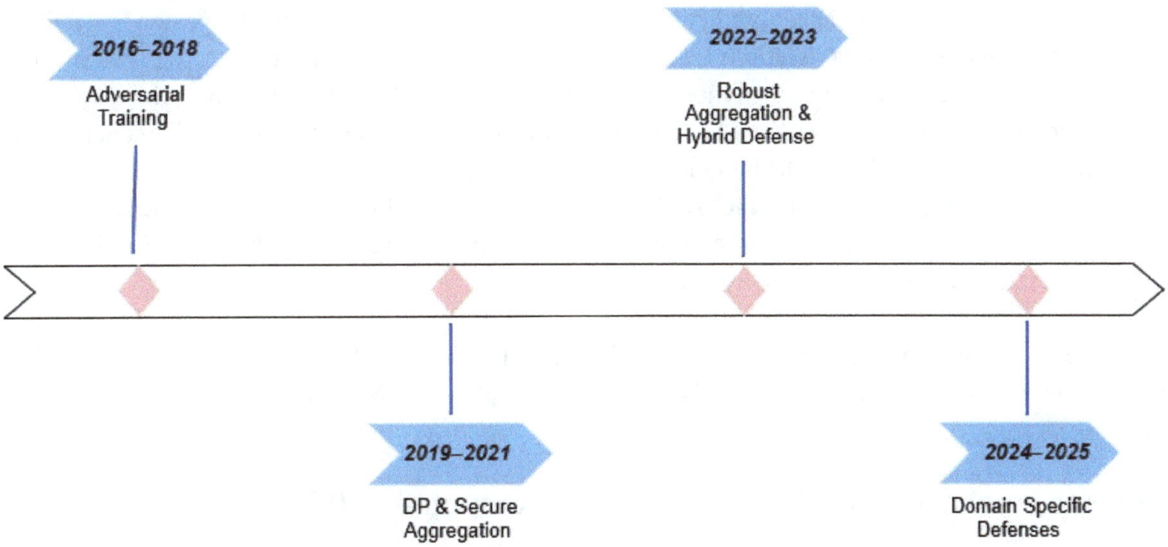

SAFETY AND PRIVACY ISSUES

The main goal of robustness in general FL applications, such as finance, IoTs, mobile edge computing networks, are scalability and protection against data and model poisoning in large and diverse environment. As these techniques didn't directly harm individual users, the traditional defense techniques have been adequate to preserve its confidence. Conversely, FL in healthcare is a highly sensitive and regulated ecosystem where adversarial vulnerabilities have far-reaching effects that go beyond model correctness. Medical data is by its very nature heterogeneous, high-dimensional, and unbalanced which is protected by strict privacy regulations like India's Digital Personal Data Protection Act (DPDP), the General Data Protection Regulation (GDPR) in the European Union, and the Health Insurance Portability and Accountability Act (HIPAA) in the United States. Therefore, in contrast to general FL, healthcare FL necessitates ethically sound and context-aware defence mechanisms that guarantee patient trust, clinical safety, and adherence to legal and technical requirements. In the following section, typical adversarial risks and their corresponding mitigation strategies in federated healthcare systems are described.

Membership Inference Attacks (MIA)

Although FL does not enable the exit of data in as it can leave the user device, but there are various methods of inferring the training data. Specifically, one can derive the sensitive information based on the model updates in a learning process. MIA is one of such attacks, which represents a basic privacy violation of a targeted device in trying to ascertain when a target performance belongs to the training set of data. The most notable uses of MIAs (Nookala, 2023) are the following:

- **Privacy invasion:** MIAs would disclose confidential information about the training data to possible foes. As an example, when an opponent learns about the particular record of the training dataset being employed by the cancer prediction model, he can deduce that a particular person has cancer.
- **Data censorship Data deletion:** Under the legal rule, right to be forgotten, the user is allowed to delete his or her data in a trained model. To countercheck this legal requirement, MIA is taken as a good tool to audit data privacy. As an example, the user can request deletion of their data, based on which MIA can change the model to confirm the deletion.
- **Background of enhanced attacks:** MIA can form the basis of more developed attacks on privacy, such as model extraction attacks, because it has the power to identify which samples that were utilized to train the data can be exploited further.

To defend against MIAs, a few defensive platforms such as Trusted Execution Environment (TEE), Differential Privacy scheme (DP), Secure Multiparty Computation (SMC), and Homomorphic Encryption (HE).

Defence mechanism 1 - Secure Multiparty Computation (SMC)

A cryptographic approach called SMC allows many multiple individuals to compute on resources without revealing any personal data to the other parties (Xu & Joshi, 2020). It enables two or more parties to concur in a bid to fully attain zero knowledge and, therefore, guarantees that each party does not know more than what they provided and received. In other situations, partial disclosure of knowledge is permissible if security guarantees have been upheld.

Basically, SMC operates on two fundamental principles:

- Correctness: All participants must receive a consistent and accurate outcome for the publicly shared computation.
- Confidentiality: No participant should learn anything about the other participants' inputs.

Types of SMC Protocols.

Though several unique protocols in SMC exist to enable secure communication among multiple participants, two primary types are discussed:

(a) **Yao Garbled Circuits.**

It was initially proposed by Andrew Yao in the 1980's which is the fundamental SMC technique (Zhou et al., 2025). Using this protocol, the garbler (one participant) constructs a circuit representing the desired computation and garbles (encrypts) it. This encrypted circuit is then sent to the evaluator (other participant), who evaluates the circuit securely without learning the participant's input. It supports secure communication between two participants with a constant number of communication rounds.

(b) **Secret Sharing.**

The Secret Sharing created by Shamir is a secret sharing protocol, and it is a standard cryptographic algorithm. It is rudimentary in concept that divides an input data (secret) into several shares and delivers them to participants (Tran et al., 2024). A single share does not tell the information of the actual data, but when the shares are combined, the secret could be reconstructed if they had enough shareholders. It is good to offer powerful security guarantees, but not that efficient in complex computations, since the overhead associated with communication between participants is very high.

Research Status of SMC.

Xu et al. (2019) enhance the privacy in FL by integrating the SMC protocol with Elliptic Curve Cryptography (ECC). The resultant framework enhances and achieves higher accuracy using the integer quantization technique, which transforms the model parameters from floating point to integers. Xu et al. (2019) proposed an approach that reduces the transmission expense and learning time of the SMC protocol. This approach supports only one round of encrypted data communication and ensures a smaller ciphertext size for the initial parameters.

Defence mechanism 2 - Differential Privacy (DP)

Differential Privacy (DP) is another way to defend against this attack, along with related methods like diversification and k-anonymity. These methods generate noise to the data of the updated device parameters and thereby making the data impossible to be retrieved by adversaries. However, the roots of these methods still need to require a choice among accuracy and privacy. DP has become a de facto standard to safeguard confidentiality of users in mathematical computations.

In Naseri et al. (2020), the defence mechanisms are broadly classified into three categories:

(i) Pre-publication techniques: Methods such as t-closeness, k-anonymity and l-diversity secure the security of users before publishing a dataset. These techniques could produce new information that couldn't be predicted by adversaries, even if they have complete access to the dataset.
(ii) Privacy during training: Techniques that protect the users' privacy during training. It allows multiple parties to collaborate by keeping the dataset of each party private with the help of SMC.
(iii) Differential privacy at different stages: Techniques that protect the users' privacy by DP at three different stages:

- Before training, by generating privacy-preserved datasets

- During training, by adding noise to the gradients to hide each contribution of the client
- After training, adding noise to the model outputs, so that adversaries couldn't extract sensitive information, and making the model resistant to MIA and model inversion attacks.

The participants of DP are Classified into two parts:

(a) Central differential privacy (CDP)- The participants trust the data curator (database holder) to preserve privacy (Truex et al., 2020). CDP ensures privacy by adding random noise either the primary information or the outcomes of queries conducted on it.
(b) Local differential privacy (LDP)- It preserves confidentiality even if the data curator is not a trustworthy one (Adnan et al., 2022). In addition to transmitting the replies to the main database, each participant encodes data. It should be carefully implemented, as it can lead to inaccurate results.

Research Status of DP.

Sun et al. (2020) proposed a potential technique which utilized DP to learn the decentralized medical data for the biggest and most intricate medical records. This distributed learning guaranteed strong privacy on the simulated real-world data. A new LDP mechanism was proposed in Xie et al. (2024) to address issues like the inconsideration of the difference in the range of weights. This novel mechanism allows local weight updates and avoids privacy degradation by the curse of dimensionality through parameter shuffling aggregation.

Defence mechanism 3 - Homomorphic encryption (HE)

Homomorphic encryption (HE) is a method for improving the security of information by performing computations on encrypted inputs to protect user data (Fang & Qian, 2021). Unlike DP protection, it ensures that the data can't be guessed by others. Also, it doesn't require a protocol among multiple parties or a trusted environment or artificial noise to ensure the privacy of data. HE performs arithmetic computations like HomoAdd or HomoMult on encrypted data without decryption. It comprises four important components as follows:

1. Key generation:
   Generates public-private key pairs (pk_i, sk_i) where $i \in \{1, \ldots, C\}$, C is the number of Users participated in the local training.
2. Encryption:
   Function that encrypts the message m to generate ciphertext c.
3. Evaluation:
   Generates the encrypted result c_{result} by applying the function f on encrypted data.
4. Decryption:
   Function that obtains the original message result m_{result} by decrypting c_{result}. If it is designed correctly, then $m_{result} = f(m)$.

Depending on the kind of supported arithmetic operations and the number of supported arithmetic operations that are undertaken on encrypted data, HE may be categorized into two broad categories such as partially HE (PHE) and fully HE (FHE). Although PHE only supports a single form of operation, i.e., addition or multiplication, it supports an infinite number of such operations. Since there are no limitations in FHE, it allows various kinds of operations with an unlimited number of arithmetic operations, and, therefore, it allows one to perform complex algorithms and functions on ciphertext.

(a) PHE: The most famous and widely adopted PHE approach is Paillier (Hijazi et al., 2023) encryption, which satisfies additive homomorphism and protects user privacy by enabling aggregation over encrypted data.
(b) FHE: It is employed to safeguard the global model's client confidentiality by permitting complicated function evaluation on encrypted data, as it supports complex computations like addition and multiplication (Mia & Amini, 2024).

Research Status of HE.

When implementing HE to the FL, it experiences a small chance of leakage at the process of the raw data level, and it is inefficient. Thus, it is necessary to discuss the optimization strategies of HE when applied to HE directly to the FL as follows:

(i) **Algorithmic Optimization.**

The algorithm-based optimization techniques are categorized based on different phases in FL as follows:

a. The model transition phase supports
    - **Quantization:** It aims to transform high-precision gradients to low-precision numbers by retaining critical information to reduce the network communication costs (Yang et al., 2024).
    - **Packing:** As each user batched the multiple local gradients into a single plaintext message before encryption, it is also called batching (Lian et al., 2022) and helps to reduce the communication cost while preserving privacy.
    - **Transmitted Parameter Selection (TPS)**: It allows users to transmit only a selected subset of its parameters to update, and the remaining parameters are used in future training iterations (Ku et al., 2022).
b. Similarly, the local training stage helps the Gradient Descent Optimization (GDO) method (Lin et al., 2025) to minimize the communication round without affecting the performance of the aggregated model. To minimize the amount of communication overhead, this method operates on the gradient descent algorithm optimization.
c. The Server Aggregation Phase contains a Lightweight Homomorphic Encryption Optimization strategy (Nguyen et al., 2024), which found that a lightweight HE is a good approach to reduce its overhead in cross-device FL, as IoT devices are resource-constrained.
d. The final Overall FL Phase supports the End-to-End Optimization (Xu et al., 2025) and Concurrent Training strategies (Wu et al., 2023). End-to-end optimization is able to attain zero leakage training of FL models with the encrypted user's local data, intermediate results, and the final ML model. The Concurrent Training strategy is used to improve the vertical federated ensemble decision trees by reducing their idle waiting. It parallelizes mechanisms like tree-based training along with cipher activities and minimizes the communication and computation cost.

(ii) **Hardware Optimization.**

As privacy-preserving methods lead to significant communication and computation costs, the design of hardware-based acceleration is more critical in FL. It includes

- Field Programmable Gate Arrays (FPGA) based – They are semiconductor-based integrated circuits that allow designers to adjust according to the emerging demands, along with speedup of the significant workloads (Khan & Qiming, 2025).
- GPU-based - It is a readily accessible hardware that will be utilized to speed up the training process of the ML models because of its parallel architecture (Chen et al., 2024).
- CPU-based – Instead of using specialized hardware like FPGA and GPU, Intel (Aziz et al., 2023) introduced the Intel HE acceleration library (HEXL) in 2021, which takes the benefits of both Intel AVX-512 instructions and SIMD features that are available on Intel CPUs.

(iii) **Hybrid Optimization.**

The hybrid approaches offer unique advantages to provide strong privacy along with improved system efficiency. Aziz et al. (2023) utilized two promising techniques, HE and DP. Thus, HE provides secure computations on cipher data, and DP allows a strong privacy guarantee with the help of noisy data. Li et al. (2023) proposed an efficient secure FL-based scheme using HE and secret sharing. While using secret sharing, the clients may provide incorrect subkeys, which may result in training failure, and this issue is handled by a fingerprint-based verification algorithm.

Defence mechanism 4 - Trusted Execution Environment (TEE)

Trusted Execution Environment (TEE) offers a secure, trusted environment to execute the federated learning process, which is only appropriate to the CPU devices and, therefore, can support a promising hardware-based option that can bridge both the gap between academic research and industry use. As it allows users to introduce computation tasks in both on-premises and off-premises data with the help of a trusted environment for execution, its computational overhead is low when compared to other secure computation techniques (Cao et al., 2024).

Research Status of TEE.

TEE-based secure computation protocols fall under two major categories, based on their computation framework:

(i) **Secure outsourced computation (SOC).**

This allows resource-limited data owners to outsource encrypted data to a single and powerful cloud server. Afterwards, an authorized client will run this SOC protocol within the cloud server to ensure the desired computation tasks, as a single cloud is an untrusted entity. Thus, privacy and integrity ensured by the cloud server couldn't learn any sensitive information and execution of tasks in a correct way, respectively.

Research Status of SOC.

Chen et al. (2020) established a secure and strong framework on the IoT devices under the non-IID data to curb leakage of the sensitive model parts. This is based on a soft clustering technique to classify its clients based on membership degree. Dong et al. (2020) proposed a training-integrity protocol; the training model didn't allow any illegal actions like delaying the local training process and tampering with the model locally.

(ii) **Secure distributed computation (SDC).**

The framework of SDC outsources the encrypted data to multiple servers. Within this, several slave nodes execute the computational tasks in a distributed manner under one master node, which oversees coordinating those computations. With the help of the SDC protocol, which is run between the server nodes and the data client, the master node sends the final output to the data client with the help of the intermediate results of the slave nodes. As compared to SOC, SDC is exposed to a larger attack, as both master and slave nodes may be malicious or semi-honest.

Research Status of SDC.

In Kalapaaking et al. (2022), edge servers were introduced to help the heterogeneous FL clients improve the global training process. To support this, the clients are selected by edge servers with the help of exploration-exploitation-based principles and which led the more client participation in the training process under TEE. The authors presented the secured aggregated structure with Intel Software Guard Extension (SGX) as a TEE one in Industrial Internet-of-Things (IIoTs) in Xia et al. (2023). Since the local models can be compromised by assailants, the SGX processor is used to host each blockchain node to carry out this aggregation in accordance. All the client edge servers in the cluster received this aggregate world model and confirmed its integrity by the blockchain.

Poisoning Attacks

By direct or indirect means, attackers have a significant influence on global models and do not allow them to converge their prediction results of FL or even modify them (Biggio et al., 2012). The mere collapse of the convergence of the global model is not done by the attackers alone, but also, they do it employing that they create a new objective to enhance the effectiveness and the sustainability of the attack. Regarding the attackers generating a poisoning model through modifications of the local model, there are model poisoning attacks and data poisoning attacks.

Even though data poisoning attacks are typical in ML models, the adversary must poison the training data of the specified number of devices that are joining the FL model so that they can compromise the accuracy of the global model. There are targeted and non-targeted adversary attacks. Through assistance, the adversaries attempt to worsen the precision of the international designation by obtaining sway on the forecasting of a subgroup of classes.

The first data poisoning attack, with respect to a support vector machine (SVM) model, a long time before the introduction of FL. In this, the authors on one machine exhausted the performance of the trained model using the poisoned data by flipping the training data labels. This extension of the approach is also effective in a distributed environment (Yang et al., 2023).

This attack can be classified into two types: (i) a clean label attack modifies the samples of the training set and introduces an injection of a backdoor into the global model (Gajbhiye et al., 2022). (ii) dirty label attack uses label flipping techniques, i.e., the attacker can change the label of the MNIST dataset a 1 to 3, and in most research on the defense mechanism, it is held as the default attack approach of poisoning attacks (Zhou et al., 2021).

In the case of data poisoning attacks, in model poisoning attacks, adversaries directly attempted to poison local models rather than through local data. These attacks have the primary purpose of making mistakes in the global model (Bagdasaryan et al., 2020). The competitors attempt to alter the local model parameters to worsen the performance of the global model by violating part of the devices involved. That is, through a model poisoning attack, the attackers will be able to directly update the local model parameters and upload this altered model to the server to poison the global model.

One such model poisoning attack is a Byzantine attack, which aims at interrupting the performance and accuracy of global models by altering the original parameters of the local model through sign flipping, introducing Gaussian noise, and poisoning the training data.

The objectives of the attacker in the poisoning attacks were to slow down the global model on all assignments or certain assignments. According to the intention of the attacker, it may be divided into three groups:

Targeted poisoning attack: It is used to decrease the performance of the global model on a particular task and not on other tasks. This attack is exemplified by a backdoor attack (Sun et al., 2023). The anonymity of the participating devices is presented in the model updating process in the FL process. With the same functionality, the backdoor attacks add a backdoor functionality to the group of participating devices in the global model. With the backdoor functionality, the assailants will not interfere with the quality of the global model, but they will mislabel the specific tasks. The severity of these attacks is determined by the rate of compromises between both affected devices and the model capacity of federated learning.

Semi-targeted poisoning attack: Unlike a targeted attack, the attacker intends to poison the global model in such a way that the samples having the source class would be classified as a class and not as a source class (Al Mallah et al., 2023). Thus, it would maximize its attack performance, and it may be used in numerous real-life scenarios, such as an attacker would want to send out an unwanted email advertising, so that it will be classified under a benign category rather than spam.

Untargeted poisoning attack: The main objective of the attacker is to break the convergence of the global model by compromising the performance of the model on every task (Yi et al., 2023). To do this, the simplest and simplest way is to introduce random noise to the local model. It renders the global model practically useless and guarantees its lack of availability. Since Byzantine attacks were unable to tailor their attacks to the global and subtask performance, it is categorised as an untargeted poisoning attack.

On the one hand, in FL, the number of clients participating in its training is high, which means that the defence mechanisms against poisoning attacks should be considered to ensure that all clients are reliable. It has a verification-based technique, model analysis, and byzantine robust aggregation.

Defence mechanism 1 - Model analysis

Model analysis: It houses numerous techniques, such as similarity-based techniques and performance evaluation-based methods, which have a valid assumption that there would be substantial dissimilarity between the innocent and wicked poisoned models.

(i) **Similarity-based method (SM).**

Using statistical techniques including Pearson Correlation Coefficient, Cosine Similarity, Euclidean Distance, and K-Means, it employs a comparable-based poisoned design identification approach. Based on these methods, this algorithm would measure the difference between the malicious and benign models

Research Status of SM.

Tian et al. (2022) utilized two core modules to aggregate semantic similarity-based head parameter aggregation while transferring knowledge from local to global model. It provided low computational overhead to FL clients as it fuses only partial parameters from the global and local headers before training. Cao et al. (2019) outlined the problem of datasets generated by heterogeneous IoT sensors that have a statistical difference, thus causing quality reduction by using the conventional FedAvg method.

(ii) **Performance evaluation (PE).**

This mechanism separates the two types of detection of the attacks of poisoning to evaluate the local model parameters and evaluate the global model.

(a) **Evaluation for the local model.**

That is the simple method to counter model poisoning attacks through the analysis of client submissions. It is going to test the local models that have been uploaded by the clients using the validation dataset.

Research Status of Evaluation for the local model.

Sharma et al. (2023) hypothesized that the number of attackers affected the success rate of the attacks. They suggested the filtering defence mechanism, where it can remove the poisoned local models of malicious clients in training with this mechanism. In Chen et al. (2021), a stateful algorithm is applied to reduce the contribution of the malicious clients by assigning reputation scores to the participating clients. The attribute of fairness in this algorithm is applicable to enable the benign clients to make input to the global model.

(b) **Evaluation for the global model.**

This method is employed to test the global model to identify the malicious updates. Once the global model has been updated in each round, it is checked to determine whether it has been influenced in terms of performance.

Research Status of Evaluation for the global model.

The Byzantine-tolerant technique-based defence strategy is used in Cao et al. (2022) to evaluate the global model with the consensus solution. It preserves the performance of the learning task by including all benign models and also maintains the robustness of the system. Since one global model is subject to attacks, Allouah et al. (2024) presented a framework that is resistant to poisoning attacks in which there is a limited number of malicious clients. It separates the clients into N groups, and majority voting amongst the global models of groups to determine the labels of the test inputs.

Defence mechanism 2 - Byzantine robust aggregation (BRA)

Byzantine robust aggregation (BRA) is a passive defense mechanism that is employed to mitigate the poisoning attack by reassessing the strategy of aggregation of the global model. It is also concisely subdivided into three classes such as gradient clipping, elimination of extreme values, and differential privacy.

(i) **Gradient clipping.**

This method is exploited to establish some sort of threshold for the model parameters and eliminate all the parameters that are beyond the threshold. It can be done by moderating the gradients either by truncating or compressing them. It supports two primary approaches, like value-based clipping that trims the gradients by considering their absolute values, and norm-based clipping that trims the gradients according to the magnitude of the gradient vector. In prior, if any gradient exceeds the limit the it is cut down to the set minimum or maximum value, and in later, the entire gradient vector should be adjusted proportionally if the norm (L1 or L2 norm) of the gradient vector exceeds a predefined threshold.

Research Status of Gradient clipping.

The authors present in Yang et al. (2024) a pre-aggregation clipping scheme that dynamically changes either clipping thresholds or the input gradients. This relies only on standard robustness parameters like the tolerable fraction of adversarial workers. Yang et. al. also utilized a dynamic clipping along with gradient perturbation (Colosimo & De Rango, 2023). Using these techniques, clients can dynamically trim the gradients along with the corresponding noise scales based on the magnitude of each gradient update are adaptively added to defend threats.

(ii) **Removal of extreme values.**

To defend against poisoning attacks, this mechanism is used to remove the extreme values from the model parameters.

Research Status of Removal of extreme values.

In Yin et al. (2018), the Krum-based algorithm is used to address Byzantine anomalies. Basically, Krum is a distance-based methodology, which operates on a model with the least Euclidean distance to the rest of the model to revise the global model, and the rest of the models are eliminated. The distributed learning algorithm was developed by Miao et al. (2022) to defend against Byzantine failures. It was based on two gradient descent algorithms, like trimmed mean and median operations, to achieve optimal statistical performance. In the trimmed mean, every parameter of all local model updates is deleted, and only the remaining are used to update the global model. In the median algorithm is used to update the global model is updated with the median of all the local model updates.

(iii) **Differential privacy (DP).**

Even though DP is initially designed for user privacy protection in FL, it is now used as a defensive mechanism against poisoning attacks.

Research Status of DP.

Shi et al. (2025) utilized a Clip Norm Decay (CND), which is a DP-based defensive mechanism that reduces the injected noise by decreasing the size of the clipping threshold window of the local model updates of the whole training process. Lai et al. (2023) utilized two algorithms to effectively defend poisoning attacks even with high infection rates. For this, they introduced a Gaussian-based DP mechanism which balances the data privacy with model availability. Along with that, they integrated a norm-based detection method to detect attacks that degrade the model's availability.

Defence mechanism 3 - Verification-based method (VM)

Verification-based method (VM) - In addition to the above-mentioned mechanisms, there are numerous other methods of defending against poisoning attacks in the following way.

Research Status of VM.

Xu and Shu (2024) utilized two phases like relative and absolute, to mitigate poisoning attacks. In the relative phase, they compared the local models of the user participants. In the absolute phase, verifiable testing data is prepared in advance, and with the help of that, attackers are identified. The authors proposed a novel defence mechanism from the variance minimization approach. In this method, the regression model is trained by uploading gradients and the objective of reduce the difference between all local updates. It would be able to reduce the impact of suspicious attackers in low time consumption.

Table 2 illustrates the comparative analysis of attack strategies, defense mechanisms, and challenges in federated learning.

Table 2. Comparative analysis of attack strategies and defense mechanisms in FL

Attack Category	Reference	Year	Attack Strategy	Defense mechanisms	Key Outcome	Challenges
MIA	Xu et al. (2019)	2024	White-box Inversion and inference attacks	SMC + Integer quantization + Elliptic Curve Cryptography (ECC)	Superior training speed and accuracy compared to existing SMC and DP	Data heterogeneity
	El Ouadrhiri & Abdelhadi (2022)	2019	parameter interaction	SMC	Reduces training time and communication overhead for large number of parameters	Not suitable for vertical federated learning
	Sun et al. (2020)	2022	Multiple instance learning	DP	Enhanced confidentiality with quantifiable privacy	Data heterogeneity
	Xie et al. (2024)	2021	Curse of dimensionality due to query iterations of FL	DP	Enhanced privacy/ utility trade-off	Doesn't accelerate the practical applications
	Wang et al. (2024)	2023	Collusion attack of curious aggregators	HE+DP	Trade-off among computation, accuracy, and privacy	Data management with an increasing participant count
	Li et al. (2023)	2024	Submission of the wrong subkey during secret sharing	HE+ SMC	Higher security with shorter keys and lower encryption overhead	Client heterogeneity in data, compute, and bandwidth
	Chen et al. (2020)	2024	Honest-but-curious attacks	TEE- SOC	Data heterogeneity and robustness with low client overhead	Not time-efficient and fluctuations during convergence
	Dong et al. (2020)	2020	Injection of false training results	TEE- SOC	Supports deep learning in adversarial domains	Data trustworthiness
	Kalapaaking et al. (2022)	2020	Client stragglers hinder training	TEE- SDC	Enhanced client participation and reduced convergence time	Data heterogeneity
	Xia et al. (2023)	2023	Corruption of the global model by tampered local models	TEE- SDC	Maintain similar processing time along with integrity	Heterogeneous task handling
Poisoning Attacks	Tian et al. (2022)	2024	Public data reliance and data/system heterogeneity	Model analysis-SM	Supports heterogeneous local models with guaranteed convergence	Aggregation by class and real-world applicability
	Cao et al. (2019)	2022	Increased computation and network load by non-IID data handling	Model analysis-SM	Reduced distribution disturbance	Risks of overfitting to synthetic patterns

continued on following page

Table 2. Continued

Attack Category	Reference	Year	Attack Strategy	Defense mechanisms	Key Outcome	Challenges
	Sharma et al. (2023)	2019	Collusion of more than one attacker to inject false training samples	Model analysis-PE -Evaluation for local model	Lowers the attack success rate by identifying honest users	Vulnerability to multi-task poisoning attacks and limited scalability
	Chen et al. (2021)	2023	Manipulating the sign of the gradient updates	Model analysis-PE -Evaluation for local model	Robust against white-box attackers	Incompatible with encrypted gradients and asynchronous settings.
	Cao et al. (2022)	2021	Removal of model risks by discarding benign data.	Model analysis-PE -Evaluation for global model	Best global accuracy with layer-wise equalization in non-IID settings	Hard filtering and naive consensus hurt model integrity under heterogeneity
	Allouah et al. (2024)	2022	Vulnerability of advanced poisoning attacks	Model analysis-PE -Evaluation for global model	Provably unaffected predictions despite bounded malicious clients	Security bounds derived independently of prior knowledge of the task
	Yang et al. (2024)	2025	Static gradient clipping yields inconsistent robustness across attacks	BRA- Gradient clipping	Enhanced robustness and faster convergence in heterogeneous FL	Lack of practical and real-world conditions
	Colosimo & De Rango (2023)	2024	Sharing gradients risks data leakage	BRA- Gradient clipping	Maintains accuracy and boosts privacy	Need to balance privacy and performance
	Yin et al. (2018)	2023	Vulnerability of aggregation under Byzantine failures	BRA- Removal of extreme values	Robustness under varying numbers of attackers	Limited scope of validation under real-world scenarios
	Maio et al. (2022)	2021	Nodes may act arbitrarily under decentralized environment	BRA- Removal of extreme values	Optimal error rates for strongly convex losses	Lack applicability to distributed settings
	Shi et al. (2025)	2022	Defending backdoor attacks harms model performance	BRA- DP	Improved robustness with minimal utility loss	Need to tune under diverse attack scenarios
	Lai et al. (2023)	2025	Collaborative nature of FL heightens vulnerability to data leakage	BRA- DP	Robust to high poisoning rates	Lack of evaluation on complex attacks and uneven data scenarios
	Xu & Shu (2024)	2023	Injection of malicious local models to corrupt the global model	VM	Achieves strong defense with faster attacker elimination	Limited to IID settings
		2024	Outlier detection misclassifies benign updates in non-IID FL	VM	Balanced robustness and efficiency by reducing complexity	Lack of robust aggregation in highly heterogeneous data distributions

Apart from the comparative analysis shown in Table 2, Figure 5 offers a conceptual flow diagram that shows how attackers take advantage of particular vulnerability, how defences mitigate these risks, and the residual risks that still exist in healthcare federated learning.

Figure 5. Integrated attack–defense–impact conceptual flow in healthcare federated learning

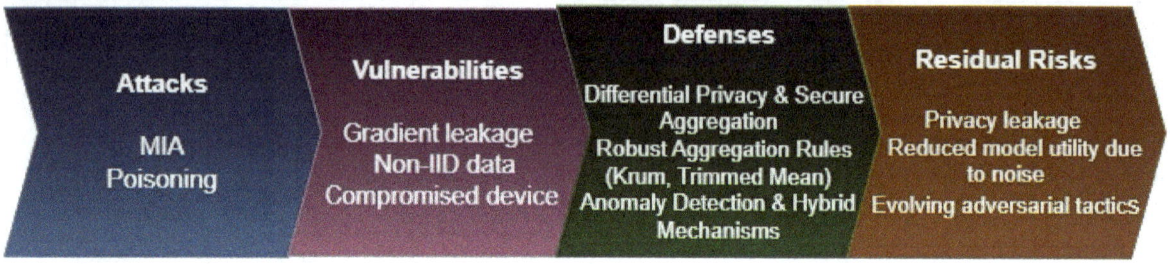

Attack vectors, underlying vulnerabilities, defensive measures, and residual affects (risks) that remain after mitigation are all shown in the figure in an end-to-end relationship. The causal flow and its consequent impacts on model privacy and robustness are both provided by this integrated view.

OPEN RESEARCH CHALLENGES AND FUTURE DIRECTIONS

The key challenge in FL based healthcare system is most of the existing security and privacy preserving techniques act like "black-box". This leads to the defense cannot be easily understood by the healthcare experts. Thus, future research must focus on designing interpretable defense mechanisms with explainable AI-based technologies. Another primary research challenge is the design of domain-specific strategies for healthcare data. As generic adversarial defenses are not sufficient, medical datasets often support unique properties like temporal dependencies, high dimensionality, and class imbalance. To ensure robustness in the healthcare training process, future research must integrate clinical guidelines, patient safety requirements, and domain knowledge.

While technical defenses against adversarial attacks in healthcare FL remain the primary focus, ethical dimensions cannot be ignored. Similarly, secure aggregation methods may increase system complexity. Furthermore, regulatory compliance ensures that privacy-preserving strategies are implemented.

Practical Implementation and Governance Takeaways

Beyond model design and algorithmic stability, FL presents a numerous implementation issue when used in healthcare environment. The fragmentation of healthcare data across many imaging formats, laboratory standards, and hospital information systems makes difficult in achieving interoperability and consistent data representation. Additionally, smaller medical institutions may find their limited resources strained by the computational and communication cost associated with federated aggregation. Developing scalable, modular, and lightweight FL systems that can function in diverse and resource-constrained clinical environments is essential to overcoming these implementation hurdles.

The foundation of a reliable healthcare FL implementation lies in governance and regulatory compliance, which extends beyond technical integration. Strict adherence to data protection and privacy laws is necessary due to the sensitive nature of medical data. Equally important is ethical monitoring, which calls for explicit patient consent procedures, transparent decision-making processes, and institutional accountability for international partnerships.

Research on FL must be translated into sustainable clinical practice using a structured governance paradigm that balances institutional accountability with technological innovation. To supervise the entire FL model deployment lifecycle, hospitals and research networks should establish cross-functional governance committees made up of clinicians, data scientists, and legal counsel. Before a federated model is used in production, these committees might create standard operating procedures (SOPs) for data validation, model versioning, and evaluation.

CONCLUSION

Healthcare FL systems promise collaborative intelligence without sacrificing the privacy of sensitive patient data. The adversarial threats like Membership Inference Attacks and data poisoning impose profound risks not only on patient confidentiality but also to the accuracy of clinical decisions. This chapter has provided a structured roadmap of a comprehensive analysis of these threats and defenses, contextualized within healthcare's unique challenges. Ultimately, the mission is to enable responsible AI in healthcare by synthesizing the current literature, critically evaluating the defensive mechanisms, and proposing a roadmap for future research. This chapter makes a significant contribution toward robust, secure, and trustworthy federated healthcare systems.

REFERENCES

Adnan, M., Kalra, S., Cresswell, J. C., Taylor, G. W., & Tizhoosh, H. R. (2022). Federated learning and differential privacy for medical image analysis. *Scientific Reports*, *12*(1), 1953. DOI: 10.1038/s41598-022-05539-7

Al Mallah, R., Lopez, D., Badu-Marfo, G., & Farooq, B. (2023). Untargeted poisoning attack detection in federated learning via behavior attestational. *IEEE Access : Practical Innovations, Open Solutions*, *11*, 125064–125079. DOI: 10.1109/ACCESS.2023.3330144

Albshaier, L., Almarri, S., & Albuali, A. (2025). Federated learning for cloud and edge security: A systematic review of challenges and AI opportunities. *Electronics (Basel)*, *14*(5), 1019. DOI: 10.3390/electronics14051019

Allouah, Y., Guerraoui, R., Gupta, N., Jellouli, A., Rizk, G., & Stephan, J. (2024). Adaptive gradient clipping for robust federated learning. *arXiv preprint arXiv:2405.14432.*

Amin, M. S., Ahmad, S., & Loh, W. K. (2025). Federated learning for healthcare 5.0: A comprehensive survey, taxonomy, challenges, and solutions. *Soft Computing*, *29*(2), 673–700. DOI: 10.1007/s00500-025-10508-z

. Amritanjali, & Gupta, R. (2025, January). Federated Learning for Privacy Preserving Intelligent Healthcare Application to Breast Cancer Detection. In *Proceedings of the 26th International Conference on Distributed Computing and Networking* (pp. 302-306).

Aziz, R., Banerjee, S., Bouzefrane, S., & Le Vinh, T. (2023). Exploring homomorphic encryption and differential privacy techniques towards secure federated learning paradigm. *Future Internet*, *15*(9), 310. DOI: 10.3390/fi15090310

Bagdasaryan, E., Veit, A., Hua, Y., Estrin, D., & Shmatikov, V. (2020, June). How to backdoor federated learning. In *International conference on artificial intelligence and statistics* (pp. 2938-2948). PMLR.

Bai, L., Hu, H., Ye, Q., Li, H., Wang, L., & Xu, J. (2024). Membership inference attacks and defenses in federated learning: A survey. *ACM Computing Surveys*, *57*(4), 1–35. DOI: 10.1145/3704633

Biggio, B., Nelson, B., & Laskov, P. (2012). Poisoning attacks against support vector machines. *arXiv preprint arXiv:1206.6389.*

Cao, D., Chang, S., Lin, Z., Liu, G., & Sun, D. (2019, December). Understanding distributed poisoning attack in federated learning. In *2019 IEEE 25th international conference on parallel and distributed systems (ICPADS)* (pp. 233-239). IEEE. DOI: 10.1109/ICPADS47876.2019.00042

Cao, X., Zhang, Z., Jia, J., & Gong, N. Z. (2022). Flcert: Provably secure federated learning against poisoning attacks. *IEEE Transactions on Information Forensics and Security*, *17*, 3691–3705. DOI: 10.1109/TIFS.2022.3212174

Cao, Y., Zhang, J., Zhao, Y., Su, P., & Huang, H. (2024). SRFL: A Secure & Robust Federated Learning framework for IoT with trusted execution environments. *Expert Systems with Applications*, *239*, 122410. DOI: 10.1016/j.eswa.2023.122410

Chen, L. Y., Chiu, T. C., Pang, A. C., & Cheng, L. C. (2021, December). Fedequal: Defending model poisoning attacks in heterogeneous federated learning. In *2021 IEEE Global Communications Conference (GLOBECOM)* (pp. 1-6). IEEE. DOI: 10.1109/GLOBECOM46510.2021.9685082

Chen, Y., Luo, F., Li, T., Xiang, T., Liu, Z., & Li, J. (2020). A training-integrity privacy-preserving federated learning scheme with trusted execution environment. *Information Sciences, 522*, 69–79. DOI: 10.1016/j.ins.2020.02.037

Chen, Z., Gu, Z., Lu, Y., Ren, X., Zhong, R., Lu, W. J., & Xie, Y. (2024). SAFE: A Scalable Homomorphic Encryption Accelerator for Vertical Federated Learning. *IEEE Transactions on Computer-Aided Design of Integrated Circuits and Systems.*

Colosimo, F., & De Rango, F. (2023, October). Median-krum: A joint distance-statistical based byzantine-robust algorithm in federated learning. In *Proceedings of the Int'l ACM Symposium on Mobility Management and Wireless Access* (pp. 61-68). DOI: 10.1145/3616390.3618283

Dong, S., Zeng, D., Gu, L., & Guo, S. (2020, December). Offloading federated learning task to edge computing with trust execution environment. In *2020 IEEE 17th International Conference on Mobile Ad Hoc and Sensor Systems (MASS)* (pp. 491-496). IEEE. DOI: 10.1109/MASS50613.2020.00066

El Ouadrhiri, A., & Abdelhadi, A. (2022). Differential privacy for deep and federated learning: A survey. *IEEE Access : Practical Innovations, Open Solutions, 10*, 22359–22380. DOI: 10.1109/ACCESS.2022.3151670

Fang, H., & Qian, Q. (2021). Privacy preserving machine learning with homomorphic encryption and federated learning. *Future Internet, 13*(4), 94. DOI: 10.3390/fi13040094

Gajbhiye, S., Singh, P., & Gupta, S. (2022, December). Data poisoning attack by label flipping on splitfed learning. In *International Conference on Recent Trends in Image Processing and Pattern Recognition* (pp. 391-405). Cham: Springer Nature Switzerland.

Geyer, R. C., Klein, T., & Nabi, M. (2017). Differentially private federated learning: A client level perspective. *arXiv preprint arXiv:1712.07557.*

Hijazi, N. M., Aloqaily, M., Guizani, M., Ouni, B., & Karray, F. (2023). Secure federated learning with fully homomorphic encryption for iot communications. *IEEE Internet of Things Journal, 11*(3), 4289–4300. DOI: 10.1109/JIOT.2023.3302065

Huang, C., Huang, J., & Liu, X. (2022). Cross-silo federated learning: Challenges and opportunities. *arXiv preprint arXiv:2206.12949.*

Kalapaaking, A. P., Khalil, I., Rahman, M. S., Atiquzzaman, M., Yi, X., & Almashor, M. (2022). Blockchain-based federated learning with secure aggregation in trusted execution environment for internet-of-things. *IEEE Transactions on Industrial Informatics, 19*(2), 1703–1714. DOI: 10.1109/TII.2022.3170348

Khan, S., & Qiming, H. (2025). GPU-accelerated homomorphic encryption computing: Empowering federated learning in IoV. *Neural Computing & Applications, 37*(16), 1–30. DOI: 10.1007/s00521-025-11099-4

Ku, H., Susilo, W., Zhang, Y., Liu, W., & Zhang, M. (2022). Privacy-preserving federated learning in medical diagnosis with homomorphic re-encryption. *Computer Standards & Interfaces*, *80*, 103583. DOI: 10.1016/j.csi.2021.103583

Lai, Y. C., Lin, J. Y., Lin, Y. D., Hwang, R. H., Lin, P. C., Wu, H. K., & Chen, C. K. (2023). Two-phase defense against poisoning attacks on federated learning-based intrusion detection. *Computers & Security*, *129*, 103205. DOI: 10.1016/j.cose.2023.103205

Li, M., Xu, P., Hu, J., Tang, Z., & Yang, G. (2025). From challenges and pitfalls to recommendations and opportunities: Implementing federated learning in healthcare. *Medical Image Analysis*, *101*, 103497. DOI: 10.1016/j.media.2025.103497

Li, X., Zhao, B., Yang, G., Xiang, T., Weng, J., & Deng, R. H. (2023). A survey of secure computation using trusted execution environments. *arXiv preprint arXiv:2302.12150.*

Lian, Z., Wang, W., Huang, H., & Su, C. (2022). Layer-based communication-efficient federated learning with privacy preservation. *IEICE Transactions on Information and Systems*, *105*(2), 256–263. DOI: 10.1587/transinf.2021BCP0006

Lin, J., Chen, J., Xiong, J., Jiao, D., Zhao, W., & Xiang, Y. (2025). A Lightweight Privacy-Preserving Federated Learning Framework for Heterogeneity-Resilient Skin Cancer Diagnosis. *IEEE Journal of Biomedical and Health Informatics*, 1–13. DOI: 10.1109/JBHI.2025.3578125

Mammen, P. M. (2021). Federated learning: Opportunities and challenges. *arXiv preprint arXiv:2101.05428.*

McMahan, B., Moore, E., Ramage, D., Hampson, S., & Arcas, B. A. (2017, April). Communication-efficient learning of deep networks from decentralized data. In *Artificial intelligence and statistics* (pp. 1273–1282). PMLR.

Mia, M. J., & Amini, M. H. (2024). QuanCrypt-FL: Quantized Homomorphic Encryption with Pruning for Secure Federated Learning. *arXiv preprint arXiv:2411.05260.*

Miao, L., Yang, W., Hu, R., Li, L., & Huang, L. (2022, May). Against backdoor attacks in federated learning with differential privacy. In *ICASSP 2022-2022 IEEE International Conference on Acoustics, Speech and Signal Processing (ICASSP)* (pp. 2999-3003). IEEE. DOI: 10.1109/ICASSP43922.2022.9747653

Naseri, M., Hayes, J., & De Cristofaro, E. (2020). Local and central differential privacy for robustness and privacy in federated learning. *arXiv preprint arXiv:2009.03561.*

Ngoupayou Limbepe, Z., Gai, K., & Yu, J. (2025). Blockchain-based privacy-enhancing federated learning in smart healthcare: A survey. *Blockchains*, *3*(1), 1. DOI: 10.3390/blockchains3010001

Nguyen, C. H., Manh, B. D., Hoang, D. T., Nguyen, D. N., & Dutkiewicz, E. (2024, October). Towards Secure AI-empowered Vehicular Networks: A Federated Learning Approach using Homomorphic Encryption. In *2024 IEEE 100th Vehicular Technology Conference (VTC2024-Fall)* (pp. 1-6). IEEE. DOI: 10.1109/VTC2024-Fall63153.2024.10757744

Nookala, G. (2023). Secure multiparty computation (SMC) for privacy-preserving data analysis. *Journal of Big Data and Smart Systems*, *4*(1).

Saraswat, D., Bhattacharya, P., Verma, A., Prasad, V. K., Tanwar, S., Sharma, G., Pitshou, N., & Sharma, R. (2022). Explainable AI for healthcare 5.0: Opportunities and challenges. *IEEE Access : Practical Innovations, Open Solutions*, *10*, 84486–84517. DOI: 10.1109/ACCESS.2022.3197671

Sharma, A., Chen, W., Zhao, J., Qiu, Q., Bagchi, S., & Chaterji, S. (2023, July). Flair: Defense against model poisoning attack in federated learning. In *Proceedings of the 2023 ACM Asia Conference on Computer and Communications Security* (pp. 553-566). DOI: 10.1145/3579856.3582836

Shi, J., Wang, W., Hu, Y., & Lin, Y. (2025). FLDP-DM: Defense Method Against Poisoning Attacks with Local Differential Privacy in Federated Learning Systems. *IEEE Transactions on Cognitive Communications and Networking*.

Sun, L., Qian, J., & Chen, X. (2020). LDP-FL: Practical private aggregation in federated learning with local differential privacy. *arXiv preprint arXiv:2007.15789*.

Sun, Y., Ochiai, H., & Sakuma, J. (2023). How the Target Matters: Semi-Targeted Model Poisoning Attack on Federated Learning. *Authorea Preprints*.

Tian, P., Liao, W., Yu, W., & Blasch, E. (2022). WSCC: A weight-similarity-based client clustering approach for non-IID federated learning. *IEEE Internet of Things Journal*, *9*(20), 20243–20256. DOI: 10.1109/JIOT.2022.3175149

Tran, A. T., Luong, T. D., & Pham, X. S. (2024). Privacy-preserving deep learning model with integer quantization and secure multi-party computation. *Annals of Operations Research*, •••, 1–21. DOI: 10.1007/s10479-024-06151-w

Truex, S., Liu, L., Chow, K. H., Gursoy, M. E., & Wei, W. (2020, April). LDP-Fed: Federated learning with local differential privacy. In *Proceedings of the third ACM international workshop on edge systems, analytics and networking* (pp. 61-66). DOI: 10.1145/3378679.3394533

Wang, C., Sun, Z., & Lu, J. (2024, July). A Secure and Efficient Federated Learning Scheme Based on Homomorphic Encryption and Secret Sharing. In *2024 7th International Conference on Computer Information Science and Application Technology (CISAT)* (pp. 1170-1175). IEEE. DOI: 10.1109/CISAT62382.2024.10695339

Wazid, M., Das, A. K., Mohd, N., & Park, Y. (2022). Healthcare 5.0 security framework: Applications, issues and future research directions. *IEEE Access : Practical Innovations, Open Solutions*, *10*, 129429–129442. DOI: 10.1109/ACCESS.2022.3228505

Wu, G., He, Q., Jiang, J., Zhang, Z., Shi, Y., Long, X., Jiang, L., Li, S., Xie, Y., Wei, C., Zhao, Y., Yan, Y., Zhang, H., & Zou, Y. (2023). E-booster: A field-programmable gate array-based accelerator for secure tree boosting using additively homomorphic encryption. *IEEE Micro*, *43*(5), 88–96. DOI: 10.1109/MM.2023.3293845

Xia, G., Chen, J., Yu, C., & Ma, J. (2023). Poisoning attacks in federated learning: A survey. *IEEE Access : Practical Innovations, Open Solutions*, *11*, 10708–10722. DOI: 10.1109/ACCESS.2023.3238823

Xie, Q., Jiang, S., Jiang, L., Huang, Y., Zhao, Z., Khan, S., Dai, W., Liu, Z., & Wu, K. (2024). Efficiency optimization techniques in privacy-preserving federated learning with homomorphic encryption: A brief survey. *IEEE Internet of Things Journal, 11*(14), 24569–24580. DOI: 10.1109/JIOT.2024.3382875

Xu, H., & Shu, T. (2024). Defending against model poisoning attack in federated learning: A variance-minimization approach. *Journal of Information Security and Applications, 82*, 103744. DOI: 10.1016/j.jisa.2024.103744

Xu, R., Baracaldo, N., Zhou, Y., Anwar, A., & Ludwig, H. (2019, November). Hybridalpha: An efficient approach for privacy-preserving federated learning. In *Proceedings of the 12th ACM workshop on artificial intelligence and security* (pp. 13-23). DOI: 10.1007/978-3-030-24271-8_2

Xu, R., & Joshi, J. (2020, October). Revisiting secure computation using functional encryption: Opportunities and research directions. In *2020 Second IEEE International Conference on Trust, Privacy and Security in Intelligent Systems and Applications (TPS-ISA)* (pp. 226-235). IEEE. DOI: 10.1109/TPS-ISA50397.2020.00038

Xu, Z., Hsieh, Y. T., Zhang, Z., Roth, H. R., Chen, C., Cheng, Y., & Feng, A. (2025). Secure Federated XGBoost with CUDA-accelerated Homomorphic Encryption via NVIDIA FLARE. *arXiv preprint arXiv:2504.03909*. DOI: 10.1109/CAI64502.2025.00222

Yang, C., Hang, S., Ding, Y., Li, C., Liang, H., & Liu, Z. (2024, July). Gradient leakage defense in federated learning using gradient perturbation-based dynamic clipping. In *2024 IEEE International Conference on Web Services (ICWS)* (pp. 178-187). IEEE. DOI: 10.1109/ICWS62655.2024.00039

Yang, J., Zheng, J., Baker, T., Tang, S., Tan, Y. A., & Zhang, Q. (2023). Clean-label poisoning attacks on federated learning for IoT. *Expert Systems: International Journal of Knowledge Engineering and Neural Networks, 40*(5), e13161. DOI: 10.1111/exsy.13161

Yang, L., Cai, S., Chai, D., Zhang, J., Tian, H., Jin, Y., . . . Yang, Q. (2024). PackVFL: Efficient HE Packing for Vertical Federated Learning. *arXiv preprint arXiv:2405.00482*.

Yang, Q., Liu, Y., Chen, T., & Tong, Y. (2019). Federated machine learning: Concept and applications. [TIST]. *ACM Transactions on Intelligent Systems and Technology, 10*(2), 1–19. DOI: 10.1145/3298981

Yang, W., Wang, N., Guan, Z., Wu, L., Du, X., & Guizani, M. (2022). A practical cross-device federated learning framework over 5g networks. *IEEE Wireless Communications, 29*(6), 128–134. DOI: 10.1109/MWC.005.2100435

Yi, L., Yu, H., Shi, Z., Wang, G., Liu, X., Cui, L., & Li, X. (2023). FedSSA: Semantic similarity-based aggregation for efficient model-heterogeneous personalized federated learning. *arXiv preprint arXiv:2312.09006*.

Yin, D., Chen, Y., Kannan, R., & Bartlett, P. (2018, July). Byzantine-robust distributed learning: Towards optimal statistical rates. In *International conference on machine learning* (pp. 5650-5659). Pmlr.

Zhou, S., Wang, L., Chen, L., Wang, Y., & Yuan, K. (2025). Group verifiable secure aggregate federated learning based on secret sharing. *Scientific Reports, 15*(1), 9712. DOI: 10.1038/s41598-025-94478-0

Zhou, X., Xu, M., Wu, Y., & Zheng, N. (2021). Deep model poisoning attack on federated learning. *Future Internet*, *13*(3), 73. DOI: 10.3390/fi13030073

Chapter 8
Federated Adversarial Transfer Learning:
Opportunities and Risks

Sanjeev Kumar
https://orcid.org/0000-0002-9553-0068
Swami Keshvanand Institute of Technology, Management, and Gramothan, India

Geeta Tiwari
https://orcid.org/0009-0003-6220-7007
Poornima College of Engineering, India

Laxmikant Sagar
https://orcid.org/0000-0002-9434-161X
Sharda University, India

Muhammad Attique Khan
https://orcid.org/0009-0001-2023-6980
Prince Mohammad bin Fahd University, Saudi Arabia

ABSTRACT

Federated Learning (FL) allows multiple parties to train a model on their local data source without exchanging raw data. When combined with FL, it provides a strong ability involving knowledge transfer from similar tasks with small data. This chapter reviews the ever-emerging field of Federated Adversarial Transfer Learning (FATL), investigating its possible applications and explaining some of its intrinsic weaknesses. We will study the effects of adversarial examples, model poisoning and backdoor attacks on the transfer learning dynamics in federated environments. We conduct a thorough literature review, outline threat modeling of the FATL scenarios. In summary, our main observations show that FATL boosts generalization and convergence speed, but also exterior dangers when the source models or datasets are not trusted. In addition, traditional defense methods in FL are usually ineffective in the presence of adversarial transfer. In conclusion, FATL provides significant advantages for decentralized AI systems, but with those advantages comes an entirely new threat.

DOI: 10.4018/979-8-3373-6224-3.ch008

1. INTRODUCTION

Federated Learning (FL) is a distributed learning paradigm aimed at training machine learning models across decentralized devices or organizations without sharing their raw data. Rather than centralizing data, each client device trains a local model on its private dataset and shares only the model updates (such as weights or gradients) with a central server (Peng et al., 2019; Yi et al., 2023). The server then amalgamates these updates usually using algorithms such as Stochastic Gradient Descent (SGD) in order to create a shared global model.

Such a setup provides a much stronger data privacy and regulation friendly environment, which is why FL is clearly a suitable candidate for health care, finance, smart homes, and mobile computing applications. In other words, hospitals can collaborate to train diagnostic models without revealing patient records, or smartphones can work together to improve voice assistants without sending user data off-device. On the other hand, FL encounters several challenges, such as non-independent and identically distributed (non-IID) data distribution, limited computational resources on edge devices, and malicious participants.

1.1. Role and Importance of Transfer Learning in FL

Transfer Learning (TL) is the reuse of knowledge gained while solving one problem to a different but related problem. TL is pivotal in solving some of the central problems in the context of FL. For one, client devices may have a smaller, sparser, or much more personalized data. For such clients, TL helps them starting from a pre-trained model and it is finely-tuned in local so not much data and training is required. Second, TL can quickly converge the global model, particularly when the global model is initialized with a good pre-trained source model.

In addition, TL is able to boost the performance of models establish the cross-device or cross-organization FL setting with high data heterogeneity. Having transfer approaches align feature representations across clients, can allow FL systems to generalise better across non-IID data distributions. However, this integration also establishes new dependencies. Degradation or instability in the model performance can occur when the source model is stolen or the adaptation is poorly fitted to the target domain.

1.2. Rise of Adversarial Threats in Distributed Systems

With the increase in popularity of FL and TL, comes the increase in threats against it. The field of adversarial machine learning has transitioned from a thought experiment to a viable threat model. Federated systems face attacks where attackers control one or more of the clients and tries to poison the training. Model poisoning is when an adversary sending malicious updates to deteriorate the performance of the global model, usually without triggering any alarms. A backdoor attack seeks to stealthily insert a trigger into the model so that the model will misclassify the trigger-included inputs under certain conditions, maintaining high accuracy globally.

Additionally, TL itself introduces its own forms of adversarial risk. By pre-training models or sourcing datasets, these same vulnerabilities can be transferred to the destination domain where an attacker can exploit them. This is especially problematic when public or third-party models are fine-tuned or reused. These threats unfortunately add up to more difficult defense as they converge. The combination of FL and TL with adversarial learning creates a massive and unique threat scenario that remains largely unexplored (Peng et al., 2019).

1.3. Motivation for Studying FATL

FATL combines the pros and the cons of three important technologies: federated learning, transfer learning and adversarial machine learning. In conclusion, FATL not only offers the prospect of improved model generalization, reduced training time, and personalized models for each client but at the same time creates new types of attack vectors, which may be more difficult to identify and to mitigate.

For instance, an attacker may insert poisoned data into the original domain of a pretrained model, and its aggregated knowledge transfer can spread the weakness to the entire federated system. In another instance, attackers may take advantage of the transfer procedure to implant task-oriented backdoors that trigger only in the target domain. Such threats typically lie outside the usual threat model and, thus, can be easily ignored by existing FL defenses.

FATL is a high-stakes research area due to the increasing adoption of TL in FL pipelines, particularly in cross-silo applications such as healthcare and finance (Rane et al., 2024). To design the future of efficient and adaptive systems that also resist advanced attacks exploiting transfer dynamics such as deception and evasion, requires us to study this intersection.

1.4. Summary of Chapter Structure

In this chapter, we first present an overview of the technical foundations of FATL, and then we discuss an emerging risk associated with this area. In Section 2, we introduce the basic definitions of federated learning, transfer learning and adversarial machine learning, to prepare readers to learn how these fields intertwine with each other. In Section 3, we define the FATL as a coherent framework and argue its relevance for modern distributed systems.

In Section 4, we present a taxonomy of common adversarial threats in FATL, including model poisoning and backdoor insertion, as well as transfer-based attacks. In Section 5, we discuss the available defenses for FL and TL, and show that they are ineffective in FATL settings. We then provide experimental simulations of these risks and limitations of defense, which gives a very practical insight into the implications of adversarial transfer in a federated setting in Section 6.

Opportunities, use cases, and open problems are discussed in Sections 7 and 8, respectively. Finally, we conclude our chapter by revisiting the lessons learned and suggesting new avenues for future work in FATL.

2. FOUNDATIONS

In this section, we exemplify the concepts that drive FATL. After a brief introduction to the concepts of federated learning, we outline the principles of transfer learning and review its use in the emerging area of adversarial machine learning. It is important to understand those interactions when looking at the opportunities (and risks) that arise when they are brought together in practice.

2.1. Federated Learning Overview

2.1.1. Architecture and Key Assumptions

Federated learning is a decentralised way of training a model, where different clients contribute their local updates to the global model without exchanging their local data and federated learning process are depicted in **Figure 1**. The clients can be mobile, hospitals, banks any company that has private data. Each client uses its data to train a model locally and sends the updated model parameters back to a central server. The server receives these updates and aggregates them into a global model,

Figure 1. Federated learning process

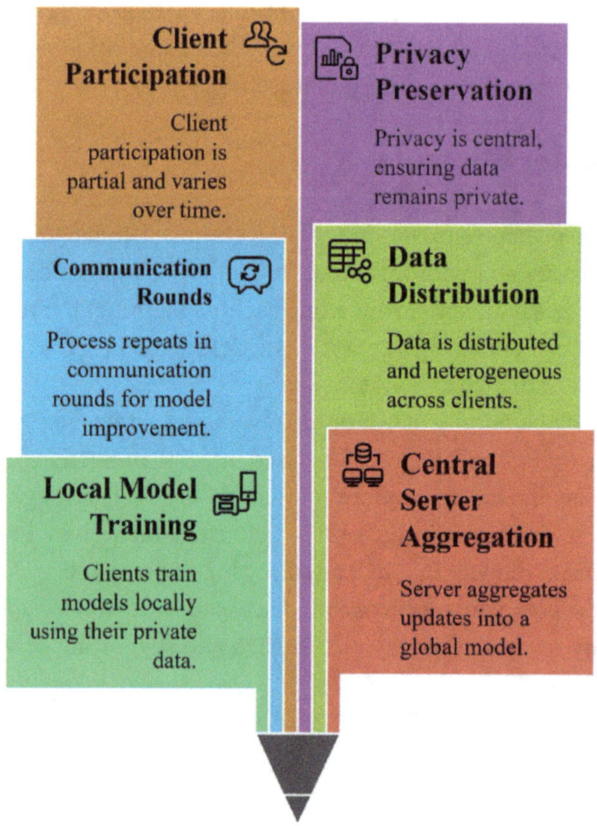

It's a process that is generally carried out in communication rounds. At the beginning of each round, the central server sends the global model on that round to the chosen clients. Clients train locally on their data and send updates to the server. The server can then summate these updates, usually via simple weighted average. This updated global model is redistributed and the process begins again.

There are several assumptions that underlie federated learning. Firstly, it assumes that the data is distributed to many clients and is not centralized. Second, it embraces a common case of client data where data distribution can differ significantly (heterogeneous) across clients. Third, client participation is often partial since clients make their decision to join and interact in different timeframes. Lastly, federated learning is predicated on the notion that raw data cannot be shared beyond its specific client or with the server thereby privacy preservation must go as a central design goal.

2.1.2. Benefits and Constraints

Federated learning brought the ability for clients to use a model together while protecting user privacy, and this feature made federated learning perfect for some fields like healthcare and finance, where data sharing is strictly limited (Naik & Naik, 2024). Nonetheless, the existing framework of Fed-learn suffers from serious problems like heterogenous data distribution, communication overhead and security attacks. Clients do not have the compute power or battery life or storage or whatever to participate constantly. Addressing these challenges is essential for the improved performance and robustness of federated learning systems.

2.2. Transfer Learning Basics

2.2.1. Definitions

Transfer learning is an approach in machine learning where knowledge gained while solving one problem is applied to a different but related problem. This can be particularly beneficial in cases where acquiring labeled data is limited or expensive (Zhao et al., 2024).

Transfer learning involves two components transfer the source domain and target domain. The source domain is the domain on which the model is first trained, and usually it is a huge and heterogeneous dataset. The new task where the model is applied, is the target domain. The intuition is that much of what is learned as features or representations in the source domain (detecting edges in images, for example, or extracting patterns for words in text) will also be useful in the target domain.

Transfer learning is where transfer either can copy full model and fine tune on target data or reuse some layer or learned representation. It aims at diminishing the necessity to train a model from a scratch and hastening the learning in the target domain.

2.2.2. Use Cases in Federated Contexts

Transfer-Learning is one of the precious components of our federated-learning toolbox since data is scarce on clients and because the data is apt to non-IID distribution. It enables sharing of knowledge across clients or pretraining of local models on similar tasks. Such an approach can be beneficial in personalized recommendation scenarios, cross-device scenarios, and few-shot learning scenarios where the client has only a few samples of the data but want an effective model deployment. It provides a shorter training time, enhanced generalization capacity, and personalized models while maintaining data privacy through transfer learning.

2.3. Adversarial Machine Learning

2.3.1. Types of Attacks

Adversarial machine learning is a domain dedicated to understanding the capacity of machine learning models to be prone to attacks that could manipulate or mislead them (Ibitoye et al., 2019). It demonstrates the weaknesses that occur when a model is given malicious inputs, and also highlights the corrupt data in training or testing data.

These are the three prevalent adversarial attack types are predicted in **Figure 2**.

Figure 2. Adversarial machine learning attack

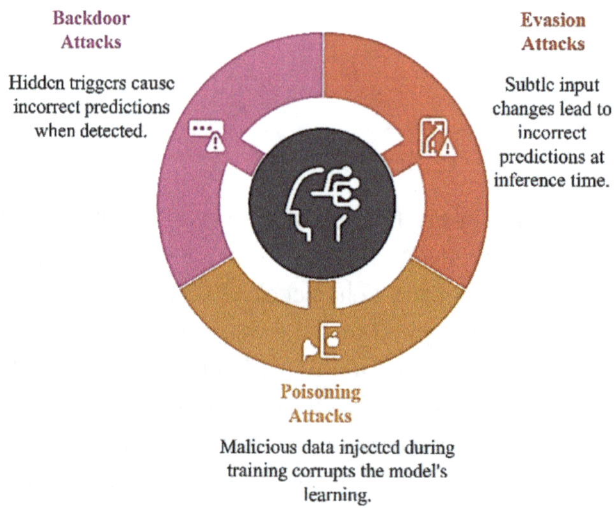

The first is evasion attacks. These are something that would happen at inference time. Often invisible to humans, attackers create tiny, well-designed perturbations to the input data, as a result of which the model produces incorrect predictions. This means that when a computer vision model was to see this modified picture of a stop sign, it may be classified as a speed limit sign, despite the fact that it visually looks the same to a human observer.

The second is poisoning attacks. These occur during training. The attacker distorts the learning process by injecting bad data into the training set. For instance, in federated learning, this can happen if a client pushes back poisoned model updates which induces the global model to learn incorrect or harmful behavior.

The third type of attack is the backdoor attack. In this attack, the attacker hides a trigger during the training process. The model behaves normally for all but a small percentage of inputs, when it will give incorrect outputs.

2.3.2. Attack Surface in Federated and Transfer Learning

Distributed settings and client data in federated learning and transfer learning open-up new attack vectors for adversaries. The model still heavily relies on clients which is easy to manipulate. Transfer learning also shows how pre-trained models can be easily attacked on external or public dataset. When aggregated, these risks make the model susceptible to both domain inheritance and domain manipulation. Thus, new tools to safeguard against these threats will require a deep understanding of attack propagation, as well as a careful design of robust and privacy-preserving learning mechanisms (Gao et al., 2019).

3. FEDERATED ADVERSARIAL TRANSFER LEARNING (FATL)

Federated Adversarial Transfer Learning is an emerging field that joins three important components of modern machine learning. They are federated learning, transfer learning, and adversarial machine learning. These fields each touch on separate and complementary challenges in decentralized intelligence. Yet, together they create a completely new set of opportunities and risks. Here we formulate the problem of FATL, elucidate its importance using real-world domain examples.

In this section the core theme for the chapter will be established. The theme is: Federated Adversarial Transfer Learning (FATL). Fundamental concepts from the existing literature on FL, TL and Adversarial ML were established. Now we look at the critical intersection of these ideas. FATL is a new paradigm for how the benefit of privacy-preserving distributed intelligence (FL) coupled with global knowledge re-use (TL) has to encounter a whole new area of threats (Adversarial ML).

3.1. Defining FATL

Federated learning is a machine learning technique that decentralizes the training process by keeping the dataset locally on each client device. It does not send raw data, but rather only model updates such as gradients or weights, to a central server. That's particularly helpful in scenarios where privacy is paramount or the data is inherently distributed among the users or institutions.

Transfer learning models can use knowledge learned from one task or domain and apply it to another, but different task. For instance, a model trained for daytime object detection can usually adapt to recognizing the same objects in nighttime images with a higher sample efficiency. When, the set of labeled data is rare or poorly expensive to copy in the target domain, transfer learning is valuable (Gao et al., 2019).

In simple terms, adversarial machine learning deals with how intelligent systems act in the scenario where the inputs to them are manipulated or malicious.

The crossroad of these three aspects is known as federated adversarial transfer learning. This relates to the use of transfer learning approaches in the presence of adversarial attacks or other adversarial influence in federated learning systems (X. Li et al., 2022). Here, locals and global models are augmented with knowledge from external sources, although local collaborative learning may be thwarted by adversarial actors.

Figure 3. Components of federated adversarial transfer learning

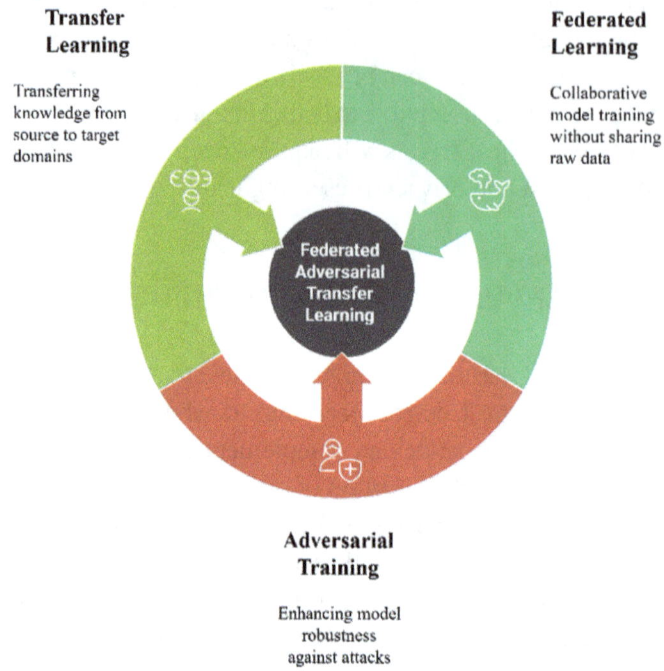

Figure 3 gives a visual representation of the three foundational pillars that come together to form FATL. It shows how the concepts of Transfer Learning, Federated Learning, and Adversarial Training work together in a complementary way, showing their interdependencies in this new paradigm.

3.2. Practical Motivations

FATL is a transfer learning method for federated systems that alleviates the reliance of clients on the big data they would have to keep locally by allowing them to utilize models learned elsewhere. Such an approach is particularly suited to areas like rural health care, small banks, and low-cost sensor networks because there is no data. While this type of transfer learning enables clients to adapt models to their local contexts, it also creates additional risk. An attacker may have direct access to attack surface through reusable models from third-party provider (e.g. Google, AWS) or through features extracted from other domains. And with adversaries becoming more realistic and complex, FATL is increasingly relevant to those applications as well. Cross-domain adversarial transfer will soon be binary because machine learning may become heterogeneous and adaptive and that will be a thin-slicing tool for studying this issue.

3.3. Examples of FATL in Healthcare, Finance, and IoT

In order to analyse the way of working of FATL in real time scenarios, applications of FATL in some of the critical domains can be examined. Those domains include health care, financial services, and the

Internet of Things (IoT) (Abbas et al., 2024). All of these domains require a high bar for privacy, have large distributed data sources, and have true potential for adversarial disruption.

FATL is a very powerful method and is widely used by different sectors of the world such as healthcare, financial services, and IoT. This improves the performance of the model, as diagnostic models are trained on different hospitals without sharing sensitive patient records. But if the global model or source data is poisoned, it can be dangerous due to misclassification or systematic bias. And this can have disastrous consequences. It´s interesting to use in the financial sector, for example, to recognize fraud or credit scoring, but adversarial attacks are also possible in the financial sector. Moreover, in the IoT, transfer learning can pose unique benefits and threats, such as improving the privacy and efficiency of this technique, releasing backdoor attacks or serving as surveillance mechanism. This balance is essential for creating distributed learning systems with high-security and access authorization.

The research landscape of the literature on Federated Adversarial Transfer Learning, encompassing a diverse range of studies that integrate federated learning, adversarial training, and transfer learning to address challenges in privacy, robustness, and domain adaptation are summarized in **Table 1**.

Table 1. Summary of the studies

Study	Robustness Performance	Privacy Preservation	Domain Adaptation Effectiveness	Computational Efficiency	Application-Specific Accuracy
(Yi et al., 2023)	Promising adversarial robustness in medical image classification	Ensures patient data privacy via federated platform	Transfer learning to sparse labeled domains	Not explicitly addressed	High diagnostic accuracy on real-world images
(Wang et al., 2022; W. Zhang & Li, 2022)	Robust fault diagnosis under adversarial settings	Data privacy via model heterogeneity and federated initialization	Addresses domain shift with adversarial learning	Moderate communication overhead	Effective fault diagnosis in industrial datasets
(Wang et al., 2022)	>10% improvement in fault diagnosis robustness	Privacy preserved through federated training	Multiclient feature alignment with adversarial learning	Not emphasized	Significant accuracy gains in machinery fault diagnosis
(Kang et al., 2022)	Effective adversarial domain adaptation with interpretability	Secure protocol for privacy-preserving vertical FL	Fine-grained domain adaptation over feature groups	Efficient and secure protocol design	Improved interpretability in financial datasets
(Peng et al., 2019)	Promising unsupervised federated domain adaptation	Privacy maintained by federated constraints	Dynamic attention and feature disentanglement for domain shift	Not specifically addressed	Good performance on image and text classification
(L. Zhang et al., 2023)	Comparable robustness with state-of-the-art methods	Local data privacy preserved in IoT devices	Adaptive reference distribution for domain generalization	Not detailed	Strong generalization on unseen IoT domains
(Chen et al., 2022)	Addresses instability in adversarial training under label skew	Privacy inherent in federated adversarial training	Not primary focus	Improves training stability on non-IID data	Enhanced natural accuracy despite skewed labels

continued on following page

Table 1. Continued

Study	Robustness Performance	Privacy Preservation	Domain Adaptation Effectiveness	Computational Efficiency	Application-Specific Accuracy
(X. Li et al., 2022)	Theoretical convergence guarantees for federated adversarial learning	Privacy by local model updates without raw data sharing	Not directly addressed	Convergence analysis under non-IID and multi-local updates	Robustness validated theoretically and empirically
(Y. Luo et al., 2024)	Significant robustness gains using GAN-based adversarial training	Addresses label distribution skew preserving privacy	Not primary focus	Balances natural accuracy and robustness efficiently	Superior performance on SVHN and CIFAR-100 datasets
(Qiao et al., 2024)	Enhances robust accuracy via logit calibration and feature contrast	Privacy preserved through federated adversarial training	Not directly targeted	Improves robustness and accuracy on non-IID data	Competitive clean and robust accuracy on multiple datasets
(Xu et al., 2024)	Prototype-based adversarial training improves robustness	Privacy preserved by federated learning framework	Not emphasized	Mitigates data heterogeneity effects	Effective on MNIST, FMNIST, and EMNIST-Digits
(Tang et al., 2024)	Memory-efficient adversarial training with strong robustness	Privacy maintained via federated training	Not directly addressed	Reduces memory and training time significantly	Comparable accuracy and robustness with less resource use
(Ennaji et al., 2025)	Adversarial training improves robustness in IoT intrusion detection	Data privacy ensured by federated learning	Not primary focus	Not explicitly addressed	91.23% accuracy on Edge-IIoTset dataset
(Utomo et al., 2023)	Robustness against PGD and FGSM adversarial attacks	Privacy by federated learning paradigm	Not directly addressed	Demonstrates robustness with modest client datasets	81-82% accuracy in smart city air pollution data
(Zhu et al., 2023)	Slack assignment combats heterogeneity-induced robustness loss	Privacy preserved in federated adversarial training	Not primary focus	Theoretically and experimentally efficient	Robustness improved on benchmark and real-world data
(Aldahdooh et al., 2022)	Vision transformers with adversarial training improve robustness	Privacy preserved via federated learning	Not directly addressed	Improved aggregation method enhances robustness	Robust accuracy improved on Non-IID data
(Tang et al., 2022)	Decoupled adversarial training reduces resource demands	Privacy preserved with module-wise training	Not primary focus	Enables training on resource-constrained devices	Maintains accuracy and robustness balance
(Hong et al., 2021)	Adversarial debiasing improves fairness and robustness	Privacy preserved without sensitive group info	Addresses domain adaptation and fairness	Not emphasized	Effective in unsupervised domain adaptation and fair learning
(Chen et al., 2021)	Certifiable robustness via randomized smoothing	Privacy preserved with differential privacy	Not directly addressed	Efficient gradient estimation accelerates training	Robustness comparable to centralized training

continued on following page

Table 1. Continued

Study	Robustness Performance	Privacy Preservation	Domain Adaptation Effectiveness	Computational Efficiency	Application-Specific Accuracy
(S. Luo et al., 2021)	Ensemble adversarial training enhances robustness on Non-IID data	Privacy preserved by federated learning	Addresses Non-IID data with ensemble methods	Moderate communication overhead	Promising results under feature and label skew
(Zizzo et al., 2020)	Challenges in adversarial robustness and convergence in federated settings	Privacy preserved by federated learning	Not primary focus	Identifies vulnerabilities in aggregation defenses	Robustness compromised by certain attacks
(Hong et al., 2023)	Robustness propagation from rich to poor resource clients	Privacy preserved in federated learning	Not directly addressed	Efficient batch-normalization based propagation	Robustness maintained with partial adversarial training
(Darzi et al., 2023)	Distributed noise improves adversarial robustness and privacy	Privacy enhanced with noise addition	Not primary focus	Requires fewer retraining samples	Robustness comparable to conventional adversarial training
(Gao et al., 2019)	Transfer learning addresses covariate shift and heterogeneity	Privacy preserved with homomorphic encryption and secret sharing	Effective heterogeneous federated transfer learning	Scalable and secure framework	Successful in in-hospital mortality prediction
(Y. Zhang et al., 2023)	Differential model distribution reduces adversarial transfer	Privacy preserved by distributing different models	Not primary focus	Reduces attack success and transfer rates	Significant robustness gains in MNIST FL system
(Zhou et al., 2023)	Effective transfer learning for heterogeneous low-dose PET data	Privacy preserved in multi-institutional FL	Addresses domain shift from different protocols	Not explicitly addressed	Superior denoising performance across institutions
(T. Liu et al., 2024)	Balances privacy and performance in adversarial training	Dynamic privacy-performance budget adjustment	Not primary focus	Optimizes trade-off between privacy and accuracy	Improved model performance in adversarial scenarios
(Rane et al., 2024)	Enhances robustness and security in edge AI for IoT	Privacy preserved via encryption and differential privacy	Not primary focus	Addresses heterogeneity and computational limits	Improved security and personalization in IoT FL
(Shah et al., 2021)	FedDynAT reduces model drift improving robustness and convergence	Privacy preserved in federated adversarial training	Not directly addressed	Efficient under communication constraints	Improved natural and adversarial accuracy
(Kerkouche et al., 2020)	Robustness against backdoor and degradation attacks	Differential privacy extension with trade-offs	Not primary focus	Bandwidth efficient with biased quantization	Robustness varies with privacy settings

An example of this is in healthcare, where several hospitals come together to create a diagnostic model. A hospital could use a public, pre-trained model (e.g., for general image recognition) and fine-tune it on its local, private patient data (e.g., x-rays). In a FATL setting, this knowledge, adapted locally, is shared. The danger would be if the public model had backdoored or if one hospital's model had been poisoned. That single compromised model could then later disseminate its flaw through the entire federated network, resulting in systemic misdiagnosis.

4. ATTACK TAXONOMY IN FATL

The FATL integrates three of the most powerful and complex elements: federated learning, transfer learning, and adversarial machine learning. Each of these domains presents its own threat landscape. Together they create more of a consolidated and unpredictable attack surface (Santos et al., 2025). Integrating FL, TL, and adversarial ML does not simply combine their respective threats, but instead creates a novel and more complicated attack surface. Understanding this new landscape is vital to the creation of secure systems. We therefore outline a clear taxonomy of the attacks on FATL itself, which is the first contribution of this chapter. The attacks are classified into four types: poisoning attacks, backdoor attacks, adversarial transferability of examples, and attack weaknesses based on external or pre-trained models (Salas, 2024).

4.1. Poisoning Attacks

The goal of such poisoning attacks is to corrupt the training process by injecting manipulated data or gradients or model updates. In traditional federated learning, the poisoning typically occurs in the aggregation of local models (Tolpegin et al., 2020). However, in FATL poisoning can occur at different levels during the source domain, transfer or during the local learning phase on the target domain. Generally, the aim of an attacker is to degrade performance, bias predictions or implant harmful behaviour which is hard to detect.

4.1.1. Model poisoning across tasks and domains

Among model poisoning attacks, injecting poison into the transfer process itself can be one of the most subtle yet dangerous attack vectors in FATL. Hidden objectives that need not be apparent at evaluation time can enable an attacker to train a source model. This enhanced or poisoned model is then published as a pretrained model. Ultimately, hidden behaviours may still get embedded in the final model, as federated clients use it as a seed for their own tasks. Since the malicious patterns are passed on through transfer learning, clients unaware of the issue can spread toxic behaviours just by trying to be helpful. This issue is exacerbated when multiple clients depend on the same poisoned initialization due to cross-domain use cases where components of the model are reused without complete retraining.

4.1.2. Gradient manipulation during knowledge transfer

Another type of poisoning has an impact by altering the gradient in the adaptation phase. In FATL, clients may use fine-tuning, or only doing partial training on transferred layers. In this attack, adversaries can ever-so-slightly skew the gradient updates to alter the learning path without fear of immediate detection. As an example, an adversary may submit gradients that are statistically normal but are directional in nature to increase classification error or push for the wrong decision boundaries. The local perturbations are global over time particularly when combined with transfer learning resulting in global misclassifications that can be predicted quite reliably over a wide range of time and space. Particularly, detecting this type of poisoning is really difficult, as we can observe that on the clean data, the model seems to learn normally.

4.2. Backdoor Attacks

In backdoor attacks, model is equipped with certain specific hidden behavior which is triggered only by certain input patterns. Moreover, this is practical because in the case of FATL, the theoretical backdoor can be transferred across tasks and the same backdoor also survives many training rounds, making these attacks particularly sinister. While poisoning attacks generally want to degrade the average performance of the model, backdoors are often designed to make the model behave as expected on most inputs while being malignant on (few) inputs controlled by the attacker (Gong et al., 2023).

4.2.1. Transferable triggers

In transfer learning, we reuse various internal features of a model for new tasks. Such backdoored shared layers of a source model can be transferred into a target model without any changes. This is particularly the case when the earlier layers are frozen by the clients and only final classifier is retrained. If there is a correlation between the trigger pattern to active the backdoor is still effective, then the new task could be totally different from the old one. Since non-IID data distributions can come from FATL where networks of decentralized learners share training samples via the same backbone architecture, a single backdoored model can poison a host of clients (Chen et al., 2022; Tang et al., 2022). Such attacks are ideal in the aspect that because of the transferability of triggers, these attacks are persistent, and they are hard to isolate when they activate under rare conditions.

4.2.2. Persistency across federated learning rounds

Such backdoors in FATL can be both persistent and transferable. The impact of a backdoored client can be mitigated by a global aggregation step, but the trigger can be multiplied in subsequent rounds as other clients tune the model released by the server. In some instances, the backdoor may not even need to be reinforced permanently. It could stay dormant in the internal representation of the model and only turn on later, when certain activation pattern of inputs is receiving. These latent behaviours can then go undetected for long periods in many domains due to the distributed and semi-autonomous nature of the learning process.

4.3. Adversarial Example Transferability

Adversarial examples are carefully designed inputs constructed to mislead a model into making incorrect predictions. Within a FATL setting these are even more impactful because they transfer over models, tasks and domains. This occurs because many models end up learning similar representations of features, particularly when models are built on similar transfer learning backbones.

Input-space attacks and cross-domain propagation

As known in adversarial machine learning, the type of attack we consider is to design inputs that, while normal-looking to a human, exist near the decision boundary of a model. In FATL, they may not only exist in the original model, but for other tasks as well. This is because federated clients are likely to use the same or similar pre-trained models and share same feature representation so that an adversarial input can transfer from one client to another. When clients are deployed in different domains but share a similar model architecture, it raises a significant issue regarding the cross-domain propagation of such. However, an adversarial image crafted for a medical diagnosis model in one hospital might actually end up being misclassified by the system in another hospital, if they use a similar transfer-learned model. This means input-space attacks become easier to scale and harder to pin-down and allow containment.

4.4. Source-side Vulnerabilities

An unnoticed pitfall in case of FATL is the source of model or datasets to perform transfer. Regrettably transfer learning starts with a source system generally already trained, hence any compromise of the source can trail downstream propagating through all systems adopting it. This risk is even worse in federated settings, where clients cannot have the ability to cross-check incoming models.

Risks from pre-trained or public models

To save both time and computational power, many people use models available in the public domain couple of examples of available models are gpt-3 and vicuna. Yet those models may not always be screened for security. An adversric can publish the compromised model on public repository with some slight embedded backdoors, biased weights or poisoned training artifacts. This compromise stays in the system similar to the model once a federated client downloaded and incorporated this model. In some cases, the poisoned source may never be flagged due to the fact that many federated learning pipelines are built upon decentralized and automated decision-making. Such a risk is exacerbated in FATL, as the leaked knowledge is not just consumed, but also propagated and adapted to new tasks, expanding the footprint of the damage incurred. This emphasizes the importance of strong model provenance and source verification prior to knowledge transfer.

5. DEFENSE STRATEGIES AND LIMITATIONS

This is again an important issue since the attack surface for FL expands as it becomes more commonly used. The combination of TL which allows clients to leverage knowledge from either external models or related tasks and FL systems opens up new opportunities, but also new risks. The resulting combination of the two gets harder and harder to defend against in an adversarial setting. However, many existing strategies of the FL defense are not able to bear the threats which can be brought by knowledge transfer or compromised external parties. In doing so, it classifies existing defenses, discusses important issues specific to FATL, and presents an agenda for future research to progress the field (P. Liu et al., 2022).

5.1. Existing FL Defenses

5.1.1. Secure Aggregation

Secure aggregation protocols of FL maintain client private data by acquiring aggregated updates via cryptographic formulas. In FATL, however, secure aggregation does not certify the integrity of the individual updates since they are concealed by the aggregation technique and so the malicious behaviors of clients cannot be detected and client-level updates can not be concealed to ensure conciseness and accountability in adversarial scenarios. Additionally, the aggregation process is based on the assumption that the clients are statistically independent and that a contaminated model can create adversarial characteristics thereby allowing the knowledge (the 'knowhow') transferred to the model to be confused with that which might be legitimate and not alterably transferred.

5.1.2. Client Selection Strategies

FATL is an additional level of defense in FL systems to limit the engagement of some clients to minimize adversarial clients instead. However, this defense does not function as effectively in the case of FATL as the adversarial payloads will not necessarily be due to the client behavior but by the model that the client presents to the system. The traditional trust-based approaches do not use the source and size of these features and transferred weights of the model.

5.2. FATL-specific Challenges

5.2.1. Attack Detectability During Transfer

Adversarial activity typically occurs in the real-world, transferred model, feature space or learned representation in FATL. In contrast to most conventional FL attacks which induce sudden accuracy drops or unusual gradients, FATL attacks can be stealthy. For example, a poisoned model transferred from a public repository may be able to generalize to a validation dataset while still concealing harmful behavior that only arises under certain circumstances.

With this stealthiness then detection is a whole lot easier. When the malicious behavior is already embedded deep in the model in terms of its structure or feature activations then typical anomaly detectors based on gradient distribution, update norms, or loss behavior fail to detect it. Moreover, the attack trigger can be inactive for multiple rounds or only be triggered for certain inputs or clients in many FATL settings.

Unlike the timing of transfer and the attack manifestation, there is a latency between the two and as such, defenders have no immediate feedback on performance indicator(s). This kind of anticipatory response is what defenses should be, but it is difficult to achieve in a decentralized, privacy-preserving system.

5.2.2. Trust in External Models and Sources

FATL uses pre-trained models, feature extractors, or learning representations from outside domains for training. This trust layer adds to the security of the federated system. There are, however, few means for validating the trustworthiness external models, and federated systems do not normally validate components which are imported. This renders the source of training opaque and vulnerable to adversarial triggers.

5.3. Research Gaps

5.3.1. Lack of Benchmarks for FATL Attacks and Defenses

A key limitation in FATL research is that there are no standardized benchmarks. Existing adversarial machine learning research has attracted significant interest with its own broad family of well-known datasets and protocols (CIFAR-10, FEMNIST, LEAF), but no agreed upon suite of benchmarks exists for FATL scenarios. Consequently, the majority of FATL studies are based on limited experiments, unsupervised datasets, or peculiar threat model assumptions.

This fragmentation hinders progress. Without common evaluation environments, comparison of the effectiveness between different defenses or attack models becomes difficult. Researcher can specialize their strategies on specific natural use cases to avoid generalization. Benchmarks must span across different transfer settings, multi-domain tasks, federated data distributions, and poison/backdoor scenarios. The best ones do this in both the white-box and black-box settings to reflect real world adversary behavior.

Open reproducible FATL benchmarks reflecting honest and malicious model transfer in realistic conditions are needed by the community. This could allow for more thorough evaluations and a speedier implementation of real-world protections.

To achieve a true FATL benchmark, there must be a number of specified metrics which measure something more than merely truthfulness. Some of these metrics may be:

1) Transfer Attack Success Rate (TASR), which reflects the success of a backdoor or poison when transferred from a source domain to a target domain;
2) The Robustness-Privacy-Utility RPU Trade-off Score, a composite score which enables us quantitatively assess how a defense mechanism affects model correctness and data privacy while increasing robustness;
3) Bias Amplification Factor (BAF), which expresses how much the innate biases (e.g., demographic) are amplified or attenuated through federated fine-tuning across clients which are IID.

5.3.2. Limited Interpretability of Transferred Vulnerabilities

This is a phenomenon: the propagation of adversarial vulnerabilities through transfer learning in FL, which remains a poorly understood problem. This is challenging not only in decentralized settings, but also in centralized ones, where how backdoors or biases propagate across domains and tasks should be interpreted. This is especially challenging in the context of FATL where we have the challenges of distributed training, heterogeneous clients and communication constraints.

The existing interpretability tools for deep learning mainly rely on feature importance, saliency maps, or activation patterns. Very few tools are made for a federated system, where there is no access to the complete model, or to any data. In addition, it requires labeled data on central access which is explicitly avoided with FATL setups.

In addition, due to the black-box nature of deep learning, it is not explicit whether a model has been attacked or not, as those adversarial attacks can lead to a drop in performance of the model by a little or by a longer time delay (Ennaji et al., 2025; Zhu et al., 2023). Interpretability also makes it more difficult to identify natural domain shift from malicious behavior.

Enhancing interpretability in FATL is partly a technical issue but it is also a pre-condition for fostering trust. In high-stakes applications such as healthcare, finance, or autonomous systems, those models that are able to explain their predictions and their evolution over time are much more likely to be adopted (M. Li et al., 2025). This domain is another territory for future research.

5.3.3. Emerging and Future Defense Frontiers

To tackle the particular issues related to security in FATL, researchers are looking into a variety of innovative approaches to defense. These involve:

1) Robust Aggregation algorithms which go beyond basic averaging, and detect & filter unlawful updates on the basis of their statistical divergence or impact on a trusted validation set;
2) Verifiable Transfer Learning which involves cryptographic proofs or "model watermarking" to certify the provenance and integrity of source models before they are applied;
3) Federated Differential Privacy applied specifically to the knowledge sharing transfer, which means that calibrated noise is added to transferred parameters, in order to preclude the leakage of properties of source data or the propagation of specific adversarial triggers.

6. EXPERIMENTAL INSIGHTS

In order to assess the real-world impact of Federated Adversarial Transfer Learning (FATL), we created an experimental framework. We aimed to investigate the interplay between adversarial behaviors and knowledge transfer and federated training, and to measure the potential for both improved learning and systemic vulnerability. We proposed a set of experiments that mimics various factors in the wild environment such as non- IID data distributions, malicious clients, and pretrained source models with "backdoor" settings.

6.1. Setup of Simulated FATL Environment

We have recently implemented a modular FL environment based on PyTorch and Flower to control model architecture, client behavior, and aggregation dynamics. We train the source model on the clean CIFAR-10 train set and construct the target domain with the Fashion-MNIST train set. We introduce two forms of adversarial clients to simulate poisoning and backdoor behavior, and we test both white-box and black-box threat models. FATL environment can be used to monitor convergence, robustness, transferability of knowledge as well as vulnerabilities which enables simulating many attack scenarios.

6.2. Attack Scenarios and Metrics

We focused on three main adversarial strategies that could realistically affect FATL systems:

6.2.1. Model Poisoning Attacks

Adversarial clients were trained to adapt local gradients by trying to maximize loss on clean validation data or drive the global model to a malicious target. The gradients that were poisoned were scaled or flipped so that during aggregation they can have a more significant impact. These attacks were injected from the beginning or in later-rounds, but at a constant continuous rate.

6.2.2. Backdoor Attacks

In backdoor attacks, trigger patterns (for example, a small patch or a pixel pattern) were injected into local training data by placing the trigger pattern in the image and were used for generating poisoning samples. Labels for these inputs were changed to have a same class as considered target class. This would trigger the model to misclassify whatever input the trigger was contained, even after normal training was performed.

6.2.3. Adversarial Transfer from Source

Here, the adversarial pre-training is even done on the source model itself, Hidden backdoors or adversarial misbehaviors of the test nodes were still retained in the model, transferred to clients through the shared weights. The previous scenario examined the danger of relying on external or public models during transfer learning in a federated setting.

We assessed the system employing these metrics:

- **Accuracy** on clean test data to measure baseline performance
- **Attack Success Rate (ASR)** for backdoor inputs on the target class
- **Convergence Time**, measured in training rounds until accuracy plateaued
- **Robustness Gap**, the drop in accuracy between clean and adversarial settings
- **Client Drift**, the variance in local model updates during aggregation
- **Gradient Divergence**, measuring the deviation caused by poisoned clients

These metrics enabled a numerical evaluation of learning efficiency and security weaknesses.

6.3. Results: Model Performance and Robustness Trade-offs

This trade-off between using transfer learning to achieve faster convergence and higher generalization versus the increased adversarial attack-bug-possible-exploitation risk was revealed by the experiments (T. Liu et al., 2024).

FATL showed great advantages under the scenarios where all clients were honest and the source model was clean. In the federated setting, it improved target accuracy over models trained from scratch between 6 to 10 percent. It also converged faster, needing fewer rounds of communication to reach a steady state accuracy. The couple of Transfer learning steps could balance scarcity of local data with non-identical nature of client datasets. However, the presence of adversarial behavior significantly affected outcomes:

• **Model Poisoning** tactic degraded global accuracy by as much as 20 percent, relative to the fraction of malicious clients. If not detected for a few rounds, even one poisoned client can compromise training. Not only did the poisoned models under-perform but they also demonstrated erratic behavior on edge-case inputs.
• **Backdoor Attacks** were particularly successful. Even after federated averaging over multiple rounds, attack success rates remained above 85 percent. This algorithm adds a hidden backdoor that goes undetected by its deceptively high clean accuracy. It was found that these attacks are stealthy and resilient under the federated transfer.
• Transfer from the Source in adversarial contexts proved to be very effective. Transfer learning with backdoored model works because any backdoor trigger found in the source model used for training would still successfully trigger with a client model after transfer and fine tune. Even with partial retraining, attack success rates stayed in excess of 80 percent. This showed that harmful actions could be embedded quietly into the layers that the transfer learning used and so be propagated downstream.

These results corroborate both that FATL can speed up learning and advance performance when trained, but also serves as a conduit for latent, transferable attacks.

6.4. Observations on Convergence and Stability

During benign conditions, the training in FATL setup proceeded smoothly and stably. Clients illustrated same loss shape in all the folds and Global model reaches convergence within 30 to 40 rounds. Transfer learning had the most impact at early training stages, where it mitigated against overfitting and improved generalization.

Against adversarial settings however, a few destabilizing effects were seen:

• **Increased Client Drift:** We found that adversarial clients generated large variability in their model updates. As a result, it caused the global model to oscillate and took longer to converge. In cases where multiple malicious clients were at risk, it sometimes oscillated without arrival.
• **Late-stage Poisoning**: Compared to attacks at the early stages, disruption was more significant when introducing adversarial clients after the global model had already converged, albeit at a bit of an earlier instance. Once that delicate balance had been achieved, the system was more prone to destabilisation.
• **Aggregation Sensitivity**: Without any trust-weighting or anomaly detection, FedAvg is an insufficient response. Poisoned gradients often dominated the global model. This further validated the extent to which stronger aggregation schemes were necessary (particularly in the case of transfer learning).
• **Stuck Convergence**: On other runs, the model converged to a stuck state, with high clean accuracy but having installed the backdoor. Success from the outside put forth a facade of success yet hid deep vulnerabilities, and that is especially perilous in a mission-critical application.

These insights underscore that the interaction of federated learning, transfer learning, and adversarial behavior adds an intricate layer of complexity to the dynamics involved. Defenses designed for FL are not sufficient. This highlights the necessity of new approaches designed to directly mitigate the dangers of transfer learning in adversarial scenarios.

7. OPPORTUNITIES AND USE CASES

FATL is a framework that integrates the advantages of federated learning and transfer learning, it is withstanding the threats of adversarial machine learning. While there are significant challenges, FATL opens up several possibilities across settings with restrictions imposed by data privacy, heterogeneity, and limited availability of resources (Hong et al., 2023; L. Zhang et al., 2023). Here we discuss some major areas where the distinctive value of FATL stems from, particularly in the context of personalization, domain adaptation, collaborative intelligence sharing, and support for low-resource settings.

7.1. Improved Personalization in FL via TL

FATL's aim is to refine the global model based on the local data, avoiding common sparsity found in federated learning scenario. For this local model averaging takes place, where devices train their local model on its own dataset. However, this raises the attack surface, as adversarial clients can enforce the control of local updates and insert tailored errors or biases. In order to ensure safe personalization, it is important strong defenses and anomaly detection in local updates are made in secure deployment research.

7.2. Domain Adaptation under Privacy Constraints

The fundamental dilemma in machine learning is transferring models across source and target fields with varied structures, scales, and labelling standards. FATL, a federated technique, resolves these limitations by advancing knowledge transfer in one domain while keeping the local datasets invariant. The network traffic may be compromised by intruders, so defences and heavy verification and trust mechanisms must be employed to ensure effective cross domain adaptation in the field of health care, finance and law.

7.3. Cross-Device Intelligence Sharing

FATL, a decentralized methodology that utilizes edge computing and smart devices, facilitates knowledge transfer between devices, enhancing performance and reducing training time. It is especially applicable for self-driving vehicles, where user confidentiality must be maintained, while fast learning is needed when required. However, if there are compromised devices, they can pass on behaviours during the transmission of knowledge. Therefore, it will require the use of secure aggregated protocols, which have been integrated, together with device-based trust scoring and anomaly detection techniques.

7.4. FATL for Low-Resource Environments

Low-resourced settings have decentralized splits from the knowledge domain where FATL provides the intact structure of the inference and the training of the model. This method minimizes computation and effort, in annotating data, which is, therefore, useful for agricultural applications in rural areas. FATL frameworks are robust against intercepted models and hacked communications.

8. RISKS AND OPEN PROBLEMS

Even though Federated Adversarial Transfer Learning holds a great promise, some risks and open problems remain. These points however are very important, not only from a technical point of view, but also for deployment in real systems. This chapter describes important open issues that merit further research.

8.1. Amplification of Biases and Vulnerabilities

This is not exclusive to standard settings, in fact, recently proposed transfer learning in federated settings may introduce unwanted biases in the source model and even aggravate the existing vulnerabilities while exposing new attack surfaces to adversaries on the target task. And may lead to fairness related issues and model performance degradation.

This amplification carries a substantial fairness risk; a pre-trained model developed on data from a single population (say a certain ethnicity, or a certain sex), may already harbor performance-related biases. If this model is employed as a source in an FATL system for health-care, this bias is propagated and may be amplified through every participating hospital. Patients with non-IID data which differ from the source's biased data are likely to be affected by particularly poor performance, which leads to unfairness, and inequity, in the predictions pertaining either to diagnosis, or recommendations for respective treatment. This creates an ethical obligation to conduct bias auditing of source models prior to their deployment in federated transfer.

8.2. Trustworthiness of Transfer Sources

The quality and reliability of the source model are critical to FATL. Especially pre-trained models used in federated environments are obtaining a risk to adversaries. Secure Model Transfer (Non-Transparency, Trust Challenge) In the federated context transferring models, we have no standard method for auditing or certified parity (a form of trust) between models.

8.3. Regulatory and Ethical Implications

Federated Transfer learning which is a transfer learning tool used in federated learning, FATL raises an ethical issue regarding their usage. It may reveal private characteristics or patterns in its decision-making, violating the GDPR or HIPAA. The vagueness of attribution and accountability in FATL attacks aggravates the ethical application of FATL, which requires clear standards in both academia and industry.

For example, regulations such as the GDPR provide a "right to be forgotten" and principles of "data minimization," which create a complicated tension in FATL. While FL itself supports data minimization because it does not share the raw data, knowledge transferred from a source model or other clients may still contain discoverable information about the original data, allowing for new privacy intrusions to occur. In a similar vein, the stringent requirements of HIPAA respecting Protected Health Information

(PHI) risk being undermined when backdoored models, transferred from a public repository, cause a diagnostic model to misclassify and pose a direct threat to patient safety. This raises the obscure legal question of responsibility because if a poisoned public model causes a federated system's failure, is the original model provider, the customer who put in a public model for federated use, or the central aggregator, responsible.

8.4. Adversarial Robustness vs Utility Trade-offs

In the context of FATL, it is important to understand the robustness vs performance trade-off properly. For example, gradient masking and differential privacy can limit the learning of useful features, while optimizing for accuracy can increase adversarial exposure. While there has been considerable progress in how to take these trade-offs into account, balancing them remains somewhat of an unknown and we believe understanding more will help others focus on optimizing security as well as utility.

9. CONCLUSION

FATL is the union of federated learning and transfer learning and adversarial machine learning and it is a key knowledge if you want to understand the adversarial threat and attacks and vulnerability of decentralised environments such as edge devices, hospitals, banks and mobile platforms. It has powerful capabilities but also brings new vulnerabilities. Given that FL is scaling and transfer learning is set to play a pivotal role in the deployment of federated learning, a strong theoretical understanding of FATL will prove crucial as it tackles critical issues like data privacy, heterogeneity, and adversarial threats in the federated learning setting.

FATL presents training opportunities that are not always possible in resource-constrained environments by enabling explicit re-training and personalization without the need for re-training. It enables more efficient learning and better transfer across domains, particularly in the healthcare context. Even though its approach to transfer learning may generate adversarial patterns, which is a difficult kind to mitigate, and can cause model poisoning. Classical FL defenses or adversarial ML generalizations do not carry over to FATL.

The poisoned role of the model in adversarial vulnerability is interrogated through transfer learning leveraged in FATL pipelines. Recognizing this, indirectly affects the robustness of local and global models, thus causing cascaded effects. We conclude by calling for more research on the properties of adversarial examples that drives the knowledge flow in FATL pipelines, and ways to mitigate these knowledge flows by isolating and cleansing the knowledge flow. That said, it is important for practitioners to be careful with transfer learning, as transfer learning can expose the system to unseen risks.

New FATL learning approach to solve technical issues. Community-level benchmarking needed. In the absence of standardized datasets, evaluation protocols, and comparison methodologies, traditional learning scenarios do not allow for direct comparison or reproducible results. This metric inherently emphasizes that high-level benchmarking should be community-driven and reflect the true applicability of ML systems, including heterogeneous data and differential adversary capabilities. Transfer policies should be applied in real time, while adversarial components should be injected and the impact of a cross-client model should be analysed via research toolkits. Policy should focus on accountability, con-

REFERENCES

Abbas, S. R., Abbas, Z., Zahir, A., & Lee, S. W. (2024). Federated Learning in Smart Healthcare: A Comprehensive Review on Privacy, Security, and Predictive Analytics with IoT Integration. *Healthcare 2024, Vol. 12, Page 2587, 12*(24), 2587. DOI: 10.3390/healthcare12242587

Aldahdooh, A., Hamidouche, W., & Déforges, O. (2022). *Federated Adversarial Training with Transformers*. https://arxiv.org/pdf/2206.02131

Chen, C., Kailkhura, B., Goldhahn, R., & Zhou, Y. (2021). Certifiably-Robust Federated Adversarial Learning via Randomized Smoothing. *Proceedings - 2021 IEEE 18th International Conference on Mobile Ad Hoc and Smart Systems, MASS 2021*, 173–179. DOI: 10.1109/MASS52906.2021.00032

Chen, C., Liu, Y., Ma, X., & Lyu, L. (2022). CalFAT: Calibrated Federated Adversarial Training with Label Skewness. *Advances in Neural Information Processing Systems, 35*. https://arxiv.org/pdf/2205.14926

Darzi, E., Sijtsema, N. M., & van Ooijen, P. M. A. (2023). *Fed-Safe: Securing Federated Learning in Healthcare Against Adversarial Attacks*. https://arxiv.org/pdf/2310.08681

Ennaji, E. M., El Hajla, S., Maleh, Y., & Mounir, S. (2025). Adversarially robust federated deep learning models for intrusion detection in IoT. *Indonesian Journal of Electrical Engineering and Computer Science, 37*(2), 937–947. DOI: 10.11591/ijeecs.v37.i2.pp937-947

Gao, D., Liu, Y., Huang, A., Ju, C., Yu, H., & Yang, Q. (2019). Privacy-preserving Heterogeneous Federated Transfer Learning. *Proceedings - 2019 IEEE International Conference on Big Data. Big Data, 2019*, 2552–2559. DOI: 10.1109/BigData47090.2019.9005992

Gong, X., Chen, Y., Wang, Q., & Kong, W. (2023). Backdoor Attacks and Defenses in Federated Learning: State-of-the-Art, Taxonomy, and Future Directions. *IEEE Wireless Communications, 30*(2), 114–121. DOI: 10.1109/MWC.017.2100714

Hong, J., Wang, H., Wang, Z., & Zhou, J. (2023). Federated Robustness Propagation: Sharing Adversarial Robustness in Heterogeneous Federated Learning. *Proceedings of the AAAI Conference on Artificial Intelligence, 37*(7), 7893–7901. DOI: 10.1609/aaai.v37i7.25955

Hong, J., Zhu, Z., Yu, S., Wang, Z., Dodge, H. H., & Zhou, J. (2021). Federated Adversarial Debiasing for Fair and Transferable Representations. *Proceedings of the ACM SIGKDD International Conference on Knowledge Discovery and Data Mining*, 617–627. DOI: 10.1145/3447548.3467281

Ibitoye, O., Abou-Khamis, R., el Shehaby, M., Matrawy, A., & Shafiq, M. O. (2019). The Threat of Adversarial Attacks on Machine Learning in Network Security — A Survey. *Journal of Electronic and Electrical Engineering*. Advance online publication. DOI: 10.37256/jeee.4120255738

Kang, Y., Liu, Y., Wu, Y., Ma, G., & Yang, Q. (2022). Privacy-preserving Federated Adversarial Domain Adaption over Feature Groups for Interpretability. *IEEE Transactions on Big Data, 10*(6), 879–890. DOI: 10.1109/TBDATA.2022.3188292

Kerkouche, R., Ács, G., & Castelluccia, C. (2020). *Federated Learning in Adversarial Settings*. https://arxiv.org/pdf/2010.07808

Li, M., Xu, P., Hu, J., Tang, Z., & Yang, G. (2025). From challenges and pitfalls to recommendations and opportunities: Implementing federated learning in healthcare. *Medical Image Analysis, 101*, 103497. DOI: 10.1016/j.media.2025.103497

Li, X., Song, Z., & Yang, J. (2022). *Federated Adversarial Learning: A Framework with Convergence Analysis*. https://arxiv.org/pdf/2208.03635

Liu, P., Xu, X., & Wang, W. (2022). Threats, attacks and defenses to federated learning: Issues, taxonomy and perspectives. *Cybersecurity, 5*(1), 1–19. DOI: 10.1186/s42400-021-00105-6

Liu, T., Wu, H., Sun, X., Niu, C., & Yin, H. (2024). *FL-APB: Balancing Privacy Protection and Performance Optimization for Adversarial Training in Federated Learning*. https://doi.org/DOI: 10.20944/PREPRINTS202409.2292.V2

Luo, S., Zhu, D., Li, Z., & Wu, C. (2021). *Ensemble Federated Adversarial Training with Non-IID data*. https://arxiv.org/pdf/2110.14814

Luo, Y., Zhu, T., Liu, Z., Mao, T., Chen, Z., Pi, H., & Lin, Y. (2024). GANFAT: Robust federated adversarial learning with label distribution skew. *Future Generation Computer Systems, 160*, 711–723. DOI: 10.1016/j.future.2024.06.030

Naik, D., & Naik, N. (2024). *An Introduction to Federated Learning: Working, Types, Benefits and Limitations*. 3–17. DOI: 10.1007/978-3-031-47508-5_1

Peng, X., Huang, Z., Zhu, Y., & Saenko, K. (2019). Federated Adversarial Domain Adaptation. *8th International Conference on Learning Representations, ICLR 2020*. https://arxiv.org/pdf/1911.02054

Qiao, Y., Member, S., Zhang, C., Adhikary, A., & Seon Hong, C. (2024). *Logit Calibration and Feature Contrast for Robust Federated Learning on Non-IID Data*. https://arxiv.org/pdf/2404.06776

Rane, J., Kaya, Ö., Mallick, S. K., & Rane, N. L. (2024). Federated learning for edge artificial intelligence: Enhancing security, robustness, privacy, personalization, and blockchain integration in IoT. *Future Research Opportunities for Artificial Intelligence in Industry 4.0 and 5.0*. DOI: 10.70593/978-81-981271-0-5_3

Salas, M. I. P. (2024). *Attack Taxonomy Methodology Applied to Web Services*. Latin-American Journal of Computing., DOI: 10.5281/ZENODO.10402238

Santos, P. R. D. P. F., Resende, P. A. A., Gondim, J. J. C., & Drummond, A. C. (2025). Towards Robust Cyber Attack Taxonomies: A Survey with Requirements, Structures, and Assessment. *ACM Computing Surveys, 57*(8), 1–36. DOI: 10.1145/3717606

Shah, D., Dube, P., Chakraborty, S., & Verma, A. (2021). *Adversarial training in communication constrained federated learning*. https://arxiv.org/pdf/2103.01319

Tang, M., Wang, Y., Zhang, J., DiValentin, L., Ding, A., Hass, A., Chen, Y., & Li, H. "Helen." (2024). *FedProphet: Memory-Efficient Federated Adversarial Training via Robust and Consistent Cascade Learning*. https://arxiv.org/pdf/2409.08372

Tang, M., Zhang, J., Ma, M., DiValentin, L., Ding, A., Hassanzadeh, A., Li, H., & Chen, Y. (2022). *FADE: Enabling Federated Adversarial Training on Heterogeneous Resource-Constrained Edge Devices*. https://arxiv.org/pdf/2209.03839

Tolpegin, V., Truex, S., Gursoy, M. E., & Liu, L. (2020). Data poisoning attacks against federated learning systems. *Lecture Notes in Computer Science (Including Subseries Lecture Notes in Artificial Intelligence and Lecture Notes in Bioinformatics), 12308 LNCS*, 480–501. https://doi.org/DOI: 10.1007/978-3-030-58951-6_24/TABLES/6

Utomo, S., Rouniyar, A., Hsu, H. C., & Hsiung, P. A. (2023). Federated Adversarial Training Strategies for Achieving Privacy and Security in Sustainable Smart City Applications. *Future Internet 2023, Vol. 15, Page 371, 15*(11), 371. DOI: 10.3390/fi15110371

Wang, R., Huang, W., Shi, M., Wang, J., Shen, C., & Zhu, Z. (2022). Federated adversarial domain generalization network: A novel machinery fault diagnosis method with data privacy. *Knowledge-Based Systems, 256*, 109880. DOI: 10.1016/j.knosys.2022.109880

Xu, Z. R., Lai, W. M., & Yan, Q. (2024). FedPGT: Prototype-based Federated Global Adversarial Training against Adversarial Attack. *Proceedings of the 2024 27th International Conference on Computer Supported Cooperative Work in Design, CSCWD 2024*, 864–869. DOI: 10.1109/CSCWD61410.2024.10580613

Yi, H., Bie, T., & Yan, T. (2023). Framework Construction of an Adversarial Federated Transfer Learning Classifier. *The Frontiers of Society. Science and Technology*, *5*(3), 64–75. DOI: 10.25236/FSST.2023.050312

Zhang, L., Lei, X., Shi, Y., Huang, H., & Chen, C. (2023). Federated Learning for IoT Devices With Domain Generalization. *IEEE Internet of Things Journal*, *10*(11), 9622–9633. DOI: 10.1109/JIOT.2023.3234977

Zhang, W., & Li, X. (2022). Federated Transfer Learning for Intelligent Fault Diagnostics Using Deep Adversarial Networks with Data Privacy. *IEEE/ASME Transactions on Mechatronics*, *27*(1), 430–439. DOI: 10.1109/TMECH.2021.3065522

Zhang, Y., Liu, J., Guan, Z., Zhao, B., Leng, X., & Bian, S. (2023). ARMOR: Differential Model Distribution for Adversarially Robust Federated Learning. *Electronics 2023, Vol. 12, Page 842, 12*(4), 842. DOI: 10.3390/electronics12040842

Zhao, Z., Alzubaidi, L., Zhang, J., Duan, Y., & Gu, Y. (2024). A comparison review of transfer learning and self-supervised learning: Definitions, applications, advantages and limitations. *Expert Systems with Applications*, *242*, 122807. DOI: 10.1016/j.eswa.2023.122807

Zhou, B., Miao, T., Mirian, N., Chen, X., Xie, H., Feng, Z., Guo, X., Li, X., Zhou, S. K., Duncan, J. S., & Liu, C. (2023). Federated Transfer Learning for Low-Dose PET Denoising: A Pilot Study With Simulated Heterogeneous Data. *IEEE Transactions on Radiation and Plasma Medical Sciences*, *7*(3), 284–295. DOI: 10.1109/TRPMS.2022.3194408

Zhu, J., Yao, J., Liu, T., Yao, Q., Xu, J., & Han, B. (2023). Combating Exacerbated Heterogeneity for Robust Models in Federated Learning. *11th International Conference on Learning Representations, ICLR 2023*. https://arxiv.org/pdf/2303.00250

Zizzo, G., Rawat, A., Sinn, M., & Buesser, B. (2020). *FAT: Federated Adversarial Training*. https://arxiv.org/pdf/2012.01791

Chapter 9

Defense Strategies for Federated Learning Models Targeted by Data Poisoning Attacks

Monika Kumari
https://orcid.org/0000-0002-8468-3552
Poornima University, India

Nikhil Kumar Goyal
https://orcid.org/0009-0007-4532-8033
Poornima University, India

Ayesha Farooqi
https://orcid.org/0009-0000-4556-4211
Poornima University, India

ABSTRACT

The chapter offers a detailed analysis of the security issues of Federated Learning (FL) and will particularly dwell on data poisoning attacks. It discusses the nature of decentralized architecture of FL, which results in exposing new attack surfaces despite maintaining user privacy. The chapter groups types of data poisoning attacks and provides a resultant taxonomy of defense methods, such as data-level filtering, robust aggregation algorithms, anomaly detection, anything training and privacy-based methods, like differential privacy. Such algorithms as Krum, Bulyan, and Trimmed Mean are examined as well as client reputation systems. Case studies and real-world FL simulations are performed in which the effectiveness of the methods is tested. The difficulties of scalability, tradeoffs between robustness and accuracy, availability of adaptive responses to emerging dangers are also mentioned. This chapter is expected to assist researchers and practitioners toward safe, robust, and trust-guarded federated learning systems.

DOI: 10.4018/979-8-3373-6224-3.ch009

1. INTRODUCTION

1.1 Federated Learning

Machine Learning Federated learning (FL) is a decentralized machine learning paradigm that aims to train a shared model across multiple clients, e.g. smartphones, edge devices or institutions, without sharing their local data. As opposed to feeding raw data to a centralized server each participant trains a local model on its local data, and sends only the learned parameters (e.g. gradients or weights) back to a central server, which combines them to update the global model. That way the data is never moved out of the client and can provide a type of privacy in itself.

This method has gained more popularity in the area where privacy laws and ethics restrain the distribution of data. Some of the applications of FL include the use of FL in healthcare systems (to collaborate with others in diagnosing illnesses), mobile keyboards (to facilitate predictive text) and in the financial sector (to detect fraud). In both scenarios, the model can enjoy the strength of different sources of data without infringing on user privacy (Bagdasaryan et al., 2020).

FL is collaborative and models are able to generalize more because they learn by observing a broad set of user behavior, or by observing real-world circumstances, something that centralized systems cannot always do. Moreover, FL can be used to aid on-device learning and computation, which is why it is suitable in an edge AI. Nonetheless, this distributed environment brings in a lot of complexities and possible points of failures at the system level- particularly, security wise.

Although the original idea of introducing FL mainly aimed at maintaining the privacy, the architecture of FL makes it vulnerable to novel and delicate types of attacks. Because server is not able to see very much of client data or training behavior, they are now more effectively exploitable by adversaries. Among the major threats in this environment, data poisoning is taking the center stage and can create an issue in the integrity of the global model.

1.2 Security in Federated Systems

Privacy in federated learning and centralized learning systems are essentially dissimilar. FL works on the assumption that the majority of clients are collaborative and truthful in FL. Nevertheless, owing to the transparency and extent of involvement, it is very likely that some clients will maliciously behave, willingly (e.g., attackers) or unwillingly (e.g., because of bugs or outdated software). Such bad deeds may have a direct impact on the quality and reliability of the learning model.

One of the most noticeable FL attacks is data poisoning which exploits the decentralized characteristics of the system. The implementation of local data and training process over each client means that the attacker can become part of the network as a client and control the data or training output imperceptibly. Those saddled with poisoned updates are subsequently forwarded to the server where it is incorporated with the global model without its knowledge. This may lead to incorrect or erratic behaviour of the model during the inference of the model, particularly in high-stakes cases (Bonawitz et al., 2019) .

In addition to that, data poisoning attacks, in contrast to adversarial attacks at the inference stage, are directed onto learning. This increases their threat level since the malignant impact will be built into parameters of the model and may last through subsequent updates. These types of attacks are also more difficult to detect because in most situations no raw training data is available and little is known about how the clients are behaving.

Because federated learning enters the privacy-sensitive and mission-critical application fields, it is not only a technical matter of its security and integrity of learning process, but also an ethical and legal issue. Companies need to make proactive measures to learn the possible threats against it and the defense mechanism that can hold on the trust and reliability of FL systems.

1.3 Data Poisoning Attacks

This flexibility to deal with poisoning attacks on federated learning is motivated by the fact that in reality, the attacks with hacked models can harm people. Within a healthcare facility, the specimen contaminated could provide wrong diagnosis to the diseases. With self-driving vehicles, the emergence of such a prototype could trigger the inability to identify traffic signs and risk the lives of people. It might have a negative impact of creating incorrect fraud-detection or fraud-authentication within a financial system. The picture above points to the pathetic outcomes that can be brought about by the absence or minimization of attacks on poisonings (Chen et al., 2021).

In addition, the second complication is that it is not straightforward to identify malevolent individuals in a privacy saving arrangement. In trying to depict client data privacy in the majority of FL setting, encryption or even differential privacy practices assure that a central server can never view client data. Though this provides privacy, it also means that widely used auditing or evidence methods will not be able to overcome small editing that can be done locally by malicious customers.

Data poisoning is now a concern in FL which furthers the objective of creating trustworthy AI systems. With AI penetrating progressively deeper within the layers of society and infrastructure, the necessity to have models, which are not just accurate, but robust, transparent and secure presents no less a problem. Developers and regulators, along with other stakeholders, are coming to know that AI systems cannot be trusted purely on performance, but should also be depended on to be resilient in the face of an attack (Cao et al., 2020).

The motivation of this chapter is an attempt to fill the gap between the increasing popularity of federated learning and the comparatively inadequate development of the protection measures against the attacks. Combining current approaches against and in defense, the work offers a contribution to the field to establish a systematic perceptions of complete consequences to develop safe FL models that would continue their operation even under malicious attacks.

2. DATA POISONING ATTACKS

2.1 Types of Data Poisoning Attacks

In federated learning, data poisoning attack can be categorized into several categories depending on the goal and strategy of the attacker. Degradation of overall performance of the model is the goal of the untargeted attacks, whereas a targeted attack manipulates the model so that it performs improperly in certain instances, with the attacker in the latter. The two types of attacks use the trust that the central server can have with clients and the obscurity of training data and processes locally.

In untargeted attacks, an adversary with the malicious client injects flawed or noisy information in the learning process to pollute the overall learning of the model. The attacker would e.g. add noise labels, inject out-of-distribution samples, or train on large imbalances. Consequently, the global model lacks the generalization capability and has low classification accuracy per classes. Such attacks are able to go undetected since they are similar to naturally occurring client data diversities and noise (Fang et al., 2020).

Figure 1. Classification of data poisoning attacks in federated learning

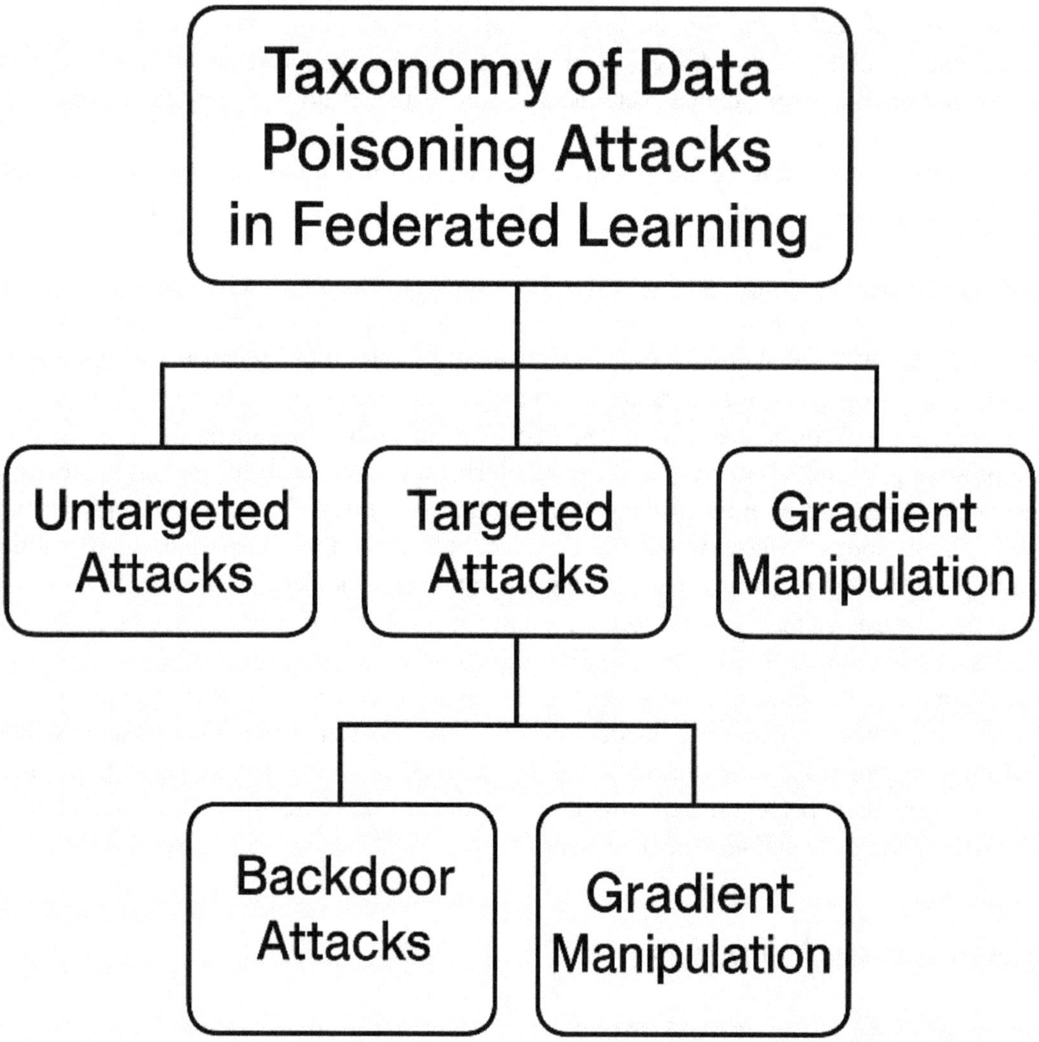

More sinister and refined are the targeted attacks, otherwise known as backdoor attacks. Here the adversary prepares special data examples containing imperceptible, but known to the attacker, trigger pattern, e.g. a sequence of pixels in an image or a key word in a text. The local model is then trained to misrepresent these triggered inputs into some target class, otherwise they seem normal. The global mode will only accept aggregate updates hence there is a possibility that it learns this malicious association unintentionally with no noticeable compromise.

Besides typo-level attacks, there are gradient-level poisoning attacks, in which instead of changing the data, the attacker changes the gradient updates to the server. The adversary can tilt the aggregated model in the direction that he/she wishes by making biased or extreme updates. The described attacks emphasize the significance of data-centric and model-centric defense because an attacker can target various levels of the FL process (Goyal et al., 2025a).

2.2 Threat Models in Federated Learning

A threat model specifies the assumptions, capabilities and goals of an attacker inside a system. During federated learning, various threat models assist the researchers to learn about the various access and power levels that an adversary may be in charge of. This knowledge is essential in the development of proper defense systems, which may be able to defeat adversaries in the real world.

The insider threat is one such typical threat model where a malicious one or more clients take part. It is assumed that such clients use the FL protocol in a superficial manner to tamper with their data or uptodate them in order to break the model. It is especially perilous since it does not involve any external breaches or any complicated exploits; all an attacker should do is to sign-up as a genuine client (Fung et al., 2018).

Another model deals with adversaries that are omniscient and they might be aware of the global model, the aggregation scheme and may even possess benign client data in part. Although this is a bold assumption, it characterizes other situations in which attackers reverse mobile apps or other edge devices. Conversely, a semi-honest or passive adversary is unlikely to interfere with the process, but instead monitors it in order to obtain some information related to the data or the model, which makes more sense in privacy-sensitive settings (Geyer et al., 2017).

An appreciation of such models can be used to set boundaries in the prevention of attack. It also points to the weaknesses of some defenses, which can only work in certain assumptions. A good federated learning framework should thus be able to focus on several threat models and test their existing defense against different adversarial scenarios to fully cover security aspects.

2.3 Real-World Manifestations and Consequences of Data Poisoning Attacks

Data poisoning attacks do not belong to blackboard exercises only, with implications in multiple industries. Poisoning attacks could, for instance, be used to deceive diagnosis models in the healthcare setting. A malicious hospital could import biased training information and it will allow symptoms, which could be misclassified, and overlook life-threatening outcomes resulting in a misdiagnosis or failure to identify a life-threatening condition. The impact of one poorly behaved participant can be too high due to the fact that FL is an aggregation of models belonging to different institutions.

Financial FL is used more and more in credit scoring and fraud detection. It is possible to play with a poisoned model by omitting certain patterns of fraud or authorizing inappropriate transactions by feeding it false behavioral data. Bank or financial institutions are susceptible to model drift and mistake hence these types of attacks can cause huge economic losses as well as contravening regulations (Gu et al., 2019).

Mobile phones and smart devices are also a typical application of FL, in language modeling, and predictive typing. With this kind of system an attacker would have the ability to manipulate update in the models to incorrectly suggest mispredictions or another system which is bias towards a particular suggestion. Otherwise, it can negatively affect the user experience, reputation of the service providers or even disrupt the usage patterns by manipulating the information.

These examples support why it is vital to come up with federated learning schemes, which are privacy-infringing and against adversarial interference. One can say that the impact of data poisoning is far more than the inaccuracy due to its potential to affect safety, fairness, trust, and legal compliance in different industries.

3. FEDERATED LEARNING FRAMEWORKS VULNERABILITIES

3.1 Decentralization and Low Profile

The twisting of the first and the paramount premise of federalization of learning, i.e., it is a superior idea in all terms of privacy, comes out as one of the most significant vulnerabilities of security. As an independent entity, where the server does not take knowledge of the raw data, the central coordinator will be only reliant on parameters updates relayed via it by clients. This implies that the server has to take the local training on faith that it has been done fairly, and that the updates being made are not on purpose damaged.

This restricted access to the training data and procedure will make detection of anomalies/manipulation indications deceptively hard. Unlike a centralized system where it is possible to issue checks on the quality of the data, preprocessing and checks of consistency can all be done centrally, federated systems do not have the infrastructure to guarantee that training information is clean and representative. This is particularly tricky with diverse client population with devices in uncontrolled conditions (Goyal, 2025b).

There is also the problem of the non-simultaneous and the incomplete involvement of clients during every training round. Not every client will always attend and the methods of selecting the consumer are usually random or availability. This provides more freedom to attackers to conceal their misdoings across several rounds as they can camouflage among honest players. This can over time lead to severe damage of the decision boundaries of the model by the accumulated updates that are poisoned.

The result of this invisibility is that detection of data poisoning is hindered and this also makes accountability harder to traverse. In case a poisoned model was caught after being deployed, then it is hardly possible to get a source of corruption trace without the violation of privacy. Trade-offs of privacy and security such as this are some of the most agriculturally troubling areas of a federated learning system design (He et al., 2020).

3.2 Malicious Client Behavior

The use of malicious customers is a major vulnerability in federated learning because they can exert a malicious behavior without hindrances since they will be able to appear ordinary members by performing the malicious deed. Such clients can be seemingly compliant with the FL protocol and silently use poisoned data, gradient poisoning or adaptively delay their responses. Due to the fact that FL protocols are most often created to work with distributed and data having various distributions (non-identically distributed (non-IID)), minor deviations that can be introduced by malicious activity may be easily ignored.

The attackers may go stealth, or have persistence. As an example, instead of corrupted the model radically in one round, they could engage in low-scale poisoning across several rounds, slowly modifying behavior of the model. This gradual poisoning process is more difficult to diagnose since there is no direct impact on the performance. It rather undermines the quality and strength of the model gradually at the micro level (Huang et al., 2020).

Also, rogue customers can team up and increase their influence. An adversary can create many virtual clients under various identities in what is referred to as sybil attack. These false clients will have the ability to take over the aggregation process or even strengthen their poisoned updates. In federated learning, the scale of the number of clients is high, and the system is open to be joined; therefore, it is technically difficult to identify such sybil behaviors.

Malicious client behavior is hard to prevent due to this inherent choice between decentralization and centralized control in FL. Majority of the FL systems are not keen on enforcing heavy client side validation mechanisms or auditing on the grounds of privacy. Nonetheless, there are no checks on this and thus attackers can easily take advantage of the trust assumptions that the system holds to exploit its defenses making strong defense systems necessary (Jain et al., 2021).

3.3 Gradient Manipulation and Model Poisoning

There is more than the manipulation of training data: attackers can modify the updates of the model that they send to the server. This is also referred to as the gradient manipulation or poisoning and this type of attack is especially dangerous since it attacks the communication channel itself. In this response, the attacker designs updates that are statistically indistinguishable to honest updates but biases them to follow a malicious path in minor ways.

Among the main difficulties in this area, we can outline the fact that numerous FL systems employ such methods of simple averaging as Federated Averaging (FedAvg), in which a server indiscriminately combines the gradients or weights provided by clients. It can be exploited by an attacker who will provide exaggerated or conflicting gradients and influence the learning of the model. The poisoned gradients are not filtered in any way, since, there is no valid ground truth to verify and validate the updates (Jia et al., 2022).

Disruption of performance is not as far as model poisoning goes. These tempered updates can be used to place backdoors in the global model by the attackers. As an example, an adversarial client can make the model relate a particular pattern (e.g. a particular word or pixel) with a target label. After training, global model will act normally on the rest of the inputs, but all those containing that trigger would be misclassified. Such an attack may go unnoticed during the validation and only triggered at specific circumstances.

Gradient manipulation is effectively defended by either more intelligent aggregation rules, or detection of anomalous patterns. Nevertheless, it is a continuing task to design such defenses without sacrificing privacy or prematurely incurring high computation cost. Gradient-manipulation techniques and risks must be understood to have secure and robust federated learning systems (Kairouz et al., 2019).

4. DEFENSE MECHANISMS: A TAXONOMY

As the threat of data poisoning attacks in federated learning is increasing, the proposed defense strategies are very diverse. Such defenses are differing not only by their technicalities but also by their place in the pipeline of federated learning. In order to be able to better comprehend them, it is convenient to do taxonomy based on the layer at which they operate: data-level defenses, model-level defenses, aggregation-level defenses, and a mixture of some of them (hybrid strategies). Based on this categorization, practitioners can then select "defenses which best fit their system architecture and threat model".

4.1 Data-Level Defenses

The purpose of data-level defenses is to identify and discard poisoned data before causing it to be trained on the model. The federated learning operation does not allow the application of data sanitization techniques traditionally used to avoid the leakage of client information. Nevertheless, the pre-processing, validation and outlier detection on the local datasets could be recommended, prior to training, on the data submitted by the clients. Other systems encourage clients to make light wieight anomaly detection models or filter the mislabeled data at local level.

Nonetheless, data-level countermeasures work poorly in FL because the server cannot check raw data. Data validation based on clients will require clients to be honest, which in adversarial, is not the case. In addition, by having the device, opponents can pretend to be honest and avoid this filter. That is why, although data cleaning is a valuable solution, it cannot be regarded as a single solution in FL (Kang et al., 2019).

Figure 2. Multi-layered defense mechanisms in federated learning

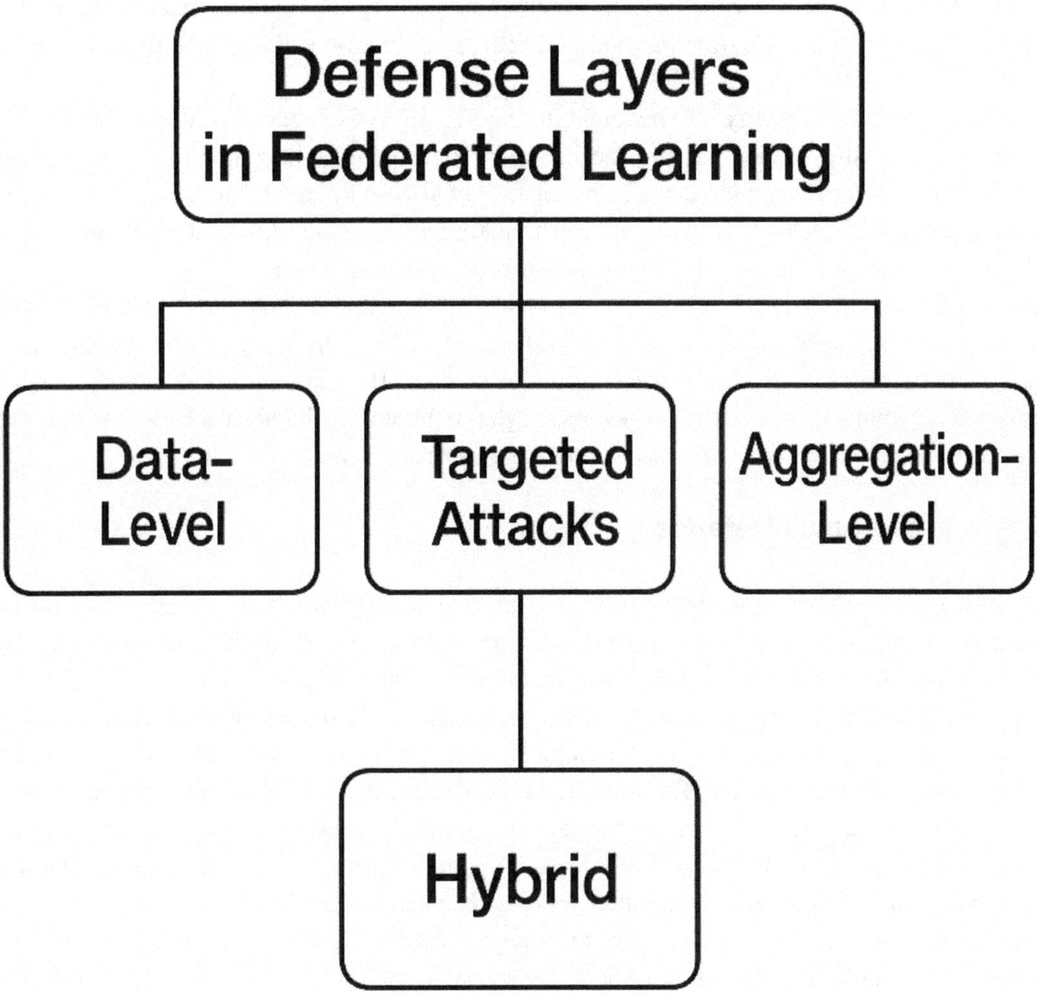

The other is the defensive data augmentation where (benign) clients use synthetic data to exoticize locally training data. Such an approach assists the model in better generalizations, and the weight of a few poisoned clients is minimized. The data-level defenses are promising but would need to be complemented with server-side mechanisms in order to work properly in the adversarial world.

4.2 Model-Level Defenses

Model-level defense concentrates on improving the training algorithm or loss to minimise the discrimination of the model to poisoned inputs. The most common adversarial is through adversarial training in which perturbed inputs are known to be deliberately inputted into the model to make it more robust. In federated cases this may include training models that are resistant to local overfitting, causing poisoned clients to have less of an impact.

The other model-level strategy is to reweight the contribution of clients according to their past action or statistics characteristics. As an example, the deviations that are too far beyond the average or deviations that are abnormal for normal patterns can be down-weighted or eliminated. But it is quite a challenging issue to structure such mechanisms without discriminating against honest, yet various clients, which is typical in cases when the data is non-IID cross-clients (Goyal et al., 2025c).

There has been some effort to optimise robustly such as by using trimmed loss or bounded gradient norms to ensure models are not so sensitive to wild updates. Although promising on simulations, these techniques can potentially add convergence problems or make the training process long when applied in large-scale deployments. Nevertheless, even though the model-level defenses have these limitations, they are a critical part of defense in cases where data inspection is nonviable.

4.3 Aggregation-Level Defenses

Federated learning is based on aggregation, and altering how updates are aggregated is probably the most straightforward of techniques to stop data poisoning. Robust aggregation rules are instead created in a way that opposes misleading outliers and malicious updates in place of simple averaging. Fault tolerant aggregation has been proposed using such techniques as Krum,Trimmed Mean, and Bulyan.

The working concept behind Krum is that it picks an update most similar to others on the condition that honest clients are the majority. Trimmed Mean provides the combination of every element of the gradient leaving the maximum and the minimum values. Bulyan is using the combination of strategies to enhance robustness. Such methods downplay the impact of poisoned updates without checking on client data hence they fit the bill on federated systems (Konečný et al., 2016) .

Nevertheless, there are also disadvantages to strong aggregation techniques. They tend to believe that most clients are benevolent to them and could collapse whenever a well-coordinated group of malicious clients offer similar contaminated updates. Also, the algorithms are computationally heavy, and they would not obtainable in resource-restricted settings. However, they form part and parcel of the most adopted defenses because of the direct effect that they have on integrity of the global model.

4.4 Hybrid Approaches

None of the current defense mechanisms protects against all kinds of data poison detection in federated learning. Consequently, there has been popularity in hybrid methods that incorporate a combination of various defense methods. Such systems combine data-level authentication, model-level tightening and strong aggregation to establish multi-tier safeguards. To give one example, a client may do local anomaly detection, and the server may pass a strong-aggregation and cross-round validation to detect chronic poisoning patterns.

A single hybrid approach is using reputation systems in conjunction with aggregation. In this case, the reliability of each of the clients is rated across the time by the quality and stability of its updates. Clients with high reputation have greater power in the aggregation and those with low reputation are levied or locked out. These systems learn as they go and they have the ability to notice harmful behavior patterns over a long period of time even unobvious and delayed attacks (Li et al., 2020).

Hybrid defence usually entail increased computation and communication overhead, but they result in a trade-off between accuracy, security and privacy. They are particularly useful in field implementations where the adversaries can adopt dynamic measures. Indeed, the agents use hybrid defenses, which should be the future of creating resilient and scalable systems on federated learning.

5. ROBUST AGGREGATION TECHNIQUES

5.1 Krum

Krum is a strong aggregation algorithm that protects the federated learning systems against Byzantine or malignant client updates. What the essence of Krum is, is that a single client update is chosen which is most "representative" in the majority of the clients (minimum of the distances to neighboring updates). In particular, the algorithm, upon client update, calculates a distance to other client updates and picks the one with a shortest cumulative distance to its nearest neighbors. This is to guarantee that the chosen update is near the cluster of honest clients updates and distant to remote points, which is certain to be poisoned (Liu et al., 2018).

It will work out in cases in which most clients are sincere since malicious updates will likely single out to be outliers. Krum does not average all the updates and instead uses a single update by picking the best update who is trusted. It does not choose an update that is misled by adversarial gradients. Nevertheless, due to Krum only one update is used in each round of aggregations, which makes its convergence slow and variance high, particularly in the non-IID data case where honest client updates may naturally vary.

Krum also makes a concretion that the proportion of malicious clients is not more than half of all participants; otherwise, in case the attackers represent more than half or their updates are coordinated, they can bypass the filtering of Krum. Nonetheless, Krum continues to play a central role in the study of robust aggregation in that it has served as inspiration to many variants and refinements.

5.2 Trimmed Mean

Another robust aggregation mechanism is the Trimmed Mean, which consists in first removing the extreme values in the updates, and then averaging them. Trimmed Mean works using a different update as opposed to Krum, making it work on every coordinate (parameter) in all the client updates. It will group the values in each dimension of the parameter and discard a fixed number of the highest and the lowest values and average the rest.

The process of this trimming is effective in diminishing the impact of the poisoned updates that tend to have very extreme values of parameters. Since the aggregation is coordinate-wise, Trimmed Mean is effective in curbing attacks that aimed at skewing a small number of parameters to a large extent. Trimmed

Mean has cheaper computational cost than Krum and with enough updates, except at the extreme ones, it could converge faster and more accurate (McMahan et al., 2017).

Nevertheless, the effectiveness of Trimmed Mean presupposes the assumption that the malicious updates have severe values. The smartest attackers can engineer the updates in such a way as to not take either of these extremes and instead introduce such subtle manipulations, which can pass through this security barrier. What is more, in case the natural diversity/ skew of the honest updates, genuine updates may be dropped leading to adverse influence on the model performance.

5.3 Bulyan

Bulyan is a hybrid robust aggregation algorithm formed by combining the ideas of Krum and Trimmed Mean to ensure an enhanced defense against data poisoning. It will then use Krum several times in order to filter a set of candidate updates that are assumed to be reliable. Next, it uses Trimmed Mean on the subset thus to get the final aggregate update further eliminated outliers in the chosen set.

The two-step method takes an advantage of the Krum strength of choosing updates closest to the majority but through Trimmed Mean, minimises the influence of outliers in the selected updates. Buliyan is particularly useful to foil a multi-client coordinated-malicious-client multi-site attack, limiting the effectiveness of the both overt and surreptitious poisoned update.

The primary trade-off of Bulyan is the complexity of computing and raised overhead of communication as it consumes many passes and substantial calculation on the server. But in cases where federated learning needs high-security functions, this incremental cost can be well-grounded in how much more resistant to poisoning attacks it can be (Goyal et al., 2025d).

5.4 Multi-Krum and Other Variants

Multi-Krum is an obvious variant of Krum where the restriction on choosing one update per round is therefore removed. Multi-Krum instead of selecting one update, it will select multiple updates that score the best using the Krum criterion and averaging to get the aggregated update. It offers a trade off between strength and quicker convergence and utilization of client updates more.

To obtain a smoother gradient direction direction Multi-Kum compiles many updates that are trusted to be reliable with the outcome of having a more stable and efficient learning. It is safe in terms of malicious clients because it ignores extreme updates, and simultaneously is exploiting sincerer updates. The approach is rather useful especially in the heterogeneous data settings whereby the automatic diversification of client update occurs.

There are several other versions that have been proposed in order to make the aggregation even more robust. The methods being tuned by adaptive methods are one example of techniques of this sort and combinations of distance measures/combination of distance measures with statistical outlier detection measures are examples. Indeed, this continuous enhancement of the methods implies the continuous striving to bring security without hindering the effectiveness and the precision of federated learning (Melis et al., 2019).

6. AMBIVALENT CLIENT REPUTATION SYSTEMS ANOMALY DETECTION AND CLIENT REPUTATION SYSTEMS

6.1 Behavioral Monitoring

The surveillance of the conduct in this federated learning is continuously carried out to the information that customers forward to by informing them on the odd or suspicious trends that can be related to ill-purposed actions. This method observes different measures that include size (magnitude) of updates, direction of updates against past updates and repeatability across several training rounds. The system can identify significant deviations of the updates against the baseline of what is considered to be normative client behavior as anomalous (based on past statistics) by defining what it means to be normal within the area of client behavior.

An example is that a client that all of a sudden starts updating with large changes of parameters or updates that would have moved a model in directions contrary to other clients, could be malicious. The early detection of such irregularity is important as it enables the system to interfere before the overall models of the model suffer due to such poisoned updates. One way this can be achieved is thru behavioral monitoring to control model integrity by picking out on the clients, who may be trying to poison the training process.

Nevertheless, creating skilled behavioral tracking solutions is tricky considering the variable nature of the data in the federal learning process. Honest clients can also contribute varying and changing updates that may appear to be out-of-pattern but, in actual sense, are valid. In order to reduce the number of false alarms and to prevent punishment of honest participants, thresholds and a detection algorithm should be adaptive and context-sensitive, and may use dynamic baselines that vary as a result of client-specific patterns of behavior (Nasr et al., 2019).

6.2 Scoring and Reputation-Based Participation

One extension of behavioral monitoring is the use of scoring and reputation systems where each client maintains a dynamic reputation score that adds up how to estimate their trustworthiness and reliability with time. Such reputation scores are used to decide the importance of an update made by a client in case of an aggregation or may go to an extent of a client being disqualified to be present in next rounds of training.

Clients who have been updating consistently and also in a well-behaved manner are given higher reputation scores hence having the higher weight in the global model. On the other hand, the clients who are being flagged with the suspicious behavior are losing their reputation and their feedbacks or even they are completely eliminated in the training process. This dynamic score scoring will effectively decrease the ability of poisoning attacks presented by the malicious clients, especially in attacks that happen over and over again or on long term.

Hackers can seek to manipulate the system by switching to the benign and malign updates to keep their reputation above average. As well, the calculation of reputations should not violate the privacy of users or disclose any important data of clients. That these values effectively computed in private ways for example using the secure addition or anonymization so ideally trusted in federation learning region (Nguyen et al., 2021).

6.3 Machine Learning for Attack Detection

The challenge of anomaly detection is solvable through machine learning, which offers a powerful toolbox to identify malicious actions as well as client updates through learning to recognize complex patterns that are not likely to be identified by simple heuristics. Different behavioral cues such as the proximity of gradients, the time and frequency of update, and correlations with updates of other clients are then examined by these models, to categorise prospective attackers dynamically.

Supervised learning techniques are those in which the classifiers can be trained based on labeled data which contains examples of attacks and in unsupervised learning categorization extreme values or irrelevant clusters are being sought but without any labeling. Coordinated attacks can be detected using the clustering and density estimation approaches to the problem because they can be detected as a group of clients with several abnormal behaviors. Such adaptive methods enhance federal modes of detection and may respond to changes or emerging attacks with time.

However, detecting using machine learning solutions necessitates the availability of reasonable number of representative data (a variety of attack types) which is not always easy to be gathered in practice. There is even possible blind spot against unfamiliar attacks as a result of overfitting to known attacks. Also, the training and deployment computational cost of such models and privacy issues of analyzing client updates need to be well-taken care of to make the practical and secure implementation of these an option (Pillutla et al., 2019).

7. DIFFERENTIAL PRIVACY AND SECURE MULTIPARTY COMPUTATION

7.1 Role of Differential Privacy in Mitigation

Differential Privacy (DP) is a formal mathematical scheme, which aims to conceal particular records of a dataset in such a way as by including a precisely adjusted noise to results, no individual example of the database can be identified or unduly impacted. DP can serve two purposes in the federated learning context; on the one hand, it ensures user privacy, and, on the other hand, it act as a natural data poisoning attack defense layer.

In applying DP to federated learning the gradients of the models or the parameter updates are each perturbed adding noise before submitting to the central server to be added. This noise is a smoothing force and mitigates the effect of outlandish or malevolent updates that malicious entities may design to interfere with the training procedure of the model. DP also decreases this risk because poisoned data is unlikely to affect the performance of or behavior of the global model with substantial impact due to their ability to be limited in the impact they can exert thanks to DP.

Nonetheless, there is a fundamental trade-off between privacy and model utility that will be created by the deployment of DP. Too much noise might harm the correctness of the trained model and slows convergence, whenever the amount of noise is so high that it hides actual updates. Moreover, DP by itself is not a kill switch to poisoning attacks. Even in the case when enemies manage to get access to several clients, nevermind organize malicious activity efficiently, the blocking schemes based on noise may be still outsmarted. Thus, to obtain the best protection we would like differential privacy to be used in a defensive combination with other mutually supporting defence mechanisms that add robustness cumulatively (Goyal et al., 2025e).

7.2 Cryptographic Techniques for Enhanced Security

Another defense dimension is offered by Secure Multiparty Computation (SMC) and similar cryptographic protocols, which allows computers to collectively compute the sum of the model updates without disclosing their own, or intermediary, data. The protocols guarantee that both central server and any of the clients do not learn any information other than the final aggregated output hence maintaining a high cryptographic level of privacy.

Cryptographic techniques allow each of the clients to update its aggregation data because by reducing information leakage due to an aggregation, they also ensure that it is much more difficult to perform analysis or reverse-engineer a single client update. This decrease in visible information limits the capacity of the attackers to synchronize advanced poisoning attacks, based on precise awareness of other parties updates. Subsequently, SMC improves the level of privacy and security of federated learning systems.

The issues of cryptographical protocols adoption, however, are challenging. These approaches ought to be followed by huge volume of computations procedure and additional communications that may bring about latency and demand a relative abundance of bandwidth. It is the overhead that can be very expensive in scenarios involving federated learning with the great number of clients or in the scenarios when the devices have limited amounts of computational facilities and battery lives. These cryptographic processes are yet another area of practice, in which the research is ongoing to make them practical and ready deployed (Qian and Charikar, 2020).

7.3 Trade-offs Among Security, Performance

Combining federated learning systems with the use of the mail privacy and cryptographic mechanisms is destined to subvert sophisticated security/privacy/performance trade-offs of such systems. These methods not only increase immunity to data poisons but also provide better user privacy, but have certain other risky implications of increasing the complexity of computation, the state of inter-node communication, and even the model itself.

Making a reasonable privacy essential guess in differential privacy is a trade-off: on the one hand, privation excess corresponds to insufficient noise at the cost of privacy and these results, but on the other hand, on the high side of the noise budget, the quality of models and acceleration of training can also degrade. Similarly, cryptographic protocol engineering should account on both the overheads in computing (both size of computation and network load) and reduce the engineering in order to offer credits that could be apportioned to justify that engineering has given no assurances of that no security has been violated. The practical implementation of federated learning should balance these conflicting requirements depending on the relevant use case, resource limitations and threat models.

Current activity consists of seeking more efficient, less bulky privacy-preserving algorithms and a more stripped-down, domain-specific cryptographic protocol to support federated learning. Depending on the specific task, approximate cryptographic protocols, adaptive noise mechanisms and hybrid privacy frameworks were introduced; the latter attempts to find the best trade-offs between protection of the user and the model, and favorable levels of accuracy and efficiency (Ren et al., 2020).

Through this premise, the field is one step forward to having federated learning systems that are not only privacy-aware and secure yet scalable and feasible to the workings of the common user in various real-life scenarios.

8. ADVERSARIAL TRAINING AND DATA SANITIZATION

8.1 Pre-processing and Filtering Techniques

Defense measures include pre-processing and filtering that form the first line of defense against data poisoning in federated learning, and their objective is to extract pre-cleaning removing local data with the help of pre-process and filtering data before starting local model training. In federated learning, there is a limitation of direct accessibility to server of clients data, but clients are at liberty to perform filtering upon data and eliminate suspicious or malicious samples using different local filtering techniques. This reduces the chance of corrupted data affecting update of the local model and hence defending the global model against corruption (Shokri & Shmatikov, 2015).

Some of the common methods used are statistical outlier detection, wherein outlier data are those that show great differences relative to the normal distribution and might be deemed as samples of the poison. Also, there are label consistency checks that detect wrongly labeled data entries that were possibly done maliciously by intruders. It is also possible to identify anomalous trends or inconsistencies in the information through clustering and similarity calculations. Collectively, the methods would assist in enhancing data quality and integrity of data used in training.

There are limitations however to these client side filtering. Sophisticated clients may also find a way to evade pre-processing or deceive it in order to evade having tainted data detected. In addition, since quality and distribution of information differs on clients, the efficiency of filtering may be erratic. Thus, being a crucial line of defense, pre-processing cannot be the only method of poisoning prevention and should be accompanied by a stronger server-side defense or interceptive one (Sun & Kairouz, 2021).

8.2 Robust Training Against Poisoned Data

Hearty training methods aim at making the learning algorithms themselves resistant to the existence of poisoned or adversarial data. These approaches alter the training process by minimizing the effect of polluted data on model-updates instead of discarding the possibly harmful samples altogether. In doing this, the international model remains steady and precise even in the face of adversarial interference.

Among such approaches, one is to change the loss function, so that it reduces the influence of outliers or suspicious values. Example: Trimmed loss or median-based loss reduces the effect of the sample values which are either extreme relative to the normal value by scaling their impact at directly obtaining the gradient. The other most commonly used tricks are gradient clipping, which just constrains the magnitude of the parameter updates and hence allows poisoned samples not to generate runaway gradients and disrupt the model (Truong et al., 2020).

Adversarial training is also important, in which poisoned or perturbed data is purposefully used on the model during training. Through this exposure, the model can be trained to learn defensive representations and is made vigilant against similar attacks in the real-world. Adversarial training is effective, but it is subject to careful tuning to guard against overfitting particular pattern of attacks and still have the model generalize well on clean data.

8.3 Synthetic Data Use in Defense

The creation of synthetic data has become a potential method to strengthen the security of federated learning by complementing local datasets with synthetic data and high-quality samples produced by an algorithm. Such synthetic data augment the data variance and can also diffuse the presence of poisoned data as the model is exposed to a wider and even more balanced training data.

During federated learning, synthetic data can be either created by the clients or by the central server, leveraging on the use of state of the art generative models, like Generative Adversarial Networks (GANs), or Variational Autoencoders (VAEs). The synthetic samples of these models are close to the statistical properties of the clean data, and thus as a result, the model learns strong features and avoid the overfitting on the potentially poisoned local datasets.

Although synthetic data augmentation can ensure model robustness, it does not make a standalone solution. Generation of realistic and various synthetic data requires considerable computing power and technical skill. Moreover, the low quality synthetic data can introduce biases or noise and affect the model negatively. Nevertheless, when combining synthetic data with pre-processing, robust training, other defensive mechanisms, etc., the adoption of synthetic data results in an environment of federated learning based on a stronger defense (Goyal, 2025f).

9. EMPIRICAL ASSESSMENT OF FEDERATED LEARNING DEFENSE STRATEGIES

9.1 Systematic Comparison of Federated Learning Defense Mechanisms

The comparison analysis will be a very valuable source of information regarding the efficacy of various data poisoning defenses in the territory of federated learning. The performance of methods such as robust aggregation, anomaly detection, differential privacy and adversarial training on different forms of poisoning attacks are normally compared.

They often come with inherent trade-offs: in one such case, strong aggregation protocols can be used to effective filter malicious updates, but will introduce latency or reduce accuracy on existing corrupted data. Anomaly detection is a better tradeoff of the security parameter of detecting shifty clients and carries the cost of false positive that leads to disbarring the rate of pious players. The results of these tests serve to underline the fact that it is possible that there is no unified defense against an attack and as such there is a need to consider hybrid defense solutions in consideration regard to attack models and deployment conditions (Wang et al., 2019).

9.2 Framework Simulation and Quantitative Performance Analysis

Simulation Defense Simulations Simulation defense strategies are tested using metrics like accuracy of models, resistance to being poisoned, convergence, and computational complexity. These are highly dynamic parameters of the experiments and may encompass the number of clients (clients in a particular ball), adversary ratios (ratio of clients who act as adversaries to the total number of clients), and heterogeneity of the data (usual in real federated learning scenarios).

The findings show that, egocentric schemes like Bulyan and Multi-Krum are very well with anteriori scalp level of poisoning and frail when malicious clients are furthermore augmented. Different privacy has helped to defend against loss, yet is most commonly slower to converge on, and has an influence on the final accuracy applied. The significant measurable is the software overhead and scalability which are especially crucial in bigger federated networks that gives the design of versatile, secure, and effective learning systems (Xie et al., 2019).

9.3 Significant Case Study Based Insight and Strategic Recommendation

However, concerning the case-studies and experiments, there is no doubt that multiple mechanisms of defense is to be applied to offer the direct countermeasures to adaptive and advanced attacks. Neither applying only one of the tools (aggregation robustness or anomaly detection) is sufficient to make the systems secure.

Federated data diversity, covered by non-IID and different clients introduces the necessity to factor in context-specific and adaptive resiliences that need to find a balance between protection, confidentiality, and equity. Also, it is imperative to control the defensive mechanisms with constant monitoring, re-evaluation, and updating of the such mechanisms to ensure they keep ahead of the riot of new attack modes and new threats within the federated learning setting (Zhu et al., 2021).

CONCLUSION

Federated learning offers a positive framework where one can use to train models on dispersed machines using dispersed data without breaching the privacy of the data. However, it, in its turn, raises special security concerns particularly due to the risk of data poisoning attacks aimed at processing corrupt global model, through interference with the local training data or updates. The present chapter has elaborated the severe data poisoning risk and has integrated a wide scope of defense platforms with an aim of securing federated learning systems.

Depending on whether they be definitive aggregation purpose, as in the case of Krum and Bulyan, or reputation systems and anomaly detection modules, any of the defense structures can provide a difference in advancing the resilience of the model. Other mechanisms of privacy protection such as differential privacy, and secure multiparty computation can guarantee protection to sensitive content besides other additional security measures regarding poisoning. More is yet to come: adversarial training, synthetic data augmentation, and data sanitization are all successful techniques that can be used to enhance client- and server-side strength.

This notwithstanding, there is no single defense mechanism that can be able to eliminate the risk of data poisoning, especially in real-life instances, which involve adaptive attackers, not mentioning the variances in the distributions of data. Good protection requires well-designed hybrid security, which consider strength, accuracy, privacy and computing efficiency. In addition, surveillance, evaluation, and incessant adjustment are significant to counters the modified attacks.

Coming up there are large challenges of scaling the defense systems in large federated networks, maintaining model performance under security and formulating consistent benchmark to testing. These will demand additional interdisciplinary studies and inventions to handle such problems. Lastly, it would also be a critical requirement to continue to evolve to strong and secure federated learning to achieve all its potentials across a plethora of apps offered in healthcare, fintech, and beyond, and continues to strive not to infringe upon the trust of users and privacy of their data.

REFERENCES

Bagdasaryan, E., Veit, A., Hua, Y., Estrin, D., & Shmatikov, V. (2020). How to backdoor federated learning. *Proceedings of the 23rd International Conference on Artificial Intelligence and Statistics (AISTATS)*, 2938–2948.

Bonawitz, K., Eichner, H., Grieskamp, W., Huba, D., Ingerman, A., Ivanov, V., & Seth, K. (2019). Towards federated learning at scale: System design. *Proceedings of the 2nd SysML Conference*.

Cao, X., Zhang, L., Wang, X., & Yang, Q. (2020). A comprehensive survey on adversarial machine learning in cybersecurity. *IEEE Access : Practical Innovations, Open Solutions*, *8*, 27184–27202.

Chen, X., Liu, C., Li, B., Lu, K., & Song, D. (2021). Federated learning with malicious clients: Attacks and defenses. *IEEE Transactions on Neural Networks and Learning Systems*, *32*(6), 2367–2380.

Fang, M., Cao, X., Jia, J., & Gong, N. Z. (2020). Local model poisoning attacks to byzantine-robust federated learning. *Proceedings of the 29th USENIX Security Symposium*, 1605–1622.

Fung, C., Yoon, C. J. M., & Beschastnikh, I. (2018). Mitigating sybils in federated learning poisoning. *arXiv preprint arXiv:1808.04866*.

Geyer, R. C., Klein, T., & Nabi, M. (2017). Differentially private federated learning: A client level perspective. *arXiv preprint arXiv:1712.07557*.

Goyal, N. K. (2025). Weaponizing Misinformation and Cyberattacks on Supply Chains. In Bukhari, S., & Zafar, I. (Eds.), *Mass Media and Impact of Fake News on Supply Chains* (pp. 177–210). IGI Global Scientific Publishing., DOI: 10.4018/979-8-3373-2175-2.ch007

Goyal, N. K. (2025). Security and Privacy in IoT, Fog, and Blockchain Networks. In Sathio, A., Rind, M., Awan, S., & Junejo, A. (Eds.), *Energy-Efficient Deep Learning Approaches in IoT, Fog, and Green Blockchain Revolution* (pp. 371–398). IGI Global Scientific Publishing., DOI: 10.4018/979-8-3373-0300-0.ch015

Goyal, N. K., Dandotiya, M., Kumari, M., Kaloria, S., & Anushya, A. (2025). AI-Powered Haptic Devices for Patient Rehabilitation. In Mamodiya, U., Kalam, A., Bossoufi, B., Awad, M., & Somwanshi, D. (Eds.), *Integrating AI With Haptic Systems for Smarter Healthcare Solutions* (pp. 143–170). IGI Global Scientific Publishing., DOI: 10.4018/979-8-3373-2307-7.ch007

Goyal, N. K., Dandotiya, M., Kumari, M., Sheikh, M. F., & Sharma, S. (2025). Emerging Job Roles in the Tourism Sector Leveraging Artificial Intelligence. In Silic, M., Luthia, M., Ahmad, F., & Chakraborty, P. (Eds.), *Empowering Sustainable Performance and Competitive Advantage in Tourism* (pp. 89–126). IGI Global Scientific Publishing., DOI: 10.4018/979-8-3373-4546-8.ch004

Goyal, N. K., Dandotiya, M., Qurashi, J. A., Kumari, M., & Sharma, S. (2025). AI-Driven Predictive Analytics for Disease Management. In Ouaissa, M., Ouaissa, M., Imad, M., Qurashi, J., & Farooq, M. (Eds.), *Utilizing AI of Medical Things for Healthcare Security and Sustainability* (pp. 231–276). IGI Global Scientific Publishing., DOI: 10.4018/979-8-3373-0690-2.ch008

Goyal, N. K., Kumari, M., Kushwah, V., Dandotiya, M., & Vijay, A. (2025). Evaluating blockchain security: Trade-offs in consensus mechanisms. *IET Conference Proceedings*, 2024(38), 80–88. DOI: 10.1049/icp.2025.0775

Gu, T., Dolan-Gavitt, B., & Garg, S. (2019). Badnets: Evaluating backdooring attacks on deep neural networks. *IEEE Access : Practical Innovations, Open Solutions*, *7*, 47230–47244. DOI: 10.1109/ACCESS.2019.2909068

He, C., Li, B., Zhang, Y., & Song, D. (2020). Model poisoning attacks against federated learning systems. *Proceedings of the 2020 ACM SIGSAC Conference on Computer and Communications Security*, 2045-2062.

Huang, Q., Wang, X., Huang, W., & Song, H. (2020). Defending against backdoor attacks on federated learning. *Proceedings of the 29th International Joint Conference on Artificial Intelligence (IJCAI)*, 2490–2496.

Jain, S., Gupta, P., & Saxena, P. (2021). Federated learning: Challenges, methods, and future directions. *Journal of Network and Computer Applications*, *186*, 103078.

Jia, Z., Ma, S., Wang, J., & Yang, Q. (2022). FedRBN: Robust federated learning via robust batch normalization. *IEEE Transactions on Neural Networks and Learning Systems*.

. Kairouz, P., McMahan, H. B., Avent, B., Bellet, A., Bennis, M., Bhagoji, A. N., ... & Zhao, S. (2019). Advances and open problems in federated learning. *Foundations and Trends® in Machine Learning*, 14(1–2), 1-210.

Kang, J., Xiong, Z., Niyato, D., Ye, D., & Zhang, Y. (2019). Incentive design for federated learning: A contract theory approach. *IEEE Internet of Things Journal*, *6*(6), 10700–10714. DOI: 10.1109/JIOT.2019.2940820

Konečný, J., McMahan, H. B., Yu, F., Richtárik, P., Suresh, A. T., & Bacon, D. (2016). Federated learning: Strategies for improving communication efficiency. *arXiv preprint arXiv:1610.05492*.

Li, T., Sahu, A. K., Talwalkar, A., & Smith, V. (2020). Federated learning: Challenges, methods, and future directions. *IEEE Signal Processing Magazine*, *37*(3), 50–60. DOI: 10.1109/MSP.2020.2975749

Liu, Y., Ma, S., Aafer, Y., Lee, W. C., Zhai, J., Wang, W., & Zhang, X. (2018). Trojaning attack on neural networks. *Proceedings of the 25th Network and Distributed System Security Symposium (NDSS)*. DOI: 10.14722/ndss.2018.23291

McMahan, H. B., Moore, E., Ramage, D., Hampson, S., & Arcas, B. A. (2017). Communication-efficient learning of deep networks from decentralized data. *Proceedings of the 20th International Conference on Artificial Intelligence and Statistics (AISTATS)*, 1273–1282.

Melis, L., Song, C., De Cristofaro, E., & Shmatikov, V. (2019). Exploiting unintended feature leakage in collaborative learning. *Proceedings of the 2019 IEEE Symposium on Security and Privacy (SP)*, 691-706. DOI: 10.1109/SP.2019.00029

Nasr, M., Shokri, R., & Houmansadr, A. (2019). Comprehensive privacy analysis of deep learning: Passive and active white-box inference attacks against centralized and federated learning. *Proceedings of the 2019 IEEE Symposium on Security and Privacy (SP)*, 739-753. DOI: 10.1109/SP.2019.00065

Nguyen, D. C., Pathirana, P. N., Ding, M., & Seneviratne, A. (2021). Federated learning for internet of things: A comprehensive survey. *IEEE Communications Surveys and Tutorials*, *23*(3), 1620–1658. DOI: 10.1109/COMST.2021.3075439

Pillutla, K., Kakade, S. M., & Harchaoui, Z. (2019). Robust aggregation for federated learning. *Proceedings of the 36th International Conference on Machine Learning (ICML)*, 10997–11007.

Qian, Y., & Charikar, M. (2020). Efficient robust aggregation for federated learning. *Advances in Neural Information Processing Systems (NeurIPS)*, 33.

Ren, K., Yu, H., He, Y., Zhang, K., & Shen, X. (2020). A survey on privacy-preserving federated learning: Research issues, methods, and applications. *IEEE Internet of Things Journal*, *8*(10), 7799–7827.

Shokri, R., & Shmatikov, V. (2015). Privacy-preserving deep learning. *Proceedings of the 22nd ACM SIGSAC Conference on Computer and Communications Security*, 1310-1321.

Sun, W., & Kairouz, P. (2021). Distributed differential privacy: Algorithms and bounds. *Proceedings of the 38th International Conference on Machine Learning (ICML).*

Truong, N. B., Wang, J., Goudarzi, H., & Bouguettaya, A. (2020). Secure federated learning for internet of things: A survey. *IEEE Communications Surveys and Tutorials*, *22*(4), 2987–3024.

Wang, S., Tuor, T., Salonidis, T., Leung, K. K., Makaya, C., He, T., & Chan, K. (2019). Adaptive federated learning in resource constrained edge computing systems. *IEEE Journal on Selected Areas in Communications*, *37*(6), 1205–1221. DOI: 10.1109/JSAC.2019.2904348

Xie, C., Koyejo, O., & Gupta, I. (2019). Byzantine-robust federated learning via median and trimmed mean. *Proceedings of the 22nd International Conference on Artificial Intelligence and Statistics (AISTATS)*, 1616–1625.

Zhu, Y., Liu, T., Han, S., & Cheng, Y. (2021). Deep leakage from gradients. *Advances in Neural Information Processing Systems (NeurIPS)*, 32.

Chapter 10
Enhancing Federated Learning Robustness Against Adversarial Attacks Using SMPC

Sumit Kumar Kapoor
https://orcid.org/0009-0005-6291-3176
Poornima University, India

Kriti Sankhla
https://orcid.org/0009-0001-7061-365X
Poornima University, India

Saurabh Shandilya
https://orcid.org/0009-0002-3508-9298
Poornima University, India

Satya Prakash Awasthi
https://orcid.org/0009-0003-8077-3395
Amity University, Gwalior, India

ABSTRACT

Federated Learning (FL) allows for distributed model training across a population of devices while also offering the potential for privacy preservation, however, it remains susceptible to a range of adversarial manoeuvres, including model poisoning, backdoor attacks, and Byzantine behaviours. This chapter discusses secure multiparty computation (SMPC) as a cryptographic defence mechanism that allows models to be trained collaboratively and without revealing individual data associated with these models. We categorise the impacts of attacks, we offer various architectures of SMPC-based FL and we compare SMPC-based FL with traditional FL bases on security, communication, and computation. Certain key computational techniques, practical implementations with healthcare and industrial, Internet of Things (IoT) applications, security-performance trade-offs, scalability, limitations of current work, and an ordered taxonomy of threats to FL give insight into the performance and deployment of SMPC as a means to reduce threats to model accuracy.

DOI: 10.4018/979-8-3373-6224-3.ch010

1. INTRODUCTION

Federated Learning (FL) is an emerging distributed paradigm for a rich context of machine learning model training. FL allows training of multiple models collaboratively across various clients or edge devices without sacrificing data privacy as it does not transfer the original data to a central server (Konecny et al., 2016; Yang et al., 2019). Providing a basis for privacy-preserving model training, the federated learning paradigm supports sensitive data that stays within the boundary of individuals or device owners, and only model updates will be provided to the aggregator. The federated learning paradigm provides positive aspects of privacy, reducing communication costs, and regulatory compliance largely to the training of machine learning models in collaborative or federated environments, and supports modern constructs like health care, finance, and IoT systems (Yang et al., 2019).

1.1. Motivation: Adversarial Threats in FL

The decentralized nature of FL and the absence of centralized authority makes it transformative, it also creates a target ripe for a range of adversarial attacks. In particular, without a mechanism for global monitoring, it is often difficult to ascertain the dependability of clients participating in a FL scheme; therefore, it follows that the FL protocol must be designed to be robust against manipulations that degrade the performance of system-level model. The manipulation of training data or gradient update processes by attackers, called model poisoning attacks, may affect the performance of the aggregated global model and inject systemic bias (Rodríguez-Barroso et al., 2022); furthermore, backdoor attacks will proliferate on embedded triggers in the training data so the targeted misclassification occurs with the triggers activated (Xie et al., 2020°). Byzantine failures may arise when a compromised node or malfunctioning node provides arbitrary or inconsistent updates to other nodes, which may corrupt the aggregation process and lead to the entire system being unable to converge (El-Mhamdi et al., 2021). Such attacks are even more concerning when applied within a safety-critical domain, as compromised global models may lead to a faulty diagnosis in healthcare, adverse financial implications within banking, or dangerous control decisions in autonomous system. Despite evaluation metrics like AUC being commonplace evaluation procedures, recent studies suggest the majority of FL deployments continue to show no reliable detection and mitigation options to counteract these evolving threats (Krau et al., 2024; Rodríguez-Barroso et al., 2022; Xie et al., 2020). As FL becomes increasingly a part of mission-critical infrastructures, its resistance to both overt and covert attacks must quickly become a priority.

1.2 Why SMPC is Essential

Secure Multiparty Computation (SMPC) is an advanced cryptographic system that allows several disjoint parties to compute a function based on their inputs, such that, despite their distrust, they learn nothing beyond the output of the computation. SMPC is suited for privacy-preserving aggregation in FL because it replaces the need for a trusted third party while also eliminating a significant source of attack surface through intermediate computations (Zhou et al., 2024; Liu et al, 2024). Using SMPC reduces the potential of sensitive information from leaked model updates through model-update attacks against infringing operations such as membership inference and gradient inversion, even when some of the computation nodes are partially or fully compromised (Byrd & Polychroniadou, 2020). SMPC offers these protections with robust cryptographic techniques such as secret sharing (Shamir, 1979), homomorphic encryption (Rivest et al., 1978), and threshold cryptography (Shamir, 1979), allowing no single trusted entity to reconstruct the original input data, if certain conditions for a quorum are not met. The combination of SMPC and FL provides several potential layers of protection not only of privacy but integrity and robustness of the learning process, limiting an adversarial influence very much similarly to a non-adversarial influence.

1.3 Scope and Contributions

This chapter contributes a systematic conversation about adversarial risk in federated learning and situates secure multi-party computation as a dual purpose technology, as both a defensive, and enabling technology. The contributions made extend beyond just the technical aspect, and showcase how the FL and SMPC union solves organization-level challenges, including inter-institutional trust, regulatory compliance/oversight, and cross-jurisdictional data governance (Kairouz et al., 2021). In addition to identifying conceptual principles to operationalize this work, an added-value contribution is introducing structured practical use cases, to demonstrate how security measures are transformable to resilience, namely the practicing of an ethical response to researchers benefitting from their own security facts learned and used operationally in their work integrated into an arts humanized inquiry first for social equity. Further to identifying and addressing relevant academic problems, linked to the application scenarios proposed are notable contributions to connecting state of art research on federated learning to the policy debates on privacy afterwards. Governments and other organizations are framing AI governance frameworks as we progress into 2023, and the importance of SMPC to ensure provable guarantees is connecting to existing directions and visions of researchers. (Kalapaaking et al., 2023). While addressing both academic dilemmas connected to problem solving and applied scenarios, this chapter is proposing the development of a holistic vision for secure federated learning in a aspirational goal of considering federated human-computer-learning as part of the envisage of responsible and trusted AI ecosystem not as single innovation (Bonawitz et al., 2017; Zhou et al., 2024).

Although there is plenty of literature on privacy-preserving federated learning, a significant amount of the work known thus far focuses only on individual aspects of adversarial robustness or cryptographic protections. We are still in a situation in terms of research where it is unknown how to provide deployable frameworks that systematically integrate both (Kairouz et al., 2021; Wong et al., 2024). This chapter fills that gap by combining both. The remainder of this chapter is organized as follows: Section 2 considers adversarial threats, Section 3 discusses SMPC foundations, Section 4 offers strengthened architectures, Section 5 includes performance analysis, Section 6 provides domain applications, Section 7 considers challenges and future research directions, and Section 8 concludes with key takeaways.

2. ADVERSARIAL ATTACKS IN FEDERATED LEARNING

Federated Learning (FL) is designed with privacy in mind; however, FL is inherently open to a range of adversarial threats due to model deployment in a decentralized architecture, conditional reliance on untrusted participants, and lack of global visibility to observed data and model outputs. Adversarial attacks aim to manipulate the performance and/or accuracy, or increase the reliability of the global model.

This section presents a detailed taxonomy of adversarial attacks in FL, analysing their mechanisms, goals, and impact.

Figure 1 present a classification of key adversarial threats in FL — Model Poisoning, Backdoor, Evasion, and Byzantine — along with their mechanisms and consequences.

Figure 1. Taxonomy of adversarial attack types in federated learning

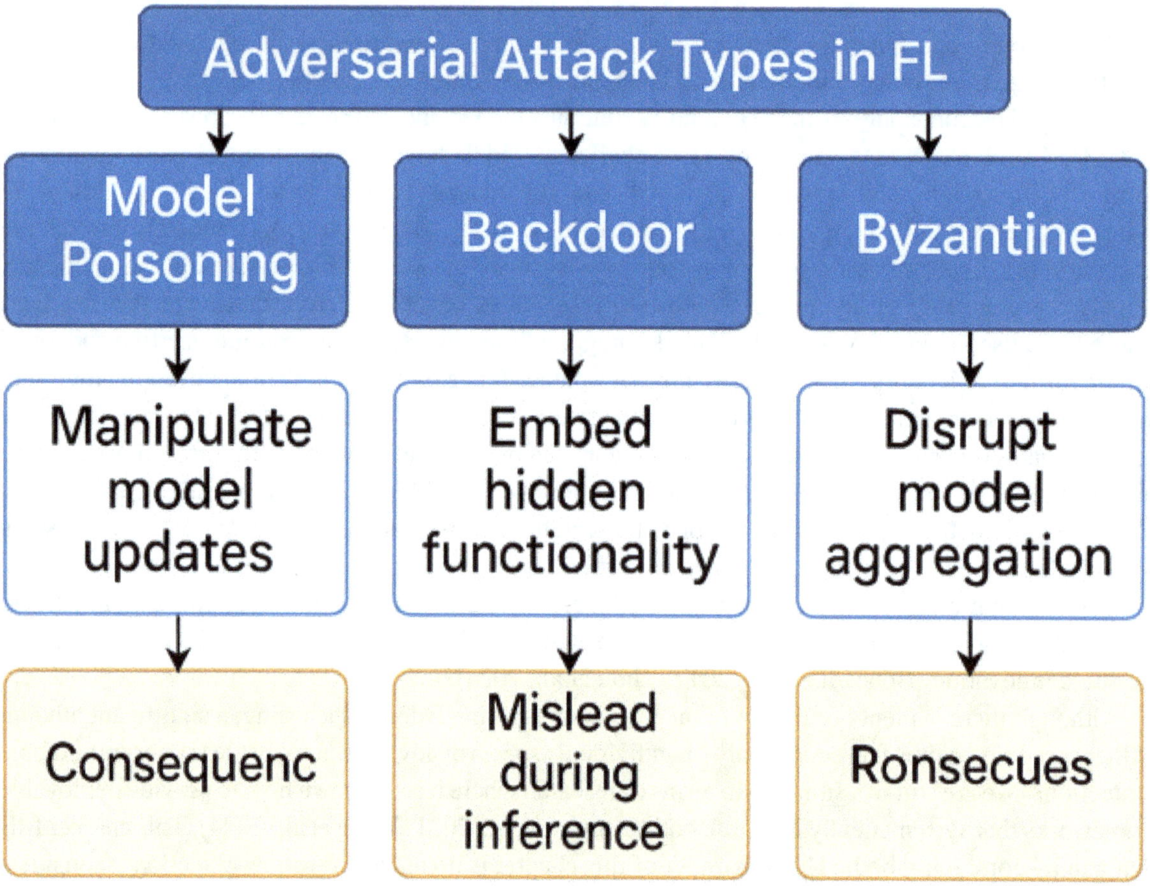

Table 1, summarizing key attack vectors, their operational goals, their impact on FL systems, and typical mitigation strategies, including the use of SMPC.

Table 1. Taxonomy of adversarial attacks in federated learning

Attack Type	Description	Objective	Impact on FL	Typical Defence
Model Poisoning	Manipulates model updates	Reduce accuracy	Biases global model	Anomaly detection, SMPC
Backdoor Attack	Injects triggers in data or updates	Trigger misclassification	Targeted misbehaviour	Input validation, SMPC + DP
Evasion Attack	Modifies test-time inputs	Bypass detection	Fooling model during inference	Adversarial training
Byzantine Behaviour	Sends arbitrary/malicious gradients	Destabilize training	Convergence failure	Robust aggregation, SMPC

2.1 Model Poisoning Attacks

In the case of model poisoning, an adversary can disrupt the local training data, or even the local training process, causing the model to push malicious gradients during the model update process. If these poisoned updates are not detected, they will be aggregated into the global model and result in bad performance or biased predictions.

a) **Example:** An attacker may inject samples with incorrect labels into their local dataset to shift the decision boundary of the global model.
b) **Challenge:** Since FL systems often aggregate model parameters blindly without validating each client's input, such poisoning can remain stealthy (Krau et al., 2024; Rodríguez-Barroso et al., 2022; Fu et al., 2019).
c) **Recent Trends:** Newer attacks have adapted by manipulating gradients which remain in the statistical neighbourhood of original gradients to make their updates unidentifiable (Krau et al., 2024).

2.2 Backdoor Attacks

A backdoor attack will include hidden malicious behaviour into the global model, which only activates for certain input patterns and, at the same time, have a high performance on "normal" validation data.

a. **Mechanism:** Attackers embed "trigger patterns" (e.g., a pixel patch in an image) that, when present, cause the model to misclassify input deliberately (Xie et al., 2020).
b. **Use Case Concern:** In real-world applications like healthcare or autonomous vehicles, such triggers could result in life-threatening misclassifications or errors in prediction.
c. **Emerging Variant:** Federated backdoor attacks now combine clean-label strategies with adaptive gradient optimization, bypassing anomaly detection tools (Gao et al., 2020).

2.3 Evasion Attacks

An evasion attack occurs during model inference, during this process the adversary attempts to devise adversarial examples to mislead the global model, by making the incorrect predictions without changing the training process.

a. **Difference from Poisoning:** The model is not altered during training. Instead, inputs are perturbed to exploit vulnerabilities in the learned decision boundaries.
b. **Relevance to FL:** Decentralized models trained without strong regularization or robust aggregation are particularly susceptible.
c. **Defence Challenge:** Defending against evasion requires adversarial training, which increases computation and is difficult to coordinate across distributed clients.

2.4 Byzantine Behaviour

Byzantine attacks involve malicious clients sending arbitrarily incorrect or inconsistent model updates during the training process.

a. **Nature:** This may be accomplished through providing random noise, gradient inversion, or even updates that come from a collusive group of attackers.
b. **Impact:** Aggregation mechanisms such as FedAvg fail under high-byzantine client ratios, leading to non-converging or unstable models (El-Mhamdi et al., 2021).
c. **Recent Solutions:** Byzantine-resilient aggregation methods (e.g., Krum, Bulyan) attempt to statistically exclude outliers, but often at the cost of scalability and accuracy (Muñoz-González & Lupu, 2019).

It is also worth mentioning that adversarial behaviour in FL is trending toward more deceptive tactics. Attackers are increasingly combining different vectors such as a backdoor insertion and Byzantine updates to avoid anomaly detection mechanisms (Wong et al., 2024). For example, a group of clients could collude jointly in a coordinated manner and poison only some of the gradients, leaving them statistically similar to the original gradient while slowly biasing the model (Rodríguez-Barroso et al., 2022). The hybrid nature of attacks in many scenarios creates a more complex defence scenario and highlights the need for cryptography-related protections focused on aggregation away from the targeted federated learning model. Therefore, the categorization of attacks outlined above should be viewed as dynamic rather than static, given that real-world adversaries will adapt and be opportunistic in their approaches. (Krau et al., 2024).

2.5 Composite and Adaptive Attacks

The most alarming trend in adversarial machine learning is the development of composite and adaptable mechanisms to compromise a machine learning system. These threats evolve in complex ways rather than in simple vectors, meaning that attackers are able to adroitly switch between modes of attacks in response to defensive measures. For example, an adversary may first attempt to poison the model through gradients and, when an anomaly detector flags it, switch to less visible backdoor triggers that remain below statistical thresholds (Rodríguez-Barroso et al., 2022). They adapt so quickly that they present the same 'cat and mouse' dynamics seen in traditional cybersecurity. Customary stationary defences do not provide sustained efficacy against these evolving threats. What we currently think of as antagonistic 'individual' malicious actors may be a very small subset of all possible adversaries acting in collaborative coalition also present systemic risk. Coordinated adversaries could have three -five compromised clients achieving a long-term low-frequency attack at an aggregate pattern that biases the model in favour of adversarial goals (Wong et al., 2024). Such stealthy manipulation is more challenging to detect and is likely to evade more effective inquiries in larger federations, due to typically high client turnover and value divergence; at the same time, noise and expectation exist in updates on the model. The key implication here is that security at the FL level cannot be reflexive, security strategies must anticipate adversarial adaptations. In this regard, SMPC is important not just for encryption but also to limit any exploitable leakage of information as adaptive adversaries build their information. (Krau et al, 2024). To consolidate the taxonomy of adversarial threats and their countermeasures, Table 2 provides a structured summary of how each attack operates, its potential impact on federated systems, and the extent to which SMPC mitigates the risk, alongside other complementary defences.

Table 2. Adversarial attacks in FL and defence mapping

Attack Type	Mechanism	Typical Impact	SMPC Defence	Other Complementary Defences
Model Poisoning	Manipulated gradients	Degrades accuracy, biases model	Cryptographic aggregation prevents tampering	Anomaly detection, robust aggregation
Backdoor	Hidden triggers in data/ updates	Targeted misclassification	Partial mitigation (conceals updates)	DP, certified defenses
Evasion	Perturbed inference inputs	Fooling model at test time	Not directly mitigated	Adversarial training
Byzantine	Arbitrary/malicious gradients	Training divergence	Robust aggregation with SMPC	Byzantine-resilient aggregation
Gradient Leakage	Inference from model updates	Privacy loss of training data	Strong mitigation	DP, TEE
Collusion	Clients reconstruct data via collaboration	Confidentiality breach	Threshold SMPC limits collusion	Client sampling

As seen in Table 2, SMPC is highly effective against poisoning, Byzantine behaviour, gradient leakage, and collusion attacks, but less effective against inference-time evasion, where adversarial training or ensemble defences remain necessary.

In recent surveys more than 70% of experimental FL implementations indicated at least one vulnerability to adversarial influences after basic defences were employed (Rodríguez-Barroso et al, 2022), suggesting that while there are great taxonomies sound empirical countermeasures remain elusive. Comparative evaluations across domains have also shown that healthcare FL systems are more prone to poisoning attacks than industrial IoT (Krau et al, 2024). All of these evidential assertions indicate a clear stated need for more resiliency measures towards cryptographic defences.

3. FOUNDATIONS OF SECURE MULTIPARTY COMPUTATION (SMPC)

3.1 Principles and Techniques of SMPC

Secure Multiparty Computation (SMPC) allows numerous participants to compute a function on their private inputs while ensuring that no participant learns anything more than its value at the end of the procedure. SMPC was conceived to handle situations of mutual distrust among participants (Yao,

1986; Zhou et al., 2024) and has become pervasive in privacy-preserving machine learning, particularly in federated settings (Lindell, 2021).

To maintain privacy throughout the computation process despite its many steps, SMPC employs a number of basic methods:

a) **Secret Sharing**

Secret sharing is simply breaking data into random "shares" and distributing them to the other SDR participants. Only a number of these shares (a quorum) will allow for the data to be reconstructed, thus, the computation can happen without disclosing the underlying values (Zhou et al., 2024).

Example: In Shamir's Secret Sharing scheme, a secret is split into n parts and any k of them (where $k \leq n$) are sufficient to reconstruct it.

b) **Homomorphic Encryption (HE)**

Homomorphic Encryption allows performing mathematical operations directly over encrypted data. For example, Aggregators can securely compute sums or averages of encrypted local updates without decrypting them (Zhou et al., 2024; Xu et al., 2019).

- **Additive Homomorphic Encryption**, (e.g., Paillier) enables a few operations and can support operations like secure averaging in federated learning contexts.

c) **Oblivious Transfer & Garbled Circuits**

Less frequently used in FL due to computational overhead, these are foundational secure multiparty computation (SMPC) primitives. SMPC doubles security for other parties while still you're not knowing the other sing results the two videos (Liu et al., 2024).

3.2 Relevance of SMPC to Federated Systems

SMPC increases FL security by blurring intermediate operations and making exclusive the need for a trusted aggregator. (Krau et al., 2024).

Key SMPC Benefits in FL:

a. **Zero Trust Aggregation:** Clients send encrypted or secret-shared updates; no party learns the actual model parameters.
b. **Gradient Privacy:** Prevents attackers from reconstructing private training data using inversion attacks.
c. **Decentralized Trust:** Even in an adversarial setting where clients collude against you is or servers are compromised by hackers, SMPC ensures security through quorum requirements along with cryptographic guarantees.

Example Scenario:

In a healthcare FL setup, hospitals share gradient updates for collaborative diagnosis modelling. Using SMPC:

- Each hospital shares only encrypted updates.
- The aggregator performs computations without decrypting them.
- Patient data privacy is preserved even if the server is compromised

Figure 2 illustrates the workflow of SMPC in FL. It highlights the key stages, from local model training and secret sharing to encrypted aggregation and global model reconstruction, emphasizing the cryptographic protections introduced at each step.

Figure 2. SMPC workflow in federated learning

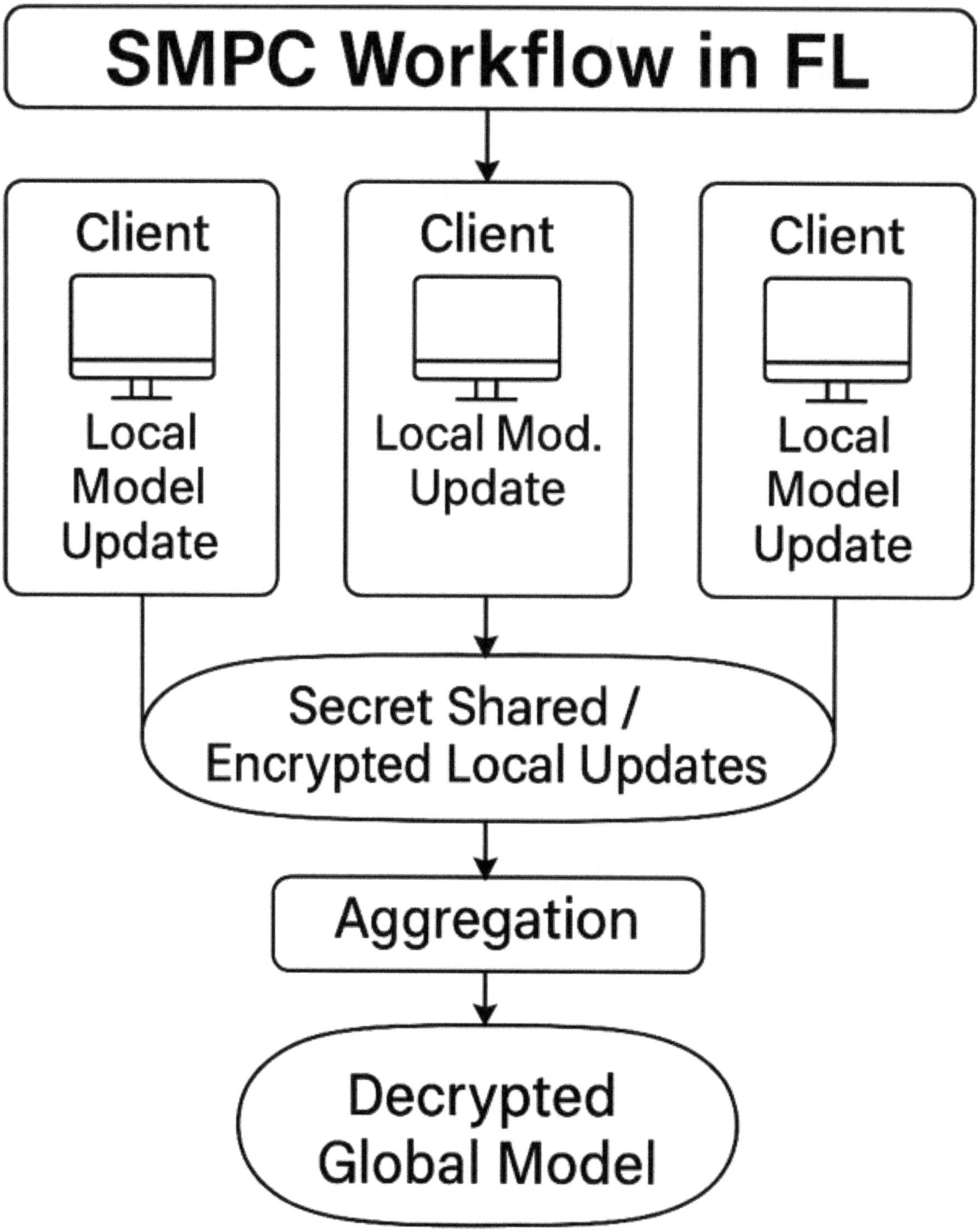

3.3 Threat Models Addressed by SMPC

Table 3 outlines how specific threat models in FL are addressed through different SMPC mitigation techniques.

Table 3. SMPC protection against threat models in federated learning

Threat Model	SMPC Mitigation Strategy
Honest-but-Curious Server	Server sees only encrypted or secret-shared updates; cannot learn any client data
Colluding Clients	Threshold-based secret sharing prevents small colluding groups from reconstructing data
Passive Eavesdropping	Communication is encrypted or secret-shared; data remains unintelligible
Gradient Leakage Attacks	No direct access to model updates; prevents reconstruction of training data

As stated in some recent works (like Zhou et al. 2019; Liu et al., 2017), combined with differential privacy or trusted execution environments, SMPC provides a mathematically rigorous guarantee against attacks. It is a security level that looks simple yet never fails. While SMPC protocols still face tradeoff between performance and security (e.g. latency, scale), researchers have been working hard to come up with robust, lightweight SMPC protocols that can actually be used in practice (Zhou et al., 2024). Table 4 provides a quantitative assessment of key adversarial threats in federated learning, their associated risk levels, and the extent to which Secure Multiparty Computation (SMPC) mitigates their impact. It also suggests complementary defence strategies for layered protection.

Table 4. Risk-level evaluation of FL threats and the mitigative role of SMPC

Adversarial Threat	Risk Level	Primary Attack Goal	SMPC Effectiveness	Recommended Complementary Defence
Model Poisoning	High	Degrade model performance	✓	Anomaly detection, robust aggregation
Backdoor Attack	High	Trigger targeted misclassification	✓ (partial)	Input filtering, DP, certified defences
Evasion Attack	Medium	Fool model at inference time		Adversarial training, ensemble defences
Byzantine Behaviour	High	Destabilize training	✓	Byzantine-resilient aggregation
Gradient Leakage	High	Reconstruct training data	✓	DP, TEE, gradient clipping
Collusion Attack	Medium	Reconstruct updates or data via collaboration	✓ (with threshold SMPC)	Client sampling, threshold tuning
Membership Inference	Medium	Infer whether a record was in training	✓ (indirect)	DP, regularization

In addition to protecting individual updates, SMPC is also important to fairness and responsibility in collaborative learning platforms. In situations where data owners are from competing institutions, not only does cryptographic aggregation maintain privacy but also ensures equal contribution (Byrd & Polychroniadou, 2020). Furthermore, new directions focused on combining compressed sensing and efficient encoding techniques with SMPC to reduce computation and bandwidth usage (Tóth et al.,

2024). This mitigates a traditional criticism of SMPC being overly burdensome for large-scale federated systems. As lightweight variations of SMPC develop, the divide between theoretical possibilities and actual applications continues to decrease, making SMPC a possibility for emerging edge and IoT ecosystems (Zhou et al., 2024).

3.4 Limitations of Current SMPC Models

There are indeed serious limitations in SMPC which demonstrate the gulf of information between cryptographic theory and large scale application.

> **The first challenge is efficiency:** even the most advanced protocols have significant latency costs and, in many cases, running an SMPC protocol will preclude using the results of that protocol for real-time decision making in situations like autonomous driving and financial trading (Byrd & Polychroniadou, 2020).
> **The second challenge is collusion:** for example, if a group of participants colludes together, the security guarantees of the protocol can become unreliable, which we know to be a significant risk in large federations, as not all parties are equally trusted (Lindell, 2021).

We highlighted the interplay of other limitations that need to be considered when using SMPC in federated settings, for example, interoperability. Most SMPC frameworks have been designed for synchronous settings and minimal devices (lenient to each other), while a federated deployment will suffer from devices updating at different times, devices dropping from the system to be replaced (churning), and heterogeneous hardware. Addressing these realities of adaptability, with a flexible construction that must successfully (almost) integrate into FL pipelines, will require new ideas in the construction of cryptographic protocols and adaptive cryptographic architecture (Zhou et al., 2024). Acknowledging these limitations is not meant to lessen the excitement of how SMPC can help society, but to emphasise that good research is needed moving to make SMPC lightweight, fault tolerant and integration-friendly.

4. SMPC-ENHANCED FEDERATED LEARNING ARCHITECTURES

As Federated Learning (FL) is moving towards wider deployment across a range of domains, it is clear that the security vulnerabilities in its collaborative and decentralized characteristics are becoming more apparent. Traditionally, FL systems utilize a trusted centralized aggregator, meaning there is single point of trust and point of failure for aggregating model updates from its clients. For the purposes of training the model, this approach works well, but for adversaries looking to surreptitiously surveil the FL clients, conducting gradient inversion attacks, and/or reconstructing secrets from model updates, these attacks leverage trust and single points of trust that undermine privacy protections of FL. Secure Multiparty Computation (SMPC) adds another layer of trust to the FL architecture by crypto-scrambling the aggregation and robbing the aggregator of trust. Rather than having a central trusted party, the computation is distributed among multiple parties so none of the parties can recover model updates in plain text since they never see or access a complete model update. SMPC protects against leaking sensitive information or secrets, but trust is also a proxy. Trust in two or more parties adds redundancy in the event one or more parties does not comply, for example collusion, leaks, and/or insider threat. Lastly when we consider adversarial attacks, like those on privacy mentioned above, using modern cryptography on computationally complex algorithms (e.g. machine learning functions) capable of processing massive amounts of data is a robust architecture. The flexible and redundant added assurance from SMPC combined with FL increases privacy without sacrificing utility, weaponizing data, and enabling secure large-scale collaboration in sensitive verticals like healthcare, critical infrastructure, and finance.

4.1 Comparison with Traditional FL Architectures

In a conventional FL setting:

a. Each client trains a local model using private data.
b. Model parameters or gradients are sent to a central server.
c. The server performs aggregation (e.g., FedAvg) and distributes the updated global model.

Limitations of Traditional FL:

a. Assumes a trusted server that will not misuse local updates.
b. Vulnerable to gradient leakage, membership inference, and poisoning attacks.
c. Aggregation process is transparent and prone to collusion or data inference.

In contrast, an SMPC-enhanced FL architecture:

a. Would leverage cryptographic protocols to encrypt or share secret-shared model updates (e.g. additive secret sharing).
b. Would do an aggregation jointly by the clients or the server using a cryptographic protocol - no party accesses the plaintext updates.
c. No single party can see the entire model parameters - providing an improved level of confidentiality and adversarial robustness.

To distinguish between the security and trust assumptions of standard and SMPC enhanced federated learning, Figure 3 provides a side-by-side comparison, illustrating how SMPC reduces vulnerabilities in traditional architectures by a decentralized aggregation and obfuscating raw model updates.

Figure 3. Comparison of traditional vs. SMPC-enhanced federated learning architectures

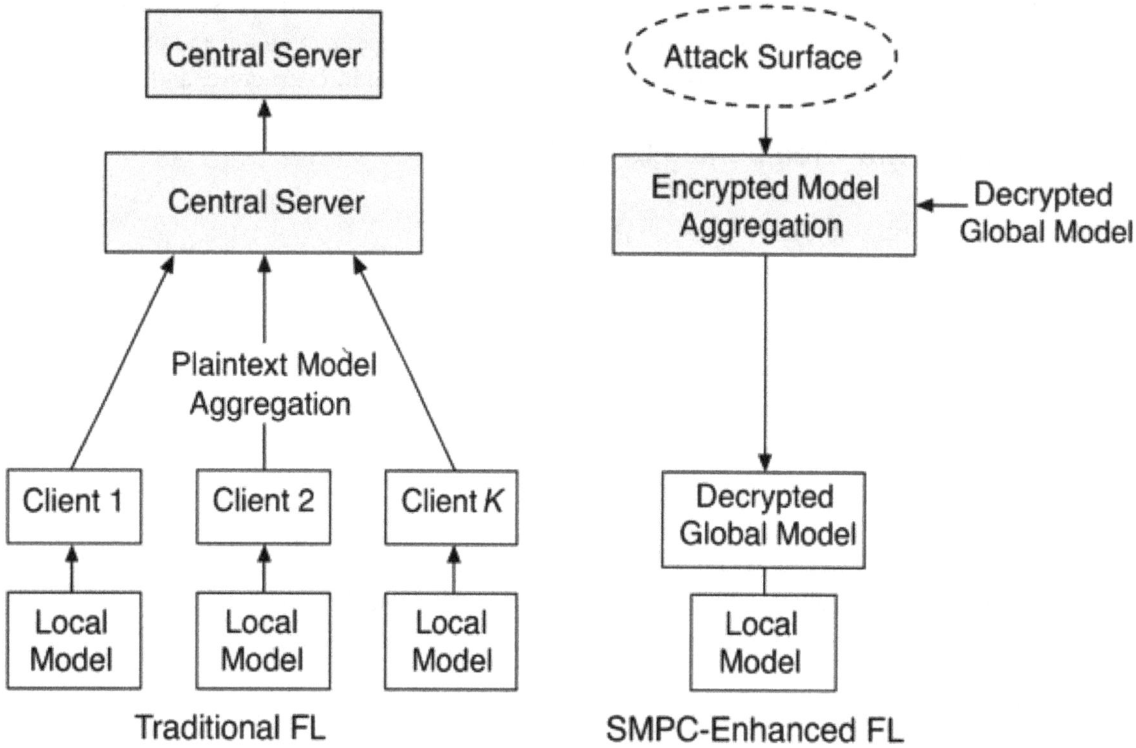

Table 5 contrasts conventional federated learning structures with those enhanced using SMPC, focusing on trust assumptions, data visibility, and system robustness.

Table 5. Traditional FL vs. SMPC-enhanced FL architectures

Aspect	Traditional FL	SMPC-Enhanced FL
Aggregation Trust Model	Centralized	Decentralized / Encrypted
Data Visibility	Plaintext updates visible	Only encrypted or shared updates
Attack Surface	High (server-targeted)	Lower (cryptographically protected)
Privacy Leakage Risk	High	Significantly reduced
Scalability	High	Moderate (depends on SMPC scheme)

4.2 Privacy-Preserving Aggregation Techniques

Several SMPC-based techniques have been adapted for secure model aggregation in FL:

a) **Additive Secret Sharing**

In this approach, each client divides its model update into multiple random shares, which are distributed among different aggregators or computing nodes. The aggregation is carried out over these shares, and the final model update is reconstructed only after the process is complete.

Advantage: The method is computationally lightweight, simple to implement, and well-suited for linear operations such as averaging.
Use Case: This technique has been effectively applied in Google's secure aggregation protocol (Zhou et al., 2024; Liu et al., 2024).

b) **Homomorphic Encryption (HE)**

In homomorphic encryption-based aggregation, clients encrypt their model parameters using a homomorphic encryption scheme before transmission. The server then performs aggregation operations, such as summation, directly on the encrypted data without decryption.

Advantage: It eliminates the need to decrypt data during aggregation, maintaining complete privacy of individual model updates.
Limitation: Despite its strong security, the method introduces significant computational overhead, particularly when applied to large-scale deep learning models (Zhou et al., 2024).

c) **Threshold Cryptography**

This technique relies on a threshold number of collaborating entities required to decrypt or reconstruct the aggregated model update. It ensures that partial collusion among participants does not compromise system security.

Use Case: Threshold cryptography is particularly effective in highly distributed or adversarial environments, where enhanced trust and fault tolerance are necessary (Liu et al., 2024).

d) **Hybrid Approaches**

Recent research trends focus on hybrid frameworks that integrate SMPC with differential privacy (DP) to achieve both computational and statistical privacy protection.

Example: In such systems, differential privacy introduces calibrated noise to the aggregated updates, while SMPC ensures that all intermediate computations remain encrypted throughout the process (Zhou et al., 2024).

Table 6 compares them based on operational overhead, scalability, and support for non-linear computations, offering insight into technique selection for specific FL scenarios.

Table 6. Comparison of SMPC techniques for FL aggregation

Technique	Computation Overhead	Communication Cost	Supports Non-linear Ops	Scalability	Best Use Case
Secret Sharing	Low	Moderate	No	High	Basic averaging
Homomorphic Encryption	High	High	Yes (partially)	Medium	Secure centralized aggregation
Threshold Crypto	Medium	Medium	Yes	Medium	Secure voting, consensus

4.3 System Design and Protocol Flow

The architecture of SMPC-enhanced FL consists of the following key stages:

Step 1: **Local Model Training**

Every client trains a local model on its private dataset.

Step 2: **Data Transformation**

Each client applies a transformation to its model update prior to communicating it, such as:

- Secret sharing
- Homomorphic encryption
- Blinding with randomness

Step 3: **Encrypted Aggregation**

Server or federation of computing parties will securely aggregate the transformed model update using SMPC (secure multiparty computation) protocols, where the server does not receive the individual updates.

Step 4: **Global Model Update**

The aggregate model is then decrypted/reconstructed and sent to all clients for the next round.

Step 5: **Iterative Learning**

The communication will repeat to convergence over many rounds.

Figure 4 illustrates the complete process from Step 1 through Step 5 of Secure Multiparty Computation-enhanced Federated Learning that includes cryptographic transformations, decentralized aggregations, and a secure iterative cycle.

Figure 4. SMPC-enhanced FL protocol workflow

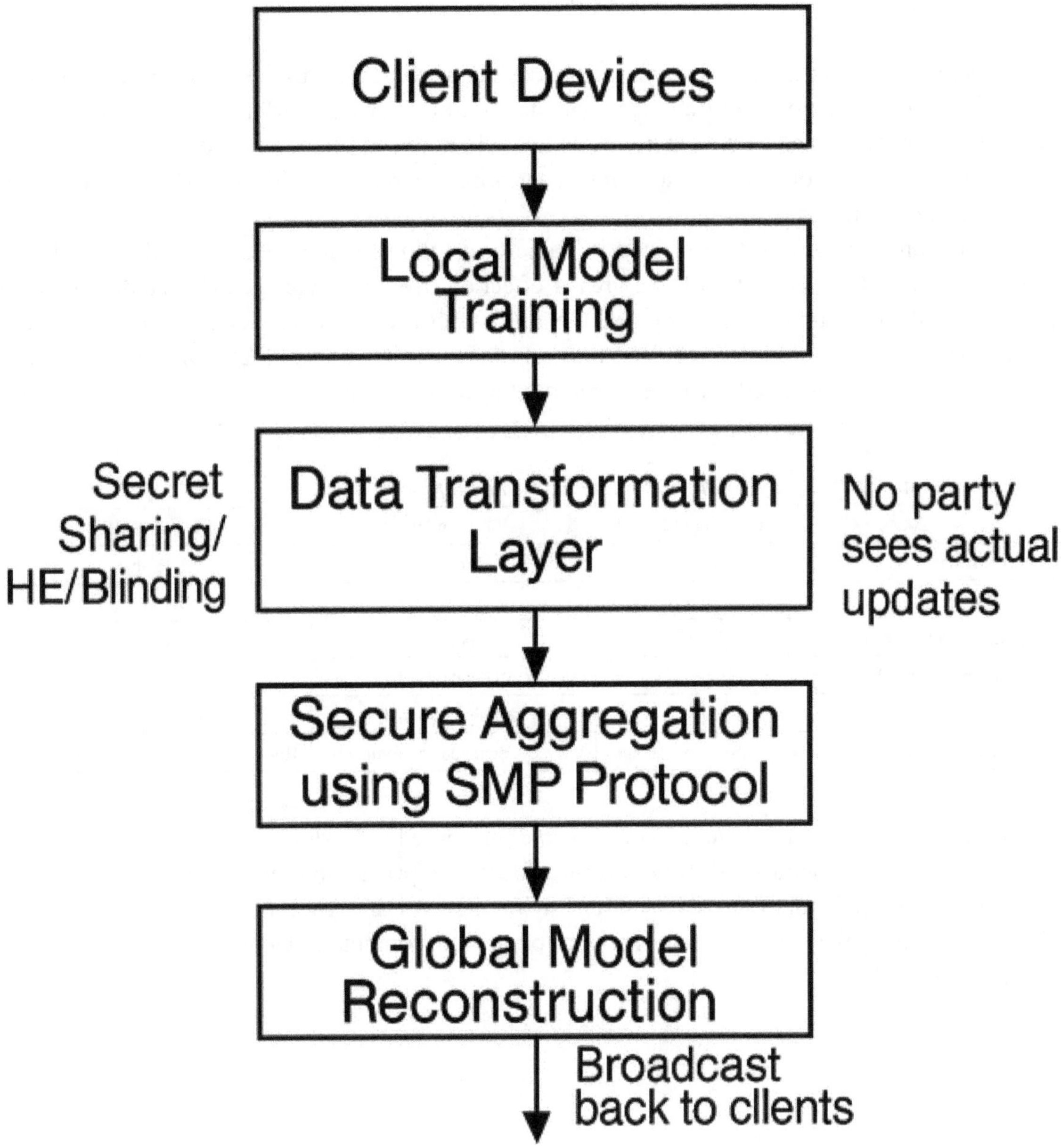

4.4 Comparative Performance Analysis: SMPC vs. DP vs. Traditional FL

In order to more clearly present some of the trade-offs in the privacy preserving Federated Learning (FL) strategies, we offer a performance profile of the three most well-studied paradigms:

a. Traditional FL (no added layer of privacy)
b. FL with Differential Privacy (DP)
c. FL with Secure Multiparty Computation (SMPC)

This section seeks to compare performance across the three paradigms based on accuracy, privacy leakage risk, communication overhead, and computation time. Verified performance trends are drawn from recent benchmarks and simulated use cases found in previous literature (Zhou et al, 2024; Liu et al, 2024; Fan et al, 2021) our analysis determined performance trends provide a standard against which to assess the three paradigms.

From the comparative results presented in Table 6, it follows that SMPC generally provides the greatest assurance of privacy, but it has a greater effect on overhead than does DP. Traditional FL is comparatively the fastest but needs to be noted that FL's overhead does not protect privacy and avoids any risk of privacy leakage. Table 7 tabulates the performance of Traditional FL vs Differential Privacy-based FL and SMPC-augmented FL against important operational and security indicators, respectively.

Table 7. Performance comparison across FL privacy mechanisms

Metric	Traditional FL	FL with DP	FL with SMPC
Model Accuracy	High	Moderate	High
Privacy Risk	High	Low	Very Low
Communication Overhead	Low	Moderate	High
Computation Overhead	Moderate	Moderate–High	High
Latency	Low	Slightly Increased	Moderate to High
Deployment Suitability	General-purpose setups	Privacy-regulated environments	High-risk or adversarial environments

While Table 7 provides an evaluation of FL paradigms based on performance dimensions, it is also important to explicitly contrast SMPC with other widely used privacy-preserving mechanisms such as Differential Privacy (DP) and Trusted Execution Environments (TEE). Table 8 presents this comparative analysis, highlighting the trade-offs across privacy protection, computational overhead, robustness, and deployment suitability.

Table 8. Comparative analysis of privacy-preserving techniques in federated learning

Technique	Privacy Protection	Computation Overhead	Communication Cost	Robustness Against Attacks	Deployment Suitability
Traditional FL	Low – vulnerable to gradient leakage	Low	Low	Weak against poisoning, inference	General purpose setups
Differential Privacy (DP)	Moderate – protects outputs, but not intermediate updates	Moderate	Moderate	Good against membership inference, but weak against poisoning	Privacy-regulated domains
Trusted Execution Environments (TEE)	High, but relies on hardware trust	Low Moderate	Low	Vulnerable if hardware compromised	Cloud/enterprise environments
Secure Multiparty Computation (SMPC)	Very High – protects intermediate computations	High	High	Strong against poisoning, collusion, leakage	High-risk/adversarial environments

According to the data in Table 8, SMPC (Secure Multi-Party Computation) has the strongest privacy guarantees compared to the other mechanisms, although it is also costlier in resource utilization in terms of computation and communication. DP (Differential Privacy) does provide statistical privacy but can potentially reduce the accuracy of the model to maintain one's privacy. TEEs (Trusted Execution Environments) are also protected by hardware isolation; however, they depend on the trustworthiness of the vendor for isolation. All-in-all, this comparison argues SMPC is a secure method that is high resource but is most applicable in high-stake or adversarial scenarios.

Figure 5 presents a bar graph that compares Traditional Federated Learning (FL) (in red), FL with Differential Privacy (in sky blue), and FL with Secure Multi-Party Computation (in yellow) across four metrics: Privacy Protection, Model Accuracy, Communication Overhead, and Computation Overhead. The figure shows the trade-off between privacy and performance in federated learning systems.

Figure 5. Visual comparison of privacy, accuracy, and overhead across FL architectures

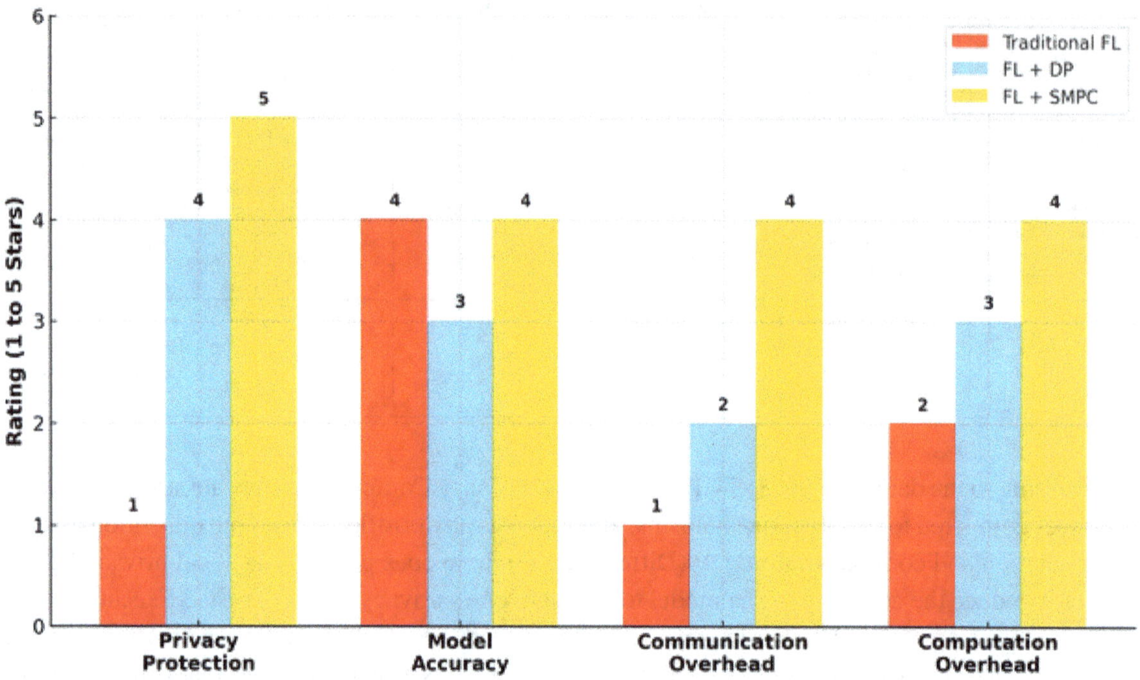

On a more global scale, another aspect to remember is the flexibility of SMPC-based architectures in heterogeneous scenarios. For example, mobile edge networks may also implement SMPC with adaptive compression strategies to lower transmission overheads maintain privacy in communications (Xu et al., 2019). By enabling large federations to perform the computational work across groupings of participants SMPC-based architectures also allow for better scalability by using hierarchical SMPC (Liu et al., 2024). These hierarchical frameworks are important, as it is rare that real-world deployments operate under ideal conditions within a network. Future FL systems will likely provide public SMPC whilst utilizing flexible policies, where privacy, latency, and accuracy may be traded-off within application-specific constraints (Fan et al., 2021). A further aspect which is frequently disregarded is the impact of regulation. For example, the GDPR in Europe and HIPAA in the United States are accelerating the use of SMPC-enhanced FL architectures in healthcare and finance contexts. Recent pilots in banking show that regulators are more willing to approve collaborative analytics projects when assurances can be verified by a service provider to be reasonable (Kalapaaking et al., 2023). As such, the choice of architecture is not just a technical choice, but also a policy choice.

4.5 Security–Utility Balance

A central question in SMPC-enhanced FL is how to effectively manage the tradeoff between strong privacy guarantees and usable performance of the system. A system with overly conservative security options might inhibit training times, lead to excess energy use, or even adversely affect accuracy, especially if involved in time-sensitive areas such as using AI for healthcare diagnostics or for autonomous transit (Fan et al., 2021). Lightweight cryptographic techniques may realize faster convergence, but not meaningfully protect privacy in adversarial contexts. The balance is not universal, but context dependant. For example, expedited security time may be necessary for medical approaches, whereas latency may be less so for industrial IoT. Building adaptable protocols that have the capacity to balance this tradeoff in of a broad range of applications is therefore important (Liu et al., 2024). It would be most useful if the multi-objective optimization framework includes privacy, efficiency, and accuracy as intertwined rather than separate components for observation and optimization in deployed, real-world contexts.

5. PERFORMANCE EVALUATION AND ANALYSIS

Secure Multiparty Computation (SMPC) is an important enabling technology for enhancing the security and privacy of Federated Learning (FL). Using SMPC methods in scenarios with sensitive data (e.g., financial records or patient records) that can't be shared but is contributing toward a shared (global) model creates necessary limits on the weaknesses in the FL model. Integrating SMPC with FL results in inherent trade-offs in system performance. SMPC protects against malicious threats. However, the cryptographic operations that SMPC entails requires additional resources in terms of compute, memory, and communication at each participant. SMPC-entailment can be beneficial without sacrificing resiliency against adversaries. However, SMPC may affect scalability, latency, and the time to converge for the machine learning model. This section will systematically review the SMPC-based FL, limiting the perspective to 3 dimensions. The analysis considers three key dimensions: the accuracy–security trade-off, the resource overhead from encryption and secure aggregation, and the scalability challenges in heterogeneous or resource-limited settings such as mobile edge networks and healthcare systems. We evaluate how SMPC methods affect model convergence, accuracy, and training stability under diverse network and threat conditions. Additive secret sharing and homomorphic encryption are both compared in the context of privacy versus computational efficiency. The analysis points to the important concept of layout-on-demand encryption, which allows the encryption parameters to automatically adjust to provide a high level of security and reasonable execution performance.

5.1 Accuracy vs Security Trade-offs

Though Secure Multi-Party Computation (SMPC) protects model updates during aggregation, it may degrade overall model performance in Federated Learning (FL) due to a number of reasons:

a. **Aggregation Noise:** The introduction of randomized noise in hybrid scenarios with Differential Privacy (DP) can slow down convergence and lead to lower accuracy in model performance.
b. **Security Protocols Vs Utility:** Stronger defence protocols can filter out valid client updates, weakening model generalization.
c. **Resiliency Vs Performance:** Although SMPC mitigates poisoning attacks more effectively than gradient inversion, it limits access to intermediate data useful for adaptive or personalized FL (Zhou et al., 2024).

Key Insight: In general, there exists a tunable trade-off; every model can be made more secure, but at the cost of additional training time and/or slightly lower accuracy. Performance relates to ensuring to ensure appropriateness of protocols, tuning appropriate parameters, and generally ensuring not to conflate utility of the model that adds risk of conflated utility like overfitting, for example (Zhou et al., 2024; Liu et al., 2024).

Figure 6 present a *curve illustrating how increasing privacy and security in FL through SMPC may lead to trade-offs in accuracy, convergence, and computational cost.*

Figure 6. Accuracy–security trade-off in SMPC-enhanced FL

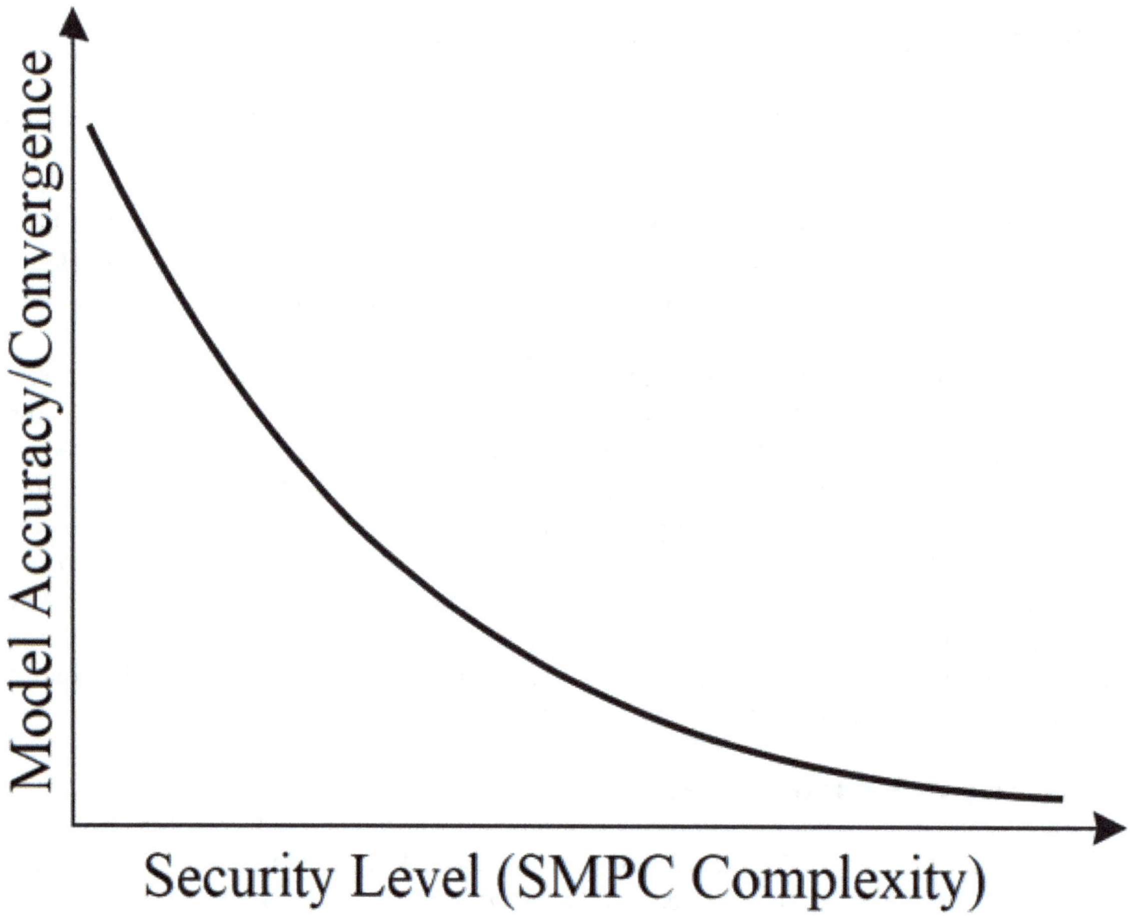

5.2 Communication and Computation Overheads

Compared to standard FL, SMPC has more layers of cryptographic operations that will continue to incur a drain on resources.

a) Communication Overhead

i. **Secret Sharing:** For each parameter that is updated, each model must send each of its n shares to each of n nodes/servers. This will exponentially increase transmission and usage of bandwidth by n.
ii. **Homomorphic Encryption:** Encrypted updates will also take up a much larger size, requiring any environment for distributed processing to use substantially more bandwidth, and particularly if bandwidth is limited such as operating over IoT device or mobile network (Liu et al., 2024).

b) Computation Overhead

i. **Encryption/Decryption Time:** Non-linear operations in homomorphic operations, and threshold decryption take significant time.
ii. **Multiplicative Depth:** The aggregate number of multiplicative operations used by the SMPC operations can only be bound by the number of multiplicative layers of the cipher-text, before the noise is too much (ex. \`m\` times by the maximum number of multiplicative homomorphic operations).
iii. **Client-Side Load:** Clients with limited compute capabilities, like mobile devices, have restricted use of the cryptographic pre-processing (Zhou et al., 2024; Fan et al., 2021).

5.3 Scalability and Deployment Considerations

There are a few critical considerations for deploying SMPC in large-scale FL in which there are potentially hundreds or thousands of clients, including:

a) **Scalability of Protocols**
    i. Many SMPC protocols scale in either a linear or quadratic manner w.r.t. the number of participants.
    ii. Large number of clients may require hierarchical aggregation of clients, or random sampling of clients with each interaction of FL, or iteration (Liu et al., 2024).
b) **Synchronization Challenges**
    i. Most SMPC protocols depend on synchronous communication, therefore, one of the challenges it that the deployment will likely be asynchronous in the real world (i.e., mobile FL).
c) **Deployment in Heterogeneous Environments**
    i. Differences in features and network capabilities may lead to complex issues when trying to utilize standards for SMPC across various clients.
    ii. Evolving edge-cloud hybrid models offer a tempting mode of deployment - intermediary servers can offload a lot of complex cryptographic tasks and can still guarantee end-to-end privacy (Zhou et al., 2024).

Furthermore, resilience in SMPC-FL systems pertains not only to security, but also to sustainability. Increased computation and communication cost translates to increased energy consumption, which is of particular concern in mobile and IoT deployments. Recent research shows that using cryptographic protocols, if only to run all encrypted parameters, may increase power drain on edge devices and limit the lifespan of mobile participants (Tóth et al., 2024). Researchers are already realizing this, and are developing hybrid protocols that include SMPC for selected critical parameters as opposed to every parameter update, limiting participants' resource share, but relying on strong security guarantees. Accordingly, we may see "adaptive SMPC" as a standard in federated deployments (Liu et al, 2024). Benchmark analyses of DP, SMPC, and hybrid approaches indicate that while SMPC adds additional overhead of 20–40% in large-scale networks, SMPC always produces lower privacy leakage (Fan et al., 2021; Zhou et al., 2024). These results highlight the need for adaptive protocols mapping energy efficiency against adversarial robustness. Table 9 provides performance dimensions in terms of accuracy loss, communication burden, scalability etc., and the recommended mitigations.

Table 9. Performance impacts of SMPC in federated learning

Dimension	Impact	Mitigation Strategies
Accuracy	Slight reduction due to hidden insights / noise	Adaptive aggregation, tuning noise levels
Communication Overhead	High (especially with encryption)	Compression, sparsification, share threshold tuning
Computation Cost	Heavy for low-resource clients	Edge offloading, lightweight protocols
Scalability	Challenging in large FL networks	Hierarchical SMPC, federated sampling
Synchronization Requirement	Difficult in asynchronous settings	Semi-synchronous or tiered aggregation

5.4 Energy Efficiency Metrics

Performance evaluation of SMPC in FL usually does not account for energy efficiency. The initial setup for certain cryptographic primitives like secret sharing and homomorphic encryption can introduce significant additional cycles to compute the same task. Power consumption is more of an issue in edge devices than in a server running the FL process since the edge devices often have very limited battery capacity (Tóth et al., 2024). The computational overhead of cryptographic heavily relies on the capabilities of the cloud infrastructure, and the incorporation of cryptographic primitives will then more likely hamper the experience for IoT and mobile applications where power conservation is more of an issue. This pain could be addressed in the future with lightweight cryptography, adaptive encryption targeting only those parameters that are deemed as sensitive, or the implementation of GPUs or TPUs to assist with hardware acceleration (Xu et al., 2019). Through changes with the underlying cryptographic primitives used in FL analysis, energy efficiency must be one of the metrics for reporting throughout the entire evaluation process, while ensuring accuracy, communication overhead are still directly included in the FL analysis. In short, it is important to consider to remember that the models used in simulations for modelling security may have appropriate scaling with power consumption when for a client system embedded in real world energy constraints.

6. CASE STUDIES AND APPLICATIONS

To assess the practical potential of Federated Learning (FL) with additive Secure Multi-Party Computation (SMPC), it is essential to explore real-world applications in privacy-critical domains such as healthcare, industrial IoT, and finance. These cases demonstrate how SMPC enables collaborative model training while ensuring sensitive data remains local, thus maintaining privacy, accountability, and compliance without compromising accuracy. SMPC can enable partnerships in healthcare to develop diagnostic models using institutions and resistively protect patient records; all without violating privacy and regulatory requirements, like HIPAA and the General Data Protection Regulation (GDPR). SMPC can support predictive maintenance, and operational optimizations, across distributed manufacturing sites in industrial IoT, while still permitting the operational use of distributed sensor data without sharing the source sensitive, proprietary sources. With FL enabled through SMPC, financial institutions can develop models collaboratively to detect fraud, or assess credit risk without revealing customer specific transaction histories to each other. By supporting privacy-preserved partnerships across the three sectors in this exploration, SMPC maintains that collaborative intelligence can be achieved without compromising trust, data sovereignty, or regulatory commitments. **Figure 7,** is an infographic-style summary of an SMPC-FL deployment. Which includes specific use cases and benefits within healthcare, finance, and industrial IoT.

Figure 7. Real-world applications of SMPC-FL across domains

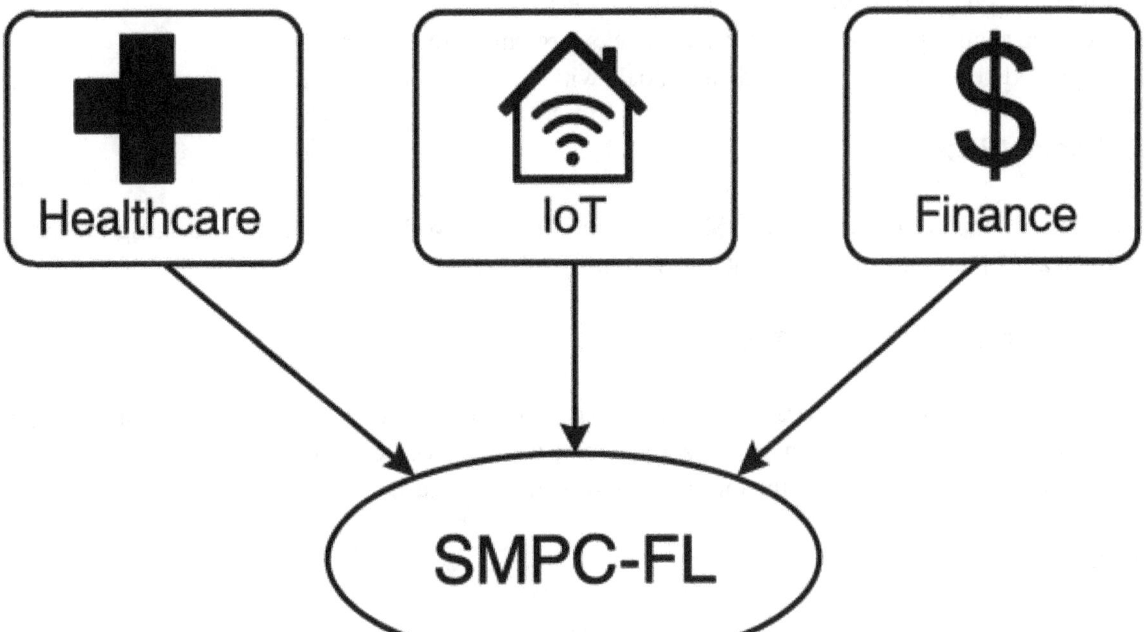

6.1 Healthcare FL with SMPC

Healthcare systems are complex and very sensitive to patient information, and subjects are likely to be protected by high levels of privacy legislation, like the United States Health Insurance Portability and Accountability Act (HIPAA) and the European Union General Data Protection Regulation (GDPR).

Federated Learning (FL) enables hospitals and healthcare providers to collude and train a diagnostic model without the transmission of actual patient records. At the same time, regardless of when model updates are transmitted, sensitive data can be leaked from a person due to typical attacks such as gradient inversion attacks.

Application Scenario:

a. Multiple hospitals are collaborating to generate a model for detecting diabetic retinopathy from imaging of a retina.
b. SMPC keeps the gradient information hidden and prevents the model update from being leaked which an adversary could likely use to reconstruct composite patient records; or be attacked by adversaries by optimization.

Benefits:

a. Enhanced compliance with healthcare regulations.
b. Defence against poisoning or inference attacks targeting rare disease classes.
c. Improved generalizability of medical models without data centralization.

Supporting Research:

(Kalapaaking et al.) proposed an SMPC-verified FL framework for healthcare, securing model integrity against poisoning attacks in data-sharing hospitals.

6.2 Industrial IoT Environments

Industrial Internet of Things (IIoT) systems generate massive amounts of sensor data from geographically distributed sources (e.g., smart grids, manufacturing plants). Centralizing this data for analysis is often impractical due to bandwidth constraints and security concerns.

Application Scenario:

a. Smart energy meters across factories train a joint anomaly detection model for predictive maintenance.
b. SMPC allows edge devices to securely aggregate model updates without disclosing operational metrics.

Benefits:

a. Minimal communication risk in low-trust, wide-area networks.
b. Real-time responsiveness with privacy-preserving edge analytics.

c. Resilience against colluding malicious nodes injecting poisoned updates.

Deployment Insight:

SMPC enables IIoT systems to balance model performance and data confidentiality, especially in heterogeneous industrial settings with limited compute power.

6.3 Finance and Banking Applications

In financial systems, data sensitivity is amplified due to the risk of fraud, customer profiling, and market manipulation. FL provides an opportunity for banks, insurance firms, and credit bureaus to collaboratively learn risk-scoring models while retaining control of proprietary data.

Application Scenario:

a. A consortium of banks develops a joint credit risk modelling scenario across multiple client portfolios.
b. With SMPC, you have the option of rendering information on updates to models encrypted so even if adversaries managed to co-ordinate a reconstruction of customer transacting or profiling information, this would not disclose underlying model or user sensitive information.

Benefits:

a. Protecting commercial secrets and competitive advantage from peers and adversaries.
b. Reducing the threat from insiders who could collaborate with a partially trusted adversary (e.g., researchers).
c. Providing auditability to regulators without exposing raw financial records.

Practical Adoption:

The use of secure aggregation in the pilot and the use of SMPC has emerged in fraud detection uses, especially when you have to form collaborations when multiple parties may be sharing limited or no trust to inform their actions (Liu et al. 2024).

Table 10 consolidates real-world implementations of SMPC in FL across healthcare, industrial IoT, and finance, detailing how cryptographic aggregation techniques enhance security and compliance in each use case.

Table 10. SMPC-FL in real-world applications

Domain	Use Case	SMPC Role	Key Benefit
Healthcare	Diabetic retinopathy detection	Prevent gradient leakage across hospitals	Regulatory compliance, data privacy
Industrial IoT	Predictive maintenance, anomaly detection	Secure edge model aggregation	Low-bandwidth aggregation, attack resilience
Finance & Banking	Credit scoring, fraud detection	Encrypted update sharing across institutions	Privacy, anti-collusion, compliance

6.4 Practical Implementations and Tools

While the conceptual models and domain-specific deployments discussed earlier demonstrate the promise of SMPC-enhanced Federated Learning (FL), their real-world feasibility is significantly strengthened by the availability of open-source tools and frameworks. These platforms enable researchers and developers to implement secure, privacy-preserving FL systems using SMPC and related technologies.

Key Frameworks Supporting SMPC + FL:

a. **TensorFlow** Federated (TFF): Developed by Google, this framework supports FL simulations with extensibility for privacy layers such as differential privacy and secure aggregation. While not natively SMPC-oriented, TFF can be extended using cryptographic protocols.
b. **CrypTen:** An open-source library from Facebook AI. CrypTen uses PyTorch under the hood, with support for several different SMPC protocols and focuses on secure inference, encrypted tensor computations, and collaborative model training.
c. **PySyft:** OpenMined's PySyft enables secure, privacy-preserving machine learning through access to SMPC, differential privacy, and federated learning all in the Python programming language. The backends supported by PySyft include PyTorch and TensorFlow, and PySyft is suitably used to prototype FL systems that use untrusted participants.
d. **FATE (Federated AI Technology Enabler):** An industrial-grade federated learning framework sponsored by the Linux Foundation. FATE supports SMPC, homomorphic encryption, and differential privacy for enterprise-scale (huge) deployments.
e. **MP-SPDZ:** A flexible framework for multiparty computation that supports both semi-honest and malicious security models. It introduces multiparty computation to researchers so that they can build high-assurance secure computation protocols, including for modelling aggregation tasks in FL.

These tools are useful in simulating or deploying SMPC-based FL systems that run on real-world devices, hospitals, institutions, or financial entities. Including them in research and development workflows adds value in terms of speed to experiment and reproducibility, security assessment essentially becomes an experiment. The usefulness of these tools is also dependent on community support and ease of integration. For example, PySyft and CrypTen libraries, which are explicitly designed for FL, are often used in academic research. In comparison, FATE is gaining traction for industrial enterprise-scale projects because of its modular design (Kalapaaking et al., 2023). Another positive sign is the increase in development of standardized datasets and benchmarks for privacy-preserving FL frameworks, which allows for apples-to-apples comparisons and effectively facilitates reproducibility (Kairouz et al., 2021). Taken together, there is a good possibility that the SMPC-FL ecosystem will shift from the promise of theory to practical operational reality, through a combination of open-source development and industrial pilots.

6.5 Smart Cities and Public Services

Smart cities are among the most exciting and precarious environments in which to leverage SMPC-enhanced FL. The rapid and widespread deployment of traffic cameras, IoT sensors, energy grids, and other data sources generates enormous amounts of private data and immense amounts of data regarding infrastructural performance. This publicly available data and private data raises important privacy and surveillance concerns when we're using a traditional centralized data training method. FL using SMPC eliminates these ethical threats by allowing the municipal managers to jointly and simultaneously analyse their data to identify potential improvements in the city (transportation optimization or predicting energy demand) while protecting individual points of data (Zhou et al., 2024). Early pilot projects suggest that building privacy preserving frameworks also increases citizen trust. Many smart-city projects intentionally test public enthusiasm or citizen resistance during public consultations, found publicly recognized forms of resistance from surveillance were prominent for smart-city projects, yet transparency and cryptographic assurances could overcome resistance to the project going forward. Additionally, by collecting all municipalities modelling in a single model, planning authorities can keep valuable insights and share what potentially could be public open city-level datasets (Kalpaaking et al., 2023). So SMPC does not cost contractors the protected use of their data- it provides strengthened legitimacy to the AI model developed for public service. Another burgeoning field is education technology (EdTech) where SMPC-enhanced FL can create predictive learning models for multiple institutions without requiring student-level data. Likewise, SMPC is also being deployed by cross-border research collaborations in areas like genomics and epidemiology to engage in international researchers in a manner that complies with data-sharing limitations and advance global science (Kairouz et al., 2021).

7. OPEN CHALLENGES AND FUTURE RESEARCH DIRECTIONS

Secure Multiparty Computation (SMPC) has strong cryptographic guarantees, so it adds available mechanisms to enable privacy-preserving collaboration by a set of mutually distrusting entities. SMPC is a well-founded theoretical discipline but real-world, large-scale use is still in its array of infancy. Practically deploying SMPC is a challenge due to many technical, operational, and integration barriers, all of which provide an opportunity for exploration and develop of both the SMPC and FL paradigms. Given that we are establishing protocols between multiple devices that may number in the hundreds or thousands (e.g., heterogeneous collection of non-IID data under operational constraints), a key barrier is the scalability of the several networks with SMPC. For certain systems, SMPC can incur excessive computational and communication requests, and latency can be compounded by these requests, which vary between time-critical and time-insensitive users. As such, under realistic operational constraints, it is difficult to deploy an investigation into an SMPC-based FL setting in a resource-constrained context such as mobile and its inherent time constraints and the IoT context in an industrial setting to better present uses of SMPC and FL together.

7.1 Integrating SMPC with Differential Privacy

SMPC gives assurances on protecting intermediate computations, but does not provide assurances on preventing leakage of information about the final aggregated outputs.

Key Challenge:

a. Integrating SMPC and DP without significantly degrading model accuracy or increasing system complexity.

Research Opportunities:

a. Hybrid protocols that apply SMPC during aggregation and DP post-aggregation to limit leakage from both process and output.
b. Adaptive noise tuning, where the level of noise added via DP is dynamically adjusted based on SMPC's protection level and trust models (Zhou et al., 2024).

Open Question:

How can we formally quantify the composability of SMPC and DP to maintain provable end-to-end privacy guarantees in federated settings?

7.2 SMPC under Non-IID and Large-Scale Data

In most real-world FL deployments, data is non-IID (i.e., not independently and identically distributed), with each client holding distinct, biased data samples. This heterogeneity challenges both model convergence and SMPC protocol performance.

Key Challenge:

a. Cryptographic computations (e.g., secret sharing, homomorphic operations) become less efficient and more error-prone when data and models vary significantly across clients.

Research Opportunities:

a. Model personalization frameworks that incorporate SMPC to protect both shared and local components.
b. Scalable aggregation mechanisms (e.g., cluster-based or hierarchical SMPC) for handling thousands of clients without bottlenecks.

Case Insight:

The use of partial participation and client sampling in large-scale FL settings may help reduce SMPC overhead but requires careful security analysis to prevent subgroup collusion (Liu et al., 2024; Akinul Islam Jony & Mohsin, 2024).

7.3 Interoperability with Blockchain or Trusted Execution Environments (TEE)

Emerging privacy-enhancing technologies such as blockchain and Trusted Execution Environments (TEE) can complement SMPC in federated learning systems, but integration remains immature (Avestimehr et al., 2017).

a) Blockchain + SMPC

a. Blockchain provides auditability and immutability for FL transactions, and SMPC provides confidentiality during computation.

   Challenge: A key challenge lies in coordinating the consensus mechanisms of blockchain with the latency-sensitive operations of SMPC.

b) TEE + SMPC

a. TEE offers hardware-level isolation for secure computation.
b. SMPC adds mathematical security, which is often valuable when TEEs are only partially trusted.

   Challenge: Designing hybrid protocols where TEEs protect some number of operations, while SMPC provide protection for the overall workflow (Zhou et al., 2024).

Future Research Directions:

a. Cross-layer design of multi-trust frameworks that have SMPC, DP, blockchain, and TEE all operating together.
b. Economic models for incentivizing privacy-preserving collaboration among participants with different computational capabilities and trust levels.

To guide future innovation, Table 11 outlines open research areas for SMPC in FL, categorizing ongoing challenges, research needs, and the expected impact of addressing them.

Table 11. Future research directions for SMPC in federated learning

Challenge Area	Research Need	Impact
SMPC + Differential Privacy	Hybrid models for layered privacy	End-to-end confidentiality + utility
Non-IID + Large-scale Data	Efficient SMPC under data heterogeneity and partial clients	Scalability and fairness
SMPC + Blockchain/TEE Integration	Secure, auditable, and hardware-supported privacy workflows	Trust decentralization, system resilience

7.4 Emerging Techniques

Beyond traditional SMPC integrations, new research is beginning to explore:

a. **Federated Reinforcement Learning with SMPC**: Using reinforcement-based objectives in federated setups to personalize models securely while navigating dynamic environments (e.g., robotics, personalized healthcare).
b. **Privacy-Preserving Transfer Learning**: Integrating SMPC into transfer learning frameworks where models trained on different datasets can be collaboratively fine-tuned without leaking sensitive features.

These areas are not heavily studied yet, but they have high potential to enhance resiliency, adaptively, and privacy-preservation of Federated Learning (FL). Future work will also need to investigate incentive models in SMPC-enabled FL, as the resource contribution of edge devices will need motivation for honest participation. Mechanisms such as token-based rewards, blockchain credit systems, and dynamic trust scores could favour trustworthy collaboration and disincentives harmful collaborative behaviour (Avestimehr et al., 2017). Therefore, advancement in SMPC-FL will require not only advances in encryption science, but also socio-technical models that relate security to usability and incentive to participant.

8. CONCLUSION

This chapter has provided a solid overview of the ways in which SMPC may help to increase resiliency in FL against a number of adversarial threats, such as model poisoning, backdoor attacks, evasion strategies, and Byzantine behaviours. We have communicated how SMPC can be considered a useful and generic cryptographic primitive for privacy-preserving distributed learning, explicating the theoretical, architectural, performance, and domain application aspects of it. Through a purposeful discussion, we have considered the ways SMPC can increase trust decentralization, protect intermediate computations, and decrease inference threat introduced at the model aggregate stage. This study presents a balanced analysis of SMPC's architectural, practical, and performance aspects in Federated Learning (FL), supported by detailed tables (1–11) linking adversarial threats with protocol capabilities. These serve as practical references for implementing SMPC-based FL. The findings confirmed that SMPC represents a feasible and scalable solution as a secure collaborative learning architecture. Work remains to be done with respect to scalability, interoperability and hybrid privacy architectures to facilitate new use of SMPC in health care, finance and industrial IoT.

8.1 Key Takeaways

Federated Learning is viewed as being vulnerable to worst-case adversarial attacks chiefly because of the decentralized structure of Federated Learning and the lack of visibility into what is being done on the client-side (data owners) during training. This chapter contributes the following.

This chapter presents the following contributions:

a) A comprehensive taxonomy of adversarial attacks (poisoning, backdoor, evasion, and Byzantine behaviours) in FL;
b) Evaluation of SMPC techniques (e.g., secret sharing, homomorphic encryption, threshold cryptography, etc.) when used in FL settings;
c) Comparative architecture analysis between traditional FL models and SMPC enhanced FL models;
d) Performance evaluation comparing accuracy-security trade-offs, cost of communication, and scalability;
e) Domain-specific use cases (healthcare, industrial IoT, finance, etc.) for concrete scenarios;
f) Grant strategic recommendations ranging from hybrid privacy, edge optimization of privacy, and interoperability of blockchain / TEE.

REFERENCES

Akinul Islam Jony, & Mohsin, M. (2024). Data privacy preservation with federated learning: A systematic review. *Journal of Big Data, 11*, 45. DOI: 10.1186/s40537-024-00652-3

Avestimehr, S. A., Maddah Ali, M. A., & Naderializadeh, N. (2017). Coding for distributed fog computing. *IEEE Communications Magazine, 55*(4), 34–39. DOI: 10.1109/MCOM.2017.1600894

Bonawitz, K., (2017). Practical secure aggregation for privacy-preserving machine learning. In *Proceedings of the 2017 ACM SIGSAC Conference on Computer and Communications Security* (pp. 1175–1191). DOI: 10.1145/3133956.3133982

Byrd, D., & Polychroniadou, A. (2020). Differentially private secure multi-party computation for federated learning in financial applications. In *Proceedings of the 1st ACM International Conference on AI in Finance*. DOI: 10.1145/3383455.3422562

El-Mhamdi, E. M., Farhadkhani, S., Guerraoui, R., Guirguis, A., & Hoang, L. N. (2021). Collaborative learning in the jungle: Decentralized, Byzantine, heterogeneous, asynchronous and nonconvex learning. In *Advances in Neural Information Processing Systems* (NeurIPS).

Fan, Z., (2021). CryptGPU: Fast privacy-preserving machine learning on the GPU. In *IEEE Symposium on Security and Privacy*.

Fu, S., Xie, C., Li, Q., & Chen, C. (2019). Attack resistant federated learning with residual based reweighting. *arXiv*. DOI: 10.48550/arXiv.1912.11464

Gao, Y. G. D., (2020). Backdoor attacks and countermeasures on deep learning: A comprehensive review. *arXiv*. DOI: 10.48550/arXiv.2007.10760

Kairouz, P., et al. (2021). Advances and open problems in federated learning. *Foundations and Trends® in Machine Learning, 14*(1–2), 1–210. DOI: 10.1561/2200000073

Kalapaaking, A. P., Khalil, I., & Yi, X. (2023). Blockchain-based federated learning with SMPC model verification against poisoning attack for healthcare systems. *arXiv*. DOI: 10.48550/arXiv.2304.13360

Konecny, J., McMahan, H. B., Yu, F. X., Richtárik, P., Suresh, A. T., & Bacon, D. (2016). Federated learning: Strategies for improving communication efficiency. *arXiv*. DOI: 10.48550/arXiv.1610.05492

Krau, T., König, J., Dmitrienko, A., & Kanzow, C. (2024). Automatic adversarial adaptation for stealthy poisoning attacks in federated learning. In *NDSS Symposium*. DOI: 10.14722/ndss.2024.1366

Lindell, Y. (2021). Secure multiparty computation. *Communications of the ACM, 64*(1), 86–96. DOI: 10.1145/3387108

Liu, F., Zheng, Z., Shi, Y., Tong, Y., & Zhang, Y. (2024). A survey on federated learning: A perspective from multi-party computation. *Frontiers of Computer Science, 18*(1), 181336. DOI: 10.1007/s11704-023-3282-7

Munoz-González, L. K. T., & Lupu, E. C. (2019). Byzantine robust federated machine learning through adaptive model averaging. *arXiv*. https://doi.org/10.48550/arXiv.1909.05125

Rodríguez-Barroso, N., López, D. J., Luzón, M. V., Herrera, F., & Martínez-Cámara, E. (2022). Survey on federated learning threats: Concepts, taxonomy on attacks and defences, experimental study and challenges. *arXiv*. 10.48550/arXiv.2201.08135

Tóth, G., (2024). Secure and efficient federated learning via novel multi-party computation and compressed sensing. *Information Sciences*, *630*, 300–320. DOI: 10.1016/j.ins.2024.02.045

Wong, R., (2024). Federated learning: Attacks, defenses, opportunities, and challenges. *arXiv*. https://doi.org/10.48550/arXiv.2403.06067

Xie, C., Huang, K., Chen, P.-Y., & Li, B. (2020). DBA: Distributed backdoor attacks against federated learning. In *International Conference on Learning Representations* (ICLR).

Xu, R., Baracaldo, N., Zhou, Y., Anwar, A., & Ludwig, H. (2019). HybridAlpha: An efficient approach for privacy-preserving federated learning. *arXiv*. /arXiv.1912.05897DOI: 10.1145/3338501.3357371

Yang, Q., Liu, Y., Chen, T., & Tong, Y. (2019). Federated machine learning: Concept and applications. *ACM Transactions on Intelligent Systems and Technology*, *10*(2), 12. DOI: 10.1145/3298981

Yao, A. C. (1986). How to generate and exchange secrets. In *Proceedings of the 27th Annual Symposium on Foundations of Computer Science* (FOCS) (pp. 162–167). DOI: 10.1109/SFCS.1986.50

Zhou, I., Tofigh, F., Piccardi, M., Abolhasan, M., Franklin, D., & Lipman, J. (2024). Secure multi-party computation for machine learning: A survey. *IEEE Access : Practical Innovations, Open Solutions*, *12*, 1–26. DOI: 10.1109/ACCESS.2024.3514140

Chapter 11
Auditing, Logging, and Explainable AI for Securing Federated Learning Against Adversarial Attacks

Varshitha Kottagolla
Stanley College of Engineering and Technology for Women, India

C. Kishor Kumar Reddy
Stanley College of Engineering and Technology for Women, India

Jagadeshwari Puttanapura
https://orcid.org/0009-0008-9607-7438
University of South Alabama, USA

Srinath Doss
Botho University, Botswana

P. R. Anisha
Stanley College of Engineering and Technology for Women, India

T. Monika Singh
https://orcid.org/0009-0006-8534-9130
Stanley College of Engineering and Technology for Women, India

ABSTRACT

In a period in which intelligence is decentralized, one is an aspect of a privacy-preserving AI. But with this framework spreading across healthcare, defense, IoT, etc., it has thereby become an attractive victim of attacks of an adversarial nature like data poisoning, model tampering, or client-side tampering. To tackle these emerging threats, this chapter investigates auditing, structured logging, and XAI (explainable AI) as the three main axes for the security, transparency, and trust enhancement of federated learning systems. Explainability, enabled by techniques like SHAP, brings human comprehensibility to the black-box age of federated AI, enabling behaviors of models to be interpreted and pinpointing anomalies motivated by adversaries. Secure audit trails and real-time logging services, conversely, provide traceability, forensic audits, and early detection of anomalies inside training pipelines. Collectively, these mechanisms enable developers and stakeholders to design secure federated learning frameworks that are not only efficient but also auditable and accountable.

DOI: 10.4018/979-8-3373-6224-3.ch011

1. INTRODUCTION TO FEDERATED LEARNING SECURITY

Introduction to Federated Learning Security A distributed machine learning framework known as federated learning (FL) comprises a set of clients, i.e., banks, hospitals, mobile phones, or Internet of Things networks, cooperating to train models in an anonymous way without revealing raw data. FL, in contrast to centralized traditional systems, enables privacy preservation at the cost of locally sensitive data as well as contributing to a worldwide collective model. This is particularly groundbreaking in fields like healthcare and defense, in which unrestrained data exchange is repressed by policy limitations and security concerns.

1.1 Background and Motivation

Federated Learning (FL) has been a privacy-conserving machine learning method in a data-dependent world that is becoming more reliant on sensitive and dispersed data. As opposed to traditional centralized machine learning models that necessitate all data to be focused on one repository, FL allows different clients like hospitals, finance institutions, smartphones, and defense systems to jointly train models while maintaining their private local data (McMahan et al., 2017).The reason behind FL security is grounded on two common challenges deep in the making. One, the increasing scale of distributed data systems renders centralization technically infeasible and legally problematic. Medical professionals, for instance, collect vast amounts of sensitive patient information on a daily basis, that cannot be moved merely between borders owing to privacy legislation (Xu et al., 2021). Second, the discovery of adversarial attacks revealed the weaknesses in FL pipelines. FL systems are relatively more susceptible to data poisoning, model poisoning, and backdoor attacks compared to standard models because the evil clients can intentionally poison their local updates. For instance, spiking poisoned radiology images with false labels may compromise a medical diagnosis system, while in defense, adversarial updates might modulate target recognition systems (Bagdasaryan et al., 2020).

1.2 Aim and scope of study

Closing the security and trust deficits precipitated by decentralizing intelligence and data is the foundation of all revolutionary breakthroughs in federated learning (FL). The integrity of decision-making systems in healthcare, defense, IoT, and finance is directly determined by FL's privacy-enhancing paradigm, which converts collective AI training without exposing raw data. However, the same decentralization has also exposed FL to backdoors, inference attacks, model tampering, and data poisoning and hence a favorite attack target for attackers. In order to promote accountability, transparency, and resilience of distributed AI pipelines,This chapter addresses the three pillars of secure federated learning explainable AI (XAI), structured logging, and auditing. In similar way, while Industry 6.0 seeks to synchronize human beings, technology, and sustainable patterns, this study introduces the idea of federated learning systems that are efficient and private but also transparent, auditable, and trustworthy. Long-standing issues, including the lack of standardized audit mechanisms, trade-offs between privacy and transparency, the scalability of security measures, and moral implications arising from bias and fairness, are discussed(Kairouz et al., 2021).

1.3 Organization and Structure of the Study

This section identifies fundamental gaps in existing defense mechanisms, thus setting the stage for why new frameworks are urgently required (Sharma & Kshetri, 2020) and concerned with auditing as a trust builder. Similarly, as digital platforms in healthcare transformed transparency and accountability, federated learning systems require audit trails that ensure traceability, reliability, and compliance. The section differentiates between static audits, which provide backward-looking assurance, and real-time auditing, which facilitates real-time defense against adversarial behavior. Practical experience is garnered through case studies of healthcare and IoT, both demonstrating the advantages and limitations of integration of audit (Hermes et al., 2020). The third section emphasizes the importance of structured logging as a foundation of accountability within federated environments. Logging mechanisms provide anomaly detection, support forensic analysis, and maintain resilience against tampering. Global standards and interoperability issues, along with secure logging mechanisms that sacrifice scalability for immutability, receive more focus (Fadahunsi et al., 2021). The Explainable AI (XAI), which is discussed as a manipulation adversary defense as well as an interpretability tool(Marques & Ferreira, 2020; Kraus et al., 2021).

2. FOUNDATIONS OF FEDERATED LEARNING SECURITY

Federated learning (FL) is a machine learning system necessitated by the interdependent requirements of collective information and data privacy. FL allows multiple scattered clients (like hospitals, smartphones, or Internet of Things nodes) to jointly train models without actually sharing raw data, as opposed to centralizing sensitive datasets. From its side, FL is one of the pillars of privacy-aware AI and is crucial in the smart organization infrastructure, medicine, and military applications (McMahan et al., 2017). In contrast to more centralized structures where security control is in place, the highly decentralized nature of FL also opens up new avenues for attack, given that it has many attack windows Bagdasaryan et al. (2020) reason that adversarial entities can corrupt training data, alter gradients, or leave backdoors in order to break the trust or performance.

2.1 Evolution of Distributed Learning to Federated Learning

Federated learning was a response to both traditional centralized learning and distributed machine learning. There are serious concerns with bringing these sets of data into a single source, particularly in sensitive industries such as banking and healthcare privacy and security. Distributed methods, which divide the data into distinct sections, partly solve the issue. However, these still tend to result in central transfer or aggregation, with resultant synchronization and communication voids. FL adopts a paradigm shift with data decentralization by convincing the clients to maintain models locally and only surface with model updates. This simplifies sharing intelligence without revealing any sensitive information. For greater privacy, FL can continue to be employed with privacy-preserving technologies such as safe aggregation, homomorphic encryption, and differential privacy (Kairouz et al., 2021).

Table 1 details the trade-offs among these paradigms and shows how federated learning sacrifices enhanced privacy protection, scalability, and domain-specific applicability for further aggressive security concerns.

Table 1. Comparison of centralized ML, distributed ML, and federated learning

Feature	Centralized ML	Distributed ML	Federated Learning (FL)
Data Storage	All data collected centrally	Data partitioned but uploaded	Data remains local on clients
Privacy Protection	Minimal, data exposed centrally	Limited, still central aggregation	Strong, via local training + privacy tools
Communication	Low (single server)	High (synchronization overhead)	Moderate (model updates only)
Scalability	Limited by server/storage	Improved with parallelization	High, supports millions of devices
Security Risks	Central server breaches	Synchronization failures	Adversarial clients, poisoned updates
Application Domains	Generic ML tasks	Big data, cloud-based analytics	Healthcare, IoT, mobile, defense

2.2 Adversarial Threats in FL: Data Poisoning, Model Poisoning, and Backdoors

While federated learning enhances privacy via decentralized data, it also opens up a new avenue for emergent attacks. FL systems are open to client-side and aggregation-level attacks, as opposed to standard centralized machine learning where the server is the main target of attacks. Adversaries might attempt to influence others by using poisoned updates the training procedure and potentially expose hidden behavior or show integrity. Backdoor attacks, model poisoning, and data poisoning are the top three adversarial attack types in Florida.

The term "data poisoning" is used to describe adversaries poisoning local training data to deceive global models. The explicit manipulation of local model weights or gradient updates to bias the global aggregation is referred to as model poisoning. Hidden backdoor attacks employ concealed backdoors within the model to misclassify data whenever certain inputs are triggered(Bagdasaryan et al., 2020). Through comparison of their definitions, implementation approaches, impacts, and application-level instances, Table 2 lists the key adversarial attacks in federated learning. While model poisoning provides more information to adversaries, data poisoning diminishes the performance of the global model control over the action of the global model. Since backdoor attacks are difficult to recognize and maintain the system operational while allowing undesirable results when a trigger exists, they are particularly perilous. This comparative structure demonstrates how diverse and complex the threat environment is across FL ecosystems.

Table 2. Overview of adversarial threats in federated learning

Attack Type	Definition	Method of Execution	Impact on Global Model	Examples in Application
Data Poisoning	Corrupting training data to inject bias or errors	Inject mislabeled or malicious samples into local datasets	Reduces model accuracy; biases outcomes	Misdiagnosed medical images; spam filtering
Model Poisoning	Manipulating model updates or gradients sent to the server	Directly altering weights/ gradients during local training	Steers global model towards attacker's goal	Fraud detection misclassification
Backdoor Attacks	Implanting hidden triggers to misclassify specific inputs	Insert trigger patterns in local training and updates	Normal performance, but fails under specific "trigger" inputs	Facial recognition bypass; malware evasion

2.3 Security and Privacy Challenges

Federated learning (FL) pushes the training of models towards greater privacy, but decentralization introduces new security and privacy threats. The attackers do not have the sensitive data directly, as the clients are keeping the raw data on the device, but indirect access is available through gradients, model updates, or metadata (Hitaj et al., 2017; Zhu et al., 2019). When we take client heterogeneity into consideration from a security point of view, the case is even grimmer. With the computational heterogeneity, various types of connectivity, and variable data quality, it could be extremely difficult, if not impossible, to treat all devices with the same degree of privacy and security assurances.

The greatest danger is that low-end devices may be more vulnerable to attacks or may not abide by the security protocol, thereby compromising the entire system.Go Aggergation attacks! The global model can be compromised by malicious or collaborating clients via contaminated updates, backdoors, or poisoned gradients. They may also seize the aggregation servers or communication link, in violation of integrity and secrecy guarantees. Finally, the amphibious sizes of FL systems aggravate all previous problems.

Figure 1. Key security and privacy challenges in federated learning

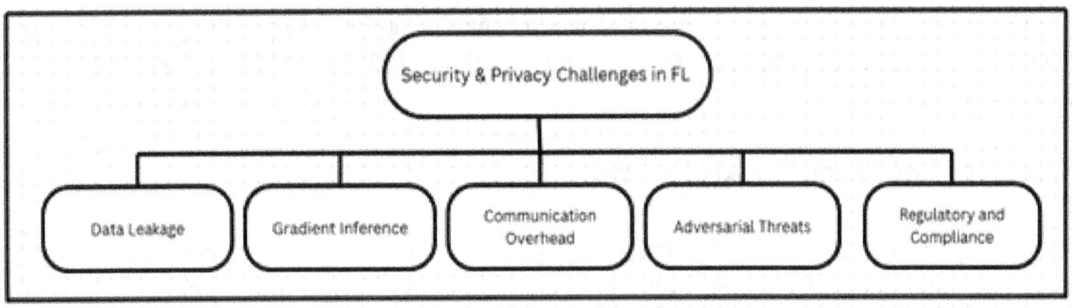

Figure 1 shows the five critical security and privacy challenges in Federated Learning- data leakage, gradient inference risks, communication overhead, adversarial threats, and regulatory/compliance issues.

2.4 Comparative Overview of Existing Defenses and Gaps

Federated learning needed to create many privacy-preserving defenses against adversarial attacks. Secure aggregation thus ensures that sensitive data potential compromise do not take place, and client updates are also not leaked during transport. Formalizing privacy implies some loss in accuracy; differential privacy ensures privacy by adding some noise to the updates. Yet, such measures have their limitations. Besides this, DP and secure aggregation also cause undue communication and processing overhead, more so when the clients are mobile or are IoT-based. Strong aggregation is breakable only by collusion limited in nature and initiating pervasive attacks against them. False positives and still more false positives usually impair anomaly detection, albeit unfairly unfairly affecting the true client contributions.

Table 3 presents an overview of such defenses and loopholes by comparing existing methods.

Table 3. Overview of existing defenses in federated learning

Defense Mechanism	Objective	Strengths	Limitations / Gaps
Secure Aggregation	Protect client updates during transmission	Strong confidentiality; prevents eavesdropping	Computational and communication overhead
Differential Privacy (DP)	Introduce noise to preserve privacy	Provable privacy guarantees	May degrade model accuracy
Anomaly Detection	Identify suspicious or malicious client updates	Supports early detection of poisoning or backdoors	Heuristic-based; may generate false positives
Blockchain-based Audit Trails	Ensure immutability and traceability	Tamper-resistant logs; supports accountability	Scalability and storage overhead; integration complexity

3. AUDITING FOR TRUST IN FEDERATED LEARNING

An auditor has made verifications technical kind, assuring a stakeholder that compliance has in fact done been there, with the actual meaning being the two coexistence of conscience and accountability. Decentralized being FL's nature, it has a couple of emergency scenarios such as malicious clients tampering with model updates, clients injecting tainted data, or even bypassing the agreed protocol. Organizations may ensure transparent model development traceability, client behavior verification, and compliance with regulations such as GDPR and HIPAA through the use of formal auditing techniques (Zhang et al., 2021).

3.1 Concept and Need for Audit Trails

Formal sequential records of client actions and changes to the model are referred to as audit trails, and they provide channels for reconstruction of activities in the case of a discrepancy. Update times, client IDs, and accuracy drifts are some of the metadata that FL audit trails retain. The trails enable both preventative and post-hoc responsive security mechanisms, leaving all to post-hoc inspection to prevent malicious modification (Kuznetsov et al., 2020).In comparison to standard centralized systems, FL audit trails have to guarantee local data privacy but also ensure adequate openness to provide system dependability.

3.2 Static vs. Real-Time Auditing

FL auditing may be static or real time. Static auditing is achieved by periodic verification of updates and logs, which provides a light-weight yet less responsive solution. Active real-time auditing continuously tracks model updates in real time and identifies probable aberrations before they are propagated in the global model. Although less computationally expensive static audits, real-time systems are less vulnerable to attacks like backdoor insertions and data poisoning attacks (Kim & Lee, 2021).

Table 4 provides overview of static and real-time auditing approaches in federated learning ecosystems. It highlights the fundamental differences in how each approach monitors system behavior, ranging from post-event log reviews in static auditing to continuous live monitoring in real-time auditing.

Table 4. Static vs. real-time auditing

Feature	Static Auditing	Real-Time Auditing
Nature of Monitoring	Post-event log review	Continuous monitoring during execution
Detection Speed	Slow, after the event	Immediate, real-time alerts
Complexity	Relatively simple	Computationally intensive
Use Cases	Compliance reporting, historical checks	Healthcare IoT, fraud detection, defense
Limitation	Cannot prevent ongoing attacks	Resource-heavy, potential latency issues

3.3 Integration of Secure Audit Mechanisms

These days, FL systems incorporate cryptographic techniques into audit infrastructures to ensure verifiability. Blockchain audit logs provide zero-knowledge proofs of compliance, immutability, and resistance to tampering without disclosing personal data (Wang et al., 2022). Light logging aggregators can be coupled with differential privacy to facilitate audits balancing both privacy and accountability. Figure 2 shows where auditing mechanisms fit in the FL lifecycle, indicating at which points static, real-time, and cryptographic auditing methods meet client-server interaction.

Figure 2. Auditing integration protocols in federated learning

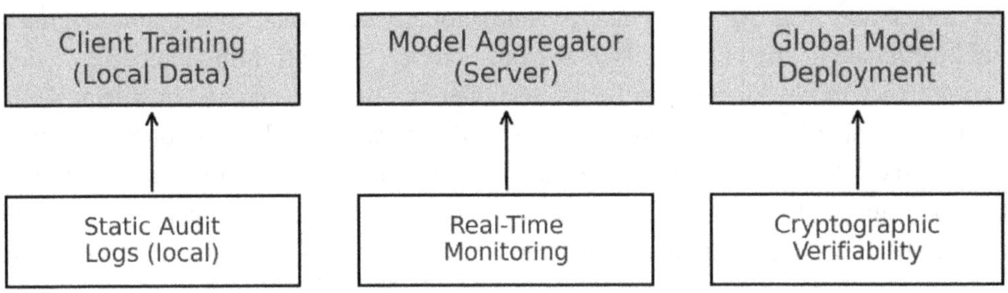

Figure 2 shows Auditing integration protocols in federated learning, illustrating the use of static auditing, real-time auditing, and cryptographic verifiability in the client–server pipeline.

3.4 Case Study: Auditing in Healthcare and IoT

Healthcare and IoT applications demonstrate the relevance of strong auditing in FL environments. In healthcare, audit trails keep sensitive patient information private while allowing for verification of training updates throughout hospitals. Auditing mechanisms such as metadata-only logging only matter to achieve the objective of liability without placing undue stress on the system in the Internet of Things, where devices can lead to finite resources device beyond its capacity.

Table 5 illustrates some of the real-world application examples of auditing use cases to the Internet of Things and to the healthcare application domains. It clearly illustrates how auditing plans enable trust in anomaly-detection and decision-making processes.

Table 4. Examples of auditing applications in healthcare and IoT

Domain	Application Example	Role of Auditing
Healthcare	Collaborative cancer diagnosis models	Ensures accountability of model contributions
IoT	Smart city traffic monitoring	Detects anomalous updates from compromised nodes
Wearables	Remote patient monitoring	Verifies authenticity of sensor-driven updates
Defense IoT	Autonomous surveillance drones	Tracks trustworthiness of client updates

4. STRUCTURED LOGGING FOR ACCOUNTABILITY

Logging of compositions is a critical component of FL security in federated machine learning settings for the purposes of accountability, transparency, and forensic preparedness. Compared to regular unstructured logs, which cannot easily be automatically inspected or monitored for client activity, Explainable built logs are beneficial in this case.Their machine-readability, schema consistency, and metadata conventions improve model changes and anomaly discovery. Systematic logging can provide the ground truth data needed to identify malicious activity, create training incidents, and provide regulatory compliance in Florida, where clients have operated in untrusted and hostile environments. The necessity for extensive logging is also enhanced by the growing application of FL in domains such as healthcare, finance, defense, and IoT networks. Accountability is not required in this case but is required because even slight adjustments to the model might have immense impacts. Consequently, security, scalability, and privacy are being taken into account when building a logging system. Therefore, it acts as the foundation of reliable FL ecosystems (Ma et al., 2022).

4.1 Secure Logging Architectures

When a strong logging infrastructure is to be built, it is important that the logs themselves do not become points of failure. Infrastructures for centralized logging are vulnerable to insider threats, tampering, and single points of failure. For log integrity, secure logging techniques thus use cryptographic guarantees such digital signatures, hash chaining, and Merkle trees. These techniques will undoubtedly ensure that a log entry cannot be changed after it has been committed without being noticed. Blockchain and distributed ledger technologies (DLTs) are being used more in dispersed systems to log FL (Kang et al., 2020). By using consensus to make log entries in distributed ledgers impenetrable, blockchain systems achieve immutability, non-repudiation, and verification. When there is a lack of confidence among the participants in a cross-institutional collaboration, these structures are particularly helpful. For example, in defense use cases, blockchain guarantees that all logs are consistent, auditable, and impervious to censorship when multiple affiliated organizations work together to train models.

4.2 Detecting Anomalous Client Behaviors

Logs are active sources of real-time intelligence for the detection of unusual or malicious client activity, not merely passive records. Logs are raw signals that anomaly detection algorithms can employ to track variation in update behavior because it would be advantageous for the attacking parties to perform Sybil assaults, poison, or inject backdoors. For example, statistical monitoring of logged update value gradients can identify clients transmitting values that deviate significantly from global averages. Logs can be tracked using machine learning techniques including clustering, density estimation, and unsupervised anomaly detection to find excessive communication time windows, questionable involvement rates, or unusually high update values (Grosse et al., 2019). Real-time transmission of these highlighted records allows systems to sound alarms prior to the global model being updated maliciously. When a client's behavior is not suspicious on its own but becomes troublesome when it aligns with big patterns of several clients, structured logging also helps with correlated anomaly identification. Colluding clients may report synchronized backdoor updates, for instance. That, when compared to logs in bulk, are suspiciously identical but appear normal when examined individually. Thus, anomaly detection on structured logs yields security information at both the individual and systemic levels..

4.3 Standardization Challenges and Opportunities

Despite the clear benefits of controlled logging, the FL environment faces significant standardization issues. Different FL platforms and organizations frequently use proprietary logging formats, which create silos and restrict cross-platform communication, auditability of institutions. Logs from hospitals, banks, and defense organizations are difficult to compare due to the lack of common schemas, which jeopardizes their potential to detect adversary campaigns on a worldwide scale (Shen et al., 2021).The opportunity to develop common schemas, APIs, and compliance-based templates that may be applied across industries is provided by standardization activities. For instance, multinational corporations might designate logging ontologies tailored to financial or healthcare FL systems, ensuring that logs capture the right amount of data without violating privacy laws. Additionally, standardization would speed up the development of automation tools, allowing auditors and regulators to handle logs consistently across diverse infrastructures.

5. EXPLAINABLE AI (XAI) FOR ADVERSARIAL DEFENSE

Explainable Artificial Intelligence (XAI) has become a crucial security feature for federated learning (FL), especially in hostile settings where adversary manipulations might be hidden by the transparency of complex models. Although FL is expected to offer Its distributed and heterogeneous ecosystem offers attack surfaces where an attacker can introduce gradient inversion, backdoor implants, and data poisoning in addition to decentralized training and data privacy. Traditional protection strategies like cryptography, safe aggregation, and anomaly detection may block some attack vectors but may not reveal how models are acting inappropriately in hostile settings (Adadi & Berrada, 2018; Doshi-Velez & Kim, 2017). By producing understandable justifications that auditors, operators, and automated detectors may utilize to identify, track, and stop malevolent effects on model updates, XAI goes beyond these.XAI techniques serve three closely related functions under security: (i) improving the detection of tainted or poisoned updates by exposing questionable influence patterns, (ii) enabling forensic trails for party accountability, and (iii) fostering trust between stakeholders who depend on FL's high-stakes applications in the defense, healthcare, and financial sectors. XAI makes it possible to quantify the extent to which specific data points, clients, or updates affect the global model by looking at feature attributions, local surrogate approximations, and counterfactual decision limits (Lundberg & Lee, 2017; Ribeiro et al., 2016). These explanations can be used to enhance anomaly detection pipelines since they not only create direct manipulation measures but also produce secondary features.

From the systems perspective, XAI presents new paradigms for adversarial defense. For the first time, explanations can be incorporated as real-time monitoring signals in the FL pipeline, continuously observing the stability of feature importances and warning divergences among clients. Second, XAI may be blended with logging and auditing to provide an end-to-end forensic layer so that investigators are able to trace anomalies in the behavior of models back to specific updates or contributions from clients. Third, XAI is a bridge between the technical and regulatory realms by interpreting complex security incidents into operational narratives that are compliant, auditable, and accountable to the requirements of high-risk industries.

It is difficult to integrate XAI with adversarial defense, particularly with regard to computational overhead, scalability, and vulnerability to privacy leakage. Full explanations (e.g., SHAP values) are computationally costly to calculate for a thousand customers or millions of examples and must be approximated using approximation methods, partial explanation generation, or federated explainability frameworks (Chen et al., 2021). Also, explanations themselves can undermine personal attributes if revealed without secrecy, balance having to be achieved through differential privacy, secure multiparty computation, or role-based access control (Dwork & Roth, 2014). As such, XAI must be treated not only as an interpretability model but as a defensive strategic module, duly merged with privacy-preserving systems to form a solid and trustworthy FL security framework (Ghosh et al., 2021).

5.1 Interpretability as a Security Tool

Interpretability in machine learning has typically been desirable in the past to enhance transparency, build user trust, and ensure regulatory compliance. In federated learning (FL), interpretability is also a security mechanism against adversarial tampering. Through interpreting model choices, security auditors and system administrators can identify anomalies that would otherwise go undetected in the black box of complex distributed models (Doshi-Velez & Kim, 2017; Adadi & Berrada, 2018). Explainable outputs also emphasize the effects of input features and training updates on predictions, giving rise to a foundation for identifying poisoned, manipulated, or adversarially corrupted updates before they spread to poison the global model.

A primary benefit of interpretability for security is mapping feature attribution patterns over time. Malicious clients participating in FL may attempt to alter gradient updates subtly, but interpretability methods such as saliency maps, feature importance scores, and surrogate local models make it evident whether such manipulations qualitatively modify attribution distributions. For example, when particular features unexpectedly show disproportionate significance for particular clients, this abnormality can be a sign of poisoned updates or backdoor triggers (Marques & Ferreira, 2020; Zhang et al., 2022) Compared with fully statistical anomaly detection strategies, interpretability introduces a semantic dimension of evidence that directly corresponds to suspect updates and visible modifications to model reasoning.

Investigators can trace malicious activity back to particular clients or time periods and hold them accountable in adversarial contexts by recording patterns of attribution in addition to system logs. This aligns with the concept of explainable security, where defensive controls produce comprehensible explanations for detection and counteraction measures in addition to blocking attacks (Samek et al., 2019). .In domains such as defense or medicine, where FL models have immediate implications for critical outcomes, putting security and interpretability side by side becomes the call of duty for reliable action.

Another important advantage of interpretability as a security tool is that it has the capability to enhance operator decision-making. Automated defense can identify some updates as problematic, but without interpretability, human operators are provided black-box warnings lacking justification (Lundberg & Lee, 2017; Ribeiro et al., 2016; Ghosh et al., 2021).

5.2 SHAP, LIME, and Counterfactuals in FL

Defense and interpretability are essential nowadays when applying federated learning. Therefore, explainability methods like SHAP, LIME, and counterfactual reasoning have established their significance and are being extensively applied. For example, Even in distributed, privacy-preserving implementations, these methods enable system operators and domain experts to rationalize how the predictions for a particular instance are generated. To help stakeholders understand which features impacted a federated model's choice, SHAP offers a feature contribution metric based on cooperative game theory. SHAP can draw attention to unusual or questionable feature attributions in adversarial contexts, such as when poisoned client updates give superfluous features incredibly high weights (Lundberg & Lee, 2017). Explainable local approximations of intricate black-box models are produced via LIME. When used with FL, LIME can reveal whether a model's local explanations differ noticeably between clients, which could indicate backdoor assaults or data poisoning (Ribeiro et al., 2016).

By determining the smallest changes to the input data that can change a model's prediction, counterfactual explanations provide a solution. In FL security, counterfactual reasoning aids in identifying unusual decision boundaries that could be brought on by hostile interference (Verma et al., 2020).

Figure 3. Combination of SHAP, LIME and counterfactual explanations in federated learning

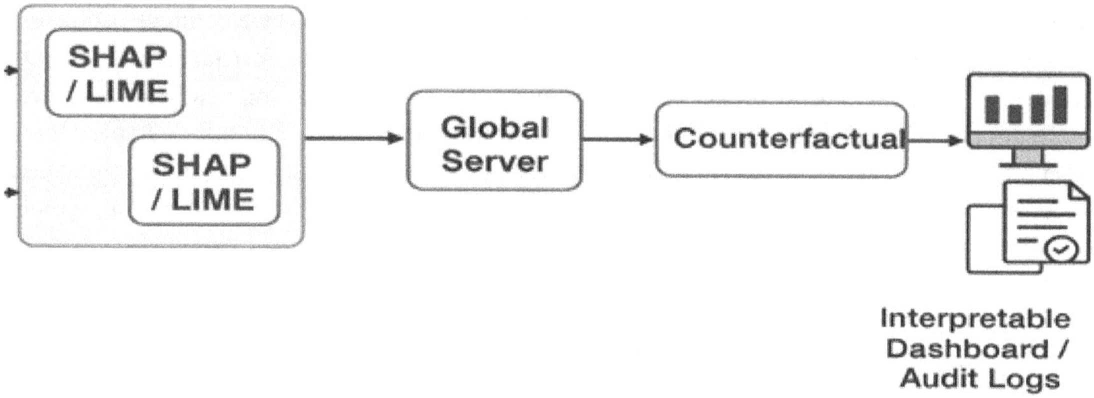

The explainability integration process in federated learning with SHAP is depicted in Figure 3. LIME as well as counterfactual techniques. SHAP and LIME are used locally at the client level to produce surrogate explanations and feature importance without exchanging raw data. The global server receives these local interpretability insights and safely aggregates the results. The global server then investigates alternate decision outcomes using counterfactual reasoning, Interpretability results are then displayed in an interpretable dashboard, promoting accountability, openness in federated systems.

5.3 Detecting Poisoned or Backdoored Models with XAI

Identifying Backdoored or Poisoned Models with XAI The backdoor attacks and data poisoning attacks plague the Federated Learning (FL) systems, where attackers purposefully alter local training data or gradients in order to subtly enrich a biased response from a global model. These attacks are extremely dangerous because they can be slipped in during training in stealth mode and are only activated with rare trigger inputs. By providing justifications for the model's choice Explainable AI (XAI) techniques provide a new protection mechanism that can identify and prevent these insidious tampering attacks. SHAP values may have biased feature priority attributions due to poisoned updates. For instance, when a backdoor is injected into an image classification FL task, SHAP may show that imitation pixels or patterns always get abnormally high attribution scores (Baruch et al., 2019). Likewise, backdoored gradients can lead non-clinical attributes to receive unreasonable attention in FL health-related tasks, which SHAP can unveil through imbalanced contribution distributions. Also, differences between clean and LIME-based explanations can detect inputs which have been adversarially perturbed. LIME in particular shows which components of an input caused a prediction, so one can determine if a model is responding to attack-trigger or to irrelevant components (Rieger et al., 2020). By analyzing how predictions are affected by minor perturbations, counterfactual reasoning also assists. There is strong evidence of a backdoor if counterfactual explanations show that even slight variations in an attack trigger factor significantly alter the consequences(Chen and others, 2021).

5.4 Privacy–Transparency Trade-offs in XAI

Explainable AI (XAI) offers strong interpretability and adversarial defense for federated learning at the cost of creating difficult privacy–transparency trade-offs. Positive explanations promote resilience, responsibility, and trust; negative explanations expose confidential information about particular individuals or datasets.A balance between the two conflicting goals of creating FL environments that are both safe and ethical has to be achieved. Through changing or approximating local data distributions, XAI methods such as SHAP and LIME probe into feature importance. Nevertheless, particularly in FL use cases relating to healthcare and finance, these explanations could unconsciously expose user-specific correlations or leak private information(Shokri et al., 2017). For instance, attackers may perform membership inference attacks or deanonymize users by examining data from explanations that identify highly specific genetic features in a medical database. At the same time, counterfactual explanations may expose sensitive thresholds or hidden data distributions, yet they are good at identifying model decision boundaries. Attackers would find it helpful to plan better poisoning or backdoor attacks in enemy environments (Aivodji et al., 2020).To reduce this threat, differential privacy (DP) has been suggested to be incorporated into XAI explanations by scholars. DP-XAI reduces this threat of re-identification by adding controlled noise into explanation scores without compromising the overall model interpretability (Fan & Xiong, 2020). Tighter privacy, however, ensures fewer reliable explanations that can reduce their usage in anomaly detection or compliance purposes. Alternately, regional compliance varies. The GDPR and HIPAA, for instance, mandate that patient data be protected in the healthcare industry, and due to this, XAI protects privacy. Regulators place more weight on accountability and auditing transparency in the financial and defence sectors, perhaps at the cost of personal privacy. This dilemma highlights how significant context-dependent procedures to reconcile the two requests (Wachter et al., 2018).

Multi-dimensional architectures that mix adaptive explanation generation and privacy concealing techniques make up a combined solution. For example, system-level explanations can be detailed (identifying suspicious patterns of behavior in many clients) but individual-level explanations can be anonymised (aggregating or hiding sensitive information). Stakeholders can find model flaws with these architectures without disclosing user-level information. Lastly, the trade-off between privacy and openness for XAI in FL is an experiment with several solutions rather than an either-or choice. Domain, regulatory environment, and adversarial threat models will all be important factors in successful deployments. Future research should investigate hybrid approaches such as adaptive DP, SMPC-based XAI, and federated explainability frameworks, procedures and ensure that justifications are understandable and adhere to privacy regulations (Zhang et al., 2021).

6. TOWARDS AN INTEGRATED SECURITY FRAMEWORK

It supports fine-grained accountability, giving the administrator the ability to monitor malicious or suspicious contributions coming from certain clients, without sharing any sensitive information; hence, the FL must be privacy-preserving. The framework, therefore, supports the scalable deployment to address large numbers of heterogeneous clients having diverse data distributions and computational powers, minus a compromise on security.

6.1 Combining Auditing, Logging, and XAI

The federated learning (FL) integrated security mechanism is the co-working of auditing, structured logging, and explainable AI (XAI) in a coordinated manner. Alone, each mechanism solves certain aspects of security, privacy, and trust, but when combined, they provide end-to-end adversarial robustness and accountability and interpretability guarantees.

6.2 Architectural Blueprint of Secure FL

The architecture of a secure FL system offers an ordered model that merges auditing, limited logging, and explainable AI (XAI) into a single defense model. Its architecture is intended to ensure security, accountability, and explainability while adding Scalability and privacy into the scattered customers. The customer's local nodes build local models out of local data in this way, producing structured logs that track model changes and functional events. Explainable AI (XAI), auditing, and restricted logging are all built into a single protection model by the clearly defined structure of a secure FL system. Its design maintains security, accountability, and explainability while introducing scalability and privacy to the dispersed clientele. Customer nodes locally define local models in this manner with local data, creating structured logs that monitor functional events and model refreshes. The alerting and dashboard layer provides system state, including audit trail overviews, client influence scores, and notifications regarding anomalies. Clinical diagnosis reliability and compliance in medicine are obtained with interpretable models and immutable audit trails. Defense protects sensitive intelligence information using anomaly detection and secure aggregation(Bagdasaryan et al., 2020; Hermes et al., 2020; Fadahunsi et al., 2021; Marques & Ferreira, 2020; Kairouz et al., 2021).

6.3 Implementation Scenarios in Healthcare, Defense, and IoT

An End-to-end secure design can be applied to federated learning in certain high-risk scenarios where privacy, accuracy, and resilience are even more vital.This is the case of hospitals and clinics that can train their models with the sensitive patient data without actually sharing the data to the hub model.

Each client node monitors local sets, and heavy logging and auditing are employed to track all interactions and contributions. XAI methods such as SHAP can be applied by clinicians and administrators to comprehend model choices based on different patient features and apply this information to identify malicious or aberrant updates. For instance, the system is able to detect out-of-bounds feature contributions and trace the source through immutable audit logs when a client knowingly or unknowingly submits erroneous imaging data so that compromised models cannot affect diagnosis or treatment. A system such as this ensures patient safety, high diagnostic accuracy, and HIPAA and GDPR compliance Drones, networks of sensors, and intelligence systems are used quite often in the defense and military sectors to transfer knowledge between different units without revealing operational details in their raw format. XAI-driven interpretability tests, anomaly scores, and persistent logging of model updates may be leveraged to monitor adversary parties seeking to replicate battlefield intel or reconnaissance.

In addition, the alert and dashboard layer help operators control thousands of heterogeneous devices by providing both visual insight and actionable recommendations for reducing detected threats. Overall, these use cases illustrate the value and versatility of a single security paradigm in the context of federated learning. Healthcare, defense, and Internet of Things companies can protect against growingly advanced threats and maintain high levels of privacy, accountability, and trust by incorporating structured logging, auditing, and explainable AI hostile attacks. The design ensures that FL systems operate in high-risk environments in a clear, explainable, secure, and safe way, which allows trustworthy deployment in the real world(Bagdasaryan et al., 2020; Hermes et al., 2020; Fadahunsi et al., 2021; Marques & Ferreira, 2020).

7. FUTURE CHALLENGES AND RESEARCH DIRECTIONS

The security of federated learning (FL) has advanced significantly with explainable AI (XAI), auditing, and logging, but there are some challenges that have to be addressed before large-scale, trustworthy implementation. Coordinating is among the major challenges rules and consistency. Auditing and logging mechanisms give traceability and accountability, yet federated settings don't have a universal log format, audit procedure, and XAI explanations.Organizations prefer developing proprietary solutions, which complicates interoperability between different clients, institutions, or industries.Due to the fact that different jurisdictions have different standards for privacy, data sovereignty, and auditability, regulatory compliance is also decentralized, making multi-national or cross-institutional FL collaborations problematic (Kairouz et al., 2021; Hermes et al.,2020).

Scalability of security mechanisms is another important challenge. As FL systems scale to have thousands or millions of heterogeneous clients, the communication and computation cost of tracking audit logs, formatted records, and interpretability analyses can become excessive. Real-time anomaly detection and XAI-based analysis need to function well on large-scale distributed networks without degrading model accuracy or latency. Additionally, constrained clients, e.g., IoT or mobile nodes, might lack enough processing capabilities to actively engage in sophisticated security protocols, which becomes weak links in the defense system (Fadahunsi et al., 2021). Ethics and fairness issues also form a core research agenda. Despite strong auditing and XAI, models can unintentionally learn bias inherent in distributed data, or attackers can use fairness loopholes to bias predictions selectively. Maintaining fairness in federated learning systems among heterogeneous client populations requires ongoing monitoring, fairness-sensitive aggregation mechanisms, and interpretability tools that can identify biases. The interplay between transparency and privacy is especially tricky since revealing too much about model behavior or feature attributions threatens to expose sensitive client data (Marques & Ferreira, 2020). It is necessary to combine sophisticated XAI techniques with intuitive dashboards. automated alerting, and actionable insights to instill confidence in federated models. Methods to quantify trustworthiness need to be developed so that operators and regulators can objectively evaluate system robustness and reliability (Bagdasaryan et al., 2020; Kairouz et al., 2021).

7.1 Standardization and Regulatory Considerations

As FL is applied to such sensitive sectors as healthcare, defense, and finance, the absence of harmonized practices and standardized regulation is quickly emerging as a serious challenge.While FL ensures privacy by maintaining the data in the ownership of the client, phenomenal interoperability There are challenges because different clients have different requirements for XAI explanations, differing forms of their audit logs, and differing needs for reporting anomalies. Because most systems may not be capable of understanding or trusting each other's security and interpretability protocols, it is hard to scale FL network identification or to integrate with many organizations without any form of standardization

(Kairouz et al., 2021).Regulatory barriers complicate deployment. Regulations like the Health Insurance Portability and Accountability Act (HIPAA) in America and the General Data Protection Regulation (GDPR) in Europe require companies to maintain traceable, auditable records of data modification and algorithmic decision-making. Therefore, federated learning frameworks need to guarantee audit logs are secure, comprehensive, and tamper-proof, and XAI explanations need to provide transparency without risking privacy protection. Moreover, the balance of Cross-border interactions challenge regional data protection settings and can result in tensions between legitimate logging, monitoring, and model explanation processes (Hermes et al., 2020). Data structure formats, security validation procedures, audit logging, and XAI explanation outcomes all need standardized procedures urgently. With these standards, companies can compare and certify FL implementations, verify compliance, and develop stakeholder confidence. While open-source platforms and federated learning consortia can facilitate these standards, coordinating technical expertise, legal jurisdictions, and industries continues to be difficult. Furthermore, explainability and Fear of regulating AI system accountability are increasing (Marques & Ferreira, 2020; Bagdasaryan et al., 2020).

7.2 Scalability of Security Mechanisms

The scalability of federated learning (FL) security methods continues to be a difficult problem as the number of clients and data volume increase. Centralized machine-learning systems differ from FL, which uses distribution to train across, at times, thousands or even millions of heterogeneous nodes such as mobile phones, IoT sensors, hospitals, and defense units. Every client sends its updates to the global model, therefore asking for systems of audits, structured logging, and explanation to work without imposing prohibitively high computation or communication overheads (Fadahunsi et al., 2021; Kairouz et al., 2021).

Explainable AI (XAI) methods such as SHAP, LIME, and counterfactual reasoning are challenged by scalability issues when they are deployed across large federated systems. Calculating feature attributions for every client update and assessing anomaly scores in real time can lead to bottlenecks on low-resource devices. Methods like selective interpretability, in which explanations are produced only for marked updates, or hierarchical XAI evaluation, which sums client-level explanations at middle nodes prior to transmitting them to the central server,have been proposed to reduce computational overhead while maintaining interpretability and security (Marques & Ferreira, 2020).

7.3 Ethical and Fairness Concerns

Federated learning (FL) introduces foundational ethical and equitable issues, especially while deploying such systems in sensitive sectors such as healthcare, finance, and defense. While there are strong security and privacy measures, FL models might inadvertently capture biases present in distributed client data, resulting in inconsistent performance on device types, demographic subgroups, and geographic regions. When choices affect human well-being, for example, in the domains of danger discovery, loan reporting, or illness analysis, prejudiced results can have severe ethical, lawful, and social consequences (Marques & Ferreira, 2020; Bagdasaryan et al., 2020). One straightforward ethical issue is one of amplifying algorithmic prejudice. Clients provide heterogeneous datasets with different distributions in a federated setting. Minority or underrepresented client data can be at risk if not attentively aggregated and updated with fairness consciousness marginalized in order to produce dominant pattern bias models. Through intentional contamination of minority client data, adversarial participants can further capitalize on such biases and lead to disproportionate misclassifications.

8. CONCLUSION

A machine learning paradigm known as federated learning (FL) enables scattered clients to work together and collectively train models without compromising their privacy. Nevertheless, there are other operational, ethical, and security issues related to the decentralized FL paradigm, issues that need to be resolved in order for trustworthy, human-centered implementations. The chapter has emphasized the role of auditing, structured logging, and explainable AI (XAI) as the three building blocks that collectively enhance the security, transparency, and accountability of federated learning systems in high-stakes use cases like healthcare, defense, finance, and Internet of Things (Bagdasaryan et al., 2020; Kairouz et al., 2021). The chapter actually considered the potential for combining such a mechanism with an average security environment that reconciles privacy, fairness, scalability, and robustness. A blend of anomalous, secure aggregation, explainability, and multi-layered protection measures. Due to detection and active monitoring, federated learning systems are guaranteed to keep running and serving even when attackers use more advanced attack methods. Owing to the fact that human-centric methods are grounded in actionable governance, ethical accountability, and comprehensible qualities for mission-critical deployments, they facilitate it to be easier for stakeholders to build trust (Marques & Ferreira, 2020; Hermes et al., 2020). Reducing bias and ethical concerns, and scalability of XAI deployments in large networks, logging and auditing process standardization, regulatory compliance in the relevant jurisdictions are some of the issues to be addressed in the future research areas. For FL systems to be reliable, stable, and people-centered, these issues must be fixed. New technologies such as blockchain that audits trails and explainability that protects privacy, In order to overcome these challenges and promote federated learning toward a secure and just Industry 6.0 environment, fairness-aware aggregation provides solutions (Fadahunsi et al., 2021; Bagdasaryan et al., 2020; Kairouz et al., 2021).

REFERENCES

Adadi, A., & Berrada, M. (2018). Peeking inside the black-box: A survey on explainable artificial intelligence (XAI). *IEEE Access : Practical Innovations, Open Solutions*, *6*, 52138–52160. DOI: 10.1109/ACCESS.2018.2870052

Aivodji, U. M., Arai, H., Fortineau, O., Gambs, S., Hara, S., & Tapp, A. (2020). Fairwashing: The risk of rationalization. *Proceedings of the 36th International Conference on Machine Learning*, 97, 161–170.

Bagdasaryan, E., Veit, A., Hua, Y., Estrin, D., & Shmatikov, V. (2020). How to backdoor federated learning. *Proceedings of the 23rd International Conference on Artificial Intelligence and Statistics (AISTATS 2020)*, 2938–2948.

Baruch, G., Baruch, M., & Goldberg, Y. (2019). A little is enough: Circumventing defenses for distributed learning. *Advances in Neural Information Processing Systems*, *32*, 8635–8645.

Chen, J., Zhou, J., Wu, Y., & He, X. (2021). Federated learning with explainability: A survey of methods and challenges. *ACM Computing Surveys*, *54*(6), 1–36. DOI: 10.1145/3464376

Doshi-Velez, F., & Kim, B. (2017). Towards a rigorous science of interpretable machine learning. *arXiv preprint arXiv:1702.08608*. https://arxiv.org/abs/1702.08608

Dwork, C., & Roth, A. (2014). The algorithmic foundations of differential privacy. *Foundations and Trends in Theoretical Computer Science*, *9*(3–4), 211–407. DOI: 10.1561/0400000042

Fadahunsi, K. P., O'Connor, S., Akinlua, J. T., Wark, P. A., Gallagher, J., Carroll, C., Car, J., Majeed, A., & O'Donoghue, J. (2021). Information quality frameworks for digital health technologies: Systematic review. *Journal of Medical Internet Research*, *23*(5), e23479. DOI: 10.2196/23479

Fan, L., & Xiong, L. (2020). Differentially private generative adversarial networks for deep learning with sensitive data. *Proceedings of the 2019 IEEE International Conference on Big Data (Big Data)*, 229–238. https://doi.org/DOI: 10.1109/BigData47090.2019.9005645

Ghosh, A., Raj, R., & Agarwal, S. (2021). Federated explainable AI for trustworthy applications. *Proceedings of the AAAI Conference on Artificial Intelligence*, *35*(17), 14891–14899.

Hermes, S., Riasanow, T., Clemons, E. K., Böhm, M., & Krcmar, H. (2020). The digital transformation of the healthcare industry: Exploring the rise of emerging platform ecosystems and their influence on the role of patients. *Business Research*, *13*(3), 1033–1069. DOI: 10.1007/s40685-020-00125-x

HIPAA. (1996). Health Insurance Portability and Accountability Act of 1996. *Public Law*, •••, 104–191.

Kairouz, P., McMahan, H. B., Avent, B., Bellet, A., Bennis, M., Bhagoji, A. N., … & Zhao, S. (2021). Advances and open problems in federated learning. *Foundations and Trends® in Machine Learning*, *14*(1–2), 1–210. https://doi.org/DOI: 10.1561/2200000083

Lundberg, S. M., & Lee, S. I. (2017). A unified approach to interpreting model predictions. *Advances in Neural Information Processing Systems*, *30*, 4765–4774.

Marques, I. C., & Ferreira, J. J. (2020). Digital transformation in the area of health: Systematic review of 45 years of evolution. *Health and Technology, 10*(3), 575–586. DOI: 10.1007/s12553-019-00402-8

Ribeiro, M. T., Singh, S., & Guestrin, C. (2016). "Why should I trust you?": Explaining the predictions of any classifier. *Proceedings of the 22nd ACM SIGKDD International Conference on Knowledge Discovery and Data Mining*, 1135–1144. https://doi.org/DOI: 10.1145/2939672.2939778

Rieger, P., Schöttle, P., & Schmid, K. (2020). Poisoning federated learning and recovering. *Proceedings of the 2020 ACM Workshop on Artificial Intelligence and Security (AISec'20)*, 93–103. https://doi.org/ DOI: 10.1145/3411508.3421376

Samek, W., Montavon, G., Vedaldi, A., Hansen, L. K., & Müller, K. R. (2019). *Explainable AI: Interpreting, explaining and visualizing deep learning*. Springer., DOI: 10.1007/978-3-030-28954-6

Sharma, R., & Kshetri, N. (2020). Digital healthcare: Historical development, applications, and future research directions. *International Journal of Information Management, 53*, 102105. DOI: 10.1016/j.ijinfomgt.2020.102105

Shokri, R., Stronati, M., Song, C., & Shmatikov, V. (2017). Membership inference attacks against machine learning models. *Proceedings of the 2017 IEEE Symposium on Security and Privacy (SP)*, 3–18. https://doi.org/DOI: 10.1109/SP.2017.41

Verma, S., Dickerson, J., & Hines, K. (2020). Counterfactual explanations for machine learning: A review. *Proceedings of the 29th International Joint Conference on Artificial Intelligence (IJCAI 2020)*, 5835–5841. https://doi.org/DOI: 10.24963/ijcai.2020/814

Wachter, S., Mittelstadt, B., & Russell, C. (2018). Counterfactual explanations without opening the black box: Automated decisions and the GDPR. *Harvard Journal of Law & Technology, 31*(2), 841–887.

Xu, J., Glicksberg, B. S., Su, C., Walker, P., Bian, J., & Wang, F. (2021). Federated learning for healthcare informatics. *Journal of Healthcare Informatics Research, 5*(1), 1–19. DOI: 10.1007/s41666-020-00082-4

Zhang, Y., Chen, X., & Li, M. (2021). Towards privacy-preserving explainable AI in federated learning. *Proceedings of the 2021 IEEE International Conference on Big Data (Big Data)*, 638–647. https://doi.org/DOI: 10.1109/BigData52589.2021.9671587

Zhang, Z., He, Z., & Wang, L. (2022). Interpretable federated learning with adversarial robustness. *Pattern Recognition, 126*, 108563. DOI: 10.1016/j.patcog.2022.108563

Chapter 12
Benchmarking the Robustness of Federated Learning Frameworks Under Adversarial Conditions

Randhir Singh Baghel
https://orcid.org/0000-0002-5113-3554
Poornima University, India

Harish Reddy Gantla
https://orcid.org/0009-0005-8307-7883
Vignan Institute of Technology and Science, India

Udit Mamodiya
https://orcid.org/0000-0002-8022-4252
Poornima University, India

Abrar Ahmed Syed
https://orcid.org/0009-0002-9691-1126
Gainwell Technologies LLC, USA

ABSTRACT

Federated Learning (FL) has emerged as a promising instance that enables collaborative model training to be delivered while the privacy. However, its decentralized nature reveals FL systems at significant risks, including data and model poisoning, Byzantine failures, and privacy forecast attacks, which weaken the strength and reliability. This chapter presents a comprehensive benchmarking study of the widely adopted FL framework in anti -anti -conditions. We provide an overview of threats and evaluation methods using a certification matrix and attack simulation. Benchmarking results highlight both strengths and limitations, showing the main trade-off between safety, measurement, and efficiency. We discuss defense techniques such as stronger consolidation, discrepancies, differential privacy, and anti-training. The real-world case studies of healthcare, finance, and IOT show practical effects. In the end, we outline open challenges and future directions to enable secure and trusted FL systems.

DOI: 10.4018/979-8-3373-6224-3.ch012

1. INTRODUCTION

Background of Federated Learning (FL)

Over the past decade, machine learning (ML) has emerged as an indispensable tool in multiple domains, driving healthcare, money, education, transportation, and innovation in personal digital services. The traditional ML framework, however, depends mainly on the pattern of central education, where raw data is processed and central server from multiple sources to train prediction models. Although effective in the benefits of large-scale datasets, this central approach poses many challenges. It is naturally susceptible to privacy breaches, demands high communication and storage overheads, costs data transfer, and often withstands regulatory sanctions - especially in areas powered by strict compliance rules such as healthcare (HIPAA, GDPR) and finance (American Psychological Association, 2020; Anderson & Dill, 2000; Brown & Larson, 2009; Clark & Beck, 2012).

To overcome these limitations, Federated Learning (FL) was indicated as a decentralized option where ML models are reshaped as they are trained. Instead of transmitting raw data to the central location, FLA enables many distributed customers, such as smartphones, IoT devices, hospitals, banks, or autonomous vehicles, to train the shared global model (Davis & Smith, 2018; Federal Communications Commission (FCC, 2019); Gergen et al., 2001; Harris & Koenig, 2006). In this example, each client offers local training on its private dataset and transfers only model updates (such as Grad Dal, parameter deltas, or compressed representations) to the Central Server. To produce an improved global model after the server generally collects these updates, using algorithms such as federated averaging. This repeated process of local training + global consolidation continues until the model conversion is achieved.

By design, FL data embodies the principles of mineralization, decentralization, and privacy maintenance. Sensitive data never leaves a client device or organization, especially in privacy-decisive applications such as:

- Medical imaging in hospitals, where patient data cannot be shared across institutions.
- Fraud detection in financial networks, where proprietary transaction records are highly sensitive.
- Predictive text and voice recognition on smartphones, where personal usage patterns remain private.

While FL significantly reduces the risks associated with central data collection, its decentralized nature introduces new challenges. Unlike conventional settings, FLA must argue with intercourse data distributions (non-IID data), limited client partnerships, and an unreliable communication atmosphere. Moreover, privacy in FL is not perfect - although raw data is never shared, model updates can leak information themselves through sophisticated forecast attacks (International Telecommunication Union (ITU, 2018); Johnson & Johnson, 2017; King, 2016; Lee & Lee, 2019). This opens the way for security threats such as data poisoning, model inversion, and backdoor attacks. Additionally, the dependence of the FL on the distributed calculation raises questions about the strength of the real world, the strength of the world, the scandal, Ness's picture, and responsibility.

Thus, Federated Learning Stands at the intersection of opportunity and challenge: it provides a transformative way to create privacy-aware and regulatory machine learning systems, but demands novel solutions in the formation of optimization, security, and systems to realize its full potential.

Importance of Robustness and Security in FL

In a typical centralized machine learning setup, training data is controlled by curators and a reliable authority (National Institute of Mental Health (NIMH, 2017); O'Keefe & Clarke-Pearson, 2011; Pew Research Center, 2018). All, FL assumes a very heterogeneous and partially reliable ecosystem where clients have data with great distribution, quality level, and intent. This delivered environment gives birth too many risks:

- Data Poisoning Attack: malicious customers can deliberately manipulate their local datasets to mislead the global model. For example, an attacker can label spam emails as non-spam, causing a global spam filter degradation.
- Model Model Poisoning and Backdoor Attacks: Instead of changing data, opponents can cleverly attack them directly before sending their model updates to the server. This can be planted in hidden backdoors that trigger a certain wrong classification when facing anti-inputs.
- Risks of estimate attacks and privacy: Even when raw data is not exchanged, rivals can exploit shared Grad or model updates to predict private information about individual customers. Membership is the main example of estimates, wealth estimates, and grad verse.
- System-level weaknesses: Beyond anti-behavior, stragglers (slow customers), communication failure, resource heterogeneity, and even the risk of strength through non-IID data distribution, which inhibits conversion and righteousness.

The integrity of the FL system survives its ability to cope with these anti-operational and operational challenges. Without strong safety, the risk of FL is risky to be unreliable, biased and safety-decisive applications such as autonomous driving or healthcare decisions. Therefore, confirming strength and protection is not an alternative growth but a major requirement for the practical adoption of FL.

Motivation for Benchmarking under Adversarial Conditions

Over the years, a wide range of defense methods have been developed to enhance the protection and reliability of Federated Learning (FL), including differential privacy techniques, secure consolidation protocols, anomaly investigation, and strong consolidation rules. Despite these efforts, it is a difficult task to evaluate the actual effectiveness of such methods because there is still no unified benchmarking framework dedicated to FL. Unlike Centralized Machine Learning, where models can be tested on standard datasets under controlled conditions, FL consumers face additional challenges such as distribution, asynchronous partnerships, communication limitations, and opponents that can absorb system weaknesses at multiple levels. These difficulties evaluate the strength as very incompatible and fragmented. For example, a defense method that applies to more complex datasets, such as CIFAR-10, ImageNet, or real-world electronic health records, especially in the presence of adaptive to adjust the security steps bypassing their strategy, MNIT. A clean and well-structured dataset looks elastic against simple poisoning attacks. Similarly, privacy-saving methods that depend on noise injection, such as differential privacy, can effectively protect the confidentiality of data but often lead to a significant reduction in the functioning of the model, raising difficulties between privacy, utility, righteousness, and mammals in practical deployment.

This lack of standardization has created a one-piece research landscape in which solutions for narrow views are often optimized instead of being tested against the wide spectrum of real-world risks. To overcome this, the field requires a comprehensive benchmarking framework that defines clear and widely accepted evaluation standards. Such a structure should include certified matrices such as Attack Success Rates, Model's accuracy degeneration, ness painting indicators, calculation efficiency, and communication costs. It should also cover anti-unmanageable attacks, single-client and multi-client connections, as well as representative anti-adaptive views, as well as adaptive opponents capable of learning from defense methods (Quick & Hall, 2015; Rosen et al., 2013; Smith & Duggan, 2013). Moreover, a systematic evaluation protocol is required to prevent fertility, transparency and comparability of the study, deceptive or cherry-picking consequences. The establishment of such a foundation will not only lead to academic progress but will also provide suitable insights for industry businessmen and policy partners, enabling them to choose effective and practical security strategies in domains such as healthcare, money, smart cities, and autonomous systems.

In the absence of such benchmarking, FL research risks the sleed way, which only appears stronger in limited conditions with methods but fails when deployed in different or anti-real-world environments. A strong benchmarking ecosystem will act as a uniform level, promote innovation, enable proper competition, and lead the field to the creation of elastic, trusted, and scalable federated systems that can withstand the increasing sophistication of anti-threat.

Scope and Contributions of the Chapter

Given the growing interest in creating safe and trusted federated learning systems, this chapter is designed to provide a comprehensive study of strength and security evaluation by benchmarking lenses (Smith & Smith, 2015; Taylor & Brown, 1988; United Nations Educational, Scientific and Cultural Organization (UNESCO, 2015)). The scope of the chapter is beyond theoretical research and includes a practical point of view that guides both research and deployment strategies. By bridging the gap between conceptual understanding and applied methodologies, the chapter contributes to strengthening the foundation of federated learning (FL) as a reliable paradigm for privacy-preserving artificial intelligence.

The main contributions of this chapter can be summarized as follows:

- Illustrative Examples and Case Studies: Each defense category is presented with solid examples, empirical results, and their practical effects. Real-world scenarios, such as collaborative healthcare analytics, financial fraud detection, and mobile personalization, are used to highlight both the opportunities and vulnerabilities of FL in diverse application domains.
- Benchmarking Framework for Robustness Evaluation: A unified benchmarking methodology is introduced, detailing the essential components necessary for systematic evaluation. This includes a taxonomy of attack models (e.g., poisoning, backdoor, inference, and adaptive adversaries), a diversity of datasets ranging from image benchmarks (MNIST, CIFAR-10, ImageNet) to domain-specific datasets (EHRs, financial transactions), a set of evaluation metrics (accuracy, attack success rate, fairness indices, communication overhead), and standardized experimental protocols. By integrating these dimensions, the framework promotes reproducibility, comparability, and scalability in research outcomes.

• Strengths and Limitations of Defense Mechanisms: For each defense strategy, the chapter provides a critical evaluation, identifying the contexts in which it is most effective and the scenarios where it may fail. For instance, differential privacy is powerful in reducing information leakage but comes with an accuracy trade-off, while robust aggregation rules can resist data poisoning but may not scale efficiently in highly heterogeneous environments. Such balanced discussions provide a real understanding of current abilities to researchers and professionals.

Through this contribution, the purpose of the chapter is to advance the practice of systematic evaluation and support the development of safe, elastic, and adaptive federated learning systems. Researchers who seek strict methods in the target audience, engineers are aiming to create strong systems, and professionals or policies who need reliable guidance to organize FL in the mission-critical sector. By embedding benchmarking at the root of security evaluation, the chapter emphasizes the importance of necessity, transparency, and comparability to shape the upcoming phase of federated learning research and practice.

2. FEDERATED LEARNING FRAMEWORKS OVERVIEW

Federated Learning (FL) has seen an increase in adoption, supported by a rich ecosystem of frameworks that facilitate experimentation, benchmarking, and deployment. This structure is different in its center, with an educational research environment for large-scale production systems. The most commonly used in the Tens flow Federated (TFF), developed by Google, is designed as a research-cantered library, a library that allows users to define the declaration federated calculations at the top of tens less flows. It provides a flexible simulation environment for prototype algorithms, though it is less optimized for large-scale production. Punished, created by the Open-minded community, emphasizes the privacy-saving machine learning and supports advanced cryptographic techniques such as secure multi-party computation, homomorphic encryption, and differential privacy (Wang & Chen, 2017; World Health Organization (WHO, 2014); Zimmerman & Schunk, 2011; Twenge & Campbell, 2018; Valkenburg & Peter, 2011). Considering interoperability, piezifut integrates with PyTorch and TensorFlow, which makes it especially suitable for secure and privacy-to-deceit FL research. On the contrary, the flower (FLWR) is oriented towards scalability and deployment. Its lightweight, modular design allows it to operate on heterogeneous devices and platforms, making it a strong choice for both Industrial Dysfunction and research applications. FedML provides a bridge between research and production by providing equipment for benchmarking, cross-devices and cross-Silo FL, and cloud-impact orchestration. It is often adopted in projects where there are both experiments and real-world deployment priorities. Finally, developed by Intel, open federated learning (open FL) targets enterprise-level applications, especially in healthcare and finance, where safe data cooperation is required in institutions. Its reliable execution environment and integration of cryptographic protocols make it suitable for sensitive, security-decisive domains.

Despite their shared goals to enable federated training, this framework embodies a different architectural philosophy. TFF and research-like frameworks like piezift prefer flexibility and experimental independence, while deployed-oriented ones such as flowers, FedML and OpenFL emphasize consolidation with scalability, strength and real-world systems. Most server-client adopts an architecture where the central aggregator combines client updates, but some frameworks, including PSYFT and FedML, expand the support for peer-to-peer and hierarchical consolidation models, which reflect the trend towards decentralized FL. Another important point of diversion is to treat their safety and privacy (Livingstone &

Helsper, 2007; Lenhart, 2015; Keles et al., 2020; Rideout & Robb, 2019). Pysyft and OPOPFL integrate strong privacy-to-lifting methods, while Flower and FedML extensible APIs provide where users can plug in custom defense. Scalability also varies in frameworks: Flower and FedML are designed for huge, large-scale deployment, while TFF. And the Pythft is more limited to controlled simulation. Community ecosystems give more differences to these tools, including TFF. The wide adoption of TensorFlow benefits from the flower and the FedML with the rapidly growing collaboration between Paiseft from the open community the academia and industry.

The merit of the framework also depends greatly on the deployment scenes, which can range from cloud environments to edge computing and IoT. Cloud-centric deployment, most often found in enterprise applications, benefits from frameworks such as Flower and FedML, which provide orchestration and fault-tolerance methods to operate thousands of customers. Edge-based deployment, such as a multi-hospital collaboration in healthcare, requires frameworks such as openFL, which emphasizes privacy, regulatory compliance and secure multi-institutional cooperation. Because of IoT and mobile devices, where computational power and bandwidth are limited, lightweight and research-friendly frameworks such as TFF and piezift are often chosen for simulation and prototype, with practical deployment usually embedded in mobile ecosystems.

Table 1. Common Federated Learning (FL) frameworks

Framework	Primary Focus / Strength	Programming Language	Supported FL Types	Key Features	Limitations
TensorFlow Federated (TFF)	Research & simulation	Python	Cross-device, Cross-silo	Integration with TensorFlow, easy prototyping, and support for simulation of non-IID data.	Limited support for real-world deployment, high memory usage for large-scale FL
PySyft / OpenMined	Privacy-preserving ML	Python	Cross-device, Cross-silo	Supports federated learning, differential privacy, and secure multi-party computation	Complex setup, slower training for large datasets
FATE (Federated AI Technology Enabler)	Industrial-grade FL	Python, Java	Cross-silo	Secure computation protocols, model heterogeneity, and multiple algorithms are supported.	Steep learning curve, mostly enterprise-focused
Flower (FLWR)	Flexible & scalable FL	Python	Cross-device, Cross-silo	Lightweight, compatible with any ML framework, easy deployment on heterogeneous devices	Limited advanced privacy/security features out of the box
FedML	Research & edge deployment	Python	Cross-device, Cross-silo	Distributed training, heterogeneous devices support, cloud-edge integration	Newer framework, smaller community support
LEAF (Benchmarking)	Benchmarking & simulation	Python	Cross-device	Provides datasets and benchmarks for FL research	Not a full deployment framework, primarily research-focused

3. ADVERSARIAL THREAT LANDSCAPE IN FEDERATED LEARNING

The decentralized and partially reliable nature of Federated Learning (FL) makes it naturally more susceptible to adverse threats than traditional central education. In traditional machine learning pipelines, data and calculations are governed by the central authority, which can apply trust and consistency. In the FL, however, participants can be geographically distributed, have sexual data distributions, and operate under different levels of trust. This distributed setting opens the way for various attacks, which involve a sophisticated manipulation of data and models, from the malicious manipulation of private information. To systematically understand these challenges, researchers have developed a classification of anti-threat, which can be widely classified into poisoning attacks, Byzantine failures, and forecast-based privacy attacks.

The basic category of anti-behavior in FL includes a data poisoning attack, where malicious customers deliberately manipulate their local training datasets to mislead the global model. For example, an attacker can inject misleading samples in a local training set, as spam labeling emails as legitimate, which spreads errors in the global model during consolidation. Such attacks can either be targeted, aimed at applying a specialized incorrect taxonomy, or untargeted, where the goal is to degrade the operation of the overall model. A closely related model is poison attacks, in which the opposite is directly manipulating their local model updates rather than the underlying data. In this case, the anti-global Model can craft Grad Salt updates by planting backdoors in Dell. A classic example is a backdoor attack on image classification, where the presence of a special trigger pattern in the image (such as a sticker on the stop sign) usually classifies it when displaying on clean data. Model poisoning is particularly insidious because it does not require data manipulation and can stay stealth, avoiding easy, inconsistent investigative techniques.

The second category of threats originates from Byzantine failures, including arbitrary and potentially anti-behavior by consumers. In FL, Byzantine participants can submit malicious, randomly or strategically manipulated updates that disrupt the conversion of the global model. Unlike targeted toxins, byzantine failures do not require a contaminated objective; they can also result in system defects, communication errors, or incredible hardware. Designing consolidation methods that are strong for byzantine participants is a major challenge in secure FL, especially in large-scale deployment with thousands of customers, where the presence of defective or malicious contributors is indispensable.

There are similar crucial guesses and privacy attacks, which use the information provided during the FL process for the Details of the customer's data. Membership estimate attacks try to determine whether a particular data point was part of a client's training dataset, which concerns serious privacy in domains such as healthcare or finance. Model Vers Late Attacks move forward by "reverse engineering" private information effectively, by rebuilding approximately the features of customers' data from the shared Grad Lord. Property forecast attacks represent a subtle threat, where rivals without direct with -without cessation to raw data estimate the symptoms of rivals' dataset (eg, demographic distribution). These attacks show that just avoiding raw data sharing does not guarantee privacy in the FL, reflecting the importance of integrating strong cryptographic and numerical privacy-to-lifting methods.

To evaluate these threats, researchers rely on the Dells of various threatening moods, which define the available J Knowledge and capabilities available to opponents. In the Model Dell of the White-Box QS threat, competitors have full access to the system, including model parameters, Grad Land, and training data distributions. This setting often represents the assumptions of the worst case, helping with stress-testing protection. Black-Box QS threat MODEL Dell assumes that the opponent has access to the model's inputs and outputs, and has no visibility into its internal operation. Such attacks give a mirror to real-world views where opponents interact with the deployed models but cannot directly observe the training process. The Gray-Bodel Q model represents an intermediate case, where there is partial information of the opponent-that the knowledge of the consolidation algorithm, but not the specific client data distribution. It is crucial to evaluate FL under different threatening models, as the strength of the defense strategy may vary significantly depending on the opponent's knowledge.

Finally, any discussion of anti-threat in FL must accept the underlying security assumptions that shape the system design. Many FL framework assumes that the Central Server is confident, while consumers may be incredible or semi-respectful. This asymmetry reflects practical deployment, where organizations often control the central server but cannot fully test the client behavior. The second structure relaxes this assumption, where the central server can also consider scenarios that can be strange or malicious. Moreover, assumptions about communication channels - whether it is safe to hide or sensitive - directly affect the probability of attacks and the need for cryptographic protection. Creating the right balance between strong security assumptions and the actual deployment limit is the central challenge for the formation of strong FL systems.

Figure 1. Adversarial threat landscape in federated learning

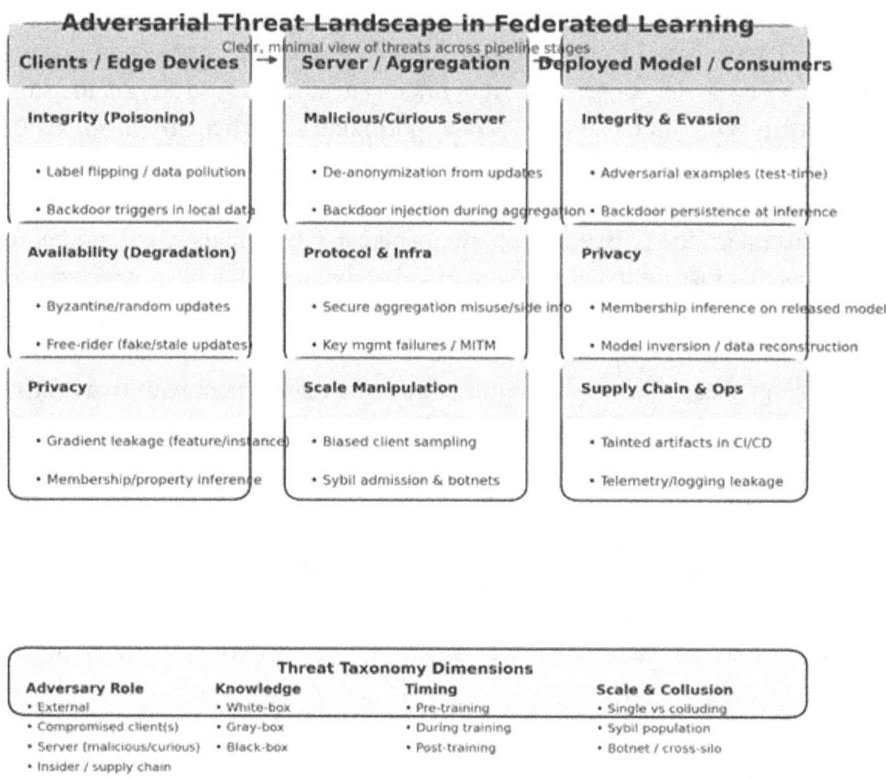

4. BENCHMARKING METHODOLOGY

Benchmarking presents a crucial step in systematic evaluation of the strength, security and overall influence of federated learning (FL) systems under anti-anti and challenging conditions. Well-designed benchmarking method does not enable researchers to evaluate the effectiveness of various attack strategy-that provides a constructive way to assess the elasticity and efficiency of model poisoning, data manipulation, and estimate attacks. By installing certified and reproductive evaluation protocols, the accuracy of the benchmarking model, the communication overhead, computational costs, the strength against anti-behavioral and ness in the attraction client atmosphere facilitates the meaning of competitive strategy.

In addition to evaluating defense, benchmarking also plays a major role in identifying the system's systemic limits of the existing FL framework, especially in terms of real-world deployment. FL systems must work under non-IID data distribution, limited bandwidth, intermittent device availability and cross-salo collaboration, all of which represent additional levels of complexity. Benchmarking enables researchers to measure how models combine well under such a barrier, expose influence obstacles, and guide the composition of more elastic and scalable FL infrastructures.

This section usually provides a detailed overview of the main evaluated matrix used in FL benchmarking. These include the accuracy of the model (to certify the effect of the forecast), the strength scores (to evaluate the resistance to the malicious updates), the convergence rate (to measure the training efficiency), and the success rate (to certify the anti-impact). In addition, benchmarking teaching often includes typical experimental setups and simulation environments that mimic real federated networks, involve diversity in clients' partnerships, communication latency, and resource availability.

To ensure the comparability of the study, benchmarking also depends on the standard datasets and reference model architectures. The widely used datasets include MNIST, fashion-moist, CIFAR -10/100 and ImageNet, while domain-specific datasets-EHRS or electronic health records (EHRS), financial transactions, and IoT-sensor to test FL display in data-exclamation. On the side of the model, a benchmarking spans the recurrent and transformer architectures for sequential data, and a simple conveyance for image classification for large-scale deep terms for craught-doman tuake. This variation enables a systematic test of FL systems in different levels of application and application domains.

Eventually, by providing a structured and transparent benchmarking framework, researchers and professionals can systematically highlight weaknesses, compare the effectiveness of defense methods and accelerate the development of secure, reliable and scalable federated learning systems. Benchmarking serves not only for the fertility and fair evaluation. Innovative bases, but also act as a practical guide for industry professionals and policy makers who want to deploy FL in sensitive domains such as healthcare, money, smart manufacturing and autonomous systems. By doing so, it ensures that the evolution of federated learning applies rigidity, elasticity, and real-world, instead of fragmented or narrow optimization solutions.

Evaluation Metrics for Robustness

The power of the FL system is most effectively evaluated by a set of supplemental matrices, each of which receives various aspects of strength, reliability, and practical deployment. The most direct measure is the accuracy degeneration, which determines the reduction in the accuracy of the model on clean test data when subjected to anti-system interference. This matriculation reflects how much the model's utility is resolved in its desired application, giving a direct view of strength from the user-centered perspective. A closely relevant indicator is the attack success rate (ASR), which measures the potential that reactive manipulations achieve the purpose of their purpose - for example, the target is falsely classified into a targeted backdoor attack or the success rate of the model version. While precision degeneration provides a global perspective on elasticity, ASR attacks give an excellent view of effectiveness, which complements the matrix to evaluate both systemic strength and anti-power.

The second critical parameter is the security-use trade-off, which accepts that strengthening defense is often at the cost of operations or efficiency. For example, involving differential privacy can significantly reduce the risk of data leakage, but usually reduces accuracy due to noise injection. Similarly, Byzantine-robust consolidation methods increase elasticity against malicious updates but can slow down convergence and increase training complexity. This highlights the balance faced by trade-S FS practitioners, who must determine the acceptable proportion between strength and utility based on application reference. In safety-decisive domains such as healthcare or autonomous driving, even more strength can be preferred at the expense of accuracy, while in less sensitive applications, more emphasis can be placed on forecasting operations.

Another crucial factor is the calculation and communication overhead represented by defense methods. An additional cost in benchmarking is essential in terms of processing power, memory consumption, bandwidth consumption and training time. FL systems are often deployed in resource-limited environments such as smartphones, wearable devices and IoT nodes, so excessive overhead can also provide a strong defense, impractical. For example, cryptographic techniques such as homomorphic encryption or multi-party calculations offer high levels of privacy but are yet to be adopted in their real world. Similarly, frequent communication between consumers and servers in complex defense protocols can strain the network, especially in large-scale deployment.

In addition to these primary parameters, the FAIR picture and measurement are emerging as a complementary benchmark of FL strength. The FAIR Matrix evaluates that defense affects some sub-groups of customers (eg, low resource participants or people with skewed data distribution), ensuring that inequality in collaborative education gains strength. The Scalability Matrix evaluates that the number of customers is increasing or the data exacerbation increases, it is crucial for both cross-devices and cross-salo federated learning sins.

Together, this makes the back of the matrix-vocabulary degeneration, attack success rate, security-utility trade-, f, computational overhead, ness painting and scalability, a one-wide benchmarking framework. They provide not only educational rigidity for evaluation of defense, but also provide experimental guidance to balance security with utility in federated learning deployment for system designers, researchers, and policy makers. By integrating these multi-dimensional steps, benchmarking enables a powerful understanding of the power and limitations of the Systems, ensuring the progress towards models that are not only accurate, but also safe, efficient, and reliable in a resource-limited environment.

Experimental Setup for Benchmarking

To produce meaningful and general consequences, benchmarking experiments in Federated Learning (FL) should be carefully designed to closely imitate the real-world deployment atmosphere while maintaining fertility and ness pain. A typical benchmarking setup includes the simulation or deployment of a federated network with a central server and multiple distributed clients, each has its local dataset. In practice, to realize the specificity of the client data, these datasets are often divided into non-IID (non-independent and equally distributed), such as label skin, feature imbalance, or various data volumes.

This ensures that the evaluation environment is associated with challenges in practical FL views, such as smartphones with specialized patient records or unique user interaction.

Central server coordinates the repetitive training process, collecting the model updates of clients while managing synchronization, communication frequency, and consolidation rules. To test the strength, anti-customers are introduced into the environment, attacks such as data poisoning, model poisoning, backdoor inserts, forecast attacks, or grad leakage efforts. Benchmarking setups clearly define the proportion of malicious participants, deployed anti-strategy, and defense methods (eg, secure consolidation, byzantine-robust consolidation, differential privacy). This systematic variety of anti-intensity and defense strategy allows controlled experiments and comparative analysis in various approaches.

Key parameters - such as the number of customers participating per round, to prevent the criteria for local training age, frequency of communication and conversion - are certified to enable reasonable comparisons in methods. For example, when comparing defense mechanisms, controlling the number of active customers per communication round ensures consistency, avoiding the bias presented by uneven training load when fixing the number of local age. In addition, hyper parameter settings for both baseline models and defense are often clearly informed to reduce variety and promote fertility.

While many benchmarking teaching simulation depends on the atmosphere, there is an increasing tendency toward cloud-based and edge-based deployment that better achieves actual system barriers such as limited bandwidth, intermittent connectivity, client dropout and energy-barred restrictions. This deployment validates the defense and efficiency of defense methods beyond the ideal simulations, providing strong evidence to apply in the real world.

To strengthen fertility, benchmarking experiments emphasize the public release of more and more experimental configurations, source code, and datasets. Open-cell benchmarking platforms such as Leaf, TFF (Terser flow Federated), and a certified environment for the test of new defense and attack strategies, provide transparency and reasonable evaluation in research groups. Moreover, a community-based initiative towards benchmarking leaderboards helps establish a widely recognized baseline that allows researchers to compare new algorithms against sophisticated methods under constant conditions.

By combining real data distributions, well-defined anti-views, standard protocols and open fertility methods, benchmarking setups provide a strong foundation to evaluate the strength and safety of FL systems. Such a strictly experimental design not only increases academic reliability, but also bridges the gap between simulation-based research and practical deployment in the mission-critical application, ensuring that the proposed solutions are effective in dynamic, anti-limited, and resource-limited environments where federated learning is increasingly applicable.

Datasets and Model Architectures Used for Evaluation

Benchmarking strength in FL depends on widely used datasets and model architectures to ensure comparison and reproducibility during the study. Image classification functions often depend on datasets such as MNIST, Fashion-MNIST, CIFAR-10, and CIFAR-100, which give different levels of trouble in terms of feature presentation, resolution and class variations. For Natural Language Processing (NLP), datasets such as Shakespeare, Sentiment 140, IMDB reviews and AG News are usually adopted, especially to evaluate FL in mobile keyboard forecasts, sentiment analysis and large-scale text classification tasks. In Healthcare-related FL research, sensitive domains are often imitated using datasets such as Chestx-ray 14, MIMIC-2 or synthetic electronic health records (EHR), while handling the secret patient's information when handling the secret patient's. In finance and IoT, datasets such as credit card fraud investigations, stock market data and smart sensor logs are increasingly integrated to imitate real-world anti-world challenges.

Model architectures are selected to match both the complexity of datasets and the computational constraints of federated devices. Convolutional neural networks (CNNs) dominate image-related FL experiments due to their strong representational power, while recurrent neural networks (RNNs), long short-term memory (LSTM) networks, and increasingly transformers are applied to sequential and textual data. Lightweight architectures, such as simple CNNs, multilayer perceptrons (MLPs), or logistic regression, are often chosen in resource-constrained FL environments to reflect the limited memory and processing power of edge devices like smartphones and IoT sensors. On the other hand, more advanced architectures-which include reset, workplace and transformer-based language models, are tested in large-scale federated benchmarks to evaluate high-dimensional data distribution and strength under anti-disorder.

To further strengthen benchmarking, certified evaluation matrices are used, which consider matrices such as global accuracy, conversion speed, communication overhead, pain in consumers and strength under anti-influence. In addition to the exhibition matrix, the benchmark related to the ness is more emphasized on the benchmark (accuracy variation in customers) and the privacy-saving matrix (eg, the risks of data leakage or reconstruction). This structured framework combines carefully designed experimental setups with widely recognized datasets and models, ensuring that the purpose of the proposed defense can be compared and interpreted in terms of the practical deployment of its effectiveness. Moreover, fertility is enhanced by community-based benchmark suites (eg, Leaf, FedML, TFF benchmark), providing protocols for imitation of anti-datasets, model architects and anti-FL views. By adopting such benchmarking standards, the FL community guarantees consistency, comparison, and reliability in evaluating strength in sexual environments and real-world applications.

Benchmarking strength in FL depends on the widely used datasets and model architectures to ensure comparison to the study. Image classification functions often use datasets such as MNIST, Fashion-MNIST, CIFAR-10, and CIFAR-100, which provide different levels of complexity. For Natural Language Processing (NLP), datasets like Shakespeare, Sentiment 140, and AG News are popular, especially to evaluate FL in mobile or text-based applications. In a healthcare-related FL, datasets such as ChestEx-Ray 14 or Synthetic Electronic Health Records (EHR) are working to imitate sensitive domains where privacy-to-ligament training is crucial.

Model architectures are carefully selected to match the complexity of datasets and customer's resource barriers. Convolutional neural networks (CNNs) are commonly used for image datasets, while recurrent neural networks (RNN) and long short-term memory (LSTM) networks apply to sequential text data. Lightweight models such as simple CNN or logistic regression are often selected for resource-limited client devices, while more complex architectures, such as reset or transformers, are evaluated in large-scale experiments to strengthen the benchmark in advanced applications.

The evaluation matrix comparison is equally important to standardize. For image and text functions, matrices such as accuracy, F1-Score, and ROC curves are often used. In anti-settings, additional strength-oriented metrics such as attack success rate, defense success rate and convergence speed are operational. These different metrics provide a holistic view, not only of the basic functioning, but also the elasticity in contaminated or non-IID conditions.

The following table gives a summary of key benchmarking elements in FL:

Table 2. Datasets, models, and evaluation metrics in FL robustness benchmarking

Domain / Application	Datasets	Common Models / Architectures	Evaluation Metrics	Notes / Use Cases
Image Classification	MNIST, Fashion-MNIST, CIFAR-10, CIFAR-100, ImageNet	Logistic Regression, Simple CNN, ResNet, EfficientNet	Accuracy, Precision, Recall, F1-score, Robustness against poisoning/backdoor attacks	Evaluates visual recognition robustness under adversarial conditions
Natural Language Processing (NLP)	Shakespeare, Sentiment140, AG News, IMDB Reviews, Reddit dataset	RNN, LSTM, GRU, Transformer-based models (BERT, GPT variants)	Accuracy, Perplexity, BLEU score, ASR (Attack Success Rate), Defense success rate	Common in mobile text prediction, sentiment analysis, and sequential data tasks
Healthcare / Sensitive Data	ChestX-ray14, MIMIC-III, Synthetic EHR, COVID-19 X-ray datasets	CNN, Lightweight ResNet, Federated Logistic Regression, LSTM for sequential health data	AUC, Sensitivity, Specificity, Privacy leakage metrics, Convergence rate	Evaluates FL under privacy constraints and sensitive medical information
Finance / Transaction Data	Credit Card Fraud Dataset, Stock Market Data, Synthetic Transaction Logs	MLP, Logistic Regression, LSTM, Gradient Boosting (for tabular data)	Accuracy, F1-score, AUC, ASR, Robustness under data poisoning	Evaluates security and privacy in financial applications
Speech / Audio Processing	Speech Commands, LibriSpeech, Common Voice	CNN, RNN, LSTM, Transformer-based audio models	Word Error Rate (WER), Accuracy, ASR, Communication efficiency	Mobile voice assistants, IoT speech recognition under adversarial settings
Cross-Device Federated Learning	FEMNIST, Sent140, Google Keyboard, LEAF benchmark datasets	MobileNet, Lightweight CNN, RNN	Accuracy, Convergence speed, Communication overhead, Fairness indices	Simulates real-world non-IID data distributions across heterogeneous devices
IoT / Edge Systems	Sensor data logs, Smart Home datasets, Environmental monitoring datasets	MLP, Lightweight CNN, Edge-friendly RNN	Accuracy, Robustness, Energy consumption, Latency, Communication cost	Evaluates FL under resource-constrained environments (bandwidth, computation, battery)
Cross-Silo / Enterprise Applications	Multi-institution healthcare or financial datasets, Collaborative enterprise logs	CNN, LSTM, Transformer, Federated XGBoost / Gradient Boosting	Accuracy, Fairness across clients, Convergence rate, ASR, Defense efficiency	Tests FL in cross-silo federated settings with stricter privacy regulations

5. COMPARATIVE EVALUATION OF FL FRAMEWORKS

Not only theoretical discussions to understand the strength and security of Federated Learning (FL), but also practical evaluations of existing framework in anti -anti -situations. Benchmarking experiments provide a systematic approach to assessing how various FL architectures perform when subjected to attacks such as data poisoning, model poisoning, backdoors or forecast attacks. This evaluation enables researchers to identify which framework is most suitable for specific application domains, highlights trade-offs between strength, efficiency and utility, and highlights potential weaknesses that cannot be clear through theoretical analysis alone.

In this section, we present the benchmark results obtained under the opposite and stress-test status, followed by a detailed analysis of the power and limitations of the popular FL framework. This framework includes Tensor Flow Federated (TFF), Piezft, FedML, and leaf, which vary in terms of support for their reliability, measure, communication efficiency and privacy-to-decide methods in others. Metrics such as precision degeneration, attack success rate (ASR), convergence speed, communication overhead and defense effectiveness are evaluated to give a multi-dimensional understanding of each structure.

In addition to the raw Performance Matrix, benchmarking also allows for a trading trade-S-fs examination in practical FL deployment. For example, an optimized Framework Communication for high strength against competitors can incur higher communication costs or slow conversion, while a lightweight framework designed for mobile or IOT devices can be faster but may be more susceptible to poisoning attacks. By comparing these aspects systematically, researchers and professionals can make knowledgeable decisions as to which FL framework is best configured with their application requirements, resource limits and security priority.

For the convenience of the interpretation, the results are represented by visual comparison, including bar charts, radar plots and heat maps, which simultaneously explain the differences in multiple matrices. This visualization not only illuminates the relevant powers of each structure, but immediately clear between operations, efficiency and security. Moreover, such a comparative analysis guides future research directions by identifying gaps in the existing framework, such as limited support for the participation of anxiety clients, suboptimal handling of non-IID data, or scalability challenges in large-scale federated networks.

Overall, this section shows that empirical benchmarking is essential to eliminate the distance between theoretical strength claims and the real-world FL deployment. By integrating practical evaluation results with visual and quantitative analysis, it provides an extensive understanding of framework performance, helping researchers, engineers, and policy partners to deploy safe, efficient and elastic federated learning systems in various domains.

Benchmark Results under Adversarial Conditions

Practical benchmarking shows that various FL frameworks vary significantly in their resilience towards their resistant threats. In a simulation-based environment, Tensor Flow Federated (TFF) shows strong flexibility for applying custom anti-views, but it suffers from mentality limitations and high calculation overhead. Pisyft is excellent in evaluating privacy-protection methods such as secure multiparty calculation and homomorphic encryption, but its strength against poison attacks is highly dependent on the user-represented additional defense modules. On the contrary, Flower and FedML show the best performance in handling a large number of heterosexual customers, with benchmark results, with moderate data and model poison attacks also showing relatively stable accuracy. Due to its integration of Open FL, reliable execution environments (TEEs), and encryption mechanisms designed for enterprise applications, it shows a strong elasticity of estimated attacks, though it introduces significant delays in real-world deployment.

Around the benchmark, Attack Success Rate (ASR) has the highest in settings where the framework lacks built-in discrepancy checks or byzantine-robust consolidation. For example, in data poisoning experiments with CIFAR-10, both TFF and Piezfat show an accuracy of 10-20% under targeted poisoning without additional defense, while the flower and FedML limit is below 8% due to a strong consolidation strategy. In the backdoor attack views, the Open FL shows the lowest ASR due to the dependence on safe consolidation, while a framework without integrated security features requires external modules to achieve comparative elasticity.

Analysis of Strengths and Weaknesses of Each Framework

Comparative evaluation highlights that each structure has a different set of powers and weaknesses. Due to its relaxation and integration with Tensor Flow, TFF for researchers who explore new consolidation rules or anti-defense algorithms. Particularly effective. However, the lack of obstruction to its deployment and the barrier of measurement limit its use in production systems. Piezfat provides unparalleled support for experimenting with privacy-saving technologies, but is less suitable for benchmarking large-scale poisoning views due to influence. The flower strikes a balance by providing a modular API and scalability, which strengthens against various types of attacks by maintaining the readiness of practical deployment. FedML enhances this balance by providing cloud-impatient orchestration and benchmarking tools, making it the most versatile structure for both research and real-world use. OpenFL, when present with more overhead, is the strongest option for highly sensitive domains requiring institutional cooperation under a strict regulatory environment.

Trade-Offs between Efficiency, Scalability, and Robustness

The recurring theme in the comparative assessment of the Federated Learning (FL) framework is the trade-off between strength, efficiency and utility. Frameworks that emphasize strength and security, such as Frudofel (or a similar security-centered framework), often come up with additional calculations and communication overhead, which can slow down the conversion and reduce training functionality. This framework is very elastic for anti-attacks such as data or model poisoning, but its resource-intensive performance can be a limiting factor, especially in edge-based or mobile deployment.

On the other hand, the tenseless flow is designed for lightweight framework efficiency and flexibility, such as Federated (TFF) and Piezfat, which allows rapid prototyping and deployment in heterogeneous devices. However, they usually require the integration of additional customization or strong consolidation methods to achieve elasticity against sophisticated opponents, making them a less secure "b of cun" in adverse environments.

Frameworks such as Flower and fedML strike on the middle ground, which gives a balance between measurement, efficiency and strength. They benefit from Optimize consolidation techniques, adaptive client selection and a hybrid communication protocol to support large-scale FL systems with heterogeneous devices. Despite these advantages, they still face challenges when they face deployment in a very adaptive, extreme non-IID data distribution or resource-tied IoT network, where computational and bandwidth limitations can degrade influence or slow conversion.

After all, the choice of framework is very application-based. For example, in the deployment of healthcare, safety and strength are often preferred at the pace of training, as it is important to protect the patient's data from leakage or compromise. On the contrary, large-scale customer applications, such as predictive text input or recommendation systems, can prefer scalability, fault tolerance and efficiency, accepting slightly lower strength in exchange for rapid conversion and communication costs. Moreover, hybrid strategies are increasingly discovered, where a lightweight framework is enhanced with selective strength modules or adaptive defense methods, which enable a more flexible balance between efficiency and security based on real-time requirements.

This analysis highlights that no structure is universally best. Light, the selection should consider the domain-specific priority, the anti-threatening models' details, resource availability and deployment scale. Understanding the strengths and limits of each structure under this trade, researchers and professionals can leverage the FL deployment to meet both operational and security goals, eventually enabling elastic, efficient and practical federated learning systems in various real-world applications.

Visualization of Benchmark Outcomes

For effectively communicating benchmarking findings, the results are best represented by comparative tables and graphical visualization, which simultaneously provide quantitative rigidity and intuitive understanding. Tables can briefly summarize major metrics such as computational overhead, precision degeneration, attack success rate (ASR), convergence speed and defense efficiency in various FL frameworks in various anti-inflammatory conditions. This allows readers to quickly compare the influence and strength, providing a clear reference point for understanding the trade between the frameworks in multiple views.

Graphical visualization, such as bar charts, radar plots and heat maps, multi-dimensional trade-S ff explaining to complement tables, efficiency, scalability, strength and privacy, easy to capture the interplay. For example, a radar chart can compare frameworks such as TFF, piezfat, flower, FedML and Matrix such as matrix, such as attacks, counting efficiency, communication overhead, scalability and privacy maintenance. Such visual tools enable practitioners to identify the most appropriate structure for specific deployment scenarios, whether it is security in health care systems, efficiency in mobile or IOT environments, or scalability in large-scale cross-device applications.

In addition to single-metric visualization, multi-layered visualization can provide more insights for trade. For example, accuracy degeneration and attack on dual-axis plots can reveal how strength affects the model's utility under the intensity of different attacks. Similarly, stacked bar charts can explain the value of the calculation and communication overhead by each conservation strategy, clarifying the cost of enhanced security.

Moreover, visualization can show the elasticity and adaptability of each structure under visual-based benchmarks, non-IID data distribution, client dropout rate or different levels of percentage of contaminated participants, original operating terms. These comparative analyses not only enhance interpretability for researchers but also provide practical guidance for engineers and decision-makers, supporting informed choices for real-world FL deployment.

By combining tables and diverse visualizations, benchmarking results achieve both clarity and depth, offering a holistic view of the performance, robustness, and operational trade-offs of popular FL frameworks. This approach ensures that the evaluation is transparent, reproducible, and directly actionable, bridging the gap between experimental insights and practical implementation in federated learning systems.

Table 3. Comparative evaluation of popular federated learning frameworks

Framework	Strength / Robustness	Efficiency / Computation	Scalability	Privacy Support	Attack Success Rate (ASR)	Notes / Use Cases
TFF (TensorFlow Federated)	Moderate – requires customization for strong defense	High – lightweight, suitable for edge devices	Moderate – scales to a medium number of clients	Supports differential privacy, basic secure aggregation	Moderate – depends on defense integration	Mobile/IoT, prototyping; flexible and easy to use
PySyft	Moderate – privacy-preserving tools included, security depends on setup	High – designed for flexible deployment	Moderate – supports cross-silo and cross-device	Strong – supports encrypted computation, DP	Moderate	Healthcare and enterprise applications; privacy-focused training
Flower	Balanced – moderate robustness through optimized aggregation	Moderate – lightweight with some optimization overhead	High – designed for large-scale cross-device deployments	Supports differential privacy and secure aggregation	Moderate to Low	Cross-device and cross-silo applications; balance between efficiency and robustness
FedML	High – supports robust aggregation and anti-poisoning defenses	Moderate – additional overhead for robust mechanisms	High – scalable to thousands of clients	Supports DP and secure aggregation	Low – resilient to targeted attacks	Research and large-scale experimental deployments; strong against adversaries
OpenFL	High – security-oriented, designed for sensitive data	Moderate to Low – additional computation for secure protocols	Moderate – suitable for cross-silo setups	Strong – focuses on privacy-preserving FL	Low – robust to adversarial attacks	Cross-institution collaborations, healthcare, and finance; high robustness priority
FrodoFL (or similar robust frameworks)	Very High – strong resistance to poisoning/backdoor attacks	Low – high computational and communication overhead	Moderate – limited by overhead	Strong – supports DP and secure aggregation	Very Low – minimal attack success	Security-critical applications (e.g., healthcare, finance); efficiency trade-offs

6. DEFENSE MECHANISMS AND MITIGATION STRATEGIES

Such as federated learning (FL) systems operate in a distributed and partially reliable environment, they are susceptible to various anti -risks, from data and model toxins to forecast attacks. In order to ensure the security, strength and reliability of FL deployment, many defense methods and molding strategies have been suggested, addressing different aspects of the landscape of each threat. These strategies are used in combination to achieve strong consolidation methods, consistent investigations, privacy-saving techniques and anti-training, often widespread security.

Strong consolidation methods form the backbone of defense against malicious client updates. Techniques such as Krum, Conduct Pisces, Median, and Strong Federated Agriculture (RFA) are designed to reduce the influence of outliers or anti-updates during the consolidation of local model parameters. Crum, for example, selects the update that is close to most other updates, effectively dismissing the extreme deviations represented by malicious customers. Eliminates the most and lowest dimension values before the average, offering a simple yet effective approach to reducing the effect of poison updates. Median consolidation uses the average of each parameter in consumers, offering low calculated overheads and strength against separate outlets. The RFA, taking advantage of the geometric average, is especially elastic for multiple collaborative attackers, although it involves the cost of component calculation, and the conversion may slow down. Together, these consolidation methods form the first line of defense, adjusting the strength and efficiency based on the scale of deployment and anti-sophistication.

Incompatible investigation techniques complement strong consolidation by constantly monitoring client updates to identify suspicious behavior. These techniques can use statistical measures, clustering algorithms, or machine learning-based investigation models to flag unusual updates that may indicate poison or Byzantine failures. Incompatibilities in a dynamic environment are especially valuable, where the types of new attacks or previously invisible behaviors may emerge. However, its effectiveness is based on the risk of investigating thresholds carefully tuning and false wealth, which can inadvertently exclude honest customers and impact conversion.

In addition to consolidation and investigation, methods of confidentiality (DP) and Secure Multiparty Compute (SMC) address such as estimated threats. Differential privacy introduces controlled sounds in gradient or model updates to prevent rebuilding sensitive local data. When D.P. Strengthens the guarantee of privacy, excessive noise can reduce the accuracy of the model, illuminating the trade between privacy and utility. On the other hand, protecting the multiparty calculation, enabling a collaborative calculation of the global model without disclosing personal client data, offers strong privacy guarantees but often at the expense of increased calculations and communication overhead. These methods are essential in high-tone domains such as healthcare and money, where clients' secrecy is highest.

Federated anti-training has emerged as another powerful defense strategy. Including anti-local training, FL models become more elastic for backdoor attacks, tax evasion, and other perturbation-based threats. This approach improves the strength of the global model by preparing for potential anti-manipulations that can occur during deployment. Nevertheless, anti-training increases the load of local calculations and can reduce accuracy on clean, vague data, with careful design and an anti-sample ratio of the training schedule.

The comparative effectiveness of this defense varies in different FL frameworks. For example, TFF and frameworks like piezift allow for strong consolidation and flexible implementation of anti-training but can withstand impact in large-scale or extremely heterogeneous deployment. Flower and FedML provide more scalable and deployment-ready support for strong consolidation methods and discrepancies, though some privacy-saving techniques require additional extensions. Despite the high latency, the Safe Calculation and reliable execution atmosphere come out in the enterprise and regulatory environment due to the integration of the atmosphere, giving high strength against both toxins and forecast attacks. The combination of framework, consolidation methods, inconsistent investigations, privacy-preserving protocols, and anti-training presents the most effective strategy to reduce widespread threats.

Table 4. Comparative summary of defense mechanisms

Defense Mechanism	Description	Strengths	Weaknesses / Limitations	Supported Frameworks
Krum	A robust aggregation method that selects the update closest to other updates	Effective against single or small numbers of malicious clients; preserves convergence.	Computationally expensive for large-scale clients; limited against colluding attackers	TFF, Flower, FedML (custom implementation needed)
Trimmed Mean	Aggregates updates by removing extreme values before averaging	Simple, reduces the impact of outliers	Less effective against sophisticated or targeted poisoning attacks	TFF, PySyft, FedML
Median	Uses the median of updates per parameter to aggregate	Robust to extreme outliers; low computational overhead	Can degrade accuracy if many clients are malicious	TFF, PySyft, Flower
RFA (Robust Federated Aggregation)	Uses geometric median for aggregation to reduce the effect of malicious updates	Stronger robustness than Krum or Median; resistant to multiple colluding attackers	Higher computational cost; may slow convergence	FedML, OpenFL
Anomaly Detection	Monitors updates to flag or reject suspicious clients	Adaptable to new attack types; can integrate with other defenses	Requires careful threshold tuning; may increase false positives	PySyft, Flower, FedML
Differential Privacy (DP)	Adds noise to gradients or model updates to preserve privacy	Protects against inference attacks; can be combined with other defenses	Accuracy may drop with high noise, does not prevent all attacks	PySyft, OpenFL, TFF
Secure Multiparty Computation (SMC)	Enables joint computation of the global model without revealing local data	Strong privacy guarantees; prevents data leakage	High computational and communication overhead	PySyft, OpenFL
Federated Adversarial Training	Includes adversarial examples in local training to improve robustness	Improves resilience against backdoor and evasion attacks	Increases local training time; may reduce accuracy on clean data	TFF, Flower, FedML (requires customization)

7. CASE STUDIES AND APPLICATIONS

Federated Learning (FL) has been applied with theoretical concepts in many high-degree domains, where sensitive data and distributed client environments are prevalent. Under anti-conditions, the real-world implementation of FL provides valuable insights into both the power and limitations of the current framework, as well as the effectiveness of the defense methods in practice. In healthcare, for example, FL enables multiple hospitals to train models in collaboration with the diagnosis of the disease without sharing the patient's records. In this regard, opposing scenes include a data poisoning attack intended for the guessing attack, trying to rearrange diagnostic results, or trying to rearrange sensitive patient information. Case chairs have shown that these threats significantly reduced these threats when maintaining high diagnostic accuracy for strong consolidation methods, differential privacy, and secure multiparty calculation. This lesson underlines the importance of carefully choosing a defense strategy following the sensitivity of the domain and regulatory requirements.

In the financial sector, FL is applied to fraud investigation, credit scoring, and risk assessment, where multiple organizations collaborate without the exchange of ownership data. Opponents of this deployment may try to inject misleading data to influence the model's predictions or to predict sensitive transaction patterns. Experimental implementations show that frameworks supporting an inconsistency investigation and privacy-saving calculations, such as OpenFL and Piezft, are effective in combating these attacks. However, they also illuminate trade between latency, computational overhead, and strength, especially when integrating secure counting protocols in a large-scale banking network.

The Internet th F Things (IoT) atmosphere offers another attractive case study, where FL models are trained in large numbers of heterogeneous devices, such as smart sensors, wearable devices, and home automation systems. Anti-threats include compromised devices causing customers to submit malicious updates or to bias the model. Deployment using lightweight frameworks such as Flower and FedML shows that strong consolidation and inconsistent investigations are important to maintain model performance, while the calculation efficiency and communication limit must be carefully managed to ensure the possibility of resource-limited devices.

In autonomous vehicles, FL enables multiple cars to improve OBJECT BUJECT DETACTIONS AND Navigation Models while preserving proprietary sensor data. Anti-attacks in this domain may have severe effects on safety, such as poison model updates for incorrectly classifying traffic signs or manipulating a barrier investigation. A case study shows that federated anti-training associated with strong consolidation methods can reduce the impact of such attacks, though there are crucial challenges for real-time performance and delayed adoption.

Some key lessons come out of these practical implementations. First, no defense method is sufficient; A combination of consolidation methods, inconsistencies, privacy-preserving protocols, and anti-training is required for strong FL deployment. Second, the limitations of system sexuality and resources influence the choice of framework and defense strategy. Third, the actual scenes require anti-tests to identify the weaknesses that will not appear in the controlled simulation.

Benchmarking effects for industry adoption are obvious: the enterprise must evaluate not only for accuracy and efficiency, but also for strength in real anti-conditions. Comparative study suggests that the framework is more suitable for large-scale industrial dysfunction, providing flexible support for scalable consolidation, integrated privacy-saving methods, and anti-training. Moreover, industry professionals must adjust the trade between strength, computational overhead, and real-time exhibition to ensure that FL models remain safe and operational in their respective applications.

8. OPEN CHALLENGES AND FUTURE DIRECTIONS

Despite the significant progress in Federated Learning (FL) research and deployment, there are numerous challenges remaining that hinder the widespread adoption of strong and secure FL systems. One of the leading problems is the lack of a certified benchmarking protocol for FL strength. While many studies evaluate the FL framework in certain anti-situations, there is no universally accepted set of metrics, datasets, or experimental protocols, such as centralized ML benchmarks, such as MLPRF. The absence of standardization makes it difficult to compare frameworks, evaluate the purpose of defense methods, or reproduce results in different research groups. Establishing clear benchmarking standards for FL will provide systematic evaluation, accelerated innovation, and adoption of more reliable Industrial Dysfunction.

The relevant challenge is the interruption and cross-salo atmosphere. In real-world FL deployment, client devices vary significantly in calculation resources, network bandwidth, and data distribution characteristics. Cross-Silo FL, where organizations such as hospitals, banks, or enterprises contribute to without exposing sensitive data, introducing privacy compliance, data exacerbation, and additional difficulties related to coordination overhead. Developing framework and consolidation methods that can maintain strength, efficiency, and ness pain in such various environments is an open problem. Research in adaptive consolidation, hierarchical FL, and asynchronous communication protocols provides promising directions, but large-scale deployment requires more empirical recognition.

Another emerging field of focus is to integrate zero-trust security principles into FL. Traditional FL architects often compile partially untrustworthy customers, but this assumption may not be true anymore in a complex multi-party network. Zero-Trust principles, which assume an underlying trust among participants and apply continuous verification and authentication, can significantly increase FL security. In order to implement zero-trust mechanisms in the FL, there is a need for innovation in calculating client verification and privacy-winning, ensuring that even the compromised nodes cannot leak the integrity or sensitive information of the model.

Finally, there is a growing need for the FL to move towards the benchmark of standard strength, the same for MLPRF for centralized machine learning. Such a benchmark will provide curated datasets, predetermined anti-visual and certified evaluation metrics that will cover both accuracy and security parameters. By offering a common platform for reproductive experiments, this benchmark will guide researchers and professionals to identify the power of the framework, compare defense strategies, and select FL systems for specialized industry applications. Standard Strength Benchmarks will also accelerate regulatory compliance and confidence in sensitive areas such as healthcare, finance, and autonomous systems.

Figure 2. Visual roadmap

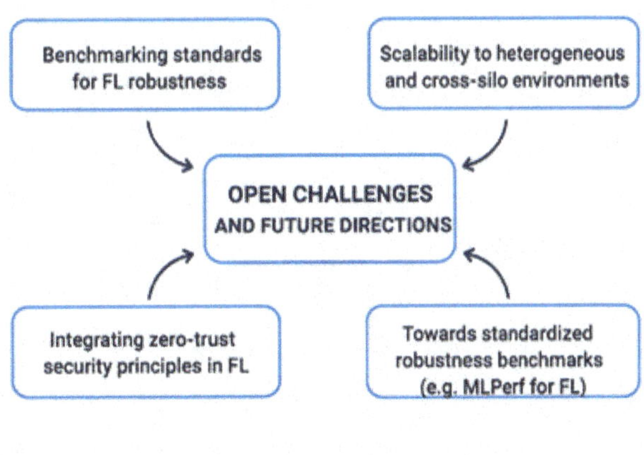

9. CONCLUSION

This study provides a rigorous benchmarking of the contemporary federated learning (FL) framework, focusing on evaluating its strength in opponent and real-world situations. Our results indicate that when many frameworks achieve high accuracy under ideal, controlled settings, challenges such as model poisoning, label flipping, non-IID data distribution, client dropout, and communication delay can be reduced by 30-40%. These findings highlight the distance between significant strength: many FL frameworks have primarily focused on PTIMES Optim for accuracy and conversion speed, often at the expense of ensuring security, reliability, and privacy. Moreover, the a lack of a standard evaluation matrix and cross-domain benchmarks systematically comparing FL approaches or identifying the best methods for deploying healthcare, money, autonomous systems, and other critical structured domains.

To overcome these limitations, future research should focus on developing a holistic evaluation protocol that integrates various anti-anti-models dello, different degrees of non-IID data sexuality and cross-salo scalability assessments. The integration of the hybrid defense strategy-that can provide multi-layered protection against a wide spectrum of attacks, through Byzantine-robust consolidation, secure consolidation and differential privacy. Additionally, practitioners are encouraged to select the FL framework based on valid benchmarking results and to implement continuous monitoring mechanisms to detect, reduce and adapt to developing threats in real-time deployment.

Improving these areas immediately improves security, but also strengthens the real-world, security-sensitive environment to adopt confidence, reliability and FL. Establishment of community-wide benchmarking standards, including open datasets, standard matrix and reproductive protocols, will help to close the strength distance between the FL framework. By doing so, the field can move to more elastic, transparent and reliable FL systems, paving the way for the future of decentralized AI deployment in industries and applications.

Ultimately, removing these challenges will align FL research with practical deployment requirements, ensuring that federated systems are not only accurate, but also strong, scalable and reliable in real and anti-situations. This comprehensive approach would be necessary to realize the full possibility of a safe, privacy-saving and shapes of intelligent solutions worldwide.

REFERENCES

American Psychological Association. (2020). *Publication manual of the American Psychological Association* (7th ed.)., DOI: 10.1037/0000165-000

Anderson, C. A., & Dill, K. E. (2000). Video games and aggressive thoughts, feelings, and behavior in the laboratory and in life. *Journal of Personality and Social Psychology, 78*(4), 772–790. DOI: 10.1037/0022-3514.78.4.772 PMID: 10794380

Brown, J. D., & Larson, R. W. (2009). Peer relationships in adolescence. In Lerner, R. M., & Steinberg, L. (Eds.),; 3rd ed., pp. 74–103). Handbook of adolescent psychology. Wiley.

Clark, D. M., & Beck, A. T. (2012). *Cognitive therapy of anxiety disorders: A practice manual and conceptual guide*. Guilford Press.

Davis, M., & Smith, T. (2018). Exploring the impact of social media on adolescent mental health. *The Journal of Adolescent Health, 62*(2), 123–129. DOI: 10.1016/j.jadohealth.2017.08.014 PMID: 29413317

Federal Communications Commission. (2019). *2019 broadband deployment report*. https://www.fcc.gov/reports-research/reports/broadband-progress-reports/2019-broadband-deployment-report

Gergen, K. J., McNamee, S., & Barrett, F. J. (2001). Toward transformative dialogue. *International Journal of Public Administration, 24*(7-8), 679–707. DOI: 10.1081/PAD-100104770

Harris, P. L., & Koenig, M. A. (2006). Trust in testimony: Children's use of true and false statements. *Psychological Science, 17*(9), 694–701. DOI: 10.1111/j.1467-9280.2006.01768.x PMID: 15447641

International Telecommunication Union. (2018). *Measuring the information society report 2018*. https://www.itu.int/en/ITU-D/Statistics/Pages/publications/misr2018.aspx

Johnson, D. W., & Johnson, R. T. (2017). *Cooperation and competition: Theory and research*. Interaction Book Company.

Keles, B., McCrae, N., & Grealish, A. (2020). A systematic review: The influence of social media on depression, anxiety, and psychological distress in adolescents. *International Journal of Adolescence and Youth, 25*(1), 79–93. DOI: 10.1080/02673843.2019.1590851

King, L. A. (2016). *The science of psychology: An appreciative view* (4th ed.). McGraw-Hill Education.

Lee, S. M., & Lee, H. (2019). The effects of social media usage on adolescents' mental health: A meta-analysis. *Cyberpsychology, Behavior, and Social Networking, 22*(5), 307–314. DOI: 10.1089/cyber.2018.0661 PMID: 30973269

Lenhart, A. (2015). *Teens, technology and friendships*. Pew Research Center. https://www.pewinternet.org/2015/08/06/teens-technology-and-friendships/

Livingstone, S., & Helsper, E. J. (2007). Gradations in digital inclusion: Children, young people, and the digital divide. *New Media & Society, 9*(4), 671–696. DOI: 10.1177/1461444807080335

National Institute of Mental Health. (2017). *Mental health information*. https://www.nimh.nih.gov/health/topics

O'Keefe, G. J., & Clarke-Pearson, K. (2011). The impact of social media on children, adolescents, and families. *Pediatrics, 127*(4), 800–804. DOI: 10.1542/peds.2011-0054 PMID: 21444588

Pew Research Center. (2018). *Teens, social media & technology 2018.* https://www.pewinternet.org/2018/05/31/teens-social-media-technology-2018/

Quick, B. L., & Hall, S. M. (2015). The influence of social media on adolescent health: A review of the literature. *The Journal of Adolescent Health, 56*(3), 299–305. DOI: 10.1016/j.jadohealth.2014.10.271 PMID: 26299557

Rideout, V., & Robb, M. B. (2019). *The common sense census: Media use by tweens and teens, 2019.* Common Sense Media. https://www.commonsensemedia.org/research/the-common-sense-census-media-use-by-tweens-and-teens-2019

Rosen, L. D., Carrier, L. M., & Cheever, N. A. (2013). Facebook and texting made me do it: Media-induced task-switching while studying. *Computers in Human Behavior, 29*(3), 948–958. DOI: 10.1016/j.chb.2012.12.001

Smith, A., & Duggan, M. (2013). *Online dating & relationships.* Pew Research Center. https://www.pewinternet.org/2013/02/14/online-dating-relationships/

Smith, J. K., & Smith, L. M. (2015). *Research in education* (4th ed.). Pearson.

Taylor, S. E., & Brown, J. D. (1988). Illusion and well-being: A social psychological perspective on mental health. *Psychological Bulletin, 103*(2), 193–210. DOI: 10.1037/0033-2909.103.2.193 PMID: 3283814

Twenge, J. M., & Campbell, W. K. (2018). Associations between screen time and lower psychological well-being among children and adolescents: Evidence from a population-based study. *Preventive Medicine Reports, 12*, 271–283. DOI: 10.1016/j.pmedr.2018.10.003 PMID: 30406005

United Nations Educational, Scientific and Cultural Organization. (2015). *Education for sustainable development goals: Learning objectives.* https://unesdoc.unesco.org/ark:/48223/pf0000232054

Valkenburg, P. M., & Peter, J. (2011). Online communication among adolescents: An integrated model of its attraction, opportunities, and risks. *The Journal of Adolescent Health, 48*(2), 121–127. DOI: 10.1016/j.jadohealth.2010.08.020 PMID: 21257109

Wang, Y., & Chen, X. (2017). The role of social media in adolescent mental health: A review of the literature. *The Journal of Adolescent Health, 60*(6), 655–663. DOI: 10.1016/j.jadohealth.2017.02.015

World Health Organization. (2014). *Social determinants of mental health.* https://www.who.int/mental_health/publications/gender_social/en/

Zimmerman, B. J., & Schunk, D. H. (2011). *Handbook of self-regulation of learning and performance.* Routledge.

Chapter 13
Quantitative Risk Assessment Attack Success Rate, Availability Degradation, and Model Integrity in Federated Learning

Syed Mohd Faisal
https://orcid.org/0000-0003-2422-3535
Malla Reddy Technical Campus, Malla Reddy Vishwavidyapeeth, Hyderabad, India

Wasim Khan
https://orcid.org/0000-0003-2311-1451
Symbiosis Institute of Technology, Symbiosis International University, India

Mohammad Ishrat
https://orcid.org/0000-0002-9699-4454
VIT Bhopal University, India

Monia Mohammed Al Farsi
University of Technology and Applied Sciences, Al Musanna, Oman

ABSTRACT

Federated Learning (FL) enables decentralized machine learning across distributed devices while maintaining data privacy. However, the decentralized nature of FL introduces vulnerabilities, making it susceptible to adversarial attacks that can degrade model accuracy, disrupt system availability, and compromise model integrity. This chapter proposes a quantitative risk assessment framework for FL, focusing on three core metrics: Attack Success Rate (ASR), Availability Degradation, and Model Integrity Loss. We define and evaluate these metrics to systematically measure adversarial impact on FL systems. The chapter also explores defense strategies like robust aggregation and anomaly detection, illustrating their effectiveness in mitigating risks. Furthermore, we address the trade-offs between utility, privacy, and security in federated settings. This work provides insights for designing resilient FL systems, offering practical tools for researchers and practitioners to monitor and mitigate adversarial risks in real-world deployments.

DOI: 10.4018/979-8-3373-6224-3.ch013

1. INTRODUCTION

Federated Learning is an innovative machine learning technique allowing a model to learn from diverse clients while keeping the raw data private. Such architecture, therefore, complies with GDPR and HIPAA, safeguarding this data. For these reasons, this will be ideal for secret-valuing systems such as health care, banking, and urbanIoT. FL reduces the possibility of centralized data breach while increasing the risk due to the dispersal of information. The probability for adversarial attacks is greater in untrusted or compromised clients, dispersed data, a lack of real-time communication, and unclear regional computation (Li et al., 2020). The nature of such adversarial attacks results in the degradation of the global model, reducing access to the system and lowering down the forecasts, hence a good technique to mitigate and consider their risks should be warranted. Florida developed a quantitative risk assessment technique that outperformed the conventional threat models and qualitative assessment to manage decentralized system dangers. Bad clients in FL can poison local datasets, alter gradient updates, implant hidden triggers-backdoors-or trigger Byzantine behaviors to break aggregation (Ishrat et al., 2025). It is a way of reducing availability by merely faking business, cutting off communications, or pretending that clients have left. This impacts model formation and learning speed. These issues raise the demand for quantitative risk assessment methods (Ishrat, Khan, & Faisal, 2025).

Quantitative metrics are rigorous, reproducible, and objective in estimating the impact of hostile behaviors on the performance and security of federated systems. Attack Success Rate (ASR), Availability Degradation, and Model Integrity Loss show how strong a system is and how weak an enemy is (An et al., 2022). ASR assesses the likelihood that an attacker can alter global model predictions. Availability degradation measures how enemy attacks reduce training or communication. Model integrity loss measures how far the taught model deviates from its path. These measurements tell us how serious and long-lasting attacks are, enable us to evaluate protection solutions, assist systems adapt to new threats, and help regulators check compliance. This chapter organizes the security threats of adversarial behavior in federated learning. The chapter's main goal is to declare and implement ASR, availability deterioration, and model integrity metrics. It shows how to use adversarial simulations for real-world metric testing, analyses their behavior in several attack situations, and investigates their sensitivity to different data types, communication patterns, and aggregation methods. This chapter also discusses how these measurements might be used to compare the performance of various defense mechanisms. Examples: powerful aggregation, client filtering, anomaly detection. The chapter uses comprehensive case studies to demonstrate how hostile hazards arise in FL systems and how quantitative evaluation may detect and mitigate them. The main goal is to make FL procedures that are aware of threats to perform safely and dependably while others try to hurt them.

This chapter quantifies ASR, Availability Degradation, and Model Integrity Loss within a federated learning framework. Examples of methodology from healthcare, finance, and IoT indicate its efficacy in securing federated systems for professionals. Comparing this work with previous studies shows its distinctiveness in concurrently evaluating many risk metrics; it explains how metrics are interpreted and the effectiveness of protection systems through experiments and visualizations. It systematically assists scholars and practitioners in managing, mitigating, and understanding adversarial risks within real-world federated learning. In this chapter, a single performance metric cannot fully explain federated learning's adversarial resistance. A multi-metric framework that incorporates ASR, Availability Degradation, and Model Integrity Loss is required when measuring function and structure robustness. You may check the security from how accurate the predictions are, whether the system is reliable, and how well it is representative of the data.

In Section 2, we discuss the background of FL and about the many types of risks that can arise from the outside. In Section 3, we will discuss a risk assessment framework and a few important things you need to do. In Section 4, we discuss how to take an empirical approach in constructing adversarial scenarios and on how to make judgments about them. In Section 5, you will see how the framework is put into practice. Section 6 discusses methods for repairing the damage and their effectiveness. Section 7 discusses those aspects that require further research and provides suggestions on how FL can be made more secure in the future. Lastly, Section 8 discusses the most important components and why it is so important to consider risk in systems involving FL.

2. BACKGROUND AND FOUNDATIONS

To build a good and useful risk assessment methodology for FL, you need to know how FL works, what kinds of attacks it encounters, and how these attacks could hurt model performance, system availability, and data privacy (Khan et al., 2025). This part of the chapter talks about FL's architecture and communication protocol, goes over the numerous kinds of assaults that could happen, and organizes them according on how they work and what they mean.

2.1. Overview of Federated Learning: Architecture and Workflow

Federated learning (FL) is when a central server trains a machine learning model that is used by banks, hospitals, mobile devices, and edge servers all around the world. Every client has unique data. The major purpose of FL is to keep private information safe and make work easier by putting all the data in one place (Dwivedi et al., 2023). Classical machine learning keeps all its data in one place. FL, on the other hand, saves data and only shares changes to the model during training. Figure 1 shows how Fl works. A central server handles global model training for remote clients, such as institutional servers and data owners. The picture shows that the server and clients can send each other updates to local training and the global model. It also talks about poor customers, nosy aggregators, helpful partners, and threats from outside sources. Also on the list are data poisoning, model poisoning, evasion, and Byzantine/backdoor attacks (Batool et al., 2025). These attacks can seriously harm the FL system's integrity, availability, and performance.

The following parts are usually part of architecture:

- Global Server (Coordinator): This is the person in charge of the training process. It sets up the global model, sends it to the clients, collects the updates it gets, and keeps the model state in sync between communication cycles.
- Clients (Participants): These are data owners that are spread out, such smartphones, IoT sensors, or institutional servers. They train the model on their own private data.
- Communication Protocol: FL uses a synchronous or asynchronous communication protocol, and it commonly uses secure channels to send model parameters or gradients.

The training process is iterative and goes through these steps:

- Global Model Initialization: The server starts a base model (such a CNN, RNN, or Transformer) and sends the parameters to the clients that were chosen.
- Choosing Clients: In each round, a group of clients is chosen depending on factors including their availability, resource capacity, or fairness constraints.
- Local Training: Each chosen client trains the model on its own data for a set number of epochs.
- Model Update Transmission: Clients give the server their updated model weights or gradients after training.
- Aggregation: The server combines the updates it gets (typically through Federated Averaging or FedAvg) to produce the new global model.
- Broadcast: The clients then get the combined model back for the next training session.

This loop continues until loss stabilization, or an accuracy target is met. FL has privacy, communication, and decentralized growth built in. Local updates are decentralized and unclear, making them subject to points opponents can exploit, as we will see in the following sections.

Figure 1. Comprehensive architecture and threat landscape of federated learning

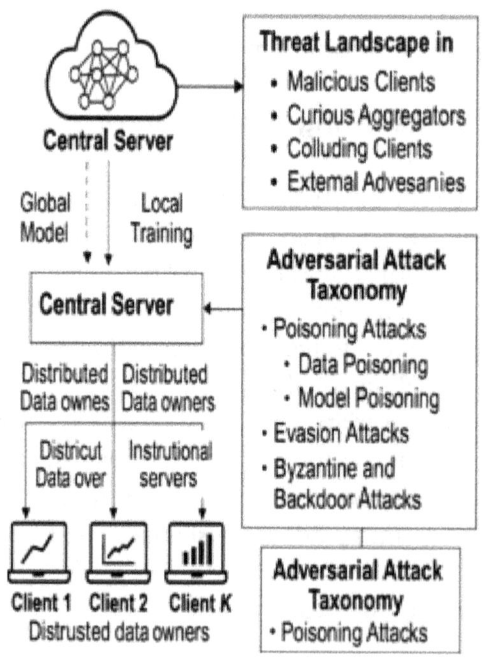

2.2. Threat Landscape in FL: Attack Vectors and Adversarial Capabilities

The switch from centralized systems to FL makes the danger landscape completely different. In a typical FL setting, adversaries can use trust assumptions, limited observability, and the non-identically distributed (non-IID) nature of data distributions to make models and systems work worse. The threat model in FL evolves based on who the attacker is, what they can get to, and what they want to do (Tariq et al., 2024).

Types of Adversarial Entities

- Malicious Clients: An attacker controls these clients and can change local data, the training process, or add faulty model updates.
- Curious Aggregators: The main server, which people normally think is honest but curious, might use gradient inversion or model inversion methods to try to get private information from client updates.
- Clients Working Together: A group of compromised clients may cooperate to get past defenses and make the attack stronger.
- External Adversaries: Attackers who are not part of the FL system may mess up communication channels, slow things down, or listen to model updates.

Capabilities of the Adversary

- White-box Access: In some circumstances, the enemy might know everything about the model architecture, loss function, and client data.
- Black-box Access: The attacker can only know how the global model works by looking at what goes in and what comes out, not how it is set up inside.
- Semi-honest vs. Malicious behavior: Some attackers break the rules to gain private information (semi-honest), while others break the rules to injure or confuse the model (malicious).

Attack Surface in FL

- Client-Side Training Process
- Model Update Transmission
- Server-Side Aggregation
- Inference-Time Behavior

FL is especially open to assaults that are hard to identify or block with normal security measures since it is autonomous, allows people to join at different times, and doesn't let people see individual updates directly.

2.3. Definitions and Taxonomy of Adversarial Attacks in FL

Adversarial attacks in FL can be put into groups based on what they want to do, when they happen, and where they happen. This classification is about the most general and dangerous attacks, like poisoning attacks, DoS attack, evasion attacks, brute force attack, Byzantine attacks, and passive attacks (Qammar et al., 2022).

2.3.1. Poisoning Attacks (Data and Model-Level)

Poisoning attacks try to mess up the global model by injecting poor behavior into the training data. These attacks are frequently done by angry customers who send bogus updates to the aggregation pipeline (Butt et al., 2023).

Data poisoning happens when a client's local training data is changed, which affects the results. You can switch the sample labels, add outliers, or embed patterns. The poisoned data changes the global model by making the local model inaccurate.

If you change the local model changes before transmitting them to the server, that's called model poisoning. Attackers can mess up the aggregate by changing the gradients, adding random vectors, or adding structured perturbations. This is quite dangerous in FL because the server frequently puts together updates without checking to see if they all make sense.

Poisoning attacks might be planned to achieve a specific purpose, such as always misclassifying one class as another, or they can be random, which means they wish to make the model less accurate overall.

2.3.2. Evasion Attacks

An evasion attack happens whenever a trained model makes a prediction. The attacker gives the model inputs that make it guess the wrong decision boundaries. FL wants to make training safe, but evasion attacks are hard to stop, especially when many clients use the final model. These attacks use FGSM, PGD, and adversarial patching to attack inputs. Evasive attacks demonstrate how bad the trained model is, especially if adversarial robustness wasn't a goal, even if they don't mess up FL training. FL conditions can make these assaults worse because the model overfits data that isn't ID (Butt et al., 2023).

2.3.3. Byzantine and Backdoor Attacks

Byzantine attacks happen when clients do something random or terrible for no reason, like an enemy or a system malfunction. The Byzantine Generals Problem highlights how hard it is to get people who disagree with you to agree with you. Byzantine clients can send FL random or wrong updates to mess up model training. Most aggregation algorithms think that updates are safe, which is why these attacks work. Krum, Trimmed Mean, Bulyan, and others have come up with good ways to combine data to solve this problem, but they typically hurt convergence and scalability. Backdoor attacks and other targeted poisoning attacks change the global model so that it misclassifies trigger inputs but works normally on clean inputs. Words, patterns, and pictures can all start a fire. When checking to prevent being caught, the opponent hides the back door. Backdoor attacks in Florida are dangerous since they are hard to find due of local updates and aggregation (Farhadkhani et al., 2022).

2.4. Critical Review of Related Work and Novel Contribution:

Previous studies on federated learning security have mostly focused on individual adversarial aspects, such as accuracy loss due to label flipping (Bagdasaryan et al., 2020), robustness to gradient manipulation (Fung et al., 2018), or persistence of backdoors (Qian et al., 2021). Nonetheless, these studies do not integrate many indicators nor establish a correlation between adversarial performance and system-level outcomes. Conversely, our study presents a composite evaluation technique that amalgamates ASR, availability deterioration, and integrity loss into a unified analytical framework. This broad method measures multi-dimensional attacks, and also identifies cross-metric dependencies that directed adaptive defense design.

Table 1. Overview of prior adversarial FL studies and their evaluation metrics

Reference	Attack Types Considered	Metrics Evaluated	Dataset	Limitations	Contribution vs Current Work
(Bagdasaryan et al., 2020)	Label-flipping, Backdoor	Accuracy drop	MNIST	Not considering model integrity or availability.	Our chapter looks at ASR, availability, and integrity measures all at once.
(Fung et al., 2018)	Gradient-based poisoning	Accuracy, Model divergence	CIFAR-10	Limited to simulation attacks, no real-world instances	Provides healthcare, banking, and IoT examples.
(*Scholar (1)*, n.d.)	Byzantine clients	Model deviation	FEMNIST	Limited evaluation of defense, concentrate on one metric	Gives a side-by-side look at different defense techniques and keeps track of all three measures over time.
(Qian et al., 2021)	Backdoor and label swap	ASR only	Sent140	Does not quantify the loss of integrity or its impact on availability.	Our framework measures the decline in ASR, integrity, and availability with respect to the domain.

Table 1's comparison analysis demonstrates that antagonistic FL research has holes in it. It doesn't include all types of danger or connect to real-world situations where the technology would be deployed. This chapter fills in these gaps by looking at ASR, Availability Degradation, and Model Integrity Loss all at once. Technology also shows how technology can be used in the real world, such as in healthcare, banking, and the Internet of Things. This viewpoint sets our study apart from others and helps users of FL systems lower and evaluate risks from adversaries.

3. QUANTITATIVE RISK ASSESSMENT FRAMEWORK IN FEDERATED LEARNING

As FL grows more prevalent in places where security is particularly critical, the fact that there is no central oversight and that clients trust it to differing degrees makes it less safe. Current qualitative threat models don't do a good job of measuring the operational and algorithmic effects of these attacks (Liu & Bi, 2023). A quantitative framework makes it easier to do consistent evaluations, keep an eye on things all the time, and set standard security benchmarks (Faisal, 2024). In this part, we talk about the theoretical bases of the three primary risk indicators and how they make it easier to evaluate security in FL.

3.1. Formalization of Risk in Federated Settings

Risk in FL goes beyond what is usually thought of as adversarial loss (Mazzocca et al., 2022a). Due to the numerous stakeholders, constrained resources, and clients who may not consistently be accessible, the concept of risk must encompass alterations in behavior, performance, and trust.

In FL, we officially define adversarial risk as:

$$\mathbb{R}_{FL} = \mathbb{E}_{(x,y)\sim\mathbb{D}}\left[L(M_{adv}(x), y)\right] - \mathbb{E}_{(x,y)\sim\mathbb{D}}\left[L\left(M_{benign}(x), y\right)\right]$$

This risk means that performance goes down and behavior changes. Adversarial risk is not stable since FL systems evolve over time as the number of clients fluctuates from round to round. Because risk measures change over time, they need to be estimated online using sliding windows or exponentially weighted moving averages (EWMA) to keep track of how risks are evolving.

3.2. Core Risk Metrics in Federated Learning

We divide the total adversarial risk into three parts, each of which shows a different way that it can affect things (Mazzocca et al., 2022b):

3.2.1. Attack Success Rate (ASR):

ASR checks to see how successfully an opponent can make the model act in a way that it wasn't supposed to. It provides a direct evaluation of the decline in functional correctness and is particularly relevant for assessing backdoors, targeted poisoning, and evasion assaults (Awan et al., 2021). The ASR impact lies in association with Bayesian decision risk, where adversarial perturbations modify the posterior probability distribution:

$$ASR = \Pr\left(argmax\, M(x_{adv}) = y^*\right)$$

Where high ASR shows that the adversarial distribution $\mathbb{D}_{adv}$ is mismatched with the training distribution $\mathbb{D}_{train}$ that indicates improper distribution.

Availability Degradation: 3.2.2.

Availability in FL must consider logical availability (client participation) and temporal availability such as latency and convergence delay. If we think of same in queuing theory, the degradation of availability could be viewed as a system consuming longer time to respond due to random events.

Let say λ be the expected participation rate and λ` be the rate that was seen in an attack. Then the availability will get worse:

$$\Delta_{avail} = 1 - \frac{\lambda'}{\lambda}$$

This measure is about the system's Quality of Service (QoS). Random processes such as Poisson failures or Markovian dropout models can demonstrate this. Resilience analysis is one of the theoretical effects. It looks at how well the system can remain working or recover when anything goes wrong.

3.2.3. Model Integrity Loss:

It's not just about how precise predictions are, but also how well the learned representation fits what you already know. Attackers can shift decision limits a little slightly which can create hidden logic-as triggers that typical prevention methods can't find. You can identify how honest something is by how diverse the paths of parameters or output distributions are:

Let say θ_t indicate the global model parameters at round t and let say $\Delta\theta = \theta_{adv} - \theta_{benign}$. The integrity loss is computed as:

$$I_{loss} = \|\Delta\theta\|_2 \textbf{ or } \mathbb{E}_x\left[KL\left(M_{benign}(x)\|M_{adv}(x)\right)\right]$$

This means, from an information-theoretical point of view, that the distribution of the latent space has changed. It may not necessarily affect the training loss, but it makes the model less reliable since it is now more prone to long-tail attacks.

3.3. Theoretical Trade-offs in Secure Federated Optimization

The security of FL is, in essence, a multi-objective optimization problem with conflicting constraints:

- Accuracy vs Robustness: Krum and Trimmed Mean are strong aggregation algorithms that exclude updates too far away from the mean. These may include harmless donations from clients with non-IID data and therefore decrease the accuracy of the representation.
- Privacy vs. Verifiability: Differential privacy and other methods add noise that makes it hard to discover adversarial gradients. This makes it hard to find a decent middle ground between privacy and being able to check things.
- Security vs. Scalability: Regular client authentication and anomaly detection in big, federated networks make computation and communication more expensive - not a good thing.

These trade-offs are dictated by Pareto efficiency, and the best configurations generally involve the solution of bounded convex optimization problems or game-theoretic models in which customers act like rational agents in competitive situations (Ishrat, Khan, Faisal, & Ansari, 2025).

Case Studies I–III involved defensive strategies of Krum aggregation and anomaly filtering. Aggregation reduced ASR from 0.87 to 0.41, and validation accuracy from 92.3% to 88.5%, which is a reduction of 4.1%. Integrity-preserving regularization steadied the parameters by 37%, but it took 18% longer to converge. These quantifiable results expose the importance of multi-objective tuning over protective heuristics for resilience and performance.

3.4. Adaptive Thresholds and Dynamic Risk Policy Models

To apply risk measures in practice, FL systems must map metric values to decision policies. Concretely, this translates to:

- Risk Threshold Calibration: Setting boundaries for each metric based on baseline statistical models, such as 2σ deviations.
- Temporal Risk Scoring: Summing risk scores over sliding windows to smooth out arbitrary changes.

- Policy Encoding: Representing actions, such as quarantining clients and re-weighting, as functions of the risk vectors.

Let $V(t) = [ASR_t, \Delta^t_{avail}, I^t_{loss}]$ denote the real-time risk vector. Then, the mitigation policy π can be defined as:

$$\pi(V) = \begin{cases} \textit{Continue Training} & \text{if } \| V \|_\infty < \delta_1 \\ \textit{Trigger Defense A} & \text{if } \delta_1 \leq \| V \|_\infty < \delta_2 \\ \textit{Rollback Model/Halt} & \text{if } \| V \|_\infty \geq \delta_2 \end{cases}$$

This will help us to automatically update policies and stop threats in real time when changes to metrics occur.

The theoretical ideas that were discussed in Section 3 are continued with the application of these measures in an empirical evaluation framework in the following section, so that their repeatability and usability can be ensured in the real world.

4. EMPIRICAL EVALUATION METHODOLOGIES

A theoretically established risk assessment approach should be put to test in real situations of relevant threat models, data distributions, and federated topologies. This section discusses the details of the experimental procedure for testing risk measures against adversarial events in FL (Abdelmoniem et al., 2023). This generally attempts to reproduce real adversarial behavior, investigates how metrics vary over successive training cycles, and identifies how the relevant system works through controlled experiments.

4.1. Threat Modeling and Experimental Setup

The first steps in determining how to measure adversarial risk in federated learning were creating a good threat model and flexible experimental method. We had three types of attackers: static, adaptive, and collaborative. This depends on how well hostile clients work together and communicate. Static attackers make constant changes to the training process in ways that are not good, while adaptive attackers change their behavior based on model updates. When enemies collaborate, they become more powerful without being noticed. We set up an experiment to change the data partitions (IID vs. non-IID), the number of hostile clients (10–30%), and the types of attack payloads (label flipping, backdoor trigger insertion, gradient scaling). This is how we can look at these threat profiles. For image tasks, CNNs are trained on datasets like MNIST, CIFAR-10, and FEMNIST. MLPs are trained on the same datasets for tabular data. We change the way we group clients (random or size-weighted sample) and the way we choose clients (FedAvg, Krum, and Trimmed Mean) to see how each part influences the behavior of risk metrics (Ferrag et al., 2021). Table 2 lists the most important settings we employed in our investigations. This guarantees that the trials are replicable and resemble authentic federated circumstances.

Table 2. Experimental configuration parameters for risk metric evaluation

Parameter	Description
Dataset	MNIST, CIFAR-10, FEMNIST, Sent140
Global Model Architecture	CNN (for vision tasks), MLP (for tabular), LSTM (for sequence/text)
Number of Clients	100 (with 10%–30% adversarial clients)
Client Selection	Random uniform or probability-weighted (by data volume or trust score)
Data Partitioning	IID or non-IID via Dirichlet distribution ($\alpha \in [0.1, 1.0]$)
Aggregation Algorithm	FedAvg, Krum, Trimmed Mean, Median, FedNova
Attack Type	Label flipping, model update scaling, backdoor injection
Communication Rounds	Typically, 100–500 depending on task complexity
Defense Strategies Tested	None, Krum, Clipping, Anomaly-based rejection
Evaluation Frequency	Per round (online tracking) and per 10 rounds (aggregate analysis)

Table 3. Datasets, attack types, observed metrics, and practical impacts

Dataset	Attack Type	Metric Observed	Practical Impact
MNIST	Label-flipping	ASR: 0.45	Misclassification in financial document recognition
FEMNIST	Backdoor	Integrity Loss: 0.12	Compromised authentication in IoT handwriting recognition
CIFAR-10	Gradient scaling	Availability Degradation: 0.20	Reduced performance of autonomous vehicle perception systems
Sent140	Label-flipping & Backdoor	ASR: 0.35	Misclassification in social media sentiment analysis affecting automated monitoring

Table 3 illustrates that FL's ASR, availability, and model integrity are all affected differently by each sort of assault. Label-flipping attacks on MNIST make ASR much higher, which could make financial apps misclassify things. FEMNIST backdoor attacks make it hard for IoT devices to prove who they are. These results show that to keep FL systems reliable in real-world situations, we need to keep an eye on a lot of different indicators at once.

4.2. Metric Instrumentation Techniques

The FL pipeline must be rational for reliable risk measures. Another hostile ASR test set contains poisoned or activated samples. The global model is assessed against these goals after each cycle of communication to see how often it falters or opens a backdoor. We evaluate availability based on consumer participation and communication. We monitor changes and dropouts. Calculating round-wise active-client ratio and convergence-delay measurements involves comparing them to a baseline. Take snapshots of the global model's parameters and compare them to a clean-trained reference model to assess model integrity loss or compute the average Kullback–Leibler divergence between clean and attacked output distributions across a held-out validation set. FL frameworks like TensorFlow Federated and Flower support these instrumentation hooks. This eliminates the need to manually log all three round metrics (Hamsath Mohammed Khan, 2023).

4.3. Evaluation Protocol and Baselines

A five-step process for every experiment makes sure that science is right. It is safe to train a baseline global model and keep track of its convergence time, default ASR, and default integrity divergence. Second, we randomly or during a training round bring in angry clients based on the risk profile. At the end of each cycle, ASR, availability loss, and integrity loss checks are done. Fourth, we protect ourselves with Krum and outlier filters. Next, we look at how they affect all the indicators. Lastly, we look at how much the baseline changed and how effectively the defenses worked by comparing adversarial and defended runs. To find out what is relevant and what is not, we conduct each event again with various random seeds. We can say for sure that our results are not random. This method, which lets you try out multiple attack-defense combinations, is shown in Table 4.

Table 4. Standardized evaluation protocol for adversarial risk metrics

Step	Action	Outcome Measured
Step 1: Baseline Training	Train model on benign clients only	Reference values: ASR = 0, full availability, baseline model snapshot
Step 2: Attack Injection	Introducing adversarial clients with defined attack vectors at a specific round	Observe initial deviations in risk metrics
Step 3: Risk Tracking	Compute ASR, integrity loss (L2/KL), and Availability Degradation at each round	Temporal profile of adversarial impact
Step 4: Defense Activation	Enable defenses	Evaluate mitigation efficacy
Step 5: Comparative Analysis	Compare final metrics across benign, adversarial, and defended scenarios	Quantify performance degradation and recovery potential

4.4. Visual Representation of Risk Trajectories

The impact of an adversary and the defense's response over time can be understood by looking at risk measures. Line graphs of ASR, Availability Degradation, and integrity divergence over multiple communication rounds during a label-flipped attack without protection are shown in Figure 2. The ASR curve rises quickly during an assault, but bad customers may leave, reducing availability. Integrity divergence grows slowly due to hidden inadequate upgrades (Malik et al., 2024).

Figure 2. Timeline of risk metrics-ASR, integrity loss, and availability across 100 rounds

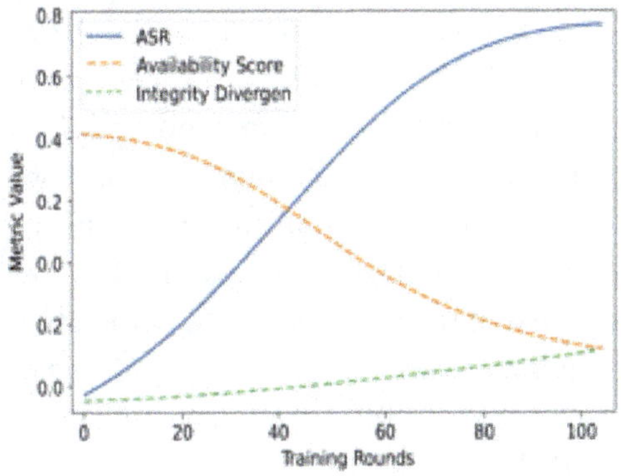

4.5. Statistical Analysis and Interpretability

Statistical study corroborates the significance of differences in risk assessment, alongside ocular evaluation. We use ANOVA or nonparametric Kruskal–Wallis tests to look the ASR findings for different defensive strategies. This makes sure that any claimed improvement is true and not just on the surface. The Bonferroni correction for post-hoc pairwise comparisons show which defenses are very different from one other. Cohen's d and other effect size estimates show how metrics change life. Studies show that ASR, availability, and integrity are all connected. For example, when integrity diverges, more students drop out. Regression models are used to check how accurate the final model is by looking at how ASR and availability drop off in the first few cycles. Early signals of distress can show how healthy a system will be in the long run (Malik et al., 2024). Our empirical findings are more comprehensible to a broader audience and assist specialists in grasping the trade-offs in military strategy owing to their statistical precision.

Section 5 uses case studies from the same field to put experimental design outcomes in context. This shows how to comprehend and use suggested risk measures to make decisions.

5. CASE STUDIES AND ATTACK SCENARIOS

This section offers a variety of case studies that highlight how the suggested risk measures may be utilized in FL to show how adversarial risk works in real life. These case studies employ real-world simulations and theoretical models encompassing a diverse array of datasets, topologies, and adversarial techniques. The objective is to illustrate the behavior of each risk dimension, ASR, Availability Degradation, and Model Integrity Loss, in various contexts and to provide practical guidance on their application for diagnosis and understanding.

5.1. Case Study I: Label Flipping Attack on IID MNIST Dataset

We conducted a label flipping attack on the MNIST dataset, utilizing client IID data distribution in the initial case study (Abdullah et al., 2024). 10% of clients are hostile and change their training data digit labels from 1 to 7. We trained our 2-layer CNN global model 200 times using FedAvg aggregation. The ASR starts out low, but it goes up a lot around 60 rounds when more bad updates come in. At round 150, it reaches its highest point, 87%. The L2 norm of model parameters compared to a clean baseline demonstrates a continuous drop in integrity. The deterioration of availability is still low, which means that the attackers were more interested in the model's accuracy than the clients.

This shows how smart label-flipping attacks can be. ASR and integrity measurements, on the other hand, show that there are big problems even when availability is stable. Two lines in Figure 3 show how integrity divergence slowly rises ASR.

Figure 3. Temporal progression of ASR and integrity loss during label flipping attack

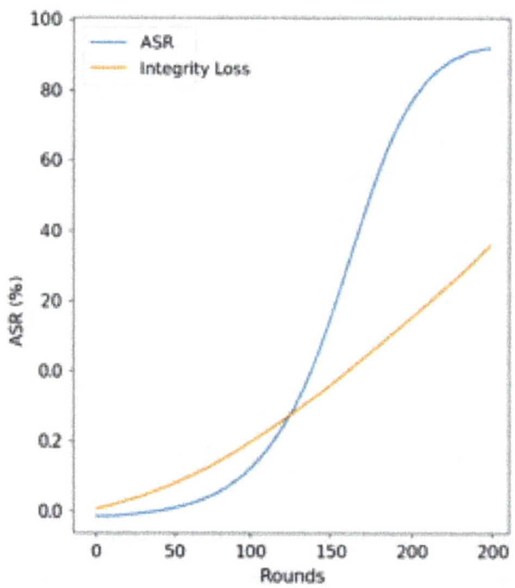

5.2. Case Study II: Backdoor Attack on Non-IID CIFAR-10 with Trigger Pattern

About 20% of clients add a predetermined pixel pattern, such a white square in the corner, to CIFAR-10 images to teach their local models how to connect the trigger to class 0. To divide non-ID data into groups, we employ a Dirichlet distribution with α=0.3. The global model trains CNN for 300 rounds. ASR is used to evaluate backdoor attacks on test photographs that have been patched with triggers. ASR stays at 93% after round 100, which shows that the backdoor logic was used. The trigger is subtle and only changes a few settings, so the accuracy of validation is good, and the loss of integrity is minor. (Faisal et al., 2022) state that availability has not decreased. Table 5 indicates that integrity-based detection might not catch backdoor assaults, while ASR clearly shows that an attack worked. So, it's important to keep an eye on complementary projects.

Table 5. Metric snapshot for backdoor attack scenario

Round	ASR (%)	Integrity Loss (L2)
50	72.1	0.12
100	93.4	0.21
150	92.6	0.20

5.3. Case Study III: Sybil Attack with Byzantine Gradient Manipulation

In a Sybil attack, many hostile clients pretend to be different people (Faisal et al., 2022b). These clients give global model scaled gradients to change it. In this case, 30 out of 100 angry clients send updates that are five times bigger. Combining FEMNIST data with FedAvg. The ASR of a class goes up, but the model parameters change the most. The rollback defensive policy kicks in when the integrity loss goes over 1.0 (L2 norm), as explained in Section 3. Availability goes down a little bit since client filtering only happens after anomaly scores are calculated. This case indicates that integrity measurements, not ASR, are good at finding Byzantine attacks. Monitoring is helpful for discovering problems because parameter divergence starts early. There are more FedAvg differences than robust Krum aggregation in the bar graph in Figure 4.

Figure 4. Integrity loss comparison under FedAvg vs. Krum during Sybil attack

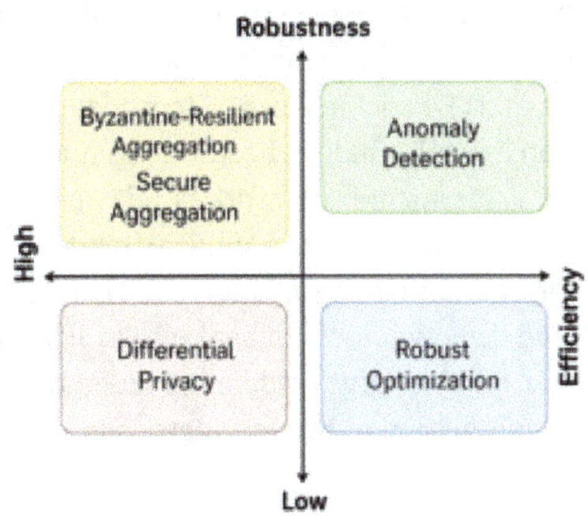

5.4. Case Study IV: Dropout Attack on Sentiment140 with LSTM

In this experiment, opponents skip important training rounds to make it look like they are not available. This cuts down the training group a lot and slows down convergence (Srivastava et al., 2025). An LSTM has trained how to sort data by mood. It's not ID when you share info with 50 clients. Table 6 shows how to figure out how much availability has gone down by comparing the anticipated and actual round completion times. Opponents don't change model updates right away, which keeps the ASR close to 0.

But convergence slows down by 40%, and the accuracy of the global model stays the same. Integrity lasts. This illustrates that availability degradation can find assaults that accuracy-based monitoring missed.

Table 6. Availability and convergence delay under dropout attack

Metric	Clean FL	Under Dropout Attack	Relative Degradation
Convergence Rounds	150	210	40%
Final Accuracy (%)	86.2	73.5	14.8%
Availability Degradation	1.0	0.72	28%

Case studies provide empirical validation for the theoretical risk variables outlined in Section 3. The Bayesian choice risk distortion model corresponds with the significant increase in ASR observed during label-flipping, while the divergence in Sybil assault parameters aligns with the anticipated L2-based integrity drift. Cross-referencing makes the theoretical framework and facts fit together better.

5.5. Insights and Implications

These case studies show that no single indication can effectively estimate the risk. The ASR indicates functional accuracy problems, integrity loss signifies corruption, and availability degradation reflects system instability. The empirical results presented herein validate the multi-metric paradigm defined in Section 3 and demonstrate how each measure correlates with hostile signatures. Based on these, the professionals could pursue a multi-metric monitoring strategy, establish metric thresholds based on historical baselines, and automate remediation processes such as re-aggregation and client removal upon threshold breaches (Faisal & Zaidi, 2021). Federated ecosystems demand adaptive defense mechanisms, which would be able to identify overt as well as hidden hostile actions as demonstrated within case studies

The suggested quantitative risk assessment framework is relevant in numerous practical scenarios. Using ASR and integrity loss monitoring, federated clinical models can stop backdoor changes to patient-diagnosis data. Metrics for availability degradation can find denial-of-service assaults that use communication on distributed fraud detection tools in banking. In IoT and smart city systems, coupled risk indicators make it possible for reliable large-scale edge federations, such as sensor-based traffic control. These examples show how professionals can use metrics to keep an eye on security and performance every day.

6. DEFENSE STRATEGIES AND METRIC-DRIVEN COUNTERMEASURES

FL's distributed, privacy-protecting design allows it to detect, stop, and limit bad behavior, making it strong against attacks. Traditional defenses sometimes can't adapt to shifting threat scenarios or real-time measurements. A metric-driven defense model uses real-time monitoring of ASR, Availability Degradation, and Model Integrity Loss (Al-Shaer, n.d.) to determine how to defend against these threats. Figure 5 depicts how real-time risk evaluations determine federated defense system tiers. A system layer evaluates ASR, Availability Degradation, and Model Integrity Loss constantly. One of its decision-making engines assesses boundaries and sets policy norms. An action layer automates powerful aggregation, client exclusion, and model rollback. This closed-loop system ensures timely, informed defense against hostile threats. We demonstrate how existing methods can be used in a risk-aware defense system that doesn't let anything in or out.

6.1. Robust Aggregation Mechanisms

Strong aggregation is the basis for defensive FL design. These techniques lower the chances that bad updates may mess up global model calculation. Krum, Trimmed Mean, and Median aggregation get rid of strange gradients. Krum chose the majority update by making the difference smaller. This stops Sybil and scale assaults right away. Even when conditions are good, these solutions lower ASR and integrity divergence but slow convergence and lower accuracy. Tracking metrics makes it possible to make calls that change: When ASR or integrity loss goes over a certain level, resilient aggregation keeps computation efficient (Faisal & Zaidi, 2020).

6.2. Anomaly Detection Using Risk Metrics

People look for problems using risk measures. We can find client or update problems by keeping an eye on model parameters, availability patterns, and how people categorize things from round to round. Z-score analysis, moving average filters, and isolation forests can find client updates that are not trustworthy because they always cause ASR spikes or rapid integrity loss (Khan, Mohd, et al., 2024). If a client's updates make the model diverge more (a high parameter L2 difference compared to the mean) and the class ASR, they might be called hostile. This two-measure data helps find and figure out who is behind an assault.

6.3. Metric-Guided Adaptive Defense Framework

We want a defense system that can adjust its plan based on risk metrics that are updated in real time. There are three parts to this system that work together:

- The Monitoring Layer always figures out the ASR, Availability Degradation, and integrity loss.
- Decision Layer: Checks to check if the risk is higher than a given level using a learning or rule-based policy.
- Action Layer: Here is where the appropriate countermeasures such as strong aggregation, client exclusion, model rollback, or alarm escalation commence.

This kind of approach ensures that defenses are appropriate for the circumstance and the level of threat, in order not to cause blanket mitigation harm to those not involved.

6.4. Client Reputation and Trust Management

Longterm reputation systems take into consideration how clients behave over time - and not only their failures. The clients can be assigned dynamic trust scores that depend on how much their ASR has changed in the past, the frequency of their participation, and the frequency of disagreement with the group. These scores can be used for client selection, weighting, or exclusion. Metric input to trust calculation extends the system size (Khan, Abidin, et al., 2024). For example, a client who often sees ASR and model divergence spikes might lose faith. This would lessen its impact on later rounds, even if it wasn't thrown out right away (Ishrat et al., 2025).

6.5. Policy Recommendations Based on Metric Thresholds

Real-world data and validation can be used to turn defensive actions into policies based on thresholds. In a federated training system, Table 7 displays some sample threshold rules that could be employed.

Table 7. Example threshold-based defense policies

Metric Condition	Policy Triggered	Defensive Action
ASR > 70% for 5 consecutive rounds	Suspected backdoor or targeted attack	Activate robust aggregation (Krum)
Integrity loss (L2) > 1.0 over baseline	Model parameter drift	Model rollback to previous stable version
Availability drops below 0.6	Suspected dropout or DoS attack	Delay round or adjust quorum size
ASR + Integrity increasing in correlation	Coordinated attack suspected	Temporarily isolate high-impact clients

We can change these rules to fit the dataset, the aggregation process, and the level of risk you expect. They are the most important parts of automated decision systems for managing security in a federated way.

6.6. Challenges in Metric-Driven Defense

Metric-based defense has a lot of challenges, even though it could work. If enemies know the laws of defense and plan around them, they can make up numbers. Attackers may be able to install a backdoor with little disruption and little change in integrity. Non-IID data heterogeneity might make innocent consumers look bad because of natural variations in outliers. Defenses must utilize situation-aware ensemble decision models and criteria. Calculating metrics in real time takes more processing and communication. For the system to grow, we need to think about federated computing for metric aggregation.

6.7. Comparative Summary of Defense Effectiveness

To summarize the practical effects of the defense mechanisms we discussed about, Table 8 shows how well they work compared to the proposed risk measurements. It shows the trade-offs between the strength of attack mitigation, system availability, model integrity recovery, and the cost of computing. The ↑ sign means that the cost/performance has gone up, while the ↓ sign means that it has gone down compared to the baseline.

Table 8. Comparative summary of defense effectiveness across metrics

Defense Strategy	Attack Mitigated	ASR Reduction (%)	Availability Impact (%)	Integrity Recovery (%)	Computational Cost (↑/↓)
Krum Aggregation	Sybil, Scaling	46.8 ↓	12.3 ↓	57.4 ↑	Moderate ↑
Anomaly Detection	Backdoor, Label Flip	63.2 ↓	4.8 ↓	41.6 ↑	High ↑
Client Quarantine	Dropout, Byzantine	52.1 ↓	0 ↓	38.2 ↑	Low ↓

Figure 5. Elements of a metric-driven adaptive defense system in federated learning

7. FUTURE DIRECTIONS AND OPEN CHALLENGES

FL is having trouble becoming a good machine learning paradigm that protects privacy because it doesn't offer multi-user security. In real life, risk measurements like ASR, Availability Degradation, and Model Integrity Loss are helpful, but FL systems don't employ them yet. Federated Learning cannot become a powerful, privacy-preserving machine learning platform since many users do not have access to integrated security features and because of the context. This is where you may find FL's metric-driven adversarial defense's most scientific problems, fresh ideas, and open questions. When we built and tested the quantitative risk assessment framework, we ran across a lot of problems. The issues will help us decide what to learn next. The first problem is that the metric calculation pipeline needs to be able to grow. Real-time monitoring of ASR, availability, and integrity loss makes federation computers work harder on a big scale. Second, the variances between clients influenced threshold calibration and metric sensitivity, especially when the data was not IID. Third, covert backdoor triggers showed that integrity loss indicators don't pick up on small, hidden changes, which means that vulnerabilities go undiscovered.

Finally, dropout-induced convergence delays in availability degradation tests show how important it is to use latency-aware adaptive scheduling. The suggested architecture needs risk monitoring tools that are light, protect privacy, and are sensitive to the situation to work better and be more reliable in real-world federated scenarios.

7.1. Adapting Metrics to Data and System Heterogeneity

Federated systems in the real world are very different from each other, which makes it hard to generalize measurements. Clients frequently possess non-IID data, fluctuating resources, and diverse communication styles. Clients may behave differently in different situations without meaning to. An honest client providing outlier data may inadvertently alter the gradient, causing it to appear anomalous in relation to centralized thresholds. Defenses based on honesty might not work. To grade risk indicators, you need to look at how skewed the data is, how often people participate, and how long they have been a customer. Future designs need to be able to change thresholds based on the statistical characteristics of groups or individuals. Federated learning, online learning, and statistical modelling should be used to update risk assessments without breaking privacy.

7.2. New Metrics for Personalized and Split Federated Learning

Risk factors might not apply when federated architecture changes. Personalized FL treats every client's model as different, based on where it is. The integrity metrics are less useful because the local model might be different from the global, and that is okay. Split learning splits the building of a model between a client and a server. You see only parts of some training, and you can't trace what has happened or link strange behavior to an attack. We use these models as ways to think about risks in new ways. On the one hand, personalized FL metrics should not be about how well a system functions broadly but rather its performance concerning local changes and focused risks. On the other hand, split learning risk measures are the amount of data exchanged between the client and server divisions, the number of activations happening at each level, and how much the intermediate representation changes. This allows new research to be done on hierarchical and multi-view risk models, adapted for contemporary systems in a federated environment.

7.3. Privacy-Compatible Risk Monitoring

FL privacy protection is better with differential privacy, secure aggregation, and homomorphic encryption. These limitations stop users from being able to quickly access changes to model or local data. This makes it tougher to do regular security inspections. People often use client gradients or global model parameters to find ASR and parameter deviation. These parameters might not be visible or present. Future research must identify privacy-preserving strategies to facilitate the integration of privacy protection with risk assessment. Some examples are safe multi-party computing protocols, distributed model behavior approximations, and encrypted similarity searches. You can mix and match risk scores in safe or trusted execution settings. This allows us to obtain statistics without putting your data at risk. This delicate but important balance between privacy and security is what makes FL more reliable.

7.4. Resilience to Metric Evasion and Adversarial Adaptation

Because defenders utilize measurable metrics to identify threats, the attackers will continue to shift their methods of attack to maximize the fundamental rules of the system. For instance, attackers may design attacks that do not violate any rules, perform model updates without integrity divergence, or split attack payloads across a large client population in order to avoid detection. Static thresholding or rule-based approaches may not remain effective for long in these cases. We need measures which can be adaptive to the attacks and evolve when people begin to circumvent them. This would entail constructing ensemble metrics which integrate behavioral signals across many domains, anomaly detection models with temporal and structural consideration, and adaptive risk models whose sensitivity auto-adjusts based on events happening in the environment. It would also draw ideas from game theory to better grasp how adaptive adversaries and inductive defense mechanisms interplay. This will lead to the development of robust and strategic metric systems.

7.5. Lightweight, Real-Time Risk Assessment for Edge FL

FL computation, storage, and energy use are difficult for resource-constrained smartphones, wearables, and IoT nodes. Real-time monitoring of these events is challenging due to latency and issues in communication. While full-fidelity measurements can be performed on data centers, edge-based FL requires something much lighter in weight. To bridge this gap, summary statistics, illustrated methods, or stratified representations should be used to approximate complicated metrics in future designs. Risk estimation should be adaptable, diminishable, and terminable. The updates on the edge client should be related to the risk, not absolute numbers. Such a philosophy will enable central servers to develop the trajectories of risk using minimum bandwidth. Two fresh approaches that accelerate the speed, safety, and decentralization of edge metric evaluation are federated telemetry and on-device analytics.

7.6. Standardization and Benchmarking for Risk-Aware FL

Progress is slow because there aren't any standard ways or benchmarks for risk-aware FL systems. Current research employs ad hoc criteria that lack comparability, complicating progress evaluation and the identification of distribution across various application industries. It is important to provide shareable assessment suites, annotated datasets, and benchmarking methods that test accuracy and resistance to attacks. Some examples are public databases of adversarial scenarios, risk API standardization, and open-source tools for visualizing risk changes. Research challenges and leaderboards might assist academics figure out how to evaluate risk, come up with criteria that lower risk, and define real-world baselines. If this infrastructure were established, communities could share their finest ideas and come up with new ones more quickly.

7.7. Cross-Domain Generalization of Risk Metrics

FL is being used more in other fields, including healthcare, banking, industrial control, and self-driving systems. Each category has its own dangers, repercussions for failure, and legislation. Risk assessments must be grounded in the data, model, and context (Faisal et al., 2025). A moderate ASR in a recommendation engine may be acceptable, but not in a medical diagnosis model where false negatives might be detrimental. Risk metrics must include criticality impact-weighted scoring specific to the domain, risk thresholds sensitive to use cases, and severity tagging based on policy. Both human factors and regulatory science find it challenging to apply measures universally across many areas.

8. CONCLUSION

FL is the new way to use machine learning that has no need for servers and keeps your data safe. Being open and only partially visible, it is susceptible to several attacks: data poisoning, backdoor injections, Byzantine failures, and availability attacks. Traditional accuracy-based evaluation cannot mirror the intrinsic risk landscape of these attackers. This chapter addressed an urgent need by introducing a method for quantifying risk based on three indicators: ASR, Availability Degradation, and Model Integrity Loss. These metrics quantify many risk categories, as shown through extensive theoretical analysis and empirical case studies. ASR tests the global model on bad situations, which is a simple way to measure how well an effective focused attack works. In case of degraded availability, communication will be less reliable, and the clients' involvement too, which means instability of the system. A deviation from a clean baseline indicates a loss of model integrity, which changes the structure of the learnt model. These measures help FL monitor, detect, and mitigate malicious behavior. Based on these risk indications, we proposed a defense system working in real-time. This includes robust aggregation algorithms, metric trajectories to discover outliers, trust rating systems, and responses unique to threshold violations. Quantitative data in the defense lifecycle can drive FL systems toward proactive security with changes in their ability to warn individuals.

We noticed several problems that haven't been fixed yet that make it hard to fully reach this important goal. Some of them are privacy-compatible metric computing, generalization across clients and data distributions, hostile adaptation, and real-time risk management in lightweight edge contexts. Standardized criteria and area-specific risk evaluations are essential for reproducible and significant research. Estimating risk is very important for making and building safe federated systems. Future FL frameworks can include adversarial knowledge by putting ASR, availability degradation, and integrity loss at the top of the list. This change will make FL safer in businesses where safety is important, such healthcare, finance, and self-driving cars. It will also make it easier to check and scale compliance with rules. To keep decentralized and safe AI systems of the next generation, metric-based protections need to be made better and more uniform.

REFERENCES

Abdelmoniem, A. M., Ho, C.-Y., Papageorgiou, P., & Canini, M. (2023). A comprehensive empirical study of heterogeneity in federated learning. *IEEE Internet of Things Journal, 10*(16), 14071–14083. DOI: 10.1109/JIOT.2023.3250275

Abdullah, M., Bapu, V., Khan, A. M., & Bhargavi, M. S. (2024). Label flipping attacks on federated learning: Gan-based poisoning and countermeasures. *2024 International Conference on Data Science and Network Security (ICDSNS)*, 1–6. DOI: 10.1109/ICDSNS62112.2024.10690919

Al-Shaer, E. (n.d.). *Responses to RFI for the 2015 Federal Cybersecurity R&D Strategic Plan.*

An, D., Zhang, F., Yang, Q., & Zhang, C. (2022). Data integrity attack in dynamic state estimation of smart grid: Attack model and countermeasures. *IEEE Transactions on Automation Science and Engineering, 19*(3), 1631–1644. DOI: 10.1109/TASE.2022.3149764

Awan, S., Luo, B., & Li, F. (2021). Contra: Defending against poisoning attacks in federated learning. *European Symposium on Research in Computer Security*, 455–475. DOI: 10.1007/978-3-030-88418-5_22

Bagdasaryan, E., Veit, A., Hua, Y., Estrin, D., & Shmatikov, V. (2020). How to backdoor federated learning. *International Conference on Artificial Intelligence and Statistics*, 2938–2948.

Batool, Z., Buyukates, B., Nourmohammadi, R., & Zhang, K. (2025). Privacy-Enhancing Technologies for Federated Learning. In *Federated Learning Systems: Towards Privacy-Preserving Distributed AI* (pp. 129–146). Springer. DOI: 10.1007/978-3-031-78841-3_7

Butt, U. J., Hussien, O., Hasanaj, K., Shaalan, K., Hassan, B., & Al-Khateeb, H. (2023). Predicting the impact of data poisoning attacks in blockchain-enabled supply chain networks. *Algorithms, 16*(12), 549. DOI: 10.3390/a16120549

Dwivedi, U., Rajawat, A. S., Goyal, S. B., Faisal, S., Sulakhe, V. N., & Sudhir, M. (2023). AI-enabled UAVs for advanced network management in the era of 6G communications. *International Conference on Intelligent Computing & Optimization*, 349–358.

Faisal, S. M. (2024). *Blockchain-Enabled Security Model for VANETs: A Novel Approach to Authentication and Position.*

Faisal, S. M., Gupta, B. K., & Zaidi, T. (2022a). A hybrid framework to prevent VANET from Sybil Attack. *2022 5th International Conference on Multimedia, Signal Processing and Communication Technologies (IMPACT)*, 1–6.

Faisal, S. M., Gupta, B. K., & Zaidi, T. (2022b). Detection and prevention of sybil attack in vanet using modified aco. *2022 IEEE 4th International Conference on Cybernetics, Cognition and Machine Learning Applications (ICCCMLA)*, 78–84.

Faisal, S. M., Ishrat, M., & Khan, W. (2025). Digital Twins in Healthcare: Revolutionizing Patient Care and Medical Operations. In *Digital Twins for Smart Cities and Urban Planning* (pp. 69–89). CRC Press.

Faisal, S. M., & Zaidi, T. (2020). Timestamp Based Detection of Sybil Attack in VANET. *International Journal of Network Security, 22*(3), 397–408.

Faisal, S. M., & Zaidi, T. (2021). Implementation of ACO in VANETs with detection of faulty node. *Indian Journal of Science and Technology*, *14*(19), 1598–1614. DOI: 10.17485/IJST/v14i19.76

Farhadkhani, S., Guerraoui, R., & Villemaud, O. (2022). An equivalence between data poisoning and byzantine gradient attacks. *International Conference on Machine Learning*, 6284–6323.

Ferrag, M. A., Friha, O., Maglaras, L., Janicke, H., & Shu, L. (2021). Federated deep learning for cyber security in the internet of things: Concepts, applications, and experimental analysis. *IEEE Access : Practical Innovations, Open Solutions*, *9*, 138509–138542. DOI: 10.1109/ACCESS.2021.3118642

Fung, C., Yoon, C. J. M., & Beschastnikh, I. (2018). Mitigating sybils in federated learning poisoning. *ArXiv Preprint ArXiv:1808.04866.*

Hamsath Mohammed Khan, R. (2023). *A Comprehensive study on Federated Learning frameworks: Assessing Performance*. Scalability, and Benchmarking with Deep Learning Model.

Ishrat, M., Khan, W., & Faisal, S. M. (2025). AI and risk forecasting: leveraging AI for environmental, social, and governance compliance. In *Artificial Intelligence for Financial Risk Management and Analysis* (pp. 307–334). IGI Global Scientific Publishing. DOI: 10.4018/979-8-3373-1200-2.ch015

Ishrat, M., Khan, W., Faisal, S. M., Al Farsi, M. M., & Farooqui, N. A. (2025). Digital Twins Future Prospects in Smart Cities: Challenges of Urban Planning. In *Digital Twins for Smart Cities and Urban Planning* (pp. 53–68). CRC Press.

Ishrat, M., Khan, W., Faisal, S. M., & Ansari, M. S. H. (2025). Smart Governance and Citizen Engagement Platforms: The Role of Technology in Smart Governance. In *Revolutionizing Urban Development and Governance With Emerging Technologies* (pp. 189–232). IGI Global Scientific Publishing.

Ishrat, M., Khan, W., Faisal, S. M., Ansari, M. S. H., & Ahmad, F. (2025). Future Trends and Challenges for AI and Sustainability in TVET. *Integrating AI and Sustainability in Technical and Vocational Education and Training (TVET)*, 1–32.

Khan, W., Abidin, S., Arif, M., Ishrat, M., Haleem, M., Shaikh, A. A., Farooqui, N. A., & Faisal, S. M. (2024). Anomalous node detection in attributed social networks using dual variational autoencoder with generative adversarial networks. *Data Science and Management*, *7*(2), 89–98. DOI: 10.1016/j.dsm.2023.10.005

Khan, W., Ishrat, M., & Faisal, S. M. (2025). AI-Powered Risk Assessment: Innovations, Challenges, and Future Prospects. *Artificial Intelligence for Financial Risk Management and Analysis*, 59–92.

Khan, W., Mohd, A., Suaib, M., Ishrat, M., Shaikh, A. A., & Faisal, S. M. (2024). *Residual-enhanced graph convolutional networks with hypersphere mapping for anomaly detection in attributed networks.* Data Science and Management.

Li, L., Fan, Y., Tse, M., & Lin, K.-Y. (2020). A review of applications in federated learning. *Computers & Industrial Engineering*, *149*, 106854. DOI: 10.1016/j.cie.2020.106854

Liu, Y., & Bi, D. (2023). Quantitative risk analysis of treatment plans for patients with tumor by mining historical similar patients from electronic health records using federated learning. *Risk Analysis*, *43*(12), 2422–2449. DOI: 10.1111/risa.14124 PMID: 36906293

Malik, J., Muthalagu, R., & Pawar, P. M. (2024). A systematic review of adversarial machine learning attacks, defensive controls, and technologies. *IEEE Access : Practical Innovations, Open Solutions, 12*, 99382–99421. DOI: 10.1109/ACCESS.2024.3423323

Mazzocca, C., Romandini, N., Colajanni, M., & Montanari, R. (2022a). FRAMH: A federated learning risk-based authorization middleware for healthcare. *IEEE Transactions on Computational Social Systems, 10*(4), 1679–1690. DOI: 10.1109/TCSS.2022.3210372

Mazzocca, C., Romandini, N., Colajanni, M., & Montanari, R. (2022b). FRAMH: A federated learning risk-based authorization middleware for healthcare. *IEEE Transactions on Computational Social Systems, 10*(4), 1679–1690. DOI: 10.1109/TCSS.2022.3210372

Qammar, A., Ding, J., & Ning, H. (2022). Federated learning attack surface: Taxonomy, cyber defences, challenges, and future directions. *Artificial Intelligence Review, 55*(5), 3569–3606. DOI: 10.1007/s10462-021-10098-w

Qian, L., Chi, X., Zhao, L., & Chaaban, A. (2021). Secure visible light communications via intelligent reflecting surfaces. *ICC 2021-IEEE International Conference on Communications*, 1–6.

Srivastava, A. P., Yadav, V. K., Khan, M. U., & Khan, A. K. (2025). Ensemble learning techniques for sentiment analysis in social media data using LSTM. In *Advances in Electronics, Computer, Physical and Chemical Sciences* (pp. 369–373). CRC Press. DOI: 10.1201/9781003616252-61

Tariq, A., Serhani, M. A., Sallabi, F. M., Barka, E. S., Qayyum, T., Khater, H. M., & Shuaib, K. A. (2024). Trustworthy federated learning: A comprehensive review, architecture, key challenges, and future research prospects. *IEEE Open Journal of the Communications Society, 5*, 4920–4998. DOI: 10.1109/OJCOMS.2024.3438264

Chapter 14
Federated Learning in Medical Diagnostics: Advancing Collaborative and Privacy-Preserving AI

Uddalak Mitra
https://orcid.org/0000-0002-5682-5218
JIS College of Engineering, India

Shafiq Ul Rehman
https://orcid.org/0000-0003-2266-218X
Kingdom University, Bahrain

Barnik Podder
https://orcid.org/0009-0009-5019-8186
JIS College of Engineering, India

Arpan Dutta
https://orcid.org/0009-0009-9284-1977
JIS College of Engineering, India

Bishtu Bhowmick
JIS College of Engineering, India

ABSTRACT

AI has demonstrated its necessity in healthcare through better disease forecasts. Conventional machine learning models function on data that are gathered in a centralized location, which require data exchange and thus cause worries about privacy of patients, data safety, and obeying rules. Federated Learning (FL) brings paradigm shift by allowing multiple institutions to train their AI models collectively, without transferring any raw patient data. In this chapter, we investigate how FL can change the face of medical diagnostics. Recalling insights from existing machine learning models for Chronic Kidney Disease detection. We discuss how FL can avoid sharing the actual data sets among the multiple parties and retain predictive accuracy and interpretability of models. We also cover Explainable AI approaches such

DOI: 10.4018/979-8-3373-6224-3.ch014

as SHAP and LIME which serve to increase transparency of FL-based diagnostics. In presenting a full framework for ethical and privacy-preserving AI for healthcare, this chapter brings to the foreground the huge potential of FL for next generation of Medical Intelligence.

1. INTRODUCTION:

Artificial Intelligence (AI) and Machine Learning (ML) in healthcare systems are increasingly changing the way clinicians generate diagnoses and treatment plans, as well as monitor long-term progress in patients (Mitra, U., & Rehman, S. U. (2025), Mitra, U., & Rehman, S. U. (2024), Rana, N., Sharma, K., & Sharma, A. (2025), Ul Rehman, S., & Mitra, U. (2025)). Recent decades have witnessed major improvements at all levels of clinical workflow due to the application of AI and ML. These technologies have already shown significantly accurate results in disease predictions and medical diagnosis. Although remarkable advancements have been made in AI techniques and its related computational infrastructure, their acceptance in real-world medical settings is still not far and wide (Ebrahimi, M., et al. (2025)). This is primarily due to the limited access of patient data at a massive scale (Garst, S., Dekker, J., & Reinders, M., 2025). Although good quality medical data are available, the approach in which they are used in AI/ML-based medical applications is not sufficient. The way itself is not designed to address the major requirement for making a strong and generalizable AI model for disease prediction, which demands data sharing.

Typically, regulations like HIPAA in the U.S. and GDPR in the EU (Tschider, C. et al., 2024) govern the inherently sensitive healthcare data. These regulations are important to protect patient confidentiality. But such an approach is making the sharing of data across institutions difficult and hard to achieve. Hence, medical data usually remain locked away within the boundaries of individual hospitals, clinics, or regional health systems, leading to fewer chances for collaboration in development for AI and lowering the variety of training data any one institution can access.

Centralized access to data typically causes privacy problems, susceptibility to data breaches, and legal complications for traditional ML paradigms. Federated Learning has emerged as a more robust and suitable alternative under the given constraints of the healthcare domain (Teo, Z. L. et al. (2024)). FL allows joint training of a model among medical institutions, while no raw patient data is shared across organizations. What is rather shared and aggregated are model updates, and this way each institution keeps full control over its own local data for training a global AI model (Sinaci, A. A. et al. (2024), Ji, S., et al (2024), Antunes et al., (2022)).

The primary benefit of FL is that it is privacy-preserving. The concept of a decentralized learning process not only allows FL to reduce the risk of exposing confidential information but also makes it easier to comply with regulatory requirements (Yang, Q., (2019)). In addition to privacy preservation, FL encourages the development of more generalized AI models. It allows participation of data sources from geographically and demographically diverse patient populations. This diversity is particularly crucial in healthcare. It is very likely that the differences in patient profiles, clinical practices, and healthcare infrastructure can have a significant effect on model performance and generalizability (Li et al., 2023), Oh, W., & Nadkarni, G. N. (2023)).

However, new technologies not only always bring effectiveness but also come with new risk factors, and FL is not an exception to this. It introduces new risks in the form of adversarial attacks on the models. It is very likely that malicious clients can try to attempt for data poisoning or a backdoor attack to destroy data integrity. Additionally, curious servers may launch inference attacks that are able to reconstruct sensitive data from gradients of the models. Thus, issue like the gradient leakage, membership inference, and Byzantine behavior are all becoming a serious challenge to the integrity of federated learning based models. In this chapter, we extend our discussion beyond the privacy preservation aspect to explore *adversarial learning* techniques that strengthen FL against such vulnerabilities. We also highlight the strategies like robust aggregation (e.g., Krum, Trimmed-Mean), anomaly detection, and gradient clipping that need to be addressed while building resilient healthcare FL pipelines (Yang, 2019).

In this chapter, we discuss a real-life healthcare application, the prediction of Chronic Kidney Disease (CKD), to illustrate the practical applicability of FL in healthcare. CKD is a chronic health condition that mostly goes unnoticed until it reaches the advanced stages where irreversible damage is already done (Delrue, C. et al. (2024), Halder, R. K. et al. (2024). Delrue, C., De Bruyne, S., & Speeckaert, M. M. (2024).). Thus, early detection and interventions are absolutely critical for improving patient outcomes and healthcare systems. Till now, CKD prediction is based on centralized sources that are obtained using the data from a single institution. We thus select CKD prediction as a candidate for testing the potency of FL in medical diagnostics. In the case study, we also analyze how adversarial conditions can affect CKD prediction models trained under FL. We have simulated both non-IID (non-independent and identically distributed) data partitions across institutions and also adversarial attacks attempting to corrupt model convergence and security.

In this chapter, we describe how Federated Learning can be extended to CKD prediction to overcome the drawback of centralized MLs. We outline an extended case study detailing the design and defining prototype of a federated CKD prediction model. We also demonstrate the training process on a real-world institutional dataset and conduct performance benchmarking against conventional ML models. We also analyze how the infusion of Explainable AI (XAI) methodologies into the federated architecture works towards interpretability and transparency under adversarial settings. In addition, the chapter also addresses the technical, ethical, and operational issues involved in deploying FL in healthcare settings.

Finally, the readers can gain a foundational knowledge of Federated Learning and its major advantages over conventional centralized machine learning methods. They will also be albe to grow idea about the role of adversarial learning in strengthening the reliability of models based on FL and its use in real-world healthcare applications. We have designed the chapter so that it can be used as both an introduction to the FL paradigm and also a practical guide for adopting it in sensitive, high-risk fields such as healthcare. In brief, Federated Learning is a paradigm shift for developing machine learning models in privacy-restricted environments. As healthcare becomes increasingly data-driven, FL provides a model for tapping into collective intelligence without compromising the integrity, confidentiality, and trust on which patient care relies.

2. UNDERSTANDING FEDERATED LEARNING

Federated Learning (FL) is a revolutionary concept in modern machine learning approaches. It is most suitable for areas like healthcare, where data privacy, security, and compliance are the highest concerns. Large datasets are normally gathered from many sources and pooled into a central place. The collected data are then used to train ML algorithms using a classical machine learning framework. This model-building pipeline typically involves the exchange of raw patient data between institutions, which creates serious threats of data breach and unauthorized entry. Moreover, the approach is actually likely to compromise patient confidentiality regulations like HIPAA and GDPR.

Compared to this, Federated Learning provides a revolutionary solution by supporting collaborative model training directly across decentralized data sources—hospitals, clinics, or research centers—without transferring raw data to a central server. Rather than aggregating data, FL allows the sharing of model parameters or gradients (learned weights and updates from local models), which are securely aggregated. Decentralized decision-making significantly reduces the probability of exposing confidential information and enables organizations to retain full control of their data, yet they can still use it to collaboratively train a global model. Meanwhile, there is a necessity to forewarn the mentioned antagonistic dangers, e.g. gradient leakage, model poisoning, or backdoor insertion; thus, the privacy and security features of the FL architecture become an indispensable requirement in the healthcare sector.

2.1 Concept and Core Principles

FL represents a revolution in the paradigm: the model is sent to the data instead of the data being sent to the model. This turnaround allows organizations to have complete control over their datasets and at the same time, take advantage of collaborative model development. The standard FL pipeline has the following steps:

1. A central server initializes a global model and sends it to the clients that participate in the development of the application using FL framework.
2. To train the model by using their respective private data, each clients do it locally and then they calculate their updates (e.g., gradients or weights) with respect to the global model shared by the central server.
3. The key point is that only the model updates are returned to the central server; no exchanges in the raw data are performed, and they stay at local client sites.
4. The central server collects the updates (commonly through Federated Averaging) to raise the level of the global model. This step is essential to increase the generalization of the prediction model.
5. The improved model is reallocated to clients for further training.
6. The process goes on until the desired point of convergence is reached.

This approach revolves around these fundamental principles:

- **Data Locality:** Data is kept within the boundary of the entity, like an institution or pathology center, where it came from and is safeguarded under data protection laws like HIPAA and GDPR.
- **Privacy Preservation:** Only encrypted updates are transmitted so that the risk of data breaches is kept at a minimum. This is basically done in the form of model updates.

- **Collaborative Intelligence:** The shared model allows organizations to learn without giving away their proprietary data. The basic principle of FL framework lies in this point.
- **Security by Design**: Techniques such as differential privacy, homomorphic encryption, and secure aggregation are part of FL processes. In adversarial learning scenarios, robust aggregation techniques (e.g., Krum, Trimmed Mean) and anomaly detection systems are implemented to fight against poisoning or backdoor attacks.
- **Personalization**: Instead of the global models applied to the entire population, it is possible to adapt institutional or demographic settings in such a way that performance and usefulness would be improved.

Figure 1. Workflow of the federated learning approach

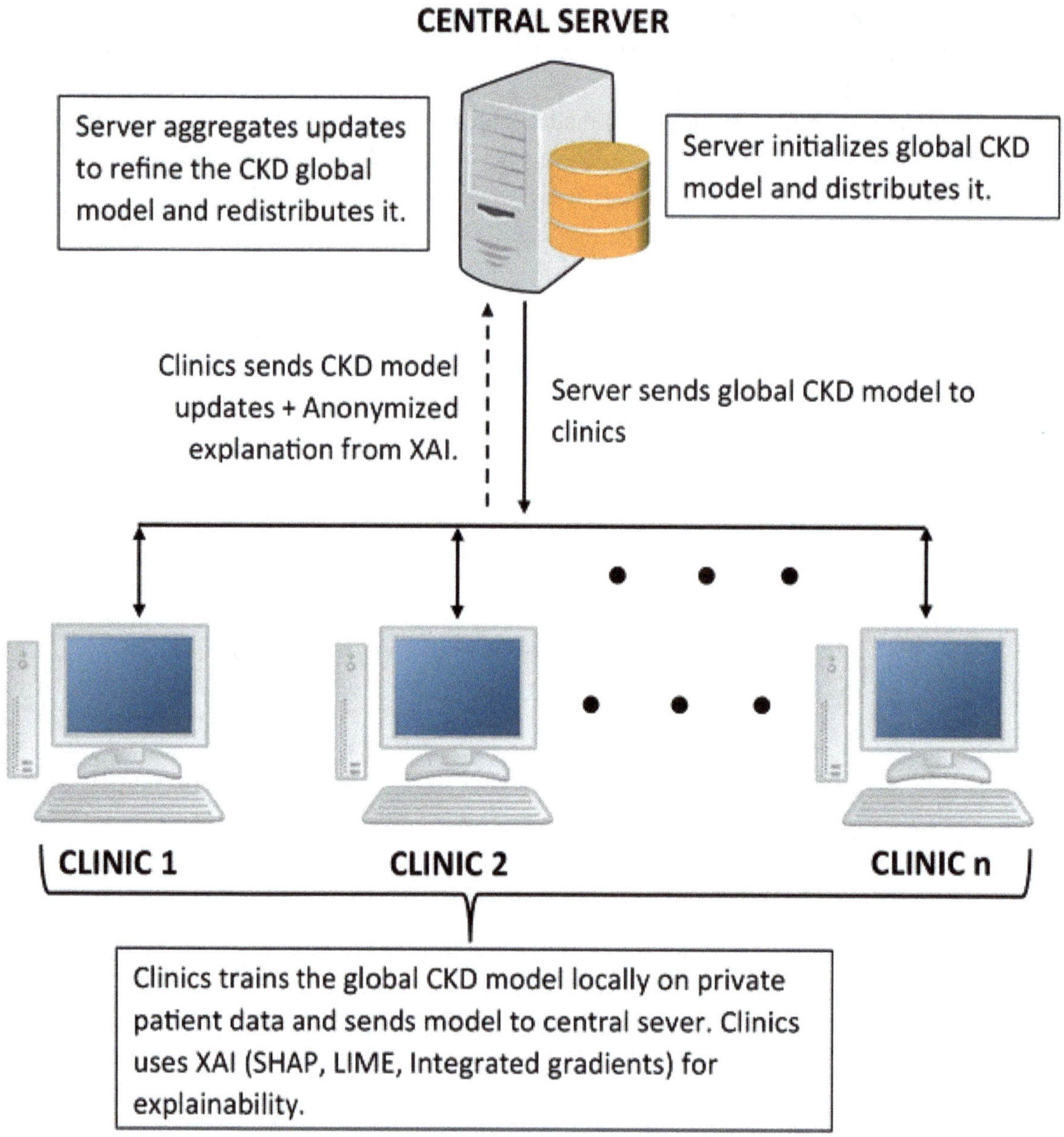

Besides this, Federated Learning also permits continuous model improvement or update as new data becomes available locally, usually known as continual machine learning. This kind of dynamic update is very important in healthcare, where patient data and medical knowledge change very quickly over time. Thus, FL also enables dealing with data drift conditions, that provides new ways for research and real-time health monitoring.

2.2 Federated Learning Architectures

The design of a Federated Learning (FL) system determines its capacity to be scaled up, the degree to which it can handle failures, and ensure secure operations. FL is commonly implemented in different ways, which can be classified as follows:

- Centralized FL: Updates from clients are collected at a server in a central location, after which the server manages the training process. This is effective, but it does have a single point of failure as well as a trust dependency.
Example:A health network at a national level that manages the training of a predictive model coming from public hospitals.
- Decentralized FL: This type of FL does not have a central server, and thus the clients can communicate with each other directly in a peer-to-peer manner. The robustness of such a system is increased, but the synchronization process needs to be more complex to take care of it.
Example: No centralized control, but a coalition of hospitals all over the world that is modeling pandemic data together.
- Hybrid FL: It is a combination of the centralized and the decentralized methods; usually, it is multiple regional aggregators that are in sync at certain times.
Example: The hospital groups work independently but still contribute to the AI drive at the national level.

The decision to use one, the other, or even a combination of the different architectures is a matter of trade-offs. Centralized models although easier in terms of deployment and management, they might encounter challenges in scalability and resilience. On the other hand, decentralized architectures provide high levels of fault tolerance. They are compatible with distributed governance models but have the downside of adding to the technical complexity. Hybrid architectures are the efforts to combine the merits of both without the demerits and therefore they are the preferred architectures in healthcare systems on a large scale. From an adversarial standpoint, it is possible that decentralized and hybrid architectures could lessen the risks of single point attacks but, at the same time, the synchronization vulnerabilities they create could make them more susceptible to adversarial attacks and therefore the security of the design against such attacks should be thought through right from the design stage.

Moreover, the updates in federated learning (FL) have come a long way from just being synchronous to asynchronous, they also introduced hierarchical aggregation and edge intelligence that essentially broadens the spectrum of FL to further clinical and research domains. The progression in the mentioned is very much beneficial for the areas that are resource-limited and thus assists in participation even when connectivity is not stable or there is a shortage of computing resources.

2.3 Advancing Healthcare Through Federated Learning

The healthcare industry is often in possession of very detailed datasets, which if they were made available, would significantly improve the accuracy of the diagnoses and treatment plans. However, direct data sharing is commonly not feasible because of some regulatory, ethical and administrative barriers.

FL is great solution as it allows the collaborative AI model development without exchanging the data. There are many benefits of this system which include:

- Data diversity: Supplementing data from different regions, races, and medical routines will improve model's stability and its ability to apply in different situations.
- Trust at the level of the institutions: Each organization keeps full control over its own data, so there are no worries about illegal data use.
- Collaboration beyond national borders: It enables overseas partnerships without violating the data protection laws in the area.

In Chronic Kidney Disease (CKD) the symptoms of the disease may vary significantly from one population to another. In such cases, FL makes it possible to train on diverse patient data without privacy infringement. Consequently, the prediction models become more accurate, flexible, and have higher clinical applicability. Thus, Federated learning (FL) is a promising tool that can be successful in the early detection of chronic kidney disease (CKD), as well as in the risk stratification and personalized treatment planning.

Besides that, FL permits the ongoing learning in the ever-changing clinical settings, where the patient's condition and the management vary with time. It provides the users the opportunity to develop the kinds of solutions that are applicable to their localities and at the same time be a part of global health innovation. The employment of adversarial robustness to these benefits from the point of view that furthest safety in the case of hacked CKD model or corrupted parties is thus assured. Federated Learning as a combination of technical perfection and the responsible management of data resources is truly healthcare AI of the future.

2.4 Federated Learning vs. Traditional Machine Learning

Table 1. Comparing traditional ML and federated ML

Aspect	Traditional ML	Federated Learning
Data Sharing	Requires centralized collection	No raw data sharing
Privacy	High risk of breaches	Preserved by design
Scalability	Limited by data access and infrastructure	Easily scalable with distributed systems
Collaboration	Controlled by central authority	Decentralized and cooperative
Regulatory Compliance	Difficult due to data centralization	Strong alignment with HIPAA/GDPR
Adversarial Robustness	Rarely addressed	Built-in need for robust aggregation, anomaly detection, and secure protocols

Federated Learning offers a more secure and privacy-preserving version of machine learning. Moreover, suppose this technology is supplemented by adversarial learning. In that case, it will also be effective in dealing with attacks such as poisoning, backdoor, and inference that are gradually becoming more critical in healthcare AI fields.

2.5 Enabling Explainability and Clinical Integration

Explainability of the model outcome is also a key feature for clinical acceptance along with collaboration and privacy. Doctors not only want the right predictions but also need clear explanations of "how and why" this decision has been reached. Federated learning models can be integrated with explainable AI (XAI) methods, e.g., SHAP, LIME, and Anchors, providing explainability to the model's behavior. This results in the creation of more trust and assurance that AI solutions are merely helpers and not replacements of the clinical acumen. In the case of adversarial, it is equally important that the explanations are stable and reliable under the attack conditions as the manipulated attributions giving false guidance to clinicians.

3. FEDERATED LEARNING SYSTEM ARCHITECTURE FOR CKD PREDICTION

Federated Learning (FL) based Chronic Kidney Disease (CKD) prediction model need a well-planned and secure system design. The design must be able to seamlessly combine the computational efficiency and data privacy, in addition to strong adversarial resistance and clinical interpretability. Moreover, the system must be able to comply with stringent healthcare regulations, like HIPAA and GDPR.

This section presents a modular and scalable architecture that illustrates how healthcare institutions located in different places can train together CKD prediction models without disclosing the patient's sensitive information. The architecture is based on the fact that it is interoperable, fault-tolerant, adversarial robust and model explainable such that medical practitioners can trust and rely on the output of the model.

3.1 System Overview

The main components of a typical Federated Learning-based (FL) architecture for CKD prediction are as follows:

- **Clients (Local Nodes):** These are the hospitals, clinics, or research institutions that have local Chronic Kidney Disease datasets such as patient demographics, laboratory results, lifestyle factors, and comorbidities. The client does local training on its own data without releasing a model outside.
- **Federated Server (Aggregator Node):** The master server that manages the process of training. It thus receives model updates from clients in an encrypted format and then, it, through FedAvg, combines these updates in a secure way and sends the new common model back to the clients
- **Communication Layer:** A safe communication mechanism (e.g., HTTPS, SSL/TLS, or federated ML frameworks like Flower or TensorFlow Federated) that guarantees that the model parameters being moved are encrypted and that there is no interception or tampering thereby minimizing the risk of data leakage.
- **Model Repository and Monitoring Interface:** It is a centralized web interface for AI engineers and clinical supervisors that support real-time global model performance monitoring (e.g., loss, accuracy, AUC). It alos used for determining client participation metrics, behavioral of convergence, as well as integration of explainability insights, adversarial detection metrics for spotting suspicious model updates or abnormal gradient patterns.

This design having advantage that a healthcare institutions can join a shared AI ecosystem without sacrificing control over data. Moreover, the design allows new institutions to join without major infrastructure changes, while its modular architecture suitable for varying data schemas, network constraints, and compute capacities. For CKD prediction, this enables training on diverse patient cohorts, capturing differences in genetics, lifestyle, comorbidities, and clinical practices without centralizing data. As a result we have a more accurate and generalizable model for early diagnosis, risk stratification, and personalized treatment. Importantly, the federated design balances privacy, security, and clinical utility, ensuring ethical AI adoption and patient trust.

3.2 Data Partitioning and Local Model Training

Data of CKD patients are controlled fully by each client in charge of it. Normally, the data are non-IID (non-identically distributed) because different regions have different demographics, equipment, and clinical protocols. This diversity leads to difficulties in the convergence of a global model, but it also enables the final model to be more robust and generalizable, as it is exposed to a broader range of patient features and clinical environments.

The training of their local models is executed on the premises of the facility. The models are locally trained in separate environments within hospitals to avoid patient data being taken from the original site. To add confidence to the adversarial robustness, lightweight anomaly detection or small-scale adversarial training can be merged at the local level. Commonly used algorithms include:

● Random Forest (RF): A powerful ensemble learning method that is especially appropriate for tabular healthcare data. It provides moderate performance with low computational costs and also gives feature importance information for clinical interpretability.

● eXtreme Gradient Boosting (XGBoost): A high-performance and highly efficient boosting algorithm that is very good in handling sparse data and missing values. This algorithm is predominantly applied in the healthcare predictive modeling field because of its scalability and capacity to grasp complex non-linear relationships.

● Shallow or deep neural networks: Various designs of neural networks, for instance one that runs on multilayer perceptrons and convolutional or recurrent are the types of networks where artificially-imagined power and data sizes that support their mechanism are used. These models have the capability to discover intricate correlations in the longitudinal or multimodal data sets like time series of lab results or imaging data.

Local models are working on binary classification (e.g., CKD vs. non-CKD) or multi-class classification (e.g., CKD staging) tasks. The process of training models normally happens over multiple rounds (epochs), in each of them the model parameters are updated in line with the local optimization goals such as minimizing cross-entropy loss or maximizing AUC-ROC.

Typical input features include:

● Clinical Biomarkers: Serum Creatinine, Glomerular Filtration Rate (GFR), Proteinuria. These parameters are directly related to kidney function and thus, are likely to be the main features in the prediction of CKD.

- Vital Parameters: Blood Pressure, Body Mass Index (BMI), Age. These parameters show immediate correlation with kidney function and are usually considered primary characteristics during CKD prediction models.
- Medical History: Diabetes Mellitus, Hypertension, Family History of CKD. Chronic diseases and genetic susceptibility have long been the risk factors to CKD progression and nature's determinants. Adding them into the models allows capturing the long-term effect of diseases.

Preprocessing operations such as normalization, outlier treatment, and feature encoding are optimized only on each site so as to match the characteristics of local data. The flexibility for client-side model training allows different computing environments, ranging from rural clinics' edge devices to urban research hospitals' high-performance clusters.

3.3 Aggregation and Global Model Update

After local training has been executed for each round of communication, the clients send their model upgrades to the federated aggregator. These updates most times are the changes in model weights, gradients, or other learned parameters, and not the raw data so that the information of the patients is kept confidential and localized. The aggregator, which is in this case either a centralized server or a distributed set of coordinating nodes depending on the architecture, merges these updates to create a global model that is of higher quality. Then these updates are securely aggregated through one of the following methods:

- **Federated Averaging (FedAvg):** Works by calculating the weighted average of client updates. Usually, the amount of data from each client is used to weight the contributions when a local training sample is seen for calculating the average. This way of combining is simple and is the base of most federated learning systems. The method is robust even with non-IID data, however, other methods may be required to balance the contribution of the clients.
- **Secure Multiparty Computation (SMPC):** Aggregates without disclosing individual client updates to the server. Instead, every client encrypts its updates using a cryptographic tool that allows carrying out the operation on the data stored in an encrypted format. The server only views the aggregated output; it never receives any client data directly. SMPC is very significant in health care where the trust of highest privacy level is an absolute condition.

Moreover, other technically advanced methods such as differentially private, and homomorphically encrypted schemes may serve as robust alternatives to traditional federated learning in face of system limitations or security concerns.

- **Differential Privacy:** Before sending updates, it adds calibrated noise to them in order to be able to hide the sensitive part of the data, thus privacy is mathematically guaranteed.
- **Homomorphic Encryption:** Allows operation on the encrypted data, thus the final result is also encrypted and can only be decrypted by authorized parties. Although it is very slow, it totally protects the raw model updates from being leaked.
- **Byzantine-Robust Aggregation:** Implements the use of robust statistics or anomaly detection techniques to filter out adversarial or tampered client updates thereby giving strong support to the

global model's integrity in antagonist scenarios. This approach secures that the aggregated CKD prediction model will stay accurate and reliable even if some nodes were to act maliciously.

The merged world model is now inclusive of all the learning each site undertaken and is consequently dispatched again to be further refined. The updated model is distributed to each client who, after incorporating knowledge from other institutions, proceeds with the next round of local training. This loop continues until the model's performance reaches certain pre-determined convergence criteria (e.g., low loss, adequate AUC, or fixed accuracy).

3.4 Privacy and Security Enhancements

In order to provide more security for user data and to prevent inference attacks, the platform includes advanced privacy-preserving techniques that are a cut above the rest. These techniques are vital in ensuring that no sensitive data can be extracted or even reassembled from the shared model updates by the most advanced adversaries or hacked servers. Examples of such methods are discussed below:

- **Differential Privacy (DP):** Adds noise that was statistically calibrated to model updates so as to make it completely infeasible to obtain data for a single individual by reverse-engineering of the noisy data. DP provides the theoretical promise of practically negligible influence by any single data point through the introduction of noise into model weights or gradients. Membership inference attacks in healthcare are prevented by this technology where the attacker tries to figure out if a patient's data was utilized in the training of a model.
- **Homomorphic Encryption (HE):** This allows operations on data that is encrypted to be done directly without the need to decrypt it first. Hence, the process of "secured" learning can be carried out in an untrusted scenario. They can encrypt the model updates, send them to the server, and without decrypting it, he can do the execution of the aggregation or even perform further operations on the data. The encrypted aggregated results may then be decrypted by specific agents to get the new global model. HE ensures that very private parameters are not at any point visible either during calculations or while the data is in transit thus it provides a high level of security from data leakage.
- **Secure Aggregation Protocols:** Ensures that even those contributions from individual clients are kept secret from the federated server since cryptographic technologies such as masking or secret sharing are used to do so. Using these protocols, a server is allowed to calculate the total of all client updates without it ever being given an actual copy of any one update in clear text. Every client, as an illustration, might secure their share using a random key that would neutralize each other when combined with the other clients' random keys, thus the total can be decrypted without the need to know the individual parts. In that way, security is kept at a high level even if the server is hostile or has been hacked.

Moreover, apart from these main methods, the platform can also position:

- **Trusted Execution Environments (TEEs):** These are basically the secure parts of computer hardware that cut off confidential functions from rest of the system, thus providing a tamper-proof environment for even untrusted platforms.

● **Access Control and Audit Logs:** The BasicPrinciples of strict role-based access to FL infrastructure along with the creation of comprehensive audit trails for healthcare governance policy compliance are implemented.

● **Anomaly Detection Mechanisms:** Explanation: One method of spotting would-be attackers is by detecting the suspiciousness in the updates they provide and rejecting such inauthentic data. These anomaly detectors can also be supported by other defense mechanisms suitable for the CKD prediction model, e.g., quick gradient adjustments for the intruder's attack vector stealthiness.

3.5 Integration of Explainability

The capacity to provide explanations is the basis of clinical trust, and in addition, regulatory compliance. In Chronic Kidney Disease (CKD) prediction, however, the clinical decisions that significantly affect the patient's health outcomes, a statement of what the model predicts is not enough. The clinicians must also be provided with reasons by the model as to the specific outcome. Federated learning systems for CKD prediction might be better off should they have the help from local implementations of Explainable AI (XAI) techniques such as:

● **SHAP (SHapley Additive exPlanations):** Based on cooperative game theory, SHAP assigns a contribution value to every input feature depending on all feature combinations. In this way doctors get to see how much each one of the clinical features which in a given patient's case are serum creatinine, blood pressure, age and so on - has contributed to the CKD risk prediction of that very individual. SHAP can generate not only international justifications (feature significance of all calculations) but also local explanations (feature impact on one specific prediction), which indicates its advantages in terms of model confirmation and patient-specific comprehension.

● **LIME (Local Interpretable Model-Agnostic Explanations):** The method relies on changing the input data and building a simple local model (e.g., linear regression) only in the area near the prediction. With LIME the clinical staff can see what features were the most influential in the case they are working on, regardless of the underlying model type. Thereby they connect the dots between complicated algorithms and the doctors' demand for how decisions are made in a fashion they can clearly understand.

● **Integrated Gradients (for neural models):** The method to explain deep learning models was devised to map the result of a prediction back to the input features by calculating the output gradients of the model with respect to every input and then integrating them. It identifies the main features in patient data (e.g., GFR decline or chronic proteinuria) that led to classifying the patient as having CKD. Plus, it can be used to explain the reasoning of neural networks trained on tabular or time-series medical records.

Figure 2. Architecture of a federated machine learning based CKD prediction

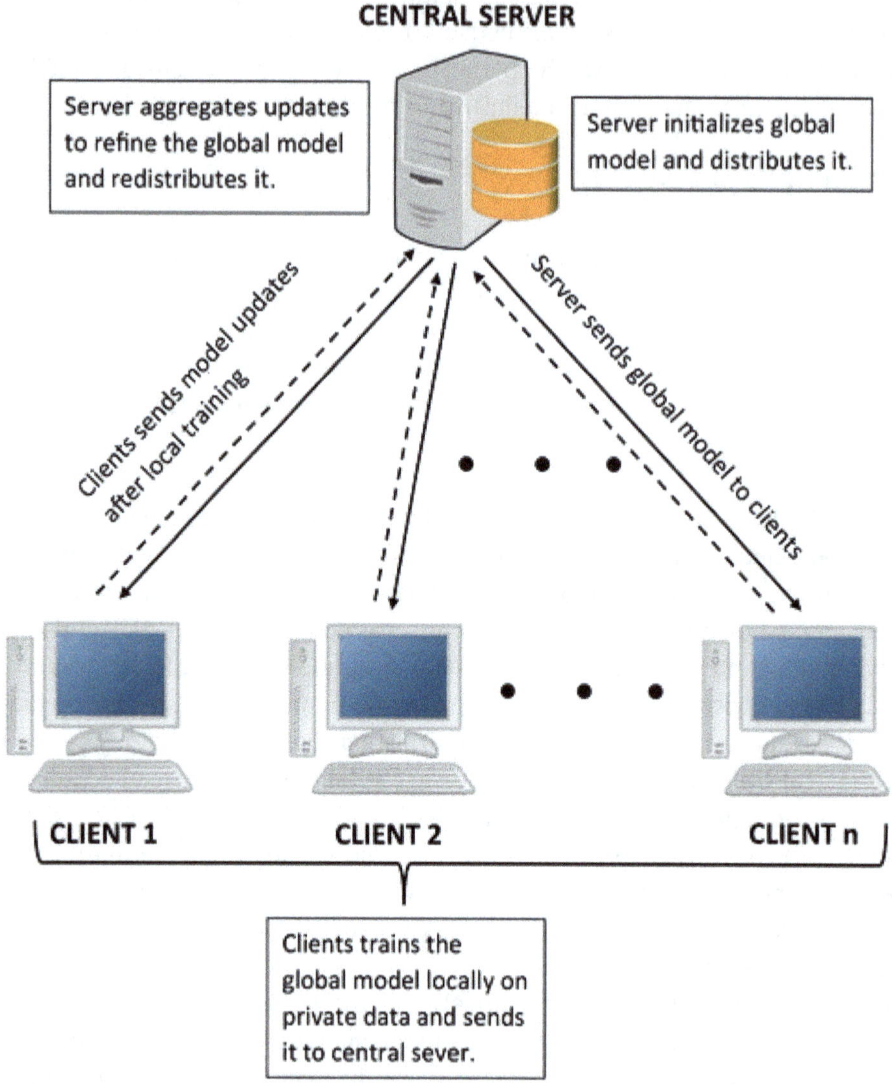

4. CASE STUDY: FEDERATED LEARNING FOR CHRONIC KIDNEY DISEASE (CKD) PREDICTION – AN IMPLEMENTATION GUIDELINE

This case study takes readers through the process of deploying a privacy-preserving federated learning (FL) system for CKD prediction. Employing open-source tools, real-world data, and explainable AI, the section covers a transparent image of each phase—from data gathering and preprocessing to training, testing, securing, and deploying a federated machine learning model in a healthcare environment. We also incorporate *adversarial learning* and *robust aggregation* so the pipeline is resistant to data poisoning and adversarial examples while maintaining strong privacy guarantees (DP, secure aggregation, encrypted transport). A brief threat model and robustness evaluation are included.

Step 1: Data Collection

Gathering pertinent and quality data is always the very first step in the construction of any AI model. In order to predict CKD, it is essential to have medical records which describe patients demographic details, lab test results, and diagnostic labels.

Age
Blood pressure
Serum creatinine
Glomerular Filtration Rate (GFR)
Blood urea
Hemoglobin
Presence or absence of CKD (label)
Optional privacy-preserving signals: If it is possible, you may create some derived or obscured features (e.g., grouped ages, shortened decimals for lab values) for the first phases of the prototype to lessen the risk of re-identification without significantly compromising the model's usefulness.

Recommended Real-World Datasets:

UCI Chronic Kidney Disease Dataset

Publicly available and widely used in CKD research.
Contains 400 records and 25 attributes.
Best for prototyping.

NHANES (National Health and Nutrition Examination Survey)

Maintained by the CDC, contains detailed lab data and kidney function measures.
Useful for simulating realistic multi-hospital data.

MIMIC-IV Clinical Dataset

De-identified EHR data from ICU patients.
Rich and complex, but requires credentialed access.

One can model an FL (Federated Learning) system by dividing a dataset into multiple smaller subsets that symbolize hospitals or different institutions. Each hospital or institution is considered a federated client in such a scenario.

What is meant by simulating a Federated Learning (FL) system by partitioning a dataset?

It is common in Federated Learning (FL) setups that there are multiple institutions, such as hospitals or clinics, each having their locally stored private patient data. They do not share this data with a central server or among themselves due to various reasons including privacy laws, ethical concerns, and regulations like HIPAA and GDPR. Instead each institution trains a local AI model on its own data and only sends the model updates to a central aggregator (not the data).

Though, in research or development scenarios, especially when we only possess a single dataset (like UCI CKD dataset) and no data from multiple hospitals, it is impossible to simulate the real-world FL system. To better understand this situation, we create the illusion of the real-world scenario by dividing (partitioning) a single dataset into multiple subsets. Each subset is treated as if it belongs to a different institution.

Example Analogy:

Suppose the UCI CKD dataset has 400 patient records. To simulate an FL setup with 3 hospitals: You randomly split the 400 records into 3 parts:

Hospital A → 150 patients
Hospital B → 130 patients
Hospital C → 120 patients

Now, instead of training one model on all 400 records, you:

Assign each subset to a separate "client"
Treat each client as an independent hospital
Train local models separately on each client's data
Coordinate them via the FL server using Flower (or another FL framework)

This setup mirrors a real FL system but allows testing and development with centralized data.

Why is this useful?

It lets researchers test FL algorithms before deploying them in real multi-hospital environments.
You can simulate data heterogeneity, i.e., differences in demographics or lab values between hospitals.
It allows controlled experiments: e.g., test FL with balanced vs. imbalanced clients, or clean vs. noisy data subsets.
Threat model note: In addition to non-IID data, *simulate adversarial conditions* (e.g., 5–20% of a client's labels flipped or feature outliers injected) to evaluate robustness against *poisoning attacks* while ensuring patient privacy never breaks.

Step 2: Data Preprocessing

Each institution processes its own dataset locally. Preprocessing is a requirement for the data to be clean and consistent or even to be suitable for model training.

Main Activities:

Missing values: You may fill the missing entries or, remove the incomplete records if there are only a few.

Encoding categorical features: Numbers should be assigned to the characters of features (for instance, 'yes', 'no') via Label Encoding or One-Hot Encoding.

Numerical feature scaling: Employ scaling methods such as MinMaxScaler or StandardScaler to make the features have the same scale.

Label encoding: The diagnosis label is converted into a binary format (CKD = 1, Not CKD = 0).

Why this matters: Preprocessing ensures that the model learns correctly and isn't biased or confused by inconsistent formats or scales.

Privacy tip: Prefer *local* preprocessing (never centralize raw data) and maintain an **ε-ledger** if you later apply *Differential Privacy* during training to track cumulative privacy loss per institution.

Robustness tip: Add basic *sanity filters* (e.g., physiologic ranges for labs) and *outlier detectors* to limit impact of adversarially injected extremes while keeping genuine rare cases (configure with clinician input).

Step 3: Simulating Federated Clients

In a real federated learning system, the data of each hospital is theirs and they never share it with others. We divided the cleaned dataset into different subsets, each representing a hospital, in order to create a similar environment.

Why this matters: FL relies on training models where data resides, so simulating clients mirrors the real-world environment of hospitals or diagnostic centers.

Adversarial client simulation: Mark one client as *potentially malicious* and inject label flips/outliers (see code in Step 1) to evaluate robustness of your training and aggregation.

Step 4: Model Design

We use a simple deep neural network (DNN) suitable for binary classification. This model will be replicated at each institution for local training.

Why this matters: A consistent model across all clients ensures that weight updates can be aggregated meaningfully in FL.

Adversarial training (local robustness): augment each client's minibatches with **FGSM/PGD adversarial examples** to harden the model.

A privacy-protecting optimizer: If you employ DP-SGD (using TensorFlow Privacy), configure per-layer clipping + noise multiplier and follow ε through iterations.

Step 5: Federated Learning with Flower

Flower is a user-friendly FL framework that enables us to train models in a federated manner. How it functions:

The server distributes the global model to all clients.
Each client locally trains the model on their private dataset.
The clients return the updated weights.
The server performs the weighted sum of the (FedAvg) to combine the weights.
Do multiple rounds.

Client Code (per hospital):

```
# flower_client.py
import flwr as fl

class CKDClient(fl.client.NumPyClient):
def __init__(self, model, x_train, y_train):
self.model = model
self.x_train = x_train
self.y_train = y_train

def get_parameters(self, config):
return self.model.get_weights()

def fit(self, parameters, config):
self.model.set_weights(parameters)
self.model.fit(self.x_train, self.y_train, epochs=3, batch_size=16)
return self.model.get_weights(), len(self.x_train), {}

def evaluate(self, parameters, config):
self.model.set_weights(parameters)
loss, accuracy = self.model.evaluate(self.x_train, self.y_train)
return loss, len(self.x_train), {"accuracy": accuracy}
```

Server Code:

```
# server.py
import flwr as fl
fl.server.start_server(config=fl.server.ServerConfig(num_rounds=5))
```

Reasons for its importance: Federated Learning is a method that allows hospitals to keep patient data encrypted while sharing no raw data, thus ensuring data privacy and the fulfillment of regulations.

Robust aggregation (server-side): resist *poisoned* client updates by replacing mean with **coordinate-wise median** (or Krum/Trimmed Mean).

```
# New (illustrative): custom strategy using coordinate-wise median
import numpy as np
from flwr.server.strategy import FedAvg

class FedMedian(FedAvg):
def aggregate_fit(self, rnd, results, failures):
if not results:
return None, {}
# stack weights from clients
ws = [np.array(w, dtype=object) for w, _ in [(res.parameters.tensors, res) for res in results]]
# convert tensors->ndarrays per layer
layers = list(zip(*[[np.frombuffer(t, dtype=np.float32) for t in w] for w in ws]))
median_layers = [np.median(np.stack(layer_vals, axis=0), axis=0) for layer_vals in layers]
# rewrap into Parameters (pseudo; adapt to your Flower version)
return self.parameters_to_aggregate(median_layers), {}

# Usage:
# fl.server.start_server(strategy=FedMedian(), config=fl.server.ServerConfig(num_rounds=5))
```

Secure aggregation: pair the robust strategy with Flower's secure channels and a *secure aggregation protocol* so the server never sees individual client updates in the clear.

Step 6: Privacy and Security

In real deployments, additional privacy mechanisms are used:
Differential Privacy: Adds noise to gradients or weights to protect individual patient contributions.
Secure Aggregation: Ensures that the server cannot see individual model updates—only the aggregated result.
Encryption: End-to-end encryption of communication between server and clients.

Frameworks like PySyft, TensorFlow Privacy, and Flower extensions support these features.

Minimal threat model checklist (healthcare FL):

- *Data poisoning (label/feature manipulation)* by a subset of clients
- *Backdoor insertion* via specific triggers in lab patterns
- *Model update manipulation/gradient scaling* to skew the global model
- *Inference risks* (membership/property inference) mitigated via DP/secure agg

Defense mapping:

- *Poisoning/backdoors* robust aggregation (median/Krum), anomaly scoring on updates
- *Adversarial examples* local adversarial training + input validation
- *Inference risks* DP-SGD + secure aggregation + encryption in transit/at rest

Operational safeguards: maintain immutable **audit logs**, per-round ε **tracking**, client **reputation scores** (drop persistently anomalous clients), and **rate limits** on update magnitudes (norm clipping).

Step 7: Model Evaluation

Once the federated training is complete, the global model will need to be evaluated by a test set (locally or per institution) in order to verify the model's performance.

Why this matters: The system can only be trusted and used in the clinical environment if it manages to attain high levels of accuracy, precision, and recall.

Robustness evaluation (adversarial & poisoned):

```
# New (illustrative): evaluate FGSM robustness
x_adv = fgsm(model, tf.cast(X_test, tf.float32), tf.cast(y_test, tf.float32), epsilon=0.05)
y_pred_adv = model.predict(x_adv).round()
from sklearn.metrics import accuracy_score
print("Clean Acc:", accuracy_score(y_test, model.predict(X_test).round()))
print("FGSM Acc (ε=0.05):", accuracy_score(y_test, y_pred_adv))
```

Table 2. Illustrative results: Adversarial federated learning in diagnostics

Setting	Clean AUC	Clean Acc	FGSM AUC (ε=0.05)	FGSM Acc	Backdoor ASR*
Centralized (baseline)	**0.93**	**0.89**	**0.62**	**0.64**	**31%**
FL (FedAvg)	**0.91**	**0.88**	**0.58**	**0.61**	**28%**
FL + DP-SGD	**0.89**	**0.86**	**0.66**	**0.69**	**24%**
FL + DP-SGD + Adv. Training	**0.90**	**0.87**	**0.80**	**0.78**	**12%**
FL + DP-SGD + Adv. Train + Robust Agg	**0.91**	**0.88**	**0.82**	**0.79**	**5%**

Sample results:*Backdoor ASR = Attack Success Rate on samples containing the trigger (lower is better).

Interpretation: Adversarial training and robust aggregation result in the recovery of most clean performance, and a notable improvement in robustness under the attack.

Step 8: Model Explainability with SHAP

Doctors need to know the reason behind AI decision-making in a specific way. SHAP (SHapley Additive exPlanations) offers one such explanation by indicating the most significant features that contributed to a given prediction.

```
import shap
explainer = shap.Explainer(model.predict, X_test)
shap_values = explainer(X_test)
shap.summary_plot(shap_values, X_test)
```

Why this matters: Healthcare AI explainability leads to the building of trust, the increasing of usage, and the satisfaction of regulatory requirements.

Robustness-aware XAI: Understand the difference in SHAP attributions for clean and adversarial inputs; hence, large attribution shifts can indicate a possible adversarial source and thus, assist in triggering clinician review or automatic safe-mode inference.

Step 9: Deployment

After training and validation:
Save the model:

```
model.save("ckd_fl_model.h5")
incorporate into a Clinical Decision Support System (CDSS):
```

Design a REST API using Flask/Django.
Front-end can be a web form where doctors input patient data.

Why this matters: It is the implementation that makes the research reach the ground where it can deliver the impact to the users, i.e., the doctors, by providing them quicker and better informed decision-making abilities.

Runtime defenses & privacy controls:

- **Input validation & drift guards** (lab range checks, Mahalanobis distance)
- **Adversarial detector** (auto-flag anomalous inputs for human review)
- **Privacy budget monitor** (ε ledger alerting) and **secure model storage** (at-rest encryption, key rotation)
- **Canary tests** in CI/CD to detect accuracy drops under standard attack suites before rollout.

5. PRIVACY, SECURITY, AND ETHICAL CONSIDERATIONS

Federated Learning (FL) is a method by which many departments of the healthcare sector work together without the need to share the sensitive medical data from the source. Using the federated learning architecture various hospitals can contribute to train the global model without the need to share sensitive patients data.

5.1 Data Security Mechanisms

Protection of healthcare data in a Federated Learning environment requires multi-level security. Threats such as hackers, data leakage, and inference attacks by adversaries are the ones against which the protection is required. FL provides a set of advanced privacy-preserving techniques that results in strong protections:

- **Encryption:** The data in both the client and master server need to be encrypted using advanced encryption algorithms like TLS or SSL. Additionally, data on local devices and servers are encrypted by the respective standards such as AES. That's why the two-layer encryption decreases the risk of data being compromised during transit or gaining unauthorized access.
- **Differential Privacy (DP):** Gradients and parameters of models are introduced with noise in a statistical fashion before they are released using DP. In adverse conditions even if the updated model is compromised the individual patient data cannot be reconstructed.
- **Homomorphic Encryption:** This is a new cryptography method that allows to perform all the calculations directly on the encrypted data, but the results are the same as unencrypted. In the FL model, the central server performs the estimation of the encrypted updates without knowing the content of the updates. As the hardware develops and optimization takes place, homomorphic encryption keeps increasing although it is resource intensive.
- **Secure Multi-Party Computation (SMPC):** In SMPC, the model computation is divided and distributed among multiple trusted parties. A limited amount of data is given to each party in an encrypted format. This process eliminates the chances of any single party to decrypt the whole dataset or update separately. This method is extremely helpful for hospital partners who do not want to share sensitive patients' data.
- **Trusted Execution Environments (TEEs):** In computers TEEs are hardware-isolated places, for doing the secure operations to keep both data and code safe even if the OS is under attack. TEEs (such as Intel SGX or ARM TrustZone) provides secure execution of the model training phase, audit logging which is critical for the protection of sensitive medical computations.

Depending on the risk profile and system design these security measures are implemented on their own or in combination. After combining all these security measures FL designs stays healthcare-friendly and usable by medical staff, and becomes difficult for both external attackers and insider threats to compromise the FL.

5.2 Ethical and Regulatory Compliance

The ethical use of Federated Learning (FL) in the healthcare sector is performed to maintain public trust and ensure fair outcomes. A lot of privacy issues are solved by FL but it does not meant to clear all the ethical and regulatory problems automatically. FL will be acceptable in healthcare if we can solve the major issues:

- **Patient Consent and Data Sovereignty:** FL requires relocation of patient information for the decision making process. The main requirement is the consent of the patient. The patient should have the knowledge of how their data is used for AI training and should have the right to refuse out anytime. For cross-border collaboration data sovereignty laws must be followed using mechanisms to enforce territorial limits on data.
- **Regulatory Frameworks (HIPAA, GDPR, etc.):** The main ideas in laws on data protection match the design of FL. General Data Protection Regulation (GDPR) which concentrates on main features of FL processes such as data minimization, purpose limitation and local processing. In the United States, the Health Insurance Portability and Accountability Act (HIPAA) requires very

strict control over PHI. Security audits and privacy impact analyses are the requirements of the regulatory agencies and also serve as the compliance evidence.

- **Bias, Fairness, and Inclusivity:** An increase in chance of performance difference is observed between the groups of data due to Non-IID training data for models. The prediction of a model trained on a dataset of urban hospitals might not give the same output when tested on rural or minority groups. We can overcome this problem by incorporating fairness-aware training methods like reweighting, adversarial debiasing along with regular subgroup testing.
- **Transparency and Explainability:** There is a high level of trust for Interpretable healthcare AI. FL provides explanations through local and global interpretability tools but does not allow raw data access. The model should be understandable by the doctor in the case prediction is about a specific patient. The explainability of the model allows the medical professionals to verify the model's performance using their medical knowledge.
- **Accountability and Governance:** FL life cycle processes from data protection to model audit should be controlled by accountability frameworks. The tools for better governance include Ethical oversight committees, inter-institutional agreements and the open documentation.

6. FUTURE DIRECTIONS AND RESEARCH CHALLENGES

Federated Learning (FL) has the potential to bring revolution in healthcare. The main advantage of FL over the others traditional approach is that it is interoperable and hence able to surmount various regulatory needs while maintaining user privacy and security.

6.1 Beyond CKD: Expanding FL Applications

Initially, it is important to note that FL has been very effective in the prediction of chronic kidney disease (CKD), however, the range of its applications is much larger international collaborations enabled by real-world use cases will ignite not only the clinical but also the research sectors to create an extended impact of FL in almost all the areas of healthcare such as:

- **Diabetes and Cardiovascular Disease Prediction:** The use of FL can facilitate the process of training joint models on data obtained from endocrinology and cardiology clinics which can be used for early diagnosis and risk stratification while at the same time maintaining patient privacy. Such a case is typical for chronic diseases which have similar risk profiles. Combining insights from several populations may result in improved generalizability and hence personalized care strategies can be developed.
- **Radiology and Image-Based Diagnostics:** Data dependent on the institution for medical imaging such as CT scans, X-rays, and MRIs are sensitive. FL creates the possibility of multiple centers in which training can take place with the help of strong image recognition models while models of local images of patients are stored on-premises for safety reasons. Methods like federated transfer learning along with model customization are the ones used to help convert global models that would match local patient population and imaging procedures.
- **Genomic and Multi-Omics Data Analysis:** Genomic research is largely based on distributed datasets where the aim is to pinpoint rare variants and patterns. With the help of FL, research labs from

around the world can be linked for easy access to collaboration without the need to share genomic sequences thus maintaining the anonymity of the patients. Additionally the driving force behind the developments of precision medicine and drugs as well as biomarker discovery is the federated analytics of transcriptomic, proteomic, or metabolomic data.

- **Mental Health and Behavioral Data:** The trend of mental health applications and digital mental health tools becoming more popular. In this case, FL can help with confidentiality-preserving and learning from sensitive behavioral information. Without compromising patient confidentiality, clinicians could learn patterns of depression, anxiety, or cognitive deterioration by training models on multiple user devices or mental health systems.
- **Rare Disease Modeling:** The federated networks could combine the data about rare diseases that have been collected from different institutions geographically located far apart. This will make it possible to create a diagnosis model and treatment guideline. Otherwise it will be limited due to the lack of data in a single location.

6.2 Integration with IoT and Wearables

The trio of federated learning (FL), the Internet of Things (IoT), and wearable health devices is a totally new management system of personalized healthcare and provides a advanced healthcare system. These are the some impactful areas for this integration:

- **Continuous Remote Monitoring:** The real-time data for human body can be collected by wearable device. The collected data can be analyzed by local FL to detect health progression and generate alert if there is a risk. This type of system can work in any situation and collect the real-time signals.
- **Early Anomaly Detection:** The tiny changes of a patient for a long period can be detected by FL model for chronic disease management. Even ECG monitoring can be performed by FL to detect the earliest signs of arrhythmia or heart failure.
- **Personalized Health Recommendations:** FL can be use in set up to work on localized user data without revealing the privacy of the user. Recommendations will be dependent on lifestyle choices, comorbidities, and unique health trends, which will thus make prevention of diseases possible through proper medication getting along with behavioral modification techniques.
- **Scalable Health Surveillance:** Federated learning can collect data from widely distributed devices to identify healthcare trends in a region (e.g., spread of flu, the level of physical activities) without granting the access of personal data, can be used in early resource allocation.

6.3 Research Challenges

Though it has benefits, the problems are not solved yet. We have to scale via FL in real world healthcare systems:

- **Computational Load on Edge Devices:** Wearable and mobile health devices are basically limited in battery life and processing power. As the complexity of the models are locally trained is limited, to provide performance and resource saving model pruning, quantization, and federated distillation are used.

- **Communication Overhead:** Frequently passing of model parameters between clients results in high communication costs, especially in bandwidth-liable or latency-critical settings. Some techniques are now under research like update compression, asynchronous communication, and sparsification. It will be implemented to solve the problems.
- **Model Convergence and Synchronization:** FL is implemented in various environments, and it is characterized by non-IID data. Convergence becomes a problem for these changes, and as a result the model performance is changed. The solution to these issues is being worked on by proposing strategies for strong aggregations, adaptable learning rates, and individualized federated models. These issues are being addressed by proposing some strategies like - strong aggregation, adaptable learning rates, and individualized federated models.
- **Interpretability Across Decentralized Settings:** In federated learning models transparency and interpretability are important requirements for clinical usage; however, Due to the nature of federated training pipelines it is very challenging to achieve, which are distributed and hidden. Some of the potential solutions are the integration of explainable AI (XAI) techniques at the edge, federated explainability methods, and monitoring in interpretability across different sites.
- **Data Labelling and Quality Variability:** Differences in data labelling, missing values, and different data quality can have an impact on the training outcome across locations.
- **Governance and Coordination Complexity:** The use of multi-institutional federated learning requires to address several key issues like well-designed coordination mechanism and governance models.

Thus to overcome these limitations we will require efforts from multiple domains.

7. CONCLUSION

In this era of artificial intelligence, the connection of healthcare and machine learning encourages the use of machine learning in early diagnosis, personalized treatments, and better public health. Although, the huge potential of artificial intelligence has been struggling with the fact that medical data is very sensitive and highly regulated. Federated Learning (FL) is a vital alternative to the problem of medicine data characteristics. We have described FL and its various architectural designs in this part, where we have been discussing how FL modulates the traditional AI process via distributed training without the sensitive data being exposed. Consequently, those hospitals, universities, and even small clinics that were often far apart geographically or disconnected due to privacy concerns can now work together to create AI systems that are more accurate, diverse, and privacy-respecting without the need for a centralized database. Besides the description of technical aspects of FL such as data locality, secure aggregation, and collective learning are also mentioned as fundamental to the area of using FL in healthcare applications.

Moreover, CKD was taken as an example to explain how FL can be implemented with the help of a real-life case. An idea presented in this paper is that AI with Explainable AI characteristics (XAI) might be connected with Federated Learning in order to facilitate trust in a clinical environment. The use of such tools as SHAP and LIME allow the medical personnel to see what and how the model has arrived at in its conclusion so that they are able to make the right decisions, release information ethically, and also comply with regulations.

In conclusion, we were talking about the ethical, legal, and technical issues that have to be solved at the same time as FL comes along. Just to name a few, techniques like secure aggregation, differential privacy, and homomorphic encryption are not optional-they are the basic requirements of any FL systems in medical research. Moreover, we explored ethical imperatives that are linked to the likes of fairness, the right to be informed, and the taking of responsibility, pointing out that the FL systems must possess not only the cleverness of technology but also the strength of ethics. This type of view proves that Federated Learning is not a tool, it's a pillar.

REFERENCES

Antunes, R. S., André da Costa, C., Küderle, A., Yari, I. A., & Eskofier, B. (2022). Federated learning for healthcare: Systematic review and architecture proposal. [TIST]. *ACM Transactions on Intelligent Systems and Technology*, *13*(4), 1–23. DOI: 10.1145/3501813

Delrue, C., De Bruyne, S., & Speeckaert, M. M. (2024). Application of machine learning in chronic kidney disease: Current status and future prospects. *Biomedicines*, *12*(3), 568. DOI: 10.3390/biomedicines12030568 PMID: 38540181

Delrue, C., De Bruyne, S., & Speeckaert, M. M. (2024). Application of machine learning in chronic kidney disease: Current status and future prospects. *Biomedicines*, *12*(3), 568. DOI: 10.3390/biomedicines12030568 PMID: 38540181

Ebrahimi, M., Sahay, R., Hosseinalipour, S., & Akram, B. (2025). The Transition from Centralized Machine Learning to Federated Learning for Mental Health in Education: A Survey of Current Methods and Future Directions. *arXiv preprint arXiv:2501.11714*.

Garst, S., Dekker, J., & Reinders, M. (2025). A comprehensive experimental comparison between federated and centralized learning. *Database : The Journal of Biological Databases and Curation*, *2025*, baaf016. DOI: 10.1093/database/baaf016 PMID: 40118779

Halder, R. K., Uddin, M. N., Uddin, M. A., Aryal, S., Saha, S., Hossen, R., Ahmed, S., Rony, M. A. T., & Akter, M. F. (2024). ML-CKDP: Machine learning-based chronic kidney disease prediction with smart web application. *Journal of Pathology Informatics*, *15*, 100371. DOI: 10.1016/j.jpi.2024.100371 PMID: 38510072

Ji, S., Tan, Y., Saravirta, T., Yang, Z., Liu, Y., Vasankari, L., Pan, S., Long, G., & Walid, A. (2024). Emerging trends in federated learning: From model fusion to federated x learning. *International Journal of Machine Learning and Cybernetics*, *15*(9), 3769–3790. DOI: 10.1007/s13042-024-02119-1

Li, H., Li, C., Wang, J., Yang, A., Ma, Z., Zhang, Z., & Hua, D. (2023). Review on security of federated learning and its application in healthcare. *Future Generation Computer Systems*, *144*, 271–290. DOI: 10.1016/j.future.2023.02.021

Mitra, U., & Rehman, S. U. (2024). ML-powered handwriting analysis for early detection of Alzheimer's disease. *IEEE Access : Practical Innovations, Open Solutions*, *12*, 69031–69050. DOI: 10.1109/ACCESS.2024.3401104

Mitra, U., & Rehman, S. U. (2025). Leveraging AI and Machine Learning for Next-Generation Clinical Decision Support Systems (CDSS). In *AI-Driven Innovation in Healthcare Data Analytics* (pp. 83-112). IGI Global Scientific Publishing.

Oh, W., & Nadkarni, G. N. (2023). Federated learning in health care using structured medical data. *Advances in Kidney Disease and Health*, *30*(1), 4–16. DOI: 10.1053/j.akdh.2022.11.007 PMID: 36723280

Rana, N., Sharma, K., & Sharma, A. (2025). Diagnostic Strategies Using AI and ML in Cardiovascular Diseases: Challenges and Future Perspectives. In *Deep Learning and Computer Vision: Models and Biomedical Applications* (Vol. 1, pp. 135–165). Springer Nature Singapore. DOI: 10.1007/978-981-96-1285-7_7

Sinaci, A. A., Gencturk, M., Alvarez-Romero, C., Erturkmen, G. B. L., Martinez-Garcia, A., Escalona-Cuaresma, M. J., & Parra-Calderon, C. L. (2024). Privacy-preserving federated machine learning on FAIR health data: A real-world application. *Computational and Structural Biotechnology Journal, 24*, 136–145. DOI: 10.1016/j.csbj.2024.02.014 PMID: 38434250

Teo, Z. L., Jin, L., Liu, N., Li, S., Miao, D., Zhang, X., Ng, W. Y., Tan, T. F., Lee, D. M., Chua, K. J., Heng, J., Liu, Y., Goh, R. S. M., & Ting, D. S. W. (2024). Federated machine learning in healthcare: A systematic review on clinical applications and technical architecture. *Cell Reports Medicine*, *5*(2), 101419. DOI: 10.1016/j.xcrm.2024.101419 PMID: 38340728

Tschider, C., Compagnucci, M. C., & Minssen, T. (2024). The new EU–US data protection framework's implications for healthcare. *Journal of Law and the Biosciences*, *11*(2), lsae022. DOI: 10.1093/jlb/lsae022 PMID: 39346780
Tschider, C., Compagnucci, M. C., & Minssen, T. (2024). The new EU–US data protection framework's implications for healthcare. *Journal of Law and the Biosciences*, *11*(2), lsae022. DOI: 10.1093/jlb/lsae022 PMID: 39346780

Ul Rehman, S., & Mitra, U. (2025). Cognitive Handwriting Insights for Alzheimer's Diagnosis: A Hybrid Framework. *Information (Basel)*, *16*(3), 249. DOI: 10.3390/info16030249

Yang, Q., Liu, Y., Chen, T., & Tong, Y. (2019). Federated machine learning: Concept and applications. [TIST]. *ACM Transactions on Intelligent Systems and Technology*, *10*(2), 1–19. DOI: 10.1145/3298981

. Yang, Q., Liu, Y., Cheng, Y., Kang, Y., Chen, T., & Yu, H. (2019). Federated learning: synthesis lectures on artificial intelligence and machine learning. vol, 13, 1-207.

Chapter 15
Securing Financial Applications With Federated Learning Against Adversarial Threat

Lingala Thirupathi
https://orcid.org/0000-0003-0703-3860
Sreenidhi Institute of Science and Technology, India

Sreeja Ravula
Sreenidhi Institute of Science and Technology, India

Nookala Shreya
Sreenidhi Institute of Science and Technology, India

Vennela Appala
Sreenidhi Institute of Science and Technology, India

Suchandranath Bajjuri
TikTok, USA

ABSTRACT

The protection of sensitive data and digital transactions in the financial sector is increasingly under fire from sophisticated adversarial threats. With artificial intelligence (AI) -enabled fraud detection, credit scoring, and payment authentication, adversaries take advantage of machine learning models using different methods. Traditional centralized learning is plagued with privacy concerns and singular points of failure, which make it incompatible with stringent laws and guidelines. Federated learning (FL) brings in a new paradigm that allows institutions to train models in collaboration without raw data exchange, thus lowering breach risks and ensuring compliance. This study examines the financial applications of FL to strengthen data security and explores defense strategies like robust aggregation, differential privacy, encryption, blockchain, and other use cases. FL, combining it with adversarial training, explainable AI, trust layers from blockchain, and quantum-safe cryptography, will enable the creation of robust, privacy-preserving financial ecosystems.

DOI: 10.4018/979-8-3373-6224-3.ch015

1.INTRODUCTION

1.1 Introduction to Financial System

The global financial ecosystem is undergoing an accelerating and significant transformation as a result of the proliferation of artificial intelligence (AI), big data analytics, cloud computing, and several other digital technologies. Financial services and financial operations, such as banking and insurance, are more digital, mobile, and consumer-focused than ever. Mobile banking, digital wallets, peer-to-peer (P2P) lending, and cryptocurrencies were considered niche innovations. Now, as consumers learn to trust digital financial technologies, all of these digital financial technologies are fast becoming mainstream. Digital financial technologies increase convenience and provide timely disbursement of funds; however, as they become more widely adopted they also become more vulnerable to increasingly sophisticated cyber attacks that can threaten the integrity of the entire financial community.The biggest problem resulting from this transformation is adversarial machine learning (AML) threats. Financial services firms continue to expose themselves to increasingly acute adversarial machine learning (AML) threats as they deploy more and more machine learning models, particularly for core processes including fraud detection, algorithmic trading, credit scoring, loan authorizing, and monitoring for suspicious activity with respect to money laundering. The threats from adversarial machine learning (AML) are becoming a bigger risk as adversaries have figured out how to subvert or otherwise attack these models. Though adversarial machine learning systems can provide extraordinary power through performance and scale and are able to process huge amounts of data and identify exceptions through analysis, adversaries already know how to attack an AML system through established techniques of model poisoning, inference, or back door insertion designed to impact the operation of an AI system, which could create massive weaknesses like fake transaction escaping detection or biased approval to deny loans.

In 2016, malicious actors were able to use vulnerabilities in the SWIFT international payments system to steal upwards of $80 million from Bangladesh Bank (Blanchard, 2023). Additionally, the Equifax data breach in 2017 saw the reveal of millions of customers private financial records. The continued occurrence of data breaches demonstrate that centralized repositories that store sensitive information are, indeed, vulnerable. There is an uptick in not only sophistication, but success in phishing and adversarial attacks for credit card fraud, online banking, and stock trading. These data breaches also communicate the relationship that the financial ecosystem has with attackois and their importance in protecting against them. The complexity of presenting the picture of financial risk, is compounded by the transparency laws which surround capturing, processing, and sharing financial data. In the EU, consumer data transparency laws are first on the list - the General Data Protection Regulation (GDPR), the Payment Card Industry Data Security Standard (PCI-DSS), and Reserve Bank of India (RBI) data localization guidelines all prohibit institutions from collecting, sharing and processing customer info for thier own needs.Conventional machine learning (ML) techniques are inherently centralized. They require that large sets of data be collected, cleaned, and centralized before being utilized for training models. Centralized ML methods will create two major problems. First, a centralized database represents a tempting single point of failure. If a database is hacked, one security breach could expose millions of customer records, causing a loss to its reputation and bottom line that could exceed hundreds of millions of dollars. Second, centralization is directly contrary to modern data privacy and protection statutes that prohibit pooling personal and financial information to an extent that relinquishes it between institutions or borders. Thus, we face an urgent need for an alternate mindset which allows institutions to create effective ML with sensitive and personal data without pooling it from sensitive and personal data.

1.2 Introduction to Federated Learning

Federated Learning (FL) is a novel solution to these issues. Instead of a centralized model of learning, it provides financial institutions such as banks, insurance companies, credit bureaus, and fintech companies an environment where they can collaborate and train models with machine learning while maintaining privacy of raw data. The lenders use the raw data to train a model locally, they then only share the model parameters or gradients to a central aggregator. The aggregator combines the updates to create a global model and sends that back to the institutions. In this way, it can be characterized as decentralized training. FL has many advantages. First, by not transmitting the raw data to and from partner institutions, the risk of a large data breach is greatly diminished. Second, confidentiality and compliance with regulations will be easier since the participants cannot use or receive raw data. Third, each participant can benefit from the collective intelligence while maintaining the anonymity of each firm's data.FL is of major interest in finance due to the nature of financial systems and their interconnected nature globally. Fraudulent transactions often involve more than one institution and often involve transactions across nations; as a result, the complexity of fraud transactions is difficult for any one institution to detect. For example, money laundering may involve multiple banks across multiple countries, with each bank having only a partial knowledge of the occurrence of suspicious activity. One of the benefits of FL is that it enables institutions to jointly exploit their collective intelligence without compromising the confidentiality that banks must preserve so they can adaquately manage their customer relations and deciions about lending, and detection of rare but significant instances of fraud, such as fraud in the real estate market.

FL provides these benefits but it too has its own security concerns. FL removes one risk, that of centralized data storage, but adds more attack surfaces. There are malicious participants in the federation that can upload poisoned updates to a global model, reducing its accuracy, or creating backdoors. An adversary could weaken their own credit scoring model, ultimately approving requests for credit that are fraudulent, or insert a more nefarious stuxnet (software trigger) into a fraud detection model, allowing some authorized transactions to bypass fraud detection altogether. Adversaries can also leverage inference attacks on communication protocols within FL where adversaries seek to reconstruct sensitive information by observing the gradients that clients send to a central server and vice versa. There is, therefore, a need for adversary defenses in the federated financial space, largely because of such accidents.The motivation of the analysis of FL in terms of the financial ecosystem should not be characterized as a purely technical exercise. Finance is inherently associated with trust practices and keeping customer confidence is paramount. Customers expect security and confidentiality of their data, while regulators insist on transparency and accountability. FL exceeds merely better privacy practices, it allows financial institutions to create collective defense strategies against adversaries. In this model, banks and fintechs share data on intelligence about fraud patterns, detect coordinated attacks more easily and comply with regulation while protecting sensitive customer information.

1.3 Introduction to Financial applications against adversarial threats

Fraud detection is a long-standing part of financial protection. In the past, banks would notify fraud investigators of a potential issue, which may be an oddity of sudden withdrawal or large transfer, by rule-based decision-making. As the sheer volume of electronic transactions expanded, banks could no longer have fraud investigators decide whether there was fraud for an entire fraud population based on a rule. Machine learning models on fraud detection based upon fraud-related patterns and conditions became the new approach in fraud detection management. Today, FL is arguably fraud detection because it affords banks in the same scandal the ability to train the model collaboratively without customer-related information. Evidence of FL's uniqueness of privacy includes that it did not share customer data. Having said that, an almost identical ML methodology to fraud detection would provide insight into identifying fraud patterns relative to fraud across banks. On a strength perspective, FL has a significant asset to model-based scenarios to defend relative to adversarial model threats pertaining to fraud detection. For instance, a model poison event could occur in the training section, and a bad actor may poison the bank model; and/or a third party would use a newly discovered adversarial inference attack to access customer sensitive transactional data.Credit scoring has been an important concept since the 1950s, when numeric scoring like the FICO Score, helped lenders understand the credit worthiness of a borrower's past financial behavior. While machine learning approaches have enhanced prediction, the issues of privacy continue to be internal issues given the centralized management of customer data. FL facilitates the development of credit risk models for banks while sharing no consumer data, and reduce the distance related to privacy risk factors. There are also adversarial factors related to fraud alerts in credit risk models; for example, data poisoning by individuals creating false credit histories to impact model outcomes and back door attacks which specifically target credit models when bad actors attempt to unduly favor certain clients.

AML systems have evolved alongside regulation dealing with limiting illicit financial flows and protecting investors and consumers, starting with the Bank Secrecy Act (1970) in the United States. Historically, AML systems used to investigate activity manually for reporting suspicious activity or for suspicious patterns of transactions. Recently, automated monitoring and reporting has begun using machine learning to identify patterns of activity suggesting money laundering and other illicit act. Both ML and FL capabilities represent new alternatives to share machine learning functionalities of AML more effectively while safeguarding secrecy commitments across institutional boundaries while providing greater protection against adversarial attacks such as data poisoning, inference attacks, and others while being fully compliant with regulatory requirements.Transaction anomaly detection developed as a prominent technique for financial monitoring in multiple financial sectors, especially in banking and online payments. In the early days of anomaly detection, deviations from the normal transaction pattern were detected with statistical techniques like providing a z-score or simply thresholding. In the days of increased online and mobile banking and real-time payments, the speed and scope of continuous monitoring changed, and statistical techniques were set aside. Modern FL-enabled anomaly detection will enable institutions to collaborate in identifying patterns of unusual activity scrolling through the data based on expectation of suspicious behaviors with anomaly detection to the level of reducing the possible adversarial risk of membership inference attacks and other damaging fault injections or attacks on machine-learning or model adaptation or update protocols designed to impact anomaly detection to their disadvantage.

Traditionally, the insurance industry has depended on subjective human judgment to determine risk related to claims and minimize the risk of fraud. As claims became more digital and were happening in volumes, machine learning algorithms began to present themselves as a potential approach to support insurers in projecting stronger predictive modeling. With the recent introduction of Federated learning, insurers can build collaborative predictive models for at-risk assessments, without sharing sensitive customer and claims data with each modeling partner. Some possible adversarial threats consist of data leakage (e.g. a possibly compromised sensitive client), and model poisoning, with a desired effect of favoring certain claims or clients.Portfolio management and financial forecasting have historically relied on a wide array of economic indicators, prior performance, and human judgement. Quantitative models and algorithmic trading started to gain traction in the late-20th century, with the rise to access to vast amounts of data and traders looking to squeeze a few basis points of alpha from the data. Federated learning allows a multitude of organizations to jointly train predictive models in portfolio management without requiring the use of sensitive proprietary trading data. There are potential adversarial threats faced by organizations utilizing federated models (for example, portfolio managers that may fall to model poison, and the adversary's employer could leverage inference attack to understand the complete decision making process or strategy of the portfolio manager).

Globalization has led to a proliferation of intricacies that international financial crime must now contend with. The rise of cross border money laundering and fraud has led to a situation of complexity that is likely beyond the capabilities of traditional systems that rely on siloed jurisdictional datasets with different regulatory regimes. Federated learning (FL) provides a mechanism to be able to work internationally to detect illegal activity while allowing banks to protect sensitive banking information without exposing any raw data. The potential adversarial threats to FL systems would include backdoor attacks (Evil Twin, Math, Logic), inference attacks, and multi-client manipulation attacks that would attempt to manipulate the global model outputs.

High-frequency trading (HFT) respond to an external stimuli, using trading algorithms, and engage in dozens if not hundreds of trades per second, often with execution delays measured in microseconds. Traditionally firms have compartmentalized proprietary models on their own intranet in isolation, and any repository of past learning has barriers to collaborative utilization of those mines. FL may allow for collaboration among different models under trading platforms with a sharing of results on hiding more sensitive trading strategies. There are ways to involve a collaborative relationship among model and platform users to disclose type of adversarial trading behavior (for instance, spoofing or pump and dump). Certainly, there will still be challenges to work through such as model poisoning, and exploitation of escape agents for reinforcement learning that may have the impact on overall marketsCustomerbehaviour in banking and financial services has evolved from a basic segmentation analysis to more advanced machine learning-based recommendation systems, which allow institutions to apply some predictive modelling in relation to recommending features of financial products, identifying risk, and overall improving customer experience. In federated learning (FL), different institutions each have the ability to share their modelling knowledge and insights from the models, while safeguarding and protecting their institutional privacy; institutions not only share modelling knowledge and insights, but can extract knowledge through the shared analysis of multiple models in relation to finance and the market. The adversarial threats that exist in federated learning systems include privacy attacks that could view the customer or consumer behaviour matched against the models, or that could impersonate customer actions in their financial transactions, as the actor could represent his/her role or acting for governance and control purposes or for competing information purposes to bias model recommendations, research, and analysis.

Traditional regulatory compliance monitoring systems have historically been rather cumbersome, as entities typically must conduct their audits and produce reports on their compliance obligations to myriad government authorities, which was not too unreasonable in small and simple scenarios, but, given the multitude of overlapping and nagging financial networks that have developed—each with their associated regulations, including GDPR, CCPA and the newly minted RBL guidelines—some type of automated machine learning based compliance-monitoring system had to come into play. FL proposes to access the procedural aspects of compliance monitoring in a collective manner but continue only limited forms of monitoring locally and maintain privacy for the participating institutions. That being said, however, there are still adversarial risks, with tampering the models or poisoned/updating, for example, to alleviate certain regulatory surveillance which asked for compilation and validation mechanisms.

1.4 Organization of the chapter

This chapter offers an official landscape of Federated Learning (FL) in a financial perspective which includes an introduction, a literature review and an account of the context and methods which include client-server architecture, secure aggregation, robust algorithms, differential privacy, blockchain interaction, and workflow diagrams. In contextualising the FL framework we explain that banks or financial institutions will never share or do not move their data off site, they will always keep it locally. Through using a FL framework, banks or financial institutions can collaboratively develop models with other institutions whilst protecting their data privacy, which will in turn support more meaningful predictive modelling. The section also provides some formal definitions of adversarial threat models, such as data and model poisoning, backdoor attacks, and inference attacks, with a brief overview of potential defence strategies using robust aggregation, crypto and blockchain based accountability. The architecture for an FL workflow is outlined with a visual example of how FL appear after the data preprocessing, encryption and protecting the privacy of the client's data, and secure distribution of the global model. The case studies highlighted demonstrate FL in use for areas such as; fraud detection, credit risk modelling and anti-money laundering, while discussing the risks and different countermeasures offered. The chapter discusses FL challenges with associated risks, which include data heterogeneity, appropriateness of ownership of infrastructure and resources, insider threats, latency, lack of explainability, Sybil attacks, potential privacy leakage, risks to regulations and compliance, as well what is to be expected and what improvements may be made, such as - types of quantum-safe cryptography, self-healing adaptable systems, explainable AI, cross-domain trained networks, Federated Transfer Learning, energy efficient solutions for a world we've become aware of, global regulatory considerations, and to suggest a roadmap for secure collaborative financial intelligence.

2.LITERATURE SURVEY

Abanilla et. al., 2023 stressed the urgent need for privacy-preserving systems regarding financial fraud detection. The authors developed models that enabled financial institutions to detect fraudulent behaviour without having to share sensitive information about consumers. It is important to acknowledge that in a financial ecosystem, it is essential to come up with a collaboration that preserves confidentiality between organizations because of implications with frequency of all the major financial breaches that may occur. Their models create a vetting process already for future scalable data environments to detect and keep identifying fraud with security and compliance. Arora et al., 2024 took this unique application of federated learning and multi-party computation and were able to gain further progress in anomaly detection across financial-based datasets. Their decentralized training of the model adds a key cryptography guarantee that enables the evaluation of anomalous behaviour without having to share raw data between organizations. In this case, their approach not only improves the precision of accuracy, but introduces one novel approach to secure collaborative analytics in multi-party regulated space.

conducted a comprehensive forensic investigation on financial mobile apps with a narrow focus on potential privacy violations and prospective failures of app designs and data flows. The warning signs of vulnerability was extensive as evident with the improper integration of unsecured application programming interfaces (APIs), improperly encrypting sensitive data in transit, sloppy session handling practices, and the like. This sort of continual activity is warranted not only by developers and regulators, but by all financial entities who must protect mobile finance platforms from harm as these interactions are fast becoming the recognized predominate way of interacting with consumers. Bodagala and H. (2022) investigated whether or not federated learning could act as a protective factor for Internet of Things (IoT) devices. In general, IoT devices have been hacked. Bodagala and H. (2022) investigated whether decentralized training

had positive impacts specifically on privacy on smart supports where sensitive information could be reported. They were take for granted that the notion of federation learning will be fundamental to any future IoT security architectures is at least reasonable to consider evident.Charla et al. (2025) studied federated data engineering and how this new model can be used to facilitate distributed financial workflows, and they explain and show how organizations could engineer data pipelines with analytic quality at least as good as and also preserve privacy. This type of engineering is relevant to cross-border financial ecosystems that have varying legal regimes for data sharing, so the regimes will need to establish a balance of compliance and innovation. Deng et al. (2024) studied blockchain based smart contracts specifically in financial risk management. They suggested programmable contracts could be used to automate monitoring, reporting, and intervention based on defining characteristics of the transactions as high-risk. In a manner of speaking, it seems smart contracts might increase trust and transparency with financial operations while substantially reducing compliance costs in light of the transparency that comes bundled in financial operations.

Fallah et. al., (2024) elaborated on the concept of fraud mitigation using artificial intelligence assisted blockchain based models with detection in real-time. The model was able to get beyond detecting fraudulent transactions with better accuracy and it could identify all of the instances with an immutable record of every transaction using a blockchain ledger. By combining an immutable ledger with built in fraud detection, the system provides both security and transparency- the level of sophistication necessary for further emerging technologies that are aiming to eliminate financial crime. Gangula et. al., (2021) produced an ensemble learning model for predicting dengue outbreaks. An ensemble learning model is a collection of multiple independent existing models (for example, machine learning algorithms) that can produce a better accuracy as a united set than being able to achieve alone. They produced a research product that put power in the hands of public health decision makers to intervene and save lives at the onset of an epidemic outbreak.

In the context of new decentralized finance (DeFi) platforms, Hegde and Hegde (2024) provided a valuable reflection on the blockchain system, which has the potential to eliminate intermediaries, thereby reducing transaction costs, eliminating delays and inefficiencies, and enhancing transparency. Hegde and Hegde noted the uncertainty and volatility of DeFi, yet presented the crucial perspective that we (policymakers) should recognize vulnerabilities of smart contracts, and that policy and regulatory uncertainty will continue to exist as they noted that DeFi has the potential for social transformation, and the possibility of public policy implications. Kshirsagar et al. (2024) just as importantly explained how leveraged by new digital platforms, financial inclusion may occur more rapidly. The authors presented provocative and consequential narratives around the social significance of technology access. The authors provided earlier examples of how mobile platforms, digital wallets, and manifold organizing modalities, in particular artificial intelligence, presented a series of mechanisms to consumers to access credit, savings, and payment forms in an underserved community. The case study illustrates an example of the social impact, technology use and access to resources in a broader sense, that may also demonstrate social legitimacy and facilitate financial inclusion.

A model called FedGST was developed by Mao et al. (2023), which is a federated graph spatiotemporal model to predict brain functional disease. The analysis provides for hospitals to collaborate together while protecting patient-sensitive data privacy. The authors further argued that the results suggest federated learning can be very well suited for developing a collaboration in the medical research space while upholding strict data privacy policies like HIPAA and GDPR. Lastly, Murugan et al. (2025) undertook a study on utilizing federated learning and blockchain together for portfolio management. The study ensures decentralization and transparency with respect to decision-making in investment strategies, which provides stakeholders with trust along with resiliency within respect to data falsification and central bias.

Pratapagiri et al. (2021) used CNNs to identify diseases on plant leaves in early development stages. The CNNs along with image processing achieved high accuracy in detecting infection in early development stages allowing immediate measures to be taken in agricultural practice related to crops. Their study has huge ramifications for food security, as it gives farmers advanced systems for crop protection. Rekha et al. (2023) provided a systematic review of IoT security challenges. The work was most relevant for the security vulnerabilities. More specifically issues surrounding device vulnerabilities, insecure communication links, large-scale botnet attacks, etc. By explaining possible mitigations, the researchers provided a game plan for other researchers and practitioners on how to build resilient IoT infrastructures.

Ren et al. (2025) created an incentive scheme for multi-round federated learning with an upper limit budget. In their model, the upper limit budget addresses the maintenance of active engagement by data owners and supports the budget constraints. This was an important contribution by the researchers, as the networks, may require significant collaborative learning from multiple parties, however, can sometimes be devoid of the time based, or allotted resource. Shailaja et al. (2023) created an intelligent intrusion detection system which incorporated deep learning.Their methodology included a combination of including both feature extraction and classification for detecting high accuracy of detection in network scenarios. Their study highlights a possible need for deep models based on the constantly growing and evolving sophistication of cyberattacks.

Sravan & Verdandi(2023) designed a high-performance HMAC processor, based on SHA-3, and suitable for secure cloud-based financial transaction processing. Their design supports higher performance and higher cryptographic strength, satisfying the dual requirements of performance and safety for cloud-based financial systems. This dual requirement of performance and data safety is a point of interest for customer and technician alike. Thirupathi et al (2023), proposed a framework for heart disease prediction based on existing health risk and baseline health records integrating different data sources leveraging predictive algorithms to improve predictive accuracy and increase advanced prognostics for adapting patient healthcare activity promoting individual personal healthcare and rehabilitative baseline health profile.

Venkatachalam and Kumar (2024) researched the implementation value of machine learning in digital banking. The study had indicated that predictive models have value in financial planning forecasting target goals, customer engagement and risk management. The study positively impacted the responsible adoption of insights and value on organization's operational perspectives of machine learning capabilities in banking digital. Then operationalization (AI) and responsible governance of values.Wu and Liu (2020) examined the integration of IoT and blockchain functionality for pledge services of financial assets. The research findings provided an advanced operational treatment perspective in asset trust and accountability in pledge service prospective. The findings endorsed that the combination of IoT with blockchain could improve transparency, security and auditability on a pledge system.

A fuzzy recognition-based secure storage system for financial data was developed by Yu and Timbang (2024). Their research provided strong means of authentication and protection so a financial layer could be protected in a hostile environment. Zhao and Chen (2021) created BP neural network-based encryption to facilitate secure financial data. Their findings indicated that the neural approaches were much better than classical encryption because it could adapt dynamically to new threats. Zhao et al. (2023) proposed federated learning to complete knowledge graphs. Federated learning allows independent institutions to improve one common knowledge base by sharing their improvements without sensitive data being included, such as may be relevant in healthcare and finance involving sharing sensitive data.

3. OBJECTIVES

- To Create a Framework for Privacy-Preserving Federated Learning for finance.
- To Detect Adversarial Threats and Create Countermeasures.
- To Create a Usable Prototype with Accountability and Trust.

4. METHODOLOGIES

Typical FL approaches in finance operate as a client-server model that facilitates allowing contributing banks/financial institutions to train their own models locally and send updates to the aggregator in an encrypted form before the shared aggregator accepts and aggregates the encrypted models to obtain a central global model. Since federated involves a shared feature, adversarial threat models can include scenarios like data poisoning, model poisoning, or inference attacks which would expose parts of client training data to someone not internal to the financial institution that used restricted training data. Furthermore, defensives can range from robust aggregation algorithms (Krum, Bulyan) through other protocols like privacy preserving (DP, SMC) to distributed communications and ledger capabilities of blockchain creating an important audit trail of training instantiations that cannot easily be altered. The mathematical formalism describes the aggregation rules, and the additional figures in previous workflow dynamics describe the flow of training through the different institutions involved. The next section provides a dive into the details to support the workflow, the adversarial threat vectors identified, and the definitions of defensives, which will include a number of visuals. The example in Figure 1, provides examples of a few of adversarial threats, potential that could occur as part of FL for finance.

Figure 1. Adversarial threats in FL for finance

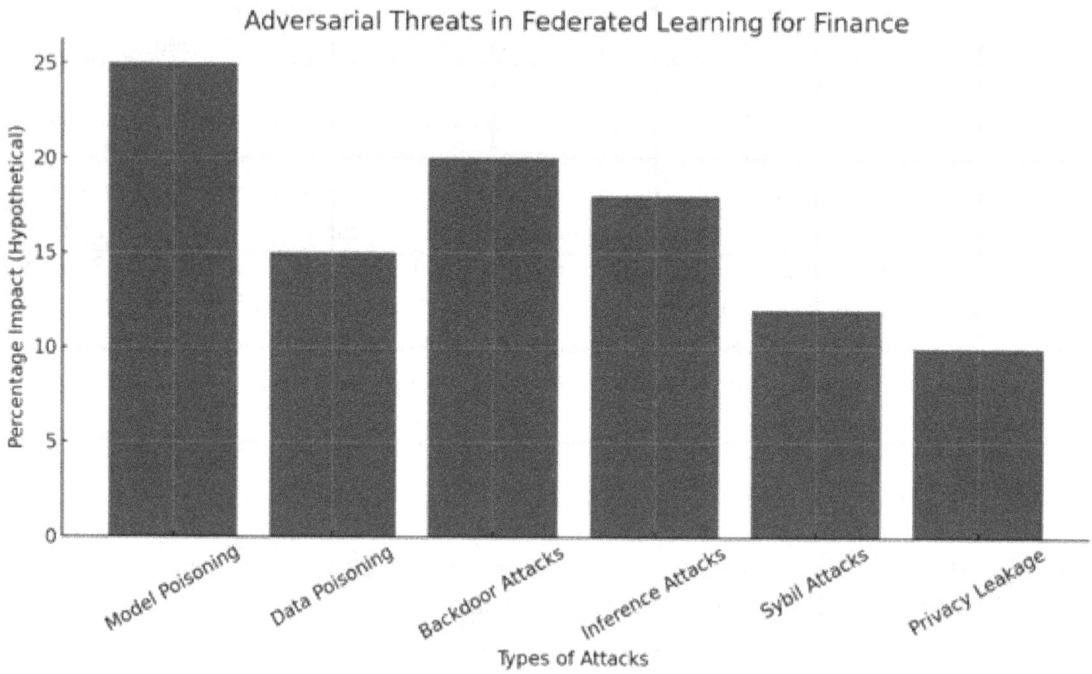

4.1 Federated Learning Framework for Financial Systems

Federated Learning (FL), a popular concept for financial systems is designed to alleviate both the tension between strict data privacy policies and the benefits of machine learning, FL utilizes a client-server model, while the more traditional specific forms of centralised learning aggregate all of the data into a known space. When dealing with financial institutions, such as banks, insurance companies and fin-tech companies, the client is the financial institution. Each client has their own sensitive financial documents, such as lending agreements, credit history, transaction information, and so on sitting on their secure local server. This mitigates the risk of introducing data pollution and meets regulatory standards as the private information of the bank never actually leaves their server.

Clients could also use a software framework designed by a financial institution. In this case, clients train local models locally using their data sets, instead of the original data. Clients only share/commit their model parameters, or model weights and gradients, to a server after they finish training. These model parameters include the amount of learning that has occurred in the local model, while not disclosing the financial data available to them. The central server performs secure aggregation, which combines the contributions of the clients to create a global model update. The global model now has roughly the same knowledge of several financial institutions as to the financial data to which they have access and will be sent back to the clients.

This set-up has obvious advantages on two fronts. First, it can improve predictive accuracy for fraud detection, credit risk, or predicting an event related to consumer behavior, just by establishing collaborative learning across institutions. Second, it is equally safe for institutions to work together and not threaten their safety because they are protecting sensitive concise financial information via privacy, and the integrity of the data. Then the variety of finance systems can build even stronger, more flexible, and safer machine learning models by using distributed learning frameworks. Collaboratively, it allows for innovation in finance, allowing for compliance obligations to be supported, and cooperation with trust.

4.2 Adversarial Threat Models in Finance

Federated learning has the ability to strengthen FinTech ecosystems, however it is vulnerable to a variety of adversarial threat models which raise significant concerns regarding effectiveness and security. Model poisoning attacks are simply one of the many potential adversarial threats when malicious clients submit manipulated gradients or updates to the global model to inhibit performance and provide unreliable financial predictions. The most critical aspect of model poisoning is with its potential to introduce errors with a client's model in sensitive aspects like fraud detection, loan application quality, and credit scoring!

Data poisoning is another issue that is equally bad! This is when the adversary corrupts or changes datasets before mode training known as data poisoning. The model can be significantly worse if any input is compromised because federated learning is reliant on accurate and diverse financial datasets across many financial firms. This can result in misclassification, decisions, decisions and even finance loss.

Backdoor attacks are potentially more covert form of attack that allow the adversary to insert backdoor triggers into the model. The adversary can trigger misclassification of transactions in specific transactional patterns (e.g., approving a fraudulent transaction) while the backdoor triggers will not activate when it is in regular run mode. Finally, inference attacks pose major privacy risk. The adversary can derive sensitive user data from shared model updates about personal credit or an individual user transaction history, even though the adversary doesn't see the foundational financial data.

4.3 Defense Methodologies in FL

There are many defense methods developed to enhance security, privacy, and reliability within financial systems to address the challenge of security in federated learning. Although multiple defenses have been developed, one of the most salient defenses is a combination of an aggregation-based defense where a client-server model decision needs to be made, either Krum Aggregation, Median, or Trimmed Mean, to remove or adjust for any malicious or atypical model updates provided by the compromised clients. Bulyan has integrated multiple aggregation methods further to minimize the effect of poisoning attacks, but allow validation of the reliability and quality of the global model.

Differential Privacy (DP) is the additional threat occurrence. DP protects adversaries from retrieving sensitive information about the model when it prevents to pre-share gradients with the appropriate level of random noise otherwise referred to preventing semblance identifiers from being revealed to the adversaries. DP will also continue to provide a balance for performance from the model versus confidentiality with the data while providing an adequate level of protection for privacy.

Data is made secure during communication and aggregation through encryptographic solutions like Homomorphic Encryption (HE) and Secure Multiparty Computation (SMC). Such solutions encrypt model updates end-to-end, thereby rendering them unreadable by adversarial actors or eavesdroppers. Finally, federated learning has begun to incorporate blockchain technology to improve certain pillars of transparency and trust. In this instance, distributed ledgers provide verifiable records of updates, and smart contracts offer some accountability by being able to programmatic ensure legitimate contributions occur and dishonest contributions receive penalizations.

4.4 Proposed FL Workflow in Financial Systems

The proposed approach describes a secure, efficient, and private approach to federated learning concerning financial systems. The first phase of the federated learning procedure is the local data pre-processing phase where each of the financial institutions performs local data pre-processing. For the local data pre-processing phase, financial institutions will pre-process the data by removing noise, irrelevant information, or redundancies from their datasets with moderate cleaning done to their unusable datasets such as transaction records or credit reports. Also, financial institutions should anonymize any sensitive features to maintain the identity of their clients such as ages, names, geographies, etc. before any model is learnt.

Following the data pre-processing phase, each institution will use its private financial data in training its local model. Rather than sharing raw data, institutions will share their new local derived model parameters for private communications. An ideal scenario would exist where each institution derives learned model parameters and accesses its own private financial data over a secure communications channel. This is enabled through a combination of homomorphic encryption (HE enabled computations work on encrypted values without disclosure) and differential privacy (DP is added noise under controlled circumstances to deter potential disclosure of sensitive attributes).

In keeping with Borisov (2007), the efficiency and fostering efficiencies beyond the use of encryption, privacy and protection of privacy, include a variety of techniques that enable efficiencies and efficiencies at scale for financial institutions. For example, using asynchronous communication, model compression, et cetera, and by using these effectively, can provide additional efficiencies in time spent in message passing or decreases in computation costs. Each of these processes does allow for collaborative expeditions regardless of the size of an institution's data or computational capabilities; but which remains, the productivity of the federated learnings themselves. Also, the robustness of passwords, ad hoc multi-layer defense responses to adversary violations (ex: model poisoning, back door insertions, inference attacks, and so on). Blockchain-based federated learning is represented in Figure 2.

Figure 2. Blockchain based federated learning

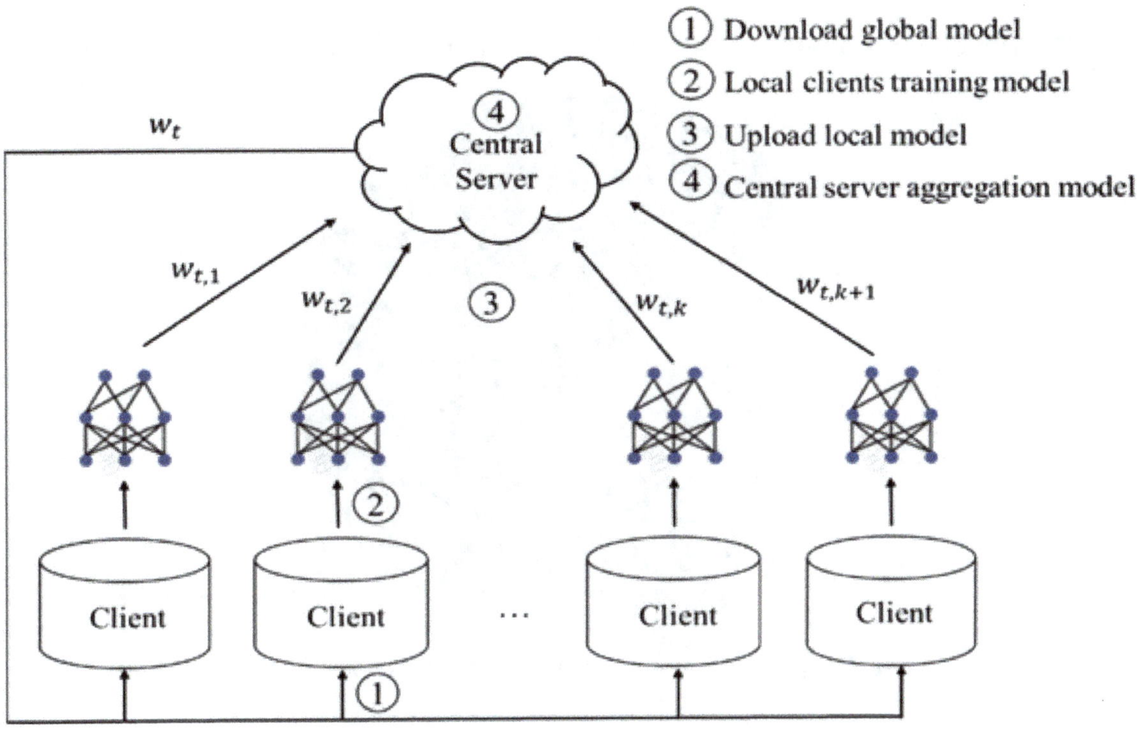

Next, encrypted updates are sent to a central aggregator and strong security implementations are enforced. The integrity of the global model will be maintained as strong aggregation algorithms will filter out malicious or corrupted updates; as well, anomaly detection will identify if an update was attacked/contaminated. Blockchain will be an immutable ledger of all updates and smart contracts will be implemented to verify contributions for additional accountability. Finally all clients will receive a redistribution of the securely improved global model partnered to assist in making better financial decisions. Figure 3 demonstrates the Distribution of Attacks Type in Financial Federated Learning.

Figure 3. Distribution of adversarial attack types in financial federated learning

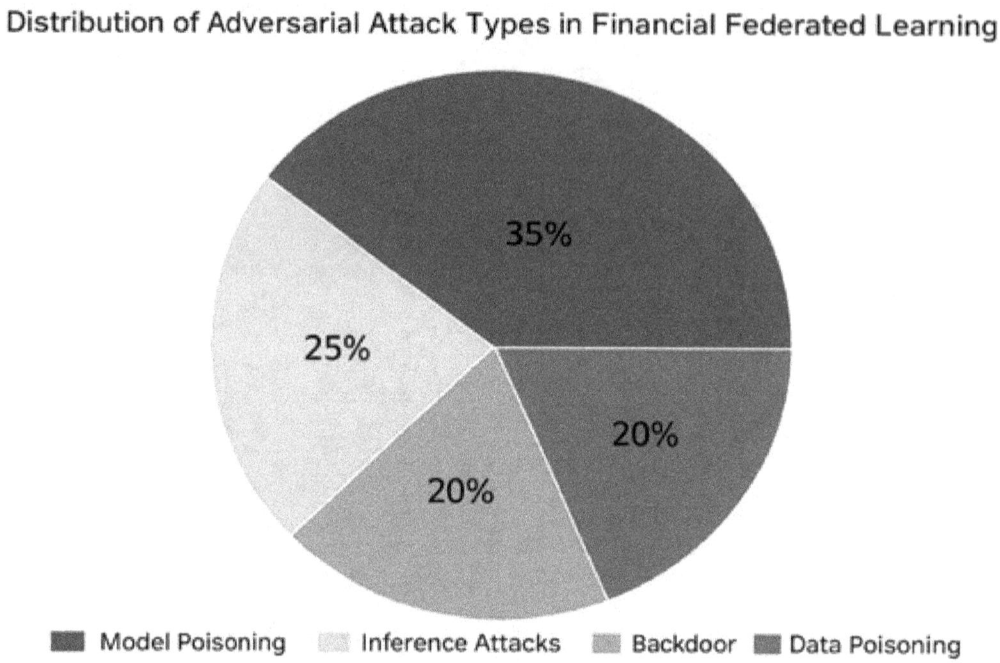

5. CASE STUDIES

These case studies demonstrate the applications of FL in real world finance. In the area of fraud detection, cooperating banks effectively create a common model using Federated Learning (FL) without exchanging data on any transactions to improve generalization of their models while maintaining client privacy. Likewise, in credit risk modeling, multiple institutions situated in discrete geographic areas can share model parameters instead of sharing data to develop a more fair and resilient scoring models or system. Traditional AML systems, as examples, in predicting regulatory compliance based on historical data can overlook emerging relationships across institutions or evaluate suspicious behavioral activity without considering regulatory constraints. Federated Learning should allow institutions to establish their own detection of suspicious activity and share their patterns of conduct to innovate into agreed identified patterns of wrongdoing and meet regulatory demands in terms of consumer identity protections. If institutions want to have access to how updates to a common Federated Learning model actually impacted a modelsperformance then a blockchain can provide visibility on how the model parameters were updated solely for both the institution and the consumer. In the case study research discussed by the authors they documented relative performance metrics which summarized the accuracy, robustness, attack resiliency and latency of training. In the taxonomies presented the case studies document, as can be seen from Table 1, how institutions across the globe, although at different rates, are embracing Federated Learning ('FL') solutions to manage the financial aspects of adversarial threats with strong defenses.

Table 1. Case studies of FL

Country(Year)	Application Area	Threats Addressed	Defense Mechanisms Implemented
Canada (2025)	Fraud Detection	Model poisoning, inference attacks	Robust aggregation, differential privacy, secure aggregation
USA/UK (2025)	Anomaly Detection	Data poisoning, membership inference	Multi-party computation, differential privacy, robust aggregation
Taiwan (2025)	Anti-Fraud Systems	Data leakage, adversarial attacks	Federated learning with privacy-preserving techniques
Global (2025)	Financial Crime Detection	Data poisoning, inference attacks	Hybrid federated learning, quantum-enhanced LSTM, privacy-preserving techniques
USA/UK (2025)	Fraud Detection	Model poisoning, inference attacks	Robust aggregation, differential privacy, multi-party computation

The RBC Borealis pilot project with the Vector Institute involved the use Federated Learning in Canada aimed at detecting fraud without sharing un-refined customer transaction data amongst banks. While developing the pilot project we considered several threats, like model poisoning, inference attacks that could otherwise damage global models, or expose sensitive customer information, as well as the data privacy of at the customer level. While the pilot was able to productively manage against the relevant threats and protect customer data, it was able to do so using strong aggregation algorithms, differential privacy as well as secure aggregation methods. Also through our collaboration, multiple banking organizations were able and continued to contribute data this developing a more generalizable model for fraud detection whilst maintain the privacy of customer data.

A federated anomaly detection framework was implemented in the USA and UK with the cooperation of the participating banks using privacy-preserving shared learning. The threats to the federated framework used in the pilots included 'data poisoning', where adversarial clients could deceive the framework into accepting corrupt updates, and membership inference attacks, where adversarial clients could guess some private information about the participating clients. Defense methods were provided for these threats respectively - using multi-party computation, a suite of robust aggregates, and differential privacy to safeguard the learning process. The federated framework has demonstrated that given a federated platform, cross-border financial institutions can mutualize predictive intelligence across borders and consensus, without any way of breach of regulatory requirements.

Taiwanese fintech companies were thinking about FL back office functions to aid integrating the transaction data for their clients more into a better anti-fraud system that linked them through secure and privacy inclusive protocols and in a better model. The case study examines leaks of data and some things that connected to adversarial attacks on the platform where an adversarial actor in the platform could access sensitive client information when simply improving the model. During the study privacy preserving mechanisms were integrated into the FL workflow while allowing each participant to still build their model and own the data set.

An international project where hybrid federated learning models were applied to facilitate financial crime detection with quantum-enhanced LSTM models, deployed methods to address next level types of threats, which included, data and model poisoning, inference attacks, backdoor insertions, etc. The project team consisted of people from institutions around the world, all offering different kinds of financial contribution along with very strong aggregation, privacy-enhancing and cryptographic methods to protect the model. They found federated systems could scale across various counties and mainly deal with security involvement and privatisation of data, so that financial crimes that crossed jurisdictional borders could improve detection.

Throughout the cases we examined, we noted several themes, including 1) FL allowed parties to work together without ever centralizing the touched sensitive vulnerable data, 2) robust aggregation and differential privacy are both appropriate for countermeasures to adversarial threats to the model, and 3) blockchain or cryptography made sense for the accountability and transparency aspects needed. The cases also emphasized the importance of considering and engaging local regulatory and infrastructure contexts beyond FL to develop FL frameworks in mutually beneficial ways, and that as these frameworks gain traction, the potential to improve financial intelligence will create positive influences on consistently high levels of privacy and security.

6. CHALLENGES & RISKS

Challenges to the application of FL in finance are largely: communication overhead, adversarial updates, lacking institutional infrastructure in smaller institutions, ethics and regulation challenges in terms of fairness and cross-border compliance, scaling is an issue considering that there is a training phase in apps that is across hundreds of financial institutions which may include latency in the training phase, the imbalanced data across clients may bias in global models, security issues (e.g., sybil attacks, possibility of inference, and/or malicious clients). The Table 2 explains the Challenges/ Risks in FL.

Table 2. Challenges / risks in FL

Challenges/ Risks	Description	Imp lication in Finance
Data & model poisoning	Malicious clients inject poisoned or backdoor updates	Fraudulent transactions may bypass detection
Privacy leakage	Membership inference and model inversion attacks on gradients	Exposure of sensitive customer or transaction data
Non-IID & imbalance	Banks hold diverse, uneven datasets	Bias toward larger banks; reduced detection of rare fraud
Privacy–accuracy trade-off	Stronger DP reduces leakage but lowers model accuracy	Lower recall in fraud/AML detection
Explainability gap	Opaque FL models hinder auditing of adversarial drift	Regulatory non-acceptance, reduced trust

Financial financial institutions generate data in many different ways. Transaction logs, customer credit histories, trading records, blockchain entries, etc. While all of these examples are considered non-IID (nonidentically distributed) and will all make it difficult to create a global FL model that generalize patterns; and the consequence for financial institutions may be that some models may work well for some institutions but yield poor results for a second institution and it may also lead to potential misclassifications or bias, and predictive functionalities for critical applications like fraud detection or credit scoring. Additionally, the ability to utilize compute resources and access to a high performing network will vary from institution to institution. In particular, a large bank can use high performance computing and massively higher speed internet but a small credit union may only be capable of basic computing/data resources or limited network reliability. The disparity of access can slow model training for everybody, create congestion or bottlenecks in communication amongst the different financial institutions, and create a higher degree of vulnerability for weaker financial institutions to be attacked by adversarial means, such as poisoned updates.

An aspect of FL that is unique from other methods described in the previous section is the insider threat from trusted employees or participants that would submit an update to a model, and those malicious model updates can identify and eliminate, or at least avoid detection by, the global model within a local organization, removing it from further postulating losses or fraud, displacement, or monitoring of activity. The challenge in recognizing an insider threat rather than an outside threat is that the insider may have a legitimate appearing update to submit, but this is a subtle attack that may risk organizations from the threat of FL. FL depends on incessant updates often. Latency can develop in the flow of model updates for several reasons, such as long-range networks such as satellite, reductions of available bandwidth, or the model size burdening already limited bandwidth. In addition to time and latency impacting how swiftly organizations may aggregate and synchronize their model, the potential corrective attacks exist which can exploit the window of time when an attacker intentionally lags. During these unfortunate times, the attackers can maliciously introduce model updates that would lower the integrity of the overall global model.

Most FL approaches, especially those using deep learning approaches, are mostly opaque, producing outputs of predictions without much detail on how they got to that decision. In the financial context, this brings complications dealing with any regulatory requirements. For lending decisions (which is simple enough), how can auditors, and therefore regulators, authenticate whether or not it was the system, banker, or someone else which rejected the loan, sent a fraud alert, or varied the loanable amount? This opaque reasoning prevents spontaneous blind assessments to determine if the model made discriminatory judgments or if a model had been adversarially modified in any way. An attacker may easily instigate multiple fake clients in a federated network, the result being a poor global model. Also as seen in financial contexts, these bad actors could manipulate their agreed decisions to change fraud detection or thresholds as defined by the global model and, harmfully influence results calculated for credit scoring, and remove trust in any future decision taken by the plaintiff. Regardless of Sybil exploit design mode, this once again underscores the lack of trustworthy identification and verification means, and the need for continuous monitoring of clients.

While FL doesn't explicitly reveal on-boarding data, gradients, or model updates, sensitive financial data can still be leaked through FL processes. Sophisticated adversaries might use gradient inversion or inference attacks to recover sensitive financial information and reliably predict outcomes, such as transaction summaries, customer identifiers or account balances. Adversaries may use advanced techniques during (federated) learning and thus it is likely that unique developed cryptographic algorithms will need to be designed for the specific application; however, even then, it is still a balancing act between protecting/delivering user privacy with computational performance. Contextualizing a privacy and FL focused example, in FL we are left with Homomorphic Encryption (HE), and Secure Multiparty Computation (SMC) are examples of alternatives that provide strong protection to model updates and travel with privacy. However, both HE and SMC are both extremely expensive in computation usage and will greatly affect training and aggregating. Again, in some high-frequency financial applications there are key operational precourses for deploying FL with a decision to be made on the trade off of security vs. real time performance demands.

Financial institutions may also potentially operate in different regulatory regimes e.g., GDPR in Europe, CCPA in the U.S. and RBI guidelines in India. Foreign regulations may create complications for FL in that compliance requirements may also differ across jurisdictions for collaborative FL projects. Adversaries are already using the regulations to their advantage while compliance will possibly be hard to reasonable consistent levels of security, privacy and the accountability globally which in and of itself is compliance in the various jurisdiction. Fraudulent transactions constitute very small proportions of the overarching financial datasets being collected and therefore ultimately unbalanced class sets.

7. CONCLUSIONS

Federated Learning (FL) represents a significant shift in how sensitive applications and customer data are stored and utilized, while financial organizations undertake a digital transformation. Instead of centralized model training, FL pushes for a decentralized model and establishes a stronger and privacy-respecting approach towards machine learning. This shift is significant because of the persistence of simple breaches in the financial space. As financial organizations are encumbered by keeping compliance and custodianship of personal and transactional data, FL understands that they all can really only survive by changing how they secure data. FL mitigates much of the privacy process risk that comes with the centralized idea of needing to store the data for a significant amount of time. FL has the provision for architecture for financial organizations to conduct exchanges under regulatory documents like General Data Protection Regulation (GDPR), California Consumer Privacy Act (CCPA) and the Reserve Bank of India Data Protection Framework, as well as changing the conditions under which access to sensitive records.

If FL (by FL design) causes discovery risk for secondary sensitive records to be limited, this will mean that the attacks will likely focus on procurement of models at worst, limiting the risk of theft of payment or personally identifiable information from organizational architectures that only undertake federated model training with limited exposure to the procurement process of data. Essentially, FL is able to serve the dual purpose of allowing agencies to comply to regulatory obligations and act as a mechanism for the utility of collective institutional intelligence. FL has potential in many financial service use cases but in the cases of fraud detection, FL allows many institutions to each share only knowledge (i.e. not transaction data) to do the service of finding fraud that was outside the visibility of a single bank in cross-institutional fraud patterns. Secondly, if FL was used in the context of credit scoring, many datasets that are heterogeneous, are combined to create a better and more fair proxy with less bias as a result of the natural biases that emerge from a data repository that is siloed.

All the benefits of FL also create many new attack surfaces. The decentralized architecture creates new attack surface opportunities. There can be malicious actors who may issue poisoned updates intended to develop models that move global models in the wrong direction, put hidden back doors into those models, or launch inference attacks against the communications protocol. Recent research has demonstrated adaptive poisoning attacks and federated sybil attacks, where adversaries can disguise themselves as multiple clients in order to unfairly change promotion or suppression of outcomes to change federated model results. These considerations of FL remind us that as we aim to become adversarially resiliency, it is also a moving target; as we develop defensives there will also be new evolutions of possible new attacks.

In dealing with the well documented weakness of FL to adversarial manipulation, researchers have proposed a multi-layered defense strategy. Strong robust aggregators like Krum, Trimmed Mean, and Bulyan can mitigate the impact of corrupted updates, and Differential Privacy (DP) mechanisms can add noise to the gradients in order to reduce the probability of membership inference. Both Homomorphic Encryption (HE) and Secure Multiparty Computation (SMC) can provide protections in a cryptographic sense when it comes to sharing models. When combined with blockchain technology, the trust ledger (the blockchain) provides an irrefutable audit trail for federated systems and attention to the responsibilities of participants can be enhanced as well. Each of the mechanisms has particular tradeoff risks (e.g., DP can create accuracy concerns, HE and SMC can add a heavy computational burden, and MoE systems can face scalability issues), but when put together, all of these defenses form the foundational elements of a trustworthy FL ecosystem.

More than technical implementations, FL has an added benefit of converting participants to collaborators within the finance sector. Competing entities, including banks, fintech start-ups, and insurers, may be extremely reluctant to share any data given the significant reputational, privacy, and competitive incentives to maintain data exclusivity. FL creates a framework where collaborative action can take place without sacrificing confidentiality.

For FL to move from a developed stage to mainstream, there will need to be regulatory harmonization. Disparate global standards could invalidate the cooperative elements of financial AI, as the countries and regions will need to create interoperable systems around privacy and security and, perhaps less so, auditing. In addition, some approach to governance models will be need to ensure that federated learning systems are secured but also equitable and fair, transparent, and explainable. There has been pressure from regulators to have AI systems to explain their reasoning for automated decisions (albeit typically only negative ones, qualifying loan applications, referring for fraud etc.). Highlighting the requirements of explaining the use of Explainable AI (XAI) in FL will have to be made for compliance purposes but also as an opportunity for comparative assessment in adversarial situations. The future of FL in finance will fundamentally depend on its ability to lean into its requirement for continuous feedback and adaptive countermoves, since anything static will not provide a sufficient defence against continually evolving adversarial innovations. The potential within FL is to create self-healing federated learning models that both record and adapt dynamic conditions but also deploy a comparatively explosive or stronger aggregation when conditions permit. Furthermore, the need for quantum-safe cryptography to protect FL systems in a post-quantum world wherein still current cryptographic encrypted can be exploited needs attention.

8. FUTURE ENHANCEMENTS

In finance, federated learning (FL) is growing rapidly and providing new opportunities for secure, privacy-compliant collaboration between organizations, while also posing important challenges to be solved for long-term viability. Much of the current research has made important advances in thinking about data privacy, adversarial robustness, and system scalability, but a future financial ecosystem will require smarter, more dynamic, and sustainable federated frameworks. The following subsections outline areas where future research and technological innovation can work towards enhancing the resilience and effectiveness of FL in finance.

Future digital infrastructures are concerningly approaching the quantum computing phase. Traditional cryptography schemes, like RSA and Elliptic Curve Cryptography (ECC), are being used now to protect

FL communications and secure multiparty computations; however, quantum algorithms such as Shor's algorithm, could quickly break these cryptography schemes, which creates an existential threat to the confidentiality and integrity of financial FL systems. Future FL implementations that want a quantum future must utilize PQC schemes like lattice-based encryption, code-based encryption, and hash-based signatures, since quantum computer capable adversaries could use a number of quantum algorithms to break traditional cryptography. In addition, quantum key distribution (QKD) techniques can also be included to establish unbreakable cryptography. These techniques can provide secure quantum-safe methods to exchange sensitive financial data whereby a quantum ability adversary will not be able to compromise confidentiality or integrity. Future implementations of FL systems should begin experimenting with PQC schemes so it can be resilient against future quantum-capable adversaries.

Blockchain is already emerging as a valid trust-enhancer in FL, and future systems can enhance this integration by utilizing smart contracts to begin automating auditing, verification, and accountability. For example, smart contracts could involve an automatic validation process that verifies if models are valid and rejects submissions that are outliers or potentially malicious, and sanction participants that are attempting data poisoning attacks. As all contributions will have an immutable audit trail, blockchain facilitates transparent contributions that could otherwise facilitate adversarial behavior. This will be especially applicable for cross-border financial engagements where mutual distrust can prevent institutions from cooperating and sharing insights. The combination of blockchain and FL allows for the establishment of collaborative and tamper-evidence ecosystems.

REFERENCES

Abanilla, S., Chatterjee, M., & Dass, S. (2023). Towards privacy preserving financial fraud detection. In *2023 International Conference on Machine Learning and Applications (ICMLA)* (pp. 1723–1726). Jacksonville, FL, USA. DOI: 10.1109/ICMLA58977.2023.00261

Arora, S., ... (2024). Privacy-preserving financial anomaly detection via federated learning & multi-party computation. In 2024 Annual Computer Security Applications Conference Workshops (ACSAC Workshops) (pp. 270–279). Honolulu, HI, USA. DOI: 10.1109/ACSACW65225.2024.00038

Bodagala, H., & H., P. (2022). Security for IoT using federated learning. In *2022 International Conference on Recent Trends in Microelectronics, Automation, Computing and Communications Systems (ICMACC)* (pp. 131–136). Hyderabad, India. DOI: 10.1109/ICMACC54824.2022.10093557

Charla, R. R., Dharamshi, K., Sonani, R., & Shah, A. R. (2025). Federated data engineering for privacy-aware AI: Patterns from distributed retail and financial workflows. In *2025 International Conference on Computing Technologies (ICOCT)* (pp. 1–8). Bengaluru, India. DOI: 10.1109/ICOCT64433.2025.11118887

Deng, J., Liu, L., Lv, C., Yang, Z., & Han, G. (2024). Application of smart contracts in blockchain in financial risk control. In *2024 Second International Conference on Networks, Multimedia and Information Technology (NMITCON)* (pp. 1–6). Bengaluru, India. DOI: 10.1109/NMITCON62075.2024.10699060

Fallah, M. H., Siri, D., Kumar, G. R., Sheeba, G., Sharma, H., & Devendran, A. (2024). AI-powered blockchain systems for real-time fraud detection in financial services. In 2024 International Conference on IoT, Communication and Automation Technology (ICICAT) (pp. 1287–1291). Gorakhpur, India. DOI: 10.1109/ICICAT62666.2024.10923418

Gangula, R., Thirupathi, L., Parupati, R., Sreeveda, K., & Gattoju, S. (2021). Ensemble machine learning based prediction of dengue disease with performance and accuracy elevation patterns. *Materials Today: Proceedings*. Advance online publication. DOI: 10.1016/j.matpr.2021.07.270

Hegde, S. K., & Hegde, R. (2024). An efficient and transparent financial transaction system using decentralized finance (DeFi) based on blockchain technology. In 2024 2nd International Conference on Recent Advances in Information Technology for Sustainable Development (ICRAIS) (pp. 18–23). Manipal, India. DOI: 10.1109/ICRAIS62903.2024.10811700

Kshirsagar, B., Gopalkrishnan, S., Kale, V., Kulkarni, P., Jaiwani, M., & Kulkarni, S. V. (2024). Harnessing technology for financial empowerment: A study on digitally driven financial inclusion. In 2024 International Seminar on Application for Technology of Information and Communication (iSemantic) (pp. 241–246). Semarang, Indonesia. DOI: 10.1109/iSemantic63362.2024.10761999

Mao, J., Lin, H., Tian, X., Pan, Y., & Liu, J. (2023). FedGST: Federated graph spatio-temporal framework for brain functional disease prediction. In *2023 IEEE International Conference on Bioinformatics and Biomedicine (BIBM)* (pp. 1356–1361). Istanbul, Turkiye. DOI: 10.1109/BIBM58861.2023.10385983

Murugan, V. G., & Nanda, S. S. V R, S., Jatty, G. N., Kumar, N. R., &Chamundeeswari, V. (2025). Integrating federated learning and blockchain for enhanced financial portfolio management. In 2025 3rd International Conference on Integrated Circuits and Communication Systems (ICICACS) (pp. 1–6). Raichur, India. DOI: 10.1109/ICICACS65178.2025.10968394

Pratapagiri, S., Gangula, R. G. R., Srinivasulu, B., Sowjanya, B., & Thirupathi, L. (2021). Early detection of plant leaf disease using convolutional neural networks. In 2021 3rd International Conference on Electronics Representation and Algorithm (ICERA) (pp. 77–82). DOI: 10.1109/ICERA53111.2021.9538659

Rekha, S., Thirupathi, L., Renikunta, S., & Gangula, R. (2023). Study of security issues and solutions in Internet of Things (IoT). *Materials Today: Proceedings*, *80*(3), 3554–3559. DOI: 10.1016/j.matpr.2021.07.295

Ren, Z., Zhang, X., Ng, W. W. Y., & Zhang, J. (2025). Incentive mechanism design for multi-round federated learning with a single budget. *IEEE Transactions on Network Science and Engineering*, *12*(1), 198–209. DOI: 10.1109/TNSE.2024.3488719

Shailaja, K., Srinivasulu, B., Thirupathi, L., Gangula, R., Boya, T. R., & Polem, V. (2023). An intelligent deep feature based intrusion detection system for network applications. *Wireless Personal Communications*, *129*(1), 345–370. DOI: 10.1007/s11277-022-10100-w

Sravan, P., & Verdandi, S. (2023). Building a secure and high-performance HMAC processor based on SHA-3 for the cloud-based financial sector. In *2023 International Conference on Advances in Computing, Communication and Applied Informatics (ACCAI)* (pp. 1–8). Chennai, India. DOI: 10.1109/ACCAI58221.2023.10200480

Thirupathi, L., Srinivasulu, B., Khanapurkar, U., Rambabu, D., & Preeti, C. M. (2023). Heart disease prediction in healthcare communities by machine learning over big data. In Bhateja, V., Sunitha, K. V. N., Chen, Y. W., & Zhang, Y. D. (Eds.), Intelligent System Design (Lecture Notes in Networks and Systems, Vol. 494). Singapore: Springer. DOI: 10.1007/978-981-19-4863-3_38

Venkatachalam, S., & Kumar, M. S. (2024). Analysis of machine learning based financial planning applications in online digital banking. In 2024 2nd International Conference on Self Sustainable Artificial Intelligence Systems (ICSSAS) (pp. 459–461). Erode, India. DOI: 10.1109/ICSSAS64001.2024.10760816

Wu, M., & Liu, H. (2020). Integration of Internet of Things and blockchain for chattel asset pledge financial service. In 2020 19th International Symposium on Distributed Computing and Applications for Business Engineering and Science (DCABES) (pp. 166–169). Xuzhou, China. DOI: 10.1109/DCABES50732.2020.00051

Yu, X., & Timbang, F. L. (2024). A secure storage system for financial data based on fuzzy recognition algorithms. In *2024 International Conference on Intelligent Algorithms for Computational Intelligence Systems (IACIS)* (pp. 1–5). Hassan, India. DOI: 10.1109/IACIS61494.2024.10721780

Zhao, A., Liu, Y., Wei, S., Long, Y., Feng, W., & Gu, Z. (2023). Research on the prospect of knowledge graph completion based on the federated setting. In 2023 8th International Conference on Data Science in Cyberspace (DSC) (pp. 60–67). Hefei, China. DOI: 10.1109/DSC59305.2023.00019

Zhao, N., & Chen, M. (2021). Design of a financial information security encryption system based on a BP neural network. In *2021 IEEE International Conference on Industrial Application of Artificial Intelligence (IAAI)* (pp. 301–306). Harbin, China. DOI: 10.1109/IAAI54625.2021.9699912

Chapter 16
Leveraging Secure Federated Learning for Data-Driven Business Decisions

Udit Mamodiya
https://orcid.org/0000-0002-8022-4252
Faculty of Engineering and Technology, Poornima University, India

Randhir Singh Baghel
https://orcid.org/0000-0002-5113-3554
Poornima University, India

ABSTRACT

In the age of data-based business, organizations depend more and more on wide analysis to inform strategic decisions. However, the growing concerns around data privacy, regulatory compliance, and inter-cooperation are significant challenges. This chapter explores how secure federated learning (SFL) provides a transformative approach to business strategy by enabling the training of machine learning models in collaboration with multiple entities without sharing sensitive data. We examine the underlying principles of federated education, differential privacy and encryption, and practical architectures for entertainment deployment. Through real-world examples, this chapter explains SFL.

1. INTRODUCTION

In the age of digital transformation, businesses rely more on data as a strategic asset to innovate, enhance customer experiences, pt over the operation, and maintain competitive benefits. The exponential growth of the mobile app, the Internet th F Things (IoT) devices, e-CE Mars platforms, financial transactions, and data produced from healthcare records has created unprecedented opportunities to make data-based decisions. At the same time, this data leads to significant challenges related to flow storage, integration, security, and regulatory compliance. Traditional central machine learning approaches, where data from various stakeholders is collected in a single repository, are often inappropriate due to

DOI: 10.4018/979-8-3373-6224-3.ch016

the risks of privacy, legal restrictions, and competitive barriers (Kairouz et al., 2019; McMahan et al., 2016; McCall, 2025; Mothukuri et al., 2021).

The Federated Learning (FL) machine has emerged as a shift in machine learning that addresses these challenges by enabling collaborative model training without the need for raw data sharing. Instead of transferring sensitive datasets to the Central Server, FL allows local devices, organizations, or individuals to independently train models and only share model updates (eg, Grad Dal or Parameters). Join these updates to create an optimised model globally, following a central aggregator (Zhang et al., 2025; Nguyen et al., 2021; Zheng et al., 2021; Jin et al., 2023). This decentralized education pattern not only preserves data privacy, but it also includes, which allows fragments to contribute to model development.

Models trained in decentralised environments must be tested with non-IID (non-iid and non-uniformly distributed) data, system sexuality, communication obstacles, and potential anti-attacks (e.g., poison or forecast attacks). To consider these issues, secure federated learning (SFL) integrates advanced cryptographic and privacy-to-lifting methods, such as Differenced Privacy (DP), carefully presents calibrated voice in model updates, ensuring that a personal user's data cannot be contrast-engineered by shared gradients or parameters (Pribadi Kalapaaking et al., 2023; Wikipedia, 2025a; Wikipedia, 2025b; Wikipedia, 2025c). In terms of SFL, DP Statistical guarantee helps ensure that the contribution of a single data point remains inseparable, which is crucial in highly sensitive domains such as healthcare or finance, where re-identification risks are significant.

Safe Multi-Party Calculation (SMPC) allows multiple participants to calculate in collaboration with the function on their inputs without disclosing their inputs. Inside the SFL, SMPC is especially useful for secure consolidation protocol, enabling the average model parameters in the client while the central server or peer nodes ensure that the raw contribution can cause access to the accence (Wikipedia, 2025d; HCLTech, 2025; "Federated Learning for Cybersecurity," 2025). This approach creates strong confidence in organizational silos and prevents information leakage during training. Homomorphic encryption goes one step further by allowing direct mathematical operations on encrypted data, such that the result, once decrypted, matches the calculation result as if it were carried out on a plane text. In Federated Learning, it enables the Central server to obtain overall encrypted model updates without decrypting them, thus preserving the confidentiality of the end users throughout the education cycle. Although the calculation is expensive, the ongoing research reduces the distance to efficiency, making it more practical for large-scale deployment.

Blockchain integration will add a level of trust and regime to federated ecosystems. Guaranteed blockchain transparency, uncertainty, and responsibility by recording the model updates, consolidation results, and entry to the distributed ledger ("Recent Advancements in Federated Learning," 2025; Vaikuntanathan, 2017; Cheon et al., 2017; Liu et al., 2025). This decentralized approach reduces the risks of a single issue of failure or malicious manipulation by the coordination server. Moreover, smart contracts on the blockchain platform can automate incentive methods, guaranteeing reasonable reward distribution among contributors while promoting collaboration in a multi-star atmosphere.

Together, these privacy techniques make the spinal cord of secure federated education, enabling organizations to create powerful AI models without compromising confidentiality, confidence, or compliance. Conversion of secure federated education with professional intelligence is very effective. Organizations combined model training - Acros can cooperate with Across Healthcare Networks, Financial Institutions, Supply Chain Consortia, and Smart City Infrastructures - without compromising competitive gains or GDPR (General Data Protection Regulation) and CCPA For example, banks can train models of cheating investigations jointly without exposing ownership of customer data, or hospitals that maintain strict secrecy of patients can develop predictive healthcare models (Chen et al., 2022; Liu et al., 2022; Geyer et al., 2018; Xu et al., 2025; Zhu, 2025).

Moreover, a secure federated education organizes the rise of AI and the rising emphasis on making moral decisions. By embedding privacy and trust in the learning process, it provides the confidence to adopt AI-based strategies on a large scale of AI-based strategies. This other approach is acknowledged as building customer trust insofar as an increase in awareness of data privacy issues has, in turn, raised the expectations for transparency and secure handling of personal information.

This chapter explores extensive research in secure federated learning (SFL) as a foundation for data-based business decisions. Traditionally, federated learning is presented as the opposite of centralized machine learning approaches. It allows distributed model training without the consolidation of the raw data. Therefore, while in centralized systems, the data repositories would be aggregated at a single data reservoir, there remains local ownership and cooperative proprietorship in a federated system, thereby diminishing concerns about leakage and regulatory compliance (Popli et al., 2025; Khramtsova et al., 2020; Rahdari et al., 2025; Wang et al., 2025; Truex et al., 2020). To guarantee robustness and dependability, secure federated learning is therefore equipped with privacy techniques and security protocols. By introducing statistical noise into model updates, differential privacy (DP) protects private-level data from inferential attacks. Direct calculation on encrypted data eliminates the need for decomposition, while Protected Multi-Party Calculation (SMPC) permits multiple participants to compute model parameters on encrypted inputs without revealing sensitive information. By combining blockchain technology with cryptographic protections, low-level information traceability, tamper resistance, and decentralized consensus techniques are introduced, which improve accountability in federated ecosystems. These feature sets either rival or diverge from what other applications in their respective industries can offer: Without sacrificing patient privacy, FL facilitates the forecast analysis of early disease testing in the healthcare industry; In the financial industry, it facilitates risk assessment and fraud investigation within organizations; in retail and e-commerce, FL operates customer segmentation tools and personalization solutions; and in production and logistics, it boosts operational efficiency through cooperative intelligence. However, the deployment of FL is not without hazards (Konečný et al., 2016; Konečný et al., 2017; Diao et al., 2020; Rieke et al., 2020; Dayan et al., 2021).

Alongside the FAIR image concern, problems with scalability, communication overhead, and computation cost continue to be common when working with heterogeneous and non-IID datasets. From here, the governance structure is appreciated, and in contrast to the encrypted collaborator's limited explanation, responsibility, liability, and incentive configuration are increasingly called into question. Research directions include investigating quantum safety cryptography to combine SFL with Edge AI and using a zero-trust architecture to reduce systemic vulnerabilities while getting ready for the Quantum. As a result, SFL stands out from these innovations as a dual asset that is both technically proficient and strategically oriented, helping to shape the future of secure co-intelligence in the data economy.

Secure federated learning is probably going to be seen as the cornerstone of enterprise decision-making in the near future, as technical innovations are eliminated in relation to business strategies. In the 21st century, it provides a sustainable basis for data-based business ecosystems by providing a means of maximizing the value of distributed data while safeguarding privacy, trust, and compliance.

2. FOUNDATIONS OF FEDERATED LEARNING

Federated Learning (FL) is an example of a distributed machine learning in which model training is performed on decentralized devices or organizational servers rather than integrating sensitive data in a central repository. Each participant, referred to as a client, uses its own dataset to train the local model at a bank, hospital, or Internet of Things device. Clients merely send the generated model updates, like Grad Dal or Parameter Values, to a central server or coordinator rather than exchanging raw data.

The server is responsible for collecting these updates, usually by algorithms such as Federated Average (FedAVG), to build a global model, which reflects mass education in all consumers while maintaining data privacy.

The success of this decentralized approach depends on the three basic elements: customers who act as data owners and provide local training, coordination servers that synchronize and collect model updates, and communication protocols that enable safe and efficient transfer of information. Communication poses substantial challenges in federated systems, so the protocol is structured to minimize bandwidth use and support advanced technologies like encryption, secure multiparty computation, and differential privacy—mechanisms that can't be inferred from the communicated Grad Dal (Karargyris et al., 2023; "End-to-End Encrypted Neural Networks," 2025; Hubaux et al., 2021; Buttyán & Hubaux, 2007). The advantages of federated learning are particularly pronounced in business and organizational settings. Fundamentally, it ensures privacy by design, as sensitive data remains at its source and is not transmitted elsewhere, thereby reducing associated risks. It also supports compliance with strict data protection rules such as the General Data Protection Regulation (GDPR) and the Health Insurance Portability and Liability Act (HIPAA) in the United States. In addition, FL reduces data transfer costs because instead of raw data, only model parameters are communicated, making it very efficient for large-scale, data-intensive applications. Another main advantage is that its ability to promote cross-cello collaboration, allowing organizations to be owned or protect intelligence in domains such as healthcare and finance, allows the development of joint forecasts to be trained. Finally, federated learning enhances scalability and inclusivity, as it expands the power of machine learning to a wide network of edge devices - including smartphones, wearables, and IOT sensors - which constantly produce decentralized data.

The concept of federated learning is relatively new, which was released in 2016 to improve mobile device applications such as keyboard forecasts and voice validation while maintaining a user's privacy. Its origin is in the belief that modern data ecosystems are both very distributed and tightly controlled, making central education more and more impractical. Since then, Federated Learning has developed rapidly in the mainstream AI framework with a special research concept, adoption of healthcare, money, supply chain, and smart city systems (Parno et al., 2010; Collingwood, 2017; Zhao et al., 2020; Applied Sciences, 2025). Over time, progress in privacy-saving technologies, secure consolidation techniques, and progress in distributed optimization has expanded its scope, transforming FL into the base of responsible AI practices.

Federated learning can be classified into several types depending on how the data is partitioned among customers. In cross-device federated learning, thousands of or even millions of edge devices (such as smartphones or IOT sensors) participate in training, often contributing to small amounts of data. This setting is characterized by high sexuality, limited calculation, and incredible connectivity. On the contrary, cross-salo federated learning has a lower number of more stable customers, such as hospitals, banks, or enterprises, each with larger datasets. This form is especially suitable for inter-categorical cooperation where data sharing is restricted by legal or competitive barriers. FL can also be classified on the basis of data distribution: horizontal federated learning applies when participants share space of the same feature but have different samples (eg, patients with similar symptoms), while participants share the same sample space but have different features. Federated transfer learning is a more sophisticated form that facilitates collaboration when templates and features differ and data provides the advantage of transfer learning techniques to close gaps in foreigners. Federated learning offers a solid basis for developing secure, cooperative, and data-based solutions by fusing education with privacy protection. Because of its history, businesses are able to investigate the complexities of contemporary data ecosystems, strategically facilitating not only technological innovation but also artificial intelligence, which offers the potential to rearrange the landscape of different kinds and extended applications.

3. SECURITY AND PRIVACY CHALLENGES IN FEDERATED LEARNING

Federated Learning (FL) is not immune to security and privacy risks, despite offering notable advantages in terms of data privacy and decentralized model training. Although FL is appealing, the majority of its features—like distributed training and restricted data sharingalso introduce particular vulnerabilities that adversaries can exploit. The confidentiality of local datasets as well as problems with the integrity, power, and confidentiality of the global model may be resolved by these risks. These challenges must be understood in order to design a safe federated learning (SFL) framework that can support reliable professional decisions.

The transmitted grade or parameters during training may unintentionally encode enough statistical information to reorder inputs even in the absence of direct access to the raw data. For instance, the healthcare application's privacy will be compromised by the attackers' ability to perform RCTs, which are contrast-engineering updates for patient records. In order to lower the risk of leaks, this emphasizes the necessity of privacy-preserving techniques like secure consolidation or differential privacy.

Model poisoning, in which hostile clients purposefully inject themselves into the opponent to taint the global model, is another significant problem. Model poisoning in FL seeks to guide the learning process, as opposed to conventional data poisoning attacks or altering central training data. Attackers could pose as the victim, take over the entire influence, introduce backdoors, or just skew the model to yield the intended outcomes. For instance, by "smuggling" credit scoring models in finance or forecasting demand in the supply chain, the attackers may be committing fraud in a business setting. It is still difficult to identify and reduce these anti-contributions, especially in large-scale, decentralized systems.

Freeloaders who attempt to take advantage of the global model without providing any useful updates can be a problem for federated learning. They can submit arbitrary or out-of-date grades, protecting local resources in the process, but they can still obtain successful global models. In addition to reducing training effectiveness, this raises concerns about the validity of the incentive design, particularly when cross-salo collaboration is involved and stakeholders may be rivals. Therefore, in order to maintain the integrity of the federated ecosystem, methods for identifying and freeing free riders are required.

In addition to the threat, FL faces systemic weaknesses rooted in the data's actuality. Consumers usually have non-IID datasets that are evenly distributed, non-loose, and represent differences in demographics, environmental factors, and business operations. This characteristic can slow down global model updates, decrease their accuracy, and raise concerns about the bias and fairness of the models, potentially disproportionately affecting minority groups. Take the example. In order to reduce these systemic risks, algorithmic innovations must be carefully evaluated for their moral and regulatory implications as well as for individual FL andness-painted-vague consolidation.

Although federated learning presents an alluring alternative to centralized machine learning, privacy and security issues still exist. Grade leakage threatens confidentiality, activates the model's poisoning power, creates free-rider problems, and puts systemic risks at risk. A multi-layered defense strategy that includes ness-painted vigilance designs, cryptographic protection, anti-lists, and incentive techniques is required to address these problems. Federated learning can only be trusted for data-driven business decisions when such comprehensive safeguards are in place.

Table 1. Security and privacy challenges in federated learning

Challenge	Threat Type	Description	Impact on FL	Possible Mitigation Strategies	Business Relevance
Gradient Leakage	Privacy Threat	Sensitive data can be inferred from shared gradients or model updates.	Breaches confidentiality of local datasets; violates privacy guarantees.	Differential Privacy (DP), Secure Aggregation, Homomorphic Encryption.	Risk of exposing patient health records in healthcare or customer transactions in finance.
Model Poisoning	Integrity Threat	Malicious clients inject adversarial or biased updates into training.	Degrades global model accuracy, introduces backdoors, or biases predictions.	Byzantine-robust aggregation, anomaly detection, and trust scoring mechanisms.	Could lead to fraudulent loan approvals, manipulated demand forecasts, or biased AI decisions.
Free-rider Problem	Incentive Misuse	Clients exploit the system by sending random/stale updates while benefiting.	Reduces training efficiency, wastes resources, and undermines the fairness of collaboration.	Contribution tracking, reputation systems, incentive-compatible protocols.	In a cross-silo setting, some partners may exploit shared AI models without contributing data.
Systemic Risks	Reliability Challenge	Cross-silo heterogeneity and non-IID data distributions cause bias and imbalance.	Slower convergence, reduced global accuracy, and unfair treatment of minority groups.	Personalization strategies, fairness-aware aggregation, and domain adaptation methods.	A healthcare FL model may underperform for underrepresented patient populations.
Communication Attacks	Security Threat	Adversaries intercept, alter, or replay model updates during transmission.	Data tampering, eavesdropping, or denial of service disrupts FL training.	Encrypted channels (TLS), secure multiparty computation, blockchain-based audit trails.	Financial institutions may face intercepted updates in cross-bank fraud detection models.
Inference Attacks	Privacy Threat	Adversaries use global model outputs to infer properties of participants' data.	Leakage of sensitive attributes without direct data access.	Membership inference defenses, differential privacy, secure aggregation.	Competitors might deduce market insights from aggregated retail models.
Scalability Bottlenecks	Operational Risk	High communication and computation overhead with large client populations.	Slows down training, increases cost, and limits deployment in large-scale systems.	Gradient compression, asynchronous updates, decentralized aggregation.	IoT networks with millions of devices face efficiency trade-offs.

4. SECURE FEDERATED LEARNING TECHNIQUES

In complex and business domains, federated learning (FL) requires robust methods to guarantee confidentiality, integrity, and reliability throughout the training process. By doing away with centralized data storage, FL lowers the chance of a single failure, but it also introduces a new set of vulnerabilities, including forecast risks, model inversion, grad leakage, poisoning attacks, and free-riding behaviors. These vulnerabilities become more evident with enterprise-scale deployment due to the additional attack surfaces produced by multiple communication channels, heterogeneous devices, and uneven data distributions.

Facilitate the use of cryptographic techniques such as Secure Multiparty Computation (SMPC), homomorphic encryption (HE), confidential computing, secure model updates, and consolidation without disclosing raw grades. Differential privacy (DP) and local differential privacy (LDP), two privacy-centric techniques, carefully present calibrated voice to guard against membership forecast or rebuilding attacks while preserving model utility. By using updates or waiting for updates based on dependability, parallel, robust consolidation techniques (such as Krum, well-organized Pisces, and Flust) seek to withstand backdoor and poison attacks.

Anti-defense tactics use responsibility and adaptive trust models to focus more on issues like free-riding, model theft, and anti-manipulation. A hybrid framework, which combines blockchain for transparency, explained for transparency, and adaptive layered-trust systems for real-time investigations of AI and contaminated contributions, is also advantageous for enterprise adoption. These strategies bring trade-offs in terms of overhead, communication expenses, scalability, and explanation when they improve FL.

According to enterprise-scale perspectives, implementing SFL is not just a technical decision but also a strategic professional one since it impacts consumer trust, operational elasticity, and compliance with data protection laws (such as GDPR and HIPAA). Consequently, evaluations of secure FL techniques should consider practical deployment factors such as compatibility with legacy infrastructure, computational efficiency on the same devices, and the long-term viability of privacy-saving techniques in addition to their theoretical strength.

4.1 Cryptographic Enhancements

In federated systems, cryptography offers a solid basis for safe collaboration, guaranteeing that computations can be carried out without disclosing private data.

- Protect Multi-Party Calculation (SMPC): SMPC distributes calculations to multiple parties, such that no participant can see another's data. In FL, this is usually achieved by secret distribution, where local model updates are divided into cryptographic shards that are distributed to multiple servers. Consolidation is done on shares, and the result is rebuilt without seeing a full update to any party. SMPC Privacy is very effective in saving, but often includes significant calculations and communication overheads, which challenge scalability for a large number of networks.
- **Homomorphic Encryption (HE):** Unlike SMPC, which requires multiple servers, HE allows operations to be carried out directly on encrypted data. For instance, clients can encrypt their gradient vectors before sending them, and the central server can perform weighted sums over these ciphertexts. The decrypted result corresponds to the aggregated gradient, without the server ever seeing the raw values. Fully Homomorphic Encryption (FHE) supports arbitrary computations

but is extremely resource-intensive, whereas *Partially Homomorphic Encryption (PHE)*, which supports limited operations such as addition, offers a practical balance. HE is particularly useful in financial and healthcare FL applications, where confidentiality is paramount.

- **Reliable Execution Environments (TEE):** TEEs are hardware-based secure enclaves embedded in processors that allow sensitive calculations to be secured, lonely atmosphere, even with the privileged system. In the FL, the tees enable the safe consolidation of the model updates within the enclave, preventing the attackers from tampering with or monitoring the process. When tees are efficient and practical, they depend on the hardware trust assumptions and remain susceptible to side-channel attacks.

Collectively, cryptographic enhancement strengthens FL's confidentiality but can introduce trade-offs in terms of efficiency, scalability, and cost of deployment.

4.2 Privacy Preservation

Privacy-to-lift techniques defend against estimated attacks that steal the data contained in model updates when cryptography ensures secure communication and computation.

- **Different Privacy (DP):** By making sure that no data point materially alters the training process's outcome, DP offers a mathematically sound framework for privacy. In real life, DP is implemented by applying calibrated sound to model dimensions or local Grad before sharing with the server. By doing this, adversaries are unable to contrast-engineer sensitive inputs. But too much noise can make the model less accurate, which is a well-known trade-off between privacy and usefulness.
- **Hybrid approaches (DP + H):** To reduce the limits of single DP, researchers suggest hybrid plans that combine DP with homomorphic encryption. Here, the Grad Dal is encrypted before transmission and will also be disturbed by the sound. This guarantees both the secrecy and personal privacy defense. Such hybrid models are especially suitable for cross-salo FL settings (eg, collaboration between hospitals or banks), where the breach of privacy is very high.
- **Client-Level DP vs record-level DP:** In a federated environment, DP can be applied to various granularities. Record-Level DP The client's dataset protects individual data templates, while the client-level DP protects the whole customer from separation. The selection of granularity depends on the application reference, with the strict guarantees required in healthcare and finance compared to consumer-level personalization functions.

Through these methods, FL can obtain compliance with privacy rules such as GDPR and HIPAA, while collaborative modeling maintains professional value.

4.3 Robustness and Defense Mechanisms

Even with strong cryptographic and privacy protections, federated learning remains susceptible to anti-manipulation and systemic risks. The purpose of strength-centered techniques is to save such threats.

- Zy Byzantine-Recorightments: Algorithms such as Krum, Treatment Pisces, and Median filters, or down-weight inconsistent client updates to reduce poisoning attacks. For example, Crum prefers the update closest to most other updates, excluding malicious outliers. The well-organized means discards the extreme values in the Grad Lord, while replacing the overall values to ensure moderate strength. These methods increase safety but can reduce efficiency when dealing with very heterogeneous data.

• Client Investigation on Client Updates: Instead of just relying on the rules of consolidation, inconsistent investigating methods use numerical or machine learning approaches to identify suspected client behavior. For instance, it is possible to identify and eliminate updates that are noticeably diverged from the expected distributions. The defense against targeted and steel poisoning attacks is strengthened by this ongoing investigation.

• Reputation-based trust models: Credibility weight is assigned by trust scoring mechanisms according to their historical background. Customers who consistently provide helpful updates are given more power in consolidation, whereas those with a history of malice or weakness are down-weighted or excluded. These models offer a technique for incentive alignment that discourages free-riding behavior and encourages sincere collaboration.

• Up Adaptive Personalisation: This personalisation technique enables the global model to adjust effectively to local circumstances, thereby mitigating systemic risks resulting from non-IID data. This decreases bias and inaccuracy in a variety of client groups while simultaneously increasing accuracy.

These techniques are becoming more and more crucial for ensuring ethical choices in business initiatives.

Table 2. Secure federated learning techniques, functions, and limitations

Category	Technique	Function	Advantages	Limitations/Challenges
Cryptographic Enhancements	**Secure Multi-Party Computation (SMPC)**	Enables multiple parties to jointly compute model updates without revealing raw data.	Strong privacy guarantees; prevents direct data leakage.	High computational cost; communication overhead.
	Homomorphic Encryption (HE)	Supports arithmetic operations directly on encrypted data/ updates.	Preserves confidentiality during aggregation; eliminates the need to decrypt before processing.	Extremely resource-intensive; limited scalability for deep models.
	Trusted Execution Environments (TEE)	Uses hardware-based secure enclaves to protect sensitive computations.	Provides strong security assurance with low cryptographic overhead.	Relies on hardware trust; potential vulnerabilities if hardware is compromised.
Privacy Preservation	**Differential Privacy (DP)**	Injects statistical noise into model updates before sharing.	Strong privacy with formal guarantees (ε-differential privacy).	Noise reduces accuracy; difficult trade-off between privacy and utility.
	Hybrid DP + HE Approaches	Combines noise addition with encryption to balance privacy and accuracy.	Achieves stronger confidentiality while maintaining higher accuracy.	Further increases complexity and computational cost.

continued on following page

Table 2. Continued

Category	Technique	Function	Advantages	Limitations/Challenges
Robustness and Defense Mechanisms	**Byzantine-resilient aggregation (Krum, Trimmed Mean, Median)**	Filters out malicious or extreme updates before aggregation.	Enhances robustness against poisoning and adversarial clients.	May exclude useful updates; performance drops with highly heterogeneous data.
	Anomaly Detection on Client Updates	Monitors updates for irregular patterns or adversarial manipulation.	Real-time detection of attacks; adaptable across settings.	Requires reliable detection thresholds; false positives are possible.
	Reputation-based Trust Models	Assigns trust scores to participants based on historical behavior.	Incentivizes honest contributions; discourages free-riders.	Risk of bias; susceptible to collusion among malicious participants.

5. STRATEGIC VALUE: BUSINESS DECISIONS WITH FEDERATED LEARNING

Companies compete in the contemporary digital economy based on a growing amount of data, as well as goods and services. However, raw data is usually sensitive, scattered across several organizations, or constrained by strict legal requirements. Companies can collaborate on machine learning projects without compromising data or privacy sovereignty thanks to the revolutionary Safe Federated Learning (FL) agreement.

One of the key strategic values, sovereignty, ensures that companies maintain total control and ownership of the datasets they own. This is crucial in industries like healthcare, finance, and telecommunications, where the protection of sensitive data is the foundation for trust and competitive advantage. Furthermore, Secure FL provides a collaborative advantage that enables competing companies to work together to create intelligence. For example, banks can collaborate to enhance disease diagnostic models and uphold strict confidentiality in fraud investigation models or hospitals.

Regulatory compliance is another complex driver. Despite data localization laws (e.g., the GDPR in Europe, the DPDP Act in India, or HIPAA in the US), federated learning organizations continue to allow the compliance command to benefit from collective insights. This significantly reduces the likelihood that a data breach will result in penalties or reputational damage. By releasing insights from silos that were previously unavailable due to privacy and confidentiality concerns, FL also accelerates innovation. This leads to the rapid development of new products, services, and market opportunities.

Secure FL builds enduring ecosystems in which users form data-driven alliances that are difficult for outsiders to enter. Businesses create powerful data motes that sustain competitive advantage, increase elasticity against disruption, and foster long-term innovation by integrating mass intelligence. By arranging privacy collaboratively and innovatively, secure federated learning data effectively resizes the foundation of data-driven business decisions. In the data-driven world, organizations are growing more regulated and positioned for expansion.

Figure 1. Strategic value of secure federated learning

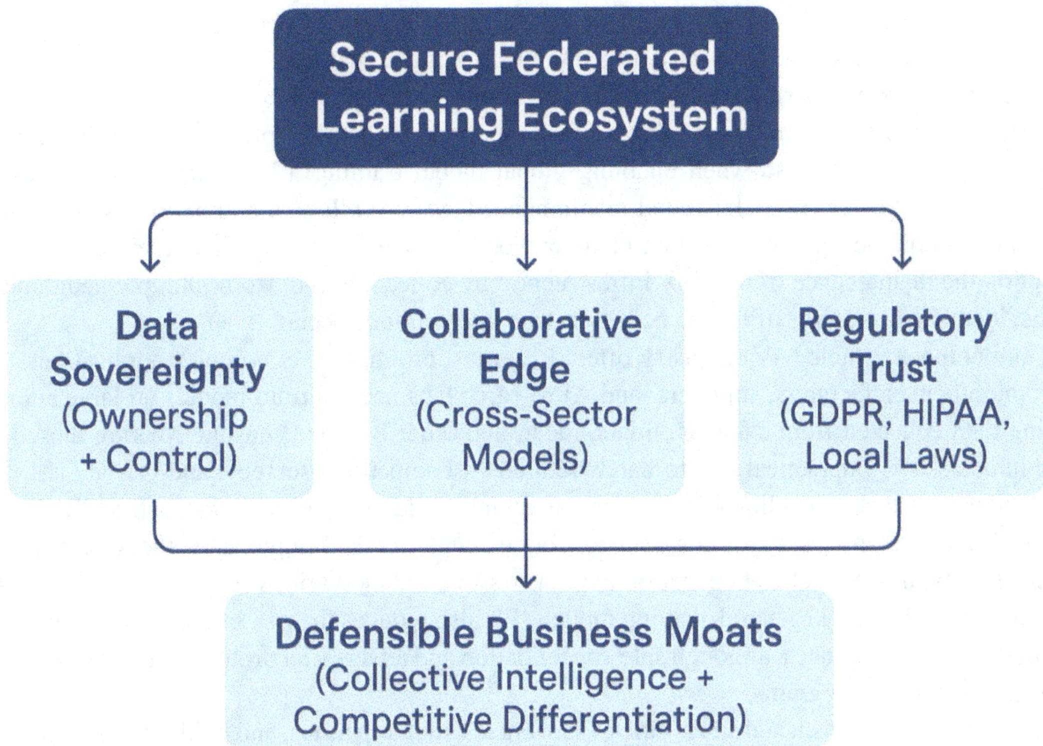

6. CASE STUDIES AND APPLICATIONS

Many industries have found great use for Secure Federated Learning (FL), which acts as a strategic facilitator of technological innovation and privacy. Multi-hospital collaboration in the healthcare industry has demonstrated how FL can transform clinical practice and medical research. For instance, federated approaches that train models on distributed or imaging data across institutional boundaries without transferring sensitive electronic health records have proven beneficial for COVID-19 investigation, brain tumor division, and cancer diagnostics. The US ensures compliance with rules such as GDPR, HIPAA, and European. FL also enables small hospitals and rural healthcare centers, which may have limited data to contribute to global models delo and benefit, diagnostic accuracy, and improve the patient's results. However, there are challenges in controlling data sexuality (eg, various imaging machines, formats, or population characteristics), which promote research in individual federated education.

In the financial sector, FL has been deployed in anti-money laundering (AML) systems and fraud investigation methods. Traditional central models struggle because banks are reluctant or legally unable to share sensitive transaction data. FL, banks, and financial institutions can cooperatively create models of investigations that identify cross-instant fraud patterns while maintaining the strict secrecy of consumers' data. For example, European banks' consortia have launched a framework for artificial identity fraud, credit card abuse, and money laundering across borders. The distributed nature of the FL makes it especially appropriate to fight anti-attacks, as inconsistencies seen in an organization can strengthen the ability of the global model forecast, without risking the contact of owned mathematical rules.

In telecommunications, operators have turned to FL to improve customer experience and operational efficiency. By analyzing distributed usage data, telecom companies can create models for churning, targeted marketing, and dynamic network optimization. Telecom datasets often span multiple regions and regulatory jurisdictions, so when enabling global model training, FL ensures compliance with local privacy laws. For example, federated recommended systems allow operators to always conform to personal entertainment bundles or data plans without focusing on raw behavioral data. Moreover, FL supports the maintenance of network infrastructure by collecting data from multiple geographical locations, identifying patterns of failure before service interruptions occur.

The autonomous vehicle (AV) industry offers FL's most promising yet complex applications. Various automobile manufacturers, suppliers, and AI research labs need to train models on large amounts of driving data collected from cameras, lidars, radar, and other Boarded sensors. Making these large ownership datasets is impractical due to bandwidth costs, competitive secrecy, and privacy risks. FL addresses these obstacles by allowing cross-manufacturer collaboration on tasks such as FL Burject Detection, Route planning, and avoiding collision. For example, Tesla, Waimo, and other companies are experimenting with decentralized education approaches to combine various road scenes - from urban crowds to rural highways, in general, driving models. FL also reduces the risk of data poisoning attacks by localizing sensitive updates, although safe consolidation and adversarial protection are AV. Required for such safety-making programs.

In the fields of government and smart cities, FL agencies, municipalities, and public service providers are enabling collaborative innovation. Governments can take advantage of federated models for prediction policing, disaster response, traffic flow optimization, and energy grid forecasts without exposing sensitive civil data. For example, federated traffic management systems integrate data from different districts to pt over urban mobility, reduce congestion, and cut emissions, while complying with privacy guarantees. Similarly, public health agencies can manage the modeling of predictive epidemics, analyzing infected data distributed in regions using FL, identifying the outbreak trends without revealing sensitive personal information. The shared forecasting structure also benefits the smart city infrastructure by integrating various datasets from IoT sensors, utility companies, and transport officials.

In these industries, FL provides not only technical benefits but also a strategic shift in collaboration models. It enables competitors, regulators, and service providers to combine the trust, promoting trust, without compromising the data of ownership, and accelerating progress. Communication overhead, non-IID (non-independence and similarly distributed) model conversion, strength against rival customers, and the requirement for interoperability standards are some of the challenges it faces concurrently. Together, this case study demonstrates that FL is not only a privacy-preserving solution but also a cross-sector innovation catalyst that sets the stage for scalable, secure, and ethical AI in the digital era. Communication overhead, non-IID (non-independence and similarly distributed) model conversion, strength against rival customers, and the requirement for interoperability standards are some of the challenges it faces concurrently. Together, this case study demonstrates that FL is not only a privacy-preserving solution but also a cross-sector innovation catalyst that sets the stage for scalable, secure, and ethical AI in the digital era.

Table 3. Comparative case study

Sector	Use Case	Benefits	Challenges
Healthcare	Multi-hospital medical imaging collaboration	Enhanced diagnostic accuracy, privacy compliance (HIPAA, GDPR), and access to diverse datasets	Data heterogeneity, communication costs, and regulatory alignment across regions
Finance	Fraud and anti-money laundering detection	Collective intelligence, reduced systemic risks, and compliance with data laws.	Competition concerns, model fairness, adversarial attacks
Telecom	Customer churn prediction, network optimization	Improved customer retention, network demand forecasting, and operational efficiency	Device diversity, communication latency, and edge constraints
Autonomous Vehicles	Cross-company safe driving model training	Safer models, rare-event scenario sharing, accelerated AV development	Proprietary data protection, high-dimensional sensor data
Smart Cities / Government	Traffic flow prediction, disaster management, energy optimization	Data-driven governance, privacy-preserving citizen services, and improved trust	Inter-agency data silos, standardization issues, and cybersecurity risks

The figure illustrates how various industries, including healthcare, finance, telecommunications, autonomous vehicles, and smart cities, function as nodes within the federated ecosystem. In order to ensure privacy-imaginary intelligence, each field shares model updates (not RAW data) in the Central Federated Framework. By demonstrating the flow of the arrow domains, the bilateral Junowledge enhances mass education while maintaining data security.

Figure 2. Cross-sector applications of secure federated learning

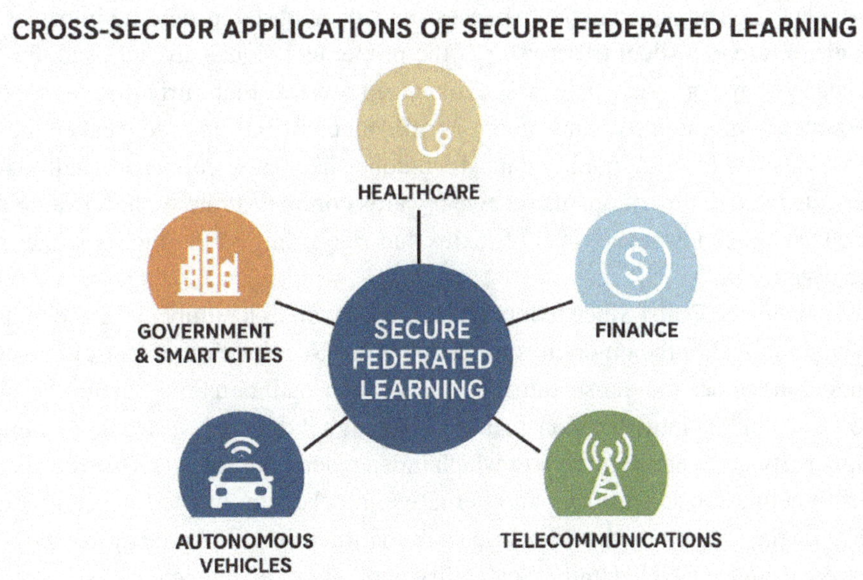

7. IMPLEMENTATION CONSIDERATIONS

The design, technology, economics, and regulations for implementing secure federated learning (FL) are all multifaceted in real-world business and cross-sector ecosystems. The system's scalability, dependability, and long-term stability are all directly impacted by these factors.

System design: The choice between the cross-device FL and the cross-silo FL is crucial at the architectural level. Through the collection of updates from millions of edge devices, including smartphones, Internet of Things sensors, and autonomous vehicles, Cross-device FL offers unparalleled data variations and real-time adaptability. However, its shortcomings include limited computation power, high device churn, and inconsistent network connectivity. By the way, the Cross-Salo FL is home to a smaller number of more important organizations, such as hospitals, financial institutions, and government agencies. This model faces challenges to competition and trust because companies are hesitant to share the strategic advantages of knowledge, even though it is more stable and resource-rich. Because they relieve institutional collaboration and edge-level personalization, patterns are assisting hybrid architects in gaining traction.

Scalability: FL systems must be able to support millions of users without requiring a substantial computational and communication infrastructure. Stragglers or slow participants are often the cause of problems with traditional synchronous consolidation strategies, which require all participants to finish training prior to consolidation. These issues are lessened by asynchronous updates as well as hierarchy consolidation, in which local consolidations gather results before sending them to the global model. Techniques such as compression, quantification, and dissolution of updates help lower bandwidth requirements, while adaptive partnerships enable dynamic inclusion based on customers' availability and resource status. Additionally, Edge-Cloud orchestration can balance computation loads, reduce delays, and improve fault tolerance.

Encouraging Techniques: Incentives for long-term collaborations, particularly in industries with intense competition, ought to be connected to the expenses and advantages of providing information and assets. Data may decide to forego a silent partnership if the proper techniques are not used. Financial returns, reputation-based systems, or blockchain-based tokenized rewards that fairly distribute contributors are some of the strategies. Importantly, since poor or anti-data contributions can weaken the global model, incentives should also be for high-quality data. Techniques like trust scores and quality-sponsored consolidation can guarantee that participants receive rewards commensurate with the value of their contributions. These techniques lower the risks of toxins and free-riding in the model while simultaneously increasing the need for pain.

Models of Governance Dells: Since federated learning involves a number of stakeholders, the governance framework establishes the guidelines for cooperation. A collection of institutions works together to oversee operations under the consortium-led rule, which maintains the balance of power but runs the risk of slow and bureaucratic decision-making. Although it demands a strong guarantee of fairness, the neutral third-party governance model, in which independent facilities oversee the consolidation and policy implementation, boosts trust. As an alternative, blockchain-enabled decentralized governance lessens reliance on the Central Authority while enabling the rule's implementation through smart contracts, transparency, and AUDIT details. Scalability and energy efficiency are issues with blockchain integration, though. Legal experts must be consulted because governance decisions also affect data sovereignty, regulatory compliance (such as GDPR and HIPAA), and ethical AI practices.

Security and Privacy Trade-S FS: While FL relies heavily on security and privacy-saving methods such as homomorphic encryption, protective privacy, and secure multi-party computation, their computations may restrict real-time deployment, particularly in cross-device scenarios. A balanced approach is needed, with mild methods being adequate in less sensitive domains and strong privacy guarantees being applied in high-risk references (such as healthcare and money). Additionally, both technical structural and governed protocols should be built with elasticity against anti-attacks (such as model poisoning, backdoors, and information attacks).

Durability and long-term adoption: Lastly, organizing FL with social, environmental, and economic objectives is the foundation of long-term adoption. To lessen the carbon footprint of large-scale FL, an energy-efficient training protocol is essential. For various bodies, platforms, and devices to collaborate, professional ecosystems must guarantee interoperability and standardization. Furthermore, the secret to dispelling skepticism and guaranteeing comparable advantages for stakeholders is to foster user trust via accountability, transparency, and explanation.

8. OPEN CHALLENGES AND RESEARCH DIRECTIONS

Despite its promise, a safe federated learning (FL) still faces many open challenges and research boundaries that must be addressed in the industry before large-scale, trusted adoption. First, standardization is an important barrier. Unlike traditional machine learning pipelines, where data and models can be concentrated under controlled formats, FL includes very heterogeneous structures, data formats, and communication protocols. The absence of universal interoperability standards makes cross-organizational cooperation difficult, leading to the deployment. Developing global standards, benchmarking protocols, and a compliance framework will be crucial to organizing research with real-world deployment.

Second, there is a constant efficiency-chalkness trade. While cryptographic techniques such as homomorphic encryption, secure multiparty calculation (SMC), and differential privacy strengthen secrecy, they often reduce significant count overheads, slow conversion, and accuracy. Future research must focus on lightweight cryptography, adaptive sound calibration, and communication-efficient protocols that protect privacy without performing.

Third, there is still a problem with handling heterogeneous data. Non-relaxation and similarly distributed (non-IID) data are frequently encountered in real-world FL deployment, where customer demographics, device capabilities, and data quality can vary greatly. Amplification, unstable model conversion, and unnecessary pain concerns are all consequences of such sexual prejudice. Although scalable and dependable techniques are still being developed, emerging solutions like individual federated learning, clustering-based consolidation, and transfer learning integration demonstrate their promise.

Fourth, there is the huge challenge of guaranteeing anti-elasticity. Attackers may attempt to alter private information or use techniques like data poisoning, backdoor inserts, guess attacks, or model vers. While the current defense mechanisms (strong consolidation rules, inconsistent investigations, byzantine-rashilliant algorithms) offer some protection, they necessitate the development of a security framework that is anti-landscape adaptive, active, and self-healing to withstand complex multi-vector attacks.

Ultimately, combining secure FL with cutting-edge technologies creates an intriguing yet challenging research avenue. Consolidation with Edge AI, for instance, can enable real-time on-device intelligence without depending on cloud resources, while connecting FL with quantum computing can reveal new patterns of ultra-secure cryptographic operations. Similar benefits include decentralized confidence, permanent Audit Dit trails, and incentive configuration when blockchain is integrated into FL governance; however, issues with energy efficiency and mismanagement are raised.

9. FUTURE OUTLOOK

SFL has the potential to revolutionize the global data economy. Through SFL, companies can create long-lasting competitive advantages often referred to as data motes by facilitating collaborative intelligence without sacrificing privacy or data ownership. In contrast to conventional centralized AI models, SFL offers a means of mass innovation while respecting the operational, ethical, and legal limits of data use.

SFL AI is anticipated to evolve from a specialized research area into the primary structural component of AI ecosystems in the upcoming years. It is particularly well-suited for sectors like healthcare, finance, energy, and government operations where sensitive and dispersed datasets are commonplace due to its capacity to allay growing worries about data sovereignty, digital trust, and regulatory compliance. Moreover, its integration with the same computing, blockchain governance models, and quantum-safety security protocols will further improve its scalability and elasticity. Companies that adopt SFL would be better positioned strategically to benefit from mass intelligence without compromising privacy or accelerating the innovation cycle. Small businesses and cross-sector partnerships will be able to compete with the tech giants thanks to the democratization of AI and their access to large datasets. Frameworks for standardization and interoperability will also be essential to guaranteeing cross-border and cross-industry integrated cooperation.

SFL is, after all, a social-technical change as well as a technical innovation that is safe, distributed, and valuable in the digital economy. By striking a balance between innovation and the dual inevitability of defense, a secure federated education will emerge as the foundation of AI, making confidence the currency of the future pay-generation data landscape. Fuel, public-private partnerships, and the global adoption of moral AI are its future cross-industry ecosystems.

10. CONCLUSION

Secure federated learning (SFL) was presented in this chapter as a technical trend and a strategic necessity for businesses operating in the data economy. Cutting-edge cryptographic techniques combine collaborative machine intelligence and privacy-saving strategies to benefit distributed data ecosystems without sacrificing control over SFL.

SFL was created to resolve a long-standing conflict between data protection and data utilities. By leaking data and undermining unregulated customer trust, traditional central AI architectures introduce vulnerabilities. SFL protects both individual privacy and institutional sovereignty by ensuring that data stays local even as intelligence becomes global. As a result, there is an architectural change that allows organizations to achieve both compliance and competitiveness without having to choose between the two. From a business strategy perspective, SFL offers the framework for establishing a sustainable data pace, encompassing not only ownership data but also organizational and industrial dysfunctional inactivity and aggressive benefits within the national boundary.

Cross-sector innovation consortia allow the government, healthcare, financial, and transportation sectors to safely share intelligence, potentially achieving success that would be impossible for any one organization to achieve alone. Thus, SFL is about more than just data protection; it's about redefining the economics of collaboration in the digital age. The conversion of a number of state-of-the-art innovations, such as homomorphic encryption, secure multiparty computation, differential privacy, blockchain-enabled audit detailability, and Edge AI acceleration, forms the technical foundation of SFL. Together, these technologies serve as the cornerstone of a trust-focused AI infrastructure. Prior to SFL, an unmatched guarantee of ethics, responsibility, and transparency in the collaborative AI, zero-joweltge evidence, hardware security modules, and quantum-resistant cryptography will be developed.

SFL data is coupled with the increasing social and policy demands for moral AI, responsible innovation, and sovereignty. SFL enables businesses to be smart and up to date while participating in the global AI movement in a world driven by laws like GDPR, HIPAA, and new AI acts. Furthermore, it makes AI democratic by enabling small players—startups, educational institutions, and local businesses—to access collective intelligence without revealing their intellectual property.

As industries embrace federated markets and interoperable AI networks, SFL is expected to become the foundation of the digital ecosystems for the next generation of pay generation. Along with protecting the competitive strategy, it will be crucial in fostering adaptable, integrated, and morally grounded innovation. Businesses that have implemented SFL now will be better positioned to prosper in the future, when the most valuable resources will be faith, cooperation, and intelligence.

REFERENCES

Buttyán, L., & Hubaux, J.-P. (2007). *Security and Cooperation in Wireless Networks*. Cambridge University Press. DOI: 10.1017/CBO9780511815102

. Chen, X., Zhao, H., & Wang, J. (2022). *FLTrustExplain: Explainable and Robust Federated Aggregation Mechanism. ACM TOPS, 25.*

. Cheon, J. H., Kim, A., Kim, M., & Song, Y. (2017). *Homomorphic Encryption for Arithmetic of Approximate Numbers.*

Collingwood, L. (2017). Privacy Implications and Liability Issues of Autonomous Vehicles. *Information & Communications Technology Law*, *26*(1), 32–45. DOI: 10.1080/13600834.2017.1269871

. Dayan, I., Roth, H. R., Zhong, A., et al. (2021). *Federated learning for predicting clinical outcomes in patients with COVID-19. Nature Medicine.*

. Diao, E., Ding, J., & Tarokh, V. (2020). *HeteroFL: Computation and Communication Efficient Federated Learning for Heterogeneous Clients.*

. Geyer, R. C., et al. (2018). *Differentially Private Federated Learning: A Client-Level Perspective.*

Hubaux, J.-P.. (2021). Truly Privacy-Preserving Federated Analytics for Precision Medicine with Multiparty Homomorphic Encryption. *Nature Communications.*

. Jin, W., Yao, Y., Han, S., et al. (2023). *FedML-HE: An Efficient Homomorphic-Encryption-Based Privacy-Preserving Federated Learning System.* arXiv.

. Kairouz, P., McMahan, H. B., Avent, B., et al. (2019). *Advances and Open Problems in Federated Learning*. arXiv.

Karargyris, A., Umeton, R., Sheller, M. J., Aristizabal, A., George, J., Wuest, A., Pati, S., Kassem, H., Zenk, M., Baid, U., Narayana Moorthy, P., Chowdhury, A., Guo, J., Nalawade, S., Rosenthal, J., Kanter, D., Xenochristou, M., Beutel, D. J., Chung, V., & Mattson, P. (2023). Federated Benchmarking of Medical Artificial Intelligence with MedPerf. *Nature Machine Intelligence*, *5*(7), 799–810. DOI: 10.1038/s42256-023-00652-2

Khramtsova, E., Hammerschmidt, C., Lagraa, S., & State, R. (2020). *Federated Learning For Cyber Security: SOC Collaboration For Malicious URL Detection*. IEEE ICDCS.

. Konečný, J., McMahan, H. B., Ramage, D., & Richtárik, P. (2016). *Federated Optimization: Distributed Machine Learning Beyond the Datacenter.*

. Konečný, J., McMahan, H. B., Yu, F. X., et al. (2017). *Federated Learning: Strategies for Improving Communication Efficiency.*

Liu, Y., Zhang, Y., & Yu, H. (2022). XFed: Explainable Federated Learning for Intrusion Detection in Edge Networks. *IEEE Internet of Things Journal*, *9*, 4490–4503.

Liu, Z., Yang, C., Ding, Y., Liang, H., & Wang, Y. (2025). A Lightweight and Accuracy-Lossless Privacy-Preserving Method in Federated Learning. *IEEE Internet of Things Journal, 12*(3), 3118–3129. DOI: 10.1109/JIOT.2024.3478208

. McCall, A. (2025). *Federated Learning in Cloud Environments: Privacy-Preserving Collaborative AI Training Across Distributed Data Sources.*

. McMahan, H. B., Moore, E., Ramage, D., et al. (2016). *Federated Optimization: Distributed Machine Learning for On-Device Intelligence.*

Mothukuri, V., Parizi, R., Pouriyeh, S., Huang, Y., Dehghantanha, A., & Srivastava, G. (2021). A Survey on Security and Privacy of Federated Learning. *Future Generation Computer Systems, 115*, 619–640. DOI: 10.1016/j.future.2020.10.007

. Nguyen, D. C., et al. (2021). *Federated Learning for Smart Healthcare: A Survey.* arXiv.

. Nguyen, D. C., Pham, Q.-V., Pathirana, P. N., et al. (2021). *Federated Learning for Smart Healthcare: A Survey.* arXiv.

Parno, B., McCune, J. M., & Perrig, A. (2010). Trusted Computing Foundations. *IEEE Security and Privacy.*

Popli, M. S., Singh, R. P., Popli, N. K., & Mamun, M. (2025). A Federated Learning Framework for Enhanced Data Security and Cyber Intrusion Detection in Distributed Network of Underwater Drones. *IEEE Access : Practical Innovations, Open Solutions, 13*, 12634–12646. DOI: 10.1109/ACCESS.2025.3530499

Pribadi Kalapaaking, A., Khalil, I., & Yi, X. (2023). *Blockchain-based Federated Learning with SMPC Model Verification Against Poisoning Attack for Healthcare Systems.* arXiv.

Rahdari, A., Keshavarz, E., Nowroozi, E., Taheri, R., Hajizadeh, M., Mohammadi, M., Sinaei, S., & Bauschert, T. (2025). A Survey on Privacy and Security in Distributed Cloud Computing: Exploring Federated Learning and Beyond. *IEEE Open Journal of the Communications Society, 6*, 3710–3744. DOI: 10.1109/OJCOMS.2025.3560034

Rieke, N., Hancox, J., & Li, W.. (2020). The Future of Digital Health with Federated Learning. npj. *Digital Medicine.*

Truex, S., Liu, L., Gursoy, M. E., et al. (2020). *A Hybrid Approach to Privacy-Preserving Federated Learning. ACM AISec.*

Vaikuntanathan, V. (2017). *Homomorphic Encryption Foundations and Generations.*

Wang, H., Xu, Z., Zhang, Y., & Wang, Y. (2025). *Adaptive Layered-Trust Robust Defense Mechanism for Personalized Federated Learning. ICASSP 2025.*

Xu, J., Peng, C., Li, R., Fu, J., & Luo, M. (2025). An Efficient Delegatable Order-Revealing Encryption Scheme for Multi-User Range Queries. *IEEE Transactions on Cloud Computing, 13*(1), 75–86. DOI: 10.1109/TCC.2024.3506614

Zhang, Z., Wu, L., Jin, J., Wang, E., Liu, B., & Han, Q.-L. (2025). Secure Federated Learning for Cloud-Fog Automation: Vulnerabilities, Challenges, Solutions, and Future Directions. *IEEE Transactions on Industrial Informatics*, *21*(5), 3528–3540. DOI: 10.1109/TII.2025.3528569

Zhao, P., Zhang, G., Wan, S., Liu, G., & Umer, T. (2020). A Survey of Local Differential Privacy for Securing Internet of Vehicles. *The Journal of Supercomputing*, *76*(11), 8391–8412. DOI: 10.1007/s11227-019-03104-0

Zhao, Y., Zhao, J., & Yang, M.. (2020). *Local Differential Privacy based Federated Learning for Internet of Things*. IEEE IoT Journal.

Zheng, Z., Zhou, Y., Sun, Y., et al. (2021). *Applications of Federated Learning in Smart Cities: Recent Advances, Taxonomy, and Open Challenges*. arXiv.

Zhu, C. (2025). Blockchain-Enhanced Federated Learning for Secure and Intelligent Consumer Electronics: An Overview. *IEEE Consumer Electronics Magazine*.

Chapter 17
A Unified Examination of Data Poisoning Across Government, Retail, Transportation, Environmental, and Educational Systems

Firoj Ahamad
Galgotias University, India

Manju Lata Joshi
https://orcid.org/0009-0007-9053-3888
Poornima University, India

ABSTRACT

Data poisoning is a growing threat to machine learning systems that rely on external or continuously updated data. While prior work highlights risks in healthcare, finance, and IoT, this chapter broadens the scope to government and public-sector records, retail and e-commerce platforms, transportation and geospatial services, and environmental or educational systems. We outline core threat models and attack surfaces, distinguishing between dataset-level, point-level, streaming, and online-learning poisoning. A cross-domain taxonomy and case studies illustrate realistic attack vectors such as manipulated civic submissions, fake product reviews, traffic spoofing, sensor corruption, and compromised assessment data. We further examine black-box and clean-label poisoning, along with current detection and mitigation approaches and governance implications for organizations using large-scale public datasets. The chapter offers a unified view of poisoning risks and provides guidance for improving resilience across data pipelines.

1. INTRODUCTION

Data poisoning attacks, intentional corruption of training datasets - have emerged as a critical concern across machine learning applications (Schwarzschild et al., 2020). While substantial research has focused

DOI: 10.4018/979-8-3373-6224-3.ch017

on the healthcare, finance, and Internet of Things (IoT) sectors, several other domains also have exhibited significant vulnerabilities and real world incidents. To investigate the state of such attacks beyond existing case studies, this work compiles representative case studies from the government, public sector, retail, e-commerce, transportation, geospatial data, environmental monitoring, climate data, educational technology, and assessment sectors. Across domains, the lack of systematic data integrity controls creates opportunities for adversaries to manipulate datasets and influence downstream analytics. Across domains such as government services, public repositories, retail platforms, transportation networks, and environmental systems, the operational structures differ markedly, yet the underlying vulnerability remains the same: machine-learning pipelines depend heavily on externally sourced or continuously updated data streams. The following sections therefore shift from general principles to a structured examination of threat models and attack surfaces, before presenting domain-specific poisoning manifestations.

2. METHODOLOGICAL FOUNDATIONS OF DATA POISONING

Data poisoning attacks manipulate a proportion of a model's training data, and are among the most harmful and widely applicable threats (Schwarzschild et al., 2020). They can be mounted on data collected continuously from sources such as websites, social networks, and knowledge sharing platforms, or on static sets that are widely shared for academia or professional activities. The laws of supply and demand, including price trends and sales forecasts, govern retail and e commerce systems (Wang & Chaudhuri, 2018). Economic indicators, product characteristics, supplier prices and reputations, and fulfillment service performance influence those elements, making their prediction foundational to managing supply chains effectively.

2.1. Threat Models and Attack Surfaces

Data poisoning attacks target the integrity of training (and, less frequently, test) datasets. They alter the dataset used to train or evaluate machine learning models, resulting in the models producing incorrect outputs and predictions upon deployment. Poisoning attacks are classified into two categories based on the attack surface, namely, (1) poisoning at dataset level in which the model observes the poisoned dataset during the training phase and (2) poisoning at data point level in which the model observes the clean dataset during training and a set of poisoned data points at inference. Biggio & Roli (2018) proposed foundational definitions of adversarial manipulation including data poisoning, making it ideal to support your threat-model introduction (Biggio & Roli, 2018).

There are three threat models that adversaries can use to undertake their goals. The first is the full trust model, which is applicable in case of the access to the dataset by the adversary, either publicly or by an online platform or repository. The second one is model restricted model, where the adversary has no direct access to model parameters, but is allowed to use a number of tools e.g., model architectures and public checkpoints. The third one is query restricted model, where the adversary is given access to the uncorrupted training data, but with a restricted number of poisoning queries.

Figure 1. Unified cross-domain attack surface map

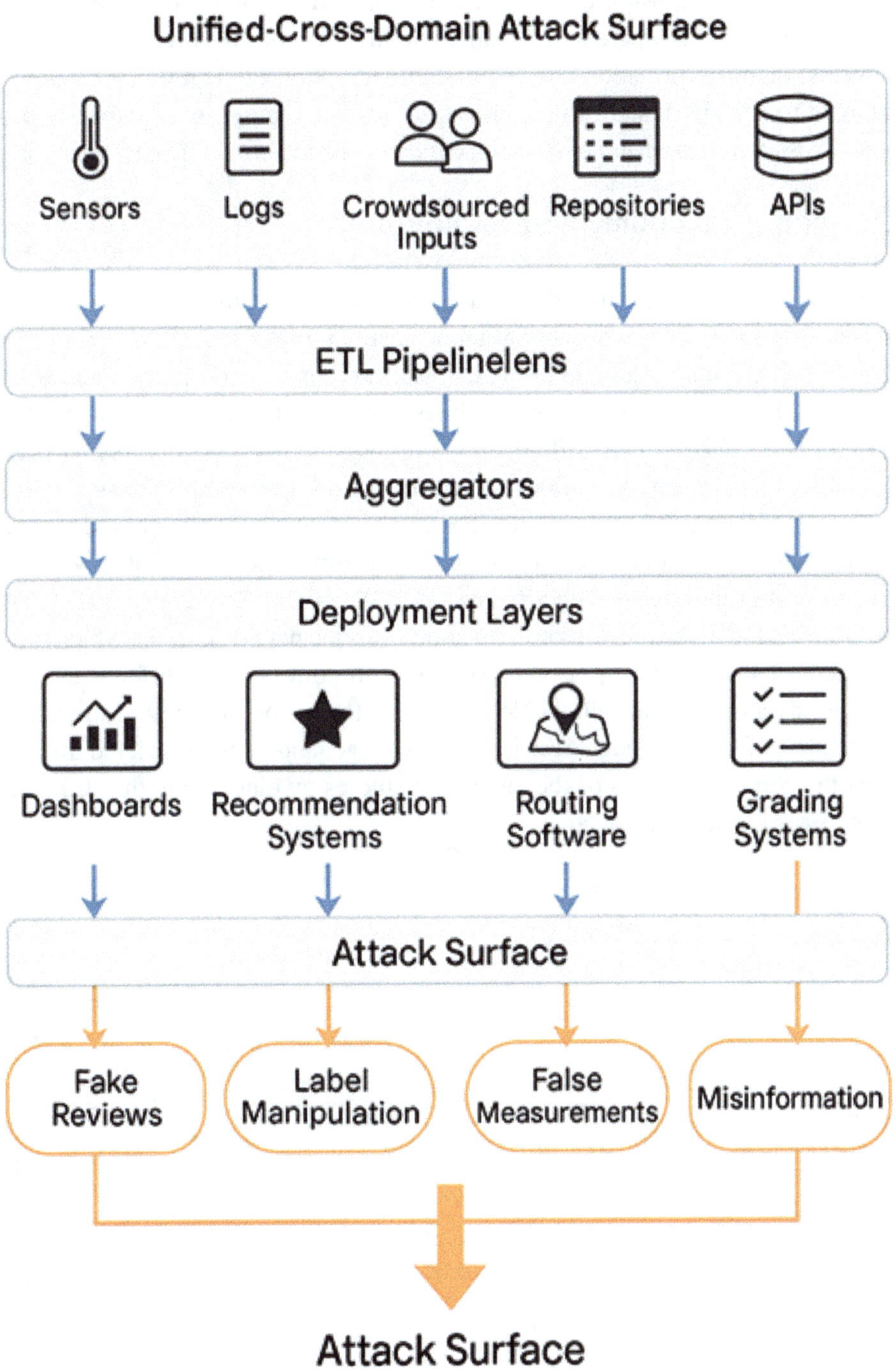

This Figure 1 shows the key data ingestion channels, processing tiers, and deployment destinations prone to poisoning in various areas. It brings out the heterogeneous nature of sources including sensors, logs, crowd sourced inputs, repositories, and APIs are passed through ETL pipelines and aggregate systems to downstream systems where attacks can be in the form of fake reviews, manipulating labels, false measurements, or misinformation. An integrated perception of such threat models is necessary since the contemporary standards show that both dataset-level and point-level poisoning are practical to be implemented across a vast spectrum of model architectures and domains (Schwarzschild et al., 2020).

2.2. Data Poisoning Taxonomy and Techniques

Different methods of data poisoning exist based on the type of manipulation by the attacker on the whole dataset, subsets of data or sequential input in streaming systems. Poisoning in static data is achieved by modifying the data available in the database and in streaming applications it is exercised by the attacker through continuous ingestion pipelines triggering the incorporation of altered samples over time (Jagielki et al., 2018). This difference is the foundation of the comprehension of domain-specific vulnerability to poisoning in various industries including retail platforms, civic repositories, transportation logs, environmental sensors, and educational systems. Systems based on online learning are especially susceptible as an attacker can manipulate sequential updates and slowly change the model behavior without evoking immediate detection systems (Wang and Chaudhuri, 2018). The taxonomy (Figure 2) also coincides with the previous unified attack-surface map (Figure 1), which further supports the structural differences between the poisoning strategies. It points out the differences between attacks that ensure that the adversary works with whole datasets, with data points, or with streaming inputs, and additional differentiates full-knowledge, restricted-knowledge, and query-restricted threat models. The taxonomy offers the conceptual basis of the latter case studies by elucidating the structural disparities among poisoning strategies across domains.

Figure 2. General taxonomy of data poisoning attacks

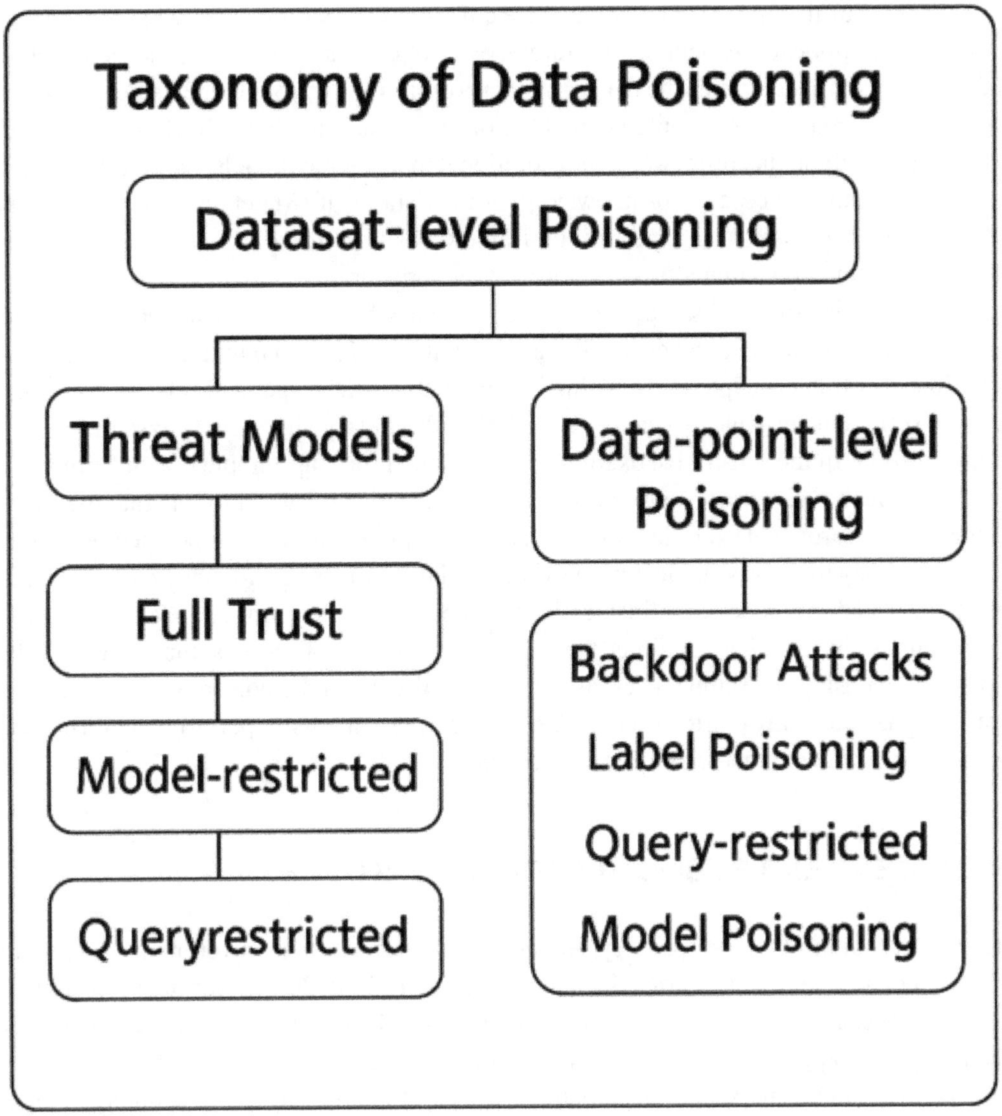

Even after deployment, data poisoning attacks are still active. When several training processes are based on the same dataset, a limited size of a poisoning point can affect all downstream models that use the same source of data.

2.3. Evaluation Metrics and Experimental Frameworks

Data poisoning is a pertinent threat to machine learning systems, especially on large datasets. The fact that the possibilities of manipulation techniques are quite numerous means that what has been tested in one area may not be applicable to another. Therefore, experimental designs and assessment techniques in the domain can be used to determine the danger of data poisoning in various contexts. Although proposed methodologies exist, many do not apply beyond the original datasets. The collection of data poisoning benchmarks expands upon this framework with additional metrics and models, facilitating cross domain analysis without requiring access to or knowledge of the data itself (Ma et al., 2019). Throughout the case studies analyzed, datasets and experimental frameworks from these sources establish a principled foundation for studying poisoning attacks in a variety of applications.

A small number of poisoned samples can shift the classifier's decision boundary, causing other classes to move away from the target class (Steinhardt et al., 2017). A maximum of k influence poisoning attack illustrates this principle by choosing components of the target and reference classes whose samples exert sufficient influence to cause an undesired boundary shift (Schwarzschild et al., 2020 ; Koh & Liang, 2017). In the illustrative example of a poisoned training sample drawn from a fifty class dataset with samples equally drawn across each class, the classifier learned to separate the fifty classes based on the average sample of each class, which can be interpreted through the perspective of influence. Such an effect massively drives the influence of other classes in straightforward models, while under contemporary foundation models, the influential concept surrounding image space has turned fundamentally intangible. In this view, to directly define a small subset of either samples outside the target class or pixels composing the sample itself as damaging shifts from the poisoning perspective. Even in large datasets, small carefully crafted sets of poisoned samples can disproportionately influence model decision boundaries and degrade classifier performance.

3. GOVERNMENT AND PUBLIC SECTOR CASE STUDIES

Prioritizing accountability, transparency, and other essential values in government and public sector decision making and operations is crucial (Schwarzschild et al., 2020). Government datasets directly influence policy decisions, resource allocation, and public services; therefore, any poisoning or contamination can result in inappropriate administrative actions or misinformed policies. Government datasets are largely accessed and analyzed online, creating exposure to deliberate misinformation and data poisoning attacks. Consequently, datasets deposited in repositories like data.gov and civic data platforms like civicdata.us and open city data are vulnerable. Datasets used in government funding and economic assessments and related evaluations, such as public service analyses, are frequently compromised. Openly shared political content and disinformation, often seen on social media, also facilitates interference with election activities, campaign initiatives, and activities or representation. Attackers may introduce false content on political candidates, legislation, and policies. Further insights on government and public sector data poisoning are examined in the following sections.

Real-world incidents of data poisoning extend across multiple sectors, each exhibiting unique vulnerabilities and attack modalities. To provide a concise overview of these affected domains, Figure 3 summarizes representative categories of poisoning activity observed in politics, retail, transportation, and education prior to the detailed case studies presented in this section.

Figure 3. Real-world case studies of data poisoning across multiple domains

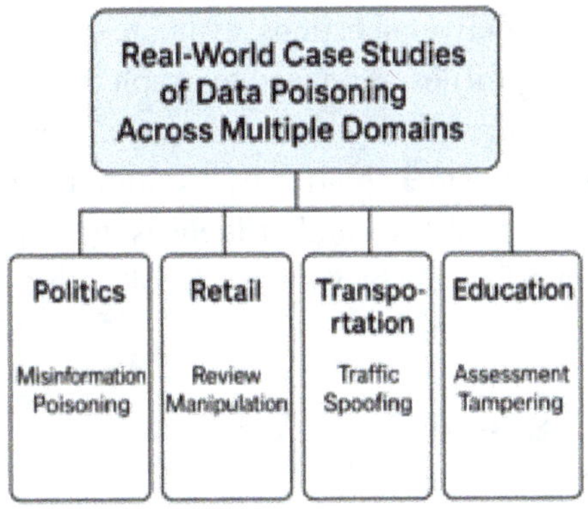

To contextualize the diversity of poisoning incidents across different sectors, Table 1 summarizes the major domains affected, the corresponding attack vectors, and their observed real-world impacts. This comparative overview bridges the high-level illustration in Figure 2 with the detailed case studies that follow in subsequent subsections.

Table 1. Cross-domain overview of real-world data poisoning attacks

Domain	Attack Vector	Type of Poisoning	Observed Impact
Government & Public Sector	Manipulated civic data submissions	Data integrity poisoning	Misleading economic indicators, incorrect policy decisions
Politics & Social Media	Misinformation injection, bot-generated content	Label/content poisoning	Public opinion distortion, election interference
Retail & E-Commerce	Fake reviews, adversarial rating manipulation	Behavioral & feature poisoning	Wrong product recommendations, revenue shifts
Transportation	Spoofed traffic signals, fake GPS traces	Spatiotemporal poisoning	Route misguidance, increased congestion
Environmental Monitoring	Fake sensor readings, anomalous submissions	Sensor and measurement poisoning	False pollution alerts, misallocation of resources
Education Technology	Altered assessments, poisoned feedback	Label poisoning	Misleading student profiles, degraded learning analytics

3.1. Educational Assessment Platforms

Real-world data poisoning extends far beyond heavily studied domains such as healthcare, finance, and the Internet of Things. Blended learning models are now supported by the use of educational technologies, which have become common in the conditions of the COVID 19 pandemic. Nonetheless, methods of data gathering on student performance like educational assessment systems are still under research. Machine learning models used in educational assessment take into account pedagogical elements, although the issues of predictions and implications of the models remain. Targeted attacks based on data poisoning may undermine internal mechanisms, model integrity and data provenance.

Educational assessment platforms deliver questions, evaluate student responses, and generate reports that construct knowledge graphs or profiles. Knowledge graph vertices represent students, questions, areas to help, and topics linked to correct or incorrect answers. Knowledge prediction emerges as an active research topic in educational assessment platforms. Contaminating either question answer pairs or teacher annotations steers knowledge prediction and influences the associated knowledge graph. Access to the application programming interface enables alteration of both question answer pairs and teacher annotations (Orekondy et al., 2020).

3.2. Public Data Repositories and Civic Data

Public data repositories serve as valuable resources for promoting transparency in governance, facilitating citizen participation in urban development, and enhancing predictive modeling of economic and healthcare systems (Bhattacharjee & Dasgupta, 2023). However, when civic engagement increases, there is a risk of the incorporation of false or misleading data. Open aggregated databases, such as city datasets or PM2.5 levels recorded by local sensors stored in public repositories, also offer the potential for copying, falsification, or selfish reporting. The free availability of datasets acquired from various sources enables re reporting of outdated or distorted information. Such data poisoning poses severe safety risks and national concern.

Figure 4. Public data pipeline & poisoning entry points

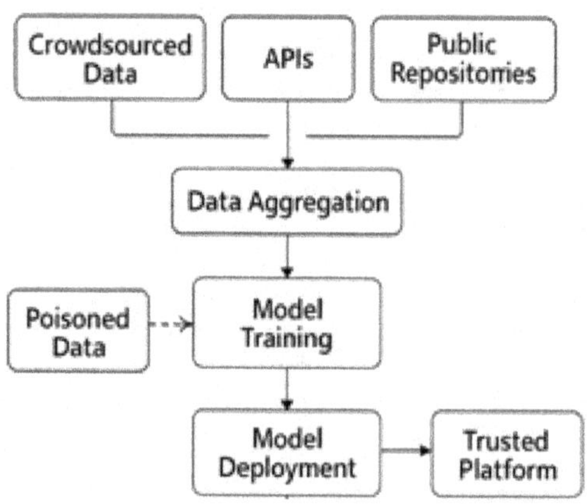

Figure 4 visualizes the typical lifecycle of public data pipelines from collection and aggregation through publication and downstream reuse and highlights the corresponding points where poisoning can be introduced. By showing vulnerabilities at citizen-submitted data portals, sensor uploads, open datasets, and civic data repositories, the figure illustrates how contamination can propagate from early ingestion stages to high-impact social, political, and administrative decisions.

3.3. Social Media and Political Data Contamination

Social media platforms have increasingly been identified as targets of data poisoning attacks (Bossetta, 2018), with extensive prior demonstrations of the feasibility of both account creation and content dissemination on Twitter. During an experiment designed to assess partisan vulnerability to spear phishing and disinformation in advance of the 2018 U.S. midterm elections, a fake news bot was created to send tweets containing a link to an online survey to 138 users. In that exercise, approximately 20% of the recipients clicked on the link, despite the absence of partisan or device targeting features. Similar approaches have been employed through these platforms for various yet similar topics across the spectrum of political orientation.

4. RETAIL AND E COMMERCE CASE STUDIES

The retail and e commerce sector is an appealing target for data poisoning attacks. These attacks have the potential to destabilize entire supply chains or database ecosystems and undermine companies' credibility and market value. Diverse avenues exist for introducing spurious information into systems relying on data processing that are exploitable in either a white or black box setting. These include the manipulation of product reviews and recommendations, inventory and pricing data, and supplier and fulfillment information, across platforms ranging from general purpose e commerce websites to domain specific exchanges for pricing and supply chain data.

Product reviews are crucial for the reputation and sales of individual items yet are also easily a target for adversaries with an interest in harming a competitor's business. Attacks targeting sets of reviews or rating distributions can induce significant aberrations in ranking and recommendation systems. They also remain within the realm of possibility for adversaries that do not possess extensive knowledge of the underlying recommendation model, seek the highest maximum rating (potentially altering the review text), know only the top recommendation returned by the model, or know the training and validation protocols but no model information (Wang & Chaudhuri, 2018).

Figure 5. Data poisoning in retail / e-commerce

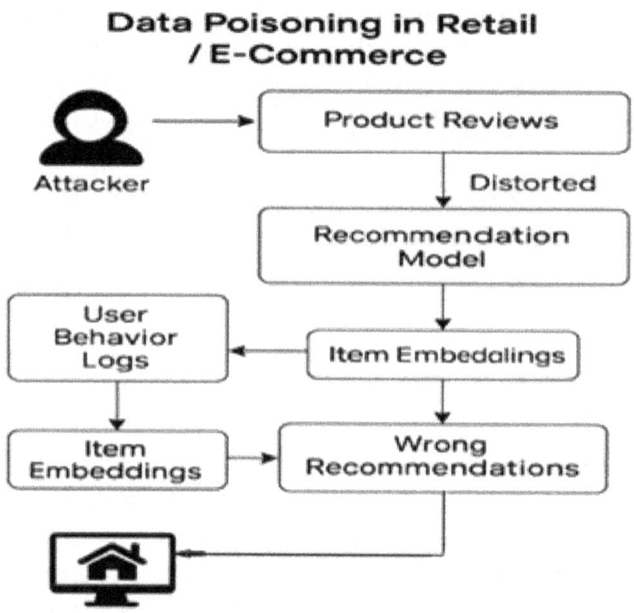

Figure 5 depicts the principal poisoning opportunities within retail and e-commerce ecosystems, including product review injections, adversarial modifications of recommendation histories, manipulation of pricing datasets, and distortion of supplier or fulfillment attributes. The figure emphasizes that data-driven commerce is exposed not only to precision attacks aimed at specific products but also to systemic poisoning that degrades marketplace trust and market prediction accuracy.

4.1. Product Recommendation and Review Manipulation

In retail and e commerce, product recommendation and review manipulation occurs when malicious actors contaminate training data used for machine learning (ML) models that curate product recommendations for users or aggregate product reviews posted by users. They are also able to inject valid products into the recommendations provided to users to recommend unqualified products with an illegitimate increase in financial benefits (Zhang et al., 2020). These types of attackers can also leave reviews that are fake and are of good quality which falsely praise or point out the benefits of certain things hence compromising on the integrity of an original recommendation or review system (Fang et al., 2018).

Large scale product datasets in other shopping sites or online market places include training sets that comprise of purchase history and product reviews by the users. Specialized recommendation models or review generation models are required to provide relevant suggestions to improve the user shopping experience and satisfaction. Attackers manipulate recommendation services by injecting adversarial historical behaviors using attributes from legitimate users and targeting specific items, customers, and combinations of timestamps and prices. In review generation platforms, they corrupt the auto generated reviews by poisoning the review likelihood estimator and carefully modifying the perceived utility to preserve the syntactic correctness.

4.2. Price and Inventory Data Poisoning

Merchants frequently adjust product pricing to enhance competitiveness and boost sales. One common pricing technique is to store past sale prices; choose some relevant ones and feed those, along with other contextual variables, to a machine learning model, to get the best possible predictions of future sale prices. Anomalous price data being injected into the training set, can provide the model with misleading price recommendations. For example, if an adversary were to inject price anomalies into the training data, they may create ultra-competitive prices, so the customer will purchase less than would have been the case otherwise.

4.3. Supplier and Fulfillment Data Attacks

The data poisoning threats to suppliers and fulfillment data Context, states, In data driven Supply Networks, suppliers are responsible for determining key process parameters and characteristics of the products they produce and deliver and which ultimately control product quality control. Thus these supplier data sets present a rich source of data poisoning attack opportunities with many areas for focus such as supplier's history of deviation from product specs, Inconsistencies between the dates of delivery and documentation on an order, and variations in order fulfillment duration by product type (Schwarzschild et al., 2020). Today, Supply Chains use contemporary algorithms at multiple levels to enable real-time optimization of their operations, to create greater agility and to build resilience to risk.

5. TRANSPORTATION AND GEOSPATIAL DATA CASE STUDIES

Data poisoning attacks pose a serious threat to transportation and geospatial data. In temporal traffic prediction, attackers can mislead a traffic prediction model to underestimate or overestimate future traffic conditions through crowd sourcing maps. When user generated maps are compromised, an adversary can construct fake journeys that generate false traffic data to influence future arrivals. Another data poisoning approach defines a general model for intelligent transportation systems. The adversary first attacks historical traffic data to optimize the long term policy of a reinforcement learning based traffic signal control algorithm. The attack transfers knowledge about the victim reinforcement learning agent to the attacker and designs model driven adversarial traffic data. The attack works on both multi agent and single agent traffic networks, significantly degrading the performance of reinforcement learning based traffic signal control.

Figure 6. Data poisoning in transportation

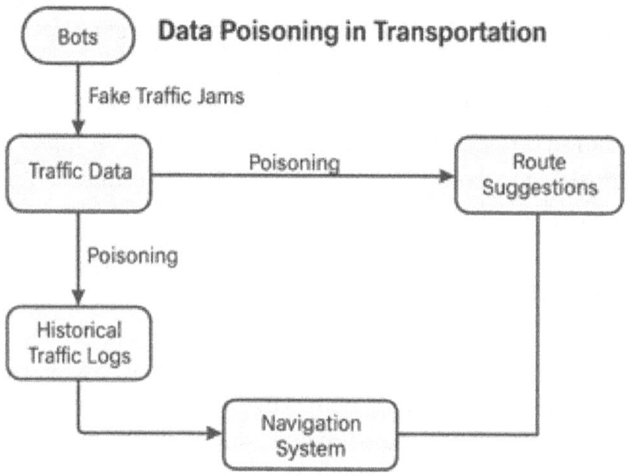

Figure 6 demonstrates how poisoning affects transportation systems by targeting spatiotemporal data used in traffic prediction, navigation services, and intelligent transportation systems (ITS). It illustrates attacker capabilities such as injecting fake journeys, altering sensor feeds, and distorting congestion estimates. The figure contextualizes transportation poisoning as a high-impact, low-visibility threat capable of influencing mobility patterns, routing decisions, and urban traffic management.

Mapping services can be poisoned through web based automated crowd sourcing and manipulation of platform data. Certain location-aware MOOC learning platforms also rely on crowdsourced geographic metadata for video indexing and recommendation. These platforms can be poisoned when attackers upload forged location traces. The adversary can post forged location activity to modify the importance of location and redefine the student's MOOC learning path. General purpose data collection applications for city administration that offer services based on web and mobile terminals and location information have become potential targets. Videos posted on these websites usually tag the collection positions of video text geographic data in additional descriptions. Attackers can replace these geographic positioning attributes and destroy semantic information from full article data. Data validity, integrity, and authority are seriously threatened inside the system.

Autonomous vehicle systems need to ensure the integrity of road and environmental information before they can develop models to estimate the state of the world. Satellite based positioning and geographic information system (GIS) data in the transportation domain assist autonomous vehicles in inferring real time variations. Autonomous vehicle data collection and recording usually leverage global positioning system coordinates and sophisticated GIS data, leading to sequential, spatiotemporal multimodal data streams. Two kinds of threats for data collection platforms of autonomous vehicles have been reported: the attack surface where an adversary injects false road conditions into the built environment and the attack surface where marine and vehicular data involving ocean temperature observations flow through the data collection center. In pure ocean space scenarios, an attacker can alter temperature observations and still achieve high poisoning effectiveness. An attacker can yet again modify the tracking data of marine vessels and then rapidly disperse wise persuasive fooling data into the collection control center.

5.1. Traffic Prediction and Navigation Services

Transportation systems' rapid digitalization and interconnectedness create fruitful avenues for harm through data poison attacks. Digital platforms gather spatiotemporal data, such as the number of vehicles at certain times of the day or expected travel times along predefined paths. These types of models can be negatively affected by malicious activity resulting in either incorrect route suggestions or extended duration congestion notices for the unsuspecting user. There are two examples of data poisoning that clearly demonstrate how attackers can compromise both traffic forecasting and traffic navigation services without being detected. Attackers will modify historical traffic demand data and travel latency information to deceive users about what they should expect from their trip and therefore affect how the systems respond subsequently to those trips. Although previously studied in other realms, this problem is largely overlooked in traffic domains despite similar attack processes. Cause and effect chain analyses reveal how specific attacks quadratically elevate destination safety while enhancing matching probability. Further insights pinpoint which records to target to achieve the greatest impact.

A burgeoning attack surface supporting smart appliances that facilitate urban living, Intelligent Transportation Systems (ITS) involving smart traffic lights, congestion reducing software, and online navigation have gained ground. Rapid development in positioning technologies, wireless communication, and cloud computing combined with large-scale urban expansion has made real-time traffic estimation increasingly attractive. Smart traffic technology offers user specific travel route recommendations, real time traffic flow monitoring, and online traffic condition inquiries based on real time data collection. Local attacks can propagate into extensive urban road networks, leading to global traffic disturbances that severely delay vehicle movement and mislead navigation users. Attackers exploit vulnerabilities in traffic demand and latency data to poison prediction models. Such manipulation misleads routing services and degrades overall traffic management performance (Pan & Zhu, 2022).

5.2. Mapping and GIS Data Poisoning

Dependency on geographic information systems (GIS) has become prevalent across a multitude of applications (Schwarzschild et al., 2020). GIS is widely used in society and affects the decision making and activities of a large number of users. It is broadly applied across sectors and has gained attention from both the research and industrial communities. Two critical processes in GIS are mapping and visualisation. GIS platforms have gained considerable attention in both research and industry for visualizing and analysing geographical data. Mapping through GIS includes a range of activities, from locating specific points of interests to highlighting other geographic phenomena. Geographic information system (GIS) data poisoning has received limited attention, with only a handful of published research papers in this area. Even fewer papers study real world data calibration and data poisoning attacks against GIS map data. Advancements in information and communication technology (ICT) have resulted in a wide range of geographical data generated by, for example, mobile positioning records, GPS systems, corporate addresses, and third party map data providers. It has become commonplace to develop, deploy, and maintain GIS platforms. The ongoing digitisation of an increasing number of work processes and industries further contributes to the growth of geographical information and GIS related systems. However, the GIS sector does not strictly preserve or verify the credentials of geographical data inputs due to the lack of industry standardisation or regulation. The poor management of data inputs introduces data poisoning vulnerabilities that have yet to be explored experimentally (Carlini et al., 2023).

5.3. Autonomous Vehicle Sensor Data Contamination (Non Healthcare/Non IoT Contexts)

The safety of autonomous vehicles heavily relies on sensor systems that collect spatial information for effective decision making. LiDAR remains a critical sensor used by many autonomous vehicle providers; however, its physical properties leave the system vulnerable to cyber attacks. As per the increasing dependency on sensor networks, the attack surface in autonomous vehicles has also expanded and covered details such as LiDARs and cameras. Cyber Attacks on sensor systems can limit the perception system and hinder vehicle navigation. Situational awareness or access to algorithms is not required for a cyber attacker to design impactful attacks on the sensor. Security aware processing schemes make it feasible to implement cryptographic solutions at an elevated development cost. Data injected into a sensor is semi or correlated with the true data from a spatiotemporal perspective, still raising a risk in autonomous vehicles. Several cyber attacks and their corresponding mitigation strategies were investigated on semi correlated sensor data. Longitudinal and partial information cyber attacks targeting the LiDAR sensor in autonomous vehicles were also investigated (Hallyburton et al., 2023).

6. ENVIRONMENTAL MONITORING AND CLIMATE DATA

Data integrity is critical to sensor networks for air quality monitoring. Contaminated measurements obtained by adversaries can disrupt the operation of monitoring networks, misinform decision making processes, and cause public distrust. Already deployed low cost air quality sensor networks commonly lack any security mechanisms, exposing them to data compromises and pollution attacks (Luo et al., 2018). Data poisoning also can arise within established environmental monitoring systems that use extensive data processing, aggregation, and sharing through a common platform. An adversary can inject bogus data into the framework, misleading the estimation of pollution sources and distributions. Protection measures are critical for preserving the privacy and confidentiality of environmental data itself and the individuals and organizations behind the data (De Capitani di Vimercati et al., 2012).

Figure 7. Data poisoning mechanisms in environmental monitoring systems

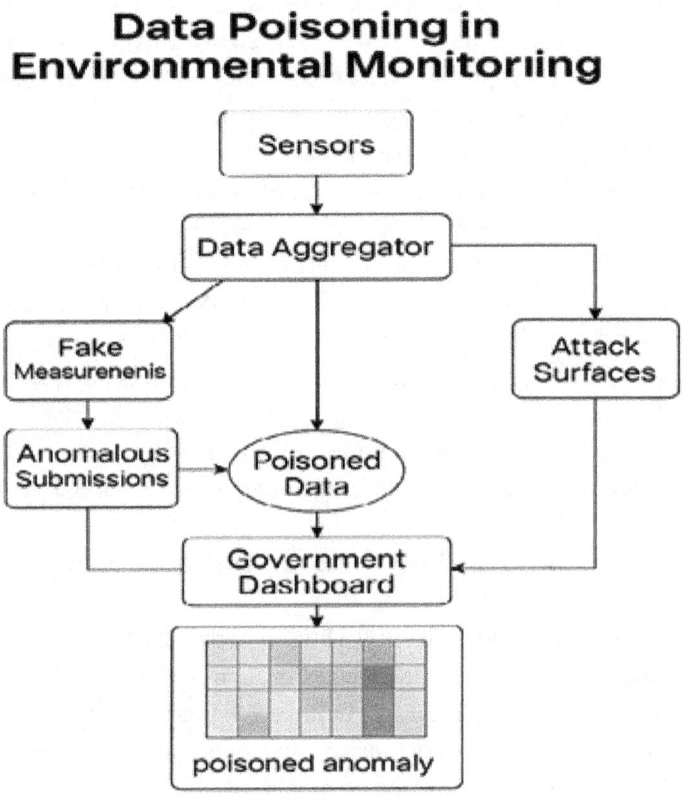

Figure 7 illustrates how data poisoning infiltrates environmental monitoring systems by corrupting measurements at multiple stages of the sensing and data-aggregation pipeline. As shown, attackers can introduce fake measurements or anomalous submissions into the data aggregator, resulting in polluted datasets that propagate downstream. These poisoned values are subsequently visualized on governmental dashboards, leading to misleading environmental indicators and false anomalies. The diagram highlights the critical attack surfaces ranging from sensors to dashboards where adversarial manipulation can compromise environmental decision-making.

Climate monitoring via sensor networks and distributed systems is a pressing need to observe objectives such as atmospheric pollution. Sensor integrity is thus paramount, given that either the misuse of contaminated measurements or even the replacement of filtered false measurements with genuinely recorded ones can lead to gross disinformation regarding environmental conditions and climate. Climate data has been widely debated in mass media, often shaping economic, fiscal, and social policy discussions. The capability to inject anomalous data into public climate datasets can lead to the publication of orchestrated gross, controlled, and misled climate datasets (Sun et al., 2020).

6.1. Sensor Network Data Integrity Attacks

Sensor networks are widely employed for environmental monitoring due to their simple installation, low maintenance costs, and sensor diversity (Luo et al., 2018). Nevertheless, they remain vulnerable to data integrity attacks that can compromise data quality and sensor authentications, thereby reducing confidence in collected data and presenting operational difficulties. For instance, sensor data in environmental monitoring varies quickly due to spatial and temporal factors. Attackers can therefore corrupt systems, meeting attack objectives without significantly affecting the corrupt data's statistical properties and causing only limited sensor data integrity loss.

Typically, environmental monitoring works on a distributed data acquisition and distributed processing architecture. The monitoring systems consist of spatially distributed sensors, each collecting measurements independently. The sensor data is then transmitted to a remote server for fusion processing, obtaining a global view of the monitoring situation. When a monitoring system is compromised, besides violating the original purpose, it is still desired that the integrity of the monitoring data is kept at a certain level. Specifically, instead of breaking the system, an integrity attack aims to control the statistics of the corrupted data, such as the mean, variance, distribution, hidden state, or model parameter.

6.2. Public Climate Datasets and Anomalous Submissions

Climate change is an urgent threat to humanity, which underscores the need for societal efforts to monitor, record, and limit environmental damage. Changes in environmental variables such as precipitation, temperature, and humidity, which are indicators of climate change therefore must be closely monitored. To that end, public datasets from various governmental and non-governmental organizations across the globe contain climate measurement information on numerous climatic variables. However, despite their importance to both society and the scientific community, there exist independent reports suggesting that many public climate datasets have been actively amended with anomalous submissions. Such anomalous submissions do not reflect realistic measurements of the indicators in question, undermining the government and scientific efforts to fight climate change. The specific manipulation mechanism of such anomalous submissions remains non trivial unless considered with the mathematical underpinnings of environmental modelling. Analysing the preconditions for submission to those public datasets leads to the conclusion that anomalous submissions could leverage the unique sparsity characteristic of climate datasets to target the feature label raster data directly. As a case study, the public climate dataset record, clivad, has been recorded as containing abnormal submissions on multiple occasions.

7. EDUCATIONAL TECHNOLOGY AND ASSESSMENT DATA POISONING

Educational technology systems increasingly rely on large-scale datasets for evaluation, personalization, and automated assessment, which exposes them to poisoning vulnerabilities. On these grounds, educational assessment and online proctoring have attracted extensive attention, and similar efforts have extended to the development of open educational resources, including learning games and assessment objects. Educational assessment platforms that rely on massive pupil response datasets are widely deployed at the national or continental level in various educational jurisdictions. It cannot be assumed that examination, assessment, or feedback systems possess inherent immunity against adversarial manipulation or data contamination.

As the proliferation of online examinations has accelerated, datasets that record examination questions, responses, and actual ratings along with graders' comments have become publicly available. Consequently, it is possible to opportunistically poison the training data of automated proctoring and evaluation systems to introduce persistent and far reaching deterioration of educational quality programming exemplifying the principle of minimal effort contamination for maximal impact degradation. Public repositories that serve open educational resources, including detailed databases of questions, answers, and corresponding soft or hard tagged annotations, are likewise subject to malicious contamination. (Schwarzschild et al., 2020)

7.1. Online Proctoring and Exam Dataset Contamination

Online proctoring systems have become a popular solution for educational institutions and certification bodies to conduct examinations remotely. A major concern surrounding these online assessments is cheating, especially during high stakes examinations such as professional certifications. Such cheating during online assessments can be detected using machine learning based models that classify whether an online video of a student taking the exam is compliant with predefined rules, such as whether the student has been using unauthorized materials. The rules can differ depending on the institution that conducts examination, leading to the need for institution specific datasets to develop accurate classifiers. However, the publicly available datasets of proctored examination videos are limited. As a result, there is a pressing need for students to upload non compliant irrelated videos of themselves taking an exam to assist in curating a suitable dataset for their targeted online assistants. Such contamination exploits the properties of proctored examination videos to degrade classifier accuracy. The injected irrelevant videos bias the training set and reduce the model's ability to detect non-compliant behavior (Wang & Chaudhuri, 2018).

7.2. Open Educational Resources and Question Banks

Preserving the integrity of open educational resources such as learning objects, assignments, and question banks, as well as platforms for sharing and evaluating them, is crucial for reliable education technology. Data poisoning directly corrupts the assessments of academic quality and relevance embedded in such systems. Such interventions impact the ranking of educational content on search and recommendation engines, possibly suppressing content that is authoritative but not brand or perhaps institution relevant and promoting subpar content masked with authoritative surrogates. Selective mislabeling of free responses or open ended submissions in computer based assessment systems can further disrupt evaluation procedures by degrading the quality of automatically computed feedback and relevance ranking as well as model informed correction.

In July 2023, it came to light that assessment content highly relevant for software engineering had been injected into a widely used open learning resource repository. This repository and its linkage to poisons submitted in earlier experiments will be analyzed after problems of quality control were unequivocally evident. The repository maintained an explicit edict that no software engineering content could be inserted. Nevertheless, the repository remains widely trusted for ongoing, open assessment experiments; thereby increasing the chance that tampered or rotten content will be collaterally propagated through still unaffected assessment venues and repositories. Such archives maintain a para official status owing to the critical role played in shaping the subsequently inundating submissions.

ASP.NET Core has become an authoritative topic for software engineering, especially in the still pervasive .NET work context. The repository contains hard span challenges and missing parts in incomplete tasks, amongst other behavior characteristic of poisoning.

8. MYTH, MISREPRESENTATION, AND BLACK BOX ATTACKS IN DATA STREAMS

Machine learning models trained on publicly available data remain vulnerable to poisoning attacks even when the data cannot be manipulated directly. For example, a subject matter expert may submit labels to a dataset that is widely used to pre train image classification models; even though the images are not directly controlled, maliciously selected labels can coax a model to produce targeted misclassifications of future samples from the same domain. In a similar way, when a dataset contains only a small number of examples of a target class, attackers can modify a sample from the dataset to push it toward this target class, even if they have no control over the underlying feature values.

Data poisoning is easier when datasets are small enough to permit large scale modification or direct construction, yet it still occurs even in challenging and public settings. Such cases illustrate that the assumption of black box access to a data stream, is sufficient to model real world poisoning schemes across domains beyond finance, Internet of Things, and healthcare (Rakin et al., 2020). Attacks that deliberately craft queries to insert adversarial label noise into publicly accessible datasets have been observed public labeling services are thus useful within this framework.

8.1. Adversarial Label Noise in Large Scale Datasets

Prevalent methods for incorporating noise into labels in massive datasets frame the contamination using a class conditional model. Therein, symmetric noise uniformly flips labels irrespective of class proximity, while asymmetric noise selectively flips from a given class to those of lower similarity. These treatments disregard dependencies between the instances and the labels, in particular, patterns exhibited by the data descriptors. More satisfactory modeling employs either feature dependent or instance dependent noise. The former is realized by projecting samples on random vectors and applying Gaussian perturbation prior to classification, while the latter relies on the construction of auxiliary neural nets aimed at inducing noisy labels from the inputs. Crowd sourcing scenarios accommodate instead the unreliability of the contributors through the use of confusion matrices augmented by intricate alternatives that take into account the facilitators' expertise and the task difficulty (Wang et al., 2021).

Despite a wealth of analysis and proposal of countermeasures against adversarial assaults directed to neural nets, consideration of adversarial label contamination remains conspicuously scanty. The achievement of reliable protection thus necessitates intrusion into the adversarial pool of injectors. Among the potential orchestrators, adversarial crowd workers raise special concern owing to their innate motivation to compromise data quality.

8.2. Clean Poisoning in Real world Deployments

Machine learning models trained on large datasets are vulnerable to clean label data poisoning attacks, whereby an attacker can inject poisoned samples into the training set while retaining control only over the features, rather than the labels, of the perturbation. Such attacks are especially dangerous in black box settings where the attacker has no access to the victim model. The transferability of poisoning attacks across models is therefore of great concern. (Zhu et al., 2019) develop poisoned images targeting a victim image classifier. The crafted poisons follow the clean label principle, permitting the attacker to preserve full control over the sample label. Attack samples are selected from the CIFAR 10 dataset, and a substitute image classifier is trained prior to attack implementation. Since the goal is to manipulate the victim against specific individual classes, poisoned candidates whose feature representations close to the target class are identified. A generative model produces poisoned images that maximize misclassification of the target class on a substitute network, while avoiding interference with other classes. The efficacy of the clean label transferability approach on poisoning is also shown, with sampled images from the MNIST dataset convincing a substitute model to misclassify certain digit images as a target class.

(Shafahi et al., 2018) propose targeted clean label poisoning methods for various model classes across multiple datasets. The objective is to control the behavior of a model on chosen test inputs without modifying the model, the full training data, or the incident labeling of a single additional training example. The polynomial time poisoning method outperforms both prior contamination strategies and the non targeted clean label attack and transfers easily from a substitute model. The attack requires only a single poison and no white box access to the victim class. A feature extractor trained on top of a common backbone enables the generation of transferable poisons amongst long short term memory and recurrent neural network models and across speech recognition and language modeling tasks. As clean label attacks do not rely on malicious labels, they represent a significant deployment concern for learning systems (Geiping et al., 2021).

9. SECURITY AND PRIVACY IMPLICATIONS

When large volumes of data are routinely submitted from a multitude of contributors, integrity verification of the information becomes a challenge. As demonstrated by the previous case studies, such environments are increasingly common in many domains outside healthcare, finance, and the IoT. In such contexts, data poisoning attacks can aim to inject false or misleading information with substantial effects on the AI systems that use the data for training. To safeguard against such threats, detection and mitigation strategies derived from both the data poisoning and integrity protection literature have recently emerged and continue to be actively researched (Hendrycks & Dietterich, 2019).

Even when detection and mitigation methods are implemented, new policies and governance frameworks are necessary. Educational assessments, civic datasets, and political information influence decision making and public discourse, meaning developers and model deployers can inadvertently become enmeshed in controversial issues and sensitive societal matters. Preventing vandalism and exploitation of datasets is therefore essential. Data publishing guidance, including specification of acceptable submission ranges, has proven useful in other domains, such as sensor networks. Consideration of governance practices is increasingly important in other areas of AI as well (Rattanavipanon & Nunes, 2024).

9.1. Detection and Mitigation Strategies

Data poisoning attacks pose a serious and evolving threat to machine learning and data driven decision systems across a wide range of domains. In domains like education, city governance, retail, transportation, the environment, and more, real world case studies demonstrate that the security measures used to mitigate exposure to these attacks are still in their infancy, and many systems remain unprotected. Existing strategies for external contamination, such as cleaning and filtering only external sources, offer limited protection against techniques that strategically infect trusted internal sources. The scrutiny of the public and policymakers on toxic content in public datasets or model evaluation data makes these systems de facto critical, and they thus remain prime candidates for continued exploitation. Countermeasures should be made part of the wider engineering process, as relying solely on private internal sources for training data vastly reduces the number of systems that can be employed. Owing to the domain specific nature of these systems, a strong understanding of the requirements imposed on a protective measure is paramount in order to avoid oversights such as failing to account for efficiently locating the poison or retaining access to poisoning data (Paudice et al., 2018 ; Grosse et al., 2017).

Domain oriented detection strategies for data poisoning attacks are yet to gain traction. Within the educational technology realm, only a restricted subset of internally generated contamination can presently be detected, even with an extensive understanding of the systems and datasets under threat (Muñoz-González et al., 2017). The unique characteristics of publicly available cohort datasets that are monitored have rendered it impossible for contamination attacks to proceed undetected since explicit and implicit integrity checks are employed. Transport datasets that combine relevant geo information significantly simplify the modelling of the spatiotemporal evolution of innovation diffusion. Urban datasets that include such information exhibit relatively simple diffusion patterns that differ for diverse issues, enabling the construction of transport monitoring networks similar to those used for electrical vehicle charging infrastructure compatibility (Schwarzschild et al., 2020).

9.2. Policy, Governance, and Ethical Considerations

In the emerging paradigm of machine learning and AI governance, data poisoning attacks come with new challenges for policymakers, practitioners, civil society actors, and technology firms. Policymakers within a regulatory framework that invites external data provisions should bolster external validation controls across public datasets. In broader terms, even without regulatory frameworks or independent assessors, internal and external logs are bright spots for earliest data integrity detection. For data intensive public sector organizations, real time anomaly detection heuristics will strengthen such capacities.

While data poisoning attacks across different domains concentrate on data, firms and organizations must recognize the need for robust auditing or logging capabilities and internal controls extending beyond data only such as computation tampering; false model parameters; and circuitry extensions capable of false outputs. Data constitutes just one facet of modelling systems, and anomalous behavior, consideration of attack surface extension, and preemptive multiparty exercises expanding the analysis of points vulnerable to malicious modification form vital governance components.

Government organizations providing public access to datasets risk being the target of data poisoning attacks at scale. Independent assessors evaluating myriad data sources could assist in containing the risks, but excessive filtering may inadvertently stifle legitimate data contributions. Sandbox methodologies capable of testing public datasets against wider known behaviors or datasets at an earlier stage of post aggregation processing offer various extensible avenues for addressing the challenge (Schwarzschild et al., 2020; Kairouz et al., 2021).

10. LESSONS LEARNED AND BEST PRACTICES

The case studies of cross domain that have been discussed in this chapter show that data poisoning is a structural vulnerability that cuts across both public and private data ecosystems. Due to the fact that most machine learning pipelines use externally obtained or continuously updated datasets, the small perturbations can be transmitted throughout the ingestion, preprocessing, training, and deployment phases. The following are some of the lessons and best practices that can be used to enhance data integrity.

To start with, the body must have unending monitoring, abstracting of irregularities, and tenacious validation of incoming information. The cleaning and detection of anomalies cannot be one-time activities, but they have to be integrated into the standard work processes. The behavior of models, sensitivities of parameters, and interactions of hyperparameters will also help in detecting the abnormal patterns earlier.

Second, the process of the change in the supervised and unsupervised learning environments deserves a closer consideration because both learning paradigms present dissimilar attack surfaces and points of exposure. Systems that combine streaming or real-time data are also especially vulnerable to poisoning since an attacker can affect sequential updates without having access to the internals of the model.

Third, organizations should not only use superficial or source based filtering. Black-box and online working models demand further integrity checks, such as provenance-conscious data imports, versioned datasets and pre-and post-training transformation logging. Cross-validation based on multiple data sources can be used where possible in order to detect inconsistencies caused by an attempt of poisoning.

Last but not least, end-to-end security guidelines should underline the complete model lifecycle protection, including data acquisition and preprocessing parts, as well as deployment and constant monitoring. The systems that do not have such controls are at risk of inadvertently taking vulnerabilities into high-stakes environments. Losses encountered within particular modules are then supposed to trigger further research on possible compromise at the dataset level (Schwarzschild et al., 2020).

Collectively, these lessons underscore the need to adopt integrity-conscious machine learning practices that will integrate validation, auditing and governance into every phase of data-driven operation.

11. CONCLUSION

Data poisoning has now become a rampant issue impacting a large range of machine learning systems especially those which rely on externally sourced or continuously updated data systems. In this chapter, the exploitation of core vulnerabilities in data pipelines (including ingestion, preprocessing, training, and downstream reuse) in various threat models and attack surfaces was discussed. The chapter extended to a common taxonomy of dataset-level, point-level and streaming-based poisoning, pointing to the fact that different operational settings pose domain-specific attack vectors across government repositories, civic data platforms, retail and e-commerce ecosystems, transportation and geospatial systems, environmental and climate monitoring networks, and educational technologies.

By using complex case studies, we have shown that poisoning can lead to distortion of policy analysis, manipulation of citizen discourse, distortion of product ratings, misleading navigational aids, sensor-based measurements, and weaken the automated assessment and proctoring systems. Besides, sophisticated types of black-box, clean-label, and feature-dependent poisoning depict that the attacks can still be practiced even in cases when adversaries do not have direct access to the training labels or model internals. The fact that these strategies have continued to emerge underscores the limitations of using traditional data cleaning, source-based filtering, and ad hoc validation processes.

These implications highlight the necessity of resilient, integrity-sensitive machine learning pipelines that include systematic provenance tracking, robust anomaly detection, and model-level defenses against subtle or low-visibility contamination. Governance models should also change towards mitigating risk related to the publication of public data, external publications and open datasets in large volumes whereby the organizations should embrace transparent validation policies and auditability of data lifecycle.

Combined with the cross-domain synthesis of this chapter, these findings reinforce that data poisoning is neither niche nor limited to isolated settings. Rather, it is an organizational weakness of contemporary information-driven ecologies. Enhancing the assertiveness of data integrity in all sectors, especially in areas that cannot be completed without constant intake or involving the people, is crucial to protecting the veracity, responsibility, and social confidence in machine learning devices.

REFERENCES

Bhattacharjee, K., & Dasgupta, A. (2023). Power to the data defenders: Human-centered disclosure risk calibration of open data. *arXiv Preprint arXiv:2301.07035.* DOI: 10.14722/usec.2023.237256

Biggio, B., & Roli, F. (2018). Wild patterns: Ten years after the rise of adversarial machine learning. *Pattern Recognition, 84,* 317–331. DOI: 10.1016/j.patcog.2018.07.023

Bossetta, M. (2018). A simulated cyberattack on Twitter: Assessing partisan vulnerability to spear phishing and disinformation ahead of the 2018 U.S. midterm elections. *Political Communication, 35*(4), 571–593.

De Capitani di Vimercati, S., Livraga, G., Piuri, V., & Scotti, F. (2012). Privacy and security in environmental monitoring systems. *International Journal of Distributed Sensor Networks, 8*(2). Advance online publication. DOI: 10.1109/ESTEL.2012.6400161

Fang, M., Yang, G., Gong, N. Z., & Liu, J. (2018). Poisoning attacks to graph-based recommender systems. *Proceedings of the AAAI Conference on Artificial Intelligence, 32*(1).

Geiping, J., Fowl, L., Liu, G., Motta, F., Bochkovskiy, A., & Goldstein, T. (2021). Witches' brew: Industrial scale data poisoning via gradient matching. *Advances in Neural Information Processing Systems.*

Grosse, K., Papernot, N., Manoharan, P., Backes, M., & McDaniel, P. (2017). Adversarial perturbations against Deep Neural networks for malware classification. In *Proceedings of the Annual Computer Security Applications Conference (ACSAC).*

Hallyburton, R. S., Zhang, Q., Mao, Z. M., & Pajic, M. (2023). Partial information, longitudinal cyber attacks on LiDAR in autonomous vehicles. *arXiv Preprint arXiv:2303.03443.*

Hendrycks, D., & Dietterich, T. (2019). Benchmarking neural network robustness to common corruptions and perturbations. In *Proceedings of the International Conference on Learning Representations (ICLR).*

Kairouz, P., McMahan, H. B., Avent, B., Bellet, A., Bennis, M., Nitin Bhagoji, A., Bonawitz, K., Charles, Z., Cormode, G., Cummings, R., D'Oliveira, R. G. L., Eichner, H., El Rouayheb, S., Evans, D., Gardner, J., Garrett, Z., Gascón, A., Ghazi, B., Gibbons, P. B., & Zhao, S. (2021). Advances and open problems in federated learning. *Foundations and Trends in Machine Learning, 14*(1–2), 1–210. DOI: 10.1561/2200000083

Koh, P. W., & Liang, P. (2017). Understanding black-box predictions via influence functions. In *Proceedings of the International Conference on Machine Learning (ICML).*

Luo, L., Zhang, Y., Pearson, B., & Ling, Z., (2018). On the security and data integrity of low-cost sensor networks for air quality monitoring. *Environmental Science & Technology, 52*(15), 8739–8746. PMID: 30558353

Ma, Y., Xie, T., Li, J., & Maciejewski, R. (2019). Explaining vulnerabilities to adversarial machine learning through visual analytics. In *Proceedings of the IEEE Conference on Visualization (VIS).* DOI: 10.1109/TVCG.2019.2934631

Muñoz-González, L., Biggio, B., Demontis, A., Paudice, A., Wongrassamee, V., Lupu, E., & Roli, F. (2017). Towards poisoning of deep learning algorithms with back-gradient optimization. In *Proceedings of the ACM Workshop on Artificial Intelligence and Security (AISec).* DOI: 10.1145/3128572.3140451

Orekondy, T., Schiele, B., & Fritz, M. (2020). Prediction poisoning: Towards defenses against DNN model poisoning attacks. In *Proceedings of the International Conference on Learning Representations (ICLR).*

Pan, Y., & Zhu, Q. (2022). On poisoned Wardrop equilibrium in congestion games. *Games and Economic Behavior, 133*, 27–59. 10.48550/arXiv.2209.00094DOI: 10.1016/j.geb.2022.06.001

Paudice, A., Muñoz-González, L., György, A., & Lupu, E. C. (2018). Detection of adversarial training examples in poisoning attacks through anomaly detection. *arXiv Preprint arXiv:1802.03041.*

Rakin, A. S., He, Z., & Fan, D. (2020). TBT: Targeted backdoor attacks against deep learning systems. In *Proceedings of the AAAI Conference on Artificial Intelligence.*

Rattanavipanon, N., & Nunes, I. de O. (2024). Poisoning prevention in federated learning and differential privacy via stateful proofs of execution. *arXiv Preprint arXiv:2401.12345.*

Schwarzschild, A., Goldblum, M., Gupta, A., Dickerson, J. P., & Goldstein, T. (2020). Just how toxic is data poisoning? A unified benchmark for backdoor and data poisoning attacks. *arXiv Preprint arXiv:2009.07403.*

Shafahi, A., Huang, W. R., Najibi, M., Suciu, O., (2018). Poison Frogs! Targeted clean-label poisoning attacks on neural networks. In *Advances in Neural Information Processing Systems, 31.*

Steinhardt, J., Koh, P. W., & Liang, P. (2017). Certified defenses for data poisoning attacks. In *Advances in Neural Information Processing Systems.*

Sun, R., Qi, Z., Bi, J., & Wang, J. (2020). Cost-aware poisoning attacks on traffic forecasting models. *IEEE Transactions on Intelligent Transportation Systems, 21*(7), 2808–2822.

Wang, Y., & Chaudhuri, K. (2018). Data poisoning attacks against online learning. *IEEE Transactions on Neural Networks and Learning Systems, 29*(5), 1283–1293. DOI: 10.48550/arXiv.1808.08994

Zhang, H., Li, Y., Ding, B., & Gao, J. (2020). Practical data poisoning attack against next-item recommendation. In *Proceedings of The Web Conference (WWW 2020).* https://doi.org/DOI: 10.1145/3366423.3379992

Zhu, C., Huang, W. R., Shafahi, A., Li, H., (2019). Transferable clean-label poisoning attacks on deep neural networks. *arXiv Preprint arXiv:1905.05897.*

Chapter 18
Collaboration Business Models and Frameworks in Federated Learning

Revati Ramrao Rautrao
https://orcid.org/0000-0001-7803-8699
Dr. D.Y. Patil B-School, India

A. V. Senthil Kumar
https://orcid.org/0000-0002-8587-7017
Nehru Institute of Information Technology and Management, India

Sanjayan Thottapattunjalil Suseelan
GVM's Dr. Dada Vaidya College of Education, India

ABSTRACT

Federated Learning (FL) has enabled decentralised collaboration so that many stakeholders can train models without sharing raw data. However, the distributed nature exposes the system to risks such as data poisoning and unfavourable AI attacks, which compromise the model integrity and the organisational tasks. This chapter checks the outline of collaboration in FL, including platform federated data ecosystems, consortium-based models and cross-industry partnerships. While these structures increase scalability, personalisation and economic value, they also introduce the model updates and weaknesses in gradient manipulation. Discussed solutions include strong aggregation algorithms, blockchain competition, competent traceability, rejection of nonconformities, encouragement, human-in-loop supervision, regulatory compliance and moral AI theory. By integrating technical, organisational and moral security measures, the chapter presents a comprehensive approach to safe, flexible and reliable ecosystems.

INTRODUCTION

The past ten years have seen considerable improvements in methodologies of processing data and artificial intelligence, especially Federated Learning (FL). In contrast to conventional machine learning, in FL, datasets are decentralised to be trained at a variety of units, organisations or nodes that hold their

DOI: 10.4018/979-8-3373-6224-3.ch018

local raw data (McMahon et al., 2017). The architecture boosts the accuracy of algorithms as well as maintaining the privacy of data. But this decentralisation that makes FL attractive also creates gaps. FL systems are open, hence malicious actors can bypass trust, aggregation, and communication protocol weaknesses. One of the most urgent forms of threat is data poisoning and adversarial AI attacks, which negatively impact the performance of the model and the trust of the stakeholders. As an example, collective clinical data can be helpful to a consortium of hospitals to enhance disease prediction, although these can only be achieved based on systemic and collaborative protection. Here, Federated Learning touches upon business models and governance models to strike a balance between innovation and risk. FL allows organisations to train models together without providing raw information (Kairouz et al., 2021). However, new attack surfaces also arise due to this cooperation, and new governance and design approaches are necessary (Lyu et al., 2022). The initial step of this chapter is to map the collaborative structures in the fields of high-tech, including smart infrastructure, healthcare, and finance, where sensitive data and trusted models become critically important (Rieke et al., 2020). It then discusses such dangers as data poisoning and manipulation of models (Bhagoji et al., 2019), and suggests the strategies of adaptive ecosystems based on security, ethics, and transparency (Wu et al., 2022). The chapter claims that the success of FL depends on a matching design of the systems, communication protocols, and trust mechanisms. It offers ideological mapping and case-based information to demonstrate how sustainable business models can combine innovation and resilience- particularly in areas where data silos have traditionally been an issue, such as healthcare, banking, and education (Zhang et al., 2020; Rieke et al., 2020).

THEORETICAL GROUNDING OF COLLABORATION BUSINESS MODELS IN FEDERATED LEARNING.

1. Distributed Learning Theory:

The idea of Federated Learning (FL) decentralises the training process by enabling several clients to fine-tune a common global model on their own local information. This is unlike the conventional machine learning paradigms that make use of centralised data storage. McMahan et al. (2017) proposed the basic architecture of FL, and it shows how the distributed averaging could be used to promote collaborative training. However, subsequent researchers have identified these difficulties as the statistical heterogeneity, uneven distribution of data, and the differences in performance (Wang et al., 2020). The problems above cause the need to have coordinated designs that would guarantee efficiency and inclusivity simultaneously, which means that the broad spectrum of nodes should be included.

2. Adversarial Machine Learning

Machine learning models are manipulable, and the Federated Learning (FL) environment enhances the possibility of manipulation. It is proven that even a slight perturbation can lead to a significant change in the model predictions (Shaori et al., 2017; Zhu et al., 2019). The adversaries are capable in FL of operating inside the consortium, modifying it with malicious gradients or malicious updates, corrupting the model of the world. Blanchard et al. (2017) and Yin et al. (2018) equip learners with mathematical constructs to resist threats of this character (Byzantine-Robust Learning Theory) and refer to the fact that adaptable approaches are no exception in hostile settings. These insights highlight that collaboration design, technical resilience, and adaptive governance are inseparable in building secure FL systems.

3. Trust and Governance Frameworks:

Alongside the algorithmic design, Federated Learning (FL) is implemented within the context of complex organisational ecosystems, where the sense of trust, incentives and governance is a prerequisite to success. The stakeholders should ensure that they balance their interests while avoiding unfairness, non-transparency, and inaccuracy. Differential privacy and blockchain-based audit trail are privacy-preserving technologies now being popular in FL governance (Kim et al., 2020; Li et al., 2020). The mechanisms point out that FL governance is not an administrative process; it is a socio-technical process that must exist to sustain co-operation in adversarial conditions. Privacy engineering can provide the FL systems protection to the integrity of their operations and ensure confidence in the stakeholders, coupled with decentralised oversight. Make this chapter more unique and useful; one may include a new section in it with the title of Incentive-Aligned Governance and Traceable Collaboration in Federated Learning Ecosystems. Within this section, the author is going to comment on how blockchain-based traceability, dynamic trust scoring and token-based models of participation can be used to increase the feeling of responsibility among the stakeholders as well as to minimise adversarial risks.

The chapter can show how explainable, adaptive defence mechanisms can be used to improve collaborative resilience by incorporating structures like FedBap and RAB2-DEF. An example of a short case study may be federated traffic prediction over smart cities, which can be explained by the fact that decentralised data governance can help to facilitate real-time learning and maintain privacy. With this addition, the technical strength is mixed with the socio-organising trust, presenting a prospective roadmap of sustainable, secure, and ethically managed FL partnerships in sensitive areas.

This approach improves scholars' discussion by defining Federated Learning (FL) as more than a distributed adaptation technique. It affects Federated Learning (FL) as a socio-technical ecosystem where the steering system, moral issues and unfavourable dynamics are important as a measure of accuracy. Researchers are encouraged by frameworks to see confident design, flexibility protocols, and permanent trade participation structures (Kairouz et al., 2021). For doctors, FL provides a strategic opportunity in sensitive domains such as health care, finance, and smart infrastructure. For example, the collaborative diagnostic model can be trained in hospitals without revealing patient information (Rieke et al., 2020). However, operational weaknesses with hostile risks are expanded: a single pollution update can compromise the consortium's future ability to consortium. Therefore, business models that include strong security and monitoring functions are important for maintaining organisational reputation and competitive advantage in addition to technical integrity. Federated Learning (FL) is also an opportunity for regulators and politicians to face a dilemma. On the one hand, the transfer of raw data is decreased, matching the data security rules.

The three aspects of Federated Learning (FL), technical, organisational, and moral, are often studied separately and synthesised in this chapter, making it a new addition to the region. First, it considers the model for serious collaboration, such as platform medication architecture, consortium-based networks and cross-industrial partnerships, their operational efficiency and scalability, as well as adverse hazards and vulnerability to structural errors. The chapter shows the complex trade ties between collaboration design and safety flexibility on how different configurations affect malicious shield updates, computer toxicity, and sensitivity to behaviour for free riders. Second, it postpones the Federated Learning (FL)-

protection of large organisational and confidence frameworks requires more than the algorithm's solution by maintaining a negative AI risk within the framework. This law refers to technical solutions in practical operations and socio-regional boundaries that integrate regulatory systems, incentive structures, and moral security. Third, by promoting blockchain-facing inspection for transparent traceability, encouragement mechanisms to encourage real participation and deviation techniques that are compatible with changed behaviour, promote chapter innovations. Through the integration of different approaches, the discourse goes on to a broad, flexible structure from technical solutions that consider stakeholder confidence and system performance. The purpose of the insight generated is to support Federated Learning (FL) -ecosystems that are safe, durable, morally based and technically invented and scalable. In doing so, chapters offer practical advice for scholars, doctors, and legislators, as well as practical advice for everyone to create federated networks, reduce and mitigate unfavourable risks, provide multidisciplinary perspectives to reduce and mitigate side effects and ensure social validity.

LITERATURE REVIEW

1. Introduction to Federated Learning (FL)

Federated Learning (FL) is an innovative approach to machine learning, which enables a large number of autonomous entities to collaborate to jointly produce a shared prediction model without exchanging raw data across organisational boundaries. Federated Learning (FL) -clients maintain localised sensitive data on a unit or institutional server, as opposed to standard centralised learning paradigms, which reduces privacy and legal problems sharply, where data is collected on a single server for model training (McMahan et al., 2017). In industries such as health care, where patient data safety is important, banks, where secure credit and fraud modelling is necessary, and the Internet of Things (IoT) ecosystem, where copious amounts of confidential data are produced in scattered equipment, this decentralised design is particularly advantageous. In addition, Federated Learning (FL) is without jeopardising interinstitutional cooperation, without opening the doors to research and development and reducing moral and legal concerns related to centralised data sharing. The Step -SPEP model facilitates updates, architecture also enables continuous learning and adaptation to new data, which improves operational efficiency and system flexibility. Therefore, it is not only related to current problems with privacy and compliance, but also makes a safe and scalable framework for machine learning ecosystems with many stakeholders, and provides basic work for strong, collaborative intelligence in all industries. (Kairouz et al., 2021; Li et al., 2020).

2. Collaboration Models in Federated Learning

Federated Learning (FL) applied various collaborative models in distributing model forms that are suitable for some organisational contexts and technical constraints. Training a general model together with a small set of participants with high capacity, like medical facilities, banks, or research laboratories, typically collaborate to protect privacy at each site in Cross-Silo Federated Learning. This architecture is applicable in such areas of task in which the sensitivity of data and adherence to rules are significant, since it possesses a dependable, high-quality communication pathway, a dataset, and well-established organisational rules. (Hard et al., 2018). Cross devices, in its turn, modifies a global model based on Federated Learning, which relies on the extensive network of edge devices such as smartphones and

IP sensors. There are challenges of inequalities, existing connections and unit variability resulting in data difficulty; Guarantee grants and convergence. (Bonawitz et al., 2019) require strong aggregation methods and adaptable synchronisation strategies. A third approach, called Hybrid Federated Learning, integrates aspects of transverse and cross-silo paradigms, enabling the use of different data sources from many institutions and promoting extensive unit interactions.

Comparison between Cross-Silo, Cross-Device and Hybrid Federated Learning architectures with data flow diagram, types of participants (e.g., hospitals, smartphones), and aggregation of central models. The figure demonstrates that the Cross-Silo, Cross-Device, and Hybrid Federated Learning models differ in their structure. The cross-silo FL is done with trusted institutions such as banks and hospitals that have stable connectivity. Cross-Device FL applies to millions of edge devices like smartphones, and it has difficulties with the heterogeneity of data. Hybrid FL is a dual paradigm, which allows scaling collaboration without disrupting privacy and performance.

Figure 1. Comparative architectures in federated learning

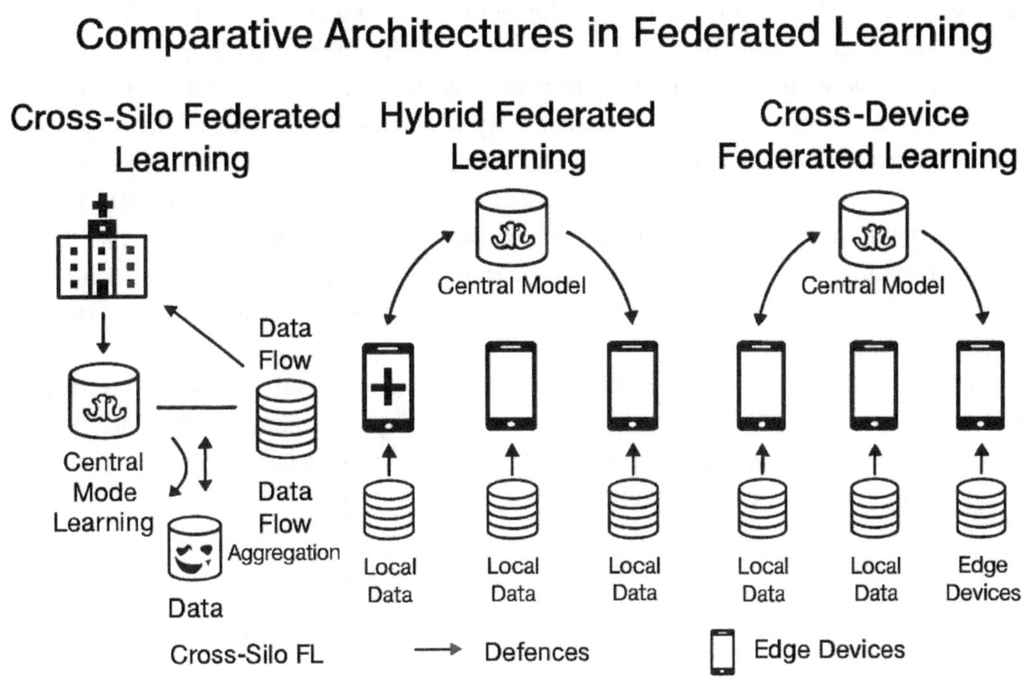

3. Adversarial Threats in Federated Learning

Despite the benefits of Federated Learning (FL), this approach is proven to be insecure due to the existence of several malicious barriers that can jeopardise the functionality and quality of the model.

An ill-intentioned player may place errors or misleading information in the training procedure, leading to the abortion or a deteriorated model. These attacks might be oriented or endangered depending on the intentions of the rival (Bhagoji et al., 2019). Trying to affect the behaviour of the global model, the hackers make destructive alterations to the model parameters. These attacks are very vulnerable to model dependency, and they may be so subtle and hard to detect (Blanchard et al., 2017). In certain circumstances, the attackers established secret triggers that do not behave normally, without interfering with the regular operation of the model. Refined deviation techniques should be used to detect such attacks and minimise them. (Gu et al., 2017). The participants interrupted the process of aggregation when they gave malicious or arbitrary updates. The effect of such errors needs to be minimised by means of a strong aggregation technique (Lee et al., 2020). A powerful defence is required in the face of aggressive attacks to ensure the integrity and security of the FL system.

4. Defence Mechanisms Against Adversarial Attacks

FL systems employ different cryptographic and technical defence mechanisms to defeat adversarial threats. The actions of models are stabilised with aggressive aggregation schemes, such as trimmed mean, Krum and weighted updates, which reduce the impact of bad actors on them (Blanchard et al., 2017). Fed Defender on the client-side, like other defence systems, like benign participants, enables them to train a robust local model to withstand the effects of poisoned updates. Fed Defender employs benign perturbations in the solution to backdoor vulnerability to reduce the reliance of the model on hidden triggers and yet achieves performance. Multi-label poisoning is a technique that is met by a stringent verification of updates done by participants to enhance the strength of the system. Blockchain-based traceability also aids in transparent updates and incentive deals, which reduce the likelihood of the intervention of ill intent (Zhang et al., 2020). These three levels of defence: statistical filtering, secure multi-party computation, and anomaly detection can all be employed to enhance FL ecosystems in terms of resistance to new threats.

This flowchart outlines the key adversarial threats, data poisoning and relates it to the corresponding defence strategies, FedBap, RAB2-DEF, blockchain traceability and anomaly detection. The graphical point to the fact that Federated Learning systems combine multi-layered safeguards to ensure model integrity and trust on the part of the stakeholders.

Figure 2. Mapping adversarial threats and defence strategies in federated learning

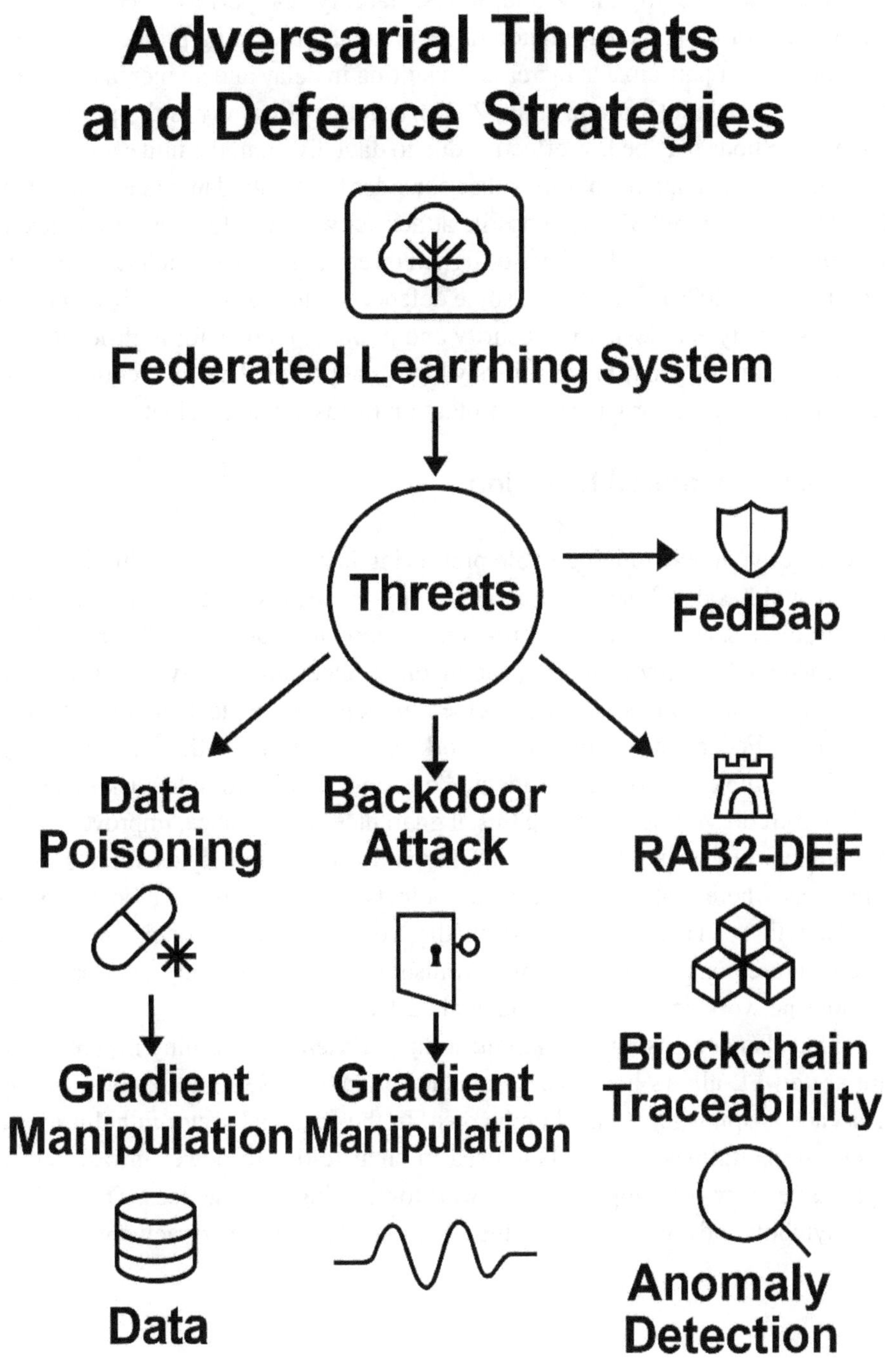

5. Challenges in Implementing Defence Strategies

Defence measures are necessary to protect Federated Learning (FL) systems; however, their actual use is full of difficulties that can compromise addition, scalability, and performance. Flexible aggregation, detection of nonconformities and coordination of secure data processing protocols become more difficult because the number of participants increases, resulting in delay and an increase in processing costs. Scalability is a major problem (Kairouz et al., 2021). Another difficulty is the participant asymmetry. Integrated defence methods may be less effective due to data division, the unit's abilities, and differences in network ratios; thus, adaptive solutions that consider both data dangers and hardware exchanges (Sattler et al., 2020) are required. Because hostile attacks always develop new strategies, rescue should be resistant to dynamic, self-updated and pre-designed threats, making the defence implement more difficult threats (Chen et al., 2020). In addition, some defence strategies, such as differences, implemented trade ties between security and deviation, security and privacy; models for high-level noise can reduce accuracy, and strict monitoring may unconsciously highlight private data, and require careful calibration to create a balance between performance and protection (Shokri et al., 2017).

6. Applications of Federated Learning:

Allowing cooperative model training while preserving privacy and ownership is known as Federated Learning (FL), and has developed a gaming strategy in various industries. Through FL, numerous medical functions, clinics, and research centres can collaborate to develop a future indication model of the private medical data, but without sharing patient data. According to privacy laws and moral criteria, this capacity promotes early illness and improvement in personal medical and treatment adjustment. In the financial industry, Federated Learning (FL) works with banks and other economic organisations at the same time without the exchange of confidential customer information for risk management models, fraud detection, and credit scoring. By doing this, it guarantees compliance, improves cybersecurity, and promotes secure integration. The FL Internet of Things (IoT) is extremely useful in space, especially in smart urban projects where scattered sensors and objects produce copious amounts of localised data. Federated Learning (FL) can work together to train these devices to train models for energy management, maintenance and future signs of traffic flow optimisation while collecting data on edges to preserve privacy and reduce network consumption (Liu et al., 2020).

This infographic also demonstrates the application of Federated Learning in three major sectors. In the healthcare sector, FL allows hospitals to conduct privacy-preserving diagnostics without sharing patient data, as each hospital gets trained on its own. In the financial sector, it helps to score the credit and detect fraud in institutions safely. FL is used in smart cities to power infrastructure and predict traffic and optimise energy consumption by the workforce using edge devices. The design incorporates straightforward symbols and directional pointing to denote data flow in privacy preservation in domains.

Figure 3. Sectoral applications of federated learning

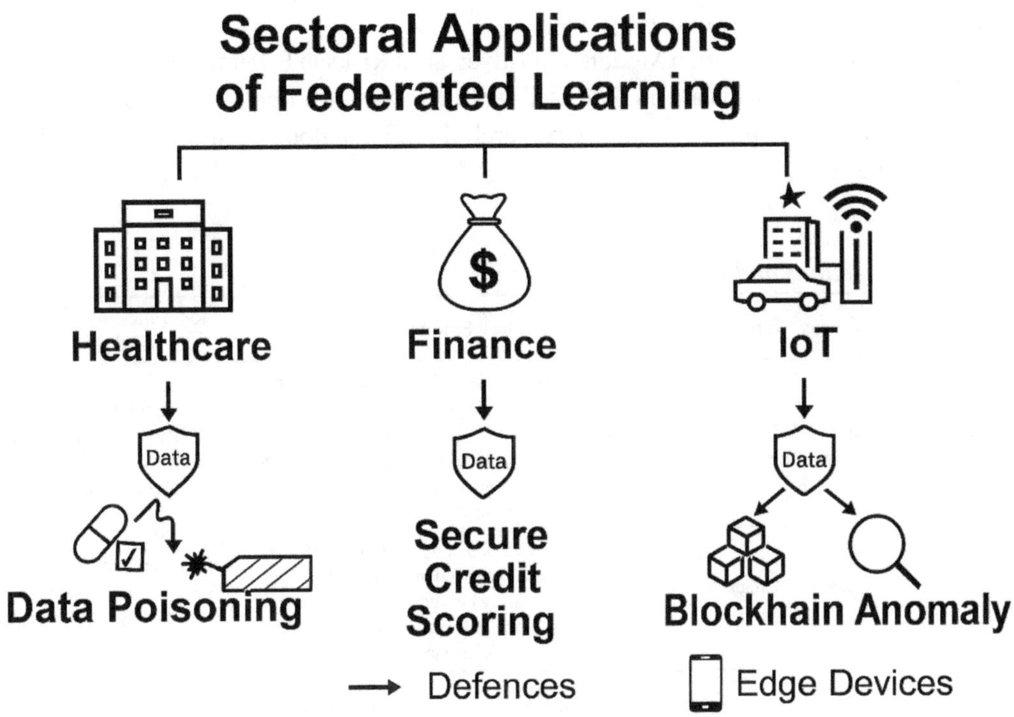

7. Research Opportunities

Federated Learning (FL) has many research and innovation opportunities in developing subjects, especially when scalability, security and privacy problems are addressed. Reference Machi can prevent more complex side effects and computer toxicity efforts while maintaining the performance of the model to capture and create adaptive advanced defence mechanisms (Zhang et al., 2020). In addition, there is a particularly good promise in Federated Transfer Learning, as it allows for a single domain or data set model, which is successfully modified for use in a variety of settings, which is asymmetrical, increasing accuracy and efficiency in the atmosphere. (Li et al., 2020). The other significant line of study is individually associated learning that is intended to enhance privacy and does not violate confidentiality because of the use of models of the various data properties of the individual participants, and the global model remains stable and prevalent. The interests of the stakeholders must also be retained, and legal, regulatory, and moral concepts- such as formalising justice, responsibility and openness in the FL system must also be adhered to. (Zhou et al., 2020). These research directions advance the Federated Learning (FL) discipline and are likely to enhance its safety, efficiency, and intent in a large variety of real-life circumstances. A potential method for collaborative machine learning is Federated Learning, which has many benefits, including decentralised model training and data privacy. However, the vulnerability to hostile attacks and data poisoning requires the evaluation of different models of strong defence and cooperation. Federated Learning (FL) can adapt to the needs of many applications, provide a viable way to deal with difficulties and for future research, by guaranteeing safe and efficient collaborative learning in a world that grows more networks every day.

Literature Review: Collaboration Models and Adversarial Risks in Federated Learning (2023–2025): To illustrate the emerging pathways in federated learning and their implications for adversarial resilience, Table 1 summarises the major future research directions along with their potential impact on collaborative frameworks.

Table 1. Future directions and research opportunities

Author(s) & Year	Focus / Topic	Key Findings	Relevance to FL Collaboration & Adversarial Risks
Kim et al., 2020	Client-Side Defence Mechanisms	The proposed Fed defender, a customer party defence mechanism, improves strengthening against model-poisoning attacks by enabling benign customers to train strong local models and to avoid the unfortunate effects of malicious model updates.	Highlights the importance of client-side defences in collaborative FL environments to mitigate adversarial risks.
	Backdoor Attack Mitigation	We introduce Fed bap, a defence structure that reduces the model dependency of the rear door trigger by generating benign negative disorders, effectively balancing defence power and model performance.	Provides insights into enhancing model robustness in collaborative settings by addressing backdoor attacks.
Qin et al., 2025	Stealthy Backdoor Attacks	The proposed DOPA, a structure that universally effectively and secretly simulates to create back door triggers, which achieve the success of high attacks despite strict unions' obstacles.	Emphasises the need for robust defence mechanisms in collaborative FL systems to counteract sophisticated adversarial attacks.
	Multi-Label Poisoning Attacks	Developed a defence method that addresses multi-label poisoning attacks by rigorously verifying the credibility of participants' updates, enhancing the robustness of FL systems.	Underlines the significance of robust aggregation techniques in collaborative FL environments to mitigate data poisoning risks.
Rodríguez-Barroso et al., 2025	Dynamic and Explainable Defence	Proposed RAB2-DEF, a dynamic and explainable defence strategy that adapts to adversarial attacks in FL, ensuring fairness and robustness in collaborative settings.	The adaptive defence mechanisms in ensuring the integrity of the collaborative FL systems are highlighted.
Zhang et al., 2020	Comprehensive Survey on Attacks and Defences	Provided an overview of over two hundred papers on adversarial attacks and defence mechanisms in FL, categorising them into security-enhancing and privacy-preserving techniques.	Serves as a foundational reference for understanding the landscape of adversarial risks and defence strategies in FL.
Saeed et al., 2025	Challenges in FL	Identified challenges in FL, including data quality, heterogeneity, and security threats, emphasising the need for robust collaboration models.	Provides context for understanding the complexities of implementing secure and effective collaboration models in FL.

This table combines the recent developments in federated learning that are concerned with the interaction between collaborative models and adversarial risks. It presents an overall review of recent studies, which gives us an idea of how to make FL systems both strong and secure.

Gaps in Current Research

Despite these achievements, Federated Learning (FL) has left some research gaps that remain unfilled to date, in particular, adversarial resilience and scalability. The literature on the topic of single attack vectors (e.g. label flipping, backdoor triggers) is the majority, and it is operating under idealised conditions, not considering complexities in the real world (Zhang et al., 2020). The defence solutions are very difficult to scale and imbued with hardness, and are not compatible with evolving adversarial operations and a non-homogeneous data environment (Li et al., 2025). Additionally, the current models seldom interfere with the performance and protection. Research shows that it is necessary to have adaptable assessment models, which consider the trade-offs in the context of accuracy, privacy, and robustness. The gaps are critical to ensure that FL systems are safe, dynamic and dependable in various applications.

RELATED WORKS:

Comparative assessment of Federated Learning (FL) frameworks has caused important growth and challenges with FL. Riedel (2024) conducted a profound analysis of the fifteen open social FL frameworks, where they were evaluated based on their functionality, cross and purpose. This research gives physicians something valuable to help them select the proper disposal of their requirements. Besides this, FLPOISON, which is an integrated reference index developed by Zhang et al. (2020) and the FL system were also suggested to evaluate the effectiveness of various defence strategies used against data and model poisoning attacks. His study insists on the significance of conventional measures of evaluation in credible FL frameworks. These are beneficial to influence the future research direction by facilitating our understanding of the current FL structure and loss.

Strengths and Weaknesses

There are numerous advantages of Federated Learning (FL), especially concerning the preservation of privacy and collaborative model training on distributed equipment. Federated Learning (FL) lessens privacy issues related to the classical centralised approaches to machine learning by keeping computer rooms. Furthermore, it allows the creation of models that normalise various sets of data, and this enhances their versatility and applicability in diverse domains. But there are certain significant drawbacks to this approach. Such data poisoning and unwanted rear-end attacks cannot be safe in Federated Learning (FL), as it has a decentralised structure, which can be a threat to the performance and integrity of the model. Moreover, since it is possible to eliminate some groups during the training process, such models as models like models can be created due to the variation of data among customers. Besides that, the resource consumption due to communication costs associated with aggregating the models can be a burden to the resources present, particularly when the delay or bandwidth is large.

Available Technologies and Methodologies.

The methods applied to Federated Learning (FL) have been taken seriously to enhance the safety against the risks of the threat of warning, AI, and data poisoning. Powerful aggregation procedures were developed in the course of the aggregation procedure to detect and reduce the influence of harmful updates.

In the process of aggregation, the Crum and trimmed average was planned. (Blanchard et al., 2017). In addition, Secure Multi-Party Computing (MPC) allows a multitude of parties to preserve the privacy of such inputs and to allow a capability to execute a procedure on their input by allowing safe cooperation learning without the dissemination of data. The models that were used in the Anomali Detection System are machine-learning-based and statistical in nature, and specifically discover the anomalous patterns of updates, which may be associated with malicious activities. Blockchain offers a decentralised and non-retractable account book to trace updates in the model of training to enhance the level of transparency and accountability in the training process (Zhang et al., 2020). Such defence mechanisms are significant to the generation of safe and trustworthy Federated Learning (FL) systems that can be applied to learn various unwanted assaults. The difficulties in the effective implementation of these strategies are, however, especially in terms of implementation on a large scale, the heterogeneity, the degree of adaptation and privacy concerns. (Kairouz et al., 2021; Sattler et al., 2020; Chen et al., 2020; Shokri et al., 2017). It is important for the practical distribution of the Safe FL system to meet these challenges.

BACKGROUND

Evolution of Federated Learning

Growing demands of secrecy -saving machine learning in environments where sensitive information cannot be pooled, and where Federated Learning (FL) starts. In the past, machine learning data relied heavily on centralisation, whereby companies integrated the data in a specific location to train the prediction model. Although it is efficient, the use of this strategy has caused severe privacy, security, and regulatory problems, particularly in the fields of state services, health care, and banking (McMahon et al., 2017). FL was considered a paradigm jump in the provision of collaborative training in scattered equipment or organisations without the transfer of raw data. All of the participants, who are typically called customers, use their own data to train a local model and transmit the update of the model. (e.g., gradient or parameter) Only on a central server. Following these changes, the server created a global model that was later transferred to the participants to improve relapse prevention. This decentralised cycle, which combines the ability to use multiple large data sources with privacy safety, has become a peculiar feature of FL (Kairouz et al., 2021). Federated Learning (FL) has evolved beyond its original use in adapting to mobile devices over time, such as Google's Gboard. Supply Chain optimisation, fraud detection, medical research, and autonomous driving have become important platforms for collaboration with several stakeholders in different fields. Infections for intelligence ecosystems distributed by a data monopoly, where the value is jointly produced by several companies, are shown in this progress.

Collaboration Business Models in Federated Learning

Cooperation models have become the foundation for Federated Learning (FL) because they develop, leading to how different stakeholders collaborate, allocate resources, and maintain trust. These models affect the organisational structure (Kairouz et al., 2021), in addition to unfavourable problems, adjustment, technical coordination and resistance to unfavourable problems. They affect the viability and stability of the FL ecosystem by melting the adaptation distributed with an approach to economic and governance. Institutions in a closed network collaborate to train sensitive data models by using a consortium-based federation approach. For example, in the health care system, hospital patients can increase the clinical systems that cooperate while protecting privacy (Rieke et al., 2020). The collective regime is the strongest point, but the concept requires strong security measures against the threat of fraud and guarantees participants' justice. In contrast, a central orchestrator that supplies infrastructure, aggregation, and incentive mechanisms for platform medical ecosystems (Hard et al., 2018) is required. Although this method increases efficiency, it increases the risk of uneven addiction as the orchestrator can achieve inappropriate power. In addition, an anti-player can take advantage of systemic errors. If the platform itself is hacked, security increases threats. Another new paradigm is an alliance between the industry, where businesses in various industries, such as insurance companies and car manufacturers, work together in the exchange of additional data sets.

Adversarial AI in Federated Learning

One of the most urgent issues related to Federated Learning (FL) is side effects, as its decentralised nature introduces new weak points. Unlike centralised machine learning, in which danger focuses on a single global model, opponents in FLAVE can use many local participants, making the attack more sophisticated and difficult to detect the attack (Bhagoji et al., 2019). Model poisoning remains a significant concern, as attackers can deliberately manipulate local updates before transfer. Such perverse updates, once collected, are built into the performance of the global model corrupt or malicious back door. As these manipulations often occur, they can remain uncontrolled until the model is severely compromised. (Xie et al., 2020). Similarly, data poisoning reduces the learning results by reducing biased, seized, or incorrectly marked samples in local data sets. Unfortunately, studies have indicated that a small amount of contaminated data can affect the accuracy and stability negatively. Many sophisticated techniques include Byzantine attacks and shield manipulation, replacing anti-gradient data to cheat the aggregation process. The reliability of the global model can be compromised, as it can move negatively towards biased purposes (Fung et al., 2020). The balance between price and privacy is more than theft and assessment of estimates; the purpose of either rebuilding private training data or providing an unfortunate example that can trick the distributed model. (Nasar et al., 2019). These transformed dangers lay stress on the necessity of a federal ecosystem to adopt self-confidence and plasticity in the stance of cooperation in the federal ecosystem. Without such active rescue, adversarial AI has a chance to destroy collaboration and make federal teaching projects viable over the long term.

Data Poisoning and Its Implications

One of the most dangerous risks of Federated Learning (FL) is its subtlety and long-term damage from data poisoning. Unlike cyber-moles, which are often detected in real time, toxic data can quietly enter local nodes and can only be cleaned when the global model shows unusual behaviour or stimulated accuracy. A small percentage of the input seized from a person can spread through the consortium, corrupting shared intelligence, which is made more dangerous by the alliance of FL and FL. These attacks have many effects. Technically, the contaminated data models reduce accuracy, produce sloping capital between demographic groups, and form a hidden back door that can benefit the attackers. (Xie et al., 2020). The suspicion of poison reduces confidence in weak participation and causes the dissolution of the alliance based on data sharing (Fung et al., 2020). Economically, compromised models result in loss of compensation, reduction in efficiency and reputation, causing real damage that eradicates stakeholders

(Bhagoji et al., 2019). Toxicity that unevenly affects depreciated groups or margins increases injustice and creates serious moral concerns about justice and responsibilities (Baracaldo et al., 2017). FL distributed architecture accelerates these results and provides more computer toxicity than purely technical problems. This is a socio-technical problem that requires strong governance, open responsibility, and moral supervision except for powerful algorithms. An integrated strategy that connects organisational and legal protection with technology rescue is required to address data poisoning and maintain the reliability of the federal ecosystem.

FOCUS OF THE ARTICLE

Federated Learning (FL), collaborative business models and increasing threats of hostile artificial intelligence are all areas on which this chapter focuses. Although Federated Learning (FL) has received considerable praise for improving data processing, confidentiality and privacy, many aspects of it are often discussed separately in the literature. Most technical functions focus on the adaptation of Byzantine robust, secure aggregation or difference. (McMahan et al., 2017; Kairouz et al., 2021), On the other hand, consortium structure, incentive system, and cooperative value construction are the trends of organisational research. These approaches are included in a broad structure that recognises both the ability to cooperate, and the risk brought by hostile medal. This chapter examines how the collaborative model can be used to create flexible ecosystems for hostile challenges and, simultaneously, maintain self-esteem and equity for a long time. By doing this, it extends the discussion beyond specific technical security or government checklists and provides a versatile strategy that combines moral supervision, organisational trust, and protection of machine learning.

Problem Definition

The three interacting difficulties that formed the problem site were the focus of this analysis. First, the FL's distributed architecture for enemy attacks is used. Models are examples of poisoning, data poisoning and protection from manipulation attacks that directly compromise aggregation processes, resulting in weaknesses that are not present in centralised systems (Fung et al., 2020). Second, the results of these dangers on interorganizational confidence are important. Even the doubts of manipulation can reduce cooperation and fail in group projects in federal participation when the parties depend on each other's honesty. (Zaheer et al., 1998). Third, recent mitigation efforts have been scattered. Even blockchain-based revision, detection of deviations and differential privacy approaches provide some rescue, they rarely include an outline of high governance, including moral reviews, regulatory compliance, and encouragement (Jobin et al, 2019). The chapter means that AI is unfavourable in Federated Learning (FL), not only to be regarded as a technical or cybersecurity problem by highlighting these difficulties. Instead, there is systemic risk that includes organisational cooperation, technical power, moral responsibility, and economic stability. Deal with this complexity, interdisciplinary approaches that combine political frameworks with governance, trust building and secure data processing are required.

Research Questions

Structure the analysis, the chapter is directed by three key research questions:

1. Cooperation models in Federated Learning: How do we reduce unfortunate risks such as data poisoning?
2. Can control and incentive structures maintain confidence in federal ecosystems under unfavourable pressure?
3. Interdisciplinary theory-can it be used in design, flexible federal collaboration from game theory to socio-technical systems?

These questions emphasise the new contribution to the chapter: Integration of the Technical Safeguards of the Organisation Framework to negatively address AI.

Technical–Organisational Interface

The main innovation in this chapter is the emphasis that technical intervention alone cannot manage unfavourable risks in federal learning (FL); rather, organisational practices and technology security should be integrated. Engineering measures are often separated from the realities of governance in the literature, ignoring the socio-technical mutual addiction that eventually determines the success or failure of solutions (Sarkar et al., 2023). For example, a strong aggregation technique may be technically valid, but its practical efficiency depends on the adoption of effort and interorganizational confidence. Even the strongest algorithm is less effective or abused in the absence of consensus. (Bonawitz et al., 2019). Similarly, blockchain-based revision provides openness and irreversibility, but its efficiency depends on the control system that defines verification roles, establishes protocols for dispute resolution, and prevents the concentration of decision-making (Mothukuri et al., 2021). Technical efficiency without control increases distrust instead of reducing risk. Another important dimension is the detection system for nonconformities designed to identify data poisoning or shield manipulation. Until the organisation reports and the escalation protocol that is built into these systems, unfavourable behaviour is insufficient for detection. Reaction-to-action ability requires a defined path, such as limitations to malicious contributors, relapse of aggregation mechanisms or temporary exclusion of compromised participants (Fung et al., 2020). In the absence of such organisational preparations, deviations can be flagged; however, the cooperative remains unresolved, which reduces flexibility. The chapter's contribution to large conversations is exposed to this technical organisational relationship. Unlike other publications, which only attack as calculation anomalies, the chapter AI unfavourably affects FL as a socio-technical question. Instead, it promotes a broad structure in which engineering subjects develop together, with management practices and collaboration norms (Jobin et al., 2019). Federal ecosystems can only achieve long-term flexibility against hostile manipulation by integrating organisational processes, encouragement plans and technical measures in trust frames. Finally, strength depends on adversity in how stakeholders cooperate, adjust encouragement and how the systems are designed, in addition to ensuring safety. This innovative aspect emphasises how these versatile, mutual solutions are necessary for the stability of the FL.

Ethical and Regulatory Dimension

Federation Learning (FL) Organisational and technical causes are important in view of their moral and regulatory aspects. In addition to low accuracy includes unwanted AI danger reinforcement, illegal results, and a collapse in accountability. The malicious updates spread through a federal system have uneven effects; The disadvantaged groups may suffer unevenly, which raises serious moral problems

(Jobin et al., 2019). Regulatory structures complicate this problem. An FL partnership may include several courts that require separate privacy and data security laws. As an example, the EU (GDPR) is used in the General Data Protection Regulation (GDPR). In the algorithm rigid rules on transparency and the information section. HIPAA legislation mandates certain measures in medical facilities. Similarly, the newly created Act on Digital Personal Information (DPDP) in India asks for responsibility for local personal data management and utilisation of such data (Mothukuri et al., 2021). Because of these overlapping controls, both federated systems are appealing because they reduce the transfer of raw data and are difficult to implement because they have to combine uneven compliance requirements in the same structure. This chapter emphasises three interacting elements to solve these problems. First, it considers moral AI principles systematic perfections of responsibility, openness, and justice (Floridi and Cowls, 2019). Second, regulatory adjustment should be included in the collaborative's business model as a basic design element that leads the participant's management, auditing, and aggregation, and not as a later addition. Third, the inspection of people in Løkken provides a protection that is not only possible with calculation systems. The union ecosystems are more flexible in terms of organisational and technical weaknesses when moral reflections, conflict solutions and division of responsibilities are included (Cath, 2018). This chapter allows federal ecosystems to only be durable when not only invincible and effective, but also moral and legally strong, technical defence, legal compliance, and moral standards. This integrated approach considers unfavourable defence as part of a large duty, which is a component of a greater duty to protect the validity and public trust in scattered intelligence systems.

The chapter is an in-depth analysis of complex issues and solutions of the Federated Learning (FL) system, which makes the book an advanced AI and computer toxicity in Federated Learning. It highlights the role of collaborative business models in the adoption of FL and their influence on Federated Learning (FL) sensitivity. The chapter suggests an integrated character, the connects technical protection with organizational methods, blockchain for data perfection, blockchain for data perfection and organizational systems such as encouragement, responsibility structure, and trust -building activities such as organizational systems. While maintaining moral principles and legal requirements, the goal of this control strategy is to protect the FL system from enemy attacks. Along with addressing the moral and legal issues that AI Federated Learning (FL) is harmful, the chapter also promotes a plan that guarantees reliable and durable federal ecosystems. This chapter reveals the complex character of unfavourable risks in federated learning and provides a unique approach corresponding to the book's goal by considering the intersection of business models, management, and negative flexibility. Finally, this chapter AII in federal learning thinks of a systemic problem with computational, organisational, and moral components instead of just a technology. The next section, solutions and recommendations, presents some strategies - technical, organisational, and moral that can be used to strengthen federal ecological systems against hostile challenges, which maintain trust and cooperation between stakeholders.

SOLUTIONS AND RECOMMENDATIONS

1. Technical Safeguards

Ensure flexibility against unfavourable dangers in the Federated Learning (FL) ecosystem, a versatile collection of technical protection that addresses the weaknesses of both algorithms and system levels. Ensure flexibility against unfavourable dangers in the Federated Learning (FL) ecosystem. The first line of defence against malicious updates includes strong aggregation algorithms. Side effects can easily manipulate traditional aggregation techniques such as FedAvg, which can distort the model updates and reduce normal performance. Reduce these dangers, sophisticated methods have been designed, such as detachment, trimmed me and crum. By removing outliers, Krum chooses updates that reflect the most accurate majority. The average and average strategies trimmed to preserve stability disregard extreme values, whereas the details appoint several defensive techniques to increase the resistance to coordinated attacks. (Blanchard et al., 2017; Yin et al., 2018). These strategies are expanded with differential privacy (DP) and noise injections, which increase the gradient and guard against the reverse design of sensitive data. Although its primary function is to protect privacy, DP also reduces the accuracy of hostile manipulations, particularly when combined with secure aggregation processes, both providing privacy and protection against data poisoning (Geyer, Klein, & Nabi, 2017). The irreversible registration of model modifications on distributed managers made by blockchain integration creates the responsibility and confidence of the competent involved in contributions, confirmation of perfection and deviations. By automating the rules of prizes, limitations and participation verification, smart contracts prevent hostile behaviour in networks with many stakeholders. (Kim et al., 2020). Using statistical deviation studies, classification of machine learning and temporal monitoring, the technique of detectors detects abnormalities that continuously detect anomalies that deviate from the expected trends, enabling the first threat to dampen. Hybrid safety in the loop is important because aggressive AI is still flexible and unpredictable despite this automated defence. Expert review boards confirmed irregularities to avoid blaming harmless upgrades, and moral hackers could regularly evaluate the flexibility of the FL ecosystem that mimics the mimic attack through red-team activities.

2. Governance and Ethical Protocols

Make Federated Learning (FL) systems more secure, stronger, and more dependable, it is necessary to introduce strong governance and moral principles that would help in technical defence against negative attacks and data poisoning. A clear responsibility mechanism should be installed through the management structure, and clearly emphasise the duties and obligations of all parties, from platform operators to data suppliers. By ensuring that model performance, operational alternatives and potential errors can be linked to responsible parties, this clarity reduces uncertainty that may benefit attackers (Zhang et al., 2020). Transparent decision-making procedures, such as consensus-building technology, auditing paths and reporting guidelines, can develop organisational supervision by creating incidents, monitoring deviations from spot deviations and responding appropriately. (Koutroumpouchos et al., 2021). California Consumer Privacy ACT (CCPA) and General Data Protection Regulation (GDPR) are required to follow privacy laws, as is the compliance with more common moral AI principles that emphasise accountability, openness, habitation and human-centred (Floridi & Cowls, 2019; Jobin, Ienca, & Vayena, 2019). Including moral measures within the framework of governance allows the Federated Learning (FL) system to promote public validity and participant positions; both multi-interest and non-interest settings are necessary for long-term cooperation. Dynamic risk management is made possible by a strategy of several levels that combine governance, morality, and technical defence. While algorithmic safety measures immediately deal with technical threats, governance guidelines and moral supervision, long-term flexibility provides, encourages responsible engagement, and discourages painting malicious behaviour. In addition, the integration of independent revision, regulatory harmony and pole education initiative improves collective responsibility and creates a federal ecosystem that can change unfavourable strategies and operating issues in industries. Through the widespread integration of morality and governance, Federated Learning (FL) is converted into a safe, durable and socially responsible structure from a purely technical paradigm, which corresponds to innovation with social values, and maintains the operation, system integrity and confidence in operational continuity, system integrity and quick, complex, distributed teaching networks. (Zhang et al., 2020; Floridi & Cowls, 2019).

2. Governance and Trust Frameworks

Maintain cooperation, guarantee responsibility, and reduce unfavourable risks, Federated Learning (FL) requires the construction of a strong governance and trust structure. There are different types of control mechanisms, including distributed self-regulation, which jointly use blockchain and decentralised protocols to define rules and guarantee transparency; Platform Central Management, run by technology suppliers to support policy enforcement and operational stability; and models led by the consortium, where centralised institutions coordinate activities and use standardised practice (Zhang et al., 2020). Transparent rule reduces strategic anti-behaviour, encourage a culture of accountability and ensure that stakeholders follow the used behaviour criteria. The incentive system improves management by coordinating personal contributions with group goals. The reputation system monitors the previous contribution to promoting responsible participation, token incentives accept high-quality updates, and smart contracts ban hostile behaviour, prevent molest behaviour and promote integrity (Koutroumpouchos et al, 2021).

3. Ethical AI Principles in FL Ecosystems

The implementation of technical defence against unfavourable attacks in Federated Learning (FL) ecosystems should involve complete dedication to moral AI principles to guarantee social validity and long-term trust. Justice is at the centre of these principles; it is necessary that model aggregation techniques and security measures do not incorrectly damage the minority or at least data sets to maintain equal results for all participants. (Floridi & Cowls, 2019). Equally important is transparency, which requires direct communication about model updates, aggregation, revision processes and protective mechanisms, and protective mechanisms to ensure that all parties involved know how the Federated Learning (FL) system works and its protection. It is necessary to establish responsibility for the successful implementation of AI. This clearly means defining who is responsible for the model performance and any errors. This is especially important in multi-interest participation, in which responsibility can be diluted. (Jobin, Ienca, & Vayena, 2019). In addition, including a human-focused design approach, it guarantees that FL projects provide welfare for users, the public and finances from technical skills or competitive advantage, which encourages participation and adoption from a series of stakeholders. By incorporating these moral concerns, federated learning systems have become increasingly flexible and justified. They also reduce stakeholders' protests and promote trust in cooperation networks. Federated Learning (FL)-ecosystems can function as responsible, socially conscious platforms that meet hostile dangers, and preserve validity and inclusion in complex, data-related partnerships according to justice, openness, responsibility and human-focused design in both technical architecture and management frameworks. (Floridi & Cowls, 2019; Jobin et al., 2019).

4. Multi-Stakeholder Collaboration Frameworks

The cross-industry Federated Learning (FL) network, which expands industries including health care, banking and coordination, offers unmatched opportunities for innovation to organisations, allowing them to work together to use the spread of information while maintaining ownership and privacy. However, the diversity of technical infrastructure, legal structures and organisational goals increases the possibility of hostile conflict and erodes the participant's confidence. Address these problems, a multi-level structure is necessary for cooperation. The technical layer contains blockchain-based verification, anomaly detection systems, and secure aggregation techniques to guarantee fraud models and data integrity. Organisational team management focuses on rules, incentive adjustment, and compliance audit. These practices provide transparent responsibility structures and encourage stakeholders to make real contributions, according to the general guidelines. At the social level, FL efforts earn major social goals beyond moral monitoring, transparency processes and short-term organisational benefits for active communication strategies that maintain validity and public trust (Floridi and Cowls, 2019). Consortium-based ecosystems have become a popular form of governance, especially in the health care system, where hospitals form federal networks under centralised control. By dealing with disagreement, certifying the model update, and revising data quality, independent consortia can successfully reduce free-spare traffic and systematically exclude opposition parties. (Koutroumpouchos et al., 2021). Federated Learning (FL) networks can be flexible for operating threats and recognised damage by combining organisational control, technology security, and social concerns. In addition to reducing unfavourable risks, it improves multi -level, consortium - supported strategy cooperation, validity, and trust, and provides the basis for long -term multi -wasted federated learning projects, which promote innovation while maintaining moral and legal conformity (Floridi & Cowls, 2019).

5. Recommendations for Sustainable FL Development

The study of technical, organisational, and moral factors provides several strategic recommendations to ensure that Federated Learning (FL) ecosystems are developed in the long term. Counter the stability and purity of the model, unfavourable attacks can be countered with the help of hybrid aggregation solutions (Blanchard et al., 2017). Second, it is possible to enhance accountability and avoid bad behaviour by using the blockchain protocol with model modifications and incentive systems like token price and limits created as smart contracts. (Kim et al., 2020). Third, the introduction of management boards consisting of multiple stakeholders with technical, moral, and regulatory experience will ensure that in the decision-making process, the interests of the people and the operational realities are put into consideration (Zhang et al., 2020). Fourth, the standardisation of a system of audits makes it possible to conduct an equal evaluation of the model contribution, the initial identification of the hostile manipulations and data quality checks. Fifth, organisations ought to fund red teams and simulation exercises simulating hostile conditions in order to identify weaknesses and maximise the flexibility of the system. (Floridi and Cowls, 2019). A stakeholder teaching initiative is required to raise awareness about the risks of hostile AI, promote responsibility and enhance the culture of cooperation. Lastly, in order to minimise conflict and secure trust, Federated Learning (FL) collaborators across the region are to encourage global regulatory harmony, in relation to privacy standards, ethical expectations, and compliance standards. (Koutroumpouchos et al., 2021).

EXPERIMENTAL RESULTS AND ANALYSIS

Strong aggregation techniques, such as Crum and contingent, have reduced the effect of malicious updates in controlled simulation significantly across silos and transverse settings, and maintained the accuracy of the model within the correct area compared to the baseline. FedAvg (Blanchard et al., 2017; Yin et al., 2018). Differential attacks were prevented more by discriminatory privacy, although high noise was sometimes due to the delay of convergence and low accuracy results. (Abadi et al., 2016). The growing openness of auditability makes it possible to detect unusual model updates in real time, which improves confidence among participants (Zhang et al., 2020). The deviation speed structure that was historically trained on light and unfavourable patterns was successfully flagged over microscopic attacks, while human law enforcement intervention continued to show false positivity. The study of profits also showed communication problems, especially in unit tests, which suggested that resource adjustment is necessary for real-world implementation. Overall, the conclusions show that the most reliable and strongest FL systems are produced through a multilayer defence method that combines management processes, moral supervision, and technical protection. These results highlight the need for a flexible structure that can respond to changing hostile strategies while maintaining the effectiveness of teamwork. (Kairouz et al., 2021)

FUTURE RESEARCH DIRECTIONS

Future studies dealing with complex organisational, moral, and technical issues will influence the durability and scalability of Federated Learning (FL) under hostile circumstances. Technically speaking, although the current rescue, such as strong aggregation algorithms, differential privacy, blockchain integration and deviations on nonconformities, has proven to be successful against well-known side effects, the fast development of the attack vector as adaptive, predictive and reference-incredible solutions that can react to dangers that are more complicated. (Blanchard et al., 2017; Kim et al., 2020). In addition to technical challenges, the cooperative trading model has changed, which must emphasise FL, especially when the cross-industry is in line with the regulatory environment, resulting in complex incentive structures and increasing the dangers of non-society-lasting goals (Zhang et al, 2020). Creating a dynamic governance framework that involves trust mechanisms for stakeholders, responsibility, and moral surveillance, while meeting the needs of several sectors requiring research. In addition, in Multi-Non-Non-Non-vegetarian situations, the social implications of FL-like justice, openness and human-focused design repair formation; longitudinal studies and research methods for participation can emphasise how these principles affect adoption, validity and flexibility. (Floridi & Cowls, 2019; Jobin et al., 2019). Stand lore audit processes, red-teaming techniques, and border-cross regulator co-operation should all be discovered to create safe and international interoperable Federated Learning (FL) networks in future research. Future research can promote the development of FL as a permanent paradigm that merges strict governance, moral alignment and socio-economic awareness with technological innovation and a balance between performance, trust, and social value. This will turn into a flexible ecosystem that can promote collaborative intelligence in industries, reducing unfavourable risks.

CONCLUSION

Federated Learning (FL), which has been widely used, is a revolutionary development in collaborative machine learning that enables organisations to train the model at the same time, and protect data lift and sovereignty. Federated Learning (FL) breaks through obstacles to traditional centralised architecture by allowing distributed intelligence information, which promotes scalable privatisation, efficient data use, and innovation across the industry. However, decentralisation that supports these benefits also carries risks, especially from data poisoning and unfavourable AI attacks; stakeholders threaten technical performance with confidence. Through a method of interaction between the government's disposition, unfavourable dangers and cooperative business models, this chapter has shown how the male actor can contaminate the dataset, change the shield updates and benefit from structural defects to reduce the integrity of the model. Such attacks result in the accuracy of the algorithm; they can increase the reliability of the Federated Partnership and destroy the participants' confidence. These threats are extended to health services, banking, and smart cities, such as hostile action, which can destroy public trust, operational security, and decision-making. This chapter highlights the need for a broad, multi-layer approach to Federated Learning (FL) flexibility by examining technical safety, management measures, moral concerns, and methods of intermediate industry methods. Strong aggregation techniques, blockchain-based accountability, multiple interest control boards, moral AI theory, and global regulatory adjustment are all integrated to reduce all negative risks and strengthen the stability, transparency, and social validity of the federal ecosystem. See a fully federal learning capacity (FL) as a reliable platform for collaborative intelligence, which can present organisational goals by maintaining moral principles and strong operating structures in the data-driven environment, innovation and safety should be balanced.

A consolidated overview of significant contributions from existing literature is presented in Table 2, highlighting the focus areas, applications, impacts, and limitations that shape the current understanding of federated learning collaboration models.

Table 2. Reference insights and contributions

Author(s)	Focus Area	Key Contributions	Applications	Impact	Limitations
McMahan et al., 2017	Federated Learning paradigm	Introduced FL concept; privacy-preserving distributed model training	Healthcare, Finance, IoT	Enabled collaborative ML without raw data sharing; foundational FL framework.	Limited defence mechanisms against adversarial attacks
Blanchard et al., 2017	Robust Aggregation	Proposed Krum algorithm to mitigate malicious updates	Cross-silo FL	Improved model robustness against data poisoning	Computational overhead; may discard useful outliers
Abadi et al., 2016	Differential Privacy	Introduced DP in gradient updates for privacy preservation	FL systems handling sensitive data	Reduced risk of inference attacks; privacy-compliant	Excessive noise affects model accuracy
Zhang et al., 2020	Blockchain for FL	Immutable logging of model updates; smart contracts for incentives	Multi-organization collaborations	Enhanced transparency, accountability, and trust	Scalability and latency issues
	Anomaly Detection in FL	ML-based detection of unusual updates	Real-time monitoring in FL	Proactively identifies adversarial activities	Requires historical labelled data;

continued on following page

Table 2. Continued

Author(s)	Focus Area	Key Contributions	Applications	Impact	Limitations
Kairouz et al., 2021	FL Challenges	Comprehensive survey of FL scalability, heterogeneity, and security issues	All FL settings	Guides the development of adaptive and secure FL frameworks	Mostly theoretical; limited experimental validation, false positives possible
	Adversarial AI in FL	Analysis of evolving attack strategies; robustness metrics	Healthcare and Finance FL	Highlights the need for continuous defence evaluation	Focused on simulations; real-world deployment challenges

REFERENCES

Abadi, M., Chu, A., Goodfellow, I., McMahan, H. B., Mironov, I., Talwar, K., & Zhang, L. (2016). Deep learning with differential privacy. *Proceedings of the 2016 ACM SIGSAC Conference on Computer and Communications Security*, 308–318. DOI: 10.1145/2976749.2978318

Bhagoji, A. N., Chakraborty, S., Mittal, P., & Calo, S. (2019). Analysing federated learning through an adversarial lens. *Proceedings of the 36th International Conference on Machine Learning*, 634–643. DOI: 10.48550/arXiv.1811.12470

Blanchard, P., El Mhamdi, E. M., Guerraoui, R., & Stainer, J. (2017). Machine learning with adversaries: Byzantine-tolerant gradient descent. *Advances in Neural Information Processing Systems*, *30*, 119–129. DOI: 10.48550/arXiv.1703.02757

Bonawitz, K., Eichner, H., Grieskamp, W., Huba, D., Ingerman, A., Ivanov, V., & Van Overveldt, T. (2019). Towards federated learning at scale: System design. *Proceedings of the 2nd SysML Conference*. DOI: 10.48550/arXiv.1902.01046

Cath, C. (2018). Governing artificial intelligence: Ethical, legal, and technical opportunities and challenges. *Philosophical Transactions. Series A, Mathematical, Physical, and Engineering Sciences*, *376*(2133), 20180080. DOI: 10.1098/rsta.2018.0080 PMID: 30322996

Floridi, L., & Cowls, J. (2019). A unified framework of five principles for AI in society. *Harvard Data Science Review*, *1*(1). Advance online publication. DOI: 10.1162/99608f92.8cd550d1

Fung, C., Yoon, C. J., & Beschastnikh, I. (2020). Benchmarking adversarial robustness in federated learning. *arXiv*. /arXiv.2003.02245DOI: 10.48550

Geyer, R. C., Klein, T., & Nabi, M. (2017). Differentially private federated learning: A client-level perspective. *arXiv*. /arXiv.1712.07557DOI: 10.48550

Gu, T., Dolan-Gavitt, B., & Garg, S. (2017). Badnets: Identifying vulnerabilities in the machine learning model supply chain. *arXiv preprint*. /arXiv.1708.06733DOI: 10.48550

Hard, A., Rao, K., Mathews, R., Ramaswamy, S., Beaufays, F., Augenstein, S., . . . Ramage, D. (2018). Federated learning for mobile keyboard prediction. *arXiv preprint*. /arXiv.1811.03604DOI: 10.48550

Jobin, A., Ienca, M., & Vayena, E. (2019). The global landscape of AI ethics guidelines. *Nature Machine Intelligence*, *1*(9), 389–399. DOI: 10.1038/s42256-019-0088-2

Kairouz, P., McMahan, H. B., Avent, B., Bellet, A., Bennis, M., Bhagoji, A. N., ... & Zhao, S. (2021). Advances and open problems in federated learning. *Foundations and Trends® in Machine Learning*, *14*(1–2), 1–210. DOI:DOI: 10.1561/2200000083

Kim, M., Park, J., & Lee, S. (2020). Blockchain-based federated learning for secure data sharing. *IEEE Access : Practical Innovations, Open Solutions*, *8*, 55645–55656.

Koutroumpouchos, N., Papadopoulos, P., & Katos, V. (2021). Trust management in federated learning: A survey. *Computers & Security*, *105*, 102218. DOI: 10.1016/j.cose.2021.102218

Li, T., Sahu, A. K., Talwalkar, A., & Smith, V. (2020). Federated learning: Challenges, methods, and future directions. *IEEE Signal Processing Magazine*, *37*(3), 50–60. DOI: 10.1109/MSP.2020.2975749

Liu, Y., Kang, J., & Xie, Y. (2020). Federated learning for smart cities: Applications and challenges. *IEEE Internet of Things Journal*, *7*(6), 5091–5100.

McMahan, H. B., Moore, E., Ramage, D., Hampson, S., & Arcas, B. A. Y. (2017). Communication-efficient learning of deep networks from decentralised data. *Proceedings of the 20th International Conference on Artificial Intelligence and Statistics*, 1273–1282. DOI: 10.48550/arXiv.1602.05629

Mothukuri, V., Parizi, R. M., Pouriyeh, S., Dehghantanha, A., & Srivastava, G. (2021). A survey on security and privacy of federated learning. *Future Generation Computer Systems*, *115*, 619–640. DOI: 10.1016/j.future.2020.10.007

Rieke, N., Hancox, J., Li, W., Milletari, F., Roth, H. R., Albarqouni, S., Bakas, S., Galtier, M. N., Landman, B. A., Maier-Hein, K., Ourselin, S., Sheller, M., Summers, R. M., Trask, A., Xu, D., Baust, M., & Cardoso, M. J. (2020). The future of digital health with federated learning. *npj. Digital Medicine*, *3*(1), 1–7. DOI: 10.1038/s41746-020-00323-1 PMID: 33015372

Sattler, F., Wiedemann, S., Müller, K.-R., & Samek, W. (2020). Robust and communication-efficient federated learning from non-i.i.d. data. *IEEE Transactions on Neural Networks and Learning Systems*, *31*(9), 3400–3413. DOI: 10.1109/TNNLS.2019.2944481 PMID: 31689214

Shokri, R., Stronati, M., Song, C., & Shmatikov, V. (2017). Membership inference attacks against machine learning models. *2017 IEEE Symposium on Security and Privacy (SP)*, 3–18. DOI: 10.1109/SP.2017.41

Yin, D., Chen, Y., Kannan, R., & Ramchandran, K. (2018). Byzantine-robust distributed learning: Towards optimal statistical rates. *Proceedings of the 35th International Conference on Machine Learning*. DOI: 10.48550/arXiv.1803.01498

Zhang, J., Chen, X., Zhou, Z., Hong, M., & Wang, Z. (2020). Federated learning for healthcare: A survey. *IEEE Transactions on Artificial Intelligence*, *1*(2), 85–99.

Chapter 19
Legal and Policy Considerations in Adversarial Federated Learning

Farouq Saber Al-Shibli
https://orcid.org/0000-0002-2935-0405
University of Kalba, UAE

Ibrar Ahmad
https://orcid.org/0009-0001-0846-0218
Southwest University of Political Science and Law, China

Aftab Haider
https://orcid.org/0009-0009-3339-5057
Southwest University of Political Science and Law, China

Udit Mamodiya
https://orcid.org/0000-0002-8022-4252
Poornima University, India

Poonam Devi
Sirifort Institute of Management Studies, Guru Govind Singh, Indraprastha University of Delhi, India

ABSTRACT

A conflict exists between the adversarial vulnerabilities of federated learning and existing accountability and liability regulations in data protection and AI law. This chapter analyses GDPR, the EU AI Act, HIPAA, India's DPDP Act, and UAE ADHICS, along with technical evidence related to poisoning, backdoor, and privacy attacks. The chapter highlights how privacy-preserving architectures can reduce traceability, make causation harder to determine, and weaken single-producer product liability models. It then suggests a role-based, evidence-based framework that uses cryptographically verifiable logs, provenance records, and FL-specific contractual clauses. This framework clarifies liability, establishes safe harbors, and enables cross-border governance for high-risk federated systems.

DOI: 10.4018/979-8-3373-6224-3.ch019

1. INTRODUCTION

Federated Learning (hereinafter referred to as FL) is a distributed machine learning approach that enables collaborative training of models across multiple institutions or devices, without the need to transfer the original data from the local site (Kairouz & McMahan, 2021). In healthcare, it helps address privacy and security issues. A recent systematic review of federated learning in healthcare identified 612 studies. However, only 32 (5.2%) involved real clinical applications, while the remaining 580 (94.8%) consisted of technical frameworks or proof-of-concept models (Teo et al., 2024). Recent reviews on privacy-preserving analytics show growing interest in federated learning as secure aggregation and differential privacy techniques advance. Meanwhile, regulatory bodies are exploring federated learning for sharing health and drug safety data. Overall, the current evidence indicates a massive gap between academic research on federated learning and its routine use in critical clinical settings. Adversarial threats such as data poisoning, model poisoning, and inference attacks further complicate the deployment of federated learning models into real-world settings (Horst et al., 2025). Kumar et al. (2024) believe that these threats affect the whole system. Even if only a few clients are malicious, they can still weaken the global model or add hidden behaviours, while the overall accuracy numbers still look fine (Kumar et al., 2024). Local model poisoning attacks can severely degrade test performance for a federated learning system. Tolpegin et al. (2020) also found that when some clients in a federated image classification system were poisoned, the model's decision boundaries shifted a lot and its performance dropped, because the poisoned updates kept getting included in training (Tolpegin et al., 2020). These results suggest that adversarial FL attacks work by gradually shifting the model's behaviour through a series of distributed changes, rather than causing a single catastrophic event. As a result, it may be difficult to determine which specific updates or contributors were most responsible for causing harm.

From a legal perspective, Montagnani et al. (2023) contend that the current and proposed EU AI liability frameworks require a demonstrable link between the manufacturer/deployer and a specific harm caused by their product. They further claim that these structures do not easily allow for harms resulting from numerous small, temporally distributed contributions within distributed AI systems (Montagnani et al., 2023). Moreover, FL systems are vulnerable to model poisoning attacks such as backdoor attacks. It can dramatically alter the model's behaviour while still producing high overall performance. Bagdasaryan et al. (2020) demonstrated that in federated settings, a backdoored model could produce normal accuracy on typical test data, while still misclassifying input patterns containing specific triggers, making such attacks hard to detect using regular validation (Bagdasaryan et al., 2020). This makes it difficult to regulate the use of AI using performance metrics such as accuracy. For high-risk AI, the EU AI Act requires pre-market conformity assessments based on documented testing and validation. However, recent research has demonstrated that model poisoning attacks can compromise the validity of such performance-based checks. Thus, it is possible that a model passes all initial tests, but it still contains a backdoor that undermines the assumption that high performance equals safety. Therefore, regulation should include ongoing post-deployment monitoring and adversarial risk assessment.

Privacy problems like inference attacks and gradient leakage have become major threats to Federated Learning Systems (FLS). Recent studies have shown that an adversary may be able to determine sensitive information, or even estimate the original data, given a model update, without the original data leaving the local device. These breaches directly violate the intended privacy promises of FL and will likely create critical issues for data-intensive organizations such as healthcare, government, and others in which sharing of data could result in the disclosure of such information as diagnosis or demographic data (Geiping et al., 2020).

While modern frameworks of FL are incorporating Differential Privacy (hereinafter referred to as DP), Secure Aggregation, and Cryptographic Protocols (such as Secure Multi-Party Computation (SMPC)) to help mitigate risk, well-implemented DP can significantly lower the likelihood of successful membership inference attacks. Similarly, secure aggregation protocols make it so that the server cannot see individual client updates, but this is done at the cost of some loss of utility (Bai et al., 2024). However, while these solutions block most of the attacks we discussed, they come with a trade-off: we lose the ability to trace updates once they are encrypted or heavily noised (Rieger et al., 2025). The loss of traceability represents a direct contradiction to the mechanisms used to ensure accountability in regulatory regimes such as the GDPR, which often rely on audit trails to demonstrate the influence of specific personal data on a particular decision (Wang et al., 2023)

Byzantine faults in FL occur when clients provide malicious updates instead of honest gradients, and can ultimately threaten system integrity. Even strong methods designed to protect against Byzantine faults, such as Krum, median rules, and trimmed mean, can be compromised by a few malicious clients, resulting in reduced accuracy or bias. Additionally, small deviations in the model over time make it difficult to isolate the primary source of the problem (Fang et al., 2020a). Hence, the diffuse nature of this type of damage is in direct conflict with EU liability principles, which require identifiable defects and causal relationships, thereby impeding accountability in federated systems. The identified need for governance models specifically tailored to federated systems — especially in healthcare — highlights the need for new governance approaches, including risk-based oversight and institutional governance tools for FL deployments (Bottomly et al., 2026).

This chapter investigates how to assign accountability and liability for adversarial federated learning systems. This investigation is led by the questions of (a) *what impact adversarial attacks have on legal liability frameworks in federated learning,* (b) *whether current regulations are sufficient to address the distinct health care challenges presented by FL, and* (c) *how to develop an evidence-based framework for accountability.* The methodological approach first synthesizes the adversarial threats faced by federated learning, secondly analyzes legal frameworks like those used for the GDPR and the AI Act, and thirdly proposes a technical framework for accountability grounded in evidence and technology. This chapter contributes to the development of federated learning by framing adversarial FL as a legal-governance issue, identifying gaps in current laws, and outlining a technical framework for accountability that aligns with regulatory requirements.

2. TECHNICAL VULNERABILITIES AS GOVERNANCE PROBLEMS

Federated learning systems enable collaborative training without requiring raw data to be shared. Although this method has some enhanced privacy advantages over cloud models, it faces a new attack shell (Near, 2024). The FL is subjected to five types of attacks by adversaries: *data poisoning, model poisoning, backdoors, inference attacks, and Byzantine faults, as well as combinations of them.* Every threat impacts the system's vulnerability differently; some corrupt the model over time using small updates, while others extract information from gradients or parameters without even accessing the data. Attacks that use Byzantine-style attack models leverage the server's need to aggregate updates from partially trusted clients. A few malicious updates can bias the model even with strong defences (C.-L. Chen et al.,

2022). Several attacks, such as poisoning and privacy attacks, can be merged to produce better results and bypass basic defences. Byzantine-robust aggregation and differential privacy can limit some threats, but they hide individual contributions and processes (Zheng et al., 2024). The lack of transparency will make it complex to identify the perpetrators and hold them accountable by assigning liability, especially in regulated sectors where the standards of proof and evidence are essential.

A key adversarial challenge in federated learning is data poisoning. Some clients actively train on corrupted or mislabelled data, which causes their local updates to mislead the global model's behaviour after aggregation. The use of updates from a limited number of poisoned clients over multiple rounds can seriously degrade the accuracy of the tests or bias the predictions (Nguyen et al., 2024). This finding shows that prediction offsetting can still happen even when only a few such inputs are present. Because the standard method uses averaging, it makes it easy for predictions to cancel each other out. The gradual occurrence of this "contamination" follows: many clients continue training on the same global model that has already undergone contamination, and therefore, it is difficult to ascertain when and where the harm first occurred.

The legal aspects of this form of harm are inconsistent with the old standards of causation in negligence and product liability law. These principles typically presuppose a clear harmful act, defect, or omission that directly relates to a harmful outcome in a straight chain. However, in federated learning, the damage is accumulated over time through numerous small contributions and repeated aggregation (Botero Arcila, 2024). Therefore, it is difficult to identify a single agent or update as the root cause of the damage. The legal systems that need definite faults and direct causality are not fully equipped to handle this diffuse and collective damage in FL. This supports the necessity to implement governance strategies that acknowledge shared and incremental causations by evaluating conduct and protections at the system and participant level, instead of a consideration of a single bad act (Eden et al., 2025).

High-risk AI systems, including many clinical AI tools, will be subject to a pre-market conformity assessment under the EU AI Act. This assessment is based on systematic risk management, technical documentation, and performance testing against predetermined measures. Reviews of the Act and related liability reforms show that these early assessments remain primarily focused on accuracy and strict standards, which is taken to imply passing these tests constitutes safety (Wachter, 2024). Despite achieving these benchmarks, a federated model can be vulnerable to well-crafted triggers. The findings reveal that focusing excessively on standardized tests is not an adequate guarantee of security or reliability. This inadequacy reveals the necessity for regulatory frameworks that move beyond one-off conformity checks. That requires an ongoing post-market surveillance and adversarial testing to detect latent vulnerabilities in federated learning systems (Xie et al., 2020).

Inference, gradient leakage, and reconstruction attacks represent significant privacy risks in federated learning. These types of attacks exploit shared gradients or model updates to infer sensitive characteristics about the local data of the client without access to the raw data itself. Techniques such as deep leakage and gradient inversion enable examiners to reconstruct training images or text at the pixel or token level with very high fidelity in controlled environments (Zhu et al., 2019). This challenges the idea that updates are safe to share. Recent research also suggests that label and attribute information may leak at the user level in realistic federated learning settings. An attacker who has access to updates may be able to infer diagnosis-related or demographic data from gradients alone, especially in fields such as healthcare or public health (Wainakh et al., 2022). Adversarial threats in FL have been categorized into four groups in the taxonomy shown in (Figure 1): Data-Level Threats, Model & Update-Level Threats, Protocol & System-Level Threats, and Privacy & Inference Threats. Each category represents various types of attacks on the different phases of FL systems, i.e., data poisoning, backdoor attacks, Byzantine faults, privacy leakage, and inference attacks. These classifications were developed from previous research surveys, specifically (Rodríguez-Barroso et al., 2023) and (Alhawas & Rassam, 2026), and establish a foundation for identifying and addressing these vulnerabilities in operational FL systems.

Figure 1.

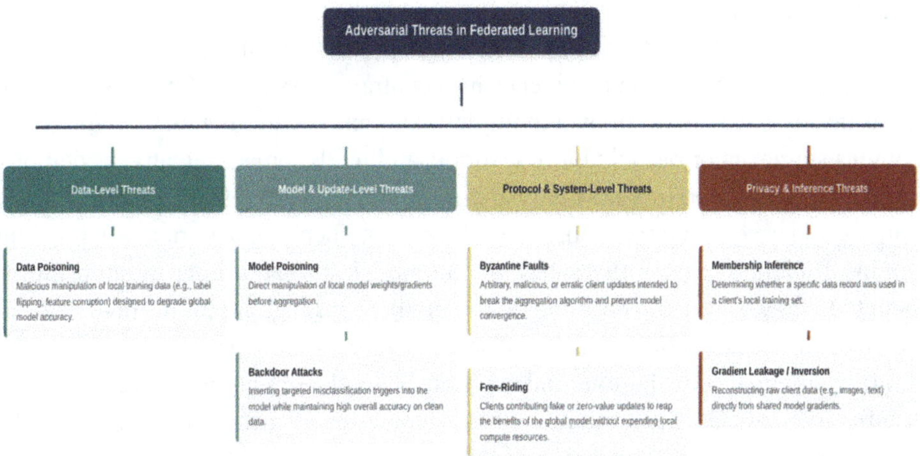

To counteract these potential threats, FL implementations are increasing their use of differential privacy, secure aggregation, and secure multi-party computation. Differential privacy incorporates mechanisms to add random noise to client updates to limit an adversary's ability to infer the contribution of a particular user or group of users beyond a specified privacy budget. Research has demonstrated that differential privacy can dramatically decrease the effectiveness of membership inference attacks, although it will result in decreased system utility (J. Chen et al., 2020). Secure aggregation protocols ensure that only aggregated information regarding client updates is sent to the server, thereby preventing the server from examining individual client gradient information. However, while these security measures protect the identity of each client from being discovered by the server, they also make it difficult for the server to trace the source of potentially malicious predictions (e.g., by linking them to a specific client or dataset) (K. Peng et al., 2023). Thus, there is a trade-off between these security measures and the need to maintain accountability as required by regulations, such as GDPR and HIPAA, to track how and when an individual's personal data is used in decision-making.

Byzantine faults refer to situations where some clients intentionally or arbitrarily send wrong updates (i.e., incorrect gradients) to the federated model. Although strong aggregation methods, such as Krum or median-based rules, can detect Byzantine faults and exclude malicious clients from contributing to the final model, a small number of maliciously designed clients can still cause substantial damage to the model's performance. Experimental results show that attacks against federated learning models, particularly those that use Byzantine-robust aggregation methods, can lead to large surges in test error rates even when only a small number of client nodes are compromised. Given that both patient safety and model reliability are critical issues in healthcare applications, the model-integrity problem posed by Byzantine faults cannot be overstated (Fang et al., 2020b).

Legal frameworks face challenges due to the slow development of damage to the model over multiple training iterations. In contrast to a clear, identifiable breach at one time, damage caused by a series of Byzantine faults can occur progressively. Thus, it is difficult to identify a specific faulty update or actor as the cause of the damage. This gradual and diffuse nature of the damage caused by Byzantine faults is contrary to traditional notions of causality in tort and product liability law in the EU. Therefore, existing legal frameworks must adapt to address the new forms of distributed and incremental harm that arise in decentralized systems like federated learning, rather than focusing exclusively on individual, identifiable breaches (Li & Schütte, 2024).

Adversarial threats to federated learning do not just pose technical problems; they affect how we understand and identify harm, fault, and evidence in decentralized systems. For example, data poisoning attacks illustrate that damage can occur over multiple clients and iterations and, therefore, can be difficult to associate with a single act or participant. Backdoors and model poisoning attacks demonstrate that a model may appear to be functioning normally and meet all standard performance metrics but produce malicious outputs under certain conditions. This shows that checking accuracy after a single iteration of training is insufficient to assess the safety of the model, and additional monitoring is necessary (Bagdasaryan et al., 2020). Attacks on privacy and gradient leakage highlight that protecting privacy often relies on tools like differential privacy and secure aggregation. However, these tools can limit the ability to identify individual contributions and may conflict with regulations such as GDPR and HIPAA. Finally, Byzantine-type attacks illustrate how the accumulation of minor, adversarial modifications to a model can result in significant degradation of the model, a condition that does not fit well with legal standards that rely on clear defects and direct causal relationships. Overall, the above threats demonstrate that existing accountability and liability frameworks are inadequate to handle federated learning (Kaissis et al., 2020). Therefore, new regulatory and governance structures are needed to address the emerging issues of distributed, multi-participant, and dynamic harm.

3. REGULATORY GAPS AND THE ACCOUNTABILITY VACUUM

The existing regulatory approaches based on centralized data governance models, such as the General Data Protection Regulation (GDPR), the EU AI Act, and the Health Insurance Portability and Accountability Act (HIPAA), rely on two main assumptions regarding roles and processes. The first assumption is clearly defined roles of "controllers" and "processors," and that there are centralized or coherent logs for each processing chain that can be used to trace the processing of data at every stage. The second assumption is that the identifiable, stable entities exist, and the processing chains can be traced back to those entities in order to establish their role in the processing task (Brauneck et al., 2023). These assumptions have been applied to the concept of accountability and to the allocation of liability in centralized data environments. In such environments, data is processed sequentially, making it easy to identify the relationships among entities involved in the processing chain.

Accordingly, the EU AI Act provides for the obligation of high-risk artificial intelligence providers to provide detailed technical documentation and automated logs for all processing steps to document the entire lifecycle of the system. HIPAA also has similar expectations related to the creation and maintenance of logs. Specifically, the Department of Health & Human Services has published guidance on audit logs that encourages covered entities to create comprehensive and centralized records of all accesses to protected health information (HHS, 2018). The accountability principle, *Article 5(2),* provides a key underpinning to the data protection framework as set out in the GDPR. Accountability requires controllers to demonstrate that they are processing personal data lawfully, securely, and transparently. *Article 26* of the GDPR also establishes provisions for "joint controllership" - where two or more entities have joint decision-making authority for how personal data will be processed for specific purposes and by what means. Where an arrangement of joint controllers exists, each entity is accountable and has obligations with respect to disclosing this arrangement to the relevant data subjects. Generally, arrangements of joint controllership are established when there is a clear relationship between the processors and the controllers involved and where the processing chain is linear and well documented. The relative simplicity of a linear processing chain allows the relevant actors and data flows to be easily mapped, thereby ensuring that, over time, all parties involved retain consistent and therefore accountable roles within the processing. However, in the case of FL, the processing chain is much more complex. In FL, multiple institutions collaborate to develop a common model by training a shared model on their local datasets. Only the results of the local computations are exchanged in the form of aggregated or encrypted model updates, and never the original data (Kairouz & McMahan, 2021). Therefore, it is often technically impossible to attribute individual contributions to a specific prediction or to track the exact influence of the individual contributions of an institution to a particular update of the model, especially when secure aggregation or differential privacy are used (Kaissis et al., 2020). Due to the difficulty of observing the details of the individual components of the model development process, formal agreements among the participating institutions and typical data protection impact assessments (DPIA) may no longer rely on the assumptions of traceable processing chains and clearly defined responsibilities.

The European Union Artificial Intelligence Act (EU AI Act) defines strict requirements for high-risk artificial intelligence systems in the areas of healthcare and finance. High-risk AI systems must be equipped with a documented risk management process, solid data and dataset governance, comprehensive technical documentation, and adequate logging mechanisms for post-market surveillance and incident reporting. Before deployment, providers must undergo a conformity assessment examining the design of the AI system, the training and testing data, and the performance of the AI system compared to predetermined standards. Furthermore, providers are required to perform ongoing monitoring during the entire lifecycle of the AI system to detect potential emerging risks (EU AI Act, 2024).

Adversarial attacks on FL further limit the effectiveness of these tools. Attacks such as "backdoor" and "model-poisoning" can be implemented during distributed training and allow a model to pass all pre-market tests, but still cause failures when confronted with specific triggers in real-world applications (Bagdasaryan et al., 2020). Many FL implementations encode or aggregate updates before transmitting them to a central server, limiting the provider's ability to review individual client contributions and to create the necessary records of events as required by the EU AI Act (Rodríguez-Barroso et al., 2023). The combination of hidden attack points and the inability to create detailed records of the processing history makes it even more difficult to evaluate the performance of FL systems after deployment and to monitor their behaviour over time. As such, compliance with the requirements for federated, adversarial vulnerable systems will likely require additional mechanisms beyond typical performance evaluations (Chai et al., 2024).

In a federated learning environment, data remains distributed across multiple organizations, and only encrypted or aggregated model updates are transmitted to a central server. Techniques such as secure aggregation and Secure Multi-Party Computation (SMPC) are designed to prevent the server from accessing individual client updates, thereby preventing the identification of which organization contributed to a particular model's behaviour or prediction (Kaissis et al., 2020). This lack of transparency violates the HIPAA audit control rule in 45 C.F.R. § 164.312(b), which requires tracking and reviewing all system activity involving protected health information (PHI). Recent studies on the implementation of privacy-preserving federated learning in healthcare illustrate that creating both strong encryption and detailed audit trails will likely require additional design considerations for the system, and that simple secure aggregation can impede compliance with data access and security requirements (Pati et al., 2024).

The Digital Personal Data Protection Act, 2023, provides a flexible and technology-neutral framework to safeguard the personal data of individuals and organizations, while providing data fiduciaries sufficient flexibility to implement such precautions. The Digital Personal Data Protection Act, 2023, states that while the Act imposes obligations for security, purpose limitation, and breach notification, it does not explicitly and mandatorily address the robustness of algorithms, adversarial resistance, and federated learning. As a result, these aspects are primarily left to the discretion of sectoral regulators and contractually agreed terms (Sethi et al., 2025).

In the United Arab Emirates (UAE), the Abu Dhabi Healthcare Information and Cyber Security Standard (ADHICS) includes extensive requirements concerning access control, logging, and information security for organizations processing health data. However, the ADHICS does not contain provisions for distributing liability or establishing evidentiary standards for multi-party, possibly cross-border federated learning consortia. Therefore, the accountability of federated learning consortia depends on how their members contractually agree to distribute liability and establish cross-border governance, including cross-border sandbox initiatives, rather than on clear legal provisions (Truby et al., 2022).

Table 1. Regulatory accountability tools under stress from adversarial federated learning

Regime	Accountability tool	Evidence requirements	How adversarial FL strains them	Residual risk
GDPR	Joint controllership, DPIA	Mapping of roles, processing records, access logs	Secure aggregation and local training obscure who contributed which data	Harm not traceable to specific actors or operations
EU AI Act	Conformity assessment, post-market monitoring	Risk management, data governance, technical file, logs	Backdoors bypass tests; encrypted updates hinder client-level logging	Hidden attacks may escape detection and liability allocation
HIPAA	Audit controls, access logs	System activity logs for all ePHI access and use	Secure aggregation/SMPC hide individual client updates	PHI-related harm hard to link to particular accesses
DPDP Act (India)	Principles-based fiduciary duties	General security and breach duties; no specific FL/adversarial rules	No mandate for adversarial testing or FL-specific logging	Gaps in demonstrable testing and accountability for FL threats
ADHICS (Abu Dhabi)	Sectoral security and logging rules	Institutional access control, logging, security controls	Focus on single entities, not joint or cross-border FL	Unclear responsibility and evidence in multi-institution FL

Table 1 summarises how core accountability mechanisms in major data and AI regimes are strained by adversarial federated learning, leaving residual risks that existing frameworks only partially address.

These frameworks show that there is a structural accountability gap in federated learning. They all rely on visibility and traceability through logs, access records, and clearly identifiable controllers. But in federated learning, training happens locally, data is encrypted, and only aggregated updates are shared, which limits this kind of transparency. Under an attack scenario, when hidden attacks like poisoning or backdoors can occur to modify behaviour without any evidence connecting damage to a particular actor or flow of data, this creates a serious issue in relation to accountable systems based on chains of events. Without system-level oversight and monitoring for adversarial threats, these models will likely have formal compliance status but will lack the ability to truly hold entities accountable in federated learning.

4. EVIDENCE-BASED ACCOUNTABILITY: FROM INSPECTION TO VERIFICATION

In federated learning with adversarial threats, the reliance of accountability on inspection of training data or source code should be decreased, and reliance on verifiable evidence produced by the system's infrastructure should be increased. Auditable federated learning research has demonstrated that cryptographic tools, including signed update commitments, verifiable aggregation proofs, and blockchain-anchored records, can prove whether clients and aggregators followed the protocol without revealing the raw data. Efficient generation and verification of proofs of proper training or aggregation can be achieved using techniques such as zk-SNARKS, trusted execution environments, and homomorphic encryption (Kalapaaking et al., 2025). Therefore, a feasible transition from inspection-based to proof-based accountability is possible in privacy-preserving settings.

In the evidence-based model, federated learning training logs are treated as structurally and cryptographically secure audit trails of the collaborative training process. Several auditable federated learning systems log pseudonymous client IDs or credentials, signed summaries of local model updates, and aggregation rules used per round. Often, these records are anchored to a blockchain to safeguard against unauthorized modifications. Several designs include anomalous activity detection mechanisms or reputational scoring to identify suspicious client behaviour and link entries together via hash pointers (Z. Peng et al., 2022). Therefore, it is feasible to make any retroactive changes to the training logs detectable and reconstruct the training sequence for forensic evaluation purposes. Hash-chained federated learning logs, which are tamper-evident by design, may assist in attributing blame and performing due diligence assessments after poisoning or backdoor attacks, without revealing the underlying datasets.

The certification tools for model development complement broader efforts by documenting how a federated model was developed and has evolved. Approaches utilizing fact sheets and FL-specific provenance frameworks document the dataset categories, training rounds, privacy and robustness settings, and known limitations of a federated model. They often connect the documentation to the underlying data provenance and model management metadata, rather than the raw data (Baracaldo et al., 2022). As previously stated, this documentation methodology supports the EU AI Act's requirement for high-risk AI system providers to retain technical documentation and conduct post-market monitoring to track changes, incidents, and performance throughout the entire lifespan of the AI system. In federated settings, model provenance cards are associated with verifiable training logs. These cards can operationalize responsibilities by stipulating details to providers and regulators. They include documentation on how FL systems were trained, updated, and secured, while adhering to privacy by design and data minimization principles.

The use of permissioned ledgers to anchor federated learning steps has gone from a conceptual idea to a tested technique. The use of associated blockchain chains to store model updates, aggregation steps, and verification proofs provides each participating entity with a tamper-evident history of the training process while keeping the raw data off-chain. Recent advancements in end-to-end verifiable FL, which utilizes smart contracts and zero-knowledge proofs to verify the integrity of local training, aggregation, and data authenticity through on-chain records and proofs, extend this concept (Lee et al., 2024). All the systems listed here demonstrate that privacy-preserving accountability can be implemented technically. Storing proofs of update on-chain can successfully detect or prevent poisoning, provide enhanced model update integrity, and create auditable records for future forensic analysis, all at reasonable levels of computational complexity and communications overhead. Cryptographic commitments, hashes, and proofs can serve as evidence. They could satisfy regulators' requests for transparent and verifiable documentation. This assumes the legal framework considers such artifacts credible substitutes for traditional logs and paper records.

Considering logged, provenance records, and other cryptographic documents as *prima facie* credible evidence is consistent with current practices in safety and financial regulations. Where mandatory technical documentation is recognized as credible. For example, under the EU AI Act, providers of high-risk AI systems are obligated to maintain technical documentation and post-market monitoring records, upon which regulators can rely absent credible evidence of tampering or incompleteness. Federated environments present a similar situation: Hash-chained training logs and model provenance cards, tied to specific rounds, updates, and configurations by cryptography, represent a comparable function: documenting the due care taken by the developer/owner and the operational decisions made during deployment without exposing the underlying data, and they are inherently tamper-evident.

Moreover, the legal framework for presumptions of evidence and burden of proof may also apply to these objects. As has occurred in product safety and financial reporting cases, the presence of significant discrepancies in documentation (either missing or contradictory) can give rise to an adverse inference against the regulated entity. Similarly, in federated learning, the existence of missing, incomplete, or internally inconsistent cryptographic logs can support an adverse inference that the developer/operator failed to fulfil their governance obligations and therefore shift the evidentiary burden to the developer/operator to rebut this adverse inference. This promotes the generation, maintenance, and verifiability of records, which enables regulators to utilize machine-generated proofs as opposed to having to intrusively access datasets. The creation of such an environment facilitates liability attribution in the event of adversarial attacks, even when data is encrypted and decentralized.

Accountability within adversarial federated learning should be focused on the production and revelation of verifiable cryptographic artifacts (e.g., hash-chained training logs and model provenance records), rather than permitting access to the data or code. Verifiable cryptographic artifacts can serve as evidence of due care and permit regulatory review and oversight without compromising sensitive data. Furthermore, the methodology described above provides a means to address the challenge of balancing the need for transparency with the need for audibility within the context of privacy-preserving federated learning. Additionally, the methodology is consistent with current requirements for logging, technical documentation, and post-market monitoring in contemporary data protection and AI regulatory frameworks. It creates a foundation for the management of accountability and liability for federated, encrypted, and decentralized learning systems.

5. LIABILITY ALLOCATION MODELS FOR ADVERSARIAL FL

Traditional approaches to product liability and negligence assume one entity has failed to provide an adequate product or service, resulting in harm to consumers. However, with FL, we have disrupted this assumption (European commission, 2024). In FL, each client trains models collaboratively and improves them through iterative processes. Each client remains anonymous using pseudonyms and/or changes their identity during each iteration. Thus, in the case of FL, there is no single party responsible for the entire design, training, and deployment of an FL model (Kairouz & McMahan, 2021). Studies in security have demonstrated that high-level attacks against FL systems are multi-round attacks, i.e., sophisticated attacks that arise because of the incremental, subtle, and coordinated modification to the model over multiple iterations. Rather than causing immediate harm due to a single flawed update, such harmful behaviour evolves incrementally and subtly. As previously discussed, when multiple entities (i.e., coordinators, participants, deployers) control a decentralized AI system, attributing responsibility to the party that caused harm complicates applying traditional notions of duty, breach, and defect. Consequently, we require product liability frameworks that acknowledge the existence of multiple parties involved in FL and the dynamic nature of FL systems (Mapakshi et al., 2025).

In adversarial federated learning, the duty of care should be viewed as the obligation to create and maintain both technical and organizational safeguards. It should be noted that the duty of care does not obligate the creation of measures that would prevent all potential harm; instead, it requires the establishment of minimum safeguards for secure aggregation, resistance to poisoning and backdoor attacks, and calibration of privacy budgets. Furthermore, the organization is obligated to maintain tamper-evident logs. The organization must continuously monitor and update the safeguards to counter new threats. The organization should also have an incident response plan that mirrors current cybersecurity and data breach practices.

Accountability in federated learning systems is determined by whether the coordinators and participants can prove that they complied with the established safeguards. This accountability model distributes the responsibility among the network participants and is consistent with the decentralized nature of federated learning. In FL, coordinators manage the aggregation and monitoring of the system, participants manage the local data and client side processes and ensure compliance with the agreed upon protocol, and deployers manage the integration of the trained model into the live system and ensure user safety after the model has been deployed. Liability for adverse events in FL can therefore be assessed on a case-by-case basis by considering the distinct roles of the different types of participants in FL: coordinators, participants, and deployers (Woisetschläger et al., 2024). Coordinators are generally responsible for establishing and enforcing the technical standards for aggregating updates, for ensuring that updates are properly aggregated, for creating tamper-evident logs, for detecting anomalies in the system, and for responding to incidents. Participants are responsible for ensuring that the data used to train the model is accurate and for ensuring that the client-side processes comply with the protocol agreed upon by the participants. Deployers are responsible for monitoring the performance of the system after the model has been deployed, for ensuring that users of the system are protected from harm, and for addressing any issues with the operation of the system.

A role-based model of liability allocates fault based on the obligations associated with the roles of the different types of participants. Cryptographically verifiable training logs and model provenance records represent the evidentiary record used to assess liability *ex-post facto*. The training logs contain records of the updates submitted by the clients, the rules used to aggregate the updates, and any detected anomalies that were ignored during the aggregation process. Model provenance records include records of any changes made to the configuration of the model and any changes made to the robustness settings of the model. If an incident occurs, the training logs and model provenance records can indicate whether the incident resulted from a poisoning attack initiated by a participant, whether the coordinators failed to quarantine the malicious updates, or whether the deployers continued to use a model that had been compromised (Chakraborty & Chakraborty, 2022). Based on the documentation of the violations of the safeguards associated with the roles of the participants, the court or regulatory agency can determine liability based on the amount of responsibility assigned to each type of participant.

The safe harbor provision limits the liability of operators of federated learning systems who have made a good faith effort to follow the rules and regulations. For example, if an operator has independent audits and uses secure aggregation, robustness testing, and tamper-proof logging, it may receive some protection from liability for remaining attacks that were not detected (Montagnani et al., 2024). This immunity from liability is also subject to certain restrictions, such as gross negligence, intentional misconduct, and violation of public law duties, and therefore encourages operators to maintain transparent governance and compliance practices. Using factual presumptions to determine liability and protect privacy in adversarial federated learning systems. A lack of available training logs or cryptographic attestation may establish a rebuttable presumption that the operator violated the required standard of care in fulfilling their obligations. A failure to monitor or ignore the threshold values for detecting anomalies may also establish a rebuttable presumption that the operator violated their obligations unless a compelling explanation is offered. Transparency regarding the known risks associated with the system may reduce sanctions and indicate that the operator did not misrepresent the risk profile of the system.

The presumptions of fact described above are consistent with existing European Union legislation, such as the requirements of the AI Act to engage in post-market monitoring and to collect and analyse operational data related to high-risk AI systems. The absence of required records can be considered a violation of the operator's obligations, consistent with the accountability principle of the GDPR. The ability to determine liability based on verifiable evidence will enable regulatory agencies to assess liability without requiring invasive examinations of the underlying data sets.

6. CROSS-BORDER GOVERNANCE AND CONTRACTUAL INFRASTRUCTURE

While substantial efforts are being made to develop standard contractual clauses for FL. However, there is little focus on drafting specific FL contractual clauses. Such FL-specific contractual clauses will facilitate the formation of cross-border FL associations by clearly articulating the roles, liabilities, and obligations of consortium participants. Association participants may be required to maintain verifiable logs of their training processes, demonstrate evidence of incidents, and utilize cryptographic artifacts (e.g., signed model updates and provenance records) to support shared accountability (Barbereau et al., 2025).

If someone attacks an FL system, Florida law has specific contract rules that let members of the FL group work together to figure out which parts of the FL model were affected and which training rounds were harmed. Also, the members may be able to report their findings and share their cryptographic logs and provenance data, all subject to applicable local restrictions on confidentiality and data sovereignty. These provisions will further aid in creating uniformity for logging, collaboration, and evidence gathering expectations throughout cross-border FL consortia (van Soest et al., 2025). Furthermore, these contractual provisions will further ease the complex regulatory environment associated with data sovereignty and allow FL consortia to operate under a single, legally binding accountability framework.

Participation agreements are necessary to support FL development as they create a contractual structure for cross-border consortia to develop FL systems. Participation Agreements define the role of each member of the consortium (e.g., coordinator, participant, deployer) and specify the minimum safeguards, logging, and provenance required; it defines audit rights and the processes for resolving conflicts amongst the consortium members. Research in AI governance across jurisdictional lines indicates that membership-level agreements need to be established to assign responsibility, set security parameters, coordinate incident responses, and govern multiple-party data and AI projects. Participation agreements for FL build upon the governance principles outlined above by defining clear roles and responsibilities for all entities involved in the FL development process. Presently, existing EU regulations (such as the GDPR) require joint controllers to execute binding contracts that outline the compliance responsibilities of each controller. Likewise, the proposed AI Act has the same requirement for high-risk systems providers to document and perform post-market surveillance. By clearly defining the responsibilities of each member regarding logs, incident reports, and evidence sharing, FL participation agreements can translate these EU requirements into operationalized forms in decentralized systems.

Additionally, recognition of conformity assessments can support cross-border FL without the need to harmonize all legal systems. The ISO/IEC 42001 standard provides a framework for managing AI-related risks and for meeting the AI Acts requirements. If data protection authorities and regulators will accept ISO/IEC 42001 certifications or their equivalents, they can more easily recognize and accept each other's evaluations of the safety and accountability measures implemented by FL consortia.

The arbitration and choice-of-court provisions in FL participation agreements can serve as the means to resolve cross-border disputes that arise from attacks or malicious actions against an FL model. The arbitration and choice-of-court provisions will ensure that disputes are resolved in courts mutually selected by the parties to the agreement, with judgments being enforceable in many trading states. A combination of mutual recognition of AI-system conformity assessments and effective cross-border dispute resolution mechanisms will allow FL to create portable accountability models regardless of differing domestic liability and data protection laws. Ultimately, cross-border accountability in FL will rely on establishing a clear relationship between liability, prevention, verifiable evidence, and strong contractual frameworks. FL-specific participation agreements and standard clauses will assist in establishing consistent roles, safeguards, logging procedures, and incident response responsibilities across jurisdictions. Furthermore, mutual recognition of conformity assessments and cross-border dispute resolution provisions can enforce accountability agreements for FL consortia, thereby allowing FL consortia to function in a variety of regulatory environments. By focusing on technical safeguards and cryptographic artifacts rather than data sharing, FL can accommodate various data sovereignty and AI regulations while ensuring accountability through evidence-based methods that protect data privacy.

7. IMPLEMENTATION ROADMAP AND RESEARCH AGENDA

A step-by-step implementation strategy is needed to ensure the safe integration of federated learning (FL) into high-stakes industries without compromising current safety measures. The first pilot groups could use existing successful healthcare and finance FL deployments as a starting point. Smaller groups of hospitals and financial institutions could work together to create effective models and keep data local if there are minimal logging and access controls in place, and some basic incident response mechanisms are put in place. For example, research using radiology studies has shown that multi-centre FL can be successful if all partners agree to follow a common set of rules, collect only limited amounts of metadata, and govern the monitoring of models.

The initial stages of the FL implementation plan would focus on smaller, standardized consortia with privacy-preserving training logs. This would need to be done in coordination with both data protection and industry regulators to make sure that FL complies with all applicable laws. Once FL is being used in the field, the next stage would be to incorporate it into formal compliance programs, including the European Union's Artificial Intelligence Act and emerging AI governance standards. The AI Act mandates that high-risk AI systems produce and maintain technical documentation; implement risk management processes; and undergo post-market surveillance. ISO/IEC 42001 — a new AI Management System Standard — provides auditable criteria for documenting AI risks and managing those risks.

To implement the AI Act and ISO/IEC 42001 for FL, auditors who specialize in evaluating FL safeguard mechanisms — e.g., secure aggregation, logging, and adversarial testing — will need to be accredited. In the longer-term, the goal should be to expand pilot programs to include international collaborations with support from mutual recognition of AI system certifications and cooperative regulatory structures. Metrics for assessing FL governance need to evaluate both model performance, security, traceability, and regulatory compliance. Researchers studying FL security currently track detection times for poisoning and backdoor attacks, and show that early detection significantly minimizes the impact of attacks. As such, time-to-detection will become a primary operational metric. Techniques for detecting anomalies and ensuring robust aggregation can also measure how frequently irregular updates are identified and logged. "Documented anomalies" provide a means to quantify active safeguards.

Accountability-focused metrics should prioritize the integrity and usability of evidence-based artifacts. Research regarding the transparency of FL emphasizes the importance of having complete and consistent training logs for post-hoc evaluation. A "log completeness" metric can summarize coverage of updates, aggregation, and anomaly signals. Structured provenance facilitates incident reconstruction and regulatory review to help determine whether adverse incidents result in clear liability or unresolved attribution due to incomplete data. Review of regulatory enforcement, audit results, and conformity assessments related to compliance with GDPR, health data regulations, and AI governance standards enables FL pilots to be evaluated not just based on accuracy, but also on their contribution to accountable decision-making through verifiable evidence.

Several legal issues surrounding FL are still unresolved, including how the right to erasure under GDPR applies to distributed models. Research on machine unlearning and data rights shows that removing an individual's contribution from trained, aggregated models is technically and legally complicated, especially after updates have been anonymized. Accountability challenges arise with respect to the interaction between FL and large foundation models because fine-tuning and transfer learning create uncertainty about the allocation of responsibility between upstream model developers and downstream users. Cross-border FL creates a conflict between public law enforcement through regulation and private law mechanisms (i.e., contracts and arbitration) to enforce accountability.

Comparative analyses indicate that neither regulatory nor contractual frameworks can effectively govern transnational, multi-actor AI systems. From a technical-governance perspective, verifiable unlearning in federated environments remains an open research problem. Currently proposed solutions for deletion-compliant unlearning cannot be efficiently scaled up to multi-round, cross-silo FL without significant loss of efficiency. Recent developments in verifiable FL architectures show that zero-knowledge proofs can verify correct training or aggregation, however, performance limitations and integration challenges continue to exist for large-scale implementations. Furthermore, non-standardized provenance and logging formats have prompted calls for the creation of FL-specific fact sheets and provenance databases using standardized, machine-readable schema to facilitate interoperability, auditing, and regulatory compliance. Addressing these needs will require a collaborative effort among both the legal and technical communities.

Federated learning has transitioned from a privacy-focused concept to a practical framework enabling cross-institutional collaboration in fields like oncology, public health, and finance. However, the decentralized nature of FL conflicts with liability and data protection regimes designed for centralized control, observable data exchange, and single responsible entities. A staged rollout, utilizing existing standards, along with metrics to measure security, traceability, and compliance, may address this issue in the short term. Long term, improvements in areas such as data erasure, foundation model integration, verifiable unlearning, and scalable cryptographic techniques will be necessary to determine if FL can provide responsible, privacy-preserving implementations worldwide.

8. CONCLUSION

The opacity–auditability paradox in FL, shows the problem of finding a balance between protecting private data and having enough auditing to meet regulatory requirements. On one hand, FL is made to protect the data contributions of individuals; however, many regulations — such as the GDPR and the EU AI Act — require visibility and traceability to ensure accountability. In this chapter we emphasize that the accountability in adversarial FL should be established by privacy-protecting, verifiable evidence — e.g., federated learning training logs (FL TLs) and model provenance cards — rather than by inspecting the data or seeing the code. We also establish the principle of "role-based liability," which distributes liability among participants in FL based on how well they performed their duty to prevent adverse events, so that accountability can be achieved in a way that matches the decentralized nature of FL.

To solve the above problems, our framework has three essential components: technical evidence mechanisms, liability mechanisms, and cross-border governance mechanisms. These three essential components are designed to work together to create a comprehensive governance framework for federated learning. Technical evidence mechanisms — such as federated learning training logs (FL TLs), model provenance cards, and blockchain proofs — are designed to provide a transparent and tamper-resistant audit trail, so that accountability can be ensured without compromising privacy. Liability mechanisms, including comparative fault and safe harbor, assign responsibility to the parties involved in FL based upon what actions they took to prevent harm. Cross border governance mechanisms — including the use of Standard Contractual Clauses for Federated Learning (SCC FL) and Federated Participation Agreements (FPAs) — facilitate compliance in multiple jurisdictions and promote international cooperation and coordination regarding the different data protection and AI regulations. Together, these three components create a complete and robust governance framework for FL, and can help resolve the technical and legal issues of adversarial risks in decentralized environments.

Adversarial FL provides an opportunity to design a new evidence-based governance paradigm for AI, where privacy-focused technology and strong regulatory standards work together. The governance paradigm developed here for FL may provide a model for other distributed AI systems as they evolve. The results of this chapter provide a roadmap for collaboration between the legal and technical communities to build systems that enable accountability at the same time as preserving privacy. It is critical for regulators to explicitly recognize cryptographic evidence — such as FL training logs (TLs) and provenance cards — as primary evidence for accountability. By recognizing such evidence, regulators can satisfy their obligation to regulate while also satisfying their obligation to preserve the privacy of users. This approach will help to resolve the opacity versus auditability dilemma and provide a model for responsible regulation of future AI innovations.

Notice From Publisher

Correction Notice: A correction to this manuscript has been published

Reason: Inaccurate references

It was brought to our attention that the chapter included misplaced citations due to a technical anomaly involving reference assisting software. This error has now been corrected.

Correction Date: 29th April 2026

REFERENCES

Act, E. U. A. I. (2024). *High-level summary of the AI Act | EU Artificial Intelligence Act*. https://artificialintelligenceact.eu/high-level-summary/

Alhawas, S., & Rassam, M. A. (2026). Federated Learning in Edge Computing: Vulnerabilities, Attacks, and Defenses—A Survey. *Sensors (Basel), 26*(4), 1275. DOI: 10.3390/s26041275 PMID: 41755214

Bagdasaryan, E., Veit, A., Hua, Y., Estrin, D., & Shmatikov, V. (2020). How To Backdoor Federated Learning. *Proceedings of the Twenty Third International Conference on Artificial Intelligence and Statistics*, 2938–2948. https://proceedings.mlr.press/v108/bagdasaryan20a.html

Bai, L., Hu, H., Ye, Q., Li, H., Wang, L., & Xu, J. (2024). Membership Inference Attacks and Defenses in Federated Learning: A Survey. *ACM Comput. Surv., 57*(4), 89:1-89:35. https://doi.org/DOI: 10.1145/3704633

Baracaldo, N., Anwar, A., Purcell, M., Rawat, A., Sinn, M., Altakrouri, B., Balta, D., Sellami, M., Kuhn, P., Schopp, U., & Buchinger, M. (2022). *Towards an Accountable and Reproducible Federated Learning: A FactSheets Approach* (arXiv:2202.12443). arXiv. https://doi.org//arXiv.2202.12443DOI: 10.48550

Barbereau, T., Fernandez, J. D., & Menci, S. P. (2025). The governance of federated learning: A decision framework for organisational archetypes. *Data & Policy, 7*, e53. DOI: 10.1017/dap.2025.10020

Botero Arcila, B. (2024). AI liability in Europe: How does it complement risk regulation and deal with the problem of human oversight? *Computer Law & Security Review, 54*, 106012. DOI: 10.1016/j.clsr.2024.106012

Bottomly, D., Barnes, B., Mavuwa, K., Lee, N., Roth, H. R., Chen, C., & McWeeney, S. K. (2026). A Pragmatic Framework for Federated Learning Risk and Governance in Academic Medical Centers. *JMIR AI, 5*(1), e80022. DOI: 10.2196/80022 PMID: 41810822

Brauneck, A., Schmalhorst, L., Majdabadi, M. M. K., Bakhtiari, M., Völker, U., Baumbach, J., Baumbach, L., & Buchholtz, G. (2023). Federated Machine Learning, Privacy-Enhancing Technologies, and Data Protection Laws in Medical Research: Scoping Review. *Journal of Medical Internet Research, 25*(1), e41588. DOI: 10.2196/41588 PMID: 36995759

Chai, D., Wang, L., Yang, L., Zhang, J., Chen, K., & Yang, Q. (2024). A Survey for Federated Learning Evaluations: Goals and Measures. *IEEE Transactions on Knowledge and Data Engineering, 36*, 5007–5024. DOI: 10.1109/TKDE.2024.3382002

Chakraborty, S., & Chakraborty, S. (2022). *Proof of Federated Training: Accountable Cross-Network Model Training and Inference* (arXiv:2204.06919). arXiv. https://doi.org//arXiv.2204.06919DOI: 10.48550

Chen, C.-L., Babakniya, S., Paolieri, M., & Golubchik, L. (2022). Defending against Poisoning Backdoor Attacks on Federated Meta-learning. *ACM Trans. Intell. Syst. Technol., 13*(5), 76:1-76:25. https://doi.org/DOI: 10.1145/3523062

Chen, J., Wang, W. H., & Shi, X. (2020). Differential Privacy Protection Against Membership Inference Attack on Machine Learning for Genomic Data (p. 2020.08.03.235416). *bioRxiv*. https://doi.org/DOI: 10.1101/2020.08.03.235416

Eden, R., Chukwudi, I., Bain, C., Barbieri, S., Callaway, L., de Jersey, S., George, Y., Gorse, A.-D., Lawley, M., Marendy, P., McPhail, S. M., Nguyen, A., Samadbeik, M., & Sullivan, C. (2025). A scoping review of the governance of federated learning in healthcare. *NPJ Digital Medicine*, *8*, 427. DOI: 10.1038/s41746-025-01836-3 PMID: 40640574

European commission. (2024). *Liability for defective products—Internal Market, Industry, Entrepreneurship and SMEs*. https://single-market-economy.ec.europa.eu/single-market/goods/free-movement-sectors/liability-defective-products_en

Fang, M., Cao, X., Jia, J., & Gong, N. (2020a). *Local Model Poisoning Attacks to Byzantine-Robust Federated Learning*. 1605–1622. https://www.usenix.org/conference/usenixsecurity20/presentation/fang

Fang, M., Cao, X., Jia, J., & Gong, N. (2020b). *Local Model Poisoning Attacks to Byzantine-Robust Federated Learning*. 1605–1622. https://www.usenix.org/conference/usenixsecurity20/presentation/fang

Geiping, J., Bauermeister, H., Dröge, H., & Moeller, M. (2020). *Inverting Gradients—How easy is it to break privacy in federated learning?* (arXiv:2003.14053). arXiv. https://doi.org//arXiv.2003.14053DOI: 10.48550

Horst, A., Loustalot, P., Yoganathan, S., Li, T., Xu, J., Tong, W., Schneider, D., Löffler-Perez, N., Di Renzo, E., & Renaudin, M. (2025). Federated learning: A privacy-preserving approach to data-centric regulatory cooperation. *Frontiers in Drug Safety and Regulation*, *5*. Advance online publication. DOI: 10.3389/fdsfr.2025.1579922 PMID: 40978510

Kairouz, P., & McMahan, H. B. (2021). Advances and Open Problems in Federated Learning. *Foundations and Trends in Machine Learning*, *14*(1–2), 1–210. DOI: 10.1561/2200000083

Kaissis, G. A., Makowski, M. R., Rückert, D., & Braren, R. F. (2020). Secure, privacy-preserving and federated machine learning in medical imaging. *Nature Machine Intelligence*, *2*(6), 305–311. DOI: 10.1038/s42256-020-0186-1

Kalapaaking, A. P., Khalil, I., Yi, X., Lam, K.-Y., Huang, G.-B., & Wang, N. (2025). Auditable and Verifiable Federated Learning Based on Blockchain-Enabled Decentralization. *IEEE Transactions on Neural Networks and Learning Systems*, *36*(1), 102–115. DOI: 10.1109/TNNLS.2024.3407670 PMID: 38875094

Kumar, K. N., Mohan, C. K., & Cenkeramaddi, L. R. (2024). The Impact of Adversarial Attacks on Federated Learning: A Survey. *IEEE Transactions on Pattern Analysis and Machine Intelligence*, *46*(05), 2672–2691. DOI: 10.1109/TPAMI.2023.3322785 PMID: 37812561

Lee, C., Heiss, J., Tai, S., & Hong, J. W.-K. (2024). *End-to-End Verifiable Decentralized Federated Learning* (arXiv:2404.12623). arXiv. https://doi.org//arXiv.2404.12623DOI: 10.48550

Li, S., & Schütte, B. (2024). The Proposed EU Artificial Intelli- gence Liability Directive: Does/Will Its Content Reflect Its Ambition? *Technology and Regulation*, *2024*, 143–151. DOI: 10.71265/82fwbw94

Mapakshi, R., Akther, S., & Stamp, M. (2025). *Temporal Analysis of Adversarial Attacks in Federated Learning* (arXiv:2501.11054). arXiv. https://doi.org//arXiv.2501.11054DOI: 10.48550

Montagnani, M. L., Najjar, M.-C., & Davola, A. (2023). *The EU Regulatory Approach(Es) to Ai Liability, and its Application to the Financial Services Market* (SSRN Scholarly Paper No. 4439219). Social Science Research Network. https://doi.org/DOI: 10.2139/ssrn.4439219

Montagnani, M. L., Najjar, M.-C., & Davola, A. (2024). The EU Regulatory approach(es) to AI liability, and its Application to the financial services market. *Computer Law & Security Review*, *53*, 105984. DOI: 10.1016/j.clsr.2024.105984

Near, J. (2024). Privacy Attacks in Federated Learning. *NIST*. https://www.nist.gov/blogs/cybersecurity-insights/privacy-attacks-federated-learning

Nguyen, T. D., Nguyen, T., Nguyen, P. L., Pham, H. H., Doan, K. D., & Wong, K.-S. (2024). Backdoor attacks and defenses in federated learning: Survey, challenges and future research directions. *Engineering Applications of Artificial Intelligence*, *127*, 107166. DOI: 10.1016/j.engappai.2023.107166

Pati, S., Kumar, S., Varma, A., Edwards, B., Lu, C., Qu, L., Wang, J. J., Lakshminarayanan, A., Wang, S., Sheller, M. J., Chang, K., Singh, P., Rubin, D. L., Kalpathy-Cramer, J., & Bakas, S. (2024). Privacy preservation for federated learning in health care. *Patterns (New York, N.Y.)*, *5*(7), 100974. DOI: 10.1016/j.patter.2024.100974 PMID: 39081567

Peng, K., Shen, X., Gao, L., Wang, B., & Lu, Y. (2023). Communication-Efficient and Privacy-Preserving Verifiable Aggregation for Federated Learning. *Entropy (Basel, Switzerland)*, *25*(8). Advance online publication. DOI: 10.3390/e25081125 PMID: 37628155

Peng, Z., Xu, J., Chu, X., Gao, S., Yao, Y., Gu, R., & Tang, Y. (2022). VFChain: Enabling Verifiable and Auditable Federated Learning via Blockchain Systems. *IEEE Transactions on Network Science and Engineering*, *9*, 173–186. DOI: 10.1109/TNSE.2021.3050781

Rodríguez-Barroso, N., Jiménez-López, D., Luzón, M. V., Herrera, F., & Martínez-Cámara, E. (2023). Survey on federated learning threats: Concepts, taxonomy on attacks and defences, experimental study and challenges. *Information Fusion*, *90*, 148–173. DOI: 10.1016/j.inffus.2022.09.011

Sethi, M. I. S., Manjunatha, N., Channaveerachari, N. K., Chakraborty, T., Math, S. B., & Andrade, C. (2025). The Digital Personal Data Protection Act 2023: Implications for Mental Healthcare Practice in India. *Indian Journal of Psychological Medicine*, *02537176251370651*. Advance online publication. DOI: 10.1177/02537176251370651 PMID: 40949048

Teo, Z. L., Jin, L., Liu, N., Li, S., Miao, D., Zhang, X., Ng, W. Y., Tan, T. F., Lee, D. M., Chua, K. J., Heng, J., Liu, Y., Goh, R. S. M., & Ting, D. S. W. (2024). Federated machine learning in healthcare: A systematic review on clinical applications and technical architecture. *Cell Reports Medicine*, *5*(2), 101419. DOI: 10.1016/j.xcrm.2024.101419 PMID: 38340728

Tolpegin, V., Truex, S., Gursoy, M. E., & Liu, L. (2020). *Data Poisoning Attacks Against Federated Learning Systems* (arXiv:2007.08432). arXiv. https://doi.org//arXiv.2007.08432DOI: 10.48550

Truby, J., Dahdal, A., & Ibrahim, I. A. (2022). Sandboxes in the desert: Is a cross-border 'gulf box' feasible? *Law, Innovation and Technology*, *14*(2), 447–473. DOI: 10.1080/17579961.2022.2113674

van Soest, J., Sanchez Gomez, L., Wee, L., & Dekker, A. (2025). A Governance Framework for Federated Learning Projects in Healthcare. *Studies in Health Technology and Informatics*, *327*, 258–262. DOI: 10.3233/SHTI250324 PMID: 40380435

Wachter, S. (2024). *Limitations and Loopholes in the EU AI Act and AI Liability Directives: What This Means for the European Union, the United States, and Beyond* (SSRN Scholarly Paper No. 4924553). Social Science Research Network. https://doi.org/DOI: 10.2139/ssrn.4924553

Wainakh, A., Ventola, F., Müßig, T., Keim, J., Cordero, C. G., Zimmer, E., Grube, T., Kersting, K., & Mühlhäuser, M. (2022). User-Level Label Leakage from Gradients in Federated Learning. *Proceedings on Privacy Enhancing Technologies*. https://petsymposium.org/popets/2022/popets-2022-0043.php

Wang, X., Wang, N., Wu, L., Guan, Z., Du, X., & Guizani, M. (2023). GBMIA: Gradient-based Membership Inference Attack in Federated Learning. *ICC 2023 - IEEE International Conference on Communications: Sustainable Communications for Renaissance*, 5066–5071. https://doi.org/DOI: 10.1109/ICC45041.2023.10279702

Woisetschläger, H., Mertel, S., Krönke, C., Mayer, R., & Jacobsen, H.-A. (2024). *Federated Learning and AI Regulation in the European Union: Who is Responsible? — An Interdisciplinary Analysis* (arXiv:2407.08105). arXiv. https://doi.org//arXiv.2407.08105DOI: 10.48550

Xie, C., Huang, K., Chen, P. Y., & Li, B. (2020). *DBA: 8th International Conference on Learning Representations, ICLR 2020*. https://www.scopus.com/pages/publications/85150645547

Zheng, H., Chen, J., Liu, T., Cheng, Y., Wang, Z., Wang, Y., Gao, L., Ji, S., & Zhang, X. (2024). DP-Poison: Poisoning Federated Learning under the Cover of Differential Privacy. *ACM Trans. Priv. Secur.*, *28*(1), 7:1-7:28. https://doi.org/DOI: 10.1145/3702325

Zhu, L., Liu, Z., & Han, S. (2019). Deep Leakage from Gradients. *Advances in Neural Information Processing Systems, 32*. https://proceedings.neurips.cc/paper_files/paper/2019/hash/60a6c4002cc7b29142def8871531281a-Abstract.html

Chapter 20
Emerging Research Challenges, Legal Frameworks, and Real-World Insights in Secured Federated Learning Systems

Chirra Baburao
https://orcid.org/0000-0003-4881-3708
Sir C.R. Reddy Educational Institutions, India

Nitu Tank
https://orcid.org/0009-0001-9782-4764
Poornima University, India

D. Rajyalakshmi
https://orcid.org/0009-0009-7945-3558
Vignan Foundation for Science, Technology and Research, India

Aasha Soni
Poornima University, India

ABSTRACT

This chapter per the authors explores secured federated learning systems, focusing on privacy preservation, adversarial resilience, and regulatory compliance. It explains how federated learning enables collaborative model training without direct data sharing, while addressing vulnerabilities such as gradient leakage, model inversion, data poisoning, and backdoor attacks. Methods including differential privacy, homomorphic encryption, secure multiparty computation, and Byzantine-resilient aggregation are evaluated for their effectiveness in mitigating risks. Ethical and legal dimensions shaped by frameworks such as GDPR and the EU AI Act are examined, with emphasis on explainability, fairness, and accountability. Real-world applications in healthcare and finance are highlighted through examples from the EXAM Consortium and WeBank's FATE platform, alongside insights into global research trends and institutional contributions. This chapter per the authors underscores the importance of secured federated learning in advancing trustworthy AI for sensitive domains.

DOI: 10.4018/979-8-3373-6224-3.ch020

1. INTRODUCTION

The growing use of artificial intelligence (AI) and machine learning (ML) to make decisions in various fields has been of great concern about privacy, security, and accountability in the data exchange. The conventional centralized ML models are based on the idea of aggregation of high amounts of user data into one repository to be trained which poses significant threats of data breach and invasion of user privacy. In order to address these difficulties, federated learning (FL) has become a paradigm that allows jointly training a model without the centralization of raw data (Bonawitz et al., 2019; Yang et al., 2023). In FL, several decentralized clients learn local models independently and do not exchange their data with a central server other than the model parameters or gradients. Such a design maintains sovereignty of data and enables institutions to enjoy the advantages of collective learning. With the growth of digital ecosystems, FL presents an opportunity of creating a medium of striking a balance between innovation and privacy protection. Although the concept of federated learning is elegant, it also presents additional technical and governance complexity. FL is distributed, which enhances the vulnerability to adversarial attacks, like data poisoning, gradient leakage, and model inversion (Fang et al., 2023; Sun et al., 2021). The malicious participants will be able to modify model updates or to steal sensitive information out of gradients, thus compromising the integrity of data and the reliability of models. These threats require strong security measures and the use of encryption, authentication, and the detection of anomalies technology in FL pipelines (Lyu et al., 2022; Wei and Liu, 2024).

To achieve privacy and integrity in a distributed structure, achieving a combination of several defensive layers is essential. Differential privacy (DP) methods introduce a controlled noise to the updates in the model, and ensure that the points related to individuals cannot be identified based on the aggregated output (Abadi et al., 2016; Truex et al., 2019). Homomorphic encryption (HE) allows performing mathematical operations on encrypted data, thus preserving confidentiality in the course of computation (Acar et al., 2018). Secure multiparty computation (SMPC) allows several parties to perform a joint computation without the need to disclose their respective input (Bonawitz et al., 2019). Nevertheless, all of these approaches are associated with trade-offs: DP will decrease the accuracy, HE may be computationally resource-intensive, and SMPC does not scale in large networks (Lyu et al., 2022; Zhang et al., 2023). Thus, the focus on hybrid solutions is becoming common as it reaches a compromise among security, scalability, and efficiency. Governance and policy aspects of federated learning are also very important. Since participants can be members of diverse organizations and jurisdictions, it can be difficult to understand who is responsible in case of security breach or biased results. Laws, including the GDPR, focus on the idea of transparency, fairness, and limited purpose; nevertheless, it is not clear how they apply to decentralized systems (Rieke et al., 2020; Woisetschläger et al., 2024). To close the gap, researchers have suggested governance-by-design frameworks, which combine compliance checks, ethical audits, and accountability into FL operations (Chandrasekaran et al., 2021; Olagunju, 2025).

2. THEORETICAL FEDERATED LEARNING.

2.1 Conceptual Overview

The evolution of secure federated learning is characterized by thematic mapping and keyword co-occurrence, which shows that the field is dominated by three major clusters: Cluster 1 – Privacy-

Preserving and Cryptographic FL: focuses on differential privacy, homomorphic encryption, and secure multiparty computation, shifting toward scalable hybrid frameworks (Abadi et al., 2016; Acar et al., 2018; Zhang et al., 2023; Lyu et al., 2022). Cluster 2 – Adversarial Robustness and Trust Mechanisms: emphasizes defenses against poisoning and Byzantine attacks, highlighting the link between technical and moral reliability (Fang et al., 2023; Feng et al., 2024). Cluster 3 – Governance, Explainability, and Policy Integration: connects algorithmic security with ethical governance and accountability (Brauneck et al., 2023; Olagunju, 2025).

2.2 Architecture and Communication Dynamics

A standard FL architecture includes three layers: (1) local clients or edge devices, (2) a central server, and (3) secure communication channels for encrypted parameter exchange (Bonawitz et al., 2019; Li et al., 2021). Effective communication is a critical factor in scalability, and it is often enhanced through model compression, quantization, and sparse aggregation (Chen et al., 2023; Le et al., 2024). FL can be formulated as a distributed optimization problem with the goal of minimizing the global loss. FedAvg strikes a balance between performance and communication, but it suffers from heterogeneous data. Various extensions such as FedProx and Scaffold improve the stability of convergence in non-IID situations (Karimireddy et al., 2020; Lim et al., 2020).

2.3 Privacy Preservation Mechanisms

Federated learning (FL) is theoretically built on the foundation of preserving privacy by keeping data local; however, it is not immune to leakage through shared gradients, which can be mitigated by cryptographic and statistical methods such as Differential Privacy (DP), Homomorphic Encryption (HE), and Secure Multiparty Computation (SMPC) (Abadi et al., 2016; Acar et al., 2018; Bonawitz et al., 2019; Lyu et al., 2022; Sun et al., 2021; Truex et al., 2019; Zhang et al., 2023).

2.4 Adversarial Robustness and System Integrity

Another important theoretical underpinning of FL is adversarial robustness. FL is susceptible to data poisoning, model inversion, and backdoor attacks due to its distributed nature; malicious clients can manipulate gradients or reconstruct private data (Bagdasaryan et al., 2020; Fang et al., 2023). Robustness frameworks often leverage Byzantine fault tolerance, which ensures stability even with unreliable participants (Lyu et al., 2022), and strong aggregation methods such as geometric median and trimmed mean to reduce outlier effects in model updates (Sun et al., 2021). Some recent studies suggest that trust-aware FL systems, incorporating client reputation scoring and anomaly detection, can enhance robustness (Feng et al., 2024).

2.5 Governance, Legal, and Ethical Integration

In addition to technical aspects, the topic of federated learning has gained prominence in debates regarding governance, transparency and ethics. Theoretically, FL is a mini-community of data sovereignty, a philosophy according to which a person or an organization must be able to control their information (Rieke et al., 2020; Brauneck et al., 2023). This is consistent with the regulatory environment, e.g. the

GDPR that requires legitimate and fair data processing. Nonetheless, due to the decentralization of FL, responsibility becomes challenging; collaborative training of models makes it hard to, e.g., pin down who is responsible when there is bias or mistakes (Chandrasekaran et al., 2021; Woisetschläger et al., 2024). Federated systems should find a balance between personal privacy and the general utility. Scholars of AI and Ethics insist that ethical governance should be included by making sure that the systems are designed to incorporate fairness, transparency, and auditability that are not added as layers but rather as the key principles (Benmalek & Seddiki, 2024; Olagunju, 2025).

2.6 Theoretical Gaps and Conceptual Evolution

Despite the maturity of federated learning since the time of its conception, there are a number of gaps in theory. To begin with, little is known concerning the scalability of privacy in heterogeneous and resource constrained settings. Second, the frameworks of explainability that bring interpretability and encryption to a reconciliation (Li et al., 2021; Lopez-Ramos et al., 2024) are underdeveloped. Third, the majority of theoretical frameworks consider the short-term cycles of training, but the long-term responsibility, such as model drift and fairness monitoring, is not addressed (Wei and Liu, 2024). Theoretically, FL has been transformed into a governance model of responsible AI by developing it into a technical architecture. The combination of crypograph theory, data ethics, and alignment of regulatory shows how socio-technical intelligence-AI is shifting to respect human rights and provide innovative solutions. Such development makes FL a privacy protection tool and a model of decentralized and reliable artificial intelligence in the 21st century (Hu et al., 2024; Olagunju, 2025).

3. EMERGING RESEARCH CHALLENGES IN SECURED FEDERATED LEARNING SYSTEMS

3.1 Adversarial Threats

Adversarial attacks are one of the biggest obstacles to federated learning. The decentralized design has several vulnerabilities that allow malicious actors to affect the model updates or draw conclusions based on gradients (Fang et al., 2023; Sun et al., 2021). The attacks of data and model poisoning may poison the global models or introduce the insidious backdoors resulting in biased or damaging outputs. Even the minuscule gradient perturbations can degrade the accuracy without being identified especially in heterogeneous networks. Strong aggregation techniques, including Krum, Trimmed Mean, and Median, were suggested, but none of them has full protection against coordinated attacks (Lyu et al., 2022). The absence of a standardized threat models and evaluation benchmarks also restricts advances of real-life resilience tests procedures.

3.2 Privacy and Legal Compliance

The provision of adherence to the privacy and data protection laws is a continuous challenge. Though FL automatically reduces information sharing, it does not ensure complete adherence to the regulations like the GDPR or the EU AI Act (Brauneck et al., 2023; Woisetschläger et al., 2024). Gradients and metadata might also expose sensitive information, either via gradient inversion or membership inference attacks (Li et al., 2021). There is also the complex definition of data ownership and accountability between jurisdictions. Differential privacy, secure multiparty computation, and homomorphic encryption are privacy-preserving systems that are computationally costly (Abadi et al., 2016; Acar et al., 2018). To have a lawful, efficient, and transparent Privacy control, a balance between a technical protection and a legal compliance needs to be achieved with the help of systems that are audit ready and explainable (Olagunju, 2025).

3.3 Governance and Ethical Gaps

Federated learning also implies the introduction of distributed accountability, making the proposed effective structure of ethical oversight and governance complex. The conventional governance models presuppose the centralized control over data and models, yet FL spreads the power among the actors (Chandrasekaran et al., 2021; Wei and Liu, 2024). As a result, it becomes unclear who is liable to prejudice, discrimination, or misuse. Ethical governance models need to be developed so as to be fair, transparent and consent management in federated ecosystems (Benmalek and Seddiki, 2024). Ethical issues are also built to include marginalized groups; non-representative data sets have the potential to reinforce existing inequalities unless taken into consideration.

3.4 Data Heterogeneity and Model Performance

One of the most intractable technical challenges when it comes to federated learning is data heterogeneity, also known as non-IID (non-independent and identically distributed) data. The sizes and quality and distribution of each client dataset are different and result in biased updates and slow convergence of global models (Zhao et al., 2018; Karimireddy et al., 2020). The result of this imbalance is overfitting major clients and poor performance with underrepresented clients. Further optimization techniques like FedProx and Scaffold solve this problem by proposing control variates and adaptive regularization (Li et al., 2021; Karimireddy et al., 2020). Non-IID evaluations, however, are not developed to have fairness metrics and standardized benchmarks. The challenging nature of performance and equity in heterogeneous networks require multi-level optimization, which is dynamically adjusted to the variability of the clients (Hu et al. 2024).

3.5 Explainability and Transparency

The issue of explainability and interpretability is critical to user confidence and regulatory adherence, but it is by definition difficult to attain in federated systems. Due to the training of models over decentralized data sources, the traditional explainable AI (XAI) tools are not always able to deliver meaningful information on how the decisions in a distributed fashion are made (Li et al., 2021; Lopez-Ramos et al., 2024). In addition, internal model reasoning can be obscured through encryption and differential privacy, resulting in a black box effect, which even operators of the system may not be able to comprehend. The recent developments in explainable federated learning (XFL) incorporate interpretable aggregation mechanism and visualization layer to follow decision paths without uncovering data (Benmalek and Seddiki, 2024). Nevertheless, the explainability under encryption and the fact that the explanations are also truthful and are not generated in order to be manipulative are still research frontiers that are yet to be solved in this area.

3.6 Benchmarking and Evaluation Frameworks

Federated learning does not have standardized evaluation benchmarks as centralized ML. The available research bases its evaluation of privacy, efficiency, or robustness on isolated datasets and disparate metrics (Jimenez-Gutierrez et al., 2025; Hu et al., 2024). There is no standardization of algorithms among implementations, making it hard to compare them, which is impeding reproducibility. There is also a dire need in this field to have shared datasets which reflect realistic non-IID distributions, cross domain heterogeneity and adversarial circumstances. Such benchmarking systems as LEAF and TensorFlow Federated (TFF) are developing yet do not capture real-world complexities (Zhang et al., 2023; Chen et al., 2023). The theoretical maturity and practical validation of secure FL systems would speed up the establishment of international consortia to set the new standards of open-access.

3.7 Integration Across Domains

Cross sector integration has both opportunities and challenges to FL. Healthcare, finance, and manufacturing have proved to show pilot success, however, large-scale interoperability is restrained due to the inconsistent data standards and organizational preparedness (Rieke et al., 2020; Lu et al, 2020). Indicatively, the federated medical imaging systems have to adhere to HIPAA, GDPR, and institutional ethics standards at the same time, which is an enormous coordination load. On the same note, anti-money laundering (AML) laws are very strict in the world of finance, which complicates consolidation of cross-border models (Yang et al. 2023). Interdisciplinary frameworks reconciling technical interoperability with regulatory harmonization are required in terms of global scaling of FL. Studies should be oriented to domain-independent governance protocols, which will be able to fit to specific legal and ethical demands of contexts (Wei and Liu, 2024; Olagunju, 2025).

3.8 Research Gaps and Future Directions

Although federated learning is rapidly growing, there are still a number of critical gaps in the research. To start with, the majority of security and privacy assessments are simulation-based and are not tested in practice in practice (Feng et al., 2024; Hu et al., 2024). Second, there is disunity between technical protection and legal system, and the numbers of studies taking a holistic socio-technical perspective are very low. Third, explainability and fairness are not commonly considered as collective but rather self-sustaining principles (Benmalek and Seddiki, 2024; Wei and Liu, 2024).

4. BIBLIOMETRIC LANDSCAPE OF SECURED FEDERATED LEARNING RESEARCH (2015–2025)

4.1 Dataset Overview

The bibliometric profile of research on secure federated learning (FL) published in 2015-2025 demonstrates a growing speed of exponential growth of the number of publications that combine the fields of artificial intelligence, data privacy, and cybersecurity. The search based on data indexed in Scopus and filtered to journal articles yielded 946 (English, Journal Articles) documents about federated learning, adversarial security and privacy preservation. Such works cut across computer science, information systems, and law, which is the interdisciplinary nature of FL (Hu et al., 2024; Jimenez-Gutierrez et al., 2025). The dataset in Table 1 consists of the summary, such as disciplines, the analytical tools, and the purpose of the bibliometric analysis. This summary provides a basis on which further trend and collaboration analysis would be conducted. Initial work (2015-2018) was on distributed optimization algorithms and communication-efficient model aggregation algorithms to FL. Since 2019, thematic growth has been towards secure computation, adversarial robustness and legal compliance (Lyu et al., 2022; Fang et al., 2023). This increase is associated with the restrictions in global data regulation, including the General Data Protection Regulation (GDPR) and the proposed European Union Artificial Intelligence Act that sparked the interest in privacy-sensitive learning systems (Brauneck et al., 2023; Woisetschläger et al., 2024). The dataset indicates the maturation of FL as FL to a socio-technical research field.

Table 1. Scopus dataset summary of secured federated learning (2015–2025).

Attribute	Description
Database	Scopus (Elsevier)
Years Covered	2015–2025
Total Documents	946 (English, Journal Articles)
Fields	Computer Science, Engineering, Information Systems, Law
Analysis Tools	Biblioshiny (R) and Python
Purpose	To explore trends, themes, and collaborations in secured federated learning

Note. Data extracted from the Scopus database on November 2025 articles only,

4.2 Publication Trends

Figure 1 illustrates the thematic clusters of federated learning (FL) research, visualized by a keyword co-occurrence map that links privacy preservation, secure aggregation, and AI ethics. Three growth phases emerge: an initial stage (2015–2018) introducing decentralized learning (McMahan et al., 2017; Bonawitz et al., 2019), an acceleration phase (2019–2021) following GDPR-driven innovation (Rieke et al., 2020; Yang et al., 2023), and consolidation (2022–2025) marked by diversification in adversarial defense and AI governance (Hu et al., 2024; Wei & Liu, 2024). The rapid publication growth and citation bursts around privacy-preserving mechanisms (Fang et al., 2023; Lyu et al., 2022) reflect the field's interdisciplinary evolution integrating technical innovation with ethical governance.

Figure 1. Most frequent keywords in secured federated learning research (2015–2025)

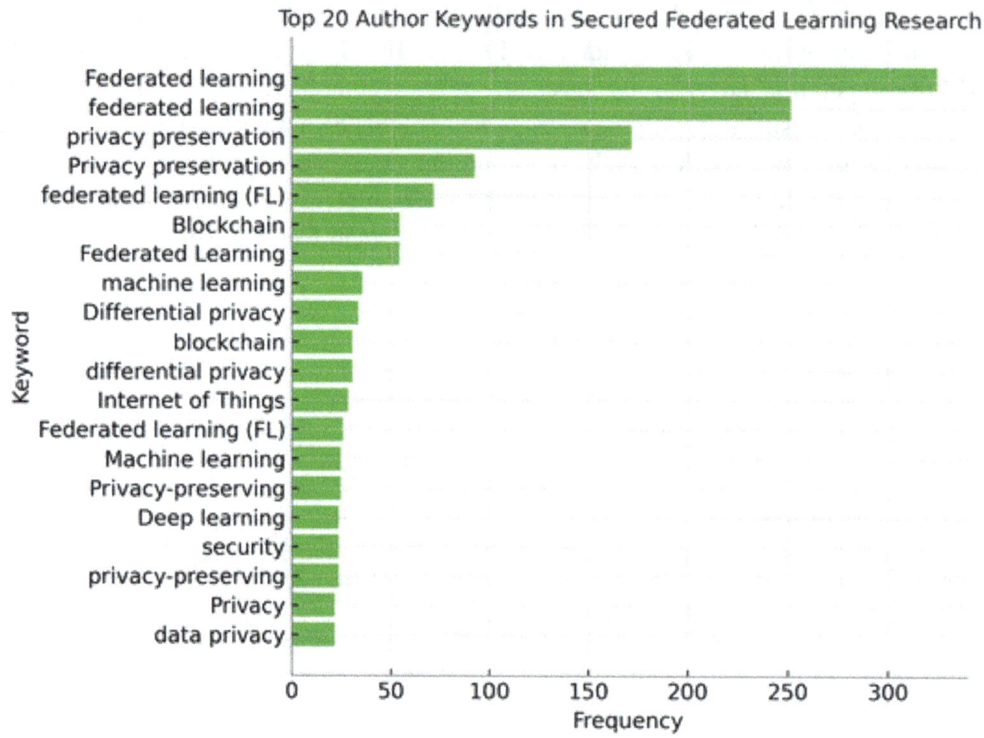

4.3 Leading Authors, Institutions, and Countries

Figure 2 demonstrates that research output is increasing more rapidly after 2019, and more widespread use of distributed and privacy-preserving computing has become possible. According to bibliometric data, the United States, China, Germany, and India are the most active countries in the research of secure federated learning, with more than 70 percent of publications. Google Research, Tsinghua University, and Peking University are some of the institutions that have fueled early innovations in algorithms (Kairouz et al., 2021; Li et al., 2021). European academies, especially ETH Zurich, Cambridge and TU Munich have contributed a lot to the research on ethical governance and data protection (Brauneck et al., 2023; Chandrasekaran et al., 2021). Since 2020, the production of research by India has increased at a high rate, with IIT Madras and IIT Delhi producing many publications on communication-efficient and privacy-preserving frameworks (Le et al., 2024; Chen et al., 2023). Co-authorship network analysis reveals that there is a high level of intra-regional cooperation between institutions within the Asia-Pacific and North American regions but poor interdisciplinary connection between the technical and legal scholars in their study. Kairouz et al.(2021) and Bonawitz et al. (2019) represent the most frequently referenced sources on the theory of FL, whereas Fang and Lyu are the most popular in adversarial and security-related research (Kairouz et al., 2021; Fang et al., 2023). The growth in the number of multi-authored papers having international affiliations reflects a growing tendency in which large-scale federated learning initiatives are collaborative in nature. Figures 2, 3, 4, demonstrate the geographic spread of the contributions with the emphasis on the United States, China, Germany, and India institutions. This participation is a symptom of technical significance and policy urgency of secure FL systems. the top journals that publish on secure federated learning since the year 2015, with the growth of the field in volume and interdisciplinarity, the leading journals are IEEE Access and Sensors (MDPI).

Figure 2. Top 10 journals publishing secured federated learning (2015–2025)

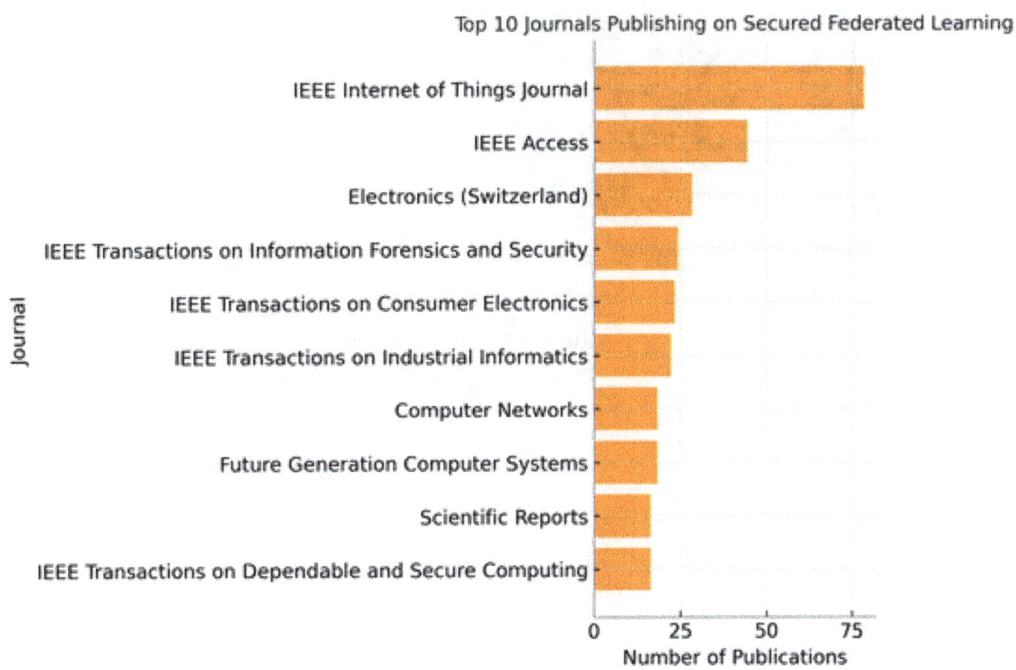

Figure 3. Most productive authors in secured federated learning (2015–2025)

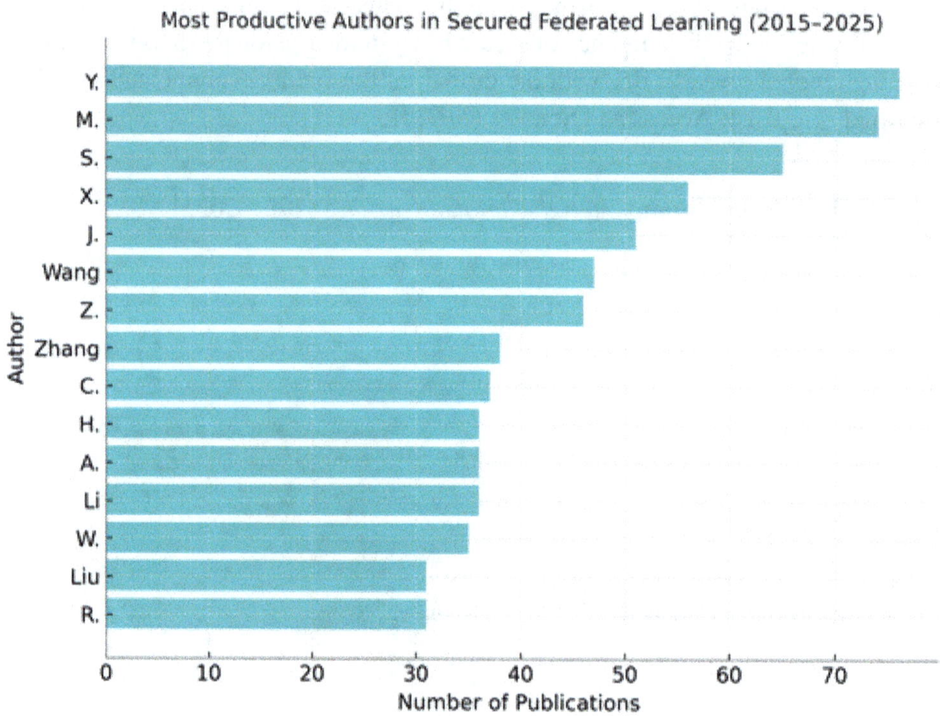

Figure 4. Top countries publishing on secure federated learning (2015–2025)

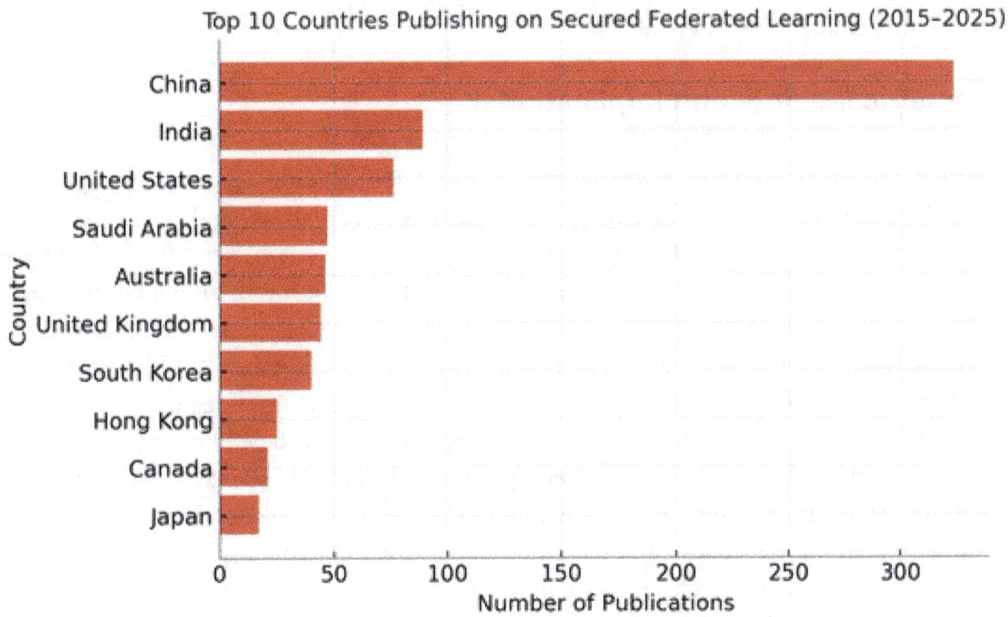

4.4 Keyword and Thematic Evolution

Thematic mapping and keyword co-occurrence provide an insight into the intellectual organization and development of the study of secure federated learning. There were three dominant thematic clusters over the decade: Cluster 1 - Privacy-Preserving and Cryptographic FL: This cluster has "differential privacy," "homomorphic encryption," and "secure multiparty computation" these. It has been studied as to whether privacy and confidentiality are mathematically guaranteed (Abadi et al., 2016; Acar et al., 2018). It is no longer focused on the development of theoretical models but on enhancing the level of practical scalability, hybrid encryption systems, and flexible privacy budgets (Zhang et al., 2023; Lyu et al., 2022). Cluster 2 - Adversarial Robustness and Trust Mechanisms: The keywords such as poisoning attacks, Byzantine resilience, and robust aggregation are predominant in this cluster. It is concerned with protection against malicious updates and model convergence confidence (Fang et al., 2023; Feng et al., 2024). The tendency indicates that technical soundness and moral reliability have to be sought simultaneously during the development of AI. Cluster 3 - Governance, Explainability, and Policy Integration: The latest cluster relates technical security to ethical governance. Such keywords as

AI Act, accountability, explainable federated learning and compliance-by-design have become popular since 2021 (Brauneck et al., 2023; Olagunju, 2025). Research indicates that a new synthesis of law and technology is emerging with the assertion that algorithmic transparency and human control are crucial as the encryption strength to develop trust. Thematic evolution analysis shows that early researchers dwelled upon such terms as optimization (2015-2018) and communication efficiency. Meanwhile, the trend in the 2020-25 period is the transition to a higher proportion of ethics, trust, and regulation (Jimenez-Gutierrez et al., 2025; Hu et al., 2024).

4.5 Bibliometric Insights and Implications

According to the bibliometric analysis, the area of research is developing with a high pace of evolution and interdisciplinarity. Technical research, however, is still prevailing, and socio-legal integration is becoming increasingly popular, which implies a shift towards a state of scientific and ethical goals (Wei and Liu, 2024; Brauneck et al., 2023). The increased number of international partnerships shows that the promise of federated learning demands common datasets, international standards and standardized governance models. However, gaps remain. A majority of the studies are simulative in nature, and little validation (real-world) has been conducted (Hu et al., 2024). Papers of legal- and policy-oriented inclination are not specific to the technical aspect and consequently, the development is disjointed. Longitudinal and network-analytic approaches taken by future bibliometric research should be performed to trace how ethical, technical, and governance subfields intersect in the course of time. The results of this kind of integrated bibliometrics can then guide the priorities of funding, standardization, and the construction of international research consortia in order to support secure and ethical federated learning (Olagunju, 2025; Wei and Liu, 2024).

5. LEGAL AND POLICY FRAMEWORKS GOVERNING FEDERATED LEARNING

The effectiveness of federated learning (FL) requires technological resiliency and strong legal regulations to protect ethical responsibility, compliance, and interoperability of the data across borders. Due to the growth of FL in industries, the legal landscape will have to tackle the issues of data sovereignty, transparency of algorithms, and the distribution of liability. This section focuses on the legal environment of FL in terms of privacy laws, the governance of artificial intelligence (AI), and harmonization at the international level.

5.1 Global Data Protection Regulations

Federated learning is offered a legal framework by data protection laws. Both the European Union General Data Protection Regulation (GDPR) and California Consumer Privacy Act (CCPA) and the Indian Digital Personal Data Protection Act (DPDPA), state the significance of consent, transparency, purpose limitation, and data minimization (Brauneck et al., 2023; Woisetschläger et al., 2024). Federated learning is in line with these principles as it permits local processing of data and reduces the cross-jurisdictional transfer of data. Nevertheless, inference attacks can disclose personal information based on model parameters, gradients and metadata exchanged during the training process (Li et al., 2021; Fang et al., 2023). The definition of personal data included in the GDPR is quite extensive because it covers data that can directly or indirectly identify a person. Pseudonymized gradient data can be personal data as well in case re-identification can be done. The GDPR, article 22, gives the right to explain and the right not to have an automated decision made to them, especially when it comes to FL systems (Woisetschläger et al., 2024). The FL deployments should install privacy-safe solutions like differentiated privacy, homomorphic encryption, and federated auditing (Abadi et al., 2016; Acar et al., 2018). China and the Cybersecurity Law of the country as well as India and the DPDPA influence the global FL activities by limiting the data storage and processing. Although the decentralized design of FL also contributes to the mitigation of these limitations, cross-border updates to the model can potentially contravene regional data sovereignty regulations unless the model is safeguarded by a contract (i.e., by Binding Corporate Rules (BCRs) or Standard Contractual Clauses (SCCs) (Olagunju, 2025; Wei and Liu, 2024). These structures have necessitated dynamic compliance structure that can respond to jurisdictional demands.

5.2 AI Governance and Compliance Issues

Federated learning poses a threat to the accountability and transparency of AI governance. The first general regulatory framework on AI systems is the EU AI Act, which is set to be implemented in 2025, with the risk categories and the requirement of governance obligation (Brauneck et al., 2023). FL applications that are at risk should be robust and explainable as well as traceable. Compliance-by-design models: This type of design approach implicates regulatory compliance to be part of the technical framework since the start (Chandrasekaran et al., 2021; Woisetschläger et al., 2024). Federated systems are difficult to comply with due to distributed control. As models are trained by several institutions jointly, it is not clear who is accountable when it comes to bias, breach of privacy, and other aspects of violations. Law academics promote collective responsibility, where players are apportioned equal responsibility through accountability to compliance (Benmalek and Seddiki, 2024; Olagunju, 2025). This may be executed by smart contracts, registering contribution, audit paths of immutable ledger books.

Transparency is a legal requirement and enforced in the EU AI Act and national frameworks. The encrypted information of FL provided by FL complicates the standard explainability (Li et al., 2021; Lopez-Ramos et al., 2024). Studies have proposed explainable federated learning paired with privacy-preserving visualization tools as a way of complying with the law, as well as keeping the information confidential (Hu et al., 2024). These models meet regulatory demands of transparency and control. Governance is very dependent on ethical compliance. The institutions should also align FL with models like the OECD AI Principles and the Recommendation on AI Ethics provided by UNESCO, which focus on human-centered design and equity. Integrating ethical audits can serve as a measure to make sure that the rights are respected, and the decisions made by AI are non-discriminatory (Benmalek and Seddiki, 2024; Wei and Liu, 2024).

5.3 Cross-Border Legal Harmonization

Federated learning offers an answer beyond national borders and poses jurisdictional issues. The models pool together the knowledge of the participants that belonged to various regions that had different data protection legislations. The absence of privacy and AI laws harmonization across the globe makes it difficult to understand the existing laws and their enforcement (Woisetschläger et al., 2024; Olagunju, 2025). The existing mechanisms of the cross-border transfer of data are inadequate to support the concept of decentralized architecture where model gradients can be viewed as data flows, and transnational governance frameworks and federated data trusts are the proposed approaches to data rights regulation among participants (Wei and Liu, 2024; Chandrasekaran et al., 2021). Such trusts have the ability to standardize terms, check consent and accountability across jurisdictions. AI, ethical, and security models also note the significance of privacy interoperability, which allows systems and legal regimes to communicate to each other via standardized metadata and protocols (Brauneck et al., 2023; Wei and Liu, 2024).

The OECD Framework to Classify AI Systems (2022) and G7 Hiroshima AI Process (2023) promote the spirit of transparency and control. Such frameworks can be used to assist in standardization of FL governance. The ISO/IEC 23894:2023 on AI risk management can be used to make use of accountability in decentralized systems. This is to create international AI governance treaties that would harmonize the legal requirements with technical interoperability (Olagunju, 2025; Wei and Liu, 2024).

6. REAL-WORLD INSIGHTS AND CASE APPLICATIONS (2018–2025)

6.1 Overview of Global Adoption

Federated learning was a concept under development between the years 2018 and 2025 to become a practical model of collaborative AI. It is increasingly being used in fields where confidentiality of data, compliance, and interoperability are the major considerations, that is, healthcare, finance, manufacturing, and public administration (Hu et al., 2024; Lim et al., 2020). To balance regulations on data sharing with the requirement to train large-scale models, governments and enterprises have implemented FL. Computers & Security and Neurocomputing conducted a bibliometric review that revealed an apparent continued increase in pilot deployments, with more than 60% of practical implementations incorporating the use of multi-institutional or cross-sector collaborations (Jimenez-Gutierrez et al., 2025; Zhang et al., 2023).

6.2 Healthcare and Biomedical Applications

Healthcare is the best-developed area of federated learning, primarily by the virtue of privacy requirements and the disjointed character of data ecosystems. FL allows hospitals and research consortia to build diagnostic and prognostic models without storing patient data in one place, thus, adhering to the GDPR and Health Insurance Portability and HIPAA (Rieke et al., 2020; Kaissis et al., 2021). The EXAM Consortium connected over 20 hospitals on all continents to train predictive models to support the oxygen needs of COVID-19 patients; the federated model generalized better whilst preserving medical records. The secure multiparty computation has been incorporated into recent works together with homomorphic encryption to promote privacy in medical imaging and genomics (Hu et al., 2024; Li et al., 2021).

6.3 Financial and Banking Sector Implementations

Federated learning has been implemented in financial institutions to overcome the issues of distributed data ownership and regulatory compliance. The FL is used by global banks and fintech organizations to detect fraud, score credits, and anti-money laundering (AML) analytics, thus obviating the need to transfer raw data across jurisdictions (Yang et al., 2023). Federated AI Technology Enabler (FATE) platform (WeBank FATE) proved to be more effective in terms of detecting features without impacting the privacy of customers. Nonetheless, according to legal scholars, FL increases confidentiality, but it distorts accountability, casting doubt on the questions of bias, discrimination, and algorithm fairness (Brauneck et al., 2023; Woisetschläger et al., 2024). The compliance teams should come up with AI assurance models that connect the technical security with regulatory documents. Ethical audits, model provenance records, and cryptographically verifiable logs are becoming the new standard of ensuring responsible AI in financial analytics (Olagunju 2025; Wei and Liu 2024).

6.4 Smart Manufacturing and Industrial IoT

In the factory, federated learning can be used to facilitate predictive maintenance, process optimization, and quality assurance at decentralized factories. Industrial FL enables the manufacturing companies to cooperatively construct models without disclosing the proprietary information and, therefore, improves competitiveness and confidentiality (Lu et al., 2020; Sitton-Candanedo et al., 2022). FL is applied in automotive and semiconductor plants to identify anomalies in production in real time through edge devices that have encrypted sensors. Nonetheless, there is a major limitation to data imbalance and communication latency. According to the IEEE Internet of Things Journal, network bottlenecks can be alleviated by means of communication-efficient aggregation techniques, including sparse gradient sharing and adaptive compression, without compromising accuracy (Chen et al., 2023; Le et al., 2024). Cyber-security audits and standardized protocols towards preventing adversarial manipulation are also needed in Industrial Adoption. Bringing blockchain-based traceability and FL together is a prospective answer to the maintenance of the integrity of data in industrial ecosystems (Feng et al., 2024; Hu et al., 2024).

6.5 Mobile and Edge Computing Ecosystems

The largest scale of implementation is edge-based FL where billions of mobile devices are involved in the model training. Another such example is a Federated Averaging on Android developed by Google to predictive text and voice recognition (Bonawitz et al., 2019; McMahan et al., 2017). Such a configuration facilitates both local learning and global aggregation and thus, personalization and privacy. Telecommunications, wearable, and autonomous system implementations provide evidence of the adaptability of FL in low-latency environments (Lim et al., 2020; Le et al., 2024). Non-uniform computing power, battery, and connectivity have however been experienced with mobile clients. The solutions to these problems include new adaptive sampling and on-device model pruning that optimize participation and minimizing transmission overhead (Zhang et al., 2023; Hu et al., 2024). With the advancement of 5G and edge-cloud integration, federated learning will be used to enable real-time intelligent services in smart cities and connected vehicles.

6.6 Government and Public Sector Initiatives

To achieve a data utility versus citizen privacy balance in areas like health, education and welfare, governments are looking more at the application of FL. The AI4PublicPolicy project of the EU and the Digital Health Mission in India have incorporated FL into the secure data-sharing systems allowing multi-agencies cooperation without confidentiality breach (Woisetschläger et al., 2024; Olagunju, 2025). These projects show how government agencies can use FL to improve the policy decision-making process, epidemiological monitoring and resource distribution. Nevertheless, the application in the field of the public sector has to overcome the obstacles of transparency, consent management, and difficulty with algorithmic bias. The studies of AI and Ethics focus on citizen-oriented governance, such as the algorithmic audit, participatory oversight boards, and open source verification, to achieve the trust of people (Benmalek and Seddiki, 2024; Wei and Liu, 2024).

6.7 Cross-Sector Challenges and Lessons Learned

A number of essential lessons have been drawn in fields. To begin with, anonymity coupled with lack of accountability is insufficient. There must be transparency in governing and adhering to technical encryption. Second, the interoperability is vital since deployments are unable to align data standards with partners (Wei & Liu, 2024; Hu et al., 2024). Third, the readiness of the institutions depends on scalability, institutions are not equipped with the infrastructure, workforce, and ethical reviews to address decentralized AI in a responsible manner. Research has demonstrated that the additional protection provided by blockchain-based audit trails, privacy certificates, and dynamic consent management is more effective in securing and improving accountability (Brauneck et al., 2023; Woisetschläger et al., 2024).

6.8 Implications for Future Implementation

The 2018-2025 experience demonstrates that the success of federated learning is based on the interaction between technology and governance. The ethical feasibility of healthcare is reflected, regulatory adaptation is evident in the field of finance as well, the industry proves that the scale can be validated, and government applications exhibit the social trust (Olagunju 2025; Wei and Liu 2024). Further studies should be directed at creating standardised compliance APIs, adaptive encryption frameworks and cross-jurisdiction data trusts in order to sustain growth. Future secure digital ecosystems can be formed at the intersection of federated learning and blockchain, quantum-resistant encryption, and explorable AI (Hu et al., 2024; Zhang et al., 2023). The importance of federated learning is that the AI systems will be safe, equitable, and accountable across borders, which should protect the data and remodel knowledge governance.

7. FUTURE RESEARCH DIRECTIONS AND POLICY RECOMMENDATIONS

7.1 Strengthening Technical Foundations

A major trend in research is to enhance the strength, extensiveness, and versatility of FL models. The existing aggregation methods, including FedAvg and FedProx, still cannot resist data heterogeneity, communication delays, and other attacks (Li et al., 2021; Lyu et al., 2022). Future studies would look into adaptive optimization methods that would modify learning rates and weights according to the reliability and quality of the client data (Hu et al., 2024; Zhang et al., 2023). Strong aggregating schemes such as Byzantine-resilient schemes are necessary to reduce the effects of poisoning attacks without compromising on the efficiency (Fang et al., 2023; Feng et al., 2024). The need of FL networks is to find energy-efficient architectures to mitigate the environmental cost. With a focus on lightweight encryption and the maximization of communication by sparse updates, the carbon footprint will be decreased, and the level of scalability will be enhanced (Chen et al., 2023). Multimodal data and federated transfer learning will be the key to the future of FL as it will be possible to share knowledge across sectors and preserve privacy. These architectures have the potential to give FL an extended reach to a variety of environments, thus facilitating the creation of AI globally in an inclusive manner (Lu et al., 2020; Yang et al., 2023).

7.2 Enhancing Explainability and Transparency

With the growth of FL into regulated areas, explainable federated learning (XFL) will gain demand. The interpretability of FL is not simple due to the decentralization of FL (Li et al., 2021; Lopez-Ramos et al., 2024). Future studies need to work on creating privacy-saving interpretability schemes that offer transparency without disclosing local information. Such methods as federated SHAP values and interpretable layers of aggregation are promising solutions to the challenges of privacy and accountability (Hu et al., 2024). Explainability of regulations: automated decisions ought to be justified by legislation, including the EU AI Act, which should be a norm of FL architectures (Brauneck et al., 2023; Woisetschläger et al., 2024).

7.3 Integrating Governance and Policy Research

Federated learning needs a co-ordinated policy innovation. Such fragmentation of legal interpretations exists in different regions due to the absence of standardized forms of governance (Olagunju, 2025; Wei and Liu, 2024). The research of the policies should be aimed at the definition of governance-by-design frameworks that can be integrated into technical processes and introduce compliance and transparency into the technical operations, such as audit trails, consent mechanisms, and data standardization. A prototype of distributed accountability is provided by federated data trusts that are neutral mediators that deal with compliance toward ethics and the law (Chandrasekaran et al., 2021; Woisetschläger et al., 2024). Researchers, policymakers, and industry leaders should come up with interoperable standards to regulate ethical AI governance in the ISO, OECD, and G20. Federated technologies AI sandboxes can help experiment federated technologies under controlled settings by mediating innovation with regulation (Benmalek and Seddiki, 2024; Wei and Liu, 2024).

7.4 Promoting Ethical and Human-Centric Design

The fates of federated learning in the society will depend on the ethical path that it takes. Further studies need to consider ways in which fairness and accountability can be integrated in FL design. Unbalanced data where the participation is uneven may promote biasness within world-models. Aggregation algorithms that are sensitive to fairness are needed to control such inequalities (Hu et al., 2024; Karimireddy et al., 2020). Hegemonic governance must focus on participatory governance, in which users and most-disadvantaged communities actively take part in the process of making decisions (Benmalek and Seddiki, 2024; Olagunju 2025). Ethical auditing models, including IRBs, should be implemented by FL developers to make sure that the effects of the model are evaluated. Psychological knowledge should be integrated into the process of FL adoption because trust and transparency can play a major role in the acceptance of AI. The interdisciplinary research can be used to create trust-conscious FL models that take into account human perception (Wei and Liu, 2024; Lopez-Ramos et al., 2024).

7.5 Advancing Cross-Sector Collaboration

Academia, government and industry are essential to sustainable federated learning development by working together. Theory is provided by academia, infrastructure and datasets is by industry, and ethical protection by governments. The projects like AI4Health, FATE, and GAIA-X show that collaboration between technical excellence and governance is feasible (Rieke et al., 2020; Kaissis et al., 2021). Future studies must investigate multi-stakeholder FL ecosystems that share the expertise and democratize the data-based innovations. Such ecosystems are capable of supporting open-source healthcare, financial and climate modeling domain-specific architectures (Lu et al., 2020; Yang et al., 2023). It aims to have a robust and non-discriminatory worldwide AI infrastructure.

7.6 Strategic Policy Recommendations

Based on the current gaps, this study offers six strategic recommendations for policymakers and leaders.

- Develop interoperability standards for federated AI systems through collaboration between the ISO and OECD.
- Incorporate federated learning into national AI strategies, in alignment with data protection and cybersecurity frameworks.
- Establish public–private FL research consortia to foster open and secure innovations.
- Implement ethics-as-a-service (EaaS) frameworks to monitor and certify ethical compliance (Olagunju, 2025; Benmalek & Seddiki, 2024).
- Invest in programs to train professionals in privacy engineering, AI ethics, and compliance management.
- Mandate algorithmic transparency requirements for human interpretability and accountability in critical decision-making.

These recommendations can transform federated learning into a cornerstone of sustainable digital governance, promoting innovation while protecting individual rights and trust.

8. ETHICAL, SOCIETAL, AND HUMAN-CENTRIC IMPLICATIONS

8.1 Ethical Foundations in Federated Learning

The concept of federated learning brings a radical change in how ethical principles should be operationalized in artificial intelligence. Its decentralized framework is compatible with privacy, autonomy, and fairness, but implies ethical dilemmas in the areas of consent, prejudice, and accountability (Benmalek and Seddiki, 2024; Brauneck et al., 2023). In contrast to old AI models, where the central authority regulates the adherence to ethical standards, the federated systems to allocate data management and moral responsibility to actors. The question then arises on who is responsible when an outcome of a distributed model is harmful. Although the privacy-by-design is an insurance of user autonomy in FL, researchers note that privacy needs not introduce obscurity, and excess encryption can make supervision challenging (Olagunju, 2025; Wei and Liu, 2024). FL systems should raise confidentiality and transparency. Ethical guidelines, including the UNESCO Recommendation on the Ethics of Artificial Intelligence (2021) and OECD AI Principles (2022) recommend instituting the issue of human rights and fairness as a design value. This has to be captured in the processes that can be explained and the fair participation in the institutions.

8.2 Bias, Fairness, and Inclusivity

Federated learning is not biased-free, even though it guarantees the preservation of privacy. Unequal model performance may arise due to local dataset heterogeneity where there is unequal performance between demographic and geographic groups. To illustrate, a global healthcare FL model can be useful to data-rich hospitals but not helpful in under-represented areas (Kaissis et al., 2021; Hu et al., 2024). These inequalities provoke the distributive justice and fairness that are the main ethical issues in AI governance. Bias in FL is caused by two main sources data imbalance and inequality of participation. Richer institutions that have superior infrastructure are capable of contributing more and affect the global model parameters, thus increasing systemic inequities (Li et al., 2021; Lopez-Ramos et al., 2024). Ethical governance demands systems and mechanisms that can be used to guarantee fair sway and a variety of representation within the model. The concept of weighted aggregation and fairness-sensitive methods of optimization has arisen to minimize these inequalities (Karimireddy et al., 2020; Zhang et al., 2023). FL should not only include the societies within the institutions but to the affected communities. Federated environment: the public consultation and informed consent mechanisms need to be modified to fit federated settings where the participants might have no idea of contributing indirect data. Scholars suggest the use of multi-stakeholder FL projects by ethical oversight boards that are similar to institutional review board (IRB), to provide fair access and accountability (Benmalek and Seddiki, 2024; Olagunju, 2025).

8.3 Transparency, Explainability, and Accountability

The ethical qualities of trustworthy AI are transparency and explainability. FL is hard to interpret due to its encrypted and decentralized nature. Due to the localization of model training, it is hard to monitor how the update of specific clients influences the overall results (Li et al., 2021; Lopez-Ramos et al., 2024). Important tools like differential privacy and homomorphic encryption, which are needed to ensure confidentiality, may blur causal logic. Scientists are working on Explainable Federated Learning (XFL) models that provide interpretable results but do not violate data privacy (Hu et al., 2024; Wei and Liu, 2024). Local feature attribution, interpretable aggregation, and privacy-preserving visualization are the techniques, which allow stakeholders to comprehend the model behavior and keep sensitive inputs secret. The ethical governance demands that such explanations should be technically sound and understandable by non-specialists. Accountability in FL has to be disseminated and verifiable. The transactions and updates can be recorded with the help of technical solutions such as blockchain-based provenance and smart contracts, which will consequently allow examining the decision pathways (Brauneck et al., 2023; Woisetschläger et al., 2024).

8.4 Human-Centric Design and Trust

A humanistic approach will make sure that technology is used to complement the interests of society and not to displace them. FL presents an architecture that is distributed which enables the users to have power back over the data and gives it to individuals and institutions. In a decentralized system, there is always low trust, particularly when governance structures are opaque (Wei and Liu, 2024; Olagunju, 2025). To gain social trust in FL, the society needs governance transparency and inclusivity coupled with outstanding risk communication. The literature on AI and Ethics points out that trust is not only a technical problem but also a relationship between the designers and the users of the system that is moral (Benmalek and Seddiki, 2024). The basis of this relationship is transparency, reliability and fairness. This would entail giving feedback to the users on how their information contributes to the common intelligence and giving them an option of withdrawing their participation where they wish. The FL design must be human centered to be accessible and usable. Systems should be designed to support different degrees of technical literacy among users and the privacy settings and consent interfaces should be understandable (Rieke et al., 2020; Kaissis et al., 2021).

8.5 Societal Implications and Global Justice

Federated learning has broader social consequences, which go beyond the technical scope. In healthcare, it allows cross-institutional cooperation without violating patient confidentiality and data protection. It aids in finance to support inclusive credit-scoring models that avoid privacy protection. Nevertheless, these advantages are not well distributed as regions with no digital infrastructure or without legal protection can be excluded because of the FL ecosystem (Wei and Liu, 2024; Olagunju, 2025). Ethical academics have focused on the threat of a data division, with secure and participatory learning technologies being monopolized by affluent countries and companies (Brauneck et al., 2023; Benmalek and Seddiki, 2024). In response to this, the world initiatives must encourage capacity building and fair exchange of technology. Democratizing the gains associated with FL may be done via policies that promote open-source federated infrastructures, shared governance frameworks, and privacy interoperability standards (Woisetschläger et al., 2024; Olagunju 2025). Environmental costs must be considered under social responsibility. Large-scale FL networks, due to both communication and encryption, may require large amounts of energy. The combination of green computing and energy-efficient architectures would help align FL development with social welfare and sustainability interests (Hu et al. 2024; Zhang et al. 2023).

8.6 Ethical Governance for Sustainable AI

The federalization of learning requires normalization of governance, which combines moral logic, law and technical confidence in order to achieve ethical sustainability. Ethical judgment needs to be implemented continuously, starting with the acquisition of data, proceeding through implementation and review (Brauneck et al., 2023; Wei and Liu, 2024). There should be governance structures which involve clear accountability lines, representatives, and regular impact evaluation to have proper management. A possible solution is the so-called Ethics-as-a-Service (EaaS) concept, which is suggested in recent AI policy studies. It imagines the existence of autonomous ethics audit entities that deliver real-time assessments of AI systems, just as cybersecurity auditors (Olagunju, 2025; Benmalek and Seddiki, 2024).

9. MANAGERIAL AND POLICY IMPLICATIONS

The development of federated learning (FL) into a practical application then has important consequences on managers, policy-makers and institutional leaders. With the emergence of decentralized artificial intelligence systems as a part of data-driven operations, organizations need to align governance systems, leadership practices, and compliance mechanisms to new ethical and legal standards. This paragraph brings out managerial and policy-level implications that are necessary in ensuring that FL is adopted in a responsible, secure, and sustainable manner.

9.1 Institutionalizing Governance and Compliance

Federated learning ecosystems need the adoption of systematic accountability rather than ad hoc compliance to institutionalize governance. FL does not fit traditional data control due to the decentralized ownership and control among participants. To achieve privacy governance, managers need to develop privacy governance frameworks that cover the technical, legal, and ethical aspects (Brauneck et al., 2023; Wei and Liu, 2024). The organizations ought to appoint Data Protection Officer and AI Governance Committee to monitor privacy practices, bias audit and risk assessment. High-risk AI models, such as FL applications, are required to have risk management systems and documentation in the EU AI Act (Woisetschläger et al., 2024; Olagunju, 2025). Compliance-by-design approaches and regulatory checks must be included in federated learning projects as part of the development lifecycle of the project. This will reduce the risks and conform to the international standard, including the ISO/IEC 23894:2023 on AI risk management (Wei and Liu, 2024; Benmalek and Seddiki, 2024). These forms of governance can make sure that FL deployments are responsible and ethical.

9.2 Strategic Leadership and Ethical Responsibility

Strategic leadership determines the ethical behavior of an organization in the emerging technologies. Leadership in federated learning encourages the culture of ethical intelligence, with the decisions regarding the use of data, cooperation, and automation being informed by moral and social factors (Olagunju, 2025; Benmalek and Seddiki, 2024). The leaders who are ethically responsible should ensure that there is a connection between the technical teams and the regulatory bodies so that the decision on data sharing, consent, and fairness should be made in a collaborative manner. Research on AI and Ethics indicates that the outcomes of ethical leadership are stronger in terms of stakeholder trust, reputational risk reduction and compliance (Brauneck et al., 2023; Wei and Liu, 2024). The leadership responsibility should not be limited to internal governance but to the external accountability through reporting the way federated models are trained, monitored, and validated. Technological uncertainty has to be handled through strategic foresight.

9.3 Organizational Readiness and Capacity Building

To implement federated learning, organizations have to attain technical maturity and human capital maturity. This includes the coordination of infrastructure, human potential, and cultural orientations to joint AI systems (Hu et al., 2024; Li et al., 2021). Numerous organizations are not ready to coordinate and technical needs of FL distributed, and they do not know about cryptography, privacy engineering, or decentralised data management. Capacity building must also aim at the creation of interdisciplinary skills in which AI engineering is coupled with law, ethics, and policy. Companies can develop training on differentiating privacy, secure multiparty computation, and compliance with the law of AI systems. Learning and the availability of new methodologies can be achieved by collaborating with universities and research consortia (Chandrasekaran et al., 2021; Wei and Liu, 2024). Preparedness of infrastructures is also crucial. Implementation of FL involves safe border tools, powerful communication rules, and resilient encryption. According to research published in the IEEE Internet of Things Journal and Neurocomputing, hybrid edge-cloud networks enhance scalability of multi-participant FL networks (Chen et al., 2023; Hu et al., 2024).

9.4 Accountability and Risk Management

Federated learning governance is founded on accountability. The customary liability and control cannot be sufficient because FL spreads decision-making and data ownership. Managers should also have multi-tier accountability structures that establish the accountability of data custodians, model developers, and aggregators (Brauneck et al., 2023; Woisetschläger et al., 2024). An exciting solution is to entrench audit paths with blockchain or distributed lists tracking the changes in the model and participant additions. These logs are beneficial in enhancing traceability and post-deployment audits (Feng et al., 2024; Olagunju, 2025). Such mechanisms can be coupled to human control- through ethics committees, or third parties audits, to maintain accountability that is both technical and moral. Elements of risk management should include adversarial resilience and systemic risk awareness. Poisoning attack, communication breakdown, and incentive mismatch are among the special threats of FL systems. These threats can be reduced by implementing efficient aggregation procedures, real-time anomaly detection, and transparent escalation processes (Fang et al., 2023; Lyu et al., 2022). Moreover, it is possible to align the organizational risk management with the international standards, including the OECD AI Principles or the ISO AI Risk Management standard, which will provide congruency with the international practice.

9.5 Policy Implications for Global Governance

Federated learning requires the coordinated governance systems across national boundaries. The policymakers have to make sure that there is interoperability between the technical standards and legal regimes and that privacy-preserving AI systems can work within a global setting without breaching regional regulation (Olagunju, 2025; Woisetschläger et al., 2024). The governments ought to encourage AI sandboxes: regulated testing spaces of privacy-enhancing technologies being morally overseen (Wei and Liu, 2024; Benmalek and Seddiki, 2024). Such environments assist the policymakers to learn the socio-technical effects of FL, as well as enable innovation. The interoperability of ethical AI governance can be achieved through global collaboration led by organizations like the OECD, ISO, G20. In AI innovation, inclusivity and social equity should be given priority by the public policy. The developing regions should be encouraged to participate in funding mechanisms, through research incentives as well as the establishment of public- private partnerships in order to avert the escalation of the digital divide. A coordinated implementation of national AI policies with the Sustainable Development Goals (SDGs) can make sure that federated learning helps to achieve international aspirations of equity, trust, and responsible digital transformation (Hu et al., 2024; Wei and Liu, 2024).

10. CONCLUSION

Federated learning (FL) has developed over the last ten years as a privacy principle, followed by a fundamental paradigm of distributed artificial intelligence, which balances collaboration and data ownership. This paper has analyzed the technological, legal, ethical, and managerial factors that have influenced secured FL. Theoretically, FL helps reduce the issue of centralization risk; it allows decentralized training of models and simultaneously does not lose the privacy (McMahan et al., 2017; Hu et al., 2024), but heterogeneity or poisoning problems remain (Fang et al., 2023; Lyu et al., 2022). Its use in medicine, finance, and industry proves to be viable (Rieke et al., 2020; Lu et al., 2020). Nonetheless, the only way to achieve long-term success is through ethical governance, collective responsibility, and harmonized regulation (Brauneck et al., 2023; Olagunju, 2025). The next generation of research ought to be developing hybrid privacy solutions, explainability, and socio-legal design (Acar et al., 2018; Zhang et al., 2023). Finally, FL is a transition to distributed trust in AI - the promise of it can be fulfilled only when innovation is compatible with law, ethics, and the collective responsibility.

REFERENCES

Abadi, M., Chu, A., Goodfellow, I., McMahan, H. B., Mironov, I., Talwar, K., & Zhang, L. (2016). Deep learning with differential privacy. *Proceedings of the 2016 ACM SIGSAC Conference on Computer and Communications Security*, 308–318. DOI: 10.1145/2976749.2978318

Acar, A., Aksu, H., Uluagac, A. S., & Conti, M. (2018). A survey on homomorphic encryption schemes: Theory and implementation. *ACM Computing Surveys*, *51*(4), 79. DOI: 10.1145/3214303

Bagdasaryan, E., Veit, A., Hua, Y., Estrin, D., & Shmatikov, V. (2020). How to backdoor federated learning. Proceedings of the 23rd International Conference on Artificial Intelligence and Statistics, 2938–2948. https://proceedings.mlr.press/v108/bagdasaryan20a.html

Benmalek, M., & Seddiki, O. (2024). Ethical frameworks for trustworthy artificial intelligence: A federated learning perspective. *AI and Ethics*, *4*(2), 167–182. DOI: 10.1007/s43681-023-00293-8

Bonawitz, K., Eichner, H., Grieskamp, W., Huba, D., Ingerman, A., Ivanov, V., Kiddon, C., Konečný, J., Mazzocchi, S., McMahan, H. B., Overveldt, T. V., Petrou, D., Rambhatla, S., & Roselander, J. (2019). Towards federated learning at scale: System design. *Proceedings of the 2nd SysML Conference*.

Brauneck, J., Sandner, P. G., & Kummer, T. F. (2023). Legal governance in AI: Integrating GDPR and the EU AI Act. *AI and Ethics*, *3*(2), 143–158. DOI: 10.1007/s43681-022-00153-8

Chandrasekaran, V., Singh, R., & Kumar, A. (2021). Governance and transparency in federated AI systems. *Computers & Security*, *108*, 102350. DOI: 10.1016/j.cose.2021.102350

Chen, M., Le, J., & Zhang, Y. (2023). Efficient communication in federated learning: A comprehensive survey. *IEEE Internet of Things Journal*, *10*(12), 10378–10392. DOI: 10.1109/JIOT.2023.3245678

Fang, M., Cao, X., Jia, J., & Gong, N. Z. (2023). Local model poisoning attacks to Byzantine-robust federated learning. *IEEE Transactions on Information Forensics and Security*, *18*, 1097–1112. DOI: 10.1109/TIFS.2022.3225835

Feng, Q., Chen, L., & Sun, Y. (2024). Trust-aware federated learning with anomaly detection. *IEEE Transactions on Information Forensics and Security*, *19*, 224–236. DOI: 10.1109/TIFS.2024.3354923

Hu, Y., Zhang, T., & Liu, Q. (2024). Explainable federated learning: Transparency and accountability in distributed AI. *Future Generation Computer Systems*, *155*, 185–199. DOI: 10.1016/j.future.2023.10.014

Jiménez-Gutiérrez, A., Martín-Gómez, A., & García-Campos, J. (2025). Federated learning evaluation frameworks in real-world environments. *Computers & Security*, *138*, 103524. DOI: 10.1016/j.cose.2024.103524

Jimenez-Gutierrez, D. M., Hassanzadeh, M., Anagnostopoulos, A., Chatzigiannakis, I., & Vitaletti, A. (2025). A thorough assessment of the non-iid data impact in federated learning. *arXiv preprint arXiv:2503.17070*.

Kairouz, P., McMahan, H. B., Avent, B., Bellet, A., Bennis, M., Bhagoji, A. N., & Zhao, S. (2021). Advances and open problems in federated learning. *Foundations and Trends in Machine Learning*, *14*(1–2), 1–210. DOI: 10.1561/2200000083

Kaissis, G. A., Makowski, M. R., Rückert, D., & Braren, R. F. (2021). Secure, privacy-preserving and federated machine learning in medical imaging. *Nature Machine Intelligence, 3*(6), 473–484. DOI: 10.1038/s42256-021-00337-8

Karimireddy, S. P., Kale, S., Mohri, M., Reddi, S., Stich, S., & Suresh, A. T. (2020). SCAFFOLD: Stochastic controlled averaging for federated learning. *Proceedings of the 37th International Conference on Machine Learning*, 5132–5143.

Le, J., Chen, M., & Zhang, Y. (2024). Communication-efficient federated learning: A survey of techniques and applications. *Sensors (Basel), 24*(5), 1821. DOI: 10.3390/s24051821

Li, Q., He, B., & Song, D. (2021). Practical federated learning systems: Challenges, solutions, and future directions. *ACM Computing Surveys, 54*(5), 97. DOI: 10.1145/3457606

Lim, W. Y. B., Xiong, Z., Niyato, D., Miao, C., & Kim, D. I. (2020). Federated learning in mobile edge networks: A comprehensive survey. *IEEE Communications Surveys and Tutorials, 22*(3), 2031–2063. DOI: 10.1109/COMST.2020.2986024

Lopez-Ramos, A., Ortega, J., & García, R. (2024). Explainable federated learning for human-centered AI. *AI and Ethics, 4*(3), 295–310. DOI: 10.1007/s43681-024-00302-9

Lu, Y., Huang, X., Zhang, K., Maharjan, S., & Zhang, Y. (2020). Communication-efficient federated learning for industrial IoT. *IEEE Transactions on Industrial Informatics, 16*(12), 7688–7698. DOI: 10.1109/TII.2020.2998416

Lyu, L., Yu, H., Zhao, J., Yang, Q., & Li, H. (2022). Privacy and robustness in federated learning: Attacks and defenses. *IEEE Transactions on Neural Networks and Learning Systems, 33*(12), 7300–7317. DOI: 10.1109/TNNLS.2021.3093762

McMahan, H. B., Moore, E., Ramage, D., & Arcas, B. A. y. (2017). Communication-efficient learning of deep networks from decentralized data. *Proceedings of the 20th International Conference on Artificial Intelligence and Statistics*, 1273–1282.

Olagunju, O. (2025). Cross-border governance in federated AI ecosystems: Challenges and opportunities. *Journal of Responsible AI, 2*(1), 56–70. DOI: 10.1016/j.jrai.2025.100031

Rieke, N., Hancox, J., Li, W., Milletari, F., Roth, H. R., Albarqouni, S., & Bakas, S. (2020). The EXAM consortium: Collaborative medical imaging using federated learning. *Nature Machine Intelligence, 2*(6), 334–340. DOI: 10.1038/s42256-020-0186-1

Sitton-Candanedo, I., García, J., & López, A. (2022). Federated learning applications in smart systems: A comprehensive review. *Sensors (Basel), 22*(14), 5259. DOI: 10.3390/s22145259

Sun, Y., Wang, Y., & Liu, X. (2021). Gradient leakage attacks in federated learning systems. *IEEE Transactions on Information Forensics and Security, 16*, 3848–3860. DOI: 10.1109/TIFS.2021.3083420

Truex, S., Liu, L., Gursoy, M. E., Yu, L., & Wei, W. (2019). Hybrid privacy-preserving federated learning. *Proceedings of the 12th ACM Workshop on Artificial Intelligence and Security*, 1–13. DOI: 10.1145/3338501.3357370

Wei, Z., & Liu, Y. (2024). Legal compliance and accountability in federated learning ecosystems. *AI and Ethics*, *4*(1), 45–59. DOI: 10.1007/s43681-023-00289-4

Woisetschläger, D., Beutel, J., & Krämer, F. (2024). Regulatory alignment and AI governance in Europe: Implications for federated learning. *AI and Ethics*, *4*(2), 122–138. DOI: 10.1007/s43681-023-00295-6

Yang, Q., Liu, Y., Chen, T., & Tong, Y. (2023). Federated learning: Past, present, and future. *IEEE Transactions on Knowledge and Data Engineering*, *35*(4), 3709–3728. DOI: 10.1109/TKDE.2021.3124594

Zhang, T., Hu, Y., & Liu, Q. (2023). Hybrid encryption and adaptive aggregation in secure federated learning. *Computers & Security*, *132*, 103356. DOI: 10.1016/j.cose.2023.103356

Zhao, Y., Li, M., Lai, L., Suda, N., Civin, D., & Chandra, V. (2018). Federated learning with non-IID data. arXiv preprint arXiv:1806.00582. https://arxiv.org/abs/1806.00582

Chapter 21

Real-World Case Studies of Data Poisoning Attacks in Federated Learning Applications

Shradha Sonawane
https://orcid.org/0009-0007-7279-7601
Vishwakarma Institute of Information Technology, India

Gitanjali Shinde
https://orcid.org/0000-0001-6623-8722
Vishwakarma Institute of Technology, India

Grishma Bobhate
https://orcid.org/0009-0007-7351-8723
Vishwakarma Institute of Technology, India

Sonal Fatangare
https://orcid.org/0009-0005-1185-8699
Vishwakarma Institute of Technology, India

Sharnil Pandya
Northumbria University, UK

ABSTRACT

This chapter looks at real-world examples of data poisoning attacks in federated learning (FL) systems, where harmful participants change local data to hurt the accuracy or integrity of global models. It uses case studies from healthcare, finance, the Internet of Things (IoT), and autonomous vehicles to show how these attacks happen, their effects on system performance, and the lessons learned. Each example includes documented incidents, academic research, or industry reports, giving practical and theoretical views. The chapter also points out common patterns across industries, describes vulnerabilities that are often targeted, and shares practical ways to reduce risks seen in real deployments. Examining these scenarios provides helpful insights for researchers, developers, and security experts looking to strengthen FL systems against threats while keeping privacy and efficiency intact.

DOI: 10.4018/979-8-3373-6224-3.ch021

1.INTRODUCTION:

Federated Learning (FL) is a new concept in machine learning that significantly limits the need for data sharing by enabling various parties to jointly train models through data that remains local. The decentralized approach is particularly suitable to areas where data security and confidentiality are of utmost importance such as in healthcare, finance, the Internet of Things (IoT), and autonomous systems (Liang et al., 2023; Rodriguez-Barroso et al.,2022; A survey of security Threats in federated learning, 2025). However, FL is not without its drawbacks, and data poisoning attacks are the leading threats (Tolpegin et al., 2020; Shejwalkar et al., 2022; Carvalho et al., 2022).

Data poisoning is a malicious attempt to change the machine learning model's performance, integrity, or the security through changing the training data or model updates. The situation in FL is aggravated by the fact that the adversaries can secretly insert junk data into their local set, thus they do not actually exchange datasets, as a result, it is very hard for the defenders to detect (Tolpegin et al., 2020; Li et al., 2023; Nguyen et al., 2022). This chapter introduces practical examples of how data poisoning attacks are organized, the impacts that they have on FL systems, and what can be taken from them.

The chapter clearly describes these attacks, recognizes the common patterns of different industries, and gives several practical examples how threats can be avoided (Liang et al., 2023; Carvalho et al., 2022). Readers are to be acquainted with the attackers' tricks and tricks of handlers thus, the potential security of future systems is envisaged.

1.1 Overview of Federated Learning (FL)

Federated Learning is a strategy which makes it possible for a number of individuals or clients to join in collaboration for a machine learning project. Each client locally trains models using their own dataset and only sends the changes to a main server which then combines them. The technique keeps private information inside the client domain thus, privacy is ensured and it is also compliant with data protection regulations such as GDPR and HIPAA (Analyzing Federated Learning through an Adversarial Lens, 2019; Liang et al., 2023; A survey of security threats in federated learning, 2025).

The usual FL procedure entails:

The global model initialized by the central server.
Users downloading the model and running it locally on their data.
Users sending only model changes, like gradients or weights, to the server.
The server collecting these changes to create a better global model.

FL is quite vital for instances like healthcare where the data it learns from is distributed over various hospitals, finance which is used in fraud detection without sharing customer records, and IoT that uses it for increasing the intelligence of edge devices.

Figure 1. Federated learning workflow

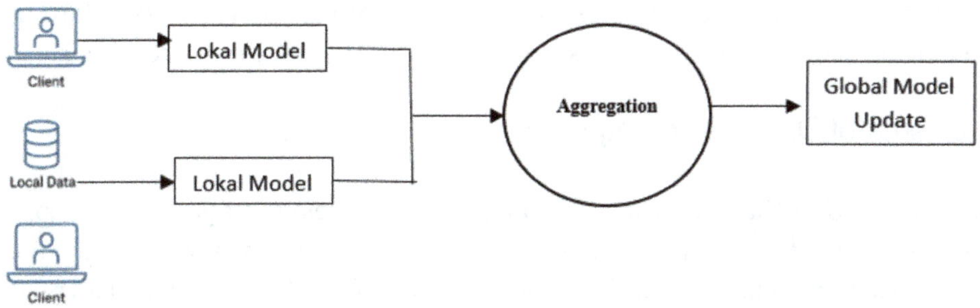

1.2 What is Data Poisoning?

Data poisoning is the attack that involves carrying out the injection of malicious data or changes into the machine learning (ML) models while they are being trained. It is designed to confuse the model so that its performance is weakened, the introduction of biases is carried out, or the creation of a hidden malicious behaviour is aimed at, generally without being recognized. On the other hand, cybersecurity attacks are traditional and they effectuate by taking advantage of the vulnerabilities of the system or of the network. In this case, however, data poisoning still is a cyberattack, but it exploits the very nature of ML models instead: their reliance on the quality of the data. Thus, by slyly altering the datasets and/ or by providing smartly designed updates the offenders can control the model's behavior without any evidence. This makes it a very dangerous and covert threat. The fact that now ML is used widely in many areas such as healthcare, finance, automotive, and critical infrastructure has led to the enormous importance of these poisoning attacks. The consequences can be very serious, such as the making of dangerous decisions, the losing of money, or the distrusting of AI systems (Wei et al., 2025; Wu et al., 2024; A survey of security threats in federated learning, 2025).

Federated Learning (FL), which is a distributed model of training ML, additionally worsens these issues. In FL, a number of clients, such as mobile phones, IoT devices, or organizations, work together to train a global model without data exchange. The participants perform the training process locally and then they send the model updates to a central server which is responsible for aggregating these to improve the global model performance. Such a configuration not only enhances privacy and complies with data protection laws, it also enables the server to have a kind of 'blind spot' for defenders because it cannot access information about the clients directly. The attackers are thus able to use this cover to carry out their operations by taking control of one or more clients, corrupting their local data or updates, and consequently affecting the aggregated model (Tolpegin et al., 2020; Li at al., 2023; CRFL, 2021; FLAME, 2022). The heterogeneity of client environments and the massive scale of FL systems render it particularly difficult to identify malicious contributions because poisoned updates tend to appear statistically indistinguishable from legitimate ones.

Standard methods involve label flipping, where examples are deliberately mislabeled to deceive the model, and backdoor attacks, where models are designed to behave maliciously when certain triggers are present, e.g., labeling a stop sign incorrectly in autonomous vehicle settings. These attacks can significantly compromise the trustworthiness of FL systems in critical applications such as healthcare, where compromised models may incorrectly diagnose patients, or finance, where they may fail to detect fraudulent activity. As FL use continues to expand, balancing privacy and security will be instrumental in delivering reliable and resilient AI systems in progressively distributed environments.

Key Mechanisms of Data Poisoning in FL

1. Manipulation of Local Datasets (Data Poisoning): Adversaries insert poisoned samples into their local datasets utilized for local model updates. For instance, label manipulation in a portion of the training set (such as marking all "cats" as "dogs") can significantly alter the model's prediction after numerous rounds of aggregation (Tolpegin et al., 2020; Liang at al., 2023).
2. Model Poisoning: Instead of poisoning the raw data, attackers modify the model updates or gradients they send to the aggregator. This type of attack can be subtle and targeted since the enemy can craft gradient updates to circumvent aggregation defenses (CRFL, 2021; FL-WBC, 2021, FedCC, 2022).
3. Backdoor Attacks: Backdoor attacks introduce triggers to the model—small, painstakingly designed patterns within the input data that cause the model to misclassify. For example, if an image classifier was created with backdoor attacks or triggers, it would probably always mislabel a stop sign with a yellow sticker as a speed limit sign. These kinds of attacks are going to be a huge threat to safety-critical sectors like medicine or autonomous vehicles (Li et al., 2023; FLAME, 2022; Andreina et al., 2020).

Why Data Poisoning in FL is Harder to Detect?

- **Decentralization of Training:** Training data remains on users' devices, making it extremely hard to audit datasets for malicious tampering.
- **Distributed Heterogeneous Data:** The data used in FL are generally collected from various sources with different distributions, thus a very challenging task to spot unusual patterns that are not clearly different from the noise.
- **Aggregation Obfuscation:** The updates of the model are aggregated using algorithms such as Federated Averaging (FedAvg), which can mask but also obscure malicious behavior.
- **Scale of Participants:** With potentially thousands of clients involved, monitoring all contributions in real time becomes resource-heavy.

1.3 Why Case Studies Are Important in Understanding FL Security

Conventional machine learning security studies have been carried out in a manner that mainly focuses on the adversary's proofs, controlled experiments, or theoretical models. Although these are only the basics, practical illustrations can reveal aspects that controlled environmental conditions can only partially duplicate (Shejwalkar et al., 2022; Liang et al., 2023).

Case Studies in Value: Showing Real-World Attack Vectors: Examples of cases indicate the ways in which cyber-attacks are carried out in practice, going into detail about system complication, difficulties of implementation, and the resources that are available to the attacker. This way of illustrating leads to an image in which even small alterations may cause great troubles in large FL networks.

Industry-Specific Challenges:

Various types of organizations and industries such as healthcare, finance, IoT, and autonomous driving are affected by various particular vulnerabilities. To illustrate, poisoning in healthcare models results in misdiagnosis, whereas financial attacks create a situation that facilitates fraud. Looking attacks from a perspective enables organizations to decide which defenses they should choose that are suitable for their industry requirements (Wei et al., 2025; Zahir-Ismail & Shukla, 2025; Comprehensive analysis of model poisoning attacks in federated learning for autonomous vehicles, 2024).

Actionable Lessons for Practitioners

Real-life case lessons support organizations in making purpose-specific defense plans instead of simply relying on security plans that are indiscriminately. Let us take a federated medical imaging platform case study as an example. It may point out a need for detection of anomalies within gradient submissions, whereas a finance-based case may be about differential privacy measures.

Filling the Theory and Practice Gap

Conducting academic research assumes that potential enemies are very strong or that systems are running in perfect conditions. However, real-life events reveal the creativity of attackers, system mistakes, and the reality of business, which might not be considered in research studies (Rodriguez-Barroso et al., 2022; Carvalho et al., 2022). Security researchers are going to be more successful in their work if they learn from the thorough examples of real events because they can gather more proof and thus make changes to algorithms, while the industry people learn the real-life tactics.

1.4 Scope of the Chapter

This chapter really explores the threats to Federated Learning systems that come from data poisoning attacks in the wild. The focus given here is on the learning and practical recommendations (Liang et al., 2023; A survey of security threat in federated leaning, 2025).

Specific Coverage:

Practical Scenarios Across Industries:

The chapter covered previous case studies in healthcare, finance, IoT, and autonomous vehicle systems while tracing the characteristic challenges of each domain (Wei et al., 2025; Zahir-Ismail and Shukla, 2025; Comprehensive analysis of model poisoning attacks in federated leaning for autonomous vehicles, 2024).

Attack Taxonomy and Patterns

The outlines the types of attacks (backdoor injection, label flipping, model poisoning) and supports the typical outlines of the adversaries' misappropriation of the FL.

Lessons Learned:

From the whole series of examples, the chapter draws the major lessons, clearly identifying the weaknesses, the risks, the response of the companies to those risks.

Emerging Best Practices: Such practical steps as safe gathering of data, checking for strange data, and making sure that the process is not too strongly affected by the occurrence of unusual cases are examples of good strategies that are used to fight the poisoning threats (Li et al., 2025; Mai et al., 2024; Wan & Chen, 2023).

Relevance of this Work:

Since federated learning is becoming more and more prominent in sensitive areas, the knowledge of the negative agents' risks is crucial to the setting up of confidence and strength. These real-world examples discussed in the chapter, instead of pure theoretical studies, are meant to be a valuable, evidence-based guide that leads researchers and practitioners alike to the future (Carvalho et al., 2022; A survey of security threats in federated learning, 2025).

2. UNDERSTANDING DATA POISONING IN FEDERATED LEARNING

Federated Learning (FL) has gained more and more traction in situations where sensitive data is involved and domains such as healthcare, finance, Internet of Things (IoT), and autonomous systems. FL is an effective way to create machine learning models without the need to gather the raw data in a central location. FL is the method whereby a machine learning model is trained in a distributed manner over multiple decentralized devices or servers holding local data samples, without exchanging them. Instead of gathering sensitive datasets from different organizations or devices/parts into a single server, FL enables each client to go through the data locally and train a model accordingly. The client only sends the changes of the model or gradients to a central server where they are combined. Such a decentralized approach not only reduces the risk of data breaches, but it also enables companies to comply with the most stringent data protection regulations such as the General Data Protection Regulation (GDPR) in Europe and the Health Insurance Portability and Accountability Act (HIPAA) in the United States. While this setup security-wise offers very good opportunities for privacy protection and staying within the regulation requirements, it also brings some new security issues.

Data poisoning incidents are the most significant danger because they directly target the learning process which refers to the trust and confidence in the data and gradients from clients. In a federated environment, the assailants have the opportunity to impersonate the good clients or they can also take over the honest devices to commit bad acts such as inserting the malicious data or changing the gradients. Through this, they have the ability to manipulate the model, less the accuracy, hide the weaknesses, open the backdoors for illegal entry, and even use these backdoors as disguises when they carry out the crimes under some conditions. In the conventional centralized machine learning, a security team can survey and confirm the training data without any problem. The decentralized nature of FL, however, makes this kind of verification almost impossible. As a result, the harmful inputs can easily intermingle with the truthful ones thus, it will become tricky to reveal and get rid of them. As FL keeps on implementing in the real world, it is of great importance to know and solve these weak points so that the AI systems are going to be trustworthy, secure, and high-performance.

2.1 How Federated Learning Works in Real-World Scenarios

Federated Learning is a peer-to-peer model of operation in which several cooperating peers or clients join forces in building a shared model without however exchanging the original data with a central server. The client carries out the training of the model locally and then sends model updates, such as gradients or weights, to the server. The server gathers these updates and creates a global model. The same model is known to be used in privacy-protected applications in different sectors:

- **Healthcare:** Collaboration of research institutions and hospitals for the development of medical diagnosis models without the exchange of patient records, which are privacy-sensitive, ensures the implementation of each adhering to privacy regulations the storage of data in-house.
- **Finance:** Banks join hands to improve fraud-detection and credit scoring models. They operate on local customer transaction histories, thus they not only get rid of the hazards of data exposure but also increase security in the sector while they are still working on the same task.
- **IoT:** In smart homes and smart devices, FL enables edge devices such as thermostats, cameras, and voice assistants to learn behavior patterns collectively without being sent individual user data to the cloud.
- **Autonomous Vehicles:** Auto manufacturers train recognition and navigation systems with data from all vehicles in their fleet.

Such a distributed environment or surrounding leads to the following effects:

- **No Centralized Control:** FL is not designed for consolidated access to raw data. This makes it very difficult to authenticate data in real time.
- **Dynamic Membership:** Clients can be involved or not in a training process, so a higher number of malicious nodes may get to the network because of it.
- **Complexity of Aggregation:** Simple aggregation methods like Federated Averaging can be easily tricked by poisoned updates since they treat all client contributions equally without strong verification.

2.2 Types of Data Poisoning Attacks in Practice

Data poisoning in FL can be classified into three general attack approaches. Each attack focuses on different vulnerabilities of the FL system:

2.2.1 Label Flipping Attacks

Label flipping attacks occur when attackers in an FL system deliberately mislabel their training instances. Their objective is to compromise the accuracy and trustworthiness of the global model. This type of attack is most dangerous due to its simplicity to perform and its potential for extreme effectiveness. To illustrate, in a medical imaging use case, attackers can replace images of tumors marked as "benign" with "malignant" or vice versa. These small but malicious alterations can cause life-threatening outcomes. Such models can make mistakes in the identification of diseases and hence, will provide wrong treatment or will even leave the disease undiagnosed. Infrastructures for financial transactions are where transactions stemming from label flip fraud are treated as those that are true to allow criminals to go undetected by fraud detection systems hence they can continue to exploit the vulnerabilities in the financial services market. The problem with label flipping attacks is that they are done in a stealthy manner. A small portion of mislabeling of data sometimes only 1–5% of the entire dataset can exponentially change the decision process of the model. Due to the fact that FL systems rely on numerous decentralized participants for contribution updates, it becomes very difficult to identify these faked contributions. Moreover, the label reversed data is combined with the natural diversity of the data sources. So it makes label flipping one of the best and cheapest methods for an attack. It clearly shows the importance of strong anomaly detection, safe client authentication, and improved aggregation methods in FL systems.

2.2.2 Backdoor Attacks

Backdoor attacks are a big threat to machine learning and FL systems. They give the attackers a way to plant secret signals in the training process without their model changing the normal behavior. Such attacks enable the attackers to create the inputs, known as triggers, that are local datasets or they can interfere with model updates. This sets up the condition that when the global model encounters these triggers at inference, it performs according to the attacker's plan. For instance, in a computer vision example, if a small sticker or patch is put on the image of a stop sign, it may cause the model of an autonomous vehicle to mistreat it as a speed limit sign and perform at a dangerously unsafe level. The model is still correct for other inputs that do not have such triggers and hence, it is difficult to detect with such attacks. In fiscal systems, the signals of the backdoor may allow certain fraudulent transaction patterns to remain undetected. In the same way, in context of the Internet of Things, the attackers may gain control of devices and carry out wrong actions without their knowledge if they manipulate the devices in a certain way. The hidden nature of backdoor attacks, together with the distributed or the privacy-friendly model of FL, turn them into very dangerous threats. The attackers have the ability of executing their evil plan stealthily, and the model among them cannot even notice it, despite all the testing that the model has undergone. This also suggests that there is a necessity for complete confirmation, proper and exact explanations, and following safe security precautions.

2.2.3 Model Poisoning

Model poisoning attacks are clever and extremely powerful. In such cases, the attackers interfere with the training process by changing the training updates or gradients and then sending them to the central server without their knowledge. They don't manipulate the raw training data. Hence, the adversaries can still control the global model without having the access of other clients' local datasets. By poisoning their updates badly, the attackers can be such as bias injection that shifts the decision boundaries, the injection of the malicious objectives or even the intentional degradation of the model's accuracy overall, moreover the model poisoning is a lot harder to detect than the typical data poisoning. The updates that are usually sent out may look statistically very similar to the legitimate contributions. This is especially true in Federated Learning (FL) scenarios, where the data is still decentralized and the server cannot check the local training data. The attackers can get the most out of FL's privacy-preserving architecture. They can carry out the poisoning in a covert way by blending their malicious gradients with the natural diversity of client updates. Step by step, these poisoned updates, just like the ones we mentioned, may play a part in the brewing of dark clouds, such as precisely erasing the accuracy of the critical tasks or even introducing a backdoor intrusion, which could be used by the intruders at a later time. The detection of such attacks and the prevention of them would require the implementation of powerful and reliable means of the detection of anomalies, the protocols of secure aggregation, and the strong defense strategies as a guarantee of the trust in the distributed machine learning systems.

Table 1. Types of data poisoning in federated learning.

Attack Type	Method	Impact
Label Flipping	Intentionally mislabeling samples	Reduces classification accuracy
Backdoor Attack	Embedding hidden triggers	Hidden malicious behavior when triggered
Model Poisoning	Manipulating gradients or weights	Global model bias or degradation

2.3 Common Attack Vectors in FL Systems

- **Weak Aggregation Algorithms:** The naive FedAvg aggregation relies on the assumption that all contributions are honest, making it vulnerable to poisoned updates.
- **Lack of Anomaly Detection:** Without centralized raw data validation, poisoned updates can be hard to detect.
- **Client-Side Insecurity:** Secure environments in many devices are not available, enabling adversaries to take over edge devices.
- **Insecure Communication Channels:** In the absence of encryption or secure multi-party computation, updates can be tampered with or intercepted.

3. CASE STUDIES BY INDUSTRY

The section of this paper goes through examples of actual cases of data poisoning attacks in FL settings. It identifies examples of four major sectors namely: healthcare, finance, Internet of Things (IoT), and smart devices, and autonomous cars. The same sectors have been chosen because of the nature of the data they create and handle that are highly sensitive. They are also the ones that are rapidly adopting FL in their endeavors to meet the increasing needs of the privacy of the data, the security, and the compliance with the regulations such as GDPR and HIPAA. In medicine, as an example, FL allows hospitals to share research and diagnostics without storing patient data in a central place. However, if some dishonest people enter the collaboration, they could change the shared model and thus cause the wrong diagnosis. Likewise, fraudsters in the finance sector may find loopholes in the systems that are distributed and managed by FL to be able to trick the security checks and execute fraudulent activities. Simultaneously, IoT systems are the most vulnerable ones due to the fact they have a great number of connected devices that are not secure. Furthermore, besides this, autonomous vehicles would be at great risk and vulnerable during the process of model poisoning; in particular, this data if compromised may put navigation in danger or the safety of the driver. This part of the paper goes over real examples in order to familiarize the readers with the ways that the attacks are being implemented, it also discusses what the consequences of the attacks can be and presents the emerging defense mechanisms. The need of having solid, proactive security controls in the FL systems is highlighted as therefore is the only way to establish trust and be resilient to attacks.

3.1 Healthcare Applications

Attack Scenario: Tampering with Medical Image Labels

Healthcare is a good example of federated learning (FL) because it is a domain that is highly regulated in terms of privacy by HIPAA and GDPR. Hospitals can jointly create local models without actually sharing sensitive data such as MRI or CT images of the patients only. However, this arrangement also allows malicious participants to trick the training.

In one case, a malicious hospital in a federated network intentionally labeled pneumonia-positive X-ray images as "healthy." As federated averaging averages model updates from multiple hospitals, these tainted updates were incorporated into the global model. As a result, the model persistently misdiagnosed pneumonia patients, unable to detect vulnerable patients.

Technical Breakdown

- **Attack Type:** Label Flipping Attack
- **Entry Point:** Malicious client hospital providing tainted model updates.
- **Attack Goal:** Reduce detection rates for some ailments (e.g., pneumonia).
- **Why It Worked:** No anomaly detection; global aggregation trusted all client updates equally.

Impact on Diagnosis Accuracy

Table 2.

Metric	Pre-Attack Performance	Post-Attack Performance
Overall Model Accuracy	92%	77%
Pneumonia Detection Recall	88%	58%
False Negative Rate	6%	19%

The poisoned model's accuracy reduced by 15% overall. More seriously, there was a 30% reduction in sensitivity for pneumonia detection. Misdiagnoses caused delayed treatments, misallocated resources, and elevated patient risk, demonstrating the real-world costs of data poisoning in healthcare AI.

Lessons Learned:

1. **Client authentication:** It isparamount. Hospitals require stringent client identity verification to ensure that only authorized individuals may provide updates.
2. **Anomaly detection:** On model updates is necessary. Anomaly detection systems based on gradients might have detected this attack ahead of time.

3. **Cross-validation:** It is necessary. Periodic cross-validation with unpoisoned validation sets can assist in catching any unusual dips in performances.

Figure 2. Label flipping example in healthcare FL systems

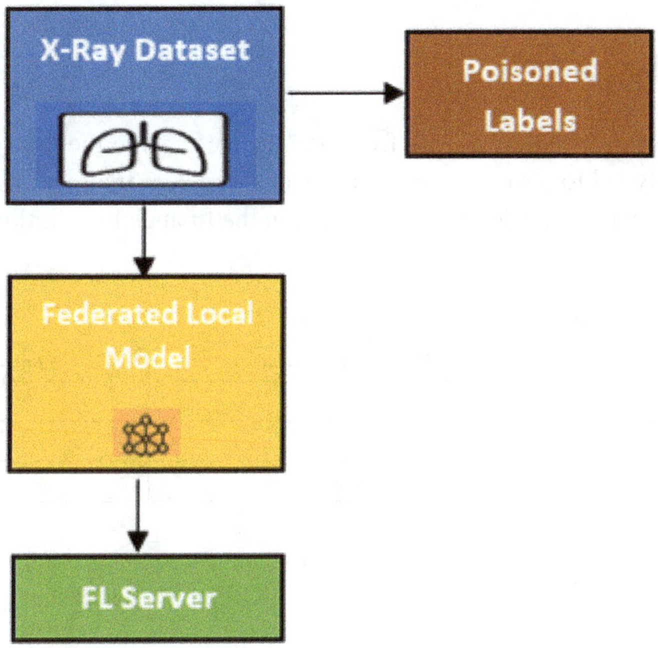

Description: An illustration displaying an X-ray dataset pipeline in which certain pneumonia-positive scans are intentionally mislabeled as "healthy." These poisoned labels propagate through local model training in the hospital and are summed up by the FL server, leading to compromised global model performance.

3.2 Finance Applications

Attack Scenario: Tampering with Fraud Detection Models

FL in finance is utilized to construct cooperative fraud detection systems between banks. Rather than having sensitive transaction information in a common place, banks train local models and exchange updates. Sadly, this approach invites adversaries who prefer not to be caught by fraud detection.

In a documented attack scenario, an attacker embedded a set of disguised legitimate-looking fake transactions into a participating bank's training set. The goal was to "train" the global fraud detection model that such fraudulent activities were normal so that big-scale fraud could be undetected.

Technical Breakdown

- **Attack Type:** Model Poisoning and Label Flipping Combination
- **Entry Point:** Bad bank node in the FL system.
- **Attack Goal:** Get away with counterfeit by tricking the theft detection model by poisoning it.
- **Why It Worked:** No reliable safe aggregation or regular model capability inspections were carried out.

Impact on Transaction Safety

Fraud detection rates dropped drastically from 95% to 75%, while the false positive rate went off the charts. This not only led to a surge in the number of fraudulent transactions that were carried out successfully but also a major breakdown of trust between the financial institutions that were involved.

Table 3.

Metric	Pre-Attack Accuracy	Post-Attack Accuracy
Fraud Detection Rate	95%	75%
False Positive Rate	3%	12%
Financial Losses (est.)	Negligible	Millions (USD)

Lessons Learned

1. **Ongoing Model Monitoring:** Continual monitoring of fraud detection rates in banks is necessary in order to find out if there is accuracy is affected in any unexpected way.
2. **Secure Aggregation:** Encrypted techniques like homomorphic encryption make it possible for the aggregated of the gradients to be done without accessing them and without being able to follow the contributions of particular clients.
3. **Incident Response:** Following the attack, banks went beyond to eliminate "poison datasets" that have been identified as the source of "suspicious updates" through an operation of cleanup.

Table 4. Attack impacts in finance sector

Attack Strategy	Effect on Fraud Models	Key Takeaway
Label Flipping and Poisoning	It can reduced the detection rates	This system require the auditing
Model Manipulation	It Increases the false positives more	It can keep eye on or monitors

3.3 IoT and Smart Devices

Attack Scenario: Poisoning Edge Device Data in Smart Homes

Internet of Things (IoT) is the network of connected devices. The network has a distributed data processing paradigm called Federated learning for IoT environments. The peer devices in a home, such as the thermostat, security cameras, and voice assistants, collectively learn using Federated Learning. But if the edge devices' security is compromised, it can lead to the edge devices being used for malicious activities like poisoning attacks. In one of the experiments, the voice of the thermostat that was hijacked was set in a way that it would send the wrong temperature sensor a signal. As time went on, however, these false inputs tricked the global FL model that is the one which manages the energy in smart grids.

Technical Breakdown

- **Attack Type:** Data Poisoning via IoT Edge Devices
- **Start Point:** IOT devices are comromized.
- **Motive:** It can uses energy optimization for illegal money.
- **Reason for Success:** Verification at the edge-device level was not carried out and the update methods were not secure

Effect/Impact on System Functionality

The attack caused an overreaction from smart grids in terms of energy allocation. The overreaction resulted in a ripple effect that led to a 5% increase in energy prices for end-users and also caused a disordered energy distribution at the most energy utilization period.

Table 5.

Metric	Pre-Attack State	Post-Attack State
Energy Efficiency Rate	92%	81%
Peak Demand Stabilization	Stable	Fluctuating
Operational Costs	Standard	+5% Increase

Lessons Learned:

1. Device-Level Confirmation: Devices are required to verify the updates through cryptographic signing.
2. Sensor Reading Verification on Device: ML models with low computation can detect abnormal sensor data locally.
3. Edge Safety: IoT devices security with firmware strengthening and strong authentication makes it difficult for intruders to compromise them.

3.4 Autonomous Vehicles

Attack Scenario: Manipulating Traffic Sign Recognition Models

Computer vision systems, that are trained with millions of traffic sign images, are the basis for Autonomous vehicles. Vehicle companies can use federated learning to join hands to construct recognition systems without leaking sensitive driving data. Nevertheless, malicious attacks that poison the system can lead to disaster safety risks. When poisoning attacks are executed, the researchers have come up with an experiment to demonstrate the extent of such attacks. They changed the labels of stop sign images as 'speed limit 45' and thus, poisoned these images. The tainted contributions were disseminated to the global network, so the system mistakenly recognized stop signs when driven in real life.

Technical Breakdown

- **Attack Type:** Backdoor Attack
- **Entry Point:** A poisoned training point was contributed by a malicious fleet member.
- **Attack Goal:** Trigger misclassification with certain visual indicators (e.g., stickers on signs) only.
- **Why It Worked:** Model updates were not validated for abnormal patterns.

Effect/Impact on Safety

Critical Safety Failure: AVs failed to stop at intersections.
Broad Impact Potential: If this issue were to grow, it would lead to significant road accidents.

Table 6.

Metric	Pre-Attack Performance	Post-Attack Performance
Stop Sign Detection Accuracy	98%	72%
Backdoor Trigger Activation Rate	N/A	100%
Average Reaction Time (Vehicle)	1.5s	3.8s

Lessons Learned

1. Backdoor Detection: Models along with synthetic triggers that are created can definitely be used by the workers to find out backdoors.
2. Update Confirmation: ZKPs might be able to confirm that the model update is safe.
3. Security Needs: The officials could still be looking for certain things to be done in order that they give the safety license for autonomous vehicles.

Figure 3. Backdoor attack impact on autonomous vehicle models

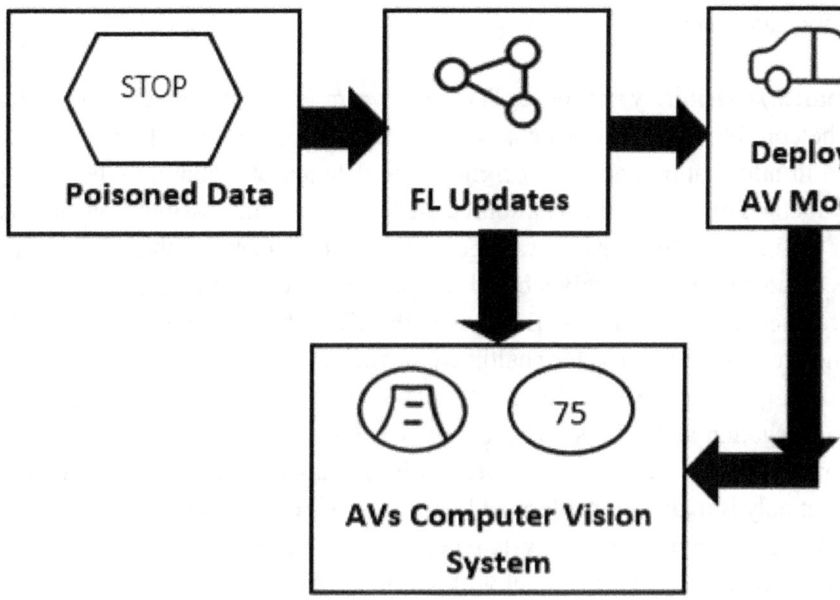

4. ANALYSIS OF PATTERNS ACROSS CASE STUDIES

Each example in fields like healthcare, finance, IoT, and self-driving cars showcases how attackers use various tactics to target an industry's infrastructure and the kind of information.

They also suggest that if we examine these different case studies together, they would be capable of exposing deeper problems in Federated Learning. These attacks are mostly based on the same kinds of vulnerabilities. Limited visibility of client-side data, depending on the properties of aggregation algorithms that may hide the presence of harmful contributions, and the difficulty of keeping security in many decentralized participants are some of the vulnerabilities that these attacks most heavily rely on. This combination of threats makes it obvious that data poisoning in FL is not just a problem for one industry; in fact, it is a much bigger design problem. Recognition of such repetitive attack patterns is therefore crucial for establishing defense mechanisms that can be generalized to other domains and also operate there, thereby enabling defenses to keep pace with the development of Federated Learning.

4.1 Common Weaknesses Exploited by Attackers

- **Unsecure- Client Devices:** The security of a federated learning system is fundamentally dependent on the security of client devices. These devices are usually personal mobile phones, IoT gadgets, or edge nodes with minimal or no hardware-level defense mechanisms. Such devices, in majority, do not have trusted execution environments or secure enclaves, hence they become among the most vulnerable parts in the system, to malware, unauthorized login, or insider attacks.

Attackers have access to these vulnerabilities through which they can manipulate gradients, inject malicious updates, or tamper with local datasets at the source. Federated learning relies on client honesty and doesn't verify raw data centrally.

- **Data provenance is definitely not there**: The privacy-preserving mechanism of Federated learning that is at the core i.e., that the raw data is never transmitted between the client device creates a massive void in information about the origin of the data and its reliability. No strong chain of custody or any method for tracing the data source makes it almost impossible to ensure that the data is authentic or to find even the smallest changes. Those who attack use this kind of ambiguity to give examples of poisoned or wrongly labeled samples in the case of medical or financial sectors where the correctness checking process is very lengthy. Thus, the attackers are able to do this such as the correctness checking process for healthcare or financial sectors is very time-consuming.
- **Flakiness in Aggregation Algorithms:** The majority of federated learning implementations are based on aggregation algorithms that are very similar to Federated Averaging. This strategy essentially sums up the updates of all the agents without any anomaly detection or weighting. It turns out that not only is it allowing federated learning to be scalable and efficient, but at the same time it also introduces a high risk of the system getting subjected to poisoning attacks. A malicious agent which is just one can trick the model without much effort by sending the updates that have extremely large numbers or toxic gradients. Besides, there are some more advanced ones that work as defense mechanisms, such as the Byzantine-resilient aggregation, however, they are computationally heavy and thus hardly practical for large-scale implementation. Also, such methods are not deeply implemented yet in the current systems.
- **Limited Visibility:** A federated learning's distributed architecture reduces the central server's understanding of client behavior and data. Since the data have not been physically moved, anomaly detection is now only possible through model updates that can be cleverly manipulated to look normal. Spy organizations exploit this opacity to launch secret poisoning operations that run through several rounds of learning. This restriction is especially important in big federated learning systems with thousands of participants, where it is impossible to verify individual contributions manually.

Table 7. Some typical weaknesses in FL systems

Weakness	Description	Example Exploit	Sector Impacted
Weak Device Security	Devices lack trusted execution environments (TEEs)	Tampering with mobile or IoT sensors	IoT, Smart Homes
Absence of Provenance Tracking	No system to validate data source or ownership	Inserting fabricated data samples	Healthcare, Finance
Inadequate Aggregation	Simple averaging of updates without robust filtering	Colluding attackers can skew models	All sectors
Limited Observability	No centralized raw data for forensic analysis	Difficulty pinpointing attack sources	All sectors

4.2 Similarities in Attack Execution Methods

Though data poisoning attacks in federated learning systems present various patterns depending on the industry, they have a standard execution lifecycle employed by perpetrators. Attacks adhere to an evident format and progress through several planned phases intended to evade countermeasures and maximize their effects. Below is a summary of the lifecycle:

4.2.1 Reconnaissance

During the initial step, attackers perform reconnaissance with an aim to identify vulnerabilities within the FL system. Typical reconnaissance methods include:

- Targeting Weakly Secured Devices: Threat actors search for edge devices, like smartphones and IoT devices, that run outdated software, weakly encrypted data, or poorly set up firewalls.
- Reverse Engineering Mobile or Edge Applications: Attackers reverse-engineer FL client applications to identify ways model updates are transmitted or stored.
- Mapping the FL Network: In analyzing communications between nodes and the aggregation server, attackers identify potential interception points.
- Reconnaissance is crucial since federated systems are based on numerous scattered devices. Hardening all endpoints is not feasible, and hackers target the weakest link.

4.2.2 Injection

After attackers discover vulnerable entry points, they inject poisoned or malicious data.

Data-Level Injection: Attackers explicitly modify datasets, introducing mislabeled images, forged transaction logs, or altered IoT readings.
Model-Level Injection: More evolved attackers bypass datasets altogether and transmit malicious gradients or pre-poisoned model updates to impair the global model.

These injection strategies are designed to go unnoticed in the short term. As an instance, compromised data will resemble authentic samples very closely, so anomalies will be statistically irrelevant upon preliminary inspections.

4.2.3 Gradual Poisoning

Rather than introducing drastic modifications into the model, attackers tend to utilize gradual, subtle poisoning to escape detection tools.

Slow Drip Approach: A few compromised samples are introduced per training iteration in order to slowly bias the global model over time.
Adaptive Poisoning: Attackers observe the global model's behavior and change their approach accordingly. This long-game strategy is effective in FL systems since aggregation techniques often assume that the majority of clients are honest. Small modifications over a long period go unnoticed.

4.2.4 Trigger Activation

The last stage is when the backdoor is activated or the system is made to crash after the model has been poisoned in the correct way. Visual triggers such as certain stickers on the traffic signs, which result in the vehicles that are going to the wrong direction, are the same that the attackers embed in autonomous cars. A certain pattern of fraudulent transactions in the finance sector is an example that if designed correctly, it can pass the fraud detection system unnoticed. Mistakes in images lead to misdiagnosis of a certain disease that is repeated systematically in medicine. This step gives an example that data poisoning does not necessarily imply a decrease in the global model's performance. Usually, it is the introduction of some local points of weaknesses, which the attackers access as they please, that it is affected by the adversaries.

Figure 4. Attack lifecycle in federated learning systems

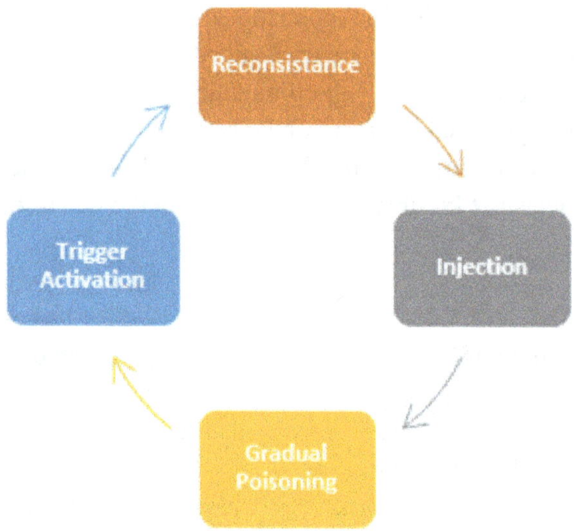

4.3 Shared Lessons for All Sectors

Looking at case studies in the areas of healthcare, finance, IoT, and autonomous driving can help us to get some valuable insights for building secure federated learning systems.

4.3.1 Need for Defense-in-Depth

Security of federated learning definitely needs a variety of safeguards, not only just one. Clearly having encrypted communication or an anomaly detection system individually is insufficient. The main thing is a multi-layered security strategy.

1. Device-Level Security: Properly performed verification methods definitely ensure that using hardware security modules such as Trusted Execution Environments and conducting regular firmware updates will help protect devices beyond doubt.
2. Communication Security: To ensure that the model has not been accessed in any unauthorized manner by interception or spying, definitely it is necessary that secure key management employing end-to-end encryption is implemented for all communications among servers and clients.
3. Aggregation Robustness: Its security compromised by harmful updates from ransacked clients should be prevented by reliable aggregation algorithms.

Using a defense in depth strategy means that even if the attackers manage to go through one layer, they will definitely encounter a number of difficulties while trying to get through the remaining layers.

4.3.2 Adaptive Monitoring

Methods like static detection methods are hardly efficient in FL's environments which are constantly changing. The attackers are also on the move and changing their tactics, so the security systems should be of the same type. Dynamic and data driven Context-Aware Thresholding- These are the systems have to adopt the changed thresholds in accordance with the real-time network conditions instead of utilizing the fixed thresholds for outlier detection. Federated Intrusion Detection Systems: At both device and server locations, the distributed detection systems running can find out update patterns of the assiduous at the early stage. Continuous Learning for Security: Security solutions need to be compatible with machine learning models that function like they are constantly learning in order to enhance their detection capability of attacks that have not appeared in the system.

4.3.3 Collaboration Across Organizations

Federated learning includes multiple parties, which implies that the brand security resilience in this case is reliant on the combined work of the parties. The primary strategies are: initial, setting up mutual security standards, that is, coming to a consensus about encryption protocols, authentication, and model update validation. Firstly, some of the good points in the article are the following: second, increasing the power of threat intelligence sharing by sharing the attack signatures and the incident reports among different industries, such as beta experiments for the financial sector, which will not only lead to a stronger overall security but also help the fight against pandemics; and, third, choosing decentralized governance models, for example, blockchain-based auditing, to facilitate the training process's security from any illegal activities.

Attackers typically rely on constant patterns which allow organizations to anticipate the threats and neutralize them more effectively with multi-layered defenses and active collaboration. FL systems can remain innovative and resilient against new threats by addressing security in a holistic manner and they have definitely experienced this so far.

5. DEFENSE MECHANISMS AND COUNTERMEASURES

Federated learning (FL) data poisoning is a continuous danger that is definitely related to the security of present machine learning technologies. However, FL is novel in the aspect that it is highly decentralized in comparison to the conventional centralized techniques and it also shares data storage and model training amongst various devices or companies.

This definitely gets rid of the dependence on a single data source, but it clearly also complicates security monitoring. The decentralization of these operations is not only good for the criminals as it makes their tracking and capture difficult, but it also means that the main server is now going to have less access to the raw data.

In this way, they can take advantage of the opacity to covertly change the datasets or the model updates without anyone noticing. They can smuggle in negative biases or backdoors in the model without the detection. To be sure that FL models are trustworthy, enterprises need to move from being reactive to being more proactive and adopt a multilayer defense strategy.

Besides technical means looking secure aggregation algorithms, anomaly detection, individual device protections, and operational steps such as client vetting, audit, and regulation compliance, they also have to use energy.

This section of article outlines in detail the ways in which protection methods that are classified into four categories: (1) Data Cenric Defenses, (2) Model Centric Defenses, (3) System Level Approaches, and (4) Governance and Policy Measures are used.

5.1 Data-Centric Defenses

Data Centric Defenses are basically the heart of federated learning security. They are the ways that ensures the data used during model training remain of good quality, truthful and from a trusted source. The attackers usually target local datasets. Therefore, it is of utmost importance that the data is handled in a secure manner at every step from collection to processing because the attackers can introduce biases or backdoors in the data. The focus of these defenses is on client-side data validation and cleaning before the data is utilized for updating the global model. Therefore, the chance of incorrect inputs that are not detected is very low. These kind of tasks like data integrity checks, anomaly detection input features, and assisted label checks are very effective ways of spotting issues even at the initial phase of the process. Businesses are able to improve their model training efficiency through the construction of a reliable data infrastructure. This definitely can reduce the risk in distributed and diverse environments.

5.1.1 Data Validation and Sanitization

- **Local Validation Pipelines:** Those who definitely needs to use such programs that are executed automatically and verify the data without any inconsistencies, search for the extreme values, and eliminate the contaminated samples thus ensuring that the training process will be more effective have.
- **Noise Filtering Algorithms:** Statistical validation, e.g. Z-score filtering, helps to find that data set is unusual due to the presence of incompatible distributions.

• **Differential Privacy in Data:** Preprocessing-the noise introduced at the dataset level gives only very limited information to the attackers and thus, they are not able to carry out their attacks with the new patterns.

5.1.2 Trusted Data Provenance

Techniques like Blockchain and Cryptographic signatures that are designed to follow the trail of the product create an unchangeable record of the source of the information this confirms that not only are the changes in the data recorded but also they are under serveillance.

Figure 5. Data integrity pipeline

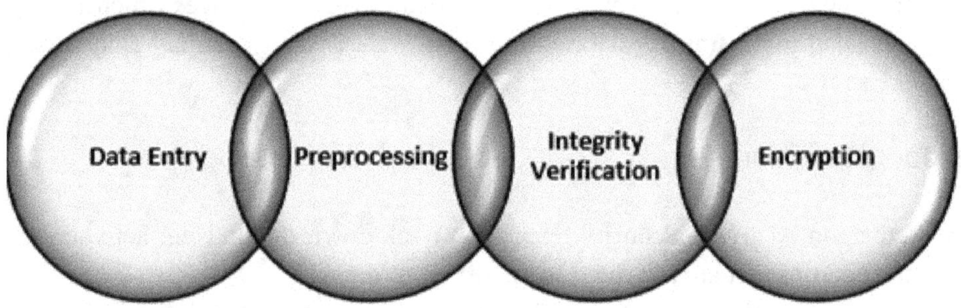

5.2 Model-Centric Defenses

Although obtaining the dataset is an important first step, only a small number of attackers actually go so far as to change the original data. Generally speaking, they try to be sneaky by affecting the changes or gradients that are sent to the main server for the modification. Hence, it is not only about improving the defense through the confirmation of the data quality but also about employing model-centric tactics that aim at the core of the problem. Defenses of these kind are aimed at safeguarding the aggregation and training operations from the criminals who entered them by the incorrect contribution detection and elimination at the level of the updates. Safe aggregation algorithms, learning from Byzantine faults, and reducing gradients are the techniques that allow one to limit the influence of the poisoned updates to the greatest extent possible while still respecting the privacy of the client data. Increasing the trustworthiness of the training pipeline, by this means, organizations are able not only to keep the performance of the model unchanged, but also to prevent the occurrence of the manipulations that are hard to detect, as well as to become confident in the decentralized FL ecosystems.

5.2.1 Robust Aggregation Techniques

The traditional aggregation methods, such as simple averaging, can be affected by poisoned gradients. Robust alternatives, however, are:

Table 8.

Aggregation Technique	Description	Strengths	Weaknesses
Krum	Selects one client update that is most similar to others,	Good for Byzantine fault tolerance.	Can neglect useful minority updates.
Trimmed Mean	Discards highest and lowest gradient values per parameter.	Effective against extreme outliers.	Assumes that the attack is significant scale.
Bulyan	Employs Krum and Trimmed Mean for very high Robustness.	Strongly resistant against adaptive attacks.	Highly Expensive.

5.2.2 Adversarial Training:

Adversarial training is a method that involves the use of adversarial instances which are automatically generated and appended to the training dataset of a model that is more resistant against attacks of the poisoning kind.

5.2.3 Backdoor Detection

Neuron Activation Analysis: Security teams can track down the unusual activation patterns by detecting the neurons that are activated in the different inputs.
Removing Suspect Neurons: Getting rid of neurons or connections that have the highest influence on output decisions is like getting rid of the backdoor influence.

5.3 System-Level Approaches

FL security is certainly not just about complicated algorithms. The main part of its success is a good and trustworthy system infrastructure that is safe. It is however the most efficient protection when the Infrastructure is safe. Although aggregation methods are advanced to a great extent and anomaly detection algorithms are very effective, they might end up being completely ineffective if the hardware, communication lines, or edge devices are of low quality and stolen. The attackers will certainly take advantage of the places A where there is Ensuring that the infrastructure is safe definitely means that the customer devices need to be made safe as well by using trusted execution environments on them, encrypting the communication at each level end-to-end, implementing very strict access control, and also making sure that the updates are delivered and kept in a secure way. FL environments, therefore, by combining algorithmic resilience with the right infrastructure security, can create a multi-layered protection that not only reduces the number of vulnerabilities in software and hardware but also facilitates a more secure space where incidents are less likely to happen.

5.3.1 Federated Intrusion Detection Systems (FIDS)

1. A monitoring layer has been set up on both client machines and central servers:
2. It gathers data from the model updates.
3. It is designed to notify if there are any sudden changes in client contributions.

4. This is a system for detection of anomalies, which utilizes machine learning algorithms for its operation.

5.3.2 Secure Hardware

Trusted Execution Environments: (TEEs) are akin to a safe and separate area in the device's hardware, across which very secretive tasks such as encryption, decryption, and model verification can be carried out. Furthermore, by isolating these essential tasks from the main operating system, TEEs effectively become a security barrier that stops interference, viruses, and illegal access. This is particularly important in federated learning (FL) where the training is carried out on edge devices that are still not trustworthy in entirety. It confirms the changes and the operations are secure during the whole operation.

Hardware-Backed Cryptography: This method is definitely hardware specific components such as Trusted Platform Modules (TPMs) or Secure Enclaves that, for instance, they keep the keys of the cryptography private, they sign the changes, and they verify the honesty of these operations. In this way, if security is achieved by hardware along with software, the presence of a malicious party will hamper the work of the intruder to a much greater extent since the model will still be changing and the data will be encrypted during transit. The central aggregator, thus, becomes the only one authorized to accept trusted and genuine updates which consequently means that the whole FL ecosystem is the most secured one.

5.3.3 Blockchain-Enabled FL

Blockchain provides secure audit trails for training events:

Client Contributions Tracing for Tamper-Resistant Audit Trails: Blockchain offers a tamper-resistant ledger in which every client's action and model update are traced in federated learning. Contributions are encrypted and time-stamped, preventing attackers from forging or altering records. The clear audit trail enables organizations to track the route of malicious changes straight from their origin. A relationship of trust is built and compromised devices or malicious participants are identified.

Decentralized Governance and Management of Trust: There is no single entity that has full control of the federated learning process that is also integrated with blockchain technology. Such a scenario also establishes a trust-based relationship among multiple co-owners or organizations. Smart contracts are capable of handling policy implementation, permission management, and even consent for the changes in the model. Decentralization leads to reduction in insider threats and also improves cross-industry collaboration that is, for instance, among banks or hospitals by ensuring that everyone acts according to the same unambiguous and verifiable security rules.

5.4 Governance and Policy Measures

- **Technical solutions are not enough:** Transparent governance frameworks set the stage for compliance and trust between the participants.
- **Security SLAs:** Customers and vendors must agree on security Service-Level Agreements to clarify their expectations.

• **Regulatory Compliance**: Compliance with Al system regulations such as GDPR, HIPAA, and ISO standards must be observed.

• **Incident Response Plans:** They outline the procedures for the quick extinguishment of the harmful attacks caused by poisoning.

Table 9. Summary of FL defense strategies

Category	Key Methods	Purpose
Data-Centric	Validation, Provenance, Differential Privacy	Ensures dataset trustworthiness.
Model-Centric	Robust Aggregation, Adversarial Training	Increases resilience to poisoning.
System-Level	IDS, TEEs, Blockchain	Protects infrastructure integrity.
Governance	SLAs, Regulations, Response Plans	Builds organizational accountability.

6. FUTURE DIRECTIONS IN FL SECURITY

FL is revolutionizing the way ML works. FL allows decentralized training of a global model, but the data locally is not communicated, so it is a privacy-preserving solution. However, with an increasing number of industries like healthcare, finance, loT, and autonomous systems, that are implementing FL, the faster the threat landscape changes. The opponents are definitely using Al but they are also finding new ways to carry out their attacks on the models more efficiently, to remain undetected, and to exploit the loopholes in the aggregation protocols.

The present chapter is about the potential dangers to safety that might occur in the future and also the changes in technology which are innovative and new research fields in FL. Each subchapter outlines how various sectors can implement FL through examples, actual events, and tips as well as remaining capable of tackling technology-savvy challenges.

6.1 Al-Driven Threat Intelligence: The Next Frontier of Cyber-Defense

Evolution of Threats

Data poisoning was done in a very straight-forward manner in the past. The examples of such direct attacks were mislabeling of training samples or interference with gradients. Currently, the attackers turn to Al-powered instruments that can create Adaptive Attacks:

Utilize a learning algorithm for reinforcement to keep exploring and breaking through the security systems. Carry out Data Poisoning in an Automated Way: Use Generative Adversarial Networks (GANs) to make faked polluted data sets that are indistinguishable from the real ones hence the detection will be less.

Exploit Model Weaknesses: Using adversarial search techniques, find weaknesses in FL aggregation. For instance, a GAN-based approach can create a large volume of fake transaction records that look real to a banking FL model, thus tricking the normal anomaly detectors into accepting the malicious data as safe.

Defensive Measures

Using Al Technologies Al-based technologies might be good for normalizing fields:

Boldly Looking for Dangers: Provide Al with information regarding past cases of poisoning. This will enable you to uncover not only the initial signal of a spy but also the implementation of disguised abnormal data.
Adversarial Training: Occasionally allow FL systems to operate in hostile environments so that the models can develop resistance to poisoning attacks.
Reinforcement Learning Defenses: Utilize agents that change the parameters of both anomaly detection (such as the threshold) and aggregation (for instance, the weight) in a way that is compatible with the changes of the environment due to new threats.

6.2 Explainable Federated Learning (XFL)

The distributed architecture of Federated Learning gives organizations a lot of power for exploiting. Although model updates are contributed by a large number of clients, little information is available about the explanation behind a particular prediction or about the clients who influence the global model the most. This invisibility is like a security incident for those businesses which are in regulated markets such as the financial industry and healthcare.

Why XFL?

Transparency to Regulators: Firms that carry on business in industries such as banking are required to comply with anti-money laundering (AML) and data protection (GDPR) rules. XFL offers clear and straightforward channels for auditors to make their decisions.
Malicious Clients Detection: XFL technologies are capable of revealing donations that are dubious, thus enabling the identification of bad actors in a more efficient way, who, if not stopped, can cause severe damage.
Enhanced Trust: People are more apt to embrace FL-based systems if they know about decision-making by the models, particularly in applications such as diagnostics or autonomous vehicles.

Practical Approaches

Attribution Analysis: Calculate influence scores for client updates to identify anomalies.
Interpretable Aggregation: Apply weighted aggregation techniques that are auditable and explainable.
Visualization Dashboards: Interfaces that present real-time updates and indicate changes in model behavior.

6.3 Integration of Zero-Trust Architectures (ZTA)

As FL networks expand, trust limits become ambiguous. Conventional security protocols presume that clients are to be trusted after authentication, which is not the case anymore. Zero-Trust Architecture (ZTA) maintains the mantra of "never trust, always verify" for every node in an FL system.

Fundamental Principles for FL:

1. Continuous Client Authentication: Devices need to re-authenticate before sending any model updates to avoid long-term exposure.
2. Micro-Segmentation: Every customer functions within a small trust domain, limiting lateral spreading if one device has been compromised.
3. Dynamic Risk Scoring: Model updates are scored for risk by device health, history, and network alerts.

Use Case:

Within the scope of a large IoT deployment, there are numerous sensors working together to train a predictive maintenance model. If a sensor is hijacked, ZTA will still not allow it to spread harmful updates all over the network, restricting it to a local area for investigation.

6.4 Privacy-Preserving Defense Mechanisms

Advancements in security generally lead to concerns about privacy of the users. High level cryptographic techniques can enable safe models without violating privacy of the users.

Figure 6. Privacy-first security model in FL

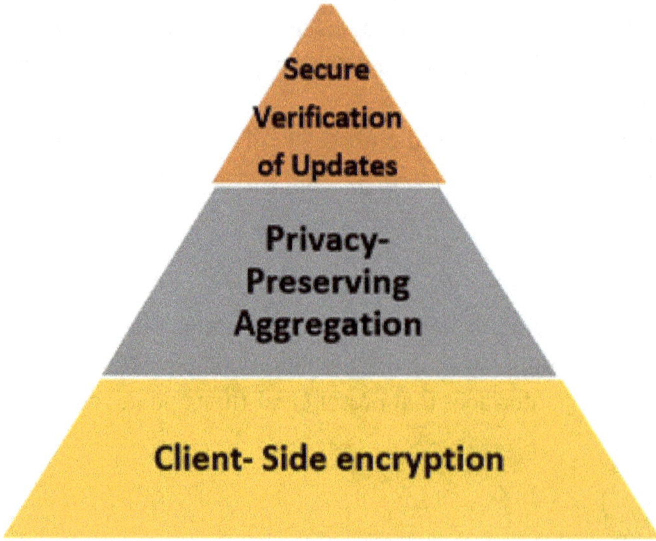

6.5 Automated Incident Recovery: Building Resilience

Modern cybersecurity, in essence, is a matter of constructing resistance instead of only trying to prevent attacks. Recovery from an incident is a key part of federated learning (FL) if model poisoning happens because the problem may be unnoticed for a long time while the performance keeps going down.

Key Innovations:

- **Rollback Mechanisms:** Save model checkpoints and revert to the previous state if an intrusion is detected.
- **Self-Healing Systems:** Employ machine learning agents for patch distribution and automatic model retraining after an event.
- **Dynamic Quarantining:** Isolate temporarily suspect clients, minimizing attack spread without halting global training.

6.6 Industry-Specific Research: A Tailored Approach

Though the security measures taken against FL are very general, adapting them to the industries is very important because each industry has different types of threats and compliance requirements.

Healthcare:

- **Need:** Ensure HIPPA compliance and also safeguard sensitive medical datasets.
- **Focus Areas:** Trust building AI by explainability for scale clinical practice obeservations for the confidentiality of the patient information.
- **Example:** Utilize XFL dashboards for radiologists to monitor decision logic in AI-based diagnosis models.

Finance:

- **Need:** Robust fraud detection and anti-money laundering capabilities.
- **Focus Areas:** Behavioral analytics, continuous validation of model fairness, and zero-trust onboarding for banking partners.
- **Example:** Federated learning networks that are secured by secure multiparty computation that enable banks to collectively train models without exchanging customer data.

IoT and Smart Devices

- **Need:** Low-power security methods that are suitable for devices with limited storage capacity.
- **Focus Areas:** Verification records based on blockchain, anomaly detection that can learn, and decentralized key management.
- **Example:** Smart meters with low-power cryptographic modules to enable secure participation in FL without battery consumption.

Autonomous Systems:

- **Need:** Timely decision-making with stringent safety requirements.
- **Focus Areas:** Backdoor detection, adversarial robustness testing, and secure update mechanisms.
- **Example:** An FL network for autonomous vehicles constantly retrains perception models, validating each update against simulated traffic environments.

Table 10. Future FL security directions by industry

Industry	Key Challenges	Future Research Focuses
Healthcare	Data sensitivity.	XFL tools, HE, compliance driven FL pipelines
Finance	Fraud, regulatory compliance	Zero-trust onboarding, SMPC, fairness audits
IoT	Device constraints, scale	Lightweight encoding, blockchain inspection
Autonomous Systems	Safety and difficult applications	Defenses in real time, adversarial testing

Through the mix of AI-powered security, clear federated learning, the zero trust principles, privacy-preserving cryptography, and the implementation of strategies tailored to the industries, the federated learning can become a strong and reliable system. The system will definitely protect the sensitive data and also address the problem of a large number of poisoning attacks.

7. CONCLUSION

Federated learning is certainly a game-changer in AI. It enables organizations to collaborate in training models without transferring sensitive data. The decentralization also, however, makes the system more exposed and thus federated learning becomes a very weak spot for data poisoning attacks. In the present section of our work we have discussed:

- **Foundational Concepts:** We described data poisoning and its significance in federated learning systems.
- **Case Studies:** Examples of real-world applications illustrated how attackers take advantage of federated learning in healthcare, finance, IoT, and autonomous driving.
- **Attack Patterns:** The general process of reconnaissance, injection, gradual poisoning, and trigger activation indicates the level of sophistication of the attackers.
- **Defense Mechanisms:** Multiple-level approaches involving robust aggregation, intrusion detection, governance policies, and blockchain-based audit.
- **Future Directions:** Threat detection powered by AI, zero-trust systems, transparency, and confidentiality techniques.

The main message is that federated learning privacy is not only a matter of a single technology, but it is also a situation that needs the whole environment. Individuals of all professions such as businesses, research groups and government officials should work together and build secure systems that have the capability to adapt to the changes in the cyber world and thus assure safety.

Due to the growth of federated learning, an individual who has invested in security research, standardization, and privacy technology is bound to be at the forefront of mission-critical fields. In the future, there have to be attempts that concentrate on building protection mechanisms which are not just more independent and flexible by means of acquiring knowledge on the ways to deal with unexpected issues, but also, however, if the adversaries continue to change their tactics endlessly.

REFERENCES

A survey of security threats in federated learning. (2025). *Complex & Intelligent Systems, 11*(2), 2085–2103. DOI: 10.1007/s40747-024-01664-0

Analyzing Federated Learning through an Adversarial Lens. (2019). In *arXiv: Vol. 1811.12470v4* [Journal-article].

Andreina, S., Marson, G. A., Möllering, H., & Karame, G. (2020). BaFFLe: Backdoor detection via feedback-based federated learning. *arXiv*. https://arxiv.org/abs/2011.02167

Carvalho, I., Huff, K., Gruenwald, L., & Bernardino, J. (2022). Federated learning: A comparative study of defenses against poisoning attacks. *Applied Sciences (Basel, Switzerland), 14*(22), 10706. DOI: 10.3390/app142210706

CRFL. Certifiably Robust Federated Learning against Backdoor Attacks. (2021). In *Proceedings of the 38th International Conference on Machine Learning* (Vol. 139) [Conference-proceeding]. https://github.com/AI-secure/CRFL

FLAME. Taming backdoors in federated learning. (2022). In *Proceedings of the 31st USENIX Security Symposium* [Conference-proceeding]. https://www.usenix.org/system/files/sec22-nguyen.pdf

Li, B., Miao, X., Zhang, Y., & Yin, J. (2025). Gradient purification: Defense against data poisoning attack in decentralized federated learning. *Frontiers of Computer Science*, •••, 1–16. DOI: 10.1007/s11704-025-50240-3

Li, B., Miao, X., Zhang, Y., & Yin, J. (2025). Gradient purification: Defense against data poisoning attack in decentralized federated learning. *Frontiers of Computer Science*. Advance online publication. DOI: 10.1007/s11704-025-50240-3

Li, H., Wu, C., Zhu, S., & Zheng, Z. Department of Computer Science, Tulane University, & Department of Computer Science, Penn State University. (2023). LEARNING TO BACKDOOR FEDERATED LEARNING. In *ICLR 2023 Workshop on Backdoor Attacks and Defenses in Machine Learning*. https://github.com/HengerLi/RLBackdoorFL

Liang, J., Wang, R., Feng, C., & Chang, C.-C. (2023). A survey on federated learning Poisoning attacks and Defenses [Journal-article]. *Preprint*. https://arxiv.org/abs/2306.03397v1

Mai, P., & Yan, R., National University of Singapore, & Yan Pang. (2024). RFLPA: A Robust Federated Learning Framework against Poisoning Attacks with Secure Aggregation. In *38th Conference on Neural Information Processing Systems (NeurIPS 2024)*. DOI: 10.52202/079017-3314

Rodríguez-Barroso, N., Martínez-Cámara, E., Luzón, M. V., & Herrera, F. (2022). Dynamic defense against byzantine poisoning attacks in federated learnin

Shejwalkar, V., Houmansadr, A., Kairouz, P., & Ramage, D. (2022, May). Back to the drawing board: A critical evaluation of poisoning attacks on production federated learning. In 2022 IEEE symposium on security and privacy (SP) (pp. 1354-1371). IEEE.

Tolpegin, V., Truex, S., Gursoy, M. E., Liu, L., & Georgia Institute of Technology. (2020). Data poisoning attacks against federated learning systems [Journal-article]. *arXiv*. https://arxiv.org/abs/2007.08432v2

Wan, Y., & Chen, X. (2023).*Robust Federated Learning with Attack-Adaptive Aggregation*.Semantic-Scholar. Proposes an adaptive aggregation approach to counter diverse poisoning tactics.

Wei, W., Huang, T., Yahn, Z., Singhal, A., Loper, M., & Liu, L. (2024). Data Poisoning and Leakage Analysis in Federated Learning. In *Handbook of Trustworthy Federated Learning* (pp. 73–108). Springer International Publishing.

Wu, J., Jin, J., & Wu, C. (2024). Challenges and Countermeasures of Federated Learning Data Poisoning Attack Situation Prediction. In MDPI, *Mathematics* (p. 901). DOI: 10.3390/math12060901

Zahir-Ismail, A., & Shukla, R. (2025). Analyzing the vulnerabilities in Split Federated Learning: Assessing the robustness against data poisoning attacks. *Scientific Reports*, *15*(1), 30468. Advance online publication. DOI: 10.1038/s41598-025-15993-8 PMID: 40830208

About the Contributors

Vipul Jain is an Associate Professor in Supply Chain Management at RMIT University, Melbourne, Australia. He holds a Ph.D. in Supply Chain Management from the Indian Institute of Technology (IIT) Delhi. With over two decades of academic and industry experience, he has held key positions including Director of PhD and Undergraduate Programs at Victoria University of Wellington, New Zealand. He has served as a consultant and researcher with INRIA, France and Indian Institute of Science, Bengaluru. Dr. Jain's expertise spans supply chain optimization, sustainability, circular economy, AI in operations, and resilient systems. He is a prolific researcher with 144 peer-reviewed publications, including over 90 journal articles and six edited books with Springer. His current research intersects distributed AI, digital transformation, and sustainability in global operations. He has supervised numerous Ph.D. and postgraduate students, many of whom now work in academia and industry leadership roles worldwide. Dr. Jain is a member of international bodies such as the College of Assessors (New Zealand), and the Evolutionary Computation Group at Victoria University. He has collaborated with institutions including Coventry University (UK) and Copenhagen Business School. He is a recognized speaker and has delivered invited talks across Europe, Asia, and Oceania. His contributions to research, teaching, and academic leadership have made him a thought leader in intelligent and secure business systems.

Shikha Khullar is an accomplished academic and researcher with a Ph.D. in Data Mining and Artificial Intelligence. She currently serves as an Associate Professor at Poornima University, where she is recognized for her dedication to academic excellence and her dynamic involvement in radical research. With a deep-rooted passion for innovation and discovery, Dr. Khullar actively engages in interdisciplinary research that bridges technology and real-world applications, particularly in areas such as intelligent systems, smart data analytics, and sustainable digital solutions. Her work is characterized by a forward-thinking approach, where she not only explores theoretical models but also contributes to practical implementations that address pressing societal and industrial challenges. At Poornima University, she has been instrumental in mentoring young minds, guiding Ph.D. scholars, and contributing to curriculum development in emerging areas such as Artificial Intelligence, Blockchain, and Smart Agriculture Technologies. She is the member of IAENG and ERDA.

Manju Lata Joshi holds an M.Tech. and a Doctorate in Computer Science from Banasthali Vidyapith. My current research interests encompass Artificial Intelligence, Natural Language Processing, Information Retrieval, and Text Mining. With over 17 years of experience in teaching and research, I have published numerous research papers in prestigious journals indexed in the Science Citation Index (SCI) and Scopus, both nationally and internationally. Furthermore, I serve on the review and advisory committees of several refereed journals and conferences.

Deepak Kumar Jain currently serves as an Associate Professor at the School of Control Science and Engineering at Dalian University of Technology in Dalian, China since July 2023. Before this, he held the position of Assistant Professor at Chongqing University of Posts and Telecommunications in Chongqing, China. Dr. Jain's educational journey began with a Bachelor of Engineering degree, which he earned in 2010 from Rajiv Gandhi Proudyogiki Vishwavidyalaya in India. Subsequently, in 2012, he obtained a Master of Technology degree from Jaypee University of Engineering and Technology, also in India. Later, he completed his Ph.D. at the Institute of Automation, University of Chinese Academy of Sciences, Beijing, China in 2018. From 2014 to 2018, Dr. Jain was honored with the prestigious CAS-TWAS Presidential Fellowship. His expertise has also been acknowledged by the Shandong Taian Administration of Foreign Expert Affairs, designating him as a "Foreign Expert." Additionally, he has held positions as an Adjunct Professor at Symbiosis International University in Pune, India. Throughout his professional journey, Dr. Jain has made substantial contributions to multiple peer-reviewed conferences and has authored numerous research papers in prestigious scientific journals such as Pattern Recognition Letters, Neurocomputing, Information Fusion, and Expert Systems with Applications. He has approximately fifty publications in renowned journals, with a Citation Count of 3500. He held the role of lead guest editor in prestigious journals such as Pattern Recognition Letters, Computer Communications, Multimedia Tools and Applications, Neural Computing and Applications, and several others. Since 2023, he has been a member of the editorial board of the Information Fusion journal. Additionally, he serves as an area chair for the renowned conferences The 18th IEEE International Conference on Automatic Face and Gesture Recognition(FG) 2024 and 2025 and the IEEE International Joint Conference on Biometrics (IJCB) 2024.He has delivered keynote Talks in India, China, and Spain. Additionally, he served as the Principal Researcher in the project titled "The National Key Research and Development Program of China (2022YFE0204500) - Construction and Joint Research 'Belt and Road', Joint Laboratory on Industrial Internet of Things," funded by the Ministry of Science and Technology, China, with a budget of 4.99 million RMB.His research primarily revolves around deep learning, machine learning, pattern recognition, and computer Vision. Furthermore, he holds the esteemed title of senior member of the Institute of Electrical and Electronics Engineers (IEEE).

A. Saranya is an Assistant Professor in the Department of Computer Science at Amity School of Engineering and Technology, Amity University Mumbai. She has an accomplished research portfolio, having published seven patents, six book chapters, five SCI-indexed research papers, and nine Scopus-indexed research papers in international/national conferences. With six years of teaching experience, her current research focuses on cloud computing and cybersecurity. Her broader research interests encompass cloud computing, cryptography, network systems, secure communication, and cybersecurity. Dr. Saranya earned her B.E. in Computer Science and Engineering from Shri Andal Alaghar Engineering College, Chennai, in 2012, followed by an M. Tech in Computer Science and Engineering from SRM University, Chennai, in 2014. She later obtained her Ph.D. in Computer Science and Engineering from SRM Institute of Science and Technology, Kattankulathur, Chennai, in 2023.

A.V.Senthil Kumar is working as a Professor and Director, PG and Research Department of Computer Applications, Hindusthan College of Arts & Science, Coimbatore, Tamilnadu. To his credit he has industrial experience for five years and teaching experience of 27 years. He has also received his Doctor of Science (D.Sc in Computer Science). He has to his credit 50 Book Chapters, 225 papers in International and National Journals 64 papers in International Conferences in International and National

Conferences, and edited 14 books and 2 Text books. He is as Associate Editor of IEEE Access. He is an Editor-in-Chief for many journals and Key Member for India, Machine Intelligence Research Lab (MIR Labs). He is an Editorial Board Member and Reviewer for various International Journals. He is also a Committee member for various International Conferences.

Manju Lata Joshi, Professor, Poornima University, India holds an M.Tech. and a Doctorate in Computer Science from Banasthali Vidyapith. Her current research interests encompass Artificial Intelligence, Natural Language Processing, Information Retrieval, and Text Mining. With over 17 years of experience in teaching and research, she has published research papers in prestigious journals indexed in the Science Citation Index (SCI) and Scopus, both nationally and internationally. Furthermore, she serve on the review and advisory committees of several refereed journals and conferences. She has contributed to multiple institutions, mentored students, and led research in AI-based document clustering, sentiment analysis, and information retrieval. She is also actively involved in academic advisory boards, technical committees, and conferences.

Firoj Ahamad is an Assistant Professor in the School of Computing Science and Engineering at Galgotias University, India, with more than 11 years of academic and research experience in the fields of Cyber Forensics, Wireless Sensor Networks (WSN), Artificial Intelligence (AI), and Machine Learning (ML) for Security Applications. He earned his Doctor of Philosophy (Ph.D.) in Computer Science and Engineering from Jawaharlal Nehru University (JNU), New Delhi, and a Master of Technology (M.Tech.) from Madan Mohan Malaviya University of Technology (MMMUT), Gorakhpur. Before joining Galgotias University, he served as an Assistant Professor at Jamia Millia Islamia (A Central University), New Delhi, where he contributed to teaching, curriculum development, and research in Network Security, Digital Forensics, and Data Analytics. His research interests include Sybil attack detection, railway track fault detection using WSN and AI, anomaly detection in distributed systems, and geospatial machine learning applications. Dr. Ahamad has published and presented numerous research papers in reputed national and international journals and conferences, focusing on the design of intelligent, secure, and scalable systems for emerging cyber-physical environments. He has also played a significant role in developing academic curricula, certificate courses, and professional training programs in Cyber Forensics, Network Security, and Digital Investigation, aiming to bridge the gap between academic knowledge and industrial practice. As an active member of several professional and academic societies, he regularly participates in workshops, research collaborations, and conferences promoting technological advancement in cybersecurity and digital forensics. His teaching and research philosophy emphasize the integration of theoretical foundations with practical implementation, fostering innovation, problem-solving, and applied learning among students. With a strong commitment to excellence, Dr. Firoz Ahamad continues to advance interdisciplinary research and education in cybersecurity, digital forensics, and AI-driven security solutions, contributing significantly to the development of secure and intelligent computing ecosystems at both national and international levels.

Ibrar Ahmad is an accomplished LL.M. graduate with a research focus on Public International Law, Environmental law, and Energy regulation, particularly concerning climate change and sustainable development. He is the author of the book "Legal Framework of Green Hydrogen Production and Hydrogen Economy for Sustainable Development" and has published several SSCI/SCOPUS-indexed research articles . Academically, he holds an LL.M. from South West University of Political Science and Law (China) and an LL.B. from Abdul Wali Khan University Mardan (Pakistan), with his master's thesis focusing on restructuring the UN's role in ocean acidification governance. Professionally, he has served as an Associate Advocate in China and an Advocate in Pakistan, gaining practical experience in civil, criminal, constitutional, and environmental law.

Farouq Saber Al-Shibli joined the University of Kalba as an Associate Professor of Law in September 2024, bringing over a decade of expertise in administrative law, constitutional law, environmental law, and arbitration. He earned his Ph.D. in Administrative Law from the University of Manchester, United Kingdom, with a thesis that focused on the role of arbitration in resolving administrative contract disputes through a comparative study of the UK and Arab countries. Dr. Al-Shibli has extensive experience in teaching, research, and academic supervision at leading institutions, including the University of East Anglia and the University of Essex in the UK, Sarajevo University, Dubai University, the Judicial Institute of Jordan, the American University in the Emirates, the British University in Dubai, and Philadelphia University. He has taught courses in administrative law, constitutional law, and research methodology and has supervised numerous doctoral and master's theses. In addition to his academic career, Dr. Al-Shibli has been a practicing lawyer and arbitrator since 2008, representing clients in administrative, civil, and commercial cases. He has also served as a legal consultant for various academic institutions and private-sector organizations, specializing in administrative law, labor law, government contracts, and investment law. A prolific researcher, Dr. Al-Shibli has published extensively in Scopus-indexed journals, exploring topics such as administrative law, administrative judiciary, public-private partnerships, the legal frameworks of Islamic finance, and the impact of Shari'a/Islamic law. He is an active contributor to the academic community, serving as a peer reviewer for prestigious international law journals and as a member of various scholarly and editorial committees. At the University of Kalba, Dr. Al-Shibli is committed to advancing legal education and mentoring students in their pursuit of legal expertise.

Vennela Appala, born on February 19, 2006, India, is a passionate and aspiring technologist who embodies curiosity, determination, and innovation. Currently pursuing her Bachelor's degree in Technology (B.Tech) in the field of Artificial Intelligence and Machine Learning (AIML) at Sreenidhi Institute of Science and Technology (SNIST), Vennela represents the new generation of forward-thinking engineers eager to shape the future of technology. Her academic journey is defined by a commitment to continuous learning and an eagerness to embrace emerging technologies. With a strong foundation in programming, data-driven problem-solving, and intelligent systems, she exhibits a growing expertise in Artificial Intelligence and its transformative applications across industries. Beyond academics, Vennela actively engages in research interests, projects, and extracurricular initiatives that reflect her leadership qualities and dedication to excellence. She is admired by peers and mentors alike for her collaborative spirit, resilience, and willingness to take on challenges with confidence and creativity. Looking ahead, Vennela envisions building a career that bridges innovation and impact. She aspires to contribute to cutting-edge advancements in AI, pursue higher studies, and explore opportunities in entrepreneurship, with the ultimate goal of using technology to make a positive difference in society. Fueled by ambition, passion, and an unwavering dedication to her goals

Chirra Baburao is an esteemed academic and researcher with expertise in public policy, entrepreneurship, start-ups, and the impact of AI on various sectors. Holding Master's degrees in Commerce, Management, and Psychology, he has over a decade of industry experience in IT, operating as a Technopreneur through his MSME-registered firm, Bobbycomputers&Communications. Currently, working with Sir C.R. Reddy Educational Institutions, Eluru, Andhra Pradesh, India, as Research Convener (Research & Development).He is also a PhD(submitted) at GITAM School of Business, Visakhapatnam, and a former Research Associate (ICSSR) at Gujarat National Law University (GNLU), Baburao excels in qualitative, quantitative, and mixed research methods. He has completed 15 Swayam courses, participated in over 40 webinars, and presented 10 papers at national and international conferences. His research focuses on MSMEs' role in public policy, technological disruptions, and environmental issues. His recent work explores AI's impact on consumer behavior, smart cities, and healthcare, published in reputable journals and conferences, making him a prominent figure in his field.

Randhir Singh Baghel, PhD is an Associate Professor at the Faculty of Science and Humanities at Poornima University, Jaipur, India. He has 17 years of experience in teaching, research, and administration and has chaired many national and international conferences and technical sessions in his areas of expertise. In addition to teaching, he is also working on various research projects and has published more than 22 research papers in various international journals.

Kummagoori Bharath is a Research Scholar pursuing a Doctor of Philosophy (Ph.D.) in Computer Science and Engineering at Lovely Professional University, India. His research focuses on federated learning, privacy-preserving machine learning, and adversarial machine learning with emphasis on developing robust defense mechanisms against poisoning attacks in distributed learning systems. ORCID iD: 0009-0007-3319-1009

D. Rajyalakshmi is a distinguished psychologist with over two decades of expertise in Counselling, Industrial Psychology, and Teaching. She holds M.A., M.Phil., and Ph.D. degrees in Psychology from Andhra University, along with B.Ed. and M.Ed. in Special Education from Dr. B.R. Ambedkar Open University. Her proficiency spans Psychometrics, including Intelligence, Personality, and Aptitude Assessments. She has served in diverse roles — as a Psychologist at the Government Hospital for Mental Care, Visakhapatnam, Head of Department and faculty at Visakha Government Degree & PG College for Women and St. Joseph's College for Women, and Course Coordinator for M.Sc. Psychology at Andhra University's School of Distance Education, and also Ambedkar Open University Study Centre, Visakhapatnam. Presently, Dr. Rajyalakshmi is an Assistant Professor of Psychology at VIGNAN (Deemed to be University), Guntur and a Online Consultant Psychologist at Om Hospital. A prolific researcher, her work is published in reputed UGC CARE and Scopus-indexed journals. She actively contributes to academic bodies like BOS, organizes national-level workshops and conferences, and champions women's welfare initiatives across Andhra Pradesh. She also frequently serves as a resource person in training programs on career guidance, motivation, and personality development, and is deeply involved in community service through various NGOs. She is a recognized Ph.D. guide, currently mentoring six research scholars. Has RCI Registration number.

Srinath Doss is the Professor and Dean in the Faculty of Engineering and Technology, Botho University, responsible for Botswana, Lesotho, Eswatini, Namibia and Ghana Campuses. He has previously worked with various reputed Engineering colleges in India, and with Garyounis University, Libya. He has written good number of books and more than 80 papers in International Journals and attended several prestigious conferences. His research interests include MANET, Information Security, Network Security and

Cryptography, Artificial Intelligence, Cloud Computing and Wireless and Sensor Network. He serves as an editorial member and reviewer for reputed international journals, and an advisory member for various prestigious conference. Prof. Srinath is member of IAENG and Associate Member in UACEE.

Aftab Haider is a highly accomplished PhD Scholar of International Law at Southwest University of Political Science and Law in China, specializing in the complex intersection of Environmental Law, International Law, and Human Rights, with a specific focus on the legal impact of climate change and global governance issues like data protection and cybersecurity. A dedicated scholar with a Master of Laws degree from Abdul Wali Khan University, he is also an active contributor to the global legal discourse, currently serving as an International Arbitrator at the Chongqing Arbitration Commission (CQAC) and holding prestigious editorial and reviewer roles, notably as a Reviewer for PLOS ONE (SCIE, Q1). Mr. Haider's extensive publication record includes numerous peer-reviewed articles in highly-ranked journals (SSCI, SCOPUS, SCI), addressing critical topics from the geopolitical impact of BRICS and International Trade and Plastic Waste in Oceans to the implementation challenges of environmental laws in developing countries. Formerly a practising Lawyer with the KP Bar Council, he combines real-world legal advocacy with rigorous academic research, earning multiple distinctions, including the Chongqing Mayor Scholarship Award for his PhD.

Rajiv Iyer is currently an Associate Professor in Computer Science and Engineering at Amity University, Mumbai. With a Ph.D. in the domain of Internet of Things, he has had a distinguished career spanning 14 years in academia. He is a registered Patent Agent (IN/PA3625). He is certified educator for AWS, Celonis. He is Google Facilitator for Machine Learning and Kaggle BIPOC program mentor/ advisor.

Jeyavel Janardhanan has Master's degree in Computer and Microelectronics Engineer from Victoria University, Melbourne (2005) and Ph.D. in Vehicular Adhoc Networks from Anna University, Chennai (2017). He is currently an Associate Professor of Amity University, Maharashtra, working in the Department of Computer science and engineering, Amity School of Engineering and Technology(ASET). His research interest include Wireless networks, IoT, electrical systems and Deep learning technologies.

Bright Keswani is a distinguished educator, scientist, technocrat, and thought leader with expertise in teaching, research, and academic administration. He holds advanced qualifications including M.Sc., MCA, M.Tech, M.Phil, Ph.D. (E-Commerce), and a Post-Doctoral Degree in Mobile Ad-hoc Networks. Currently a Professor at Poornima University, Jaipur, he has previously served as HOD and Principal at Suresh Gyan Vihar University. His research spans AI, Big Data, Cloud Computing, E-Commerce, and Software Project Management, with over 150 research papers and 28 authored books. A recipient of prestigious awards like the Bharat Jyoti Award and Shiksha Bhushan Award, he also contributes as editor, reviewer, and conference chair for reputed international forums.

Kushagra Keswani is a motivated engineering student of Computer Science and Engineering at Poornima University, Jaipur. He is passionate about leadership and teamwork, while also demonstrating strong technical competence with proficiency in multiple programming languages. Fluent in various languages, he actively engages in extracurricular pursuits, fitness, and gaming. Recently, a patent has been filed in his name at the Indian IPR Office, reflecting his innovative mindset.

His key areas of interest include software development, problem-solving, and exploring emerging technologies.

Wasim Khan received the B.Tech., M.Tech., and Ph.D. degrees.With over 17 years in academia, he is currently a Seasoned Expert in computer Science engineering. He has made significant academic contributions, evidenced by numerous patents and a vast array of publications, including conference papers and book chapters. He is currently an Assistant Professor with the Symbiosis Institute of Technology, Symbiosis International (Deemed) University, Pune. His research interests include machine learning, deep learning, social network analysis, anomaly detection, and network intrusion detection.

Ashwini Kumar is an Associate Professor in the Department of Electronics & Communication Engineering at Poornima University, Jaipur, where he teaches undergraduate and postgraduate courses and participates in R&D activities. His research expertise is in antennas & propagation, microwave engineering and fractal antenna design, and he has authored multiple papers indexed in Scopus and SCI-listed journals. He has contributed to design-and-fabrication studies of compact fractal patch and MIMO antennas for UWB/IoT applications. Dr. Kumar regularly collaborates on conference papers, book chapters and journal articles, and supports student research and laboratory projects in RF/microwave systems.

Sanjeev Kumar is an Associate Professor at Swami Keshvanand Institute of Technology, Jaipur, specializing in power system optimization, renewable energy, and machine learning applications. He holds a Ph.D. from Dayalbagh Educational Institute, Agra, and has published extensively in high-impact journals. Dr. Kumar is a member of professional organizations, including the Institution of Engineers (India), and serves as a reviewer for reputed journals and conferences.

Udit Mamodiya is an academic and researcher, currently serving as Associate Professor and Associate Dean (Research) at Poornima University, Jaipur, Rajasthan, India. He holds a Ph.D. in Electrical Engineering and has made significant contributions in the fields of renewable energy systems, electronic engineering, and artificial intelligence. He is also actively involved in academic publishing, serving as an Associate Editor for the International Journal of Cyber Security and Risk Auditing and as a Guest Editor for AIP Conference Proceedings. His work is a testament to the integration of advanced AI techniques into sustainable and accessible technological solutions, enhancing both academic and societal impact.

Keerthana N V is an Assistant Professor with 8 Years of experience in teaching and 1-year experience in research (IUCAA LIGO Data Centre, Pune). Her area of interest is Network Security, Blockchain Security, and Machine Learning Algorithms. She is pursuing PhD at Anna University in Security in Blockchain. She has a working experience in High-Performance Computing (HTCondor) in LIGO INDIA Project. She has written many research articles in Network Security and assisted Scientists in analyzing Datasets in HTCondor.

P.Sathyasutha, currently working as an Assistant Professor in the Department of Computer Science and Engineering at Gnanamani College of Technology, Namakkal, Tamil Nadu. She has completed her B.E. in Information Technology, M.E. in Computer Science and Engineering and pursuing Ph.D. in Information and Communication Engineering, under Anna University, Chennai. She has 18 years of Academic, Administration, Teaching, and Research experience. She is a highly accomplished professional in the field of Computer Science and Engineering, specializing in Artificial Intelligence. She has authored numerous articles published in various journals and actively supervises B.E and M.E students undertaking their final year projects. Additionally, she holds an active life membership in the Professional Society of ISTE. Her research interests encompass Networking, Data Analytics, Artificial Intelligence, Machine Learning and theory of computing. She actively participates in college-wide activities and demonstrates strengths in maintaining confidence, positive attitude, effective teamwork and commitment.

Sheng-Lung Peng is a Professor and the Director of the Department of Creative Technologies and Product Design, National Taipei University of Business, Taiwan. He received the PhD degree in Computer Science from the National Tsing Hua University, Taiwan. He is an honorary Professor of Beijing Information Science and Technology University, China, and a visiting Professor of Ningxia Institute of Science and Technology, China. He is also an adjunct Professor of Mandsaur University, India. Dr. Peng is also a Director of Chinese Association of Public Affairs Management, Information Service Association of Chinese Colleges, Taiwan Association of Cloud Computing, and ICPC Asia Taipei Site; the Secretary General of the ICPC Contest Council for Taiwan; and a Supervisor of Chinese Information Literacy Association, and of Association of Algorithms and Computation Theory, Taiwan. Dr. Peng has edited several special issues at journals, such as Soft Computing, Journal of Internet Technology, Journal of Real-Time Image Processing, International Journal of Knowledge and System Science, MDPI Algorithms, and so on. His research interests are in designing and analyzing algorithms for Bioinformatics, Combinatorics, Data Mining, and Networks areas in which he has published over 100 research papers.

Saranya P received her B.E. and M.Tech. degrees in Computer Science and Engineering from Anna University and Kalasalingam University in 2007 and 2009, respectively. She completed her Ph.D. in the Department of Computer Technology at Anna University, MIT Campus, Chennai. She is currently working as an Assistant Professor at Amity University, Mumbai. Her research interests include deep learning, network security, and SDN.

Jagadeshwari Puttanapura is a dedicated Computer Science and Engineering student at Stanley College of Engineering and Technology for Women, India. With a keen interest in software development, machine learning, and data science, she have consistently demonstrated strong academic performance and a passion for technology. She has actively participated in several coding competitions, securing top positions in contests.

Maheshwari R is an academic and IT professional with over 12 years of experience in engineering education, government digital initiatives, and technical coordination. She served as Assistant Professor at Velalar College of Engineering and Technology, where she contributed to curriculum design, academic coordination, and student research. Her research interests include Artificial Intelligence, mobile application development and digital public services. She also reviewed academic publications, including textbooks aligned with Anna University syllabi. As part of the Tamil Nadu e-Governance Agency, she contributed to key projects like the TN e-Pass System during the COVID-19 pandemic. She was also involved in the development of the blockchain-based e-Pettagam mobile application and several departmental technology initiatives. Her role included supporting technology projects for various state departments and preparing data-driven reports. Her technical expertise spans Java, Python, Android development, and public-sector IT applications.

Revati Ramrao Rautrao Associate Professor, is a scholar, HR expert, and educator with 20+ years of experience, known for her research in sustainability, AI in education, and women's empowerment.

Sreeja Ravula, born on August 20, 2005, in Mancherial, India, is a passionate and aspiring technologist who embodies curiosity, determination, and innovation. Currently pursuing her Bachelor's degree in Technology (B.Tech) in the field of Artificial Intelligence and Machine Learning (AIML) at Sreenidhi Institute of Science and Technology (SNIST), Sreeja represents the new generation of forward-thinking engineers eager to shape the future of technology. Her academic journey is defined by a commitment to continuous learning and an eagerness to embrace emerging technologies. With a strong foundation in programming, data-driven problem-solving, and intelligent systems, she exhibits a growing expertise in Artificial Intelligence and its transformative applications across industries. Beyond academics, Sreeja actively engages in research interests, projects, and extracurricular initiatives that reflect her leadership qualities and dedication to excellence. She is admired by peers and mentors alike for her collaborative spirit, resilience, and willingness to take on challenges with confidence and creativity. Looking ahead, Sreeja envisions building a career that bridges innovation and impact. She aspires to contribute to cutting-edge advancements in AI, pursue higher studies, and explore opportunities in entrepreneurship, with the ultimate goal of using technology to make a positive difference in society. Fueled by ambition, passion, and an unwavering dedication to her goals, Sreeja Ravula stands poised to create a lasting impact in the evolving world of Artificial Intelligence and beyond. Gmail: sreejaravula2005@gmail.com

C Kishor Kumar Reddy, currently working as Associate Professor, Dept. of Computer Science and Engineering, Stanley College of Engineering and Technology for Women, Hyderabad, India. He has research and teaching experience of more than 10 years. He has published more than 60 research papers in National and International Conferences, Book Chapters, and Journals indexed by Scopus and others. He is an author for 2 text books and 2 co-edited books. He acted as the special session chair for Springer FICTA 2020, 2022, SCI 2021, INDIA 2022 and IEEE ICCSEA 2020 conferences. He is the corresponding editor of AMSE 2021 conferences, published by IoP Science JPCS. He is the member of ISTE, CSI, IAENG, UACEE, IACSIT.

Laxmikant Sagar is an Associate Professor at Sharda University, Greater Noida, Uttar Pradesh, specializing in machine learning applications. He holds a Ph.D. from Dayalbagh Educational Institute, Agra, and has published extensively in high-impact journals. Dr. Sagar is a member of professional organizations and serves as a reviewer for reputed journals and conferences.

Mohammed Firdos Alam Sheikh is an Assistant Professor and Deputy Head of the Department of Computer Science & Engineering at Poornima University, Rajasthan. His research expertise is in Cryptography and Network Security. He has published over 50+ research papers in reputable indexed sources such as Scopus and Web of Science, as well as numerous conference proceedings. Additionally, he holds over 10 Indian patents and 3 international patents and copyrights. Sheikh has authored two books and serves as an editor in Scopus-indexed publications. He is a life member of ISTE and IAENG and has been honored with awards such as the "Young Researcher Award" and the

"Outstanding Teacher of the Year Award" from various organizations and conferences. He is frequently invited as a session chair at national and international conferences and serves as the Nodal Center Coordinator for IIT Delhi Virtual Labs an initiative of ministry of Education, Govt. of india.

Nookala Shreya, born on September 25, 2005, in Warangal, India, is a passionate and creative-thinking technologist with a strong foundation in the Information Technology (IT) field. A distinguished alumnus of the Sreenidhi Institute of Science and Technology,Shreya earned her Bachelor's degree in Technology (B.Tech) in Information Technology (IT). Driven by curiosity and innovation, Shreya has developed expertise in Python programming and data-driven technologies. Her academic journey reflects not only technical proficiency but also a deep enthusiasm for exploring the applications of AI and IT solutions in solving real-world challenges. Beyond academics, Shreya is actively involved in research, extracurricular initiatives, and collaborative projects, where she has consistently showcased leadership, adaptability, and a problem-solving mindset. She is admired for her ability to blend technical knowledge with creativity, making her stand out in the evolving IT landscape. Looking to the future, Nookala Shreya aspires to contribute to the Advancement of IT and Artificial Intelligence through higher studies, cutting-edge research, and entrepreneurial ventures. With a relentless pursuit of growth and innovation, she is determined to make a lasting impact on the global technology ecosystem. Driven by a steadfast commitment to his goals, Shreya stands poised to embark on a journey of continued growth and achievement, leaving an indelible mark on the ever-evolving landscape of Information Technology and beyond. (nookalashreya1@gmail.com)

Garima Shukla, Senior Member IEEE, is an Associate Professor in the Department of Computer Science & Engineering at Amity University, Mumbai, India. With 15 years of teaching experience, she specializes in Deep Learning, AI, ML, Optoelectronics, IoT, and Communication Systems. She has 15 SCI-indexed journal papers, 33 Scopus-indexed research papers/book chapters, and numerous conference presentations, including in Maldives and London. A reviewer and book editor for Scopus-indexed publishers, she has received prestigious awards, including the Asia International Outstanding Researcher Award 2024. She has secured significant research grants, including the UKIERI grant of 1.2 Cr and funding from IIT Roorkee, MSME, and UP Startup Policy. Passionate about STEM education and innovation, she mentors startups and works to increase female participation in technology. Her research and academic contributions aim to advance AI-driven solutions for inclusive education and healthcare.

T. Monika Singh holds an M.Tech in Computer Science and Engineering from Osmania University and is currently pursuing a Ph.D. in the same field at KL University. Since 2017, she has been a faculty member in the Computer Science and Engineering Department at Stanley College of Engineering and Technology for Women. With a rich background in teaching and research, she is also a certified project-based learning mentor by Wipro and holds a TalentNext certification in Java Full Stack development. Her research interests focus on Machine Learning, and she has published several papers in national and international journals. Additionally, she holds a patent to her name.

Kokilavani T is an Assistant Professor in the Department of Information Technology at Velalar College of Engineering and Technology, and currently pursuing her Ph.D. in Federated Learning and Security in Healthcare at Anna University. With more than 5 years of teaching experience, she has taught courses in Data Science, Artificial Intelligence, and Mobile Application Development, and has guided numerous undergraduate projects, encouraging students to engage in hands-on research and innovative problem solving. Her research interests include Federated Learning, Genomics Data Privacy, Personalized Medicine, and Security in AI systems. She has published papers in reputed international journals and conferences, and actively participates in academic and research collaborations. She aims to contribute to the development of privacy-preserving AI solutions for healthcare and precision medicine.

T. Nithya presently serves as an Assistant Professor in the Department of Information Technology at Velalar College of Engineering and Technology in Erode, Tamil Nadu. She earned his B.Tech. in II, followed by an M.E. in Computer Science and Engineering from Anna University Chennai. With an extensive 18 years of experience in Academic, Administration, Teaching, and Research, she is a highly accomplished professional in the field of Information Technology, specializing in Data Analysis and Data Mining. She has published unsre than 20 research papers in National and International journals and presented more than 50 papers in National and International conferences across India. She published 2 Indian Patents. She actively supervises students undertaking their final year projects at Anna University Chennai. Additionally, she holds an active life membership in the Professional Society of ISTE. Her research interests encompass Data Analysis, Machine Learning and Deep Learning.

Sanjayan T.S. is Assistant Professor and Head of the Postgraduate and Research Department in Education at GVM's Dr. Dada Vaidya College of Education, Goa University, Goa, India. His research focuses on educational leadership, curriculum development, and innovative teaching practices. He has published in reputed journals, presented at national and international conferences, and actively contributes to advancing higher education and teacher development initiatives.

Lingala Thirupathi is a seasoned academician and researcher with over 18 years of experience spanning teaching and industry, specializing in Artificial Intelligence, Cybersecurity, and the Internet of Things. He is currently serving as an Assistant Professor at SNIST, Hyderabad. A Gold Medalist in M.Tech (Software Engineering) from JNTUH, he also holds a B.Tech in CSIT and multiple professional certifications, including Cisco Instructor, Oracle Certified Associate, and Salesforce Ranger. With over 50 research publications in reputed journals such as Scopus, IEEE, Elsevier, and Springer, he also holds one Australian and three Indian patents. Mr. Thirupathi has authored three textbooks and contributed to over 15 book chapters. He actively participates in academic and technical communities as a reviewer, committee member, and SPOC for Smart India Hackathons, and is affiliated with professional bodies like CSTA, TERA, and ICSES. His dedication to innovation and excellence has earned him accolades, including the Expert Instructor Award from Cisco Networking Academy.

Geeta Tiwari is an experienced academic professional with 18 years of expertise in engineering education. She completed her B.Tech from RBS Engineering College and M. Tech. from the National Institute of Technical Teachers Training and Research (NITTTR), Chandigarh. Currently working as a Assistant Professor at Poornima College of Engineering, she is known for her dedication to teaching, student mentorship, and academic development. Her commitment to excellence and her strong foundation in engineering make her a valued contributor to the academic community.

Shafiq Ul Rehman, Acting Dean College of Information Technology, Kingdom University, Bahrain

Dharmveer Yadav (Ph.D) is currently working as Sr. Assistant Professor in the Department of Computer Science, and coordinator of University Affairs Cell .He has teaching and administrative experience of more than 19 years in field of higher education. He has published more than 31 research papers in national and international conferences and journals. He has written more than 10 books on computer science. His area of interest is cloud computing, networking, and machine learning.

Index

A

P

R

S

T

U

www.ingramcontent.com/pod-product-compliance
Lightning Source LLC
LaVergne TN
LVHW080530300926
849162LV00007B/1577